ECONOMICS
AND CONTEMPORARY ISSUES

FOURTH EDITION

ECONOMICS
AND CONTEMPORARY ISSUES

FOURTH EDITION

MICHAEL R. EDGMAND
Oklahoma State University

RONALD L. MOOMAW
Oklahoma State University

KENT W. OLSON
Oklahoma State University

THE DRYDEN PRESS
HARCOURT BRACE COLLEGE PUBLISHERS

Fort Worth   Philadelphia   San Diego   New York   Orlando   Austin   San Antonio
Toronto   Montreal   London   Sydney   Tokyo

Publisher	George Provol
Acquisitions Editor	Emily Barrosse
Product Manager	Kathleen Sharp
Developmental Editor	Stacey Sims
Project Editor	Sandy Walton
Art Director	Bill Brammer
Production Manager	Carlyn Hauser
Cover Image	Rick Smith Illustration

ISBN: 0-03-024667-9

Library of Congress Catalog Card Number: 97-67942

Copyright © 1998, 1996, 1991 by The Dryden Press

Address for Orders
The Dryden Press, 6277 Sea Harbor Drive, Orlando, FL 32887-6777
1-800-782-4479

Address for Editorial Correspondence
The Dryden Press, 301 Commerce Street, Suite 3700, Fort Worth, TX 76102
Web site address:
http://www.hbcollege.com/

THE DRYDEN PRESS, DRYDEN, and the DP LOGO are registered trademarks of Harcourt Brace & Company.

Printed in the United States of America

7 8 9 0 1 2 3 4 5 6   039   9 8 7 6 5 4 3 2 1

The Dryden Press
Harcourt Brace College Publishers

THE DRYDEN PRESS SERIES
IN ECONOMICS

Baldani, Bradfield, and Turner
Mathematical Economics

Baumol and Blinder
Economics: Principles and Policy
Seventh Edition (Also available in
Micro and Macro paperbacks)

Baumol, Panzar, and Willig
Contestable Markets and the Theory
of Industry Structure
Revised Edition

Breit and Elzinga
The Antitrust Casebook: Milestones
in Economic Regulation
Third Edition

Brue
The Evolution of Economic Thought
Fifth Edition

Edgmand, Moomaw, and Olson
Economics and Contemporary
Issues
Fourth Edition

Gardner
Comparative Economic Systems
Second Edition

Gwartney and Stroup
Economics: Private and Public
Choice
Eighth Edition (Also available in
Micro and Macro paperbacks)

Gwartney and Stroup
Introduction to Economics: The
Wealth and Poverty of Nations

Heilbroner and Singer
The Economic Transformation of
America: 1600 to the Present
Third Edition

Hess and Ross
Economic Development: Theories,
Evidence, and Policies

Hirschey and Pappas
Fundamentals of Managerial Eco-
nomics: Theories, Evidence, and
Policies
Sixth Edition

Hirschey and Pappas
Managerial Economics
Eighth Edition

Hyman
Public Finance: A Contemporary
Application of Theory to Policy
Fifth Edition

Kahn
The Economic Approach to Envi-
ronmental and Natural Resources
Second Edition

Kaserman and Mayo
Government and Business: The Eco-
nomics of Antitrust and Regulation

Kaufman
The Economics of Labor Markets
Fourth Edition

Kennett and Lieberman
The Road to Capitalism: The Eco-
nomic Transformation of Eastern Eu-
rope and the Former Soviet Union

Kreinin
International Economics: A Policy
Approach
Eighth Edition

Lott and Ray
Applied Econometrics with Data
Sets

Mankiw
Principles of Economics
(Also available in Micro and Macro
paperbacks)

Marlow
Public Finance: Theory and
Practice

Nicholson
Intermediate Microeconomics and
Its Application
Seventh Edition

Nicholson
Microeconomic Theory: Basic Prin-
ciples and Extensions
Seventh Edition

v

Puth
American Economic History
Third Edition

Ragan and Thomas
Principles of Economics
Second Edition (Also available in
Micro and Macro paperbacks)

Ramanathan
Introductory Econometrics with
Applications
Fourth Edition

Rukstad
Corporate Decision Making in the
World Economy: Company Case
Studies

Rukstad
Macroeconomic Decision Making in
the World Economy: Text and Cases
Third Edition

Samuelson and Marks
Managerial Economics
Second Edition

Scarth
Macroeconomics: An Introduction to
Advanced Methods
Third Edition

Stockman
Introduction to Economics
(Also available in Micro and Macro
paperbacks)

Walton and Rockoff
History of the American Economy
Eighth Edition

Welch and Welch
Economics: Theory and Practice
Sixth Edition

Yarbrough and Yarbrough
The World Economy: Trade and
Finance
Fourth Edition

PREFACE

Economics and Contemporary Issues takes an issues approach to introductory economics, creating a user-friendly textbook that illustrates that knowledge of economics will help make more sense of the world. The global economy affects us personally and socially. An understanding of it is crucial in personal planning—regarding education, careers, and families—and in political and social decision making.

This book examines major issues pertaining to education, health care, social security, unemployment, inflation, and international trade, answering such questions as: Is education a good investment? What causes inflation? What are the benefits and costs of international trade? It also examines social and political phenomena that will have continued importance in the twenty-first century—the collapse of communism and central planning, the role of government in a modern economy, crime and drugs, poverty, and the failure of economies to grow.

This textbook maximizes the advantages of the issues approach by examining issues that interest students, while developing core economic principles that provide penetrating insights and a basis for lifelong learning. An economic analysis of contemporary issues will often challenge students' deeply held beliefs regarding such topics as poverty, free trade, and the causes of inflation. Such challenges combined with the analytical framework provided by economic theory make this textbook ideal in a curriculum emphasizing critical thinking.

Students who study this textbook will develop an increased interest in economics, seeing it as important in understanding issues that affect them personally, as well as in understanding today's headlines. Many students will study additional economic issues as a result of using this book.

NEW TO THIS EDITION

Economic problems and issues change so rapidly that new editions of an issues book should reflect many changes. The fourth edition of *Economics and Contemporary Issues* clearly illustrates this process. Accordingly, this is not a superficial update but a substantial revision.

The authors have updated all of the data, tables, and figures; improved the exposition throughout the text; included more real-world examples and illustrations; provided more suggestions for further reading; and developed new questions at the end of many of the chapters.

The book now contains two types of material in the boxes (17 of which are new) that are separate from but complement the main text. The information in these boxes provides (as indicated by their labels) "**Additional Insight**" and a fuller "**International Perspective.**" The latter reflect the authors' commitment in writing a textbook that both broadens the readers' knowledge of the United States and makes them more informed citizens of the world.

The overall structure of the book is unchanged, with one exception: Chapter 17, "Prospects for Development of the Third World," in the third edition has been dropped. Chapter 16, "Poverty Growth: Poverty Reduction Par Excellence," has been thoroughly rewritten, however, to place the development problem in the broader context of differences in growth rates among nations.

Chapter-by-Chapter Changes to the Fourth Edition:

• In Chapter 1, "Economic Systems: Why Do They Matter?," has been rewritten and updated with a concentration on the material on Transitions to a Market Economy to reflect the rapid changes taking place in the former planned economies of Eastern Europe.

• Chapter 2, "Markets or Government? The Cardinal Economic Choice," has been completely rewritten. It is essentially a new chapter that should have much greater appeal to both students and instructors than the old version.

• Chapter 3 has a new title, "U.S. Farm Policy: How Is It Changing?," to reflect increased emphasis on farm policy, including the 1996 Farm Bill.

• Chapter 4, "Market Power: Does It Help or Hurt the Economy?," provides a fuller discussion of the pros and cons of market power, including the issue of Market Power and Economic Growth.

• Chapter 8, "College Education: Is It Worth the Cost?," now contains an explicit treatment of the present value and rate of return approaches to investment evaluation.

• Chapter 9, "Social Security: Where Are We? Where Are We Going?," contains the latest projections of the Social Security Trust Funds and considers the reform alternatives recommended by the President's Advisory Commission on Social Security.

• Chapter 10 has been retitled "Poverty and Discrimination," to indicate that the chapter now contains an analysis of market discrimination and the relationship between poverty and discrimination. This chapter also contains a discussion of the recently enacted Federal Welfare Reform legislation.

• Chapter 11, "Tracking the Macroeconomy," contains new material on the relationships between Nominal and Real GDP and the GDP Deflator.

• Chapter 12, "Unemployment: A Recurring Problem," is updated to reflect the new Minimum Wage Law and the Earned Income Tax Credit as an alternative. It also contains an expanded discussion of the problem of Unemployment in Europe and of job listings on the Internet.

- Chapter 13, "Inflation: A Monetary Phenomenon," includes a discussion of inflation rates in other countries.
- Chapter 14, "Deficits and Debt: What Legacy?," includes a discussion of budget deficits in other countries and has an update of Deficit Reduction Plans in the Clinton Administration.

THE INTENDED AUDIENCE

One audience for this textbook is students enrolled in the growing number of one-term issues courses offered by economics departments, often as general education courses. This book contains enough economic theory, however, for the traditional one-term survey course in economics. It is also appropriate for use as a supplement in traditional two-semester principles courses or as a text for the economics part of social science survey courses. If the instructor adds other readings, it can also be used as a core text in an upper-division issues or capstone course.

FEATURES

Economics and Contemporary Issues has several features that are important in an issues-oriented text:

1. Effective aids to self-learning
2. A balanced treatment of microeconomics and macroeconomics
3. A basic theory core
4. Up-to-date, comprehensive background information on each issue
5. Flexibility in the sequencing of topics and issues

AIDS TO SELF-LEARNING   The most important aid to self-learning is clear, concise exposition of basic concepts. *Economics and Contemporary* Issues is readily understood by beginning students. Every sentence has been rewritten to eliminate confusing or excessive prose.

To understand economics, students must master its basic vocabulary. To facilitate this, key terms are highlighted when they first appear and defined in three places: the body of the text, the margin, and the end-of-book glossary. In addition, each chapter begins with a list of key terms from previous chapters and ends with a list of the key terms introduced in the chapter. Boxed material is used to stimulate additional interest and insight.

To help students master the standard tools of economic analysis, there is a judicious use of graphs and tables, which are carefully explained both in the text and in accompanying captions. Graphs are constructed initially from accompanying data to help the beginner master this important tool of economic analysis.

Self-testing is an essential component of self-learning. Each chapter contains review questions (with answers in the *Instructor's Manual*), and a carefully constructed *Study Guide* is available. Each chapter provides a summary of important points.

MICRO–MACRO BALANCE   The analysis of macroeconomic issues is often slighted in issues books. Not here, however. After discussing economic systems in Chapter 1 and the role of government in Chapter 2, 7 of the 14 remaining chapters cover macroeconomic issues, including unemployment, inflation, the federal budget and balance of payment deficits, and economic growth. The microeconomic aspects of agriculture, monopoly power, health care, crime, pollution, education, social security, and poverty are also examined.

BASIC THEORY CORE   Both the micro and macro parts of this book use a small number of understandable, yet powerful, economic concepts and models.

In the microeconomics chapters, supply-demand and marginal analysis are used extensively. Models of competitive and monopolized markets are developed. The distinctions between social and private benefits and costs are used to analyze market and government failures.

The basic macroeconomics tool is the model of aggregate supply and demand. Use of this versatile model enables beginning students to understand the forces that determine output, employment, price level, and the effects of alternative policies.

CURRENT, COMPREHENSIVE INFORMATION   Our experience shows that most beginning students know too little about economic history, data, and institutions. An issues course must fill this void by providing the information necessary for understanding the nature and significance of the problems addressed.

Essential information can be provided by both the instructor and the textbook. Although there is no perfect substitute for an instructor who seeks new information and provides it to students, this book simplifies the instructor's quest by providing current and comprehensive background information on each issue.

FLEXIBILITY IN SEQUENCING TOPICS   This book is structured so that microeconomic issues are examined before macroeconomic issues. The macroeconomic issues can be studied first, however, because the micro chapters (Chapters 1 through 10) have been designed to be independent of the macro chapters (Chapters 11 through 17). Instructors who prefer to teach macro first, following an introduction to the market system, can do so by assigning Chapters 1 and 2 before beginning Chapter 11.

Chapters 1 and 2 provide the foundation for Chapters 3 through 10. Chapter 11 provides the foundation for the macro section of the book. A one-term principles survey course would include Chapters 1 through 4, 11 through 13 (plus appendices), and other selected chapters to fit the instructors' interests.

SUPPLEMENTARY MATERIALS

Students will greatly benefit from working through the *Study Guide,* prepared by Professor Kim Andrews of Central Missouri State University. Each chapter in the *Study Guide* includes a review of key terms, true/false and multiple-choice questions, and practice problems.

Instructors will find the *Instructor's Manual and Test Bank* helpful in planning their courses and preparing exams. This aid was written jointly by Professor Andrews and the textbook authors. It includes chapter overviews, learning objectives, teaching suggestions, additional references for each issue, detailed lecture outlines, answers to questions in the textbook, a variety of exam questions and problems, and transparency masters.

The Dryden Press will provide complimentary supplements or supplement packages to adopters qualified under its adoption policy. Please contact your sales representative to learn how you may qualify. If as an adopter or potential user you receive supplements you do not need, please return them to your sales representative or send them to:

Attn: Returns Department
Troy Warehouse
465 South Lincoln Drive
Troy, MO 63379

ACKNOWLEDGMENTS

This book is a joint product of three authors who are long-time colleagues—and still friends after working on this project. We did not produce this book alone, however, and we greatly appreciate the contributions of users, colleagues, reviewers, students, and the staff of The Dryden Press. We appreciate all comments that we receive and rely on them as we make revisions. Let us know how we can improve our book.

Many of the changes in this edition were made in response to the careful reviews and thoughtful suggestions of Eric Brooks (Orange County Community College), Philip J. Lane (Fairfield University), John Merrifield (University of Texas, San Antonio), and Paula Smith (University of Central Oklahoma).

The book still reflects, however, the substantial contributions of Michael Applegate and the suggestions of Steven Petty (Oklahoma State University), and the reviewers of previous editions: John P. Blair (Wright State University), Bruce Domazlickey (Southeast Missouri State University), Robert B. Harris (Indiana University—Purdue University at Indianapolis), John Scott (Northeast Louisiana University), Charles Stull (Western Michigan University), Millicent Taylor (University of Southern Colorado, Ugur Aker (Hiram College), Gale Blalock (University of Evansville), James R. Frederick (Pembroke State University), Christopher Lingle (Loyola University, New Orleans), Edwin A. Sexton (Virginia Military Institute), Ranbir Varma (Long Island University), Pauline Fox

(Southeast Missouri State University), Neil Garston (California State University, Los Angeles), Doug McNeil (McNeese State University), John Pisciotta (Baylor University), Steve Smith (Rose State College), Barbara Street (Chaminade University of Honolulu), Hyung C. Chung (University of Bridgeport), Emily Hoffman (Western Michigan University), George Murphy (University of California, Los Angeles), Larry Sechrest (University of Texas, Arlington), and Alden Smith (Anne Arundel Community College).

Former editor Liz Widdicombe insisted that Dryden was the right company for this project. We're glad she persisted, and we gratefully acknowledge the guidance provided by the Dryden staff, including Gary Nelson, Stacey Sims, Susan Van Buren, Sandy Walton, Carlyn Hauser, Bill Brammer, Kathleen Sharp, and Cristin Westhoff.

Michael R. Edgmand
Ronald L. Moomaw
Kent W. Olson
March 1997

TO THE STUDENT

Welcome to *Economics and Contemporary Issues*. This book will teach you how the U.S. economy works and how economic incentives and institutions are related to important social problems. In the process of learning these things, you will also sharpen your critical-thinking skills.

The issues and problems you will study command the attention of concerned citizens and policy-makers. Many of them will continue to be important long after you finish this book. The principles you learn here, however, will also help you to understand new problems and issues as they appear.

In examining each issue, we develop and apply the principles essential for understanding its economic dimensions, and then evaluate current and alternative approaches to dealing with it. The first step is the province of positive economics; the second is the focus of normative economics. Positive economics explains and predicts economic phenomena; normative economics selects social goals and evaluates policy alternatives according to how well they achieve these goals. This approach reflects the dual purpose of economics: discovering how the world works and determining how it can be improved.

The basic normative questions posed throughout this book are whether government action is necessary to solve social problems and, if so, what policies should be adopted. For example, the chapter on air pollution considers whether curbing pollution—a social goal—can be accomplished efficiently by the private sector alone, and concludes that it cannot. Existing regulations and proposed policies are then evaluated to determine which of them are most likely to improve the situation. We use a similar approach in examining the other issues. We hope the net result will be a greater appreciation of the strengths and weaknesses of both the private and public sectors of the economy.

To achieve lasting benefits from economics, and to do well in your course, plan to go beyond merely memorizing this material. Learn, in addition, how to apply the principles and models developed in the text.

We have strived to write clearly and concisely so that you will understand the important principles. You will greatly enhance your ability to apply these principles by answering the questions at the end of each chapter and by working through the *Study Guide* accompanying this book.

Brief Contents

DETAILED CONTENTS

ECONOMIC SYSTEMS:
WHY DO THEY MATTER?

Experience shows that market economic systems are superior to other economic systems in organizing a nation's economy. The collapse of the centrally planned systems in the former Soviet bloc has led to attempts to create market economic systems from the wreckage of these planned systems. The collapse of Soviet communism is a central feature of the 20th century; the successful construction of market systems a central hope of the 21st. According to *The Economist*, "Across the whole region [Central and Eastern Europe and countries formed from the Soviet Union], the possibility and desirability of creating capitalism has now been accepted, even by the laggards."[1] The most decisive reason "has surely been a simple recognition of the superiority of capitalism as an economic system."[2]

Because market (capitalist) economic systems have evolved without anyone actually deciding to create them—like Topsy, "they just grew"—it is sometimes difficult to know their essential features. The explicit decision to abandon central planning in favor of market systems provides a laboratory for the study of these features. This chapter uses that laboratory to discuss two fundamental questions: What do economic systems do, and why do market systems perform better than alternatives?

MARKET ECONOMIC SYSTEMS: AN INTRODUCTORY LOOK

The changes undertaken by countries trying to establish market economic systems imply much about these systems' essential features. These countries are establishing a legal system consistent with private ownership of most business operations—particularly, agriculture, manufacturing, retailing, wholesaling, and business and personal services. They also are allowing individuals to establish the terms by which they engage in economic transactions—that is, allowing prices to be set in markets by individual action. Finally, they are allowing economically successful people to benefit from the wealth they create and unsuccessful people to suffer the consequences of deficiencies in wealth creation—using market rewards and penalties as incentives. This suggests three essential features of a market system: private ownership, market exchanges, and market incentives.

For the price system that emerges to work well, it must be based on *voluntary exchanges* between *informed* people. Knowing the price of a good helps people decide if they want to purchase it. For price to be most helpful in a purchase decision, it should be thought of as a relative price. A **relative price,** the price of one good in terms of another good, measures what must be given up to purchase an item. It is an exchange value. For instance, if the price of a compact disc (CD) is $15, an individual sacrifices the best alternative use of the $15 to buy the CD. Perhaps the best sacrificed alternative is attending a concert. In deciding whether to purchase the CD, the individual would then compare the benefits of owning a CD to the benefits of the concert. If prices do not change much over time, peo-

Relative Price
The price of one good in terms of another good. It measures what must be given up to obtain a good.

---

[1]"After Communism," *The Economist* (December 3, 1994), 27.
[2]Ibid.

ple become aware of prices as exchange values—what must be given up of one thing to get another. This awareness greatly simplifies their decision making. They know what they are sacrificing to get another CD—a concert.

If the average of all prices is increasing rapidly over time, prices might not inform people well about exchange values. (Such a continuous increase in the average of all prices over time is called inflation, which is analyzed in Chapter 13.) Consider three examples. First, suppose that the price of a CD doubles to $30 and that all other prices do not change. If the price of a CD goes to $30, the sacrifice for a CD would then be two concerts. In this case, the price change signals that a greater sacrifice—at least the benefits from two concepts—is required for a CD. As a result, people buy fewer CDs.

Second, suppose that the price of a CD doubles to $30 from its original price and that all other prices double. The best alternative sacrificed is still one concert, which now also has a $30 price tag. If all prices change in the same proportion, exchange values do not change. Thus a moderate and steady rate of inflation may not seriously damage the usefulness of the price system as a signaling device.

Often, however, inflation accelerates and decelerates over time and has different effects on prices in different sectors of the economy. In this third instance, with erratic inflation, people can no longer rely on experience to evaluate prices as exchange values. Suppose some prices do not change, others double, and others triple, causing the average price level to double. Now to find the sacrifice for a $30 CD, consumers would have to study all prices to find the best alternative to a CD. As erratic inflation continues, people have to evaluate alternatives in detail each time they consider a purchase. With a stable average price level, it is much simpler for consumers to be informed about market alternatives. Such stability makes prices an even better source of information.

In addition, a well-functioning market system requires that individuals be willing and able to trust other individuals with whom they deal. A major step in this direction is the establishment of a clear and understandable legal system creating private property rights. The system must create all types of ownership structures: proprietorships, partnerships, and corporations. Besides property law, the legal system must include contract, criminal, tort, and other types of law. Many problems must be dealt with: fraud, theft, counterfeiting, misrepresentation of a product's attributes, the failure to mention safety problems, and so on. These laws encourage economic transactions because they make them feasible and binding. For the laws to be effective, however, people must generally agree with and obey them. If not, more government resources will be devoted to law enforcement. In addition, people will devote more personal resources to the protection of their person and their property and to the evasion of laws and regulations. A market system becomes less effective because resources are devoted to nonproductive activities, such as tax avoidance and evasion.

Besides formal rules of conduct, well-functioning economic systems also require informal rules. People must be able to rely on each other's word; no legal system can regulate all situations in which honesty is an important stimulus for good economic performance. For example, suppose that when you asked other people the time of a meeting, some gave you the correct time but others did not.

It is hard to imagine a law requiring that we tell each other the correct time. If we cannot rely on a correct answer, however, inconvenience is added to our lives.

To conclude, a market system is one in which rights to private property are defined, established, and protected by law. Furthermore, private property must constitute a significant portion of the economy. Given private property, individuals decide what to produce and consume, based on what they see as their self-interest. People make career and production decisions considering their interests, opportunities, and talents, and in light of what other people will pay for their labor or their products. Having decided what to produce or where to sell their labor, people exchange what they produce or what they earn for goods and services produced by other people.

A market economy eases these voluntary exchanges by establishing prices for goods and services that allow individuals to purchase from others rather than directly exchanging what they produce. People do not have to trade bread for wine; they can sell bread for money and use the money to buy wine. For example, the use of money and prices allows college professors to teach without worrying whether students will pay them with house painting, baby-sitting, house cleaning, or farm products. As you well know, students pay colleges money; colleges in turn pay the professors, who then buy what they want and can afford. Prices provide information that simplifies voluntary exchange between individuals; they inform and motivate people in their economic decision making. For a price system to work smoothly, people must generally obey the law and behave in a mutually trustworthy manner.

WHAT DOES AN ECONOMIC SYSTEM DO?

An economic system consists of a set of economic, political, social, and other rules. Given the rules, people make choices that taken together determine five interrelated economic outcomes: (1) the quantities of various goods and services produced in an economy, (2) the methods of production, (3) who gets the goods and services, (4) the overall employment level of the economy and whether it produces at its capacity, and (5) the growth of the economy. Consider some specific points. How will business firms produce? Will automobile producers, for example, make extensive use of robots, or will they move away from assembly-line production to team production? How-to-produce questions are among the easier ones that an economic system deals with, because they are partly answered by engineering considerations.

More complex questions include the following: How much and what types of food, clothing, and various other products should be produced? Reasonable answers depend on the talents and desires of the 265 million people and 130 million workers in the U.S. economy. What goods and services are they adept at producing? What goods and services do they wish to consume? The questions are difficult because people do not wish to consume everything they are adept at producing and are not adept at producing everything they want to consume. Therefore consumption must be coordinated with production.

The distribution of goods and services to people also raises difficult issues. To achieve a high level of economic output, people must be rewarded for what they produce so that they have incentive to continue and perhaps to increase their production. Compassion or justice, however, requires that those who cannot produce an adequate amount be taken care of in some way. The contradiction between the distribution of material goods as incentives and their distribution for compassion is troubling. People in most societies are unwilling to accept a distribution of goods and services based entirely on what one produces. Many people engage in voluntary redistribution (charity) and support government in its mandatory redistribution.

Periods of high unemployment or rapid inflation disrupt an economic system. If many people are unemployed, we lose what they could have produced. This loss can never be recovered. As discussed above, rapid inflation makes it harder for an economic system to operate. Because an unregulated market system apparently is subject to recurring episodes of unemployment and inflation, many economists believe that governments must promote economic stability.

Because the U.S. economy has grown slowly for the last quarter century, the relationship between economic growth and economic policy has become more important. Promotion of economic growth is complex and controversial. Economic growth is attained by sacrificing in the present to provide for the future. Thus economic growth policy is a feature of the conflict between generations. To complicate matters, economic growth depends, among other things, on satisfactory outcomes in the other four areas.

This book introduces you to a market economic system, particularly the U.S. system, and its performance. Although the different performance measures are interrelated and difficult to discuss in isolation, different parts of the book emphasize different issues. Chapter 2 expands on this chapter's brief discussion of government's role in a market economic system. Each following chapter incorporates the role of government in the issues examined. Chapters 3 through 8 explore aspects of what goods to produce. Chapters 9 and 10 focus on distribution: social security and poverty. Chapters 11 through 14 deal with unemployment, inflation, and other issues regarding the overall economy. Chapters 15 and 16 examine international economics and economic growth.

All of these issues involve the central problem of coordination. We next examine why coordination is so complex in a modern economy. After identifying what an economic system must do—*coordinate*—we begin the discussion of how a market economic system does its job. Later we compare market and centrally planned (command) economic systems.

THE DIVISION AND SPECIALIZATION OF LABOR

As early as 1776, when Adam Smith published his trail-breaking treatise in economics, *The Wealth of Nations*, economists recognized the importance of the division of labor. Smith meant two things by the division of labor. One is the specialization of labor in a particular production process—today, that might be the person in a service station who specializes in changing oil. The second is the specialization of firms in a few activities—the automobile service station that only does mufflers. Division of labor implies specialization of economic activity.

Smith argued that the division and specialization of labor gave "modern" economies a tremendous wealth advantage over "traditional" subsistence economies. He illustrated the division of labor in a firm by describing the specialized tasks done by workers in producing straight pins. One worker "draws out the wire, another straights it, a third cuts it, a fourth points it, a fifth grinds it at the top for receiving the head; . . . and the important business of making a pin, is divided into about eighteen distinct operations, which in some manufactories are all performed by distinct hands."[3] Smith estimated that, in factories with extensive division of labor, the daily production of pins per worker might be 4,800 times the production of a single worker who did all of the tasks.

Although you might think producing a textbook does not involve extensive division of labor, both types of specialization are important. The production of this book required tens of thousands of specialized people and many specialized business firms—the economists who researched the topics; the editors, publishers, and printers; the loggers and manufacturing employees who produced the paper; the people who invented and produced the computer hardware and software; and so on. The enormous availability of books today would have been unimaginable to Middle Age monks, who manufactured books by hand, copying and beautifully illustrating manuscripts. Dramatically increased division of labor has made books incredibly inexpensive today compared with what they cost in the Middle Ages.

Smith's insights about the advantages of the division (specialization) of labor remain relevant. He discussed three ways in which it increases output of goods and services. First, specialization allows people to become highly skilled in particular tasks. Today, we would say that specialized workers become more skilled through higher education, vocational training, and on-the-job training. Second, specialization reduces the time wasted as people shift from one task to another. Smith referred to the time wasted by subsistence farmers as they switched from one farm task to another. Time-management experts currently make a similar point. They recommend that workers complete one task—responding to the mail—before they switch to another task—scheduling production. By reserving large blocks of time for each task, people avoid losing time because of (a) mental shifting of gears, (b) putting materials away (for those who do that), (c) getting out new materials, and so on. The fewer the tasks—that is, the greater the specialization—the more time saved. Third, Smith observed that specialized workers made many inventions and innovations in the early Industrial Revolution; because they were concentrating on just a few tasks, these workers could see easier ways to do them. Although some inventions and innovations today are made by people specializing in such ac-

---

[3]Adam Smith, *An Inquiry into the Nature and Causes of the Wealth of Nations* (Indianapolis: Liberty Press, 1981), a reprint of the edition published by Oxford: Clarendon Press, 1979, Book I, Chapter 1, p. 15.

tivity, itself an example of greater division of labor, specialization still eases innovations because it is easier to automate a simple task than a complex one. Furthermore, just as in Adam Smith's day, contemporary workers invent and innovate in a search for new and better ways of doing their jobs. As we do our jobs, we gain knowledge. Often that knowledge is tacit knowledge, which is knowledge that we can use but cannot explain easily to others. For instance, an expert at video games, cannot teach—through a lecture or a book—someone else to play the games equally well. Other people have to learn by doing, just as the expert did. Because we cannot easily explain tacit knowledge to other people, it must be used by the people who have it. Given the opportunity, workers use this knowledge to invent and innovate.

Greater division and specialization of labor are not unmixed blessings. The monk responsible for illuminating a beautiful manuscript had a great feeling of accomplishment. He could see the product of his labor. With increased specialization, many workers cannot see their accomplishments. Work that requires repetitive, monotonous actions leads to worker discontent. Besides promoting division of labor, economic systems may need ways of avoiding overspecialization.

Specialization based on division of labor is an integral part of any economy.[4] If we specialize, however, we produce more of some things than we want to use and less of other things. We must trade, which means that society has to have a way to coordinate the activities of vast numbers of *specialized* people.

ECONOMIC COORDINATION AND THE MARKET SYSTEM

The successful coordination of economic activity through a market system relies on a simple proposition. The proposition is that *voluntary exchange* between two individuals occurs only if each individual expects to benefit from the exchange. For the exchange to be truly voluntary, both parties must (a) be responsible individuals who can make rational decisions, (b) have reasonable access to information, and (c) have reasonable alternatives to the exchange. Suppose Chris wishes to trade his time as a bassoonist for income. If Kate's orchestra is the only place of employment for bassoonists, Chris is in a perilous position. If he has no other way to earn income, any agreement that Chris makes to work for Kate is hardly voluntary. Fortunately, we do not face many situations where there are no alternatives for essential products. (Monopoly, which is a situation in which buyers have limited alternatives, is discussed in Chapter 4.)

A major exception to the purely beneficial effects of voluntary exchange arises if a third party is negatively and involuntarily affected. Suppose Chris, the bassoonist, obtains the job if he practices at home five hours a day. If his neighbors can hear his practicing, it could cause them involuntary harm. Such involuntary harm is a *neighborhood effect*. If such effects are important in particular exchanges, the harm experienced by third parties must be considered

---

[4]Comparative advantage, developed in Chapter 15, is also an important reason for specialization.

along with the advantages gained by the trading parties. A real example is air pollution. Producers and consumers of paper benefit from their voluntary exchanges, but a paper mill's air pollution may harm people who live in its vicinity. (Chapter 7 deals with issues surrounding air pollution.)

THE PRICE SYSTEM AS COORDINATOR

One of any society's most important tasks to ensure that the quantity produced of any good (such as apartments) is the quantity that consumers want to purchase. If more is produced than consumers demand, resources are wasted in producing apartments—resources that could be used to produce something else. If less is produced than consumers demand, they will be dissatisfied; implicitly too much of something else is being produced. In *competitive markets*, which are markets with many buyers and sellers, the interaction of demand and supply determines the quantity of the good produced. This section discusses the demand and supply using the market for apartments as a familiar example.

DEMAND Consider the market for apartments of a given size and quality in a particular city, say, Gotham City. Gotham has a population of 5 million, income per person is $16,000, and the price of the standard owner-occupied house is $80,000. Assume that population, income, and the price of a house are three of the four things that affect how many apartments people want to rent. The fourth thing is the rental price of an apartment. How many apartments will people plan to rent at different rental prices, holding income, population, and house price constant?

To answer, we develop the *demand schedule* for apartments—the number of apartments per month that people demand at each alternative price. The demand schedule exists for the given values of income, population, and house price. If any of these values change, the demand schedule changes. If the price of an apartment is $500 a month, Table 1.1 shows that Gothamites demand 400,000 apartments. If the price were $450 a month, they would want 475,000 apartments. Thus, if the price falls from $500 to $450, the quantity demanded of apartments increases from 400,000 to 475,000.

Suppose we plot the demand schedule. Because we use diagrams throughout the book, you will find it helpful to learn by doing: plot the demand schedule on a separate sheet of paper. (Later you can compare your plot with a figure that we provide.) Place price (rent) per apartment per month on the vertical axis (in $100 increments) and the number of apartments per month on the horizontal axis (in increments of 100,000). Assume that all apartments are of equal size and quality. To plot the **demand curve,** a visual of the demand schedule, take each point from the demand schedule and locate it in your figure. (Note that the demand "curve" can be a straight line.) For instance, at point E in Table 1.1, the price is $300 and the quantity demanded is 700,000. Find $300 on the vertical axis of your diagram and draw a horizontal (dashed) line at that price all the way across the diagram. Now find 700,000 on the horizontal axis and draw a vertical (dashed) line from there to the top. The intersection of the two dashed lines is a point on the demand

Demand Curve
A curve (line) showing the quantity demanded of a good for each possible price, holding other factors that affect demand constant.

A DEMAND
SCHEDULE
FOR APARTMENTS
IN GOTHAM CITY

	TABLE 1.1	
Price (Monthly Rent per Apartment)		**Quantity (Apartments per Month)**
A	$500	400,000
B	450	475,000
C	400	550,000
D	350	625,000
E	300	700,000
F	250	775,000
G	200	850,000

The demand schedule shows the quantity demanded of apartments at each different price. For instance, if the price is $500 a month, the quantity demanded is 400,000 apartments. At a lower price of $450, the quantity demanded would be greater: 475,000 apartments. The demand schedule exists for a given income, population, and price of a house.

curve. Find another point, maybe B, in the same way. Because this is a straight line, the two points can be connected to give the demand curve.

Suppose now that the market price is $400. Draw a horizontal dashed line from $400 to the demand curve; at the intersection drop a vertical dashed line to the horizontal axis. The point where the dashed line hits the axis gives the quantity demanded of apartments: 550,000. So the demand curve gives the quantity demanded, the quantity that consumers plan to buy, at each alternative price, assuming all of the other demand factors do not change. Of course, only one price can exist at any particular time.

The demand curve can be looked at in another way. Suppose 400,000 apartments are on the market. The **demand price** is the price at which consumers will buy exactly that quantity, the price at which the market would clear. To find it, draw a vertical dashed line from the horizontal axis (start at 400,000) to the demand curve and then draw a horizontal dashed line to the vertical axis. The demand price for 400,000 apartments per month is $500 per month. The demand price has an important interpretation. Some consumer rents the last apartment, the 400,000th, if the actual price is $500 per month. So the apartment is worth at least that much to some consumer. If the actual price were slightly higher, $501 per month, no one will rent the last apartment. It is not worth $501. So the 400,000th apartment is worth at least $500, but no more than $500; thus, it is worth exactly $500. The demand price shows the maximum price that some consumer will pay for the last unit.

The demand-price concept helps us to understand the **law of demand.** The law of demand says that the quantity demanded of any good is negatively related to its price, holding other things such as population, consumer income, consumer preferences, and the prices of other goods constant. Figure 1.1, which like your plot is based on Table 1.1, shows that a lower price—$300 rather than $400—

Demand Price
The price at which consumers will buy the exact quantity on the market. The maximum price that anyone will pay for the last unit.

Law of Demand
As the price of some good changes with other factors constant, the quantity demanded for that good changes in the opposite direction.

A DEMAND CURVE
FOR APARTMENTS
IN GOTHAM CITY

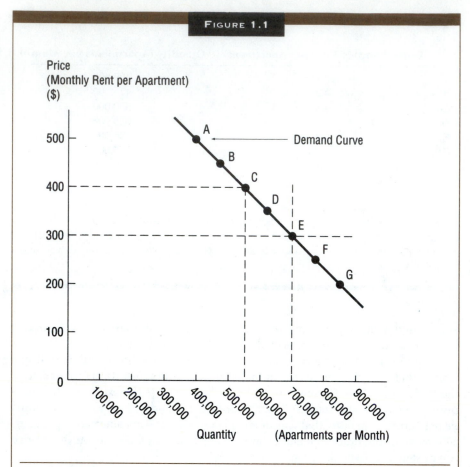

FIGURE 1.1

The demand curve shows the quantity demanded of apartments per month at each alternative price. Only one price can exist at a time, so only one quantity demanded can
exist in a particular month. The demand curve is plotted from the demand schedule in
Table 1.1. At point E, price is $300 per apartment per month and quantity demanded
is 700,000 apartments per month. Put this and other points in the diagram. Then con-
nect them to get the demand curve. If the market price is $400, the demand curve says
that the quantity demanded is 550,000 apartments. Or if there are 400,000 apartments
on the market, then the demand price, the price at which 400,000 apartments could
just be filled, is $500.

results in a larger quantity demanded. Equivalently, the greater the quantity of
apartments that consumers have, the lower is the value that consumers place on the
last unit purchased—the lower the demand price. Therefore, to induce consumers
to buy a larger quantity, price must go down. Price must go down because the value
of one more unit is less than the value of the previous one. Why is this so? Why
does the demand price fall? In the market for apartments, the demand price falls
because the first apartments are rented by people that place the greatest value on

them. If the price is $500, the only people willing to rent apartments are those who value them at a minimum of $500. To get more people to want to rent apartments, to increase the quantity demanded, people who value them at less than $500 must want to rent them. But that happens only if the price is less than $500.

In this regard, it is helpful to think about individual demand. For instance, as you consume additional scoops of ice cream per day, what happens to your demand price? How much do you value the fourth scoop of ice cream compared to the first scoop? A thought experiment tells us that the most that we would pay for an additional scoop falls as the amount that we have already consumed rises. So as quantity increases, the demand price falls, implying that an individual's demand curve for ice cream has a negative slope. It makes sense that the market demand curve, which is made up of all of the individual demand curves, also would have a negative slope.

The demand schedule, the demand curve, demand price, and the law of demand help us to understand one side of a market. To understand market coordination, it is also necessary to understand the other side—the supply side.

SUPPLY   To understand the supply of apartments in Gotham City, suppose that construction technology and the prices of land, construction materials, and labor are fixed. Suppose also that the alternatives available to people who might build and place apartments on the market do not change. For instance, the profitability of supplying office space is assumed to be constant. Holding these and other variables affecting cost constant, the number of apartments that landlords plan to supply depends upon the monthly rent that they expect to receive.

The *supply schedule* gives the number of apartments per month that landlords plan to supply at each alternative price. Like the demand schedule, the supply schedule exists for the given levels of other variables—here, construction technology, resource and materials prices, and profitability of other alternatives available to landlords and potential landlords. Changes in these other variables create a new supply schedule. The supply schedule in Table 1.2 shows that landlords plan to supply 400,000 apartments if the rental price is $300 per month and to supply 475,000 apartments if the price is $350. If the expected price increases from $300 to $350 per month, the quantity supplied increases from 400,000 to 475,000.

The **supply curve** is constructed and interpreted in the same way as the demand curve. (It will be useful for you to use the supply schedule to draw a supply curve, which you can later compare with Figure 1.2.) Suppose the market price is $450. The supply schedule or curve shows that the quantity supplied is 625,000. If the market price is $450, landlords would supply any quantity up to 625,000. They will not voluntarily supply more than 625,000.

The **supply price** aids in understanding why landlords are willing to supply fewer than 625,000 apartments, but not more than that quantity. The supply price—$450—is exactly sufficient to get landlords to supply a specified quantity. If the actual price is less than the supply price, say $449, the quantity supplied will be fewer than 625,000 apartments. At an actual price of $450, the 625,000th unit will be supplied. The lower price is not sufficient to get any landlord to supply the 625,000th apartment because it does not both cover the cost of production and provide an acceptable surplus (rate of return) to anyone who might

Supply Curve
A curve (line) showing the quantity supplied of a good for each possible price, holding other factors that affect supply constant.

Supply Price
The price that is exactly sufficient to get producers to sell a specified quantity. It is the minimum acceptable price for the last unit, just covering its cost of production.

A SUPPLY
SCHEDULE OF
APARTMENTS IN
GOTHAM CITY

TABLE 1.2

	Price (Monthly Rent per Apartment)	Quantity (Apartments per Month)
A	$500	700,000
B	450	625,000
C	400	550,000
D	350	475,000
E	300	400,000
F	250	325,000
G	200	250,000

The supply schedule gives the number of apartments per month that landlords would supply at each alternative price. It exists for given values of other variables: construction technology, resources and materials prices, and profitability of alternatives. If the price is $300 per month, the quantity of apartments supplied per month is 400,000. If the price is $350 per month, the quantity supplied is 475,000.

supply the apartment. The supply price, $450, is the price that is just sufficient to get the last unit to the market. It exactly covers the opportunity cost (which includes an acceptable surplus or rate of return) of producing the last unit. The **opportunity cost,** in turn, is the value of what the resources—land, labor, construction materials, the owners' contribution, and so on—could have produced in their next best use. So the supply price is the minimum price that any producer would accept for supplying the last unit. The producer would be happy to receive a price higher than the supply price for the last unit because that would provide a greater return than necessary.

Opportunity Cost
The value of the best alternative given up when a choice is made.

Inspection of the supply curve in Figure 1.2 shows that the supply price increases as quantity increases. Thus the greater the quantity supplied, the greater the opportunity cost per unit. An example helps to understand why this happens. Suppose that more apartments are built and rented in Gotham City. In the process, workers and materials would be attracted from the production of other things and perhaps from other cities. The opportunity cost of these new workers and materials is the value of what they currently produce. Workers and materials would be attracted first from the least valuable of their current uses. Perhaps they are attracted from building yet another amusement park that would just barely be profitable. Both the opportunity cost and wages necessary to attract the new workers might not be much higher than those of the workers currently producing apartments. But as apartment construction increases even more, workers and materials might be attracted from the construction of new health care facilities that are in greater demand than the amusement parks. Opportunity costs would be higher and the wage necessary to attract the workers would also be higher. The opportunity cost of producing additional apartments increases because the addi-

FIGURE 1.2

A Supply Curve for Apartments in Gotham City

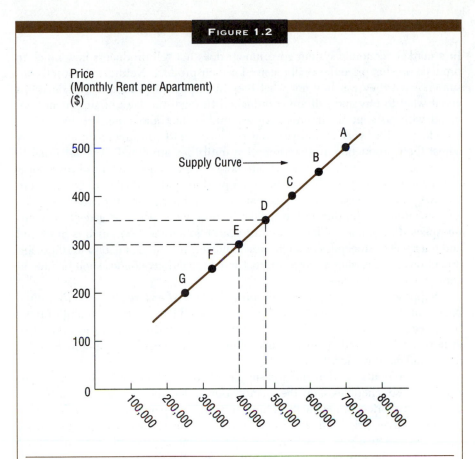

The supply curve shows the quantity supplied of apartments per month at each alternative price. It is plotted from the supply schedule in Table 1.2. At point E, price is $300 per apartment per month and quantity supplied is 400,000 apartments per month. The diagram can also illustrate the supply price. The supply price is the price that would have to be paid to put a certain quantity of apartments on the market. If 400,000 apartments are on the market, the lowest price that any supplier would accept for the 400,000th apartment is $300. If the price were $299, the 400,000th apartment would not be supplied. The supply price therefore is $300.

tional workers must be attracted from uses with increasingly higher values. It is this relationship that leads to the **law of supply**—namely, holding other variables constant, the quantity supplied of a product is positively related to its price.

Now we put our understanding of the supply side of the market—the supply schedule, the supply curve, the supply price, and the law of supply—together with our understanding of the demand side. The two parts of a market interact to coordinate the plans of consumers and producers.

Law of Supply
As the price of some good changes with other factors constant, the quantity supplied for that good changes in the same direction.

PUTTING THE PIECES TOGETHER: DEMAND AND SUPPLY

In a market economic system government does not tell producers how much to produce or what price they will receive for their product. Neither does it tell consumers what they can buy nor what they must pay for products. The decisions about what to buy and sell are coordinated through the laws of supply and demand with no central direction. An astounding fact about market economies, therefore, is that year in and year out producers and consumers simultaneously adjust their production and consumption until they are equal. It is *not* usual to have excessive stockpiles of fruit or automobiles at the end of a typical year; nor is it usual to have people willing to pay for a product and be unable to get it. There are exceptions, however, because producers sometimes get their plans wrong. Examples often pop up during the holiday season, when a toy or gadget becomes unexpectedly popular. (What was it last year?) Sometimes too much is produced and unexpected stockpiles of an item accumulate. In a market economy, these are exceptions; history shows, however, that in command economies such failures of coordination are the rule.

Suppose a supercomputer were programmed to ensure that the 15 million people of the New York metropolitan area received the great assortment of fresh fruit, vegetables, and milk that they desire to buy, and that this was done with little waste. We would be amazed and rightly so. Yet a market economy does this day in and day out. How?

Table 1.3 puts the demand and supply schedules from Tables 1.1 and 1.2 together. These schedules show the quantity demanded and supplied of apartments at alternative prices. Individuals in the Gotham City apartment market do not affect the market price. They are like the potato farmer who can produce from fence row to fence row or withhold all of her potatoes from the market without changing the price of potatoes. They are also like the shopper who can spend all or none of his money on potatoes, again without affecting the price of potatoes. They are *price takers*.

Excess Demand
A situation in which quantity demanded exceeds quantity supplied at a given price.

If the market price is $300 a month, the quantity demanded of apartments is 700,000 a month and the quantity supplied is 400,000. At $300 the quantity demanded by consumers is greater than the quantity supplied by producers; this is an example of **excess demand.** People want more apartments than are available; landlords notice that they have unsatisfied customers. Someone will ask or offer a higher price (rent). Landlords will find that they are still able to rent their apartments at the higher price. As the price increases, the quantity demanded decreases—the law of demand. In addition, as the price increases, landlords will figure out ways to supply more apartments. The quantity supplied increases. As price goes up, the quantity that people plan to buy decreases and the quantity that other people plan to sell increases. Initially, the plans of consumers and producers were not coordinated. But as the price increases, the plans converge. At a price of $400 per month, the quantity demanded and the quantity supplied of apartments are equal—550,000. (Work out on paper what happens if the market price is $450 a month.) The excess demand that exists at the lower price is auto-

TABLE 1.3		
Price (Monthly Rent per Apartment)	Quantity Demanded (Apartments per Month)	Quantity Supplied (Apartments per Month)
$500	400,000	700,000
450	475,000	625,000
400	550,000	550,000
350	625,000	475,000
300	700,000	400,000
250	775,000	325,000
200	850,000	250,000

The demand and supply schedules for apartments help us see how the plans of consumers and producers are coordinated in a market economy. Each individual consumer or producer assumes that the market price is outside his or her control, so these consumers and producers adjust their quantity demanded or quantity supplied to the market price. Suppose the market price is $250. Consumers wish to rent 775,000 apartments per month. But landlords will not place that many on the market. They are willing to supply only 325,000. Excess demand of 450,000 will push price up. As price increases, quantity demanded falls and quantity supplied increases. The originally inconsistent plans of consumers and producers come together as price adjusts. At a price of $400, the plans are exactly coordinated. Quantity demanded equals quantity supplied. The equilibrium quantity exchanged is 550,000 apartments.

DEMAND AND SUPPLY SCHEDULES FOR APARTMENTS IN GOTHAM CITY

matically eliminated if the price of apartments is flexible. The price system coordinates the plans of consumers and producers.

Figure 1.3 puts the demand and supply curves of Figures 1.1 and 1.2 together. Suppose the market price is $500 a month. Table 1.3 shows that the quantity demanded is 400,000 apartments per month and that the quantity supplied is 700,000 per month. The situation is one of **excess supply** because quantity supplied exceeds quantity demanded. The excess is 300,000 apartments: 700,000 minus 400,000. In the figure it is measured by the distance from A to B—AB. Many landlords have vacant apartments. Although the apartments are vacant, the landlords have to pay taxes and perhaps make mortgage payments. They will try to entice consumers into the apartments by offering a lower price. The quantity demanded will increase. Some young people, for example, might decide to establish independent households because of the lower price. As the price falls, some landlords might decide to use their buildings for something other than apartments. The quantity supplied decreases.

Suppose the existing price is $300. As an exercise, use Figure 1.3 to explain to yourself why the price will increase. Your exercise and the example in the previous paragraph show that if the market price results in excess demand, the price

Excess Supply
A situation in which quantity supplied exceeds quantity demanded at a given price.

DEMAND AND SUPPLY CURVES FOR APARTMENTS IN GOTHAM CITY

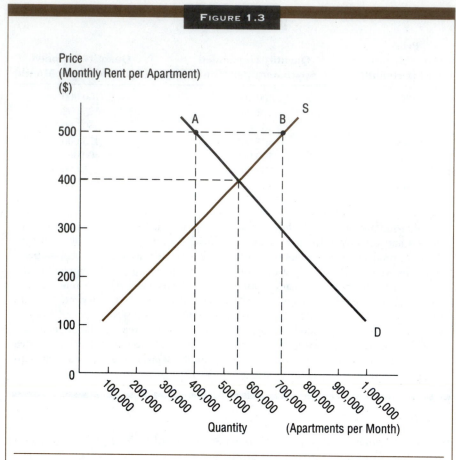

FIGURE 1.3

Suppose the price is $500 per apartment per month. The figure shows that the quantity supplied at that price is 700,000 apartments per month and that the quantity demanded is 400,000. The difference is an excess supply of 300,000 apartments. This excess supply can be measured by the distance from A to B—AB.

Equilibrium
A state of rest for the economy or market. Market equilibrium occurs at the price at which quantity demanded equals quantity supplied—the equilibrium quantity exchanged.

will increase and if it results in excess supply, the price will decrease. The market price continues to adjust until the quantity demanded equals the quantity supplied—until the market is in **equilibrium.** An equilibrium is a situation that will continue indefinitely unless some outside force affecting the situation changes. The price, $400, which equates the quantity demanded and the quantity supplied, is the *equilibrium price*. The quantity demanded and supplied (550,000) at that price is the equilibrium *quantity exchanged*.

This emergence of equilibrium is the essence of market coordination. It allows a market system to determine how much of each good to produce and how to produce it. Moreover, the market system accomplishes these tasks without a central plan. The essence of a command economy—a planned economy—is that government orders individuals to produce certain goods and services. These orders are laws. In other words, in a command economy a central plan puts legal obligations on people to obey it. In a market economy, on the other hand, government establishes rules of behavior. Given these rules of behavior, individuals decide what goods to produce and how to produce them.

COMPARATIVE SYSTEMS: AN INTRODUCTORY SKETCH

This section discusses coordination through the price system in a market economy and compares it with coordination in a command economy. In addition, it shows that many coordination problems of a command economy are similar to problems that arise if government prevents price adjustments in a market economy. The chapter then turns to a discussion of the transition of the former planned economies to market economies.

THE PRICE SYSTEM

A comparison of a market economy with a command economy—capitalism versus centrally planned socialism—is *not* a comparison of no planning with planning. Planning occurs in any economy. The difference is who does the planning that coordinates economic activity, and how plans are enforced. In a command economy, government plans what and how to produce. The plan is enforced by law. In a market economy, individuals plan. As students, you plan your education: courses, major, and graduate school. In a command economy, your choices might not be allowed if they were inconsistent with the plan. Similarly, as consumers, you plan what to buy, given the prices of consumer goods, your income, and your preferences. In a command economy, your choices might not be permitted if they are not consistent with the plan. In the former Soviet Union, you could have wanted to buy a car and may have had the money to pay for it, but you might have waited ten years to get one because the plan did not call for enough new cars. As a producer, you plan how and how much to produce based on expected profitability. In a command economy, the manager of a state-owned enterprise produces according to the central plan and uses techniques imposed by the central planners.

We assume that in a market economy consumers attempt to maximize their satisfaction, and producers attempt to maximize their profits. A competitive market has many consumers and producers. No single consumer or small group of consumers has any noticeable effect on the market price. Consequently, a single consumer does not worry that the price of a good, say, housing, will go up if he or she buys more housing. In competitive markets, consumers are price takers, which means that they accept market prices as given.

Similarly, competitive producers attempt to maximize their profits. They also are price takers. No single housing producer or small group of housing producers has any noticeable effect on market price. Consequently, a competitive producer does not worry that the price of housing may fall if he or she attempts to sell more.

There are two exceptions. First, suppose there is only a single producer of a product in a market, such as electricity. This single producer realizes that to sell more electricity, the price must fall. Consequently, a single producer affects the price when he or she decides how much to sell.

Second, what applies to a single competitive producer does not apply to all producers. One housing producer does not noticeably affect the price of houses, even by increasing production by 10 percent. Suppose, however, each of 10,000 producers puts 10 percent more on the market. To sell this many more houses, the price must fall. This fact, however, will not affect the output decisions of individual producers. Whether an individual producer produces more or less will have no effect on the production decisions of other producers because no one expects a single producer to be able to affect market price. Because a producer decides what to produce based on market price, producers do not respond to what another producer does. For instance, suppose that Henry decides to produce 20 percent more houses. His decision does not affect how many houses Anne or other housing producers plan to produce. Consequently, the individual competitive producer is a price taker even though all producers acting together affect market price.

In a competitive market, all participants are price takers. They take the market price as given. Given their circumstances, their economic choices are simply how much to produce and consume.

INFORMATION, RATIONING, AND MOTIVATION IN A MARKET ECONOMY

PRICES AS INFORMATION   In a market economy, prices play several roles: they inform, they ration, and they motivate. These roles are crucial elements in the coordination of consumer and producer plans. The price system informs producers and consumers about underlying changes in the economy. For instance, an increase in price signals that a good has become more valuable; it does not matter if this price increase is because consumers demand more or producers produce less. The price system also provides incentives that motivate consumers and producers to adjust to those changes. These incentives provide the motivation for change: conservation and increased production.

Suppose the apartment market in Gotham City is in equilibrium. In Figure 1.4, the equilibrium price and quantity are P_0 and Q_0. Now suppose demand increases unexpectedly from D_0 to D_1. Perhaps population increases. In any city, some people are moving out while others are moving in. Consequently, it will not be immediately obvious that population and therefore demand have increased. The immediate effect of the increased demand for apartments may be simply that they rent more quickly and vacancy rates fall. Excess demand of $Q_1 - Q_0$ develops.

The effect of the increase in demand is to raise the demand price for the quantity Q_0 from P_0 to P_1. There may be no immediate increase in the quantity supplied. If we assume no change in quantity supplied, the market price will rise to P_1, the demand price. The excess demand disappears. This price increase informs people that apartments have become more scarce.

FIGURE 1.4

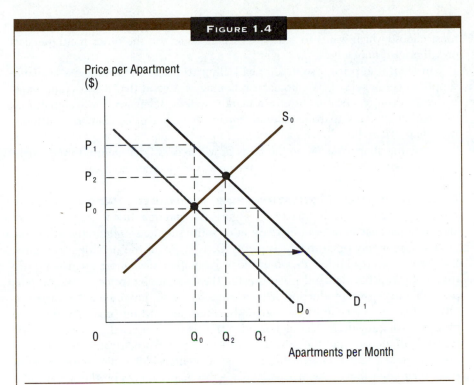

With the demand and supply curves D_0 and S_0, the equilibrium price and quantity in the apartment market are P_0 and Q_0. An increase in demand to D_1 disturbs the original equilibrium. The immediate effect may be no change in quantity and an increase in price to P_1. The increased price rations the original quantity of apartments to consumers who are willing to pay the most for it. P_0, however, is the opportunity cost of producing an additional apartment. With the market price, P_1, above the opportunity cost, producers can profit by expanding output. Ultimately, the price increase motivates producers to expand output.

RATIONING OF EXISTING APARTMENTS   The higher price informs consumers that housing is now more expensive. If they expect the price increase to be permanent, the original residents of the town will reduce the quantity they demand of housing. Similarly, the new residents will demand a lower quantity at the higher price than at the lower price. In short, consumers automatically respond to more expensive apartments by reducing the quantity demanded. They conserve because it is to their advantage to do so.

People will choose to live in more crowded conditions, but this does not mean that excess demand exists—it means that increased scarcity has caused the equilibrium price to go up.

The distinction between excess demand and increased scarcity is important. **Scarcity** is the economic condition common to all societies. It simply means that,

Scarcity
The common situation for all economies: aggregate wants exceed the ability to meet them.

in the aggregate, our wants exceed our abilities to meet them. Consequently, we must choose which wants to satisfy. Excess demand, on the other hand, persists only if price cannot adjust.

Ration
To allocate a limited supply of goods and services to people.

In short, the price system automatically **rations,** or allocates, the available supply to consumers. This automatic rationing of a good that has become more scarce is a controversial feature of a market system. It means, for example, that the market allocates apartments impersonally. A higher price changes consumption plans. Those people who are willing to pay the most for the good get it. But the rationing of apartments on the basis of willingness (and ability) to pay might result in people living in what others perceive as inadequate housing.

PROFITS AS THE MOTIVATION FOR INCREASED PRODUCTION OF APARTMENTS

At a price of P_1 (Figure 1.4) and quantity of Q_0, provision of an additional apartment—an increase in quantity supplied—generates economic profits. The supply price for the quantity Q_0 is P_0. With the new demand curve D_1, the new demand price, P_1, would clear the market, if no more apartments are supplied. With the demand price greater than the supply price, however, it is profitable to expand production. This is because the supply price is the opportunity cost of one more unit. Consequently, either an existing producer or a new producer will provide it. The higher price signals the increased scarcity of apartments to producers, and the possibility of earning profits *motivates* them to produce more apartments. Producing more apartments yields a higher return than producing other things. As producers place more apartments on the market, the price falls.

So long as the demand price is greater than the supply price, profits are made by producing more. The increase in quantity supplied moves the market to a new equilibrium with price P_2 and quantity Q_2. The producers compete for profits by producing more apartments. As they produce the additional apartments, price falls; beyond the quantity Q_2, profits cannot be earned by producing additional housing. It is ironic that the pursuit of profits under competitive conditions eventually eliminates the opportunity for additional profits.

The increased demand in the apartment market automatically causes increased demand in input markets. Increases in construction wages, for instance, signal greater job opportunities, motivating people to become construction workers. If input prices change, the cost of production of other goods changes. So the effect of the increased demand for and therefore increased scarcity of apartments ripples into other markets. In each market, as price changes, individuals adapt their plans to new conditions. Price changes are the signals for individuals to change their plans; profits are the motivation.

INFORMATION, RATIONING, AND MOTIVATION IN A COMMAND ECONOMY

In a command economy, even if the central planners want to respond to the desires of consumers, adjustment to changes in demand and supply is necessarily slower and subject to larger error than in a market economy. If the demand for apartments in a particular area increases, the central planners could respond, as the market does, by allowing rent to increase and building more apartments. But such a price increase would meet political resistance from existing tenants. Furthermore, price increases would be necessary for the inputs, such as bricks and mortar, used to produce apartments. This, in turn, would require price changes for other products. So, excess demand develops.

RATIONING OF EXISTING APARTMENTS   In the former Soviet Union the State Committee on Prices set about 500,000 prices. It was not feasible to change the price of some products without changing other prices. Because it is inordinately expensive to set 500,000 prices, prices there did not change often. Many prices did not change more than once every ten years. Thus, prices could not provide appropriate information about scarcity and opportunity cost to consumers and producers, and they could not ration available supply. Excess demand and excess supply did not disappear because prices did not adjust. For instance, in the Soviet Union excess demand for apartments persisted for years. Young couples, even those who could afford separate housing, had to live with their parents and perhaps others in small apartments. There were exceptions. The Communist Party and the government took care of their own. People with political influence got apartments. It was who you knew that counted, not what you would pay, unless you were willing to pay bribes.

The market price system, by contrast, is anonymous. An increase in demand causes price to rise automatically and leads the economy to a new equilibrium. Since the price increase is the result of the adjustments of many individual planners, no single entity can be blamed for the price increase. In a command economy, on the other hand, a price increase must be permitted by the central planners. The central planning agency or the government, therefore, will be blamed for it.

For at least two reasons, prices do not change often in a command economy. First, it is costly to change prices, because even a single price change leads to many other price changes. Second, it can be costly politically to increase the price of such things as apartments. Thus, in a command economy, the central planners often make no price response to an increase in demand.

THE MOTIVATION FOR INCREASED PRODUCTION OF APARTMENTS
Problems would persist in a command economy even if the planners allowed price to rise. It would take a long time to set the new prices. The higher prices would result in economic profits. But in a command economy producers usually do not share in these profits, which undermines their motivation to increase production. One of the reforms often tried in command economies is to let producers share in profits so they will be motivated to follow price and profit signals.

Alternatively, the central planners could order the production of more apartments. They first must be sure, however, that the demand increase is permanent. If not, they could make a serious error. In a market economy, if an individual planner expands production, that planner bears the consequences. If the decision is a good one, the person profits. If not, the person bears the loss. Normally, the effects on the market would be inconsequential because one producer has little effect on the entire market. When central planners make a decision, however, they necessarily affect the entire market. If the decision is a good one, the planners get little credit. (The politicians take the credit). If they err, there could easily be too many apartments. Moreover, the error is easily traced to their planning decision, making it easy to penalize them. As a result, central planners may be reluctant to make significant changes. The risks associated with inaction may be less than the risks of action. In other words, for the market producer, it's heads, I win; tails, I lose. For the central planner, it's heads, other people win; tails, I lose.

The ability of a command economy to adjust to economic changes is limited. Political factors limit the price or output adjustments that can be made, and the information requirements for adjusting to economic changes are enormous. They include information about the market in question and about related markets. Because profits usually do not go legally to planners or production managers, the motivation for change is often political rather than economic. On the other hand, a market economy with decentralized planning based on a price system does not require a large bureaucracy for central planning. It does not need centralized information about individual markets. And it has a built-in incentive system. Nevertheless, in some cities in market economies people have the same trouble renting apartments as others had in the former Soviet Union. Some people in New York City are unable to rent the apartments they want, although they are willing to pay the asking price. Some people are prevented from renting apartments because of their race, and others get them through bribes. Such situations arise most frequently in command economics and market economies with price controls.

INFORMATION, RATIONING, AND MOTIVATION: PRICE CEILINGS

Price Ceiling
A government law or regulation that sets a maximum price that can be charged for a good or service.

In many cities throughout the world, excess demand for apartments is a way of life. It is no coincidence that most of these cities have price ceilings. A **price ceiling** is a government law or regulation that sets the highest price that can legally be charged for a good. In apartment markets, a price ceiling is often called a rent control.

Rent controls in New York City and Cairo, Egypt, cause shortages in those cities. Apartment shortages do not exist in Atlanta, Georgia, or Cairo, Illinois, cities that do not have rent controls.

If they are imposed, rent controls usually are imposed during periods of increasing scarcity. Scarcity can increase with unexpected increases in demand because new construction does not immediately accompany a demand increase. This increases market price. When the price of rental housing goes up, renters either have to pay the higher rent or leave their apartment homes.

Renters, of course, object. They receive no increase in the amount or quality of their housing; the landlord adds no new appliances, and no free day care center becomes available. The landlord simply profits. Not surprisingly, enough political support often develops to get rent controls enacted. The intent may be to help renters, particularly low-income renters, have decent housing. But what are the consequences?

Figure 1.5 represents an apartment market. The demand for rental housing is D_0 and its supply is S_0. In equilibrium, the price is P_0 and the quantity is Q_0. Landlords make no profits on the last unit produced. Suppose now that the city council has passed a law that the highest price that can be charged for an apartment is P_0. The law has no effect because P_0 is the equilibrium price.

But suppose demand increases to D_1. At the price P_0, the quantity demanded of apartments is Q_1. The number of apartments demanded is greater than the number supplied, Q_0. Excess demand of $Q_1 - Q_0$ exists. But no one will supply more. The demand price is greater than the supply price, meaning that there is a profitable opportunity to increase quantity supplied. By law, however,

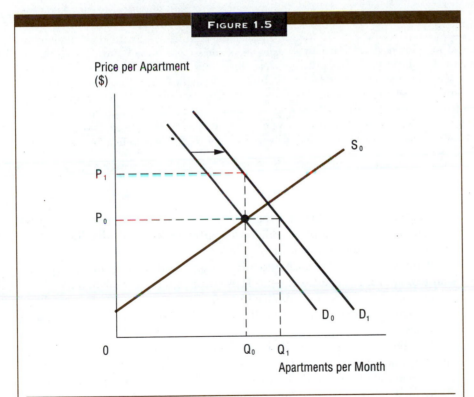

FIGURE 1.5

RENT CONTROLS IN THE APARTMENT MARKET

Suppose the market is at equilibrium with price and quantity of P_0 and Q_0. Then a law is passed that price cannot be above P_0. Now suppose demand increases to D_1. The price control is effective, and an excess demand of $Q_1 - Q_0$ exists. Landlords can ration on the basis of personal characteristics. If the price control is evaded, the under-the-counter price may increase to P_1.

CAN SOCIALISM USE THE PRICE SYSTEM?

Some leaders of former communist countries want to keep elements of central planning while moving their economies to a price system. Presumably, they are searching for the benefits of the price system—coordination, motivation and incentives, information, and rationing—while maintaining the political power that comes from central planning. Or perhaps they want to maintain the power to reduce income inequality—a major stated goal of socialism.

THE COORDINATION PROBLEM

The early opponents of socialism doubted that a centrally planned economy (CPE) could calculate prices that cleared markets. The ability to clear markets is one of the great achievements of a price system. Indeed, the price system can be thought of as a supercomputer calculating prices that coordinate plans of producers and consumers. Today, many people argue

that appropriate ingenuity combined with the great capacity of supercomputers means that CPEs can solve the calculation problem.

But CPE history is not encouraging. For instance, excess demands for housing and some kinds of food were characteristic of the former Soviet Union. Planners were unable or unwilling to set equilibrium prices. Even if modern computers enable the computation of appropriate prices, central planners may have political reasons for not using them.

THE INCENTIVE PROBLEM

Suppose that a socialist system solves the coordination problem. Can it have incentives that motivate people to respond appropriately—to reallocate resources to consumers' most desired uses? First, prices must reflect opportunity costs. Under central planning, Poland, in Northern Europe, exported semitropical flowers. It priced energy so low that it was profitable to grow flowers in artificially heated greenhouses. The opportunity cost of these flowers was greater than their market price. But they were grown and exported

no tenant can pay more than P_0, the supply price, for another unit. Because of the price ceiling, the cost of an additional apartment is greater than the revenue that can legally be received from it.

Many people who are unable to rent because of the excess demand place a value greater than P_0 on an apartment. These frustrated renters might offer existing tenants more than the controlled price to sublet their apartments. Although illegal, this happens in market economies with price ceilings just as it does in command economies.

The actual operation of a market with rent controls is much more complex and has various associated costs. One cost is limited mobility. Over time, some of the rent-controlled apartments become vacant. People move to other cities or decide to buy a house. They die. But people do not move to other apartments in the city. Why? Because the excess demand means they may not be able to find another apartment at such a low rent. If they stay in their apartment, they have a good deal, even if the apartment is "too small" or "too large" for the family. If they move to another apartment, their housing costs may rise substantially.

Another cost is illegal activity. Something other than the price system must ration the available supply to consumers, given the price ceiling. Landlords will because the subsidized energy prices hid their opportunity cost.

Second, people must be rewarded for following price signals. That is, CPEs must pay people according to the value of what they produce and allow them to make huge profits in return for developing lower-cost production methods or new products. Because one purpose of socialism is to narrow wage and income differences, it has difficulty with such an incentive system. In short, socialists are often unwilling to adopt policies that guide people toward economically appropriate behavior.

THE INFORMATION PROBLEM

Giant strides in economic growth in capitalist economies have raised the material condition of ordinary people beyond that of the upper class two centuries ago. This growth has occurred in economies where entrepreneurs *respond* to market prices that relay appropriate information about profitable opportunities. Relaying appropriate information, is the essence of solving the coordination and incentive problems.

Entrepreneurs take the information and develop new processes and products. The price system then relays information to potential users about the new processes and products. This information flow—derived from prices—is essential for economic growth.

Perhaps CPEs can solve the calculation and incentive problems, but the information problem is the most challenging. Many economists argue that if the leaders of former CPEs want economies that generate progress, these leaders must abandon the idea of salvaging elements of central planning. Only in economies where the price system relays accurate information have entrepreneurs like Walt Disney, Henry Ford, Bill Gates, and Oprah Winfrey initiated persistent economic growth.

---

*Source: see Don Lavoie, "Computation, Incentives, and Discovery: The Cognitive Function of Markets in Market Socialism" in *Privatizing and Marketizing Socialism*, special ed., Jan. S. Prybyla, ed. Richard D. Lambert, *The Annals of The American Academy of Political and Social Science* 507 (January 1990), 72–79, for a detailed discussion.

---

accept some price above P_0. Consumers are willing to pay a price up to P_1. If the transaction takes place at a price above P_0, it will be illegal even though it is voluntary and makes both parties better off. Making voluntary exchanges between buyer and seller illegal has created criminals for centuries. The Roman emperor Diocletian imposed price controls in A.D. 301. His Edict of Maximum Prices set maximum prices, wages, and transportation costs throughout the Roman Empire. Incentives to violate the edict were so great that Diocletian used capital punishment in an effort to enforce the controls. Similar penalties were sometimes used in the former Soviet Union.

Under rent controls, landlords and consumers have incentives to break the law. The simplest action is under-the-counter payments. Other devices to evade the law include key money, furniture rental, and security deposits. (Perhaps you can figure out how these normal business practices can be used to evade the law.) In short, the available supply might be rationed on the basis of who is willing to make the largest illegal payment.

Discrimination is a third cost. Landlords are in a position to ration based on the personal characteristics of potential tenants. Because of the excess demand in a rent-controlled market, they have many prospective tenants for each vacancy.

They can reject many applicants and still rent their apartments without delay. Given excess demand, even if it is illegal to do so, they might reject applicants on the basis of racial or national origin, sex, religion, marital status, presence of children, or the practice of alternative lifestyles.

Of course, they also can do this in an uncontrolled market. The rejection of prospective tenants in such a market, however, has a cost. The waiting list is not as long. Rejecting an applicant means that the apartment may remain vacant. It costs money to refuse financially qualified applicants.

The price control sidesteps the automatic rationing of the uncontrolled price system. Just as in apartment markets in the former Soviet Union, the automatic rationing of the price system is replaced with nonprice rationing. The latter provides incentives for sellers and buyers to circumvent the price control with actions—illegal payments, fake security deposits, and so on—that violate the spirit if not the letter of the law. Nonprice rationing also results in rationing on the basis of buyers' personal characteristics. Discrimination based on race, religion, and family characteristics replaces the impersonal rationing of the uncontrolled price system.

Finally, in the controlled market, no legal incentive exists to motivate producers to produce more housing. The purpose of price controls is often to eliminate profits. But profits provide the motivation for increased production. Although the existence of excess demand provides a signal to producers, the elimination of profit destroys their motivation to increase production.

In reality, the imposition of rent controls usually takes place in a different manner. After a period of rapid rent increases, government rolls back the rent increases to some earlier, "normal" level. Some producers then find that they are unable to make a normal rate of earnings. Over time, they find it advantageous to shift their investment to other activities. To do so, they receive rents but put nothing, or as little as possible, into maintenance and repair. This reduction in quality is equivalent to a price increase for a unit of constant quality. This is a common response to price controls, similar to keeping the price of a chocolate bar constant and reducing its size. Finally, as the unit gets closer to being unrentable—either for legal reasons or because no one will pay to live in it—the owners stop paying the property tax. After several years, they simply abandon it. They have taken as much out of the house as possible. It then is vacant, becoming a firetrap or a crack house.

Another alternative for landlords is to convert apartments into condominiums.[5] After the landlords have done some remodeling, they sell the units to people who want to own rather than rent. Doing so evades the price or rent controls, which usually apply only to rental housing. The condominium prices can be quite high. Although the existing renters usually have an option to buy, they frequently do not want to or financially cannot. Often the political support for rent controls comes from the unwillingness to let high rents push people out of their apartment homes. But condominium conversion has exactly that effect. So, in the end,

---

[5]Some cities with rent controls prohibit this conversion. This prohibition is an example of the additional legislation that becomes necessary when governments impose price controle

a policy designed to keep renters from being priced out of their apartment homes does so anyway.

The city government often recognizes that the excess demand for rental housing is serious. It also recognizes that the rent controls cause the excess demand. It may respond by exempting new apartments from the rent-control law. But once a city has imposed rent controls, potential builders of new apartments often fear future rent controls, causing them to charge higher rents in order to get their return while the getting is good.

Systems and Coordination

This discussion of the provision of apartments in different economic systems shows that a market system provides goods to people based on their willingness (including ability) to pay. Command economies and market economies with price controls are much less successful in coordinating demand and supply. They run into similar problems of excess demand (shortages) and of allocation of apartments and other goods to people in response to bribes or on the basis of personal characteristics rather than what they will pay.

Market systems successfully coordinate economic activity. Price falls in response to excess supply and rises in response to excess demand so as to equate the quantity demanded and supplied of a good. A market system coordinates the interdependent actions of specialized producers; it does not require a legally imposed central plan to do so. It fosters the division of labor that is responsible for increasing the "wealth of nations."

Historical experience shows that command economies have great difficulty in coordinating economic activity. They do not have a market economy's ability to automatically and inexpensively collect information about consumer preferences and production capabilities. Neither do they share the capability to automatically and inexpensively provide incentives and motivation for people to make wealth-promoting decisions. Prices do all of this in a market economy. The imposition of government price controls, however, eliminates much of a market economy's capability to coordinate economic activity. The next section briefly discusses experiences of some former communist countries in their struggle to transform their command economies to market economies.

Transitions to a Market Economy: Some Experiences

This chapter identifies five pieces of a market economic system that the former centrally planned economies must put together to become market economies. Unfortunately for these so-called transition economies, these are not five easy pieces and all pieces have to be in place at about the same time. To work well, a market economy or price system must have reasonably stable prices. Second, it must have a system of private property rights that defines the rules of economic transactions. Third, and remember that the order is unimportant because all pieces must be in place, it must allow the rewards and penalties of the price system to motivate decision makers—market incentives. Fourth, prices must be allowed to fluctuate in response to demand and supply, so that they convey information accurately and ration available supplies. Finally, its legal system must be broadly obeyed and its culture must generate a climate of trust.

We discuss the progress of several transition economies in terms of these five pieces. We must recognize that many of these countries are still in the transition phase and the situation that we describe now (in late 1996) may change by the time you read this. Several countries in Central Europe, including the Czech Republic, Hungary, and Poland, have created market economies. Others, including Belarus, Kazakhstan, and Ukraine, have a long way to go. Russia lies between the extremes. These countries' different rates of transition depend upon history, politics, tradition, and the economic situation when the transition began.

INFLATION

Many of the countries that abandoned communism did so in the presence of extreme economic distress. Economic growth had stagnated, and there was excess demand for many products—apartments, cars, and so on—because of inflexible prices. Inflation and unemployment, however, were generally low under central planning. Inflation was low because prices were held down by law, by plan, and by inertia. Prices did not reflect the scarcity of goods and services. Unemployment was low because many people had make-work jobs where the value of what they produced was less than the cost of production. As prices were freed, the suppressed inflation exploded, hidden unemployment became open, unemployment grew, and production fell drastically. These countries faced extremely difficult and painful economic problems. Initially, they had the pain of the transition without the rewards of a market economy. It is only recently that some countries have begun to see the rewards.

Figure 1.6 describes the transition for Poland and Romania. Poland attempted a rapid transition to a market economy. In 1990, in the early part of the transition, its annual inflation rate was almost 600 percent. If the price of potatoes, say, was 10 zlotys (the Polish monetary unit) per pound at the end of 1989, at the end of 1990 it was 70 zlotys. This rapid inflation damaged the information function of prices. As Figure 1.6 shows, the annual inflation rate in 1991 was below 100 percent—prices didn't quite double—and has continued to fall gradually to about 20 percent. This rapid inflation followed by a reduction in inflation is characteristic of using the "shock treatment" to transform the economy. The negative growth—decline—in output and the rise in unemployment are characteristic of an economy in transition from central planning to markets. Starting in 1992, Poland's output has increased every year through 1996. The shock treatment initially was very costly, but output growth began quickly. The Czech Republic, Estonia, and Slovenia have followed a pattern similar to Poland's.

Romania has followed a more gradual path to a market economy. Its output fell more in 1992 than in 1991 or 1990. It was also not until 1992 that Romania's

FIGURE 1.6

THE TRANSITION:
SELECTED
COUNTRIES

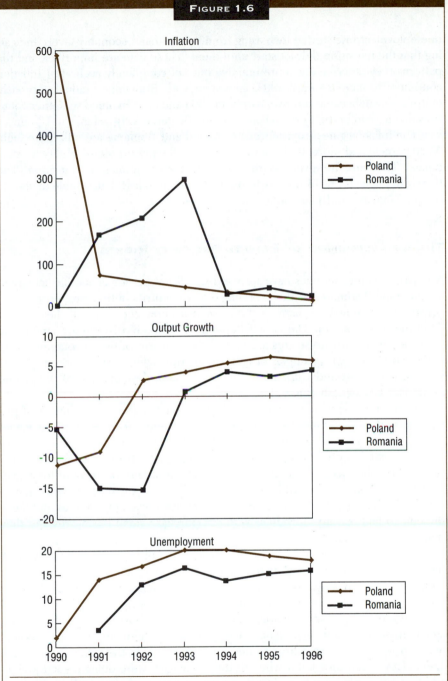

The three panels provide a snapshot of the transitions of the Polish and Romanian economies. The top panel shows that Poland quickly brought inflation down, whereas Romania had increasing inflation followed by a cut in the inflation rate. Perhaps because its transition began earlier, Poland's output growth rate recovered faster, but both economies have experienced high unemployment rates since the beginning of the transition.

unemployment rate started increasing from its command economy levels, indicating that the transition did not start until then. (These data are imperfect, and the patterns they describe are representative but not completely accurate.) Inflation continued to increase until 1993, consistent with Romania's gradual approach. Output growth became positive, barely, in 1993 and has remained so. Other countries that have followed a gradual path include Bulgaria, Kyrgyzstan, and Ukraine.

The inflation rates experienced by Poland and Romania are still quite high. At 20 percent and more, they continue to erode the price system's ability to coordinate. They are, however, on the low side for economies in transition. The Czech Republic is one of the few to reduce inflation to less than double digits.

THE ESTABLISHMENT OF PRIVATE PROPERTY RIGHTS

Many transition economies have sprouted significant private economic activity in a short time. Estimates of the percentage of a country's output produced in the private sector show that many of these countries now get over half their output from the private sector. The Czech Republic, Poland, and Russia are among the countries whose private sectors account for large shares of their economies. Bulgaria and Croatia are examples of countries with smaller, but important, private sectors. In Belarus and Ukraine, on the other hand, development of the private sector is still at an early stage.

There are at least two aspects to privatization and the establishment of private property rights. One is creating these rights and encouraging the development of new private businesses. Most of these former command economies have been successful in promoting and fostering new, small private businesses. Restaurants, repair shops, small manufacturing operations, and so on account for significant parts of their new private sectors. Similarly, many small state-owned enterprises (SOEs) have been turned over to private ownership. It has not been difficult to find private individuals who can purchase small businesses and then manage them effectively.

The second aspect, however, is the privatization of large SOEs. This is much more difficult. Imagine a society in which most people are completely unfamiliar with the idea of owning stock in a company like General Motors (GM). Imagine also that the people who currently manage GM were stripped of their authority and that ownership responsibilities were given to people with absolutely no management or ownership experience. The problems would be enormous. Where would people get the resources to buy stock? How could they choose new managers? How could they know whether their managers were doing a good job? In addition, many of these large SOEs provided their employees with health care, education, and recreation. It would be difficult to privatize such enterprises because they might then discontinue the social services and lay off many workers. As a result, privatization of large SOEs has been slow in many countries and almost nonexistent in others. The continued existence of large state-owned enterprises has created significant incentive problems for many transition economies.

INCENTIVES

A major problem of command economies is motivating the managers of SOEs to make sound economic decisions. A central plan might provide a target of a certain number of suits of clothes. The enterprise would be allocated workers and cloth. To ensure meeting the target, managers would have an incentive to make suits of only one size—small. Although it might seem unbelievable, such things happened under central planning. Consequently, it is important to provide the managers of these enterprises with appropriate incentives. This is also why it is so important for the transition economies to privatize their SOEs. If the enterprises are privatized, the owners presumably will be interested in profits.

Different countries have used different schemes to achieve privatization. Managers and workers have been given partial ownership of their enterprises. Citizens have been given ownership shares in enterprises. Enterprises have been sold to foreign investors. In all these situations, the owners want profits. Enterprises earn profits by producing what consumers want in a cost-effective way. If managers share in the profits through ownership, performance contracts, or in other ways, they will have an incentive to be responsive to consumer wants. They will also have incentive to use appropriate production techniques to monitor workers and to try to figure out better ways of doing things.

FLEXIBLE PRICES

Most of the countries of Central and Eastern Europe have allowed the prices of many goods to adjust to demand and supply conditions. Some countries have freed prices all at once and others have done it gradually, but, according to *The Economist* magazine, almost all have done so. Belarus and Ukraine are exceptions, having made little progress. The transition countries, however, have been slow in freeing prices of such items as electricity, housing, and public transportation. In addition, they have subsidized SOEs. Prices of essentials have been held down for humanitarian and political reasons. Allowing these prices to increase to market-clearing levels might cause distress and could cause political unrest. Nevertheless, price controls limit market coordination and impede economic restructuring. This failure to free their prices is not unique to the transition economies. As discussed in Chapter 3, government fixes many prices in the United States, including the prices of peanuts and sugar.

One purpose of the subsidies to SOEs is to prevent unemployment from increasing beyond its already high rates. Another purpose is to ensure that the SOEs continue to provide social services, such as health and education, to their employees, as they did under the previous system. Some SOEs are completely wasteful; the value of what some of them produced under central planning was actually less than the value of the resources that they used. This is probably still true in some transition countries. To keep such enterprises in operation results in significant waste and impedes economic restructuring.

INTERNATIONAL PERSPECTIVE

COWBOY CAPITALISM IN RUSSIA?

Criminal activity in Russia reminds some people of lawlessness in the Old West. After all, rustling, land grabbing, bank robbing, and other criminal activities are part of the western saga, just like the cowboy. Perhaps a new capitalist economy breeds criminal and gang activity. Certainly Russia has a significant crime problem. It might be reassuring for Russians to know that the chaotic criminal conditions that exist today are just a stage of capitalism.

Numerous gangs operate in Russia. They deal in illegal goods, they smuggle, they bribe government officials, and they force legitimate businesses to pay for protection. They divert resources, such as oil, which they get at below world-market prices, from legitimate uses and sell them on the world market. Blackmail, threats, and murder to prevent competition or to learn business secrets occur with some regularity.

It is an insult to the early settlers, however, to compare contemporary Russian lawlessness to conditions in the Old West. Because law enforcement did not spread west as fast as the settlers, criminal activity probably exceeded the norm in more established parts of the United States. Although there was respect for the rule of law that derived from a long history of established property law, vigilante groups, consisting of community leaders, operated outside the law. Superficially, this appears like gang activity. Unlike the Russian gangs, however, vigilante groups attempted to enforce the law, not victimize honest citizens.

In the early stages of capitalism in the United States, most prices were unregulated and few regulations prevented people from doing what they wanted, so long as other people were not harmed involuntarily. Unlike the situation in a command economy or in a society with price controls, unexploited gains from voluntary exchange did not exist and thus could not generate profits for gangs. Government officials did not have the power to prevent profitable activities; consequently, there was no reason to bribe them.

LEGAL SYSTEM

Each country must develop and enforce a system of contract, criminal, property, and tort law to carry out its economic transformation. These systems will differ from country to country; the different approaches to privatization provide an example of these differences. Bankruptcy law is an example of a type of law that must be developed.

Many transition economies have made little progress in creating legislation to allow private and state enterprises to become bankrupt. Bankruptcy is unpleasant. When it happens, the owners *and* their debtors lose. Financial institutions suffer. Employees of the bankrupt enterprise may lose their jobs. But bankruptcy is an important part of a market economy. It is a way that economic resources can be moved from owners who are not using them profitably to other owners who may do a better job.

One analyst claimed that too few bankruptcies is a weakness of the Czech economy. A new bankruptcy law was enacted in early 1993, but critics claimed "that the government has bought political peace by allowing inefficient and overstaffed industries to continue production. The government has certainly played a role in the lack of bankruptcies: first, by delaying the implementation of the law and sec-

Russian history is different. Bribery of government officials was routine in the Soviet Union, and it was not considered wrong. It was a way to get things done. Evading price controls also was a way of life. As a result, the respect for and trust of the legal system necessary for capitalism to work well was not generated by life in the Soviet Union to the same extent as in a society with fewer restrictions and longer experience with the rule of law.

Rather than being like the Old West, the situation in Russia is more like what began to develop in the United States during Prohibition. Prohibition made gang activity extremely profitable in the 1920s. Criminals profited from selling alcohol, some otherwise honest citizens enjoyed its consumption, and government officials profited by turning a blind eye to the situation.

No, gang activity in Russia does not result from an early state of capitalism; it is not cowboy capitalism. Furthermore, it is not something that will automatically go away. The gangs that prospered during Prohibition in the United States outlasted Prohibition by decades. They moved into illegal gambling and drug sales, and they corrupted some labor unions. Furthermore, gang activity can harm an economy as well as the individual victims. As the wealth and power of gangs increase, they are more likely to infiltrate legitimate businesses and labor unions. Investors who can invest in areas where gangs are less prevalent will be reluctant to invest in gang-ridden areas. There is evidence that areas of southern Italy with the highest growth rates have the lowest crime rates and vice versa. Although this is not conclusive, it is hard to disagree with the scholar who said gangs "can therefore have serious consequences for the economic growth of the legitimate economy. . . . [They] may create monopolies in local enterprises, control entry, . . . [and collect] protection payments. New investment may be discouraged and old investment driven out."

---

*Source: This box was suggested by Annelise Anderson, "The Red Mafia: A Legacy of Communism," Chapter 10, in *Economic Transition in Eastern Europe and Russia* (Stanford: Hoover Institution Press, 1995), p. 343.

---

ond by giving firms other options."[6] Although it seems odd to criticize an economy for having too few bankruptcies, the reason for the criticism is simple. Allowing inefficient enterprises and managers to operate prevents the economy from moving to a higher level of production.

Finally, the disruptions caused by introducing a new system have created a climate of lawlessness in some transition economies. Violent crime, financial frauds, and a failure to follow contracts are prevalent in Russia, China, and other countries. A recent example of a possible failure to follow contracts occurred in Beijing. McDonald's had a long-term lease on land and a building near Tiananmen

---

[6]Sharon Fisher, "Czech Economy Presents Mixed Picture," *RFE/RL Research Report* 3 (July 22, 1994), 34. The discussion of transition economies is based on several sources including *OECD Economic Surveys: The Czech and Slovak Republics* (Paris: Organization for Economic Cooperation and Development, 1994); "The Polish Economy under the Post-Communists," *RFE/RL Research Report* 3 (August 26, 1994); Ben Slay, "Rapid versus Gradual Economic Transition," *RFE/RL Research Report* 3 (August 12, 1994), 31–42; and "After Communism," *The Economist* (December 3, 1994), 23–27.

Square. They sold many hamburgers. It is hard to imagine a location with more potential customers. But the contract may not be honored because developers from Hong Kong are willing to pay more for the location; McDonald's may have to find a new location.[7] Capricious actions like this take place in several transition economies. Sometimes they are private actions allowed by government, and other times they are public actions. Regardless, they reduce the security of property rights and inhibit economic activity by domestic and foreign investors.

ADDITIONAL THOUGHTS ON TRANSITION ECONOMIES

Transition economies have had diverse experiences on their different paths to market economic systems. They had different starting points. Some had well-performing economies and others decided to change their systems because their economies were doing poorly. Some had a significant private sector and recent experience with a market economy; others had neither. Some had a functioning government; others had to establish national sovereignty and also a new economic system. In all cases, the transition has caused severe economic problems in these countries.

Some countries, such as Poland, have attempted a quick transition to a market economy, while others, such as Hungary, have taken a more gradual approach. Although they all have had extremely high unemployment and rapid inflation, some, such as the Czech Republic, have quickly stabilized their economies; others, such as Russia, have a long way to go. Similarly, almost all of the transition economies have freed most prices, but they are reluctant to free the prices of necessities, such as food and shelter. Poland, perhaps, has the freest price system, while Belarus and Ukraine have retained the most control over prices. The Czech Republic and Poland have established vigorous private sectors, while Belarus and Ukraine have just begun to develop their private sectors. Similarly, the transition economies recognize the need to improve incentives, particularly for the remaining state-owned enterprises, but they differ in their willingness to adopt market incentives. The establishment of institutional and legal systems to undergird their embryonic market systems has also been slow. An example is the slow development of bankruptcy law and procedures. As new economic, legal, and political institutions evolve in the transition countries, they have marvelous opportunities to reap the benefits of market systems, while perhaps avoiding some problems of established market economies. Mounting evidence suggests that the economies that have reformed the fastest have had the most economic growth since 1989.[8]

---

[7]*Tulsa World*, Business Section, February 21, 1995.
[8]Jeffrey D. Sachs, "Reforms in Eastern Europe and the Former Soviet Union in Light of the East Asian Experiences," National Bureau of Economic Research, Working Paper 5404 (January 1996).

SUMMARY

Market economic systems must have a legal and institutional framework that supports private property and the validity of contracts. These systems work by allowing individuals to make voluntary exchanges; a price system evolves. For voluntary exchanges and a price system to work well in organizing an economy, prices must be free of government control and inflation must be avoided. Finally, because a market system does not have centralized control, incentives based on prices encourage and motivate people to respond to other peoples' abilities and desires when they choose what to produce and consume.

Division of labor results in specialization that creates a need to coordinate the interdependent actions of the people in an economy. A market economy accomplishes this coordination with a decentralized price system. In understanding this coordination, it is crucial to understand the basic demand and supply analysis. Prices coordinate by informing producers and consumers about alternatives, by rationing existing supplies, and by motivating people to respond to market incentives. In a command economy and in a market economy with price controls, prices are often unable to perform these functions.

Transition economies are making uneven progress in the transformation of their economic systems. Some countries have stabilized their economies, freed prices, established private property rights, developed market incentives, and have created the beginnings of legal and institutional systems necessary for a market economic system. Most other countries have freed prices (to one degree or another), but there are great differences in the extent to which they have transformed other elements of their systems.

KEY TERMS

Relative price	Supply price	Equilibrium
Demand curve	Opportunity cost	Scarcity
Demand price	Law of supply	Ration
Law of demand	Excess demand	Price ceiling
Supply curve	Excess supply	

REVIEW QUESTIONS

1. What are three essential features of a market economy? Explain.
2. Why is average price stability important in a market system?
3. What are five questions that an economic system must answer?
4. Why is the division of labor important? Why does an increased division of labor make the coordination problem more difficult?

5. State the law of demand and illustrate it with a diagram. Show an example of a demand price on your diagram and explain why it falls when quantity increases.

6. The supply price of corn increases as more corn is produced. Illustrate this fact with a diagram and explain why it happens.

7. The operation of the laws of demand and supply ensures that the market for apartments will be in equilibrium.
   a. Define equilibrium.
   b. Draw a diagram with demand and supply curves. Illustrate the equilibrium price and the equilibrium quantity exchanged.
   c. Suppose the market price is above the equilibrium price. Show the quantity demanded and the quantity supplied on your diagram. What will happen to cause this market to return to equilibrium?

8. Explain how price acts as a signal for consumers and producers. Explain how it acts as a motivator.

9. Why is coordination difficult to achieve in a command economy?

10. College students pay $400 for a standard two-bedroom apartment in Stillwater, Oklahoma. Students can rent apartments without delay, and most apartments are rented by the beginning of the fall semester. The chamber of commerce believes that apartments at that price will discourage students from enrolling at the university; if students are not enrolled, they will not shop in Stillwater. So the chamber convinces the town council to set a maximum price (rent), a price ceiling of $300 per month per apartment.
   a. Use a diagram to illustrate this situation. Show the new quantity demanded and supplied of apartments. What coordination problem arises?
   b. What other problems may arise as individuals try to solve the coordination problem?
   c. Does this plan make Stillwater more attractive for students?
   d. Suppose enrollment at the university increases substantially. Discuss the effects of this in the apartment market. Under what conditions would people be willing to build new apartments? What reassurances would they need?

11. Draw a demand curve D_0 and a supply curve S_0 for apartments. Show the equilibrium. Now draw a new demand curve D_1 to the right of D_0; the new demand curve is caused by an increase in population. Explain how the price system will operate to signal and motivate producers and consumers to react to this new situation. What is the role of profits?

12. What have transition economies had to do in their attempts to create market economic systems?

13. Discuss the success of the transition economies in creating market economic systems.

14. According to the box titled "Can Socialism Use the Price System?" what are the three problems solved by the price system?

15. According to the box titled "Cowboy Capitalism in Russia?" is the gang activity in Russia typical of the early stage of capitalism? Discuss.

SUGGESTIONS FOR FURTHER READING

"A Survey of the Chinese Economy." *The Economist*. November 28, 1992. This is an excellent survey of Chinese economic reforms. This magazine's country surveys are a useful source of information regarding events in the transition economies.

"A Survey of Eastern European Economies." *The Economist*, March 13, 1993. The magazine's in-depth look at the transition economies of Eastern Europe.

"A Survey of the Soviet Economy." *The Economist*, April 9, 1988. Although this survey of the former Soviet economy is no longer current, it describes the historical problems experienced by a command economy.

Economic Reform Today, http://www.CIPE.org/ert.html. This Internet source is published jointly by the Center for International Private Enterprise, an affiliate of the U.S. Chamber of Commerce in Washington, D.C., and the United States Information Agency. It is published four times a year and contains articles about economic reform written by leading scholars. All articles are available on line.

Friedman, Milton. *Capitalism and Freedom.* Chicago: University of Chicago Press, 1962. Chapter 1 in this classic discusses essential features of a market economy and argues that a market economy—economic freedom—is necessary for political freedom.

Galbraith, John Kenneth. *The Affluent Society.* Boston: Houghton Mifflin, 1958. Galbraith is an influential critic of the workings of modern capitalist systems. In this and other works he argues that modern capitalism biases people toward private material goods at the expense of such goods as education, parks, highways, and so on. He also argues that the competitive economic system discussed in this chapter no longer describes the operation of an industrial economy.

Kennett, David, and Marc Lieberman. *The Road to Capitalism: Economic Transformation in Eastern Europe and the Former Soviet Union.* Fort Worth: The Dryden Press, 1992. This collection of accessible readings is a must for anyone who wants in-depth treatment of the problems of command economies, the operation of markets, and economic transition.

OECD Economic Surveys: The Czech and Slovak Republics. Paris: Organization for Economic Cooperation and Development, 1994. OECD country surveys are a source of detailed information about many Eastern European countries.

2

MARKETS OR GOVERNMENT? THE CARDINAL ECONOMIC CHOICE

TERMS YOU SHOULD KNOW

Supply (Chapter 1)

Demand (Chapter 1)

Opportunity cost (Chapter 1)

Equilibrium (Chapter 1)

Although the U.S. economy is often described as a market system, it is actually a "mixed" economy, one in which both the market system and an extensive system of federal, state, and local governments play key roles. In fact, in 1994, U.S. governments

1. spent enough money—more than $2,430 billion—to buy 35 percent of the nation's output of goods and services,
2. employed more than 19 million people—one sixth of the employed labor force,
3. produced over 10 percent of national output,
4. borrowed nearly 42 percent of all funds lent in credit markets, and
5. imposed more than $600 billion in costs on U.S. businesses and consumers through a vast array of regulations.

A government this large does not meet the universal approval of U.S. voters and policy makers, and there is a continuous debate in this country regarding the appropriate size and composition of government economic activity. We do not try to cover all aspects of this debate in this chapter; our objective instead is to present some of the basic analysis that economists use when they participate in this debate. This analysis is in two parts. First, we examine instances in which the market fails to provide what economists believe society wants from the economy. Second, we explore some of the more important problems created when government tries to supplement or supplant market-based economic activity.

In Chapter 1 we explained the virtues of the market system. Here we explain its defects. In Chapter 1 we perceived a very small role for government—essentially that of establishing and enforcing property rights. Here we prescribe a much broader role for government, but we also acknowledge the problems that often accompany an expansion of this role.

ECONOMIC GOALS

Market Failure
An instance in which the market system fails to achieve one of the nation's economic goals.

As noted, the first thing that we want to identify are the instances of market failure in the U.S. economy. **Market failure** occurs whenever the market system fails to achieve one of the nation's economic goals. Thus, the logical starting point is a discussion of these goals.

There is no official list of economic goals, but the policy agenda of the past 40 years suggests the following: (1) full employment of labor, (2) a low rate of inflation, (3) economic growth, (4) economic security for selected groups, (5) cost-minimization, and (6) allocative efficiency.

The full employment of labor has had a prominent place on the nation's policy agenda ever since the Great Depression of the 1930s. The inflation goal has played a lesser role in the policy arena, presumably because the United States has had a history of moderate long-run increases in the price level. Rates of inflation for much of the 1970s and the early 1980s, however, were high enough to elevate this issue to, and recent enough to keep it on, the policy agenda. In the long run, the United States also has a record of significant economic growth, but the rate of growth slowed enough during the 1970s and 1980s to stimulate a sustained interest by policy makers in how fast the economy is growing.

The United States has a relatively unequal distribution of income and wealth, but U.S. policy makers have never shown much interest in, nor has there been much political support for, equalizing this distribution. Rather, in this country most of the concern about distribution has manifested itself in programs designed to alleviate economic insecurity for specific groups. There is a long list of such groups, but abiding attention has been paid primarily to the poor and to the elderly. Thus, the nation's goals include a reduction in the poverty rate and adequate provision of income and health care to the elderly.

In a general sense, the goal of **cost minimization** is the same as achieving an objective at lowest possible cost. The most often assumed objective is the production of a unit of some good or service; so the goal of cost minimization is often assumed to be simply that of producing at lowest cost. But the goal could be anything—such as reducing poverty, processing claims, getting to the moon—and achieving any of these objectives at lowest possible cost is a desirable goal.

Allocative efficiency is achieved when the resources allocated to an activity produce the highest value to all of the individuals affected by that activity. This goal appears on the policy agenda often in the form of doing an activity only if the benefits it provides exceed the costs.

Cost Minimization
The goal of achieving an objective at the lowest possible cost.

Allocative Efficiency
The goal of allocating resources so that the highest value is produced.

MARKET FAILURE

As noted, market failure occurs whenever the market system is unable to achieve the nation's economic goals. In this section we explore the ways in which the market system appears to fail to achieve the goals just described.

FULL EMPLOYMENT

The output of goods and services in the U.S. economy, like that in other advanced industrial economies, fluctuates around a rising trend. These fluctuations, generally known as business cycles, have been documented for at least the last 140 years. In fact, there have been 30 cycles of expansion and contraction since 1854 and 9 since the end of World War II. Each contraction, or recession, in the economy is accompanied by rising unemployment. Thus, the U.S. economy has a clear record of failure to achieve full employment on a sustained basis

This record has led many economists to conclude that a market system is incapable of achieving full employment on its own, and, therefore, that government must play an active role in offsetting the market's tendency toward periodic recessions. The offsets advocated, as explained further in Chapter 12, are appropriate increases in government spending or tax reductions, or timely increases in the nation's money supply.

LOW RATE OF INFLATION

It is difficult to tell from the pronouncements and actions of policy makers exactly what rate of inflation is too high, but the current threshold of concern seems to be a rate in excess of 4 percent. If the goal is to keep the rate of inflation below this level, the U.S. economy has failed to achieve the goal in 19 of the last 35 years.

Although many of these 19 years occurred during expansionary phases of the business cycle, economists are less inclined to blame high rates of inflation than they are to blame high rates of unemployment on the market system, per se. As noted in the following section on government failure, many economists attribute inflation, instead, to misguided government monetary policies. Regardless of cause, the cure advocated most often is for the nation's money managers (the Board of Governors of the Federal Reserve System) to effect a reduction in the money supply.

ECONOMIC GROWTH

In the 79 years from 1869 to 1948, U.S. real output (output after inflation) per person grew at an average annual rate of 1.7 percent—a pace sufficient to double the nation's standard of living every 41 years. From 1948 to 1973, the economy literally broke this mold, achieving an annual rate of growth of 2.3 percent in real output per person—a rate that doubles the standard of living in only 31 years. In 1974, however, annual growth virtually stopped, and although it recovered after a couple of years, the economy averaged only 1.1 percent annual growth from 1973 to 1980. The economy picked up again in the 1980s and early 1990s, with growth averaging 1.5 percent per year from 1980 to 1994, but it never has returned to the path that many thought was its destiny based on the performance achieved in the first quarter century of the post–World War II era, or even to the path marked by the pre–World War II economy.

If the nation's goal is to attain the rate of growth achieved in either of the two pre-1973 periods (1869–1948 or 1948–1973), then the U.S. economy has failed to grow rapidly enough for the last two decades. As explained more thoroughly in Chapter 16, economists are still uncertain, however, about how much blame to assign to the market system or to government. There is, moreover, no firm consensus about the appropriate actions for government to take, if any, as means of helping the economy to achieve more rapid growth. Some economists advocate more government investment in human capital, physical infrastructure, and research and development; others advocate reductions in government regulations and taxes.

ECONOMIC SECURITY FOR SELECTED GROUPS

THE POOR   Taking the very long view, the United States has made great strides in reducing the percentage of the population that is poor. One study has estimated, for example, that the proportion of families in poverty fell from 67 percent in 1896 to around 25 percent in 1960. Starting in the early 1960s, the federal government made a concerted effort to reduce the poverty rate further. As noted in Chapter 10, the income provided by this effort has helped greatly to reduce the official poverty rate in the United States—to the neighborhood of 13 to 14 percent over much of the last 20 years. Unfortunately, however, the data indicate that over 22 percent of the population would be poor if these expenditures were not devoted to poverty reduction. This suggests that the market system generates almost as much poverty on its own today as it did more than 30 years ago and that continuous government action may be necessary to correct this particular market failure.

THE ELDERLY   Families headed by persons age 65 or older in the two lowest income quintiles (the lowest 40 percent) receive over half of their income from Social Security and Medicare. This suggests that what is true of the poor in general appears to be true of the elderly in particular; namely, economic insecurity among the elderly would rise dramatically if the benefits provided by programs such as Social Security and Medicare were eliminated. The extent of the increase would be difficult to determine, because families would probably save and invest differently during their working lifetimes in the absence of these programs, and a greater share of the burden of financing the needs of the elderly would probably come from extended families and private charities. It is not likely, however, that the problem of poverty among the elderly could be solved completely by the elderly themselves, even with the help of their families and private charities. Thus, there appears to be a need for some government action to address the problem of potential poverty among the elderly.

COST MINIMIZATION   One of the principal accomplishments claimed for the market system is that it tends to produce goods and services at lowest cost per unit. The logic behind this claim is simple. In a market system only firms that make a profit survive. Since profit is the difference between revenue and cost, the firms that are more successful in constraining costs will have a survival advantage, other things being equal, over the firms that are less successful in constraining costs. Thus, there is relentless pressure on firms to search for ways to reduce costs.

Cost minimization is especially important for a firm that faces many actual or potential rivals capable of satisfying consumer demand; the competition among rivals essentially becomes cost competition. The number of actual or potential rivals in many markets of the U.S. economy is large enough to produce such cost competition, but the evidence reviewed in Chapter 4 suggests a potential lack of competition in several. Thus, there may be a need for some government action to offset this market failure.

ALLOCATIVE EFFICIENCY

Consumer sovereignty
The production of goods and services according to individual demand.

Another virtue of the market system is that resources tend to be allocated to the production of goods and services in response to individual demand. Such **consumer sovereignty** generally directs production toward the combination of goods and services with highest value, that is, toward an efficient allocation of resources. Economists have noted many instances, however, in which the market system fails, or would fail, to achieve allocative efficiency. We will now explain several of these cases in some detail, beginning with a fuller explanation of what is required to achieve allocative efficiency.

As noted, allocative efficiency requires the production of the highest-value combination of goods and services. Value in this regard is measured in terms of the amounts people are willing to pay. The amount that an individual is willing to pay for a good or service is used by economists as an indicator of the benefits that the individual gets from that good or service. The rationale for doing this is that the individual would not be willing to pay the amount that he or she does unless the benefits were perceived to have a value at least as high as the amount paid.

With limited resources and limited goods and services, individuals must compete for what is available. Allocative efficiency requires that, as a result of this competition, the available goods and services be allocated to the individuals who value them most highly. These individuals include both those who have actual possession or actually use a good or service—the direct beneficiaries—and those who benefit indirectly—the indirect beneficiaries—from the goods or services possessed or used by the direct beneficiaries.

Marginal Private Benefits (MPB)
Direct benefits of a unit of a good or service.

Marginal Private Costs (MPC)
Direct costs of a unit of a good or service.

Marginal External Benefits (MEB)
Indirect benefits of a unit of a good or service.

Marginal External Costs (MEC)
Indirect costs of a unit of a good or service.

Marginal Social Benefits (MSB)
The sum of marginal private and marginal external benefits.

Marginal Social Costs (MSC)
The sum of marginal private costs and marginal external costs.

A simple condition must be satisfied for allocative efficiency to occur: the amount that the direct and indirect beneficiaries are willing to pay for a unit of a particular good or service, such as a bushel of wheat or a year in college, must be greater than, or at least equal to, the amount that others are willing to pay for the highest valued alternative uses of the resources used to provide the bushel of wheat or the year in college. The amount that others are willing to pay for the highest valued alternative uses are the opportunity costs, or simply "costs," of the bushel of wheat or year of college. Costs may be confined to the direct benefits from the alternative uses—let us call these direct costs—but they may also include indirect benefits from alternative uses, or indirect costs.

In economics, direct benefits and costs of a unit of a good or service are called **marginal private benefits (MPB)** and **costs (MPC).** The term "marginal" denotes a unit of a good or service. The use of the term "private" reflects the fact that transactions in the private, or market, sector of the economy reflect only direct benefits and costs. In economics, indirect benefits and costs of a unit of a good or service are called **marginal external benefits (MEB)** and **costs (MEC).** Market transactions do not reflect indirect benefits and costs created by, but "external" to, market transactions. Economists refer to the sum of marginal private and marginal external benefits as **marginal social benefits (MSB),** and to the sum of marginal private costs and marginal external costs as **marginal social costs (MSC).**

Given these new terms, the condition for achieving allocative efficiency can be restated: allocate resources to the production of a unit of a particular good or service only if MSB is greater than or at least equal to MSC. If this rule is followed, then the value gained by all who benefit from a particular unit is at least as large as the value given up by all who sacrifice something because that unit is produced.

COMPETITIVE MARKET To understand market failure, it helps to understand first a case in which the market does not fail. This can then be used as a benchmark for comparison.

The case in point is that of the competitive market introduced in Chapter 1. There we illustrated such a market in terms of the demand for, and supply of, apartments in Gotham City. The relevant diagram, Figure 1.3, is reproduced here as Figure 2.1. We have added new labels, however, to the demand (D) and supply (S) curves.

The demand curve in Figure 2.1 illustrates the behavior of consumers: they buy more apartments when the price per apartment falls. The supply curve in Figure 2.1 illustrates the behavior of suppliers: they provide more apartments when the price per apartment rises. The intersection of the demand and supply curves indicates the number of apartments that will be bought and sold and the price that will be paid.

The demand curve has been labeled MPB (for marginal private benefits), because the demand curve tells us the amount that someone is willing to pay for each apartment, and the amount that someone is willing to pay is the economic indicator of benefits. The demand curve has also been labeled MSB (for marginal social benefits) to reflect the assumption that there are no marginal external benefits from apartments.

The supply curve has been labeled MPC (marginal private costs) because the supply curve tells us the price the supplier must receive to cover costs. The supply curve has also been labeled MSC (marginal social costs) to reflect the assumption that there are no marginal external costs associated with apartments.

As noted, the market will provide 550,000 apartments—where the quantities demanded and supplied are equal, or S = D. This is the quantity that market participants choose based upon considerations of their own, or private benefits and costs. That is, it is the quantity where MPB = MPC. It is by coincidence also the quantity where MSB = MSC. Thus, the competitive market for apartments efficiently allocates resources to apartments, even though the market participants are pursuing their own interests and don't care a whit about achieving this goal. At any level less than 550,000 units, MSB > MSC and society would experience benefits from additional apartments greater than benefits from the alternative uses of the resources required to supply additional apartments. Thus, more units should be provided. At any level greater than 550,000 units, MSC > MSB and society loses more benefits from sacrificed alternatives than it gains from additional apartments. Thus, fewer units should be provided.

Many markets are similar to the market depicted here in the sense that they are reasonably competitive and free of externalities. The essence of the competi-

A COMPETITIVE
MARKET FOR
APARTMENTS WITH
NO EXTERNAL
BENEFITS OR
COSTS

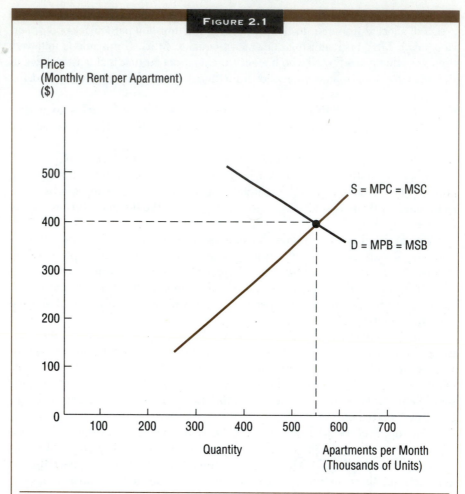

FIGURE 2.1

This figure illustrates a competitive market for apartments in Gotham City. Market equilibrium occurs at 550,000 units, where S = D or MPB = MPC. There are assumed to be no external benefits or costs in this market; hence, MSB = MPB and MSC = MPC.

tive case is that no individual market participant has the ability to affect price; thus, the price that is established is the market clearing price where MSB = MSC.

MONOPOLY   If some market participants have market power in the form of the ability to affect price, the allocation of resources will generally be allocatively inefficient. In monopoly, where one seller supplies the market, the seller has the ability literally to set the market price. As explained in Chapter 4, the price consistent with the monopolist's goal of maximizing profit is higher than the price where $MSB = MSC$. This makes the monopoly allocatively inefficient in the sense that too little is produced and too few resources are allocated to the monopolized market. Alternatively, the monopolist denies consumers the opportunity to buy additional units from which they would reap benefits greater than costs. If the market for apartments in Gotham City were controlled by one seller, for example, the quantity sold would be less than 550,000 units and MSB would exceed MSC.

There are not many pure monopolies, but there are many markets in which a few firms have market power. In these markets there is market failure, although to a lesser degree. The pure monopolies are those to whom government has given the exclusive right to supply a product. The most familiar of these are the public utilities from which many people get their water, electricity, and natural gas.

We have assumed in the basic competitive model for apartments in Gotham City that there are no external benefits or costs. This example, and Figure 2.1, can be easily modified to illustrate the effect on allocative efficiency if there are external benefits and costs.

EXTERNAL BENEFITS Suppose that the apartment buildings in Gotham City are particularly attractive; in fact, they are so attractive that they draw visitors from around the world just to view them. Each viewer is willing to pay something for the visual properties of the apartment buildings. The amount the viewers are willing to pay per unit is a measure of the marginal external benefits (MEB) provided by each unit.

Now, although each unit produces MEB, neither the owner nor the renter can charge the viewer anything. Thus, apartment market participants ignore MEB in making their decisions about how much to buy and sell. They base their decisions solely on the benefits they perceive—marginal private benefits (MPB). The consequences of this situation for allocative efficiency can be visualized by modifying Figure 2.1 to incorporate the new assumptions we have made. This is done in Figure 2.2.

In Figure 2.2, we leave the MSC curve alone and retain the label MPC as well to remind you that it is also an MPC curve—that there are no external costs in this example. We distinguish, however, between MPB and MSB. To understand this distinction, recall that MSB is equal to MPB plus MEB. The distance between MSB and MPB represents MEB, the benefits per unit to viewers.

Market participants will continue to buy and sell 550,000 units; this is still the amount that is in their own best interests. It is, however, no longer the amount that is in the social interest. That is the amount at which $MSB = MSC$, or 700,000 units. In this case, the market fails to provide enough apartments to satisfy the willingness to pay of both the apartment dwellers and the viewers.

This may be a fanciful illustration, but it underscores an important point: anytime there are benefits that cannot be appropriated by market participants, the market tends to allocate too few resources to the production of the good or service. Less fanciful examples are primary and secondary education and public health. Primary and secondary education enhance the earning power of the persons educated (a private benefit) and probably turn them into better citizens

A COMPETITIVE
MARKET FOR
APARTMENTS
WITH EXTERNAL
BENEFITS, BUT
NO EXTERNAL
COSTS

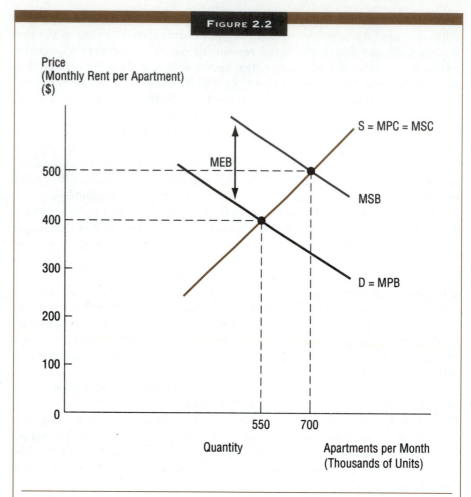

FIGURE 2.2

Price
(Monthly Rent per Apartment)
($)

This figure illustrates the market for apartments in Gotham City with the assumed presence of marginal external benefits. The market equilibrium is 550,000 units, where MPB = MPC. This is less than the efficient quantity where MSB = MSC.

as well, to the benefit of those not educated (an external benefit). Certain public health measures, such as immunization, provide protection to the party immunized (a private benefit) and also some protection to people not immunized (an external benefit).

In cases like these, some type of government action is necessary to ensure that the efficient amount is provided. One option is for the government to subsidize the provision of the extra units, using tax dollars.

PUBLIC GOODS Goods and services differ in terms of the relative importance of private and external benefits. At one end of the spectrum would be a good where all benefits are private except for the external benefits of one individual. At the other end of the spectrum would be a good where, if one individual were to provide it, a large number of people would benefit from its provision even if they paid nothing for it. The latter goods are called public goods.

National security is the classic example of a public good. It is "public" in the sense that if it is provided at all it bestows benefits on the public in general. That is, no one can be effectively excluded from the benefits of national security. In such a case there is the danger that each individual will fail to reveal his or her true willingness to pay, hoping to get a "free ride" after other people pay for it. If everyone reasons this way, of course, there will be no national defense even though the aggregate true benefits from it may be very high. In such a case, there appears to be a clear need for government to levy taxes and use the proceeds to provide what the market cannot provide; that is, for the government to act on behalf of individuals.

EXTERNAL COSTS Now suppose that there are no external benefits associated with apartments in Gotham City. Assume instead that each apartment burns coal and that pollution from this source drifts across the city. People who are particularly sensitive to this pollution suffer physically. Some become ill and miss work. Many see the doctor more frequently. Some curtail their outdoor activities. Some buy filtration systems for their homes. The income they forgo, the money they spend at the doctor, the value to them of the activities they give up, and their outlays for filtration systems are all examples of external costs imposed by apartment dwellers.

The existence of external costs implies a difference between social and private costs. Figure 2.3 shows two cost curves; one for MSC (marginal social costs) and another for MPC (marginal private costs). The vertical distance between the two is MEC (marginal external costs).

As before, apartment buyers and sellers will decide to buy or sell solely on the basis of private benefits and costs. This means that 550,000 units will be bought and sold because this is where MPB = MPC. The efficient quantity, where MSB = MSC, is only 400,000 units, however. Thus, the market overallocates resources to apartments in the presence of external costs.

In cases such as this, the government may have to take action to reduce the quantity of apartments rented. Some of the actions they may take are reviewed in Chapter 7 for real world cases of air pollution.

NONEXISTENT MARKETS Life is full of risks—risks that might lead to poor health, dying, accidents, poverty, fire, inflation, unemployment, disability, natural disasters, and so on. The market system responds to these risks whenever it can by offering insurance. In some cases, however, it cannot provide insurance—for example, the market does not insure against events like inflation, unemployment, and poverty. In these cases, the market fails totally and it is necessary to provide insurance through government if it is to be provided at all.

A COMPETITIVE
MARKET FOR
APARTMENTS WITH
EXTERNAL COSTS
BUT NO EXTERNAL
BENEFITS

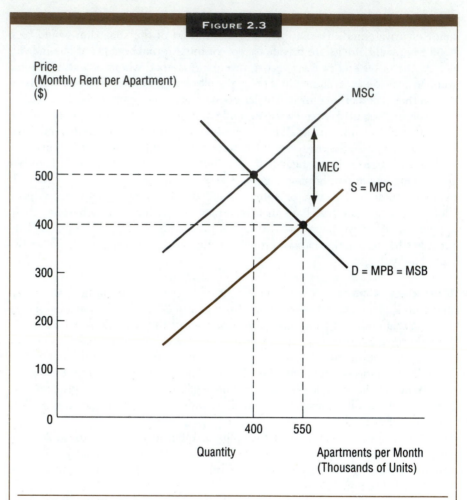

FIGURE 2.3

This figure illustrates the market for apartments in Gotham City with the assumed presence of marginal external costs. The market equilibrium is 550,000, where MPB = MPC. This is greater than the efficient quantity of 400,000 apartments, where MSB = MSC.

MORAL HAZARD   Another type of market failure also characterizes insurance markets. The fact that insurance compensates insurees for the cost of the adverse consequences of an act may make some of the insured less careful to avoid the act. For example, the protection of automobile accident insurance may induce insurees to drive less carefully, or the protection of medical insurance may induce insurees to engage in behavior that is conducive to poor health. Economics refers to cases such as these, where insurance increases the probability that claims will be made or that the claims made will be more expensive, as examples of **moral hazard.**

Moral Hazard
The danger that insurance will make insured parties more likely to engage in risky behavior.

Moral hazard occurs because the individual insuree who causes it can shift the increased costs associated with his or her acts to others who are insured. Thus, moral hazard creates external costs, driving a wedge between the private and social costs of various activities. When it does, the market system produces too much of those activities. It is questionable, however, if government action is necessary to correct for this particular market failure. The market can correct itself to some extent. For example, medical insurance companies can reward behavior that is conducive to wellness, such as refraining from smoking, and auto insurance companies can reward practices that produce safer driving, such as driver education. The mere existence of market failure does not always mean that government action is desirable.

IMPERFECT INFORMATION   Finally, there are cases in which the market system may fail to provide the right quantity of goods and services simply because consumers have imperfect knowledge about the benefits or costs. Four general cases are possible. First, consumers may underestimate true benefits and do too little of the activity. This is often alleged to be the case for saving for retirement, where households are charged with failure to appreciate the long run benefits of systematic saving starting at an early age. Second, consumers may overestimate true benefits and consume too much of a good or service. This may happen, for example, in the market for medical care, where, for reasons outlined in Chapter 5, consumers willingly undergo tests or procedures of little benefit. Third, consumers may underestimate costs and consume too much. This would probably be the case for many new drugs and products that pose a safety risk. Fourth, consumers may overestimate costs and consume too little; risks can be exaggerated as well as understated. In all of these cases, the government may have a role to play in providing, or in ensuring the provision of, more accurate information.

GOVERNMENT FAILURE

One would hardly get a balanced view of the defects of the U.S. economy by examining only cases of market failure. Numerous instances of government failure exist as well. In a manner parallel to the concept of market failure, **government failure** occurs whenever government activity is inconsistent with achieving one of the nation's economic goals.

Government failure
An instance of government activity that is inconsistent with achieving one of the nation's economic goals.

FULL EMPLOYMENT

As noted in Chapter 12, the federal government certainly has the means, through fiscal and monetary policy, to help avoid or offset recessionary tendencies in the market sector of the economy. Basically, fiscal policy relies on increasing government purchases and reducing taxes to reduce unemployment; monetary policy relies on increases in the money supply. Both policies have been used with some success in the past to moderate recessions.

Unfortunately, the federal government can deepen, or even initiate, a recession by inappropriate or ill-timed policies. Perhaps the classic instance of the former was the significant reduction in the money supply that took place during the first four years of the Great Depression of the 1930s. While a severe contraction in economic activity probably could not have been avoided, many economists now believe that the decline would not have been so severe if the money supply had not been reduced so much. A clear case of the government initiating a recession is the 1981–1982 recession. The culprit here was also a reduction in the money supply; initiated in this instance to reduce high rates of inflation. These are extreme examples, of course. Most of the time, the difficulty lies with getting Congress to act (in the case of fiscal policy) in a timely manner or in accurately predicting the reaction to changes in monetary policy.

LOW RATE OF INFLATION

As noted in Chapter 13, the federal government also has the means to reduce the rate of inflation in the U.S. economy. The fiscal and monetary policies used to cure a recession can simply be reversed; that is, Congress could cut government expenditures or raise taxes, or the monetary authorities could reduce the money supply; most economists favor the use of the latter.

On the one hand, monetary policy has been used successfully to reduce high rates of inflation; a good example is the 1981–1982 period referred to previously. On the other hand, equal-size changes in the money supply do not affect the economy uniformly; sometimes the effects are felt quickly and sometimes only after a considerable period of time, and the magnitude of the effects varies as well. In fact, this combination of potential power and variability is too disquieting for some economists, and it has led them to advocate that the monetary authorities be allowed to vary the money supply only within a relatively narrow range.

ECONOMIC GROWTH

Productivity
A measure of the performance of a resource used in production. Labor productivity is measured in terms of output per hour of work. Productivity of capital is measured in terms of output per unit of capital.

Economic growth results from having more resources—land, labor, and capital—with which to produce output. It also results from getting more output from available resources, that is, from improvements in the productive capabilities, or productivity, of these resources. In an economy where output is tilted heavily in favor of manufactured goods and services, such as that in the United States, increases in the amount and productivity of land play a minor role in driving total output upward. The key to economic growth in the United States, then, is what happens to the total number of hours worked and the **productivity** or output per hour worked, and to the size and productivity of the capital stock.

The contributions of three of these ingredients—productivity per hour worked and the size and productivity of the capital stock—depend heavily on the amounts invested in labor and capital. Improvements can be achieved in labor productivity by investing in activities that improve individual capabilities, such as education and health care. Increases in the size of the capital stock can be achieved by investing in new factories and equipment and basic infrastructure such as highways, seaports, and airports; and the capital stock can be improved by investing in research and development. High rates of investment require that society refrain from using income to purchase consumption goods. This can happen only if society saves a significant share of its income.

U.S. governments can claim many positive contributions to these determinants of economic growth. They have invested heavily in basic infrastructure, education, research, and health care. They have provided a host of tax incentives and subsidies for business investment and private expenditures on education and health care. But they have thwarted growth, as well, via tax, expenditure, borrowing, and regulatory policies.

TAXES AND GROWTH The primary objective of the tax system, from the government's perspective, is to raise revenue. Taxes do affect behavior, however, and in ways that may be detrimental to economic growth. Tax rates on income from work, such as those in the federal and state personal incomes taxes and the payroll tax for Social Security, may be high enough in combination to reduce the number of hours that some people are willing to work. Tax rates on income from savings may be high enough to discourage some people from saving. Tax rates on business income, such as those associated with federal and state corporate income taxes, may be high enough to reduce the level of business investment in plant, equipment, and research.

EXPENDITURES AND GROWTH Government expenditure programs may also adversely affect peoples' incentives to work, save, and invest. This country has a host of programs, such as Aid to Families with Dependent Children, food stamps, housing allowances, and Supplemental Security Income, that provide benefits to the poor where the benefits to eligible recipients are reduced as their earned incomes rise. Economists call these benefits **income-tested transfers.** Sometimes the reduction in these benefits may be great enough to discourage people from working as much as they would have in the absence of this penalty.

Income-tested transfer A transfer that becomes smaller as income increases.

Adverse effects of government expenditures on hours worked are not, however, confined to income-tested transfers for the poor. Social Security is a good example. It provides for a reduction of $1 in benefits for every $3 earned by retirees above a certain level.

Social Security also provides incentives for early retirement. But the primary concern about Social Security in an economic growth context is the possibility that it has had a significant adverse effect on the amount saved in the United States. This possibility and the aforementioned aspects of Social Security are explored in greater detail in Chapter 9.

DEFICITS AND GROWTH So far we have written about how specific taxes and expenditures may adversely affect economic growth. The overall relation of taxes to expenditures may also adversely affect economic growth. The problem of

INTERNATIONAL PERSPECTIVE

DOES MORE GOVERNMENT MEAN LESS GROWTH?

One of the concerns about a growing government sector is that it may lead to a slowdown in a country's rate of economic growth. Several reasons why this might happen have been explained in the main body of the text. For example, a larger government sector requires higher taxes and higher taxes may reduce work effort, savings, and investment. A larger government sector may also mean more regulation and more regulation may require business firms to substitute investment in regulatory compliance for investment in goods-producing plants and equipment. More government need not mean slower growth, however, if it provides more education, research, social infrastructure, and political stability. Whether more govern-

ment will bring slower growth, then, cannot be determined on the basis of theory alone.

There is considerable variation across countries in terms of both size of government and rate of economic growth. Accordingly, several researchers have attempted to determine whether there is a relationship between government and growth by making cross-country comparisons. In the studies done to date, government's influence on the economy has been represented by either government expenditures or taxes. The research question is whether slower rates of growth have been associated with higher ratios of government spending or taxes to output.

Keith Marsden, using a sample of 20 countries for the period 1970–1979, found a statistically significant negative relationship between growth rates and tax shares: on average, a one percent increase in the ratio of taxes to output was associated with a 0.36 per-

concern is that federal government expenditures often exceed revenues (primarily taxes), generating a deficit in the federal budget. To make up the difference between expenditures and revenues, the federal government must borrow money from the private sector of the economy. The concern is that the money borrowed by the federal government would have been borrowed for private investment, or that the federal government deficit "crowds out" private investment, thereby reducing the economy's capacity for long-run growth. These matters are explored in Chapter 14.

REGULATION AND GROWTH   Finally we come to regulation. Government has hundreds of regulatory agencies. In 1992, there were 59 major federal regulatory agencies with about 125,000 employees. Among the better known are the Environmental Protection Agency, the Occupational Safety and Health Administration, the Federal Communications Commission, the Antitrust Division of the Department of Justice, and the Federal Trade Commission. Thousands of agencies with regulatory authority exist at the state and local level. The most powerful of these in most states are the agencies that regulate public utilities, which supply basic commodities such as electricity and natural gas.

Regulatory agencies account for a relatively small portion of government spending. For example, regulatory activities claimed about $12 billion, or less than 1 percent, of the federal budget in 1992. Most of the cost of regulation shows up off-budget, however, in the costs to business firms and consumers of cent decrease in the rate of economic growth. Charles Wolf and Randy Ross estimated that a 10 percent increase in the ratio of government spending to output was associated with a 1 percent decrease in the rate of growth, using a sample of 27 countries for the 1972–1982 period. Daniel Landau's study of the relationship between government expenditures and per capita economic growth shows results similar to those of Marsden and Wolf and Ross. Alternatively, Mancur Olson found no reliable connection between the size of government and economic growth in his study of long-term secular growth, and Frederic Pryor reached a similar conclusion based on his study of a broad range of market-based and command economies over the 1950–1980 period.

Based on these studies, the evidence of a relationship between the size of government and the rate of economic growth is just as ambiguous as the theory of a relationship between government and growth. This issue is such an important one in making the choice between markets and government, however, that we have certainly not heard the last word from the research community.

Sources: Keith Marsden, "Links between Taxes and Economic Growth: Some Empirical Evidence," *World Bank Staff Working Paper 605* (Washington, DC, 1983; Charles Wolf, Jr., *Markets or Governments*, 2nd ed. (Cambridge, MA: The MIT Press, 1994), 145–51; Daniel Landau, "Government Expenditure and Economic Growth: A Cross-Country Study," *Southern Economic Journal* 49, no. 3 (January 1983) 783–92; Mancur Olson, *The Rise and Decline of Nations* (New Haven: Yale University Press, 1982); Frederic L. Pryor, "Growth and Fluctuations of Production in OECD and East European Countries," *World Politics* 37, no. 2, January 1985, 204–37.

complying with government regulations, or in the adverse effects of government regulation on investment. The latter occurs either because regulation blunts individuals' willingness to invest in the more highly regulated sectors of the economy or because money that would have been used for investment is used instead for compliance. Thomas Hopkins puts the cost of complying with federal rules at $668 billion in 1995.[1] Jorgenson and Wilcoxen estimate that environmental regulations alone may be costing the United States over 3 percent of total output each year.[2]

ECONOMIC SECURITY FOR SELECTED GROUPS

THE POOR   We noted that, in spite of a large effort by government, the problem of poverty in the United States has not been solved completely. We would not necessarily call this an example of government failure, however, because the general result of these programs has been to advance the goal of poverty reduction. The government failure label here is used to indicate those features of our poverty programs that increase the poverty rate.

[1]Thomas Hopkins, "Over-Regulating America," *The Economist* (July 27, 1996), 19–21.
[2]Dale W. Jorgenson and Peter J. Wilcoxen, "Environmental Regulation and U.S. Economic Growth," *Rand Journal of Economics* 21 (Summer 1990), 314–40.

Antipoverty policy in the United States relies heavily on government transfers of money or goods and services. In most cases, the amount transferred falls as eligible recipients earn additional income. Such reductions have the same effect on recipients as would a tax levied on earned income; that is, they may induce some recipients to work less, thereby increasing the gap between a poor family's income and the poverty line.

Other features of some of the antipoverty programs may induce or facilitate divorce or separation, adding to the number of female-headed families. As explained in Chapter 10, people in such families are quite likely to have a difficult time escaping poverty.

THE ELDERLY The rate of poverty among the elderly before they receive government transfers is higher than the before-transfer poverty rate among the populace at large, but the rate of poverty after government transfers, such as Social Security, is lower among the elderly than it is among the populace as a whole. This result clearly indicates that government transfers have had an important effect in reducing the poverty of the elderly. It does not eliminate the possibility, however, of certain features that, by themselves, tend to increase poverty among the elderly.

The features at issue are those that tend to reduce hours worked, such as incentives for early retirement and the penalty for working too many hours after retirement. Both of these features were mentioned earlier in the context of the discussion of economic growth.

COST MINIMIZATION

The one government failure that most economists and noneconomists alike recognize is "waste," or the failure of government agencies to achieve the lowest possible costs in providing goods and services. This is not normally believed to be a problem in those parts of the market sector where (1) markets link the costs of an activity to the income that sustains it through the prices charged for the marketed output, (2) there is competition among producers for consumers' outlays, (3) output is measurable and the quality characteristics of products are known to both buyer and seller, and (4) there are reliable rewards and penalties in the form of profits and losses. Government provision of a good or service normally severs the link between costs and prices, however, because the revenues that sustain government activities are derived from nonprice sources such as taxes. Government output is often distributed under noncompetitive conditions; in many cases, the government is either the dominant or only supplier. Public-sector output is often difficult to measure, there are often no clearcut means of rewarding government employees for innovation, and there is a lack of termination mechanisms for government programs. These features of governmental programs blunt incentives for government officials and agencies to economize on resources or to adopt new, cost-saving technologies.

The expectation that governments provide goods and services at the lowest possible cost is similar to the expectation that business firms provide their products at the lowest cost. This is a perfectly legitimate, and important, application of the cost-minimization test, but it is not the only one. As noted earlier, the general cost-minimization goal is to achieve a particular objective at lowest possible cost, and the objective need not be limited to that of producing goods and services.

The cost-minimization test can be applied, in fact, to all means of achieving the other goals we have been discussing. That is, we ought to minimize the costs of achieving full employment, a low rate of inflation, economic growth, economic security for selected groups, and allocative efficiency. The cost-minimization test can be applied, also, to goals not on the short list of five we have stressed to this point. Such applications reveal other instances of government failure and help to identify ways that government can become more cost-effective in its activities.

Suppose, for example, that we want to minimize the cost of achieving economic security for the elderly. If that is our objective, then we are probably a long way from attaining it. The reason is simple; as noted in Chapter 9, a large share of the benefits provided to the elderly through Social Security and Medicare go to individuals who would be economically secure without those benefits. The costs of achieving economic security for the elderly could be reduced, then, by allocating a smaller amount of money to the elderly who have no real need for it.

For another example, consider the problem of environmental pollution. Ideally, the goal of the government is to achieve allocative efficiency in the face of environmental pollution, that is, to reduce output to the level where MSB=MSC. In reality, the achievement of this goal may require information that is simply not available in any practical way. Thus, the government may decide, as it has done, to aim instead at achieving certain air quality standards, such as maximum permissable levels of ozone, nitrous oxide, or particulates. This is reasonable, but government agencies often go one step further and prescribe, or limit, the choice of alternative means of achieving these standards. As explained in Chapter 7, air quality standards can often be achieved at lower cost—in fact, the nation could save several billion dollars by using emission taxes or by selling pollution permits rather than by using the means traditionally prescribed by government.

ALLOCATIVE EFFICIENCY

As noted, allocative efficiency is all about providing the right amount of a good or service; namely, the amount where marginal social benefit=marginal social cost. Allocative **in**efficiency occurs when there is either too much of something, as when pollution accompanies production, or too little, as when immunizations are provided solely according to marginal private benefits (willingness to pay of buyers only). Such cases do not occur solely in the market sector of the economy. Government decisions can also result in either too much or too little of an activity.

Several examples of allocative efficiency failures attributable to government actions are developed in subsequent chapters in this book. Collectively, these

ADDITIONAL INSIGHT

WHAT DOES GOVERNMENT REALLY COST?

In 1995, all governments in the United States combined spent more than $2.5 billion. This is a substantial sum—over 35 percent of the nation's total output. There is reason to believe, however, that the opportunity cost of government—what the nation actually sacrificed for the government goods and services it received—was considerably higher. In addition to the spending that appears in government budgets, there are several important costs that do not appear in the budget. The more important among these are the nonbudget costs of government regulation, taxation, expenditures, and borrowing.

Government regulation imposes two types of nonbudget costs: (1) the short-run costs of compliance and (2) long-run losses in potential output caused when productive capital expenditures are displaced by outlays for compliance. Government taxation and expenditures result in losses in potential output to the extent that work effort, savings, and investment are reduced in attempts to avoid taxes or reductions in government payments, or because the prospect of future government payments reduces individual incentives to work, save, and invest. Government borrowing may also result in lower potential output to the extent that it replaces private borrowing for investment.

As reported in the main text, Thomas Hopkins puts the cost of complying with federal government rules alone at $668 billion in 1995. Ballard, Shoven, and Whalley estimate that taxes cost the nation from 13 to 24 percent more than the revenue actually raised, or somewhere between $325 and $600 billion. Definitive estimates of the nonbudget costs of expenditures are not available, but those associated with Social Security alone could be as high as the costs of either regulation or taxation (see the discussion of the effect of Social Security on savings in Chapter 9). We also know of no consensus estimates of what government borrowing costs the economy in terms of long-run potential output foregone, but the discussion of this issue in Chapter 14 indicates that the cumulative effect of 20 years of federal deficits could be substantial.

Governments have always been remarkably silent on the costs borne outside the budget as a result of government activities, although the federal government began to produce estimates of the off-budget costs of federal regulation during the Bush administration. A significant extension of this kind of effort would help both the American public and its political representatives to know the true cost of government, but it will be slow in coming since it is surely in the best interests of many politicians to understate the costs of their decisions.

Sources: "Over-Regulating America," *The Economist*, July 27, 1996, 19–21; Charles L. Ballard, John B. Shoven, and John Whalley, "The Total Welfare Cost of the United States Tax System: A General Equilibrium Approach," *National Tax Journal* 38, no. 2 (June 1985), 125–40.

examples are only a very small percentage of the cases that could be developed, but they should provide the reader with a good idea of what is meant by allocative inefficiency in the public sector. Here we provide only a brief explanation of these cases.

RENT CONTROLS   As noted in Chapter 1, various local governments in the United States have adopted rent controls, effectively placing an upper limit on rents that landlords can charge. These limits commonly keep rents below the market-clearing, or equilibrium, levels. When this happens, landlords are only willing to supply a smaller number of units than the equilibrium quantity. If there are no externalities associated with the production, use, or existence of the rental units, then D=MSB and S=MSC, and the equilibrium quantity (where D=S) is the allocatively efficient quantity. It follows that the provision of less than the equilibrium quantity in response to rents controlled below the equilibrium level results in MSB>MSC, and the government induces suppliers to supply too few rental units.

These points are illustrated in Figure 2.4, which represents the market for rental units in a city with rent controls. The equilibrium price (rent) and quantity are P_e and Q_e, respectively. Since D=MSB and S=MSC, the equilibrium quantity is the allocatively efficient quantity. If landlords can charge no more than P_c

A COMPETITIVE MARKET FOR APARTMENTS WITH RENT CONTROLS

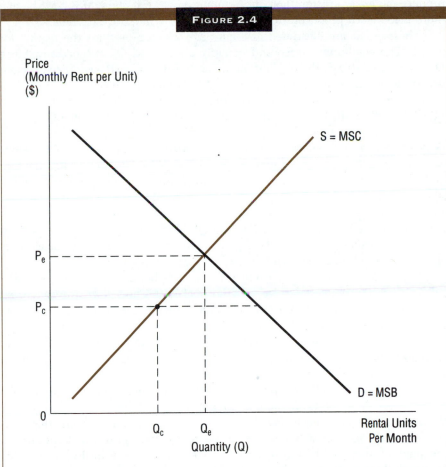

FIGURE 2.4

This figure illustrates a market for apartments with rent controls. The market equilibrium without government intervention would be at Q_e units, where S=D. This is also the allocatively efficient quantity because it is where MSB=MSC. When rent is limited to P_c, only Q_c units, less than the efficient quantity, are supplied.

because of the rent control, they will provide only Q_c units. At Q_c, MSB (as measured by the vertical distance to MSB at Q_c) clearly exceeds MSC (as measured by the vertical distance to MSC at Q_c), and too few units are provided.

AGRICULTURAL PRICE SUPPORTS   As noted in Chapter 3, the U.S. government has a series of programs designed to keep the prices of various agricultural commodities above the market-clearing, or equilibrium, prices of the commodities. Such prices induce farmers to produce at levels of output greater than the market-clearing, or equilibrium, quantities. In the absence of externalities, the equilibrium quantity is the allocatively efficient quantity—the quantity where MSB=MSC. If government price-support programs induce farmers to produce at levels greater than the equilibrium levels, then MSC>MSB, and there is too much produced from the perspective of allocative efficiency.

These points are illustrated in Figure 2.5, which represents the market for wheat. The equilibrium price and quantity are P_e and Q_e, respectively. Since D=MSB and S=MSC, the equilibrium quantity is the allocatively efficient quantity. If the government supports the price at P_s farmers will produce Q_s bushels, a quantity at which MSC is clearly greater (as measured by the vertical distance to MSC at Q_s) than MSB (as measured by the vertical distance to MSB at Q_s).

GOVERNMENT-SUBSIDIZED MEDICAL CARE   As discussed in Chapter 5, government provides large subsidies to consumers of health care through the federal Medicare and the federal-state Medicaid programs. These programs are designed to make medical care more accessible to the elderly and the poor. They do so by lowering the cost of each unit of medical care received or consumed by Medicare and Medicaid patients. For example, Medicare pays about 85 percent of the costs of a hospital stay and the patient pays only 15 percent. Medicaid pays all the costs of a hospital stay and the patient pays nothing.

From the consumers' perspective, these cost-sharing arrangements drastically reduce the perceived price of a hospital stay. They make the perceived price—what the consumer must pay for a unit of medical care—significantly less than the marginal social cost of medical care—the amount the consumer and the government together must pay to ensure the production of a unit of medical care. Acting on the basis of only that part of cost which they pay, consumers buy too much medical care.

These points are illustrated in Figure 2.6, which represents the market for medical care. MSC is the minimum amount that suppliers must receive to pay the costs of providing each unit. The line P_c represents the amount that consumers have to pay for each unit. The difference between MSC and P_c per unit is the share of costs paid by the government. Consumers will want to buy all units for which the perceived benefit per unit—the marginal private benefit (MPB)—is greater than or equal to P_c. Thus, consumers will choose to buy Q_c, or more than the allocatively efficient quantity, Q_e (where MSB=MSC).

EXCESSIVE ENVIRONMENTAL REGULATION   In Figure 2.2, we showed how the market produces an excessive quantity of the goods whose production is

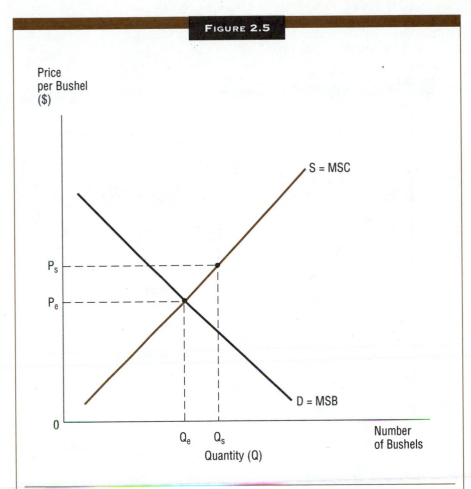

FIGURE 2.5

This figure illustrates a market for wheat with a government-supported price. The market equilibrium without government intervention would be at Q_e, the allocatively efficient quantity. When the government assures a price of P_s, the quantity supplied becomes Q_s, or more than the efficient quantity.

a source of air pollution and argued that some government action is necessary to achieve a smaller, allocatively efficient quantity. Governments in the United States have responded to this need, but their efforts have, in some cases, reduced output below the allocatively efficient level or, what is the same thing, provided more pollution control than the efficient amount. This type of government failure in providing water pollution control is discussed in Chapter 7 and illustrated in Figure 2.7.

In Figure 2.7, the horizontal axis represents pollution controlled, measured by the percentage controlled. The vertical axis represents the benefits and costs

**A MARKET FOR
MEDICAL CARE
WITH GOVERNMENT
COST-SHARING**

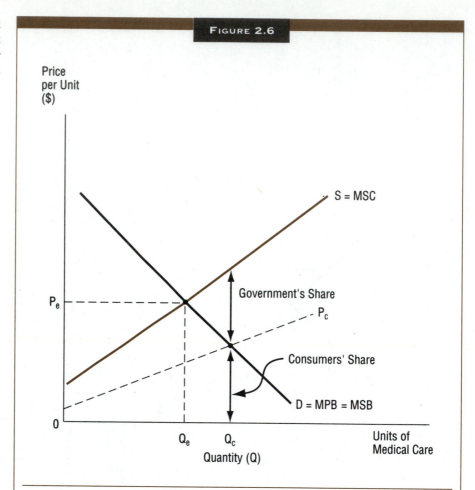

FIGURE 2.6

This figure illustrates a market for medical care in which government shares part of the cost. The market equilibrium without cost-sharing would be Q_e, the allocatively efficient quantity. When the government shares or pays part of the cost, consumers perceive a series of prices, illustrated by P_c, that are only part of the cost of providing each unit (MSC). With such cost-sharing, they buy Q_c units, or more than the efficient quantity.

of pollution control, measured in dollars. The larger the amount of pollution control, the higher the quality of water. The benefits of pollution control are derived from the uses of water of improved quality, such as drinking, swimming, boating, fishing, and species preservation. The values created by cleaner water are assumed to diminish as the water becomes cleaner, thus the downward-sloping marginal social benefit (MSB) of pollution control curve. The costs of pollution control reflect the values foregone in order to make the water cleaner. For example, to achieve cleaner water the activities of polluters, such as factories and

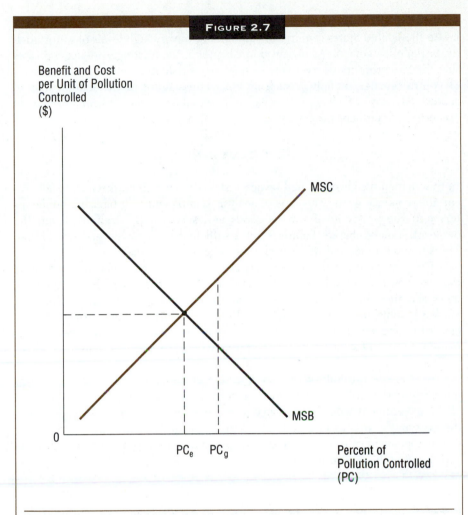

FIGURE 2.7

Benefit and Cost
per Unit of Pollution
Controlled
($)

MSC

MSB

0

PC$_e$ PC$_g$

Percent of
Pollution Controlled
(PC)

This figure illustrates how the amount of water pollution control prescribed by government is related to the efficient quantity of water pollution control. The efficient quantity, or percent, of control is where MSC (of control)=MSB (of control), or PC$_e$. Government policies require polluters to achieve PC$_g$, however, or an inefficiently large percentage of control.

farms, are curtailed. The cleaner the water, the more that the output of polluters must be reduced. The marginal social cost (MSC) of pollution control curve reflects the value of the output that must be sacrificed to achieve cleaner water. Its upward slope reflects our assumption that the higher the existing level of quality, the more expensive it is to achieve higher water quality.

The efficient level of pollution control is where MSB=MSC, or PC$_e$. A smaller amount of control than this would deny society the chance to realize benefits greater than costs on each unit up to PC$_e$. A greater amount of control than this would create a loss per unit on each unit in excess of PC_e. Water pollution law in the United States requires the attainment of very high levels of water quality, or pollution control. As reviewed in Chapter 7, the existing evidence indicates that the law prescribes excessively high levels of pollution control, that is, levels of control greater then PC_e, such as PC_g. Thus, although the market fails to achieve allocative efficiency in the face of external costs, the government may do no better—or perhaps even worse.

CONCLUSIONS

In this chapter we have outlined several instances in which markets fail to achieve certain economic goals. This type of analysis is sufficient to establish a public interest in the provision of various goods and services. By itself, however, the demonstration of market failure is not a sufficient basis for government action. The latter is justified only if we are better off as a consequence.

The premise on which our analysis is based is that we cannot merely assume that the government will succeed where the market has failed. In fact, government activities should be required to pass the same tests as those to which the market is subjected; namely, they should not be undertaken unless they move us closer to our economic goals. If they do not, then it may be better to rely on the market, for even though it is imperfect it may be less imperfect than the governmental alternative.

We think it also follows that the question of the appropriate role of government is one that will probably never be settled. The appropriate responsibilities of the government will surely change as the economy's problems change and as the economy's goals assume differing degrees of importance. The future, as we see it, appears to offer no substitute to a pragmatic approach in determining the appropriate role of government.

SUMMARY

This chapter is aimed at examining the appropriate role of government in the U.S. economy—what Charles Wolf, Jr., calls the "cardinal" economic issue. The U.S. economy is often characterized as a market economy. Government, however, plays a key, but debatable, role.

The debate about what government should do and how large it should be cannot be settled by economics alone. Economists can contribute to this debate, however, by carefully examining the strengths and weaknesses of both the market and government sectors of the economy.

The central message of this chapter is that the choice between markets and government is a choice between two imperfect alternatives—that both the market system and the government sector fail in various ways to achieve selected economic goals. The goals selected are full employment, a low rate of inflation, an acceptable rate of economic growth, economic security for the poor and the elderly, cost minimization, and allocative efficiency.

The historical record indicates that the market system may be unable to generate sustained full employment, a low rate of inflation, and an acceptable rate of economic growth. The market system has also failed in the past to provide economic security for the poor and the elderly. The market system is quite good at achieving minimum costs of production, except in the instances where one or a few firms have significant market power. The market system is also an effective means of achieving allocative efficiency, with the exception of cases of external costs and benefits, public goods, monopoly, nonexistent markets, moral hazard, and imperfect information.

Some of government's presence in the economy may be a reflection of its attempt to correct these market failures. Government has policies or policy tools that it can use in each of these instances to help the nation achieve its economic goals more fully. It does not always act in this manner, however, and it is possible to document many cases of government failure. History suggests that government can help the economy to achieve full employment and a low rate of inflation, but it also suggests that it has not always been successful in doing so; in fact, there have clearly been instances when government actions intensified the problems of unemployment and inflation. Government can enhance the rate of growth through investments in education, research, and infrastructure, but it can also reduce rates of growth by the effects of taxes, expenditures, regulations, and borrowing on work effort, saving, and investment. Government has done a lot to improve the economic security of the poor and the elderly, but various features of its poverty and Social Security programs make these clients less economically secure. Government is notorious for failing to achieve minimum costs in the provision of government goods and services, but it also fails to achieve other goals or objectives at minimum cost. Finally, government actions produce allocative inefficiency, a few instances of which we describe briefly in this chapter and more fully in other chapters of this text.

KEY TERMS

Market failure
Cost-minimization
Allocative efficiency
Consumer sovereignty
Marginal private benefits (MPB)

Marginal private costs (MPC)
Marginal external benefits (MEB)
Marginal external costs (MEC)
Marginal social benefits (MSB)

Marginal social costs (MSC)
Moral hazard
Government failure
Productivity
Income-tested transfers

REVIEW QUESTIONS

1. What is meant by market failure? By government failure?
2. What does government really cost?
3. How do we know that the market sector in the United States fails to achieve economic security for the poor and the elderly?
4. Why does the market sector appear to do a good job of minimizing the cost of producing goods and services?
5. Carefully explain two cases in which markets produce too much, and two cases in which markets produce too little, from the perspective of allocative efficiency.
6. Is there any evidence of government failure with regard to full employment and inflation?
7. How may government have moved the economy farther from, rather than closer to, the goal of an adequate rate of growth?
8. Cost minimization is a goal that applies to the attainment of goals. Explain.
9. How does government cost sharing for medical care create allocative inefficiency?
10. Based on your reading, what general principle seems to apply in making a choice between markets and government?

SUGGESTIONS FOR FURTHER READING

Friedman, Milton, and Rose Friedman. *Free to Choose: A Personal Statement.* New York: Harcourt Brace Jovanovich, 1980. An expression of the conservative case for limited government and the basis of the authors' popular television series.

Galbraith, John Kenneth. *Age of Uncertainty.* Boston: Houghton Mifflin, 1977. The liberal case for an expansive role for government in the U.S. economy.

Schultze, Charles L. *The Public Use of Private Interest.* Washington, D.C.: The Brookings Institution, 1977. An examination of the ways in which the market can "intervene" in the public sector and improve performance.

Wolf, Charles, Jr. *Markets or Governments: Choosing Between Imperfect Alternatives.* Cambridge, MA: MIT Press, 1989. Wolf's analysis of nonmarket failure in Chapters 3–5 of this book is a useful contrast to the analysis of market failure.

3

U.S. FARM POLICY: HOW IS IT CHANGING?

TERMS YOU SHOULD KNOW

Opportunity cost (Chapter 1)

Demand price (Chapter 1)

Law of demand (Chapter 1)

Supply price (Chapter 1)

Law of supply (Chapter 1)

Excess demand (Chapter 1)

Excess supply (Chapter 1)

Congress recently considered a bill called Freedom to Farm and enacted a related law, the Federal Agriculture Improvement and Reform Act of 1996, otherwise known as the 1996 Farm Bill. After reading in Chapter 1 about the efforts of formerly centrally-planned economies to transform themselves to market economies, you would probably not be surprised to find the Czech Parliament, for instance, considering "freedom to farm" legislation. But why is the U.S. Congress considering it? The answer is that massive government intervention in production agriculture arose during the Great Depression in response to three facts: (1) prices declined more in agriculture than in other sectors of the economy during the early 1930s, (2) farmers were losing their farms because of debt foreclosures, and (3) poverty was more prevalent in rural and agricultural sectors of the economy. Large price fluctuations and debt financing have been a feature of U.S. agriculture at least since the Civil War. As a result, farmers periodically have experienced high rates of bankruptcy; the early 1980s were a stark illustration.

In the desperate days of the Great Depression, the federal government increased the regulation of agriculture and other sectors of the economy. It instituted three lasting elements of U.S. agricultural policy in the 1930s. The government set price floors for some products, and to hold prices up, it, in effect, bought the output that farmers could not sell because the price floor was above the equilibrium price. In addition, government encouraged farmers to reduce production and to destroy crops and animals that were already in existence to reduce supply and increase price. Finally, the government worked with farmers to increase prices of some products by ensuring that farmers held part of their production off the market.

Federal government intervention in agriculture continued as the 20th century progressed. In the early 1990s government subsidies to farmers amounted to about $13 billion per year, or about $10,000 per farm family per year. This figure does not include the higher prices that consumers pay because of some policies and the cost of the inefficiency that results from government interference in farmers' production decision. The Organization for Economic Cooperation and Development puts the direct and the indirect costs of U.S. farm subsidies in recent years at about $30 billion per year.

Given these extensive and costly programs, you may think that U.S. agriculture needs propping up so that we can be assured of a continuing domestic food supply. Nothing could be farther from the truth. The agricultural sector of the U.S. economy is admired throughout the world. About 2 percent of the labor force feeds the entire U.S. population. In addition, agricultural exports account for approximately 10 percent of U.S. exports. Furthermore, farmers are well compensated for their efforts compared with the compensation received by the average American. In 1997, the average income of farm households is expected to be slightly above $46,000, which would be higher than the national average for all households.[1] The greater amount of poverty in agriculture compared with the rest

---

[1] "Agricultural Income and Finance: Situation and Outlook", Economic Research Service, U.S. Department of Agriculture, January 1997.

of the economy of the early part of this century had all but disappeared by the mid 1960s. By the late 1980s, the poverty rate for farm families had fallen below that for the entire population.[2]

Government farm programs are probably not the dominant reason for the positive trends in farm income and farm poverty. In 1989 most farmers—70 percent—were part time. With sales of less than $40,000 a year, these farmers receive little government subsidy; they receive most of their income from off-farm jobs. Family farmers, with farm sales of $40,000 to $250,000 per year, received about one-third ($18,000) of their $56,000 annual income from off the farm. Suppose, to use a high estimate, government subsidies accounted for one half of the average family farm-income. Even then, with complete elimination of the subsidy the income of family farmers would be above average. Large commercial farms with sales greater than $250,000 per year collect the great bulk of the farm subsidies. In fact, for all farm programs in 1988, "more than 40 percent of direct payments . . . went to fewer than 4 percent of all farms. These farms averaged almost $62,000 in payments, almost $100,000 in net cash farm income, and more than $800,000 in net farm worth."[3] Clearly, commercial farms will generate large incomes without government subsidies.

Government farm programs interfere with farmers' production decisions, provide large subsidies to the wealthy, and do little to help poor farmers while they increase food prices. In an era in which many countries are liberalizing their economies, it perhaps is inevitable that the United States would reconsider its agricultural policy. Examining how U.S. agriculture and farm programs evolved during the 20th century in more detail is necessary for understanding the support for these programs and the difficulty of reforming them. To do so we continue our discussion of demand and supply. Because we are dealing with government programs, we will also see how economics helps to explain political decisions. The 1996 Farm Bill schedules major parts of the U.S. farm programs to disappear early in the next century. Will they?

DEMAND AND SUPPLY ANALYSIS

Demand and supply analysis shows how the market determines what to produce. The law of demand states that, at a lower price, consumers would plan to purchase more of a good—say, milk—during a week.[4] (This and succeeding

---

[2]Bruce L. Gardner, "Changing Economic Perspectives on the Farm Problem," *Journal of Economic Literature* 30 (March 1992), 62–101. This is the source for subsequent information about farm income and farm subsidies.

[3]*Economic Report of the President: 1991* (Washington, DC: Government Printing Office, 1992), 133.

[4]In discussing demand and supply, it is important to include a time dimension. It would not be meaningful to say that Susan has a greater demand for milk than Henry because she plans to purchase 20 gallons of milk and Henry plans to purchase 2 gallons. For instance, Henry may plan to purchase 2 gallons a day, and Susan may plan to purchase 20 gallons a month. Henry would have the greater demand.

statements about the laws of demand and supply assume that factors, other than price of the good, do not change.) It also states the reverse. At a higher price, consumers would plan to purchase less milk per week.

The law of supply states that producers of a good—say, milk—would plan to sell less milk per week at a lower price. It also states that, at a higher price, they would plan to sell more.

In a market economy, the laws of demand and supply lead to an equilibrium. By definition, an equilibrium exists when there is no reason for a situation to change. In a market equilibrium, the quantity that people plan to buy at the market price is the same as the quantity that producers plan to sell at that price. With the plans of consumers and producers the same, no one wants to change behavior. To review this, suppose that, at the going price, consumers plan to buy more of a good—say, milk—than producers plan to sell. Consumers find their plans frustrated. They cannot buy the amount of milk they want, even though they are willing to pay the price. Producers find that they cannot satisfy their customers. Some consumer is likely to offer a higher price or some producer is likely to ask for one. The price would increase.

According to the law of demand, at the higher price, consumers will plan to purchase less. According to the law of supply, producers will plan to produce and sell more. Buyers buy less; sellers sell more. As the plans of consumers and producers converge, the market moves to equilibrium.

If this economic coordination (also discussed in Chapter 1) were accomplished once and for all, the price system's ability to coordinate might not be particularly important. Change, however, characterizes modern economies. New goods and services emerge. Consumers learn about new goods and learn more about existing goods. National population grows. Population grows in some parts of a country and declines in others. These and other changes that affect demand require an economic system to repeatedly solve the coordination problem.

Similarly, changes in factors affecting supply require the economy to adjust to new equilibriums. Supply is affected by changes in technology, in the prices of resources such as labor, and in the relative profitability of various activities. New production techniques, new goods, and new opportunities will be the trademarks of the twenty-first century, just like they have been of the twentieth. The remainder of this section examines how various factors affect demand and supply; the following section considers the effects of changes in demand and supply on equilibrium price and quantity.

OTHER DEMAND FACTORS

The amount that consumers are willing to pay for an additional gallon of milk, the demand price, depends on how much they like milk (their preferences), and their income, among other factors. It also depends on the amount of other goods, such as cheese, that they consume, which, in turn, depends upon the prices of other goods. Consequently, the demand for any good—say, milk—depends on factors other than the price of milk, such as consumers' preferences, consumers' income,

TABLE 3.1					
Original Demand		Demand with New Cheese Price		Demand with New Income	
Price per Gallon (1)	Gallons per Week (2)	Price per Gallon (3)	Gallons per Week (4)	Price per Gallon (5)	Gallons per Week (6)
$3.50	0	$3.50	0	$3.50	1
3.25	0	3.25	0	3.25	2
3.00	1	3.00	0	3.00	3
2.75	2	2.75	0	2.75	4
2.50	3	2.50	1	2.50	5
2.25	4	2.25	2	2.25	6
2.00	5	2.00	3	2.00	7
1.75	6	1.75	4	1.75	8
1.50	7	1.50	5	1.50	9
1.25	8	1.25	6	1.25	10
1.00	9	1.00	7	1.00	11

The original demand schedule for milk changes to a new demand schedule as other factors affecting demand change. The demand for milk decreases if the price of cheese decreases. The demand for milk increases if consumers' income increases.

and the prices of other goods.[5] A complete statement of the law of demand is that as the price of some good changes, keeping the other factors unchanged, the quantity demanded of the good changes in the opposite direction.

In Table 3.1, columns 1 and 2 present a market demand schedule for milk. Suppose that this demand results when the price of a pound of cheddar cheese is $5, the price of a gourmet chocolate chip cookie is $0.75, and consumers have incomes of $300 per week.

RELATED GOODS   Now suppose that the price of a related good changes. Say that the price of a pound of cheddar cheese drops to $3. As a result, consumers purchase more cheese. Eating more cheese, they purchase less of a cheese substitute, milk. Consequently, for any given quantity of milk, consumers will not be willing to pay as much for an additional unit. The demand price for the sixth gallon of milk decreases from $1.75 to $1.25. In Table 3.1, the demand

---

[5]This chapter does not discuss some of the other factors, such as expected future prices, that also affect demand. See James D. Gwartney and Richard L. Stroup, *Economics: Private and Public Choice* (Fort Worth: Dryden Press, 1995), Ch. 17, for a discussion of these other factors.

Decrease in Demand
A situation in which, at each price, consumers plan to purchase less of a good; it is depicted by a leftward shift of the demand curve. It may also be interpreted as a reduction in the value of an additional unit of the good, which emphasizes the downward shift of the curve.

Substitute
A good that is used in place of another good. An increase in the price of one good results in an increase in demand for the substitute good.

schedule changes from the one in columns 1 and 2 to the one in columns 3 and 4. This is an example of a **decrease in demand** for milk because of a decrease in the price of a related good, cheese. For any given quantity of milk, consumers place a lower value on an additional unit of milk—that is, the demand price decreases. Equivalently, for each price, consumers plan to purchase less milk.

The demand curve changes from D_0, the original demand curve, to D_1, as shown in Figure 3.1, which plots information from Table 3.1. The downward movement in the entire demand curve reflects the decline in demand prices. Its movement to the left shows that consumers plan to purchase less at each price.

Suppose the price of cookies increases. The law of demand implies that you now would buy fewer cookies. Assume that consuming cookies enhances your enjoyment of milk. Because you are consuming fewer cookies, the value that you place on an additional gallon of milk declines. Demand decreases, as in Figure 3.1.

The demand for two types of related goods—substitutes and complements reacts differently to a change in the price of a third good. Good A is a **substitute** for good B if a decrease in the price of A results in a decrease in the demand for B. The price change for one good and the demand change for the other good are in the

A DECREASE IN DEMAND

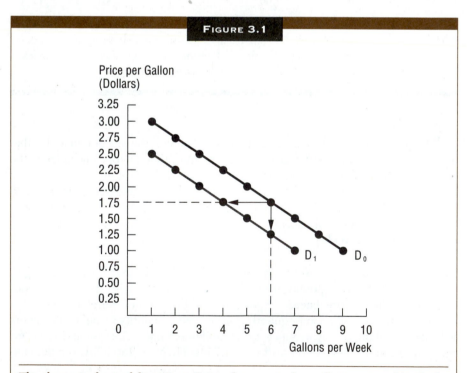

FIGURE 3.1

The change in demand from D_0 to D_1 is a decrease in demand. At a price of $1.75, the quantity purchased decreases from six to four gallons per week. Quantity demanded decreases at every price. Alternatively, the demand price for the sixth gallon falls from $1.75 to $1.25. The demand price falls for every quantity.

same direction. In this example, cheese and milk are substitutes because a decrease in the price of cheese leads to a decrease in the demand for milk. In effect, the cheese substitutes for the milk in consumers' diets.

Good A is a **complement** to good B if an increase in the price of A results in a decrease in the demand for B. The price change for one good and the demand change for the other good are in opposite directions. Cookies and milk are complements in the example because an increase in the price of cookies leads to a decrease in the demand for milk.

INCOME   Now suppose that each consumer's income doubles. With this increase in income, each consumer might place a higher value on milk. In Table 3.1, the demand schedule resulting from the increased income is shown in columns 5 and 6. Demand has changed. Originally, the fourth gallon of milk was worth $2.25. Now the fourth gallon of milk is worth more, $2.75. There has been an **increase in demand,** which means that consumers plan to purchase more at each price. For instance, at the price of $2.25, the quantity demanded is now six gallons; originally, it was four gallons.

Demand changes from D_0, the original demand curve, to D_1, the new demand curve, as shown in Figure 3.2. The movement upward in the demand curve shows that, for each quantity, demand price increases. Alternatively, the move to the right shows that, for each price, consumers plan to purchase more.

In this example, the demand for milk increased when income increased. A good for which this happens is a **normal good.** A normal good is one that consumers purchase more of when their incomes go up. Some goods—perhaps hamburger—are inferior goods. There is nothing inherently inferior about these goods; it's just that as consumers' incomes go up, they place a lower value on "inferior" goods. For instance, if your income goes up, you may decide to eat more steak dinners. If you eat more steak, there will be less room in your diet for hamburger. Thus, hamburger might be an **inferior good,** which is a good that consumers purchase less of when their incomes go up.

Other factors obviously affect demand. One is consumers' preferences. Consumers may, for whatever reason, change their minds about the benefit that they receive from consuming certain goods. If so, the demand for the goods will change. Demand in a particular market also will change if the number of consumers in the market changes. This is so because market demand is just the sum of the demands of individual consumers. In short, the demand for a good depends upon the price of the good, consumer income, the prices of related goods, consumer preferences, and the number of consumers.

OTHER SUPPLY FACTORS

The quantity of wheat that producers plan to supply depends upon the price of wheat. But it also depends upon other factors that affect the cost of producing wheat. These include the technology of wheat production, the prices of inputs, (say, fertilizer and labor) used in producing wheat and the prices of goods, (say, corn) that could be produced instead of wheat. A full statement of the law of

Complement
A good that is used with another good. An increase in the price of one good results in a decrease in demand for its complement.

Increase in Demand
A situation in which, at each price, consumers plan to purchase more of a good; it is depicted by a rightward shift of the demand curve. It may also be interpreted as an increase in the demand price, which emphasizes the upward shift of the curve.

Normal Good
A good that consumers purchase more of when their income rises.

Inferior Good
A good that consumers purchase less of when their income rises.

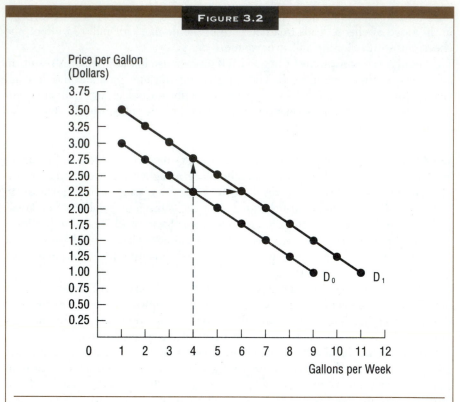

FIGURE 3.2

The change in demand from D_0 to D_1 is an increase in demand. At a price of $2.25, the quantity purchased would increase from four to six gallons per week, Quantity demanded increases at every price. Alternatively, at a quantity of four gallons per week, the demand price increases from $2.25 to $2.75. The demand price increases for every quantity.

supply, therefore, is that a change in the price of a good, keeping these other factors unchanged, results in a change in quantity supplied in the same direction as the price change.

Figure 3.3 shows the market supply curve, S_0, that exists, say, when the price of fertilizer is $0.25 a pound, the price of labor is $10 an hour, the price of corn is $4 a bushel, and a given technology exists. To find the quantity supplied for each price, choose a price on the vertical axis in Figure 3.3, say, $2.20. The corresponding point on the horizontal axis gives the quantity supplied, five bushels. The supply price for five bushels, $2.20, is just sufficient to cover the cost of the fifth bushel.

What happens to the supply curve when other factors change? Suppose that there is an advance in technology. Perhaps a new strain of wheat is developed that flourishes with less fertilizer. Clearly, the cost of wheat production falls. The

FIGURE 3.3

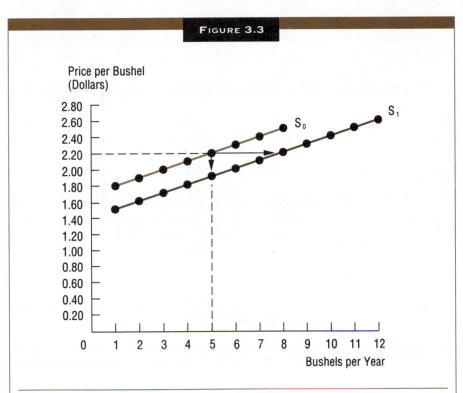

The shift in the supply curve from S_0 to S_1 is an increase in supply. At any price, the quantity supplied increases. For instance, at a price of $2.20, the quantity supplied increases from five to eight bushels per year. Alternatively, at any quantity, the supply price decreases. For the fifth bushel, the supply price falls from $2.20 to $1.90.

fifth bushel of wheat produced in the market now costs only $1.90 rather than $2.20. In other words, the supply price for five bushels falls from $2.20 to $1.90. With the reduction in cost, there is a new supply curve, S_1, in Figure 3.3. Suppose the price had been $2.20. Before the advance in technology, the quantity supplied was five bushels. But a profit is now made on the fifth bushel because $2.20 is greater than the new supply price. With the new supply curve, producers supply eight bushels at $2.20. In fact, with the new supply curve, more will be supplied at each price. The cost reduction leads to a movement of the supply curve to the right. This is an example of an **increase in supply,** where for each price producers plan to sell more.

Now suppose the price of labor rises from $10 to $15 an hour. The cost of wheat production increases. The cost of the fifth bushel of wheat, the supply price, goes from $2.20 to $2.50 (Figure 3.4). With the increase in cost, the supply curve moves up, from S_0 to S_1. With S_0, if the price had been $2.20, the quantity supplied would have been five. But with S_1, a price of $2.20 does not cover the

Increase in Supply
A situation in which, at each price, producers plan to sell more of a good; it is depicted by a rightward shift of the supply curve. It may also be interpreted as a reduction in supply price for each quantity of the good, which emphasizes the downward shift of the curve.

new supply price. With a price of $2.20, producers will supply only two bushels. In fact, the quantity supplied will be less at any given price. The cost increase leads to a movement of the supply curve to the left. This is an example of a **decrease in supply,** where for each price producers plan to sell less.

On any farm or in any agricultural area, different crops can be produced. If we are considering the supply of wheat, we also have to consider the profitability of these related crops. For instance, suppose the price of corn goes up. According to the law of supply, the quantity supplied of corn will increase. It is profitable for farmers to increase corn production. The opportunity cost of growing wheat has increased. Because the cost of wheat production is up, the supply of wheat will decrease, as in Figure 3.4.

In short, the supply of a good depends upon the price of the good, technology, the prices of inputs, and the prices of other goods that could be produced. The law of supply is that the quantity supplied increases if the price of the good increases, assuming that the other supply factors do not change. The next

Decrease in Supply
A situation in which, at each price, producers plan to sell less of a good; it is depicted by a leftward shift of the supply curve. It may also be interpreted as an increase in the supply price for each quantity of the good, which emphasizes the upward shift of the curve.

A DECREASE IN SUPPLY

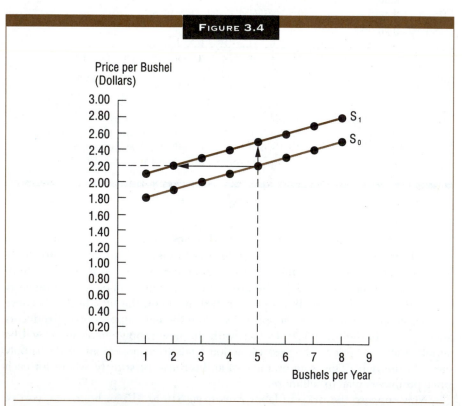

FIGURE 3.4

The shift in the supply curve from S_0 to S_1 is a decrease in supply. At any price, the quantity supplied decreases. For instance, at a price of $2.20, the quantity supplied decreases from five to two bushels per year. Alternatively, at any quantity, the supply price increases. For the fifth bushel, the supply price increases from $2.20 to $2.50.

section considers how changes in factors affecting demand and supply cause the equilibrium to change.

THE EFFECTS OF CHANGES IN DEMAND AND SUPPLY ON EQUILIBRIUM PRICE AND QUANTITY

In Chapter 1 we studied price determination in competitive markets. Competitive markets have many well-informed buyers and sellers. No single buyer or seller has a noticeable effect on market price; buyers and sellers are price takers. Furthermore, people can participate in competitive markets solely in response to their evaluation of the advantage of doing so. Potential buyers need only consider whether the expected value of a purchase is worth its opportunity cost. Similarly, people can become producers simply because they expect it to be profitable. Government laws and regulations do not prevent voluntary exchanges. In this section we study the effects of changes in demand and supply on equilibrium price and quantity exchanged.

CHANGE IN DEMAND

Figure 3.5 illustrates the market for cheese. In the initial situation the demand and supply curves are D_0 and S_0. As explained in Chapter 1, the equilibrium price and quantity exchanged are P_0 and Q_0. At P_0 consumers plan to purchase Q_0, and producers plan to produce and sell Q_0; quantity demanded equals quantity supplied. Suppose now that new medical studies, as they so often do, find evidence of much greater health dangers in eating dietary fat. Cheese is high in dietary fat, so consumers will place a lower value on cheese. Demand, as illustrated in Figure 3.5, decreases from D_0 to D_1. The reduction in demand for cheese causes both price and quantity supplied to decrease. The old equilibrium was at P_0 and Q_0; the new one is at P_1 and Q_1.

The simplicity of this change conceals the complexity of what is happening. Consumers have decided that cheese is less valuable to them. They want less at the going price. At the initial price, P_0, an excess supply develops. Without central direction, the price falls to the new equilibrium price, P_1. The decrease in demand causes the quantity supplied to fall. As the quantity supplied falls, some inputs are released from cheese production. Some labor resources (people) are forced to find jobs in other industries. Because milk is used in cheese production, dairy farmers start producing less milk. Land that had been used for dairy farming is converted to other agricultural uses. The change in consumer preferences causes resources to be reallocated to products on which consumers now place a greater value relative to cheese. Although the market accomplishes this reallocation automatically, history shows that central planning, such as existed in the former Soviet Union, is often unable to do so.

Notice that the supply curve for cheese has not changed. The quantity supplied has decreased, but there has been no change in technology, the prices of inputs, or the prices of other goods that might be produced. We sometimes read

THE EFFECTS
OF A CHANGE
IN DEMAND

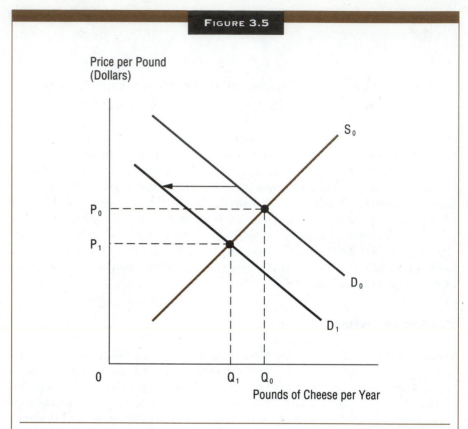

FIGURE 3.5

Price per Pound
(Dollars)

S_0

P_0

P_1

D_0

D_1

0   Q_1 Q_0

Pounds of Cheese per Year

The decrease in demand from D_0 to D_1 creates an excess supply at the original equilibrium price, P_0. This excess supply creates pressure for the price to fall. As the price falls, the quantity supplied decreases. Equilibrium is restored at P_1 and Q_1. Both price and quantity exchanged decrease.

that a reduction in demand causes a reduction in supply, but that is not true. The correct interpretation is that a decrease in demand (a leftward shift in the demand curve) results in a decrease in the quantity supplied (a movement along the existing supply curve).

Cheese producers and dairy producers may have other responses. They may advertise that cheese is a healthful food, just as beef producers now advertise that beef is a healthful food. They might support research to develop a lower-fat cheese, as pork producers have developed lower-fat pork over the years. These efforts to protect their profits through advertising and research would lead to an improved situation for consumers and producers. In the face of falling prices, however, producers might use a political approach rather than attempting to satisfy consumers' changed demand. They might use political advertising, campaign contributions, and so on to entice the government to keep the price of cheese at its original level.

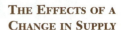

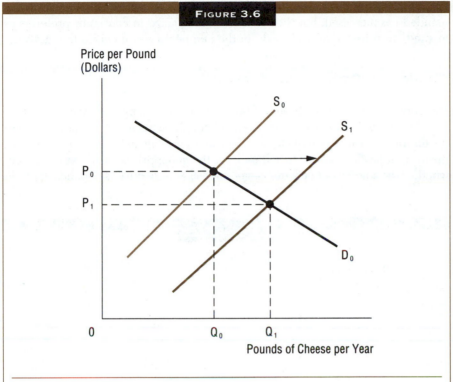

FIGURE 3.6

Price per Pound
(Dollars)

Pounds of Cheese per Year

The increase in supply from S_0 to S_1 creates an excess supply at the original equilibrium price, P_0. The price falls in response to the excess supply, causing quantity demanded to increase. The new equilibrium is at a lower price, P_1, and a higher quantity, Q_1.

CHANGE IN SUPPLY

The impact of an increase in the supply of cheese is also easy to determine. Suppose that the price of milk falls. This lowers the cost of producing cheese and therefore increases its supply. Supply, as illustrated in Figure 3.6, increases from S_0 to S_1. The increase in the supply of cheese causes price to fall and quantity demanded to increase. The old equilibrium was at P_0 and Q_0; the new equilibrium is at P_1 and Q_1.

Again, much is happening behind the scene. Producers have learned that it is cheaper to produce cheese. Fewer other things are given up to produce a pound of cheese; because its opportunity cost is less, producers are willing to supply more at the going price. At the initial price, P_0, an excess supply develops. Price falls to the new equilibrium price, P_1, without a government planner giving any orders. The increase in supply causes quantity demanded to increase. As quantity demanded increases, consumers substitute the now cheaper cheese for other foods in their diets. Because of the change in cost conditions, consumers now consume more cheese and less of other foods.

The demand curve for cheese, however, has not changed. The quantity demanded has increased, but there has been no change in consumer preferences, income, the prices of related goods, or the number of consumers in the market.

CHANGES IN DEMAND AND SUPPLY

It is somewhat more complicated if both demand and supply change at the same time. Suppose that demand decreases and supply increases. A demand decrease means that consumers wish to buy less at the going price; a supply increase means that producers wish to sell more at the going price. As you might expect, whether the amount actually exchanged increases or decreases depends upon the

THE EFFECTS OF
CHANGES IN
DEMAND AND
SUPPLY

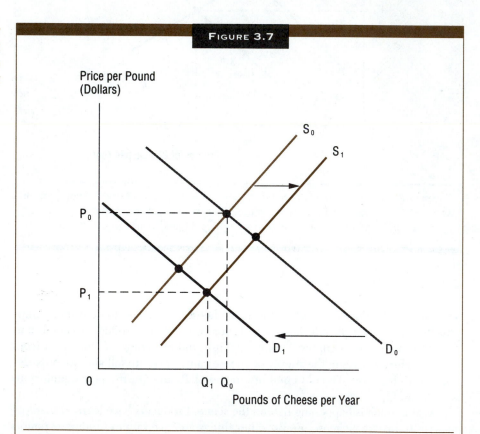

FIGURE 3.7

The decrease in demand from D_0 to D_1 and the increase in supply from S_0 to S_1 cause an excess supply at the original equilibrium price, P_0. The excess supply causes price to fall. Other things equal, the increase in supply would also cause quantity to increase. But other things are not equal. Demand has decreased. By itself a decrease in demand would cause quantity to decrease. Consequently, quantity might increase or decrease depending on the size of the supply increase compared to the demand decrease. In this example, the demand decrease is larger, so quantity falls.

relative size of the two changes. But for any quantity, consumers now place a lower value on cheese and producers are willing to accept a lower price for it. Consequently, the price will fall.

In Figure 3.7, the decrease in demand from D_0 to D_1 is a larger change than the increase in supply from S_0 to S_1. Consequently, quantity bought and sold decreases from Q_0 to Q_1, but the quantity exchanged would have increased if the supply increase were large enough. Price falls, as it must, from P_0 to P_1.

Price changes for agricultural products occur frequently because of changes in demand and supply. Over time, the prices of many agricultural products, adjusted for inflation, have fallen. This long-term fall in agricultural prices is partially responsible for federal government intervention in agricultural markets.

U.S. Farm Policy

The political support for U.S. farm policy derives from two sources. One is based on economic and historical characteristics of the industry. The other is based on the political influence of the recipients of farm subsidies. We first discuss the economic and historical characteristics of agriculture that have shaped farm policy. Then we consider the political aspects.

Economic and Historical Characteristics

As the Industrial Revolution progressed in the 19th century, household income in the small but growing industrial and urban parts of the U.S. economy surged ahead of household income in the farm sector. In 1840, slightly more than two-thirds of employed workers—3.7 million—were in agriculture. Although the number of workers in agriculture grew until the 1920s, the percentage has fallen since 1800. In 1920, more than one-fourth of U.S. workers—11.1 million—were still in agriculture, but since then the percentage of agricultural workers has dropped to about 3 percent and the number has dropped to less than in 1840—about 3 million. This massive downsizing of agricultural employment was accompanied by large reductions in the number of farms. Because of price and income instability in agriculture, fluctuations in the economy and in the weather at times forced thousands off the farm in a short time.

A massive exodus from agriculture is characteristic of economic development in most countries. Innovations in agriculture and industry, combined with education and research provided through the land-grant university system, have resulted in tremendous technical progress in U.S. agriculture. The supply of agricultural products has increased substantially. The demand for agricultural products—food—increases with income and with population. Increases in income, however, do not cause proportionate increases in demand. For instance, if your income doubles, you probably would not double food consumption or the amount spent on food. You probably would not increase your food consumption at all, but you might spend more on food—not by eating more, but by eating better. Furthermore, population has not grown nearly fast enough to counteract the huge increases in supply caused by technical progress. (To test your understanding, draw a diagram that illustrates these demand and supply changes.)

Suppose output per farmer doubles in 14 years, which is within the historical experience. If the number of farmers remains the same with this productivity growth, farm output will also double. The demand for food would have to double for farm prices to remain the same. Population and income growth are simply not fast enough to increase demand that much. If productivity grows rapidly, farm prices must fall, as they have over the past 100 years—about 0.5 percent per year. This price trend, based on farmers' greater ability to produce, is part of U.S. agriculture's success story. The falling prices indicate a greater availability of food. But because the quantity demanded is not very responsive to price changes, prices would have to plummet for all of the potential farm production to be purchased.

Farmers have responded to this price trend by leaving agriculture. Consider the demand for and the supply of labor in agriculture. Because output per worker has increased, fewer workers can produce the same amount. Furthermore, because the price of agricultural products has decreased, the market value of a given amount of output has decreased. Both the productivity increase and the price reduction cause a decrease in the demand for labor. Economic development in the nonagricultural sector affects the supply of labor. Growth in manufacturing, services, and other sectors of the economy improves opportunities outside agriculture, increasing the opportunity cost of remaining in agriculture. Thus, the supply of labor to agriculture decreases. As Figure 3.8 shows, the result is necessarily a reduction of labor in agriculture. Because of the tremendous growth of opportunities outside agriculture, the supply decrease is larger than the demand increase. Thus, wages in agriculture increase.

Farmers have also responded to the falling prices in agriculture by taking high-cost farms and farmland out of agriculture. Farms may be high cost because they contain marginal land. In many parts of the country, forests stand on land that produced crops 75 years ago. This land requires too much labor, fertilizer, and other inputs to be farmed today. In other places, buildings stand on land used for farming just a few years ago. Excellent farmland can be high cost, if it has valuable alternative uses. Farming the best agricultural land is costly, if it is also a prime site for a shopping center.

The tremendous productivity increases in agriculture have been accompanied by an enormous reallocation of labor resources (people) and land away from agriculture. This reallocation in response to the market, and in spite of government farm support programs, has left the remaining farm population better off—relatively and absolutely. The resources transferred from agriculture are now in more productive uses, increasing the total output of the economy. Although productive, these reallocations can cause pain. Some family farms no longer are viable. Agricultural families see their children migrate to urban areas, breaking the family farming tradition.

FIGURE 3.8

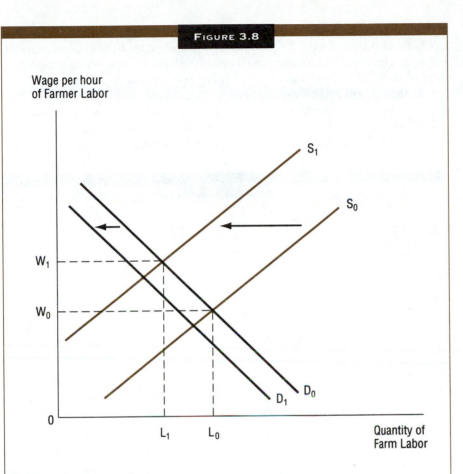

The initial wage is W_0 and the initial amount of farm labor is L_0. Because of technical change and falling output price, the demand for agriculture labor decreases. At the same time, economic development in the nonagricultural sector raises the opportunity cost of being in agriculture, causing the supply of labor in agriculture to decrease. The wage for workers in agriculture goes up although the amount of labor goes down.

PRICE AND INCOME INSTABILITY

Although long-term changes in demand and supply of agricultural products create steady pressure to leave the farm, short-term events may create crisis conditions. Most types of agriculture are risky; income for individual farmers from a single type of agriculture can fluctuate dramatically from year to year. At the beginning of a growing season, farmers must allocate their land and equipment in light of expected prices and profit. Often they borrow large amounts to buy land and to plant crops or built an inventory of livestock. Because there is a long lag between the decision to produce and the harvesting of crops or the selling of live-stock, farmers cannot even be sure they will have output to sell. Disease, pesti-lence, and localized bad weather (such as hailstorms) can wipe out a farmer's crop or herd. A run of bad luck can cause a farming operation to go under.

Besides this individual risk, farmers also face market risk. The supply of farm products is not very sensitive to price changes in a particular year—after the potato crop is planted, a price increase has little effect on the quantity produced during a year. Nor is the demand for farm products—particularly broad categories

THE EFFECT OF AN INCREASE IN SUPPLY

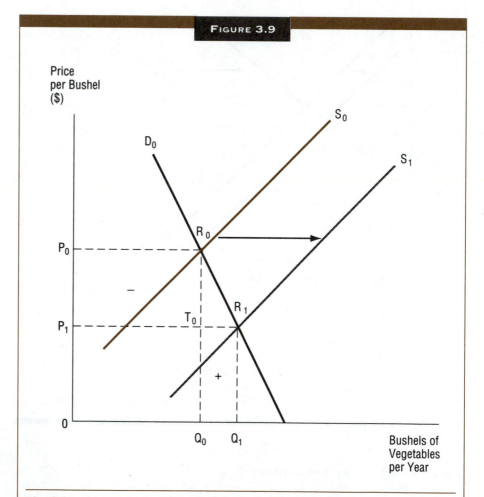

FIGURE 3.9

This figure shows a demand curve for which quantity demanded is not very responsive to changes in price. Because of this unresponsiveness, an increase in supply (perhaps caused, ironically, by good weather) pushes price down by relatively more than it pushes quantity exchanged up. In this situation the total revenue for vegetable produc-ers falls because of the supply increase. Before the supply increase, total revenue is measured by the area of the rectangle $OP_0R_0Q_0$; after, it is measured by the area of $OP_1R_1Q_1$.

of food such as meat, fruit, and vegetables—very sensitive to price changes. So in Figure 3.9 the original demand and supply curves, D_0 and S_0, for vegetables are quite steep. An increase in supply to S_1, perhaps caused by good weather, causes price to plummet from P_0 to P_1. Price falls substantially because quantity demanded is not very responsive to price change; thus, quantity exchanged increases only from Q_0 to Q_1. What happens to vegetable farmers' total revenue? Total revenue (price times quantity sold) in the original situation in Figure 3.9 is OP_0 times OQ_0. It is represented by the area of the rectangle $OP_0R_0Q_0$. In the new situation the relevant rectangle is $OP_1R_1Q_1$. By inspection, the area of $OP_1R_1Q_1$ is less than that of $OP_0R_0Q_0$. The new rectangle increases in area by $Q_0T_0R_1Q_1$ because more is sold, but the increase is more than offset by the reduction in area $(P_0R_0T_0P_1)$ due to the lower price. Although farmers sell more, they receive less revenue than originally expected because the good weather leads to a large price decrease. Such an unexpected reduction in price, particularly if accompanied by a poor harvest, can cause a large reduction in income, making it difficult if not impossible to repay loans and continue operation.

An analysis of an unexpected reduction in demand would show similar results. Because quantity supplied is relatively unresponsive to a price change, a reduction in demand causes a sharp drop in farm prices and farm income. Farmers experienced this during the Great Depression, when agricultural prices fell more than other prices in response to reduced demand. Moreover, farm products are subject to variation in demand because of foreign trade. Suppose Argentina has a bumper wheat crop. Argentine wheat may displace U.S. wheat in other countries, reducing the demand for U.S. wheat. Farmers are thought to face greater market risk because weather is unpredictable and because quantity demanded and quantity supplied are not very responsive to price changes.

Intense competition complicates the individual and market risks faced by all farmers. Because agriculture is so competitive, farmers often find that they are just breaking even. Consider the kiwi fruit. This fruit, from China via New Zealand, has exploded in popularity in the United States. But the first California farmers to grow and sell kiwis were taking a big chance. Such innovative farm products as the Belgian endive and the Ugli fruit have floundered in the U.S. market. The early kiwi farmers were successful; the price received for their product more than covered the marginal cost of production. Figure 3.10 describes the situation. As an approximation, assume that the supply curve for a particular year is vertical—$VSR - S_0$. Such a supply curve is sometimes called a very-short-run supply curve because it does not allow producers to adjust their planned production. We assume that after the production decision is made for a particular year, there is nothing that farmers can do to adjust the amount that they sell. (Weather can affect the supply curve by moving it to the left or the right.) With demand curve D_0, the equilibrium price and quantity exchanged are P_0 and Q_0. The price received by these farmers by assumption is above their marginal cost of production C_0, which includes a normal rate of earnings on the investment made by the farmers. (The marginal cost (supply price) is C_0 by assumption.) Therefore, the demand (and the market) price P_0 is above the supply price. The market price gives existing farmers **economic profits,** which are rates of earning greater than necessary to attract economic resources into the industry. If these farmers are operating

Economic Profit
A rate of earning in excess of the minimum necessary to attract economic resources into a particular use.

THE EXPANSION
OF U.S. KIWI
PRODUCTION

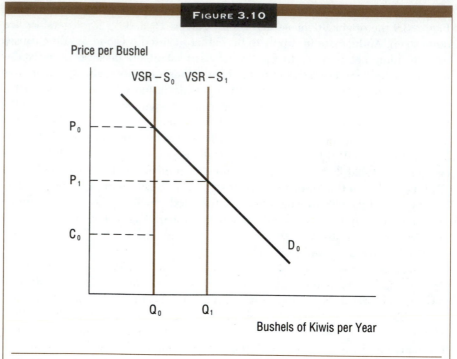

FIGURE 3.10

This figure shows that competitive farmers have incentive to supply food in response to consumer demand. At quantity Q_0, the demand price, P_0, is greater than the cost of producing an additional unit, C_0. Because a producer will receive a price greater than the cost of production for one more unit, some producer will increase profit by doing so. So long as the demand price is greater than the supply price, the very-short-run supply curve will march to the right, causing market price to fall and quantity exchanged to increase.

at capacity, this situation is stable—they will continue to earn economic profits—until other farmers start growing kiwis.

Other farmers will soon see their kiwi-growing neighbors driving BMWs; or perhaps the county extension agent will tell them about kiwis' profitability. As they become aware of the profits, they will invest in kiwi production. So long as the demand price is greater than the supply price (marginal cost of production), the very-short-run supply curve will march to the right. As supply increases, the demand price will fall. As more farms are converted to kiwi production, the supply price (marginal cost) will increase for at least two reasons. First, the new farmers and the new land may not be well adapted to kiwi production. Second, as more orange groves are converted to kiwi production, the land transferred is likely to be better and better adapted to orange production. As more orange groves are converted, the opportunity cost of kiwis (the value of the oranges given up) increases.

Suppose that when the very-short-run supply curve advances to VSR-S_1, pushing the demand (and market price) to P_1 and the quantity exchanged to Q_1, the supply price (marginal cost) rises to P_1. Because the demand and supply prices are equal, supply will stop increasing. This equilibrium will persist unless there are changes in other factors affecting demand and supply. The original kiwi farmers saw a steady erosion of their economic profits. Depending upon how long it takes to establish kiwi production, these profits may exist for a year or two or perhaps as long as five years. Farmers who take the chance of starting the industry get their rewards during this period. The economic profits eventually will be competed away; latecomers receive only a normal rate of earnings. The existence of economic profits signals people that rewards are available to those who risk putting their resources into producing the product. Besides their information role, these profits motivate people to take action that benefits other members of society.

Farmers recognize that they are in a risky, competitive industry. Some have argued that the risk and competition provide a justification for government regulations that reduce the risk. Although theoretical arguments can be made about the benefits to consumers and producers of using government action to reduce excessive risk caused by market failure,[6] too often such policies result in protecting farmers from competition and enhancing their incomes. Government and farmers could use *marketing orders* to reduce price variation, but providing an example of government failure, the program reduces competition instead. Orange production in California, for example, is strictly regulated, but it is essentially unregulated in Florida and Texas. The federal government, through a program of marketing orders, decides what percent of a California grower's crop can be sold in the primary market—fresh oranges. The remainder of the crop is sold in secondary markets—exports and for processing into juice. Often the price in the secondary market is not sufficient to cover the cost of harvesting the oranges, causing growers to allow their oranges to rot on the tree. By regulating the quantity of fresh oranges sold, the government causes the price for fresh oranges to be above market price. The price in the secondary market is pushed down. The average price, a combination of the price in the primary and secondary markets, is pushed up by the government action. Consumers purchase fewer fresh oranges because of the higher price in the primary market. Marketing orders, as they become increasingly restrictive, are one reason that per person consumption of fresh citrus fruit has dropped in the United States. In reaction to this fact, one U.S. Department of Agriculture official said, "Oranges are not an essential food. People don't need oranges. They can take vitamins."[7]

Although the marketing orders raise the average price of California oranges, they do not permanently increase growers' profits. At first, a marketing order will increase price and result in economic profits. Then, as our discussion of the kiwi market suggested, growers will expand capacity and new growers invest in developing new orange groves.[8] The increase in supply will push the price down until

---

[6]These arguments are beyond the scope of this book. For a discussion, see Bruce L. Gardner, *The Governing of Agriculture* (Lawrence, KS: The Regents Press of Kansas, 1981).

[7]James Bovard, *The Farm Fiasco* (San Francisco: ICS Press, 1991), p. 201 (quotation taken from the *Oakland Tribune,* July 27, 1984). Chapter 9 in this book, "Trampling Individual Rights," discusses marketing orders.

[8]At the request of California kiwi growers, the Reagan administration created market orders for kiwi fruit. See Doug Bandow, "Federal Marketing Orders: Good Food Rots While People Starve," *Business and Society Review* 53 (1985), 40–47.

OECD FARM POLICY: NEW ZEALAND BREAKS THE MOLD

Farm policy in the United States is not unique. Throughout the industrialized world, farmers have obtained substantial protection from their governments. This protection consists of barriers to free trade that permit domestic agricultural prices to be above world market prices, price supports, deficiency payments, and various other subsidies. The dollar support per farmer in 23 countries in the Organization for Economic Cooperation and Development (OECD), a group of developed countries, averaged about $14,000 per full-time equivalent (FTE) farmer in 1993.° In the European Community (EC) it was about $12,000; Japan, $20,000; United States, $17,000; and New Zealand, $1,000. To transfer this amount cost about $380 per capita in the OECD and the EC, $570 in Japan, $340 in the United States, and $34 in New Zealand. So in the United States a family of four gives up about $1,400 to provide a FTE farmer with about $17,000. In New Zealand, the same family would sacrifice about $140, while providing a FTE farmer with $1,000. A fundamental economic fallacy provides one part of the support for these programs. It is the all-or-nothing fallacy, and it results in a national-security argument for protecting farmers.

The argument is simple and persuasive. Food is necessary to survive. Farmers produce food. If domestic farmers go out of business, we may lose our independence, because we must rely on foreign countries for life's necessities. This argument, along with the relative and absolute decline in the number of farms and farmers in most developed countries, leads nonfarmers in some countries to want to protect agriculture. The implicit assumption is that if some farms or farmers are going out of business, all farmers are in danger of doing so.

Economic situations are rarely so cut and dried. In the United States the number of farms and farmers has declined for most of the 20th century. Does this mean that the United States is in imminent danger of becoming reliant on other, perhaps unfriendly, countries for its food supply? No U.S. farmers are producing more than ever. Only the high-cost farms and the high-cost farmers are leaving agriculture, and as they do the supply price of U.S.-produced farm products falls. The lower-cost farms and farmers would be able to supply the U.S. market at lower cost. So one example of the all-or-nothing fallacy is to think that if one farmer leaves agriculture, all farmers will leave agriculture. They don't. And as the high-cost producers leave, the remaining producers in the industry are the lower-cost ones.

Another argument is that some desirable or perhaps necessary products—say, coffee, sugar, or wool—

economic profits are eliminated. The original increase in the price of California oranges will make Florida, Texas, and foreign oranges more attractive. Not only will there be an increase in supply of California oranges, there will be a decrease in demand because of a growing use of such substitutes as oranges from other areas, other fruits, and perhaps vitamins. So the marketing order will be made more severe; the fraction of the crop that a grower can sell has to fall again. More oranges rot, and the process continues. A further complication is that the erosion of the market by substitutes results in pleas by favored producers for protection from foreign and interstate competition.

Government's attempt to raise the price of a product by holding some of it off the market will inevitably fail unless some way is found to keep out new producers. In the long term, citrus producers in California do no better than those in Florida and Texas, although marketing orders are much more important in California.

may not be produced in a country without protection. Southerners during the Civil War and Americans during World War II faced restrictions due to the unavailability of sugar and coffee. Honey, herbal teas, and toasted grain drinks were found to be tolerable substitutes. We now use corn syrup to sweeten our soft drinks; we have many other substitutes for sugar. In short, there are many different ways to obtain our fundamental nutrition, clothing, and other requirements. No one product is essential. If a country cannot produce a particular product because it is not competitive on world markets, it is likely that there will be substitutes for the product. If an unfriendly country cuts off the supply, it usually would not cause a crisis because of available substitutes.

New Zealand no longer accepts the fallacies. Although it is a small, vulnerable country, it has come close to removing government protection from agriculture. Most of its government expenditures for agriculture are spent on research, disease control, and pest control. Government payments to farmers based on production have essentially been eliminated. New Zealand has also moved away from providing relief payments to farmers because of climatic disasters, encouraging farmers to undertake risk management. New Zealand permits marketing boards to attempt to influence market price, but overall New Zealand's farmers, as we have seen, receive far less per farmer than do farmers in most other OECD

countries and New Zealanders pay far less to support agriculture.

The OECD provides another measure of support for agriculture. It is an estimate of the average amount that the price of agriculture products in a country is above the world price. From 1979 to 1986, New Zealand's domestic agricultural prices were about 28 percent above world prices. That number has dropped to just 3 percent. In comparison, the average domestic agriculture price for the OECD is about 69 percent above world prices. The same percentage for the EC is about 90; for Japan, about 200; and for the United States, about 30.

New Zealand has demonstrated that a country can eliminate most agricultural protection without causing a crisis in its agricultural economy. In 1996 the United States started toward a free market in agriculture. As the century closes, it will be interesting to see if the 1996 Farm Bill leads to fundamental changes in U.S. agriculture or if it is simply a short diversion from the policies of the 1930s. Although agreeing in principle that market agriculture would be desirable, most OECD countries have not made much progress in moving toward it.

---

*Organization for Economic Cooperation and Development, *Agricultural Policies, Marketing and Trade: Monitoring and Outlook* (Paris: OECD, 1994) is the source of much of this discussion.

Government tries to help farmers by reducing price and income risk. Marketing orders and price supports (discussed below) reduce the risk of price falling because of market considerations. Preventing price from adjusting to changes in demand and supply, however, has its drawbacks. Price changes inform consumers about which products have become relatively plentiful and which have become relatively scarce. These market signals allow consumers to adjust their spending patterns in ways that conserve the products that have become more scarce and encourage the use of those that have become more plentiful. Besides reducing the information role of prices, marketing orders become tools to enhance the incomes of farmers and protect them from competition rather than as means of reducing price and income variability.

Similarly, disaster relief protects farmers from the risk that devastating weather poses for their income. Floods, droughts, hurricanes, and hail can wipe out a farmer's crops. Federal disaster relief for those who have the bad luck to suffer financially from the weather is widely expected and accepted. This disaster relief, however, encourages the behavior that leads to the disaster. Farmers often do not buy crop insurance because they know that they can rely on the federal government to bail them out if disaster strikes. Furthermore, farming in areas prone to flooding is more prevalent because farmers expect that in the event of a flood, they will receive disaster relief.

Farmers know how to reduce risk. First, they can buy crop insurance to protect against natural disasters. Second, they can diversify. At one time the wisdom of diversification was explained with an agricultural example: "Don't put all of your eggs in one basket." By reducing risks, government programs encourage farmers away from that ancient wisdom. In the 19th century, Ireland depended heavily on one crop—one variety of potatoes—and suffered famine when it failed. South American farmers, who rely on potatoes for subsistence, have diversified for centuries. They have developed different varieties of potatoes that respond to different weather patterns and are immune to different diseases. If one potato crop fails, another will likely make it. Disaster is avoided. Third, they can use commodity market techniques to reduce their risk.[9] Fourth, some market participants, who are more willing to bear risk, may voluntarily assume other participants' risks—for a price, of course. Poultry farmers, for instance, have shifted much of their market risk to large processors like Tyson and Perdue. They used to have very unstable incomes because of the variability of their input costs and output price. Most poultry farmers now contract with the processors, with the contract making most of the payment dependent upon how efficiently the farmers convert feed into pounds of bird. The price variability still exists, but the processors, who bear the risk, are more efficient in handling it.

Although price and income variability may be a greater problem for farmers than for people in many other occupations and industries, they are not unique to agriculture. Farmers would seem to have no special claim on the government because of risk. Neither does market failure—the fact that the market helps deal with risk, but does so imperfectly—definitely provide a reason for government action. As we have seen, government efforts to perfect the market's methods of dealing with risk often fail with government protecting farmers rather than reducing risk.

PRICE SUPPORT PROGRAMS

The most visible and probably the most costly farm programs have been price support programs for such commodities as corn, cotton, milk, rice, sugar, and wheat. Although programs differ from crop to crop, the basic idea is that the government guarantees a minimum price for the product. It enforces the guarantee by buying the product if price gets below the minimum, by requiring farmers to reduce output to hold the price up, by restricting imports of the product, or by

---

[9] See Gardner, "Changing Economic Perspectives," Chapter 6, for an accessible analysis of some of these techniques. They are beyond the scope of this book.

paying the farmer the difference between the market price and the guaranteed price. Space does not permit an in-depth analysis of all variations of these programs. So we will start with the minimum price policy—a price floor—and consider two variations.

PRICE FLOOR   The price floor program was used extensively for such crops as corn. The program is sometimes sold as a way to keep prices up in good years by allowing the government to buy and store some of the bountiful harvest, which in turn would be sold in lean years, increasing availability and reducing price. Although biblical in concept, the program has not worked as sold.

PRICE FLOOR FOR CORN

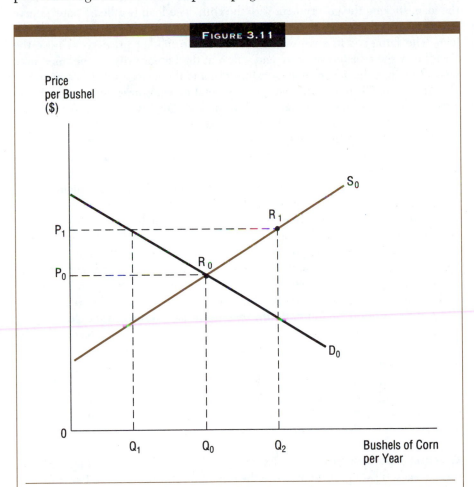

FIGURE 3.11

In equilibrium, the price of corn per bushel is P_0 and the quantity exchanged is Q_0. Now suppose the government sets a support price at P_1. Excess supply exists because quantity supplied is Q_2 and quantity demanded is Q_1. The excess supply, $Q_2 - Q_1$, will cause price to return to equilibrium unless something is done. In a price support program, the government buys the excess supply and stores it.

Price Floor
A minimum price set by government; the market price is not allowed to go below it.

Suppose the government establishes a **price floor** for corn at P_1 as in Figure 3.11. The equilibrium price is P_0 and the equilibrium quantity is Q_0. The quantity demanded of corn falls from Q_0 to Q_1, but farmers plan to supply Q_2, which is more than consumers plan to buy. An excess supply of corn, as measured by the distance from Q_1 to Q_2, or $Q_2 - Q_1$, emerges. To hold the price at P_1 someone has to buy the excess supply. The government, in effect, does so. Rather than buying the corn, in the typical program the government takes the corn as collateral in a loan to the farmer. The government lends an amount equal to the value of the corn put up as collateral, where the value per bushel is given by the price floor. If the market price stays below the price floor, the farmer defaults on the loan, sticking the government with the corn. The loan is called a nonrecourse loan, meaning that the government must accept the corn as full payment for the loan. The farmer is in a win-win situation. If the market price goes above the floor, he or she reclaims the corn and sells it at the higher price. If the price stays below the floor, the government gets the corn and the farmer gets the money.

At the equilibrium price and quantity, total expenditures by consumers and total revenues of farmers are measured by the area $OP_0R_0Q_0$. With the price support, the total revenues increase to the area $OP_1R_1Q_2$.

To purchase the quantity Q_1, consumers have to pay a price higher than the equilibrium price. To buy the excess supply, consumers as taxpayers have to pay the support price times the quantity $Q_2 - Q_1$.

Corn farmers get increased revenue because they sell more at a higher price. Consumers—both as direct buyers and taxpayers—spend more but receive less. Part of the cost of the program to consumers is the higher price they pay. Another part is the value of the consumption they give up. With regard to the milk price support program, one calculation shows that eliminating the milk price supports would result in a substantial increase in the intake of two nutrients that are consumed at rates below recommended daily amount—calcium and vitamin A. Welfare families with children would benefit the most in terms of nutrition.[10]

A price support program, if effective, eventually results in the government accumulating surpluses, which it must store. If it dumps the surplus on the domestic market during lean years, farmers become unhappy. If it tries to sell it on the world market, it has to subsidize the sale, violating free trade arrangements and upsetting friendly countries. Storing the excess supply is costly, and giving it away is difficult. Some might be sold to developing countries, which otherwise would not buy it, at subsidized prices, and some might be given away in school lunch and commodity distribution programs.

OUTPUT CONSTRAINTS   Eventually, the problems of dealing with the surplus caused by a price floor above the equilibrium price become too costly politically. Two avenues of escape appear attractive. One is to reduce the storage and disposal problem by requiring or inducing farmers to limit their production. Suppose the government sets a price support of P_1 in Figure 3.12. To participate,

---

[10]Dale Heien and Cathy Roheim Wesselk, "The Nutritional Impact of the Dairy Price Support Program," *Journal of Consumer Affairs* 22 (Winter 1988), 201–19.

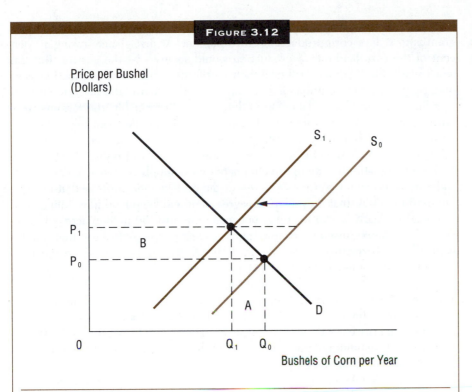

FIGURE 3.12

In equilibrium the price of corn per bushel is P_0 and the quantity exchanged is Q_0. Now suppose the government wants the price of corn to be P_1. The government can require farmers to take 15 percent of their land out of production in an effort to reduce output by 15 percent. If successful, the supply curve will decrease from S_0 to S_1, which will push the price up to P_1. The government will have established a higher price without causing excess supply. The government would not have to buy corn or make deficiency payments. Farmers, however, have strong incentives to evade the output constraints in various ways.

farmers must take land out of production shifting supply to S_1 and eliminating the excess supply.

Farmers would have higher total revenue because quantity demanded is not very responsive to price. Thus, farmers lose the revenue measured by the area of the rectangle labeled A because of the smaller quantity exchanged. But they gain the revenue indicated by the rectangle labeled B. Because their output would be less, their total cost would be less. Therefore, their profits would increase. In addition, farmers may be paid to take their land out of production.

Output constraints appeal to politicians because they shift part of the burden of supporting farmers from the taxpayer to the consumer without causing excess supply. The costs of the programs are hidden because consumers pay higher prices for many different products rather than taxes for a few large items in the federal budget. Government programs are more popular if their costs are hidden.

Output constraints rarely work as advertised. Suppose the goal of the program is to reduce corn production by 10 percent. At first glance, taking 10 percent of the corn land out of production would seem to be the answer. But this won't work. First, farmers will take their less fertile land out of production. Second, they will farm the remaining 90 percent of their corn land more intensively by using more fertilizers, labor, and other inputs. Presumably, the farmers were farming at the lowest possible cost before any land was taken out of production. So now, when they use more inputs per acre of land to produce corn, the opportunity cost of the corn is higher. Thus, the amount of corn produced will not fall by 10 percent, and the attempt to eliminate excess supply or deficiency payments will not be successful. Farmers also resent the bureaucratic controls that must be imposed to ensure that they keep the agreement and keep land idle. Idling good farmland is clearly wasteful. It was not uncommon for 50 million acres of farmland to be idle because of farm programs. Paying people not to use their land is politically embarrassing as well as wasteful. A second avenue of escape is to establish target prices and make deficiency payments.

TARGET PRICES AND DEFICIENCY PAYMENTS

Target Price
A guaranteed price for a product. The product is sold at the market price and the government pays the producer the difference between it and the guaranteed price.

Given the problems of storage and disposal, the government may tell farmers that they will be guaranteed a certain price for their crop, say, corn. This guaranteed price is the **target price.** But the government does not support this price; it does *not* buy the excess supply produced at the target price.

Farmers decide how much corn to produce on the basis of the target price. In Figure 3.13, with a target price of P_1, farmers plan to produce Q_2 bushels of corn per year. When this amount of corn reaches the market, the market price falls to P_2, the demand price for that quantity. There is no excess supply, but the price falls below the guarantee. So now the government must make good its promised target price to farmers. It makes a deficiency payment, which is the difference between the target price and the market price multiplied by the number of bushels of corn that the farmer sells.

The target price system seems to have several advantages over the price support system. First, there is no excess supply. Second, there are no direct export subsidies. Third, consumers do not pay an elevated price for their cornflakes and other corn products.

But the target price system is not really so different from the price support system. Figure 3.13 shows a potential excess supply of $Q_2 - Q_1$, just as there would be if a price support were set at P_1. The output of corn and the amount of money received by farmers are the same under both systems. The excess supply disappears because the price falls to P_2. For the last bushel produced, the supply price is P_1 and the demand price is P_2. Just as with the price support program, the cost of producing the last unit is greater than its value. Resources that could be used to produce something else are wasted. The government is, in fact, subsidizing buyers to take the potential excess supply off its hands. Thus, the target price system deals with excess supply by implicitly subsidizing buyers.

A price-floor system extracts subsidies from consumers for farmers in two ways. First, consumers pay higher prices for farm products. Second, consumers pay taxes so the government can buy the excess supply. A target price system

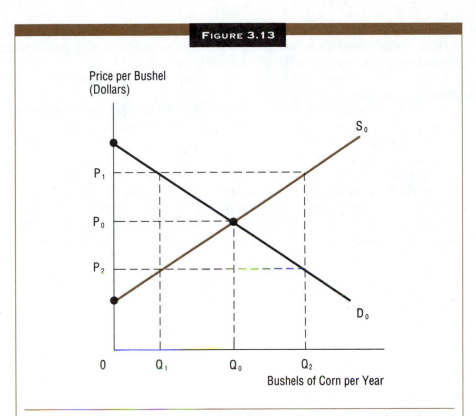

FIGURE 3.13

Price per Bushel
(Dollars)

S_0

P_1

P_0

P_2

D_0

0   Q_1 Q_0 Q_2

Bushels of Corn per Year

In equilibrium, the price of corn per bushel is P_0 and the quantity exchanged is Q_0. Now suppose the government sets a target price for corn at P_1. Farmers will produce the quantity Q_2 because the government has guaranteed the target price. But consumers will buy only the quantity Q_1 at that price. Therefore the target price will not be realized in the market. For consumers to buy the quantity Q_2, price must fall to P_2. To give the farmers the guaranteed price, the government must give farmers $P_1 - P_2$ per bushel as a deficiency payment.

results in a market price below the equilibrium price. It taxes consumers to pay farmers. With the target price system, a bigger chunk of the money for farmers comes directly from the government creating two political problems. One, the size of the subsidy to farmers is easily seen. Two, farmers clearly recognize that they are recipients of government transfer payments.

RENT SEEKING

Agricultural policies impose large costs on consumers and create difficulties for politicians and the government. You might wonder why we continue to have such agricultural programs. The answer may be political rent seeking. **Political rent seeking** occurs when people seek economic advantage through government

Political Rent Seeking
Attempt by certain individuals or groups to encourage government activity that will result in an economic advantage for them.

Economic Rent Seeking
Attempt by people to gain an economic advantage through production of new or better products or through production of products at a lower cost.

action. It is in contrast to **economic rent seeking,** which occurs when people seek economic advantage by producing new or better products or by producing products at a lower cost and selling for a lower price.

The size of the government give-away programs to farmers shows that farmers are very successful political rent seekers. Their success may seem strange because the farm population is less than 2 percent of the total population. Farmers do not seem to have enough votes to warrant such preferential treatment.

The answer may be that farmers of a particular type, such as dairy farmers, are a small group of producers with a strong interest in getting a higher price for milk. A small increase in the price of milk can generate big profits for dairy farmers. So they are willing to put a lot of time, effort, and money into convincing members of Congress to raise the price of milk. According to political humorist and author P. J. O'Rourke, the dairy industry contributes $2 million a year to congressional campaigns. Another small group—sugar producers—contributes half a million dollars a year.

Legislators weigh the gratitude that dairy farmers will have for a price increase against the reaction that numerous consumers will have to higher milk prices. There obviously are many more consumers than dairy farmers, but no single consumer or small group of consumers has a big stake in the price of milk. The increase in the cost of milk results in only a small increase in any single family's cost of living. Even if they are aware of the program and its impact, most families probably won't even be angry enough to write a letter about it to a member of Congress. Few people would make political contributions to defeat legislators simply because they voted to increase the price of milk.

A small group of committed people with a big stake in a desired political action, like getting a higher price for milk, has a good chance of obtaining that action. This is so because the cost of the action will be spread over a larger group of people. No single person will bear a large enough cost to attempt to defeat the proposed action. Consumer lobby groups, such as Ralph Nader's various enterprises, do exist, but these groups rarely have the power or resources of an industry lobby group.

Dairy farmers get Congress to give them subsidies, but their industry is important in many states and makes large donations to many politicians. Not surprisingly, they obtain favorable legislation. The dairy industry is one of many in which the benefits are concentrated in a small group, and the costs are spread over a larger group. Similarly, the 130,000 farmers who get the bulk of the corn and wheat subsidies are sufficiently concentrated to be a potent political force in several midwestern states.

But how do a few thousand rice farmers in a couple of states exert sufficient political influence to obtain the government favors? The answer is logrolling, which might be defined as the trading of votes by members of Congress to obtain passage of legislation of interest to each other. Thus, legislators from rice-producing states vote to support wheat farmers, and, in return, members of Congress, from wheat-growing states vote to support rice farmers.

So even if the peanut and rice farmers do not have sufficient clout to enact their desired legislation they can leverage their political influence through logrolling. Will the members of Congress from a state where sugar growers have political influence vote for a corn bill, in return for votes for a sugar bill? The ability of extremely small agricultural groups to obtain favorable government treatment suggests that they will—that such logrolling occurs.

The logrolling agreements do not have to be explicit—a wink and a nod will do—because of the way. Congress handles farm legislation. Every five years or so, Congress considers farm legislation in a single Omnibus Farm Bill. If you want your part of the farm program to pass, you must vote for the whole package.

Given these strong political forces supporting farm programs, it will be interesting to watch farm policy evolve under the 1996 Farm Bill. The bill establishes a path toward freeing up farm markets.

THE 1996 FARM BILL   The 1996 Farm Bill may signal a new era in U.S. agriculture. It schedules the target price and deficiency payment program for elimination in 2002. Until that time participating farmers, who had previously received deficiency payments, will receive deficiency payments based on formulas contained in the bill. Target prices no longer determine the deficiency payments; they in effect are based on deficiency payments received in the past. Wheat farmers, for instance, will receive deficiency payments for wheat even if they grow other crops. The price floor program—the nonrecourse loan system—remains in existence as a safety net. Currently, the price floors for various products are quite low, and it is unlikely that the floors will be above the equilibrium anytime in the near future.

Upon expiration of the 1996 Farm Bill in 2002, the farm program reverts to the program contained in 1949 legislation. That program would be extremely costly and provide huge subsidies to farmers. Although the U.S. farm program almost certainly will not return to its 1949 status, the expiration of the current farm bill will require that a new bill be enacted in 2002. One possibility in 2002 is that deficiency payments will be history, price floors supported by nonrecourse loans will remain below equilibrium, and government protection of agriculture will be minimal.

Another possibility is that the current farm bill is simply a continuation of the cycle of providing support for farmers in a politically acceptable way. Farm programs have moved from programs with high price floors, large surpluses, and various restrictions to programs with high target prices, large deficiency payments, and various restrictions. In the past when surpluses become a problem, deficiency payments have been introduced and when big deficiency payments have attracted political attention, price floors have substituted for price targets. The current bill eliminates most restrictions and has a schedule of declining deficiency payments. Surpluses are not expected to be a problem.

No one knows what will happen in 2002. Will farmers engage in significant political rent seeking in an effort to restore their subsidies? Will their political position, augmented as it is by log rolling, be strong enough to maintain some kind of subsidized agriculture? Will farmers, as they claim, thrive on the opportunity to be entrepreneurial and not be interested in new programs? Clearly, these questions cannot be answered now. As political and economic events unfold over the next few years, we will learn whether 1996 inaugurated a new era in U.S. agriculture.

SUMMARY

In this chapter, we first discussed how the laws of demand and supply interact to determine market equilibrium. The equilibrium price and quantity are the price and quantity that coordinate consumers' and producers' plans. The price adjusts until the quantity that consumers plan to buy is the same as the quantity that producers plan to sell—until quantity demanded equals quantity supplied.

Changes in demand and supply cause the equilibrium price and quantity to change. For instance, an increase in demand means that consumers place a higher value on a particular product. This causes an increase in the equilibrium price and quantity. As price increases, quantity supplied increases.

An increase in supply means that producers can produce the product at a lower marginal cost. This causes a decrease in the equilibrium price and an increase in the equilibrium quantity. As price decreases, quantity demanded increases.

An increase in demand and an increase in supply both cause equilibrium quantity to increase. But the demand increase causes price to increase, and the supply increase causes price to decrease. When both changes happen together, we cannot say what will happen to equilibrium price.

Federal government farm programs supposedly are designed to attack farm poverty, preserve the family farm, and stabilize farm prices and income. Although these programs provide large benefits to wealthy farmers, they are not designed in a way that particularly helps poor farmers or small family farmers.

Price support programs and target price programs give the biggest benefits to farmers who produce the most and thus surely have the most wealth. These programs are expensive for consumers. The price support programs lead to a large excess supply of farm products. Significant storage costs and waste result. Price support programs and target price programs both cause significant problems in international relations.

Farm support programs appear to exist because small groups of farmers can organize into effective political groups. They use their political influence to seek political rents, and they do so quite successfully. The next few years will show whether the United States is ready to join New Zealand in moving toward free markets in agriculture.

KEY TERMS

Decrease in demand	Inferior good	Price floor
Substitute	Increase in supply	Target price
Complement	Decrease in supply	Political rent seeking
Increase in demand	Economic profit	Economic rent seeking
Normal good		

REVIEW QUESTIONS

1. What factors will lead to a change in demand? If the good in question is a normal good, briefly explain how each factor will affect demand.

2. Use your knowledge of demand to answer each of the following questions:
   a. How would a freeze in Florida affect the demand for oranges?
   b. The price of coffee falls. How is the demand for coffee affected?
   c. Income falls. How will this affect the demand for beans, an inferior good?
   d. How will a fall in the price of peanut butter affect the demand for jelly?
   e. The media report that red apples are sprayed with a substance that allegedly causes cancer. What would be the likely effect of this news on the demand for apples?
   f. How would an East Coast hurricane affect the demand and supply of lumber in the affected area?

3. Briefly describe the difference between a change in quantity supplied and a change in supply. What will cause each of these changes to occur?

4. Use a graph of supply and demand to illustrate each of the following:
   a. Equilibrium price and quantity.
   b. An increase in demand and its effect on the equilibrium values.
   c. A decrease in supply and its effect on the equilibrium values.
   d. A relatively small decrease in demand and a relatively large increase in supply and their effect on the equilibrium values.

5. Explain in words and use graphs of demand and supply to illustrate what happens to the price and quantity exchanged of each of the following:
   a. New cars, if automobile workers receive a 20 percent increase in wages.
   b. Compact disc recordings of rock music, if the teenage population increases.
   c. Bread, if there is an increase in the price of fertilizer used to grow wheat.
   d. Fur coats, if conservation laws restrict the number of fur-bearing animals that can be harvested.
   e. Hamburgers, if strict environmental regulations reduce the profitability of raising cattle and consumers become more worried about the consumption of animal fats.

6. Cite and briefly describe some specific examples of the government's farm policy. Explain how the effects of price supports and target prices differ.

7. Suppose the government announced that it was going to treat the agricultural industry the same way that it treats the retail industry. That is, it will eliminate all price support programs and all deficiency payment programs. What would be the effect on farm poverty? On the number of farmers? On food production? On food prices?

8. Explain the risks involved with farming. Explain why government programs are not necessary for farmers to deal with these risks.

9. Some people argue that no reason exists today for government to be so heavily involved with agriculture. These people believe that agricultural programs exist to satisfy political constituencies. Given that only 2 percent

of the U.S. population is in agriculture, how does agriculture get so much political support?

10. Congress has just recently passed a farm bill. Do library research to find an example of a significant change in farm policy or a significant policy that was not changed. Does the analysis in this chapter help you to understand this aspect of the new legislation? How?

11. Based on the box titled "OECD Farm Policy," compare New Zealand's farm programs with those of the United State.

12. Explain the all-or-nothing fallacy (see the box on OECD farm policy). Can you think of other examples?

SUGGESTIONS FOR FURTHER READING

"A Survey of Agriculture," *The Economist,* December 12, 1992, 1–18. This survey of agriculture and agricultural policy in industrial economies is an excellent analysis of agriculture as an industry. In particular, it discusses costs of farm policy in various parts of the world.

Bovard, James. *The Farm Fiasco.* San Francisco: ICS Press, 1989. This book contains a wealth of information about agriculture and agricultural policy in the United States. It takes a strong position against present farm policy.

Browne, William P., Jerry R. Skees, Louis E. Swanson, Paul B. Thompson, and Laurian J. Unnevehr. *Sacred Cows and Hot Potatoes: Agrarian Myths in Agricultural Policy.* Boulder, CO: Westview Press, 1992. This group of distinguished agricultural scholars points out many misconceptions that we have about agriculture and rural America. They show the effects of current farm policy and suggest that changes are in order.

Gardner, Bruce L. "Changing Economic Perspectives on the Farm Problem." *Journal of Economic Literature* 30 (March 1992), 62–101. A balanced economic analysis of the agricultural economy and agricultural policy. It includes a discussion of the political economy of agricultural policy.

Moore, Thomas Gale. "Farm Policy: Justifications, Failures and the Need for Reform." *The Federal Reserve Bank of St. Louis Review* 69 (October 1987), 5–31. This article is a source for much information, albeit somewhat dated, about federal farm programs. Moore suggests ways that the federal farm programs might be changed. The Federal Reserve Bank reviews are excellent sources of material relevant for this course.

O'Rourke, P. J. "Agricultural Policy." Chapter 16 in *Parliament of Whores,* 142–153. New York: Atlantic Monthly Press, 1991. A sardonic, ideological view of government and agriculture.

Shepard, Lawrence. "Cartelization of the California-Arizona Orange Industry, 1934–1981." *Journal of Law and Economics* 29 (April 1986), 83–123. Although parts of the article are quite technical, it contains an excellent, nontechnical discussion of marketing orders.

Texas A&M University Agricultural and Food Policy Center—http://afpcl.tamu.edu/—contains information about the 1996 Farm Bill, other information, and useful links.

"Toward a Market-Oriented Farm Policy," *Economic Report of the President.* Washington, DC: Government Printing Office, January 1991, 131–135. Various issues of the *Economic Report of the President* deal with agricultural policy.

Wright, Brian D. and Bruce L. Gardner, *Reforming Agricultural Commodity Policy.* Washington, DC: the AEI Press, 1995. This book contains accessible policy analysis of agricultural programs.

4

MARKET POWER

Does It Help or Hurt the Economy?

TERMS YOU SHOULD KNOW

Economic profit (Chapter 3)

Economic rent seeking (Chapter 3)

Political rent seeking (Chapter 3)

Marginal benefit (Chapter 2)

Marginal social benefit (Chapter 2)

Marginal cost (Chapter 2)

Marginal social cost (Chapter 2)

Demand curve (Chapter 1)

Supply curve (Chapter 1)

Equilibrium (Chapter 1)

Economic profit (Chapter 3)

Given that government wants to promote economic efficiency *and* economic growth, appropriate policy toward market power is difficult to prescribe. Economic efficiency, as we will see, requires that market power be minimal; economic growth may require a more permissive view of market power. This tension between efficiency and growth unfolds in U.S. government policy. On the one hand, the United States has laws against firms agreeing to fix prices and laws that prohibit the purchase of one firm by another (the merger of two firms), if the purchase would create significant market power. The European Union and other industrialized countries have similar laws. On the other hand, the United States and other governments grant monopolies—give market power—to firms that invent new products and processes. The purpose of such grants is to provide incentive for research and development and other forms of economic rent seeking. Government deters the creation of market power through price fixing and mergers of independent firms, but it encourages market power associated with innovations and inventions.

Furthermore, as discussed in Chapter 3, government sometimes helps firms attain market power for reasons other than promoting invention and growth. It does so by helping firms fix prices above the competitive level, restricting new competition, and inhibiting foreign competition. Marketing orders, price floors, and import tariffs for agricultural products can be understood as government helping firms get market power.

Firms can earn profits in various ways. Microsoft, in a complex series of events, has established itself in computer software and operating systems. It has done so, although many other successful firms (Apple, IBM, and others) have fought to prevent it. Microsoft has offered a product-price combination that consumers have chosen over the alternatives. Much of its success comes from successful economic rent seeking (entrepreneurial behavior). Entrepreneurial behavior by Bill Gates and others, such as Mary Kay, Sam Walton, and Oprah Winfrey, is responsible for much economic growth and creates large economic profits. As with Microsoft, successful economic activity sometimes results in market power.

Market Power
A situation in which a firm or a few firms can affect the price received for their product, and new firms do not enter the industry in response to economic profit.

Market power lets firms earn economic profit for long periods without attracting new competitors and without improving their product or reducing their production costs. It does so because it permits a firm or a few firms to set a price higher than the competitive equilibrium price. Market power requires (1) that a few firms control the product and (2) limitations on the entry of new firms. For instance, the four firms that produce about three-quarters of all U.S. aluminum are in a different market situation than the many firms that produce personal computers. The difference is that the aluminum firms have more control over market price.

Monopoly
An industry with a single producer of a good that has no close substitutes.

Oligopoly
An industry with only a few producers or sellers of a good.

This chapter discusses market power and some of its effects on the U.S. economy. A **monopoly,** a single seller of a product with no close substitutes, is the extreme in market power; it chooses its product's price and may earn profits without attracting competitors. The chapter also explains how monopolies determine price, and then it discusses the source of market power in the U.S. economy. Most U.S. industries with market power are **oligopolies.** An oligopoly consists of a few firms selling the same or similar products. To what extent do oligopolies have market power? To answer this question, the chapter examines **cartels.** A cartel is an organized group of producers who attempt to manage their output and pricing as if they were a monopoly. The chapter first examines market power in terms of efficiency, then it examines some of the growth aspects of market power.

Cartel
An organized group of producers who manage their output and pricing as if they were a monopoly.

MONOPOLY ANALYSIS

A monopolist is the only producer of a good that has no close substitutes. The monopolist's demand curve is the market demand curve for the good. In Figure 4.1, the output chosen by the monopolist determines the price that it can receive. If the monopolist chooses to produce the quantity Q_0, the demand price, the maximum price at which it can sell that quantity, is P_0. For a larger quantity, Q_1, the demand price is only P_1. Clearly, the more the monopolist produces, the lower the maximum price that it can charge. This conclusion is simply a restatement of the law of demand.

Contrast this with the situation facing the competitive firm. A competitive firm can sell as much or as little output as it produces without affecting its price; it is a price taker. In contrast, the quantity the monopolist chooses to sell affects price. The monopolist searches for the price that will maximize profit; it is a price searcher.

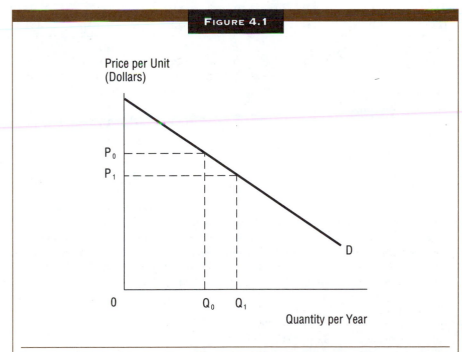

FIGURE 4.1

Price per Unit
(Dollars)

P_0

P_1

D

0   Q_0 Q_1

Quantity per Year

THE MONOPOLIST FACES THE LAW OF DEMAND

The monopolist is the only seller of its product. Suppose it is selling Q_0 at the price P_0. To sell an alternate, larger quantity, Q_1, it must accept a lower price, P_1.

Because the monopolist faces the market demand curve, its decision about how much to produce is more complicated than the competitive firm's decision. When it chooses an output, it also chooses a price. In contrast, the competitive firm chooses an output, but the market determines the price.

MARGINAL REVENUE

Suppose the monopolist faces the demand situation given by the first two columns in Table 4.1. At a price of $9, it can sell 1 unit per week; at $8, it can sell 2 units per week. At $9, its total revenue per week is $9, as column 3 shows. At $8, it is $16. By increasing its output from one to two units per week, it increases its total revenue by $7 per week. This change in total revenue with a unit change in output is **marginal revenue.** Marginal revenue is the private benefit to the monopolist of selling one more unit.

For the monopolist, marginal revenue is less than price. This is important because price measures marginal social benefit. A monopolist, like anyone else, uses marginal private benefit in decision making. For the monopolist marginal

Marginal Revenue
The change in total revenue associated with a one-unit change in the output sold by a producer.

DATA FOR THE MONOPOLY ANALYSIS

TABLE 4.1						
Q (1)	P (2)	TR (3)	MR (4)	MC (5)	TC (6)	Profit (7)
0	$10	$0	$—	$—	$0	$0
1	9	9	9	3	3	6
2	8	16	7	3	6	10
3	7	21	5	3	9	12
4	6	24	3	3	12	12
5	5	25	1	3	15	10
6	4	24	−1	3	18	6
7	3	21	−3	3	21	0
8	2	16	−5	3	24	−8
9	1	9	−7	3	27	−18

This table is based on the monopoly's demand schedule and marginal cost schedule. Given price and quantity, total revenue is price times quantity. Marginal revenue is then the change in total revenue with a unit change in output. Given marginal cost, total cost is the sum of successive marginal costs. Profit is total revenue minus total cost.

Q = Quantity per unit of time   Profit = TR − TC
P = Price per unit
TR = Total revenue = P × Q
MR = Marginal revenue = $TR_1 - TR_0$
MC = Marginal cost = $TC_1 - TC_0$
TC = Total cost = The sum of successive marginal costs

revenue is less than the demand price and therefore, marginal private benefit is less than marginal social benefit. In deciding how much to produce, the monopolist will not value an additional unit as much as it is worth to some buyer. From the buyer's viewpoint, the monopolist fails to produce an additional unit even though its value is greater than its opportunity cost. As we shall see, this fact causes the monopolist to act in a way that leads to economic inefficiency.

It is easy to see why marginal revenue is less than price for the monopolist. When it plans to sell one unit, it can charge $9. When it plans to sell two units, it must charge a lower price ($8) for the second unit *and* for the first unit. Therefore, the increase in its revenue is $8 minus the $1 lower price that it gets for the first unit, or $7.

In comparison, the marginal revenue for a competitive firm is the same as price; it is marginal private *and* social benefit. Suppose the price of wheat is $5 per bushel. A wheat farmer might sell 1,000 bushels per year and receive $5,000 per year. The wheat farmer can also sell 1,001 bushels per year and receive $5,005 per year. With a unit increase in the number of bushels sold, the change in total revenue is $5; that is, marginal revenue is $5, the same as price. Marginal revenue equals price for the price taker, because the price taker does not have to accept a lower price to sell an additional unit. Price takers, like monopolists, use marginal private benefit (MPB) in deciding how much to produce. But in a competitive market price takers use marginal social benefit (MSB) in decision making because MPB and MSB are identical. Price gives accurate information about the value of one more unit to consumers whether the seller is a price taker or a monopolist. But the monopolist uses marginal revenue (his or her MPB) rather than price (MSB) in decision making.

In Table 4.1, total revenue is in column 3 and marginal revenue is in column 4. Total revenue is price multiplied by quantity. Marginal revenue is the total revenue associated with one quantity minus the total revenue associated with the preceding quantity. The total revenue associated with three units is the price ($7) times the quantity (three units), or $21. The total revenue associated with four units is $24. Thus, the marginal revenue associated with four units is $3, obtained as $24 − $21.

If the monopolist decided to sell six rather than five units, (at $5 per unit), it would have to lower its price to $4. As a result, total revenue would be $24 rather than $25. The marginal revenue would be −$1. It can take in more revenue by selling five units than by selling six units. As the example shows, marginal revenue decreases as output increases.

THE MARGINAL PRINCIPLE

To determine the output that provides the greatest profit to the monopolist, it is necessary to include cost. For simplicity, Table 4.1 uses a special cost-output relationship. Marginal cost, the change in total cost with a one unit increase in output, is constant at $3 per unit. It costs $3 to produce the first unit; it costs $3 to produce each succeeding unit. Therefore, the marginal cost of the fourth unit is

THE MONOPOLIST
AND ECONOMIC
EFFICIENCY

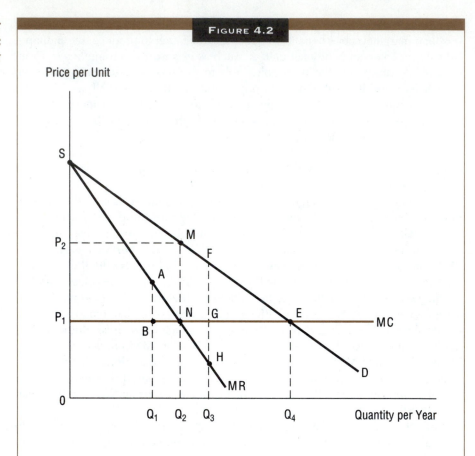

FIGURE 4.2

Following the marginal principle, the monopolist chooses the output Q_2 that equates marginal revenue and marginal cost. It charges the highest price, P_2, consistent with selling that quantity. The marginal cost of the monopolist—under certain conditions—would be the supply curve for the competitive industry. If this industry were to become competitive, the equilibrium price and output would be P_1 and Q_4. So the monopolist restricts output below the competitive output and charges a price above the competitive price. It makes a profit given by the area P_1P_2MN.

$3. The total cost of producing four units is $12—$3 each for the first, second, third, and fourth units.

Marginal Principle
To maximize profits, the producer should choose the output that equates marginal revenue and marginal cost.

The monopolist follows the **marginal principle** in choosing the output that maximizes profit. The marginal principle states that profit will be maximized if marginal revenue equals marginal cost. If marginal revenue is greater than marginal cost, the marginal principle implies that the monopolist should increase output. Because marginal revenue decreases as output increases and because marginal cost is constant, they eventually become equal.

As Table 4.1 shows, following the marginal principle leads the monopolist to an output where marginal revenue equals marginal cost. For instance, at an output of two units, marginal revenue ($7) is greater than marginal cost ($3). So increasing output from one to two units increases total revenue by $7 and total cost by $3. Profit increases by $4. At two units, profit is $10, compared to $6 at one unit. At five units, marginal revenue ($1) is $2 less than marginal cost ($3). So decreasing output from five to four units increases profit (by $2).

The profit-maximizing equilibrium may be easier to understand in a graphical analysis. Figure 4.2 shows a demand curve, a marginal revenue curve, and a marginal cost curve.[1] The marginal revenue curve, which is the monopolist's marginal private benefit curve, lies below the demand curve, which is the marginal social benefit curve. At output Q_1, marginal revenue is Q_1A and marginal cost is Q_1B. Increasing output slightly will increase profit by the distance AB. As long as marginal revenue is above marginal cost, increasing output will increase profit. Conversely, if output is greater than Q_2 (say, Q_3), decreasing output will increase profit. In summary, if output is less than Q_2, increasing it will increase profit; if output is greater than Q_2, decreasing it will increase profit. Therefore, the output that maximizes profit is Q_2.

The monopolist will sell its chosen output, Q_2, at the highest price possible, the demand price. This price P_2 is at the point where a vertical line from Q_2 intersects the demand curve. Notice that the monopolist will not want to charge a higher price than P_2, given its demand and cost conditions. It is wrong to think that a monopolist can always increase its profit by increasing price. If the monopolist increases price, it reduces the quantity sold. After a certain price is reached, it no longer pays to increase it further.

MONOPOLY AND COMPETITION COMPARED

As discussed in Chapters 1 and 3, a competitive market economy or a **competitive industry** has several properties. First, it does not require a central planning agency. Second, decisions are impersonal because there are many decision makers with no single one having a decisive influence. Third, markets are more likely to be in equilibrium than those in a command economy; thus, costs associated with the failure of markets to clear are smaller. Fourth, individuals can choose to buy products from or sell their labor to many different sellers and buyers. This freedom to choose limits the power of firms over customers and employees and vice versa. Fifth, the more firms there are in an industry, the less political power they are likely to have. Other things being equal, the smaller the number of firms, the easier it is for them to organize for political rent seeking.

Competitive Industry
An industry in which (1) there are many buyers and sellers, (2) no individual buyer or seller can affect the price of the good, and (3) equilibrium price and quantity are determined by the interaction of buyers and sellers in the marketplace.

---

[1] Here is a useful hint for drawing this diagram. For a straight-line demand curve, the marginal revenue curve is also a straight line. Furthermore, the marginal revenue curve lies halfway between the linear demand curve and the vertical axis. The marginal cost curve is a horizontal line, which is the assumption made in Table 4.1. We use the straight lines for convenience. All of the results discussed would be the same for a curved demand curve and for a curved, upward-sloping marginal cost curve.

The existence of significant market power changes many of these properties. First, it makes markets personal. If the price of refrigerators increases, consumers blame General Electric or one of the other producers. In contrast, if the price of wheat goes up, consumers do not blame specific wheat producers. Second, it limits the freedom to choose. Henry Ford supposedly said that his customers could have any color Model T that they wanted, so long as they wanted black. Only a producer with market power would dare be so unresponsive to consumer demand. Third, it increases firms' effectiveness in political rent seeking.

Although impersonal markets, free choice, and political factors are important, economists often focus on the purely economic effects of market power. Suppose that the monopoly shown in Figure 4.2 became a competitive industry with no change in the marginal cost curve.[2] The minimum price that some producer would accept for the first unit of output is its marginal cost, P_1. The minimum price would be the same for any additional unit. This minimum price defines the marginal cost curve. Thus, the monopolist's marginal cost curve is the supply curve for the competitive industry. The demand curve also would remain unchanged. Therefore, under competition, price would be P_1, quantity would be Q_4, and profit would be zero.

Figure 4.2 suggests that a monopoly harms consumers. The monopolist restricts output to Q_2, compared to the output of the competitive industry, Q_4. As a result, the monopolist charges more—P_2 rather than P_1. By restricting output and increasing price, the monopolist drives a wedge between the demand price (marginal social benefit) and the supply price (marginal cost of production) of the good. A potential gain from trade exists, but the trade is not made. The value of one more unit of the good, the demand price, is greater than the value of the units of other goods given up to produce it–the opportunity cost or supply price. So the output is less than the **efficient output.**

Efficient Output
The output where marginal social benefit equals marginal social cost.

In contrast, under competition marginal social benefit equals marginal social cost. Therefore, the value of one more unit just equals the opportunity cost of producing it. Consumers and producers make all trades that have a potential for gain because in equilibrium price measures both the value of one more unit and the cost of producing it: demand price equals supply price.

Some people object to monopoly because of monopoly profit. Unlike a competitive firm, a monopolist might earn profit in equilibrium. Monopoly profit, however, is not a loss to the economy; it is a transfer of income from consumers to the monopolist. People who dislike monopolies because of the profit they earn may be objecting to who gets the profit, not its existence. In fact, a monopolist has no guarantee of a profit. (A monopoly of slide rules probably would not be profitable.)

Perhaps the most fervent complaints about monopoly arise when the good monopolized is extremely important for its users and its producer makes large

---

[2]Later the chapter discusses a situation in which changing a monopolistic industry into one with several firms will change the cost curve.

profits—"blood money," according to an article in *Scientific American.*[3] An obvious example is the monopoly production and sale of breakthrough drugs. An example might be Prozac, the widely used and highly profitable antidepressant. The possibility exists, of course, that expectation of such profits motivates pharmaceutical companies to undertake the research necessary to discover such drugs. In the next section, we explore the extent and sources of market power in the U.S. economy.

MARKET POWER AND ECONOMIC EFFICIENCY

Market power exists when a single seller or few sellers can adjust price or output in pursuit of greater profit and when the existence of profit does not attract new firms into the industry. In the United States economy, many industries—such as the aluminium, automobile, beer, cereal, computer-operating systems, and the local telephone service—are dominated by a few firms. We raise three questions about this domination. One, has there been an increase in market power in the U.S. economy over the last 50 years? Two, to the extent that market power exists, why is it not eliminated by new competition? Three, is domination of an industry by a few firms likely to allow them to exercise market power by raising market price?

THE TREND IN MARKET POWER

Much evidence suggests that market power has decreased—not increased—in the U.S. economy over the past 50 years. It has increased in some industries; for instance, it may have increased in the beer industry as Anheuser Busch (Budweiser) and Miller have become more prominent. In contrast, it has decreased in in the computing industry as IBM's dominance of computer hardware is dissapearing in the information age. William Shepherd's comprehensive study concludes that market power in the U.S. economy fell from 1939 to 1958 and fell again from 1958 to 1980.[4]

Competition increased according to Shepherd for three reasons. The first reason is the increased competition from foreign competition in the manufacturing sector. As the European and East Asian economies recovered from the devastation of World War II and transportation costs declined, foreign competition became more intense. Government encouraged this greater competition by reducucing barriers to foreign trade. As a result, U.S. producers of automobiles, televisions, other electronic equipment, and other products became less able to raise prices without attracting competition. The intensity of global competition, if anything, has increased since 1980. Shepherd's second reason is government

---

[3] Tim Beardsley, "Blood Money?" *Scientific American* 269 (August 1993), 115–17.
[4] William G. Shepherd, "Causes of Increased Competition in the U.S. Economy, 1939–1980," *Review of Economics and Statistics* 64 (November 1982), 613–26.

deregulation of the economy. The transportation sector is much more competetive than it was, because government has eliminated some of its regulations. The transportation sector provides a good example. Interstate trucking became more competitive after the late 1970s than it was before, because no special permission or license beyond such things as safety regulation is necessary to begin a freight transport business. Air transportation provides another example. Southwest Airline, a small local carrier before deregulation, provides significant competition for other domestic airlines. Growing out of the southwest, it has penetrated California and the Mid-Atlantic states, and it is now challenging in the New England states. Airfares are usually lower at airports serviced by Southwest. This new competition would not have been permitted before deregulation. Third, Shepherd cites the federal government policies that made mergers and price fixing more difficult. All of the reasons for greater competition from 1939 to 1980 are as strong or stronger now than they were then.

A fourth reason has emerged since Shepherd's study. The information revolution has increased competition in many industries. First, easy access to information about prices and markets throughout the country, along with lower transportation cost, has reduced the power of many local monopolies. Second, fiber optics, along with deregulation, has increased competition in long-distance telephone service. Third, new products and technologies have made television much more competitive. Superstations, specialized networks, cable, and satellite dishes have created greater choice among programs, networks, and signal providers.

BARRIERS TO ENTRY

To the extent that market power persists, it does so because of barriers to entry that come from four major sources. First, technical conditions of production might be such that a technologically efficient factory operating at full capacity supplies most of the market. For instance, the output of a technologically efficient turbogenerator factory would supply about 25 percent of U.S. production. Consequently, just a few firms produce turbogenerators. The technical conditions of production create a **barrier to entry,** which is anything that prevents firms from entering an industry with the same costs as existing firms.

Barrier to Entry
Any condition that prevents new firms from entering an industry with the same cost conditions as existing firms.

Natural Monopoly
A monopoly that exists if demand and cost conditions are such that only one firm can survive in an industry.

Some industries are **natural monopolies** because, in a free market, only one firm would survive. Such a monopoly cannot be broken into several firms without causing significant, unnecessary duplication. Imagine breaking a cable television system in a small town into five systems. Surely, cost would increase. In this situation, the monopoly with its lower cost may be more efficient than an industry with several firms. Because natural monopolies seem to produce goods and services of great importance to consumers, government often regulates them and sometimes even owns them. Natural monopolies, however, account for market power in only a few industries.

Second, an existing firm or small group of existing firms might have an absolute cost advantage over potential new firms. Firms in the aluminum industry

THE BATTLE BETWEEN AMERICAN AND JAPANESE AUTOMOBILE FIRMS

The Big Three of the U.S. automobile industry emerged from World War II with over 90 percent of U.S. car sales. This dominance continued for almost three decades. Since 1975, however, the share has dropped to about 60 percent. What happened?

Perhaps Sir John Hicks, a Nobel-Prize winning English economist, had the answer when he observed that "The best of all monopoly profits is a quiet life." Or as a Chrysler executive said, "The real problem is that the U.S. car industry went to sleep for 20 years."*

History suggests that the postwar automobile industry exercised market power. It restricted output, and price increased; costs rose, and quality control faded. The industry was so lucrative that management could enjoy the quiet life. It was easier to share "monopoly" profits with the United Automobile Workers, the industry's trade union and its members, than to control costs by paying market wages. Thus, wages in the automobile industry in 1981 were over 50 percent greater than average wages in manufacturing. In addition, management allowed production methods to become obsolete and ignored quality problems. Consumers paid high prices for cars of mediocre quality. Auto workers did well, management did and does well, and stockholders did all right but could have done better.

The energy crisis of the 1970s caught U.S. car producers off guard and increased the demand for smaller cars that got better gasoline milage. Car imports, particularly, from Japan, surged. U.S. producers were not concerned about the long-run prospects of their industry. After all, General Motors, Ford, and Chrysler were industrial giants, and Toyota had only recently attempted to become an important producer. The U.S. firms complained that Toyota and other Japanese firms had a protected home market and somehow were subsidized by the Japanese government. In response, the U.S.

government provided protection for U.S. producers by convincing the Japanese government to limit exports of cars to the United States.

The Japanese cars, however, had more going for them than gasoline efficiency and perhaps government support. They had higher quality and were cheaper to produce. U.S. management could not believe that Toyota and other Japanese firms could produce a small car for one-half of what it cost them. Nevertheless, they could. Although a part of the reason was higher U.S. wages, the great shock was that the Japanese produced cheaper, higher-quality cars because Japanese management was more effective. Rather than attempting to compete with Detroit's mass production techniques, Toyota's managers developed new techniques of car production. They made assembly-line workers responsible for quality, whereas Detroit's mass production took responsiblity away from workers. To Detroit's amazement, a Japanese worker could stop the assembly line if some production problem arose. Stopping the assembly line to prevent the production of defective cars was unheard of in Detroit. U.S. firms expected many newly produced cars to be defective, but the assembly-line workers were not allowed to do anything about it. Part of a U.S. auto assembly plant was devoted to fixing cars after they came off the assembly line. Not surprisingly, many defective cars made it to consumers. In short, the Japanese adopted quality-control, inventory, and human-relations policies that led to much greater productivity than U.S. firms could achieve. Just-in-time manufacturing, quality circles, and continuous improvement are phrases that emerged from Toyota and other Japanese firms. These improved management techniques are just as much an innovation, and perhaps just as important, as many new products that have been introduced in the past 50 years.

---

*See John E. Kwoka, Jr., "Automobiles: Overtaking an Oligopoly," in *Industry Studies,* ed. Larry L. Duetsch, (Englewood Cliffs, NJ: Prentice Hall, 1993), 68. This study provides the basis for much of this discussion.

have long had an advantage over potential rivals because they control most of the high-quality, accessible bauxite.

Third, existing firms in some industries—including the automobile, beer, and cereal industries—develop and maintain market power through product differentiation. A firm whose product is subject to competition from other firms with closely related products has at least one route to market power. If it can convince consumers that its product is superior to the related products, it will be able to raise its price without sacrificing its sales completely. The product may actually be superior or the firm may be fortunate enough to convince the public that its product is superior when in fact it is not. Suppose an existing firm, say Anheuser-Busch, raises "brand" consciousness sufficiently to develop market power. Existing or potential rival firms may be unwilling or unable to invest in product development or marketing at a level that can allow them to recapture part of the Anheuser-Busch market.

Often a barrier to entry for new firms comes from the fourth source of monopoly, the government. The U.S. Postal Service, local cable companies, and local telephone services are all examples of government-granted monopolies. Technical conditions may dictate that local cable systems be monopolies. Nothing in the technology of first-class mail delivery, however, requires that it be a monopoly. The government also grants a monopoly to people who invent new products or new ways of producing products. It does so by giving the inventor the sole right to produce the product.

Furthermore, government grants protection from new firms in various other ways. For instance, taxes on goods imported from other countries—tariffs—protect domestic producers from foreign competition. Similarly, restrictions on the quantity of goods that can be imported—quotas—protect domestic producers. An example was a restriction on the number of cars that Japan could export to the United States. These restrictions allowed U.S. producers to charge U.S. consumers jacked-up prices. Governments also require that taxicab companies, physicians, and many other firms and professionals have a license to operate. Whatever its purpose, licensing has the effect of excluding unlicensed people from the industry or occupation; it is a barrier to entry.

Most U.S. industries with market power are oligopolies—consisting of a few firms—rather than monopolies. Can a few firms that dominate a market cooperate in choosing output and price? In the United States, explicit cooperation of this type is illegal. For instance, it is illegal for the owners of gasoline stations in a small town to agree to set a certain price for gasoline. Sometimes, however, the owners can achieve the same result without an explicit agreement. Perhaps they play golf together and simply come to understand that price cutting is not good manners. We examine this possibility in detail in the next section by studying the OPEC cartel.

OPEC: A Few Sellers Acting Like a Monopoly

To understand if domination of an industry by a few sellers is likely to allow them to exercise market power by raising price, we consider OPEC—the Organization of Petroleum Exporting Countries. OPEC is an organization of 12 petroleum-exporting countries.[5] In the early 1970s, these countries sold more than 90 percent of all the petroleum exported to other countries. Petroleum production in these countries—for instance, Saudi Arabia, Iran, Venezuela, and Kuwait—had been increasing at the same time that production in the Soviet Union and the United States—the largest producing and consuming countries—had begun to decline. In 1970, the average price per barrel of oil at the well in the United States was $3.18. This average price started a roller coaster ride in 1974, when it went to $7.67. The ride took it to $31.77 in 1981. Some respected analysts expected $100 per barrel prices by 1990. But the roller coaster headed down, with the price falling to $28.52 in 1982, $26.19 in 1983, and $24.09 in 1985 before it almost crashed at $12.66 in 1986. More recently, it has been between $15 and $20 per barrel.

In the mid-1980s, annual petroleum production in the Soviet Union and in the United States had increased compared to the mid-1970s. On the other hand, OPEC's Saudi Arabia—where petroleum is sometimes cheaper to pump than water in the United States—produced almost 50 percent less in the mid-1980s than it had in the mid-1970s. Other countries with reduced annual production were Kuwait, the United Arab Emirates, and Venezuela, all members of OPEC. Countries with sharply increased annual production were Mexico, the United Kingdom, and Norway.[6] These countries are not members of OPEC.

CARTEL FORMATION

These changes in petroleum prices and production are consistent with the idea that OPEC acts like a cartel. To succeed, a cartel must restrict output and prevent entry of new firms. A successful cartel requires an ACE in the hole: agreement, cooperation, and enforcement.

A cartel agreement requires that all important producers *agree* on both total output and the division of that output among cartel members. Its purpose is to restrict output and raise price above the competitive price. The agreement outlines a procedure for solving problems as they arise; it cannot, however, anticipate and solve all possible problems.

In a cartel, the members must continually *cooperate* and come to new agreements as conditions change. If successful, price will be above the marginal cost of production for each member of the cartel. For instance, the price of petroleum in 1981 averaged close to $32 a barrel in the United States. Some members of OPEC could produce and deliver a barrel of petroleum to the United States for less than $5.

Every barrel such a country shipped to the United States beyond its quota increased its profit by $27. Cheating was very profitable, as it is in any cartel. As long as a cartel member thinks it can cheat—produce more than its quota—

---

[5]The members of OPEC are countries, not business firms. They may have objectives other than profits. It is instructive, however, to study OPEC to see how cartels work.
[6]Data are from various years' issues of the American Petroleum Institute's *Basic Petroleum Data Book*.

without greatly affecting cartel price, it will be tempted to increase its profit by doing so. Therefore, a cartel must be able to *enforce* the agreement.

THE DETERMINANTS OF CARTEL SUCCESS

All members of a cartel suffer from a split personality. On the one hand, they realize that the maximization of cartel profit is probably in the best interests of each member of the cartel. Thus, they agree to a common policy and cooperate in following and adapting that policy. On the other hand, if other members keep the agreement, each member realizes that it can increase its profit by cheating. Enforcement becomes necessary.

The fewer and more similar are the firms, the easier it is to form and operate a cartel. In an industry consisting of two identical firms, the agreement that maximizes cartel profit requires that cartel output be divided evenly between the two firms. For instance, a national market might be split in two. Each firm could keep the profit it earns, and each would earn the same profit.

Furthermore, with only two members, it is easy to determine if the other firm cheats on an agreement. Suppose the market price falls below the expected cartel price. Either demand has decreased or the other member of the cartel is cheating by producing more than the agreed amount.

If cheating occurs, the noncheating firm probably will retaliate by also expanding output. The agreement will break down. Profit will decrease. Neither member wants this to happen. Because each firm can identify the cheater, the agreement may be self-enforcing. With just two identical firms in the industry, no *explicit* agreement is necessary to reach a cartel-type solution. This is why many economists think that some highly concentrated industries act as if they were monopolies, even in the absence of explicit cartel agreements.

It becomes progressively more difficult to agree on, cooperate with, and enforce a cartel policy (1) as the number of firms in the industry increases and (2) as the firms become less and less similar. With more firms it becomes more difficult for the agreement to include all or at least most of the major firms in the industry. One problem is the holdout. When Rockefeller Center was being developed in New York City, owners of a small piece of land in its midst refused to sell. Perhaps the owners had some sentimental attachment to the business that they operated on the land. Or perhaps they hoped to obtain a much higher price by holding out till the last minute.

A potential member of a cartel might behave in the same way, letting the other firms restrict their output so the holdout will benefit from the higher price without restricting its output. With such a bargaining position, the holdout firm might capture a larger share of the cartel profit. Rockefeller Center was built around the holdout, but a cartel must include all of the major players.

A second problem is that, with more firms, it becomes more difficult to detect cheating. If there are ten firms in the cartel and the cartel price starts to fall, then either there is a decrease in demand or at least one of the nine other cartel members is cheating. But which one? Thus, each firm might think that it can cheat without being detected. As the detection of cheating becomes more diffi-cult, the incentive to cheat becomes overwhelming.

If the firms are not similar, agreement also is harder to reach. Suppose there are only two firms, but one is a higher-cost firm. As you might think, to produce a given output at least cost, the lower-cost firm must produce a larger share of total output than the higher-cost firm. In the extreme case, the lower-cost firm would produce all of the cartel output. But now the initial bargaining becomes ex-tremely difficult. The higher-cost firm will demand a larger profit share than out-put share if it is to accept a lower output quota. The lower-cost firm will argue that profit shares and output shares should be the same. If the lower-cost firm has a large cost advantage, it may be able to force the other firm to accept and keep an agreement. It may do so by threatening to flood the market with output unless the higher-cost firm cooperates.

PROBLEMS OF THE OPEC CARTEL

The OPEC cartel has encountered serious problems for at least three reasons. First, there are 12 members of OPEC and 6 to 10 nonmember countries that are important producers of petroleum. Second, the demand and supply for petro-leum is different when consumers and producers have time to adjust completely to a price change. Third, the member countries of OPEC have different and con-flicting goals.

OPEC's initial success, as indicated by an increase in price from about $3 a barrel to more than $30 a barrel in less than a decade, was due to a number of factors. Political upheaval in the Middle East played an important role. OPEC also accounted for over 90 percent of the world's exports.

But OPEC did not have significant barriers to entry for new producers. As a result of major petroleum discoveries in Alaska, the North Sea, and Mexico and of numerous successful attempts to squeeze more petroleum out of existing fields, non-OPEC production grew substantially.

The petroleum pessimists thought that the supply of petroleum could be represented by the supply curve S_0 in Figure 4.3. On S_0, an increase in price from P_0 to P_1 does not cause an increase in quantity supplied. But the pes-simists underestimated both the greed and the ingenuity of business owners. The incredible profit potential of $30-a-barrel petroleum attracted a tremendous amount of resources into the industry. Given sufficient time for adjustment—five to ten years—the supply curve for petroleum looks more like S_1 in Figure 4.3. The increase in price engineered by OPEC carried the seeds of its own destruc-tion in the supply response of non-OPEC countries. Quantity supplied increased from Q_0 to Q_1.

Just as the petroleum pessimists underestimated supply responsiveness, they also underestimated demand responsiveness to a price change. The pessimists thought that demand responsiveness was almost nil. It is only a slight exaggera-tion to say that they thought that the demand for petroleum products was verti-cal. When price increased suddenly and substantially in the 1970s, consumers

THE SUPPLY OF
PETROLEUM

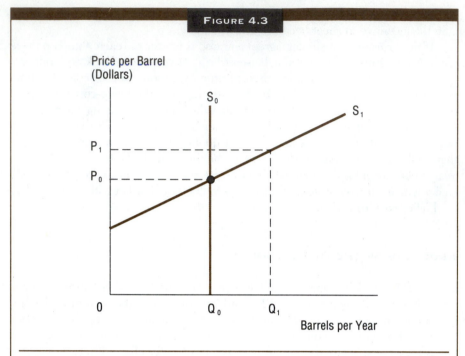

FIGURE 4.3

Price per Barrel
(Dollars)

If the supply of petroleum is similar to S_0, raising price does not induce an increase in quantity supplied. Many people believed that OPEC would be very successful because they thought S_0 was a good representation of the supply curve for petroleum. It turns out, however, that the supply curve for petroleum is more like S_1 because the price increases engineered by OPEC resulted in big increases in quantity supplied by non-OPEC producers.

were not able to adjust their purchases very much—at first. The demand for petroleum could be cut only so much by reducing (1) pleasure driving, (2) home heating in the winter, and (3) home cooling in the summer. But given time to adjust, people replaced their cars, furnaces, air conditioners, and houses with ones that were more energy efficient.

Similarly, firms adopted more energy-efficient methods of production. The amount of energy used per dollar of national output fell almost every year in the 1970s and 1980s. Thus, the demand curve for petroleum products—given several years for adjustment—is better represented by D_1 than D_0 in Figure 4.4. Here, an increase in price from P_0 to P_1 causes quantity demanded to fall from Q_0 to Q_1.

Finally, the OPEC countries differ substantially in terms of their petroleum reserves, their populations relative to their reserves, and in many other ways. They are *not* similar. Just as in any cartel, the objectives of any one country conflict with those of other countries and with the objective of maximizing cartel profit. Countries with large reserves relative to their populations want to stretch

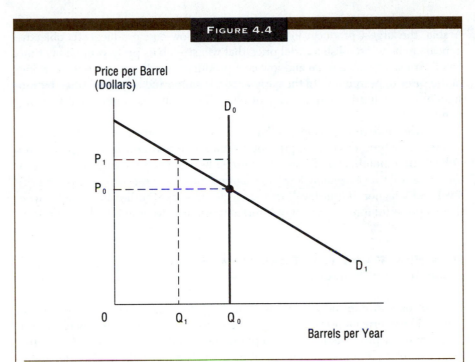

FIGURE 4.4

THE DEMAND FOR
PETROLEUM

If the demand for petroleum is similar to D_0, raising price does not induce a decrease in quantity demanded. Many people believed that OPEC would be very successful because they thought D_0 was a good representation of the demand curve for petroleum. It turns out, however, that the demand curve for petroleum is more like D_1 because the price increases engineered by OPEC resulted in large decreases in quantity demanded after consumers had time to adjust.

their sales of petroleum and their profits over a long period of time. They fear that a low-output/high-price strategy will hasten the demise of petroleum as a major source of energy, preventing them from enjoying petroleum profits in the future.

Countries with large populations and small reserves want to get their profit now with a low-output/high-price strategy. They wish to use their profit to finance economic development and to reduce political tension. They do not care that such a strategy might result in an early replacement of petroleum as a prime source of energy because they will not have any petroleum to sell in the future. The different objectives enhance the always-present incentive to cheat; thus, OPEC is "a confederacy of cheats." According to one magazine, several important producers regularly violate OPEC agreements.[7]

---

[7]"A Confederacy of Cheats," *The Economist,* June 10, 1989.

Although OPEC is currently weakened, Saudi Arabia holds it together. Saudi Arabia, the largest producer in OPEC, is a very low-cost producer. Its objective appears to be to establish a cartel price that will stretch its profit over a long time. Saudi Arabia is such a large and low-cost producer that it can cause wide swings in the price of petroleum. In the early 1980s, it supported the cartel price by substantially reducing its output. As a result, other countries could cheat with impunity.

In the mid-1980s, Saudi Arabia became an enforcer. It substantially increased its output, driving the price of petroleum temporarily below $10 a barrel. Other cartel members and perhaps nonmembers got the message: cooperate or the price will stay extremely low. New agreements were reached at a lower price level and a higher output level. It remains to be seen whether the cartel can remain a powerful force, or whether internal tensions will cause it to disintegrate.[8]

DO A FEW FIRMS THAT DOMINATE A MARKET HAVE MARKET POWER?

It is not easy to determine if a few firms that dominate a market have market power. The internal tensions caused by the entry of new producers, by the substitution of other products for the cartel's products, and by dissension and cheating in the cartel itself are not unique to OPEC. Any formal or informal agreement to restrict output and increase price is subject to similar tensions. In the absence of barriers to entry and government enforcement of agreements, formal and informal cartels are likely to be unstable. If government actively discourages cartels, it is even more difficult for them to function. In short, the market power of oligopolies is weaker (1) the greater the number of firms, (2) the more dissimilar the firms, (3) when there is no powerful firm to enforce an agreement, and (4) over time, because of the responses of consumers and other producers to high prices and large profits.

MARKET POWER AND ECONOMIC GROWTH

As we have seen, economic efficiency and a dispersion of economic and political power call for industries with little market power. Economic growth, as we will see in Chapter 16, depends upon the development of new products and new ways of doing things. Knowledge and the creation of new knowledge are the basis for much economic growth and for the growth of many firms. Knowledge-based (high-tech) firms have several features that lead to a monopoly or near-monopoly of their products, that is, market power. The development of a new medicinal drug or a new operating system for computers has huge start-up costs, and the

---

[8]Sargon J. Youhanna, "A Note on Modelling OPEC Behavior 1983–1989: A Test of the Cartel and Competitive Hypotheses," *The American Economist* 38 (Fall 1994), 78–84, finds that OPEC continues to function as a cartel.

product developed is essentially knowledge. After the knowledge of how to produce a new drug, operating system, or chip is developed, it may take a huge investment in plant and equipment to produce the product. These large up-front costs are a much bigger part of the total cost of producing a drug or a chip than are the labor and material costs. Another cost that knowledge-based firms face is the cost of development projects that fail because the search for new knowledge leads researchers to many dead ends.

Up-front costs have important implications. For example, as W. Brian Arthur says, "The first disk of Windows to go out the door cost Microsoft $50 million; the second and subsequent disks cost $3."[9] The marginal production cost of successive disks is $3, and similar situations exist for drugs, videos, and CDs. To cover the development cost of these products and other unsuccessful products, the price of a drug or a software disk must be greater than the marginal production cost.

Firms can recover the development costs only if thay can price their successful products at monopoly or near-monopoly levels. They can do so only if they have property rights in the knowledge that underlies the product. If other firms could freely copy CDs or drug formulas, the firm that created the music, the software, or the formula would be unable to raise its price much above production cost; the up-front development costs would not be covered. This is one reason government grants monopolies of new products through copyrights and patents. Even if a firm has this patent or copyright protection, however, it may be unable to capture profits and prevent quick imitation by rivals, unless it uses tactics that attract the attention of regulators. To secure first-mover advantage, one tactic is to introduce new products at low prices to expand the customer base. Netscape went so far as to give away its software. In these markets, being the first mover and having a superb product is important, but the first mover and the best product do not always win. Arthur cites Prodigy as a first mover in on-line services and the Macintosh operating system as a superb product; neither has become the dominant player in the respective markets.

If the initial product is sold cheaply or given away to create a large customer base, the firm must exploit that customer base to recover its cost. Microsoft presents several examples of how this can be done. It has extended its dominant position in operating systems to software by developing word processing programs, spreadsheets, and other software. In an attempt to capture the software market, Microsoft encourages producers of computers using its Windows operating system to load its software rather than other software on their computers. The idea is that if ultimate consumers can be enticed to learn its software, they will be locked into Microsoft's products; it will have a captive market. It is alleged that Microsoft uses persuasion and rebates to entice computer producers to load its software and not to load its rivals' software on new computers. To extend its position in software, Microsoft attempted to purchase the producer of a popular financial software package so that the package could be part of its bundle. The government discouraged this purchase on monopoly grounds, and Microsoft

---

[9] W. Brian Arthur, "Increasing Returns and the New World of Business," *Harvard Business Review* 74 (July/August 1996), 100–109. The quote is from p. 103.

developed its own financial package. Currently, Microsoft is battling Netscape in an attempt to overtake Netscape's lead in web browsers, and Netscape has alleged that Microsoft has violated antitrust laws.

Several questions come up in these knowledge-based industries. One, can we be sure that the superior product will become the industry standard? Two, what discretion should firms be given in taking advantage of their successful products? Three, should firms be allowed to extend their market dominance from one market to another? These are hard questions and different people will come to different conclusions. We do not attempt to answer these questions here, but this chapter suggests that the answers may involve a tradeoff between economic efficiency and economic growth. Given the importance of knowledge-based firms for economic growth, it is important for policy not to penalize success. On the other hand, the monopolization of necessities is to be avoided, if possible.

The dilemma is well illustrated in the pharmaceutical industry whose products are essential and whose firms often have significant market power. Sometimes a firm will have a patent on the only product useful in treating a particular disease. In the late 1980s Wellcome, a British company, sold the only drug, AZT, that seemed to help AIDS patients. It was accused of "profiting from disease" because the annual charge for using the drug was $10,000, a charge that the company reduced to $3,000 because of political pressure. Even at the lower charge, the company may have made as much as 70 percent over the costs of production and marketing.[10] Such situations cry out for government intervention. Extreme critics compare pharmaceutical profit to "blood money."[11] *The Economist* and *Scientific American* recognize that large profits on successful drugs provide incentive for private firms to do the risky and expensive research necessary to discover new drugs. In recognition of this incentive role of profits, governments grant patent monopolies to the discoverers of new drugs.

Market power in pharmaceuticals springs from patents, but the patents are necessary to induce private-sector research aimed at developing new drugs. Robert Goldberg argues that the government is incapable of performing the research. He notes that governmental pharmaceutical research in the Soviet Union was ineffective in producing new drugs. Moreover, he claims that price controls (regulations) have stifled pharmaceutical research in the United Kingdom. In short, he believes that monopoly profits are necessary to induce firms to do desirable research.[12] Although Goldberg dismisses government-sponsored research and government regulation, other economists see a government role in basic research and in regulation of private research.

In this discussion of market power and economic growth, we have seen that market power might be an unavoidable consequence of the innovative activity of

---

[10]"Profiting from Disease," *The Economist*, January 27, 1990, 17–18.

[11]Tim Beardsley, "Blood Money? Critics Question High Pharmaceutical Profits," *Scientific American* 269 (August 1993), 115–117.

[12]Robert M. Goldberg, "Race Against the Cure: The Health Hazards of Pharmaceutical Price Controls," *Policy Review* (Spring 1994). For a more balanced view of the issues, see F. M. Scherer, "Pricing, Profits, and Technological Progress in the Pharmaceutical Industry," *Journal of Economic Perspectives* 7 (Summer 1993), 97–116.

business firms. Because this innovative activity is essential for continued economic growth, limiting the market power that results from firms finding new products and better ways to produce old products could be self-defeating. A dilemma facing policy makers is what to do about the pricing of new products that are necessary for life and for which there are no close substitutes. These rare situations must be handled on a case by case basis. In the next section, we discuss government policy toward market power in other cases.

GOVERNMENT AND MARKET POWER

Economists have not reached a consensus on government's role in dealing with market power, as thay have, for instance, concerning farm policy. The conflicting implications of economic efficiency and economic growth create this lack of consensus. For instance, some economists have criticized while others have supported the U.S. Department of Justice investigation of Microsoft's tactics. Three general principles can guide policy toward market power in a way that reconciles the sometimes conflicting goals of efficiency and growth. First, government can limit mergers of firms that produce the same or similar products while prohibiting price fixing. Second, government can encourage economic rent-seeking by granting patents and copyrights while supporting basic research. Finally, it must discourage political rent-seeking so that it does not become a source of market power.

U.S. *antitrust laws* dealing with mergers and price fixing probably satisfy the principle. First, they make it even harder for oligopolies to reach formal or informal agreements to exercise market power. These laws, particularly the Clayton and Sherman Acts, prohibit explicit conspiracies to fix prices, divide markets, restrict entry, and engage in other cartel behavior. Second, they help to maintain the number of firms in an industry by preventing most mergers that would increase market power. As Shepherd argues, these laws enhance the tendencies for industries to remain or become competitive.

Given the federal antitrust laws and the existing structure of industries in the United States, many economists believe that market power is not a major problem in the U.S. economy. They recognize that it exists, but they do not advocate government action—beyond the current antitrust laws—to reduce market power.

Second, government policy should not impede and perhaps should promote economic rent seeking. The tremendous growth in industrial economies in the last two centuries depended largely upon the entrepreneur seeking profit. If progress is to be sustained, prices must be allowed to relay information about scarcity to entrepreneurs, and entrepreneurs must be allowed to reap profit from their innovation. Instead of breaking up or regulating firms that achieve market power through economic rent seeking, government can play a positive role by increasing the incentive for innovation. As the experiences of General Motors and IBM show, the market power that is created is often temporary. Market power in a market economy is like the mythical gunslinger in the Old West: it lasts only until someone faster comes along.

The third principle implies that government must take care not to make political rent seeking more lucrative than economic rent seeking. Granting patents to innovators must not lead to granting market power to existing firms and interest groups. Political rent seeking—the attempt to gain economic advantage through government action—supports much market power. License systems support the market power of accountants, some cab companies, doctors, realtors, and others. In almost every instance, the license system is requested by the industry or occupation. Moreover, the standards for getting and keeping a license are almost always set by the industry or occupation. Rarely does such activity lead to economic progress.

Summary

A competitive economy is efficient because the value of one more unit of any good (marginal benefit) is just equal to the opportunity cost of producing one more unit (marginal cost). If marginal benefit were greater than marginal cost, unrealized gains from trade would exist. This is because the value of the additional unit of a good would be greater than the value of the goods given up to produce it. The monopolist restricts output and raises price above marginal cost. Marginal benefit under monopoly is greater than marginal cost. Thus, the monopoly output is inefficient.

Yet the monopolist does not have an unlimited desire to raise price. When price goes up, output goes down. Charging more and selling less is not always a good strategy. To maximize profit, the monopolist equates marginal revenue with marginal cost.

The U.S. economy is reasonably competitive. Efficiency loss due to monopoly does not appear to be very large. Moreover, profit attracts new firms into an industry. In addition, economic rent seeking—innovation—is important in many parts of the economy, in particular the knowledge-based industries.

Monopoly occurs for four reasons: (1) technology sometimes requires that a firm be so large that it can supply the entire market, (2) a firm might have absolute cost advantages, (3) a firm might use advertising and product development to gain a dominant position, and (4) government sometimes encourages monopoly.

The OPEC cartel shows how several firms in an industry might act like a monopoly. Although numerous countries produce petroleum, OPEC has succeeded in restricting petroleum output and raising price, but cooperation is not perfect. Some countries cheat on the cartel agreement by producing more than their share. Enforcement activity by Saudi Arabia has increased cartel stability.

Analyses of cartels and of OPEC in particular show that agreement among firms—even if it is not an explicit agreement—might lead to monopoly. But cheating—which increases as the number of firms in the industry increases—and the entry of new firms make such agreements unstable. Government can promote competition through antitrust laws, but it must avoid impeding economic rent seeking.

Economic growth, as well as economic efficiency, is related to monopoly and competition. As they develop new products and processes, knowledge-based firms may achieve significant market power. If they do this without price fixing and merger, thay may promote economic growth while they are capturing a large market share. Government policy, in such circumstances, must recognize that reining in the profit seeking behavior of such firms may reduce the incentive to innovate and thus impede economic growth.

KEY TERMS

Market power
Monopoly
Oligopoly
Cartel

Marginal revenue
Marginal principle
Competitive industry

Efficient output
Barrier to entry
Natural monopoly

REVIEW QUESTIONS

1. Why does the efficient output occur where marginal benefit equals marginal cost? Analyze in detail.
2. If a firm is a pure competitor, marginal revenue and price will be equal. If the firm is a monopoly, marginal revenue will be less than price. Justify these statements.
3. Suppose you are given the information about a monopoly that appears in the following table.

Quantity	Price	Marginal Cost
1	50	20
2	45	20
3	40	20
4	35	20
5	30	20
6	25	20
7	20	20
8	15	20
9	10	20
10	5	20

   a. What is the firm's total revenue for each quantity?
   b. What is the firm's marginal revenue for each quantity?
   c. What quantity and price should the firm choose to maximize its profits?
   d. Suppose the monopolist is currently producing five units of the good. What actions should it undertake and why?

e. Use the information above to plot the demand curve faced by the monopolist, the monopolist's marginal revenue and marginal cost curves, the profit-maximizing level of output, and the profits earned by the firm.

4. "A monopolist can charge whatever price it desires for its output." Is this statement true or false? Defend your answer.

5. State and defend the general principle to be followed in maximizing profits.

6. Use graphical analysis to compare and contrast the economic outcome of monopoly with the economic outcome of pure competition.

7. "Because a monopolist can extract a higher price than a firm that is a pure competitor, the monopolist will always earn a profit." Is this statement true or false? Defend your answer.

8. List and briefly discuss the major sources of monopoly in the United States.

9. What is a cartel? What factors help to maintain a cartel? What factors encourage its dissolution?

10. "Profits on drugs are too high. Drug companies should not be allowed to profit excessively from drugs necessary to treat serious diseases." Discuss.

11. Evaluate the following statement: "Because monopoly results in economic inefficiency and in large profits for a few powerful corporations, we should enforce regulations to break up these firms or eliminate their profits."

12. According to the box titled "The Battle between American and Japanese Automobile Firms," why were the Japanese firms successful in the battle?

SUGGESTIONS FOR FURTHER READING

Adams, Walter, ed. *The Structure of American Industry.* 8th ed. New York: Macmillan, 1990. This is a classic collection of industry studies, many of which will intrigue students. The chapter on the automobile industry was useful in preparing this chapter.

Arthur, W. Brian. "Increasing Returns and the New World of Business." *Harvard Business Review* 74 (July/August 1996), 100–109. This is an accessible discussion of the economics of knowledge-based firms.

Baumol, William J., and Alan S. Blinder. *Economics, Principles and Policy,* 7th ed. Fort Worth: The Dryden Press, 1997. Chapters 11, 12, 18, and 19 provide extensive discussion of market power and monopoly.

Carr, Edward. "Onward and Upward," *The Economist,* June 18, 1994, SS11–SS14. A discussion of the future of the petroleum market and OPEC's role in it. Carr expects an upward trend in petroleum prices.

Duetsch, Larry L., ed. *Industry Studies.* Englewood Cliffs, N.J.: Prentice Hall, 1993. This is a recent collection of industry studies, many of which will be of great interest to students. The chapters on the automobile and pharmaceutical industries were particularly useful in preparing this chapter.

Friedman, Milton. *Capitalism and Freedom.* Chicago: University of Chicago Press, 1962. This classic book discusses, among other things, both monopoly and licensure. Chapter 2 discusses government and monopoly. Chapter 5, "Monopoly and Social Responsibility," argues that the social responsibility of business is to make profits, within the rules of the game. Chapter 6, "Occupational Licensure," makes a strong case for *not* licensing doctors.

Goldberg, Robert M. "Race Against the Cure: The Health Hazards of Pharmaceutical Price Controls," *Policy Review,* Spring 1994. This is a polemic against price controls and other government intervention in the pharmaceutical industry.

Griffin, James M., and Henry B. Steele. *Energy Economics and Policy.* 2nd. ed. Orlando, Fla.: Academic Press, 1986. This book has an excellent discussion of energy markets and a detailed analysis of OPEC.

Knott, David, "OPEC's Past Explains 'No Cut' Strategy," *Oil and Gas Journal* 92 (January 31, 1994), 47. This is a short discussion of problems in the OPEC cartel. This magazine is a rich source of commentary on OPEC and petroleum markets.

Scherer, F. M. "Pricing, Profits, and Technological Progress in the Pharmaceutical Industry," *Journal of Economic Perspectives* 7 (Summer 1993), 97–116. This is a thoughtful, balanced discussion of profit, innovation, prices, and regulation in the pharmaceutical industry.

ECONOMIC EFFICIENCY:
SOME EXTENSIONS

OUTLINE

Total Benefit and Total Cost

The Deadweight Loss of Monopoly

TERMS YOU SHOULD KNOW

Marginal private benefit (Chapter 2)

Marginal social benefit (Chapter 2)

Demand curve (Chapter 1)

Marginal private cost (Chapter 2)

Marginal social cost (Chapter 2)

Supply curve (Chapter 1)

This appendix presents a brief discussion of economic efficiency and shows that the equilibrium in a competitive market is efficient. It then analyzes the deadweight loss of monopoly.

TOTAL BENEFIT AND TOTAL COST

Economic efficiency exists if net benefit, which is total benefit minus total cost, is as large as possible. This section shows how economists measure total benefit and total cost. Figure 4A.1 illustrates the measurement of total benefit from a product: bicycles of a given quality. The height of rectangle A measures the most that some consumer will pay for the first bicycle. It is a measure of its benefit: the marginal private benefit. As long as the consumer receives all of the benefit from the good, the marginal private benefit is the same as the marginal social benefit. The marginal social benefit is the marginal private benefit plus any marginal benefit received by anyone other than the individual consumer. For example, suppose you have a beautiful lawn. The private benefit is the benefit you receive from your lawn. Your neighbor may also receive benefit from your lawn. If so, the social benefit is the benefit you receive plus the benefit your neighbor receives.

THE MEASURE-
MENT OF TOTAL
BENEFIT

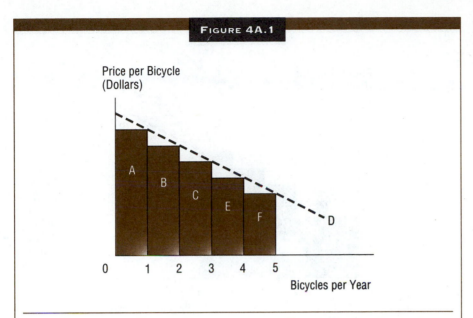

FIGURE 4A.1

Rectangle A measures the most that any consumer will pay for the first bicycle. Assuming all benefits are private, it is the marginal social benefit of the bicycle. Additional units of bicycles have lower values. The sum of the five rectangles gives the total social benefit of five bicycles. Connecting the upper right corners of the rectangles with a straight line gives the marginal social benefit curve, which is also the demand curve.

Rectangle B is the marginal benefit of the second bicycle. Rectangles C, E, and F give the marginal benefits of each additional bicycle. The sum of the areas of all the rectangles is the total amount that consumers would be willing to pay for five bicycles. Connecting the upper right corner of each rectangle, as does the dotted line, gives the marginal benefit curve. It is also the demand curve for bicycles. The area under the demand curve up to five bicycles is almost the same as the total area of the five rectangles. Therefore, in general, the area under a demand curve (from the origin to the quantity in question) is an estimate in dollars of the total benefit that buyers would obtain from that quantity of the good. Assuming all benefits go to direct users, it is the **total social benefit** of that quantity of the good.

Figure 4A.2 illustrates the measurement of cost. The height of rectangle G is the least amount that any producer would accept for producing the first bicycle. It is a measure of the marginal private cost, because it is the cost paid by the producer. As long as the producer pays all of the cost of production, the marginal private cost equals the marginal social cost. In general, the marginal social cost is the marginal private cost plus any marginal cost paid by anyone else. For example, suppose your neighbor is raising hogs. The private cost of raising the hogs is whatever cost your neighbor pays. If the odor from the hogs is offensive to you, the social cost is the private cost to your neighbor plus the cost to you of putting up with the offensive odor.

Total Social Benefit
The maximum that consumers would pay for a given quantity of a good.

**THE MEASURE-
MENT OF TOTAL
COST: BICYCLES**

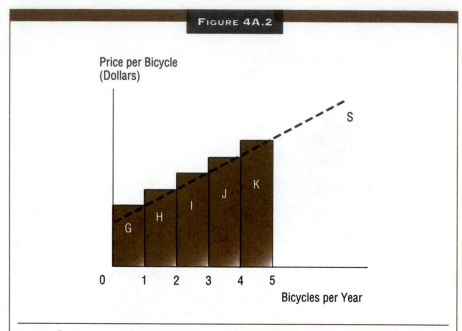

FIGURE 4A.2

Price per Bicycle
(Dollars)

Bicycles per Year

Rectangle G measure the least that any producer will accept in payment for the first bicycle. Assuming all costs are private, it is the marginal social cost of the bicycle. Additional units of bicycles have a higher cost. The sum of the five rectangles gives the total
social cost of five bicycles. Connecting the upper right corners of the rectangles with a
straight line gives the marginal social cost curve, which is also the supply curve.

Rectangle H is the marginal cost of the second bicycle. Rectangles I, J, and K
give the marginal costs of each additional unit. Assuming all costs are private, the
sum of the areas of the five rectangles gives the **total social cost** of producing
five bicycles. Connecting the upper right corner of each rectangle gives the marginal cost curve. It is also the supply curve for bicycles. The area under the supply curve is almost the same as the total area of the five rectangles. Therefore, the
area under the supply curve (from the origin to the quantity in question) is an estimate of the total social cost of that quantity of the good.

In short, the area under the demand curve measures the total social benefit
from consuming the good in question. Similarly, the area under the supply curve
measures the total social cost of producing the good.

Economic efficiency exists if total social benefit minus total social cost is as
large as possible. What type of market achieves economic efficiency?

Consider the equilibrium output in a competitive bicycle market, represented in Figure 4A.3. The demand and supply curves are for bicycles of a given
quality. At the equilibrium price—$500—consumers buy 100 bicycles. They
spend $50,000. The vertical distance from 0 to $500 is the price. The horizontal
distance from 0 to 100 is the quantity. Total expenditure is price per unit times

Total Social Cost
The minimum that
producers would accept
in payment for a given
quantity of a good.

Economic Efficiency
The state that occurs
when total social benefit
minus total social cost is
as large as possible.

FIGURE 4A.3

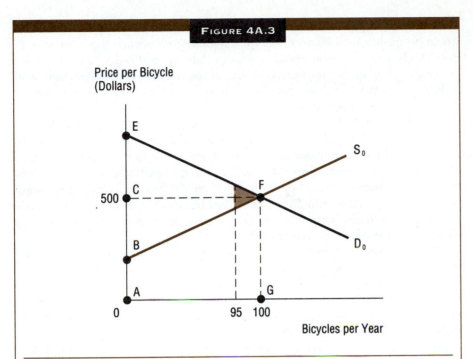

The bicycle market is in equilibrium at a price of $500 and a quantity exchanged of 100. The value of 100 bicycles is the area under the demand curve, AEFG, but consumers can buy them for $50,000, which is the area ACFG. Consumer surplus is the area CEF. Producers, of course, receive the area ACFG for selling the bicycles, but their cost is the area under the supply curve, ABFG. So producer surplus is the area BCF. Total surplus is the area BEF. Given the marginal social benefit (demand) and the marginal social cost (supply) curves, the total surplus is as large as possible.

the number of units, represented in the diagram by the area of the rectangle ACFG. Total benefit is the area under the demand curve out to the quantity 100, the area of AEFG. The net gain to consumers, known as consumer surplus, is total benefit minus total expenditure. It is the area below the demand curve and above the dotted line extending from $500 to the demand curve, the area of the triangle CEF.

At the equilibrium price, the total revenue received by producers is also the area of the rectangle ACFG. The total cost of production is the area under the supply curve from 0 to 100, the area of ABFG. The net gain to producers, known as producer surplus, is total revenue minus total cost. It is the area of the triangle BCF, which is the area below the price line and above the supply curve.

The net gain to society—consumers and producers—is measured by the triangle BEF; this area, total surplus, is as large as possible. Suppose the output were slightly smaller, say 95 units. With fewer bicycles produced and sold, both total benefit and total cost would be smaller. Total benefit would be smaller by the area under the demand curve between 95 and 100 units of bicycles. Total cost would be smaller by the area under the supply curve between these two quantities. The benefit reduction would be greater than the cost reduction; the shaded area in the diagram is a measure in dollars of the difference between the benefit reduction and the cost reduction. Net gain to society goes down by the amount measured by the shaded area.

Similarly, for a slightly larger output, the cost increase is greater than the benefit increase. Therefore, society's net gain is also smaller for a larger output than 100. (To test your understanding, use Figure 4A.3 to demonstrate to yourself that an output larger than 100 would result in a smaller total surplus.) Total surplus goes down if output is more or less than 100 bicycles. Total surplus must be as large as possible with an output of 100 bicycles. In short, the competitive output is the efficient output because it provides the largest net gain to society. Thus, competitive markets achieve economic efficiency.

The competitive output is the efficient output because the demand and supply curves are also the marginal social benefit and marginal social cost curves. Thus, the price that consumers are willing to pay measures both marginal social and marginal private benefit. Similarly, marginal cost measures both marginal social and marginal private cost. If price is greater than marginal cost, private producers increase their profit by expanding output because marginal private benefit is greater than marginal private cost. But marginal social benefit is also greater than marginal social cost, so people in society receive a net benefit at the same time that producers increase their profit. As people attempt to improve their own economic well-being, they increase the net gain to society.

THE DEADWEIGHT LOSS OF MONOPOLY

With our understanding of economic efficiency, we can now see how economists measure the efficiency loss, the deadweight loss, of monopoly. In Figure 4.2, p. 106, the competitive equilibrium price and quantity exchanged are P_1 and Q_4. Consumer surplus is measured by the area P_1SE, which is the area under the demand curve from 0 to Q_4 (total benefit) minus the area OP_1EQ_4 (total expenditure). With the horizontal supply curve, producer surplus is zero. As we saw, the monopoly price and quantity exchanged are P_2 and Q_2. Compared with the competitive equilibrium, total benefit falls by the area under the demand curve from Q_2 to Q_4. One part of that area is the rectangle Q_2NEQ_4, which measures the reduction in consumers' expenditure and also the reduction in producers' cost. Because the cost is the opportunity cost of resources, the transfer of these resources to other uses creates benefits equal to their opportunity cost. So there is no net benefit loss because of the transfer of resources to other uses.

Deadweight Loss
In general, this is a loss in total benefit because of an output restriction that is not made up by greater output in another industry.

The other part of the area measuring lost total benefit is the triangle MEN. Its area measures the **deadweight loss** of monopoly; it represents consumer surplus lost because of output restriction that is not made up by a gain in consumer surplus because of increased output elsewhere. The loss occcurs because the value of the resources in the current industry is greater than their value in their alternative use. For instance, at the output Q_3 resources used to produce a unit of output create a benefit of Q_3F, the demand price, but the value of what these resources could produce in their next best use is only Q_3G, their opportunity cost. Although the value of a unit of output of consumers would be greater than the opportunity cost, the monopolist does not produce the unit because the marginal revenue, the marginal private benefit to the monopolist, Q_3H is less than the opportunity cost.

Recall that consumer surplus for this product was P_1SE. It is now P_2SM. In addition to losing the area of the triangle MEN, consumers have lost the area P_1P_2MN, which is now part of the monopolist's total revenue. Although it is lost to consumers, it is captured by the monopolist so it is not a loss to the economy. This creation of monopoly profit, however, is one reason that some people object to monopoly.

Most estimates of deadweight loss of monopoly suggest that it is not large, ranging from $100 to $500 per person per year. Increased competition because of deregulation, new technologies, and greater foreign competition are some reasons why the loss is not greater. Another important factor is the threat of the entry of new firms, which limits the ability of firms to raise price, which in turn reduces the deadweight loss.[1]

SUMMARY

If we accept that individuals are best able to make their own choices and thus best able to judge the value of goods and services to them, demand and supply curves in competitive markets are marginal private benefit and marginal private cost curves. If individual decision makers receive all benefits and bear all costs, so that private and social values are equal, economic efficiency occurs where the marginal private benefit and cost curves intersect. But that is the equilibrium in a competitive market. Therefore, competitive markets yield efficient outcomes. In contrast, a monopoly market results in an output less than the efficient output. This inefficient output leads to an efficiency loss or deadweight loss due to monopoly.

---

[1]See Douglas F. Greer, *Industrial Organization and Public Policy*, 3rd ed. (New York: Macmillan, 1992), 609–15 for a summary of studies that show the losses in economic efficiency due to market power. Per person, these losses would be somewhere around $100 to $500 per person per year. Robert T. Masson and Joseph Shaanan, "Social Costs of Oligopoly and the Value of Competition: An Empirical Analysis," *Economic Journal* 94 (September 1984), 520–35, shows that the threat of competition from new firms—new entry—reduces such losses by as much as half as they would be in the absence of this potential competition.

KEY TERMS

Total social benefit   Economic efficiency
Total social cost   Deadweight loss

REVIEW QUESTIONS

1. What is meant by economic efficiency? Show that a competitive market yields the efficient output.
2. What is the deadweight loss of monopoly? Show it on a diagram. Is it a large loss for the U.S. economy?

5

HEALTH CARE REFORM: HOW MUCH?

TERMS YOU SHOULD KNOW

Law of demand (Chapter 1)

Marginal external benefit (Chapter 2)

Marginal private benefit (Chapter 2)

Marginal social benefit (Chapter 2)

Marginal social cost (Chapter 2)

Allocative efficiency (Chapter 2)

In 1950, Americans spent 4.4 percent of national output for health care. In 1994, health care expenditures absorbed nearly 14 percent of national output, the highest percentage among the world's industrialized nations. Growing alarm over this trend has helped to spawn a host of proposals in Congress for health care reform. Our objective in this chapter is to examine the economic basis for this reform effort.[1]

DO WE SPEND TOO MUCH ON HEALTH CARE?

Health care has been absorbing a growing share of the nation's resources. The rising concern about the size of this share suggests that we are spending too much on health care. The first step in health care reform is to determine whether this is the case.

We are spending too much on health care from an economic perspective if the things we give up for health care—the costs of health care—have a greater value than what we gain—the benefits from health care.[2] There is undoubtedly a large amount of health care that yields benefits greater than costs, but economists have identified a number of features of the health care system that may drive spending to the point where costs, at least at the margin, exceed benefits. Some of these features are the product of private health care choices and institutions; some are the result of government action.

PARTIAL-COST PAYMENTS

Health care is somewhat unusual in that much of what is purchased is not paid for directly by the consumers of health care. Much of the tab is paid, instead, with third-party payments.

Third-Party Payment
A payment made directly to the provider of a good or service by a party other than the buyer.

A **third-party payment** is a payment made directly to the provider of a good or service by a party other than the buyer. The principal "third parties" in the market for health care are private insurance companies and government agencies. Table 5.1 shows that third-party payments were 81.6 percent of the $949.2 billion spent on national health care in the United States in 1994.

Partial-Cost Payments
The difference between the full cost of the health care received and the third-party payments for that care.

When third-party payments are involved, consumers pay directly for only part of the full cost of providing health care. They make **partial-cost payments** equal

---

[1]This is not the only issue driving health care reform in the United States. In spite of the growing share of national output devoted to health care, 35 million to 40 million Americans lack health insurance, the basic means of payment used by the majority. This aspect of the problem is discussed briefly toward the end of this chapter.

[2]The readers of Chapter 2 will recognize this as "too much" from the perspective of allocative efficiency. There is another meaning of "too much" that also receives significant attention in economics, namely, costs that are higher than necessary to accomplish something. This may be an important source of excessive costs in the health care sector, but clearly outlining the dimensions of allocative inefficiency is enough of a task for one chapter.

TABLE 5.1		
Type of Expenditure	**Third-Party Payment**	**Partial-Cost Payment**
Private		
Out-of-Pocket		174.9
Health Insurance	313.3	
Other	40.2	
Government		
Medicare	166.1	
Medicaid	122.9	
Other	131.8	
	774.3	174.9

Source: U.S. Health Care Financing Administration, *Health Care Financing Review,* Spring 1996.

to the difference between the full cost of the health care received and the third-party payments for that care. Partial-cost payments are called out-of-pocket payments in official government statistics; according to Table 5.1 they amounted to $174.9 billion—only 18.4 percent of national health care expenditures—in 1994.

Although the partial-cost payment covers only part of the full costs of health care, it is perceived by consumers as the price that they pay at the point of purchase. Given this perception, a straightforward application of the law of demand indicates that they will purchase at least some care that costs more, at the margin, than the benefits it provides.

As noted in Chapter 1, the law of demand states that consumers will purchase larger amounts of a good or service at lower prices when the other factors that also influence demand are held constant. Economists have confirmed through a large number of studies that health care is no exception to this law.[3] Thus, the relationship between the price of health care and the quantity of health care demanded can be represented by a standard demand curve, such as the downward-sloping curve in Figure 5.1, which relates the price per hospital day to the number of hospital days purchased each year.

The information associated with the demand curve actually tells us two things: (1) the maximum quantity that will be purchased at each price and (2) the maximum amount that consumers will pay for each quantity purchased. In Figure 5.1, for example, a maximum of 174 million hospital days will be purchased when the price is $800; alternatively, a maximum of $800 will be paid for the 174 millionth hospital day. Economists use the maximum amount consumers will pay as a measure, in dollars, of the marginal private benefit; that is, the value placed by the consumer on the marginal unit purchased. In this example, the 174 millionth

---

[3]Many of these studies are summarized clearly in Sherman Folland, Allen C. Goodman, and Miron Stano, *The Economics of Health and Health Care* (New York: Macmillan, 1993), Chapter 7.

THE EFFECT OF
PARTIAL-COST
PAYMENTS ON
HOSPITAL
EXPENDITURES

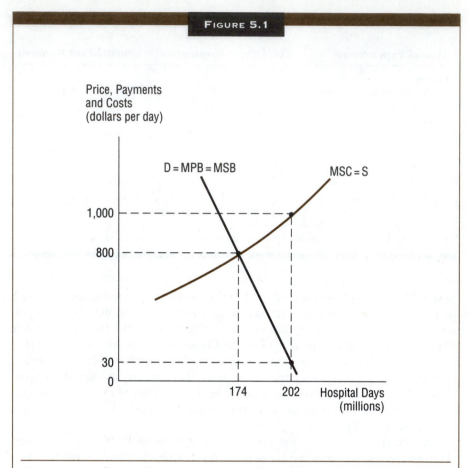

FIGURE 5.1

Consumers pay the partial-cost price of $30 per hospital day, at which they demand 202 million days. If they were charged the full cost of each day, they would purchase 174 million days at $800 per day–the price and quantity at which D = S. Moving from the partial-cost to the full-cost price would reduce costs of hospital care by $25.2 billion dollars, the area under the MSC curve from 174 million to 202 million hospital days.

hospital day is the marginal unit and the marginal private benefit of that unit is $800. This follows from the reasoning that the buyer of this hospital day, the patient, must perceive a benefit worth at least $800, since she is willing to pay this much. The application of similar reasoning to each point on the demand curve indicates that the demand curve is also a marginal private benefit curve.

If, in addition, the benefits from each hospital day are confined solely to patients, the demand curve for hospital days is an accurate measure of marginal social benefit—the value placed by consumers *and others* on the marginal unit purchased. There may be instances, of course, in which hospitalization provides benefits to individuals other than the patient. An example is hospitalization that helps to halt the spread of a contagious disease.

The benefit that each hospital day provides to others is an example of a marginal external benefit—the value placed by individuals other than the consumer on the marginal unit purchased. Thus, marginal social benefits are the sum of marginal private and marginal external benefits. In the case where benefits are confined solely to the patient, marginal external benefits are zero and the demand curve is both a marginal private and a marginal social benefit curve. That is, demand (D) equals marginal private benefits (MPB), and MPB equals marginal social benefits (MSB) if marginal external benefits (MEB) are equal to zero. This is the case assumed here; hence, the curve is labeled D, MPB, and MSB.

The other curve in Figure 5.1 is the marginal social cost (MSC) curve; it depicts the cost to the producer (the hospital) and to others of providing the marginal unit (each additional hospital day). We assume that additional hospital days can be provided only at increasing marginal social cost, primarily because hospitals differ in terms of the efficiency with which they can provide services. That is, hospitals vary in terms of cost per hospital day.

The number of hospital days that should be provided from the perspective of allocative efficiency is 174 million, where MSB = MSC. Benefits exceed costs for each day from 1 to 173,999,999; thus, they should all be provided. Beyond 174 million days, however, costs exceed benefits for each day; thus, none of them should be provided.

The MSC curve is also the market supply curve (S). The supply curve shows the maximum quantity that will be supplied at each price received by the producer. For example, if the price received by hospitals is $800 per day, they will supply patients with no more than 174 million hospital days of care. $800 is enough money to cover the cost of providing all of the first 174 million hospital days, but it is not enough to cover the cost of providing any days in excess of 174 million. Similar reasoning indicates that hospitals will be willing to provide a maximum of 202 million days of hospital care if they receive $1,000 per day.

If there were no third-party payers for hospital care and patients paid the full cost or marginal social cost of each hospital day, 174 million hospital days would be sold at a price of $800 per day—the quantity and price where demand and supply are equal. At a price of $800, the maximum amount that consumers want to buy is equal to the maximum amount that suppliers want to provide. Thus, in the absence of third-party payments, consumers would purchase the efficient quantity of hospital care.

In the presence of third-party payments, however, consumers make only a partial-cost payment at the point of purchase. In fact, the partial-cost payment for hospital care in the United States averages only about 3 percent of the full-cost price. According to data produced by the American Hospital Association, 202 million hospital days were provided in the United States in 1993 at an average cost of $1,000 per day.[4] Thus, with a partial-cost payment rate of 3 percent the partial-cost payment averaged only $30 a day.

As indicated in Figure 5.1, patients used 202 million hospital days when the price to them at the point of purchase was $30. Hospitals received $1,000 per

---

[4]As summarized in *Health Care Financing Review* 15, no. 4 (Summer 1994), 173.

day; $30 from the patient and $970 from third-party payers. The partial-cost payment created a demand for 28 million (16 percent) more days than the efficient level—a demand met by hospitals because the price they received ($1,000) covered the cost of 202 million days. Although the price to consumers, in the guise of the partial-cost payment on each of the extra 28 million hospital days, is less than the benefits received, the cost to society exceeds the benefit on each of these units. Thus, the extra 28 million days are a vivid example of "too much" health care. If the resources used to provide this extra care were released from the hospital sector, hospital costs would decrease by $25.2 billion—the area under the MSC curve from 174 million days to 202 million days.[5]

The preceding case is an example of the kind of effect that partial-cost payments have on the use of resources in the health care sector. The demands for other types of health care are also excessive because of the influence of partial-cost payments. Generally, however, excessive demands for other types of health care, such as visits to doctors' offices, surgery, and dental care, are probably less than in the case of hospitalization because the partial-cost payments are higher for other types of health care.[6] Overall, partial-cost payments probably induce consumers to buy about 10 percent more health care than the efficient level. This is not a trivial amount, given total national health care expenditures of $949 billion in 1994.

PHYSICIAN-INDUCED DEMAND

The mischief created by partial-cost payments is a good example of how consumers' behavior can be affected by the incentives they face. In the case we reviewed, consumers are merely responding rationally to the incentive of a reduced price, and the excessive quantity of resources in the hospital sector is a reflection of consumers' choices. The outcome may not be socially desirable, but the consumer is still sovereign.

In the real world of health care, the purchasing decision is often jointly determined by the patient and the physician. The physician normally recommends a course of action, but the patient is presumably free to approve or disapprove, so the consumer is ultimately sovereign in the sense that he or she has the final authority over health care expenditures. Most consumers have little knowledge of medicine, however, so they often simply accept the physician's recommendation. This appears to give physicians considerable freedom to exercise their own pref-

---

[5] To calculate the costs saved, note that the area under the MSC curve between 174 and 202 million days is actually two areas: (1) a rectangle with a base of 28 million days (= 202 − 174) and height of $800 and (2) a triangle on top of this rectangle, with a base of 28 million days and a height of $200 (= 1000 − 800). The area of the rectangle is 28 million × $800, or $22.4 billion. The area of the triangle is (28 million × $200)/2, or $2.8 billion. Adding the two areas gives $25.2 billion.

[6] According to data reported in *The Health Care Financing Review*, Spring 1996, p. 233, the partial-cost payments for physicians' services, dental care, nursing home care, and drugs in 1994 were 19, 49, 37, and 62 percent, respectively.

INTERNATIONAL PERSPECTIVE

ANOTHER HIDDEN COST OF PARTIAL-COST PAYMENTS

We have noted in the text and in Figure 5.1 that cost sharing induces consumers of health care to demand an inefficiently large amount of health care, resulting in costs that are excessive from a social perspective. This happens because with cost sharing, only a small part of the cost necessary to provide health care is imposed on buyers; the remainder is paid by third parties. Just the opposite effect can occur, however; that is, cost sharing can impose costs on consumers that are not shared by third parties. Such seems to be the case, at least, in Canada.

In Canada, most health care is paid for entirely by national health insurance and no cost sharing is required. Thus, if the government were willing to pay for it, consumers would continue to consume health care until the benefit perceived on the last unit was zero (in Figure 5.1, this is where the demand curve would cut the horizontal axis). The government is not willing to pay, however, for this much health care.

The result of such a government expenditure constraint is that the quantity of health care demanded often exceeds the quantity of health care supplied. In the face of such excess demand, patients often find that they have to wait for hospital and physician services.

Steven Globerman studied the problem of waiting for health care in British Columbia. He found that all patients together waited a total of 868,408 weeks for 10 types of hospital admissions in 1989, and that many of them experienced significant difficulty either at work or at home because of their untreated condition. To put a cost on waiting, Globerman estimated the value of productive time lost. He did this by first multiplying the total time lost waiting by the percentage of patients experiencing difficulty while waiting, giving him an estimate of the amount of productive time lost. He then multiplied this number by average weekly industrial earnings in British Columbia in 1989. The resulting number—his estimate of the value of the productive time lost due to waiting—turned out to be about 0.2 percent of British Columbia's Gross Provincial Product.

Undoubtedly, some cost is associated with waiting for hospital services in the United States, although we are not aware of any estimates. There appears to be little waiting so far at least, on the part of insured patients, but the spread of cost-containment efforts may change this situation. Currently, the waiting that does occur is concentrated on the uninsured population, which must surmount the barriers to accessing hospital care imposed by the inability to pay.

Source: Steven Globerman, "A Policy Analysis of Hospital Waiting Lists," *Journal of Policy Analysis and Management* 10 (Spring 1991), 247–62.

---

erences. At the very least, it affords physicians the opportunity to use their superior knowledge to persuade patients that particular services are necessary. If they use this opportunity to enhance their own income by prescribing health care that is ineffective or unnecessary, then they are a source of excessive health care expenditures.

Clearly ineffective health care prescribed by physicians to increase their own wealth is what we call **physician-induced demand.** This is health care that could be eliminated without materially impairing health; thus, it wastes resources. In economic terms, it is health care for which marginal social cost exceeds marginal social benefit.

At least three conditions are necessary for the existence of physician-induced demand. We have already touched upon two of these: (1) asymmetric information

Physician-Induced Demand
Clearly ineffective health care prescribed by physicians to increase their own wealth.

(information known by physicians that is superior to that of patients) regarding the efficacy of health care alternatives and (2) the desire of physicians to increase their own wealth. In addition, physicians' income must depend directly on the amount of health care that they prescribe. The first two conditions are surely present in the United States, although physicians as a group are undoubtedly motivated by more than money. The third condition is present in the majority of the market where physicians practice fee-for-service medicine (that is, where there is a fee charged for each service provided).

The existence of these conditions has prompted many economists to search for evidence of physician-induced demand. Although much literature bears on this topic, making it difficult to generalize, we interpret the reported results to indicate that there is evidence of ineffective health care but that much of it cannot be unequivocally attributed to physician-induced demand.

Two primary bodies of research suggest a significant quantity of ineffective health care. One features an evaluation of actual medical records by experts to determine if certain procedures are prescribed more often than warranted by risk-benefit considerations. Results of these studies reported in the literature indicate that as much as one-third of certain common procedures (coronary bypass surgery, coronary angiograms, pacemaker insertions, carotid artery surgery, and upper gastrointestinal endoscopy) have been judged inappropriate or of equivocal value.[7]

The other body of research that suggests a large amount of ineffective care is the studies that have documented the enormous variations in the use of care in different areas of the country or across countries. In summarizing much of this literature, Phelps argues that such differences are evident for a large number of hospital admissions and surgical procedures even after correction for factors other than physician practices that could explain the variation. That is, he attributes most of the variation in admissions and procedures to variations in physician practices.[8]

Variations in physician practices or the use of inappropriate procedures are not necessarily due, however, to physician-induced demand. They could be caused by the inherent uncertainty of diagnostic medicine and variations in training and skills of physicians. Medicine, after all, is not an exact science, and there are honest differences of opinion within the medical community about the effectiveness of various procedures.

Economists have also identified several potential limits to the pure exercise of physicians' preferences, including the following:

1. The apparent inability of physicians to close the market to competitors. Between 1965 and 1990 the number of physicians grew by nearly 110 percent while the U.S. population grew by only 28 percent. Observed patterns of physician location indicate clearly that

---

[7]David M. Cutler, "A Guide to Health Care Reform," *Journal of Economic Perspectives,* 8, no. 3 (Summer 1994), 14–15.

[8]Charles E. Phelps, *Health Economics* (New York: HarperCollins, 1992), Chapter 3.

physicians throughout the country were unable to hold on to their market shares in the face of this increase in supply.[9] This factor has apparently reduced the potential for physician-induced demand, just as the appearance of new foreign competitors attenuated the market power of U.S. automobile manufacturers.

2. The possibility that patients form a priori expectations about the conditions for which they seek medical assistance. If physicians suggest procedures that deviate significantly from patients' expectations, they may not consent to these procedures. Patients could then seek treatment from other physicians. Such monitoring by patients constrains physicians in their pursuit of wealth. Some patients may be simply put off by physicians who are too aggressive in prescribing treatment. If they are, they will seek alternative counsel.

3. The growing practice by third-party payers of requiring second opinions before they agree to pay for expensive medical care. Here, the threat of alternative diagnoses may make physicians more conservative in their diagnoses.

4. The possibility that there are limits to the amount of work that physicians want to create for themselves. Physicians are like the rest of us in the sense that maximizing their own satisfaction may be more important than maximizing their wealth, and this constrains the amount of leisure they are willing to sacrifice for the pursuit of wealth.

5. The likelihood that some physicians consider it unethical to put a patient through procedures that would have questionable beneficial effects.

Cromwell and Mitchell estimate that each 1 percent growth in the number of surgeons has resulted in only one-tenth of a percent growth in surgeons' services.[10] Rossiter and Wilensky found an effect of similar magnitude for all physicians.[11] These results suggest that although physician-induced demand exists, it is not a major source of excessive spending for health care.

DEFENSIVE MEDICINE

The popular press has directed a great deal of attention lately to medical malpractice—deviations from accepted medical standards of care that cause injury to a patient. The U.S. legal system provides compensation to patients who can prove that they have been victims of medical malpractice. To protect themselves against

[9] This is Phelps' conclusion in *Health Economics*, 186–92.

[10] Jerry Cromwell and Janet B. Mitchell, "Physician-Induced Demand for Surgery," *Journal of Health Economics* 5 (1986), 293–313.

[11] Louis F. Rossiter and Gail R. Wilensky, "Identification of Physician-Induced Demand," *Journal of Human Resources* 19 (1984), 162–72.

the financial consequences of medical malpractice suits, doctors buy malpractice insurance. This insurance is expensive—about $15,000 per year in 1991 for self-employed physicians.

In such an environment, physicians may have increased the rate at which they practice **defensive medicine,** providing medical procedures such as surgery, examinations, and laboratory tests to reduce the risk of a malpractice suit and not because they believe the procedures are of great value to their patients. The likelihood that this practice is followed is greater because of partial-cost payments; physicians are less reluctant to prescribe treatment of questionable value when they know their patients are not paying full cost.

Defensive Medicine
Medical procedures performed to reduce the risk of a lawsuit, rather than because of their medical value.

But even if defensive medicine is practiced, it need not be wasteful. It may result in higher quality care, fewer injuries, or a reduction in the number of high-risk procedures. Each of these is an outcome with value to consumers.

According to some physicians, the rise of defensive medicine is a major factor in the expansion of medical costs. The most widely cited estimate, however, indicates that it explains less than 1 percent of all medical expenditures.[12]

TECHNOLOGICAL CHANGE

American medicine has long been marked by significant technological change, in terms of new types of physical capital, such as CT scanners and magnetic resonance imagers; new procedures, such as coronary bypass grafting; and new drugs, such as successive generations of more effective antibiotics. In most industries, technological change reduces required resources; thus, it is a source of lower costs. This is apparently not the case in the health care industry, especially in the hospital segment of the industry. This has led some observers to argue that we have "too much" technological change, in the same sense that we have too much health care as a result of partial-cost payments; that is, technological change has resulted in the provision of health care for which benefits at the margin are less than costs.

Technological change in the hospital sector has been driven primarily by the competition for patients. Because only doctors can admit patients to hospitals, hospitals fiercely compete for doctors. Hospitals have lured doctors, in part, by adopting the latest technology. The quest by doctors for new technology has been driven, in turn, by patients' demands for the latest medical innovations.

It is likely that some of the care provided with the aid of new technology is wasteful simply because partial-cost payments apply to all hospital care, including that which uses new technologies. That is, what appears to be excessive spending on new technology may not be due to the technology, per se, but to the way in which hospitals are reimbursed for it. Consumers may be willing to pay, however, for new technology because of the improvement it makes in the quality of health

---

[12]Roger Reynolds, John A. Rizzo, and Martin L. Gonzalez, "The Cost of Medical Professional Liability," *Journal of the American Medical Association* (May 22–29, 1987), 257, 2776–81.

care. Thus, some of the new technology may yield benefits to consumers that are equal to or greater than the costs to society of providing the technology.

Still, it is difficult to shake the impression that it would be possible in many metropolitan areas to get by with fewer units of some of the new physical capital, such as CT scanners, magnetic resonance imagers, and cardiac catheterization facilities, with little inconvenience to consumers. They may be paying for more capacity than necessary. Thus, it seems premature to rule out the possibility that technological change is a source of excessive health care spending. We would be surprised, however, if it turned out to be a major problem in this regard.[13]

EXPERIENCE RATING OF INSURANCE POLICIES

The way in which insurance companies reimburse health care providers plays a big role, as noted, in overspending for health care. This is not the only adverse effect, however, of health insurance on efficient resource use. Another is the way in which insured populations are rated.[14]

Insurance rating is the basic procedure used by insurance companies to determine insurance premiums. Historically, health insurance was community rated, meaning that in a given community or metropolitan area, all members of each of a small number of family types paid the same premium. This arrangement proved unstable as insurers discovered they could pick out groups or companies with lower than average expected claims and offer premiums below the community rate.

Currently, most health insurance is **experience-rated insurance.** There are two types: self-insurance and insurance subject to medical underwriting. With self-insurance, premiums are large enough to cover actual losses of a group of people who insure themselves, plus the costs of administering claims. With insurance subject to medical underwriting, premiums are based on individual or group characteristics that are correlated with the use of health care. Insurance subject to underwriting is the type most people think of when there is reference to experience-rated insurance.

Many economists applaud the increased use of experience rating. What they have in mind when they do so is the ideal experience-rated system in which higher premiums act as an incentive for people to change their behavior in the direction of choices that will reduce their use of the health care system. For example, higher premiums for smokers would be viewed favorably as a means of inducing smokers to quit smoking. It appears, however, that the potential cost

Experience-Rated Insurance
Premiums are based on individual or group characteristics that are correlated with the use of health care.

---

[13]Although we do not give technology much credit for *excessive* health care spending, we do believe that it has been an important factor driving up health care costs. In our judgment, most of the costs due to technological change can be justified on the basis of benefits provided.

[14]There is a third effect, called moral hazard. Moral hazard occurs whenever the assurance of insurance coverage induces the insured party to make choices that increase the probability that the insurance will be used. An example of this in the case of health insurance would be an individual who starts smoking because he knows he is insured for the high medical costs associated with this habit.

savings from this source are small; most of the individual variation in health care use comes from factors beyond individual control, such as age and heredity.[15]

In fact, experience rating may actually impose more costs than it saves. The costs of experience rating come in several forms. First, experience rating, per se, is associated with high administrative costs stemming from the need for a great deal of individual information and monitoring. Second, experience rating leads to discrimination in the job market against workers with higher-cost health experiences or prospects, such as older, disabled, and previously ill workers. There is an economic cost of health-cost discrimination if it causes companies to bypass more productive workers. Third, experience rating produces "job lock," a situation in which an individual is afraid to leave a job because of the fear of losing health insurance coverage. There is some evidence that job lock reduces mobility rates for married men by as much as 25 percent.[16] If this is the case, and not all economists agree that it is,[17] there has been an adverse effect on the level of national output. The size of this effect is uncertain, so we do not know the economic loss attributable to experience rating.

THE FEDERAL TAX EXEMPTION FOR HEALTH INSURANCE

We noted at the beginning of this chapter that certain characteristics of the public segment of the health care sector may also lead to too much health care. One of these is the federal tax exemption for health insurance.

Employers pay for a significant fraction—over 80 percent—of the health insurance premiums of workers in the United States, but there is good evidence that they shift the cost to employees in the form of lower wages.[18] If this is the case, why don't employees just purchase their own insurance? They don't because the cost to them of a given policy is less if their employer pays for it than if they pay for it themselves. This happens because the federal tax code exempts employee compensation received in the form of health insurance from the federal individual income tax.

The size of the exemption depends on the size of the insurance premium paid and the employee's marginal federal income tax rate.[19] The marginal federal income tax rate is the tax rate levied on the last dollar of federal taxable income. Currently, it is one of five tax bracket rates: 15, 28, 31, 36, or 39.6 percent.

---

[15]Henry Aaron makes this point forcefully in "Issues Every Plan to Reform Health Care Financing Must Confront," *Journal of Economic Perspectives,* 8, no. 3 (Summer 1994), 31–43.

[16]Cutler, "A Guide to Health Care Reform," 19–20.

[17]Douglas Holtz-Eakin, "Health Insurance Provision and Labor Market Efficiency in the United States and Germany." In Rebecca Blank, ed., *Social Protection versus Economic Flexibility: Is There a Trade-off?* (Chicago: University of Chicago Press, 1994), 157–87.

[18]Phelps, *Health Economics,* 297.

[19]Actually, it also depends on the marginal tax rate on individual income in state tax codes and the rate of the Social Security payroll tax. If, for example, an individual worker is subject to a 28 percent federal rate, a 5 percent state rate, and the 7.65 percent payroll tax rate, the relevant marginal rate is the sum of the three rates, or 40.65 percent.

Suppose an individual in the 28 percent tax bracket is provided an insurance policy for which her employer pays a premium of $1,800 a year. If the worker were to buy the insurance herself, she would have to earn enough income before taxes to pay for both the insurance premium and her taxes on that income. In this example, she would have to earn $2,500 to realize the $1,800 after taxes to pay the premium ($1,800 is $2,500 minus .28 × $2,500). A worker in the 36 percent bracket would have to earn $2,812.50 to buy the $1,800 policy. Turning these numbers around, the $1,800 policy is worth $2,500 to the 28 percent taxpayer and $2,812.50 to the 36 percent taxpayer. Alternatively, both taxpayers enjoy exemptions from taxes worth $700 and $1,012.50, respectively, or their employer lowers the cost to them of health insurance by 28 and 36 percent, respectively. Had they bought the policy, remember, it would have cost them this much more in earnings before taxes.

To understand how valuable these exemptions are, it is necessary to understand how they affect the net cost of health insurance to the individual. The net cost of health insurance is not the same thing as the insurance premium. The net cost is only that part of the premium that the individual does not expect to get back in the form of insurance benefits. It is the part of the insurance premium that covers the cost of insurance administration and contributions to insurance company profits.[20] The net cost of insurance varies inversely with the size of the group insured, with larger groups paying a smaller cost per dollar of benefits. The net cost ranges from 5 to 8 percent of benefits for employee groups over 1,000 to 30 to 40 percent of benefits for groups of 10 or fewer. The average net cost of insurance is 15 to 25 percent of benefits.

The bottom line cost to the individual of health insurance is the difference between the net cost of insurance and the value of the insurance exemption. Given the net costs just indicated and the current marginal federal income tax rates, it is clear that the federal income tax exemption drastically lowers the bottom line cost of health insurance to most insured workers. In fact, the bottom line cost to many workers is negative.

This effect of the federal income tax exemption for health insurance should have the same kind of effect on the quantity of health insurance demanded as the effect on the quantity of any good or service from a marked reduction in price. As long as the demand curve for health insurance is downward-sloping, and there is considerable evidence that it is,[21] the federal income tax exemption should increase the quantity of health insurance purchased.

In fact, the cumulative effect of the federal income tax exemption of health insurance could be very large. The exemption produces a secondary effect in the market for medical care, since the increases in insurance coverage in turn increase the quantity of medical care demanded. Phelps has estimated that total medical care would decline by 10 to 20 percent among the under-65 population if the tax exemption for health insurance were eliminated.[22]

---

[20] This is called the "loading fee."
[21] Phelps, *Health Economics*, 300–302.
[22] Phelps, *Health Economics*, 302.

INCENTIVES FOR EXCESSIVE HEALTH CARE
IN MEDICARE AND MEDICAID

Any discussion of the incentives for excessive health care in the United States would be deficient without an evaluation of Medicare and Medicaid. Medicare is the federal government's program of health insurance for people who are 65 years or older. Medicaid is a joint federal-state health care program for low-income households, elderly persons in long-term nursing care, and the disabled. These programs financed $289 billion—over 30 percent—of national health care in the United States in 1994.

Medicare has two parts: Part A, which pays for hospital, skilled nursing, and home health care, and Part B, which pays primarily for physician care, ambulatory surgical services, and outpatient services. Enrollment in Part A is mandatory for every person receiving Social Security benefits. Enrollment in Part B is voluntary, although the cost is low enough that 97 percent of Part A recipients have this coverage.

Part A is financed primarily by a 2.9 percent tax levied on taxable payroll. Enrollees pay an annual deductible and a share of the remaining hospital costs. There is a lifetime limit of 150 days of hospital coverage.

Part B is financed primarily out of general federal tax revenues. Enrollees pay a monthly premium equal to about 25 percent of the cost. They must also pay an annual deductible and 20 percent of all claims above the deductible.

Although Medicare is a government insurance program, it was modeled in some respects after private insurance policies. Both types of insurance, for example, require patients to make only partial-cost payments for health care at the point of purchase. In 1991, Medicare patients paid 15 percent of their own hospital costs and 36 percent of their bills from physicians, with the remaining fees being paid by Medicare as a third party.

This feature of Medicare induces patients to purchase an inefficiently large quantity of health care, that is, to demand some health care for which benefits are less than costs. It has an effect in this respect similar to the effect of partial-cost payments for health care financed by private insurance. Excess health care as a share of total health care financed by Medicare may not be as large as excess health care as a share of total health care financed by private insurance, however, because the partial-cost payments are higher for Medicare than for privately insured health care.

The other principal source of inefficiency in Medicare is the package of insurance coverage that it provides. The theory of optimal insurance tells us that expected consumer satisfaction from health insurance is highest with a policy that provides relatively complete protection for uncertain, but costly events, such as long-term hospital or nursing home care, and relatively less insurance protection against more certain, but less costly events, such as short-term hospital stays, doctors' visits, ambulatory surgery, and so on.[23] If this is the case, Medicare is

---

[23]E. B. Keeler, J. L. Buchanan, and J. E. Rolph, "The Demand for Episodes of Treatment in the Health Insurance Experiment" (Santa Monica, CA: The RAND Corporation, Report R-3454-HHS, March 1988).

structured just the opposite of an optimal policy; it has a lifetime cap on the hospital days it will pay for, and it is very generous in covering short stays and relatively routine care. This structure provides an incentive for consumers to spend too much on the items that Medicare favors. It also suggests that if the government restructured Medicare along the lines suggested by the theory of optimal insurance, it could provide a higher level of consumer satisfaction and save money as well.

Medicaid suffers the first of the two just-reviewed defects of Medicare, but to a greater degree. Medicaid pays for all of the costs of Medicaid patients. Thus, the partial-cost payment for Medicaid patients is zero and there is bound to be overconsumption of medical services by Medicaid recipients as a consequence.

Unlike Medicare, the structure of Medicaid benefits is not biased against coverage for uncertain, costly, long-term events. In fact, Medicaid is the principal source of public support for long-term care. The chief criticism of Medicaid in this regard is that the immediate family of the long-term care recipient is often required to divest its assets before long-term care benefits will be paid. This feature contravenes another principal of optimal insurance—namely, that consumer satisfaction from insurance is higher when there is a cap on the insured's share of catastrophic expenses. If asset divestiture is viewed as the cost of receiving long-term care under Medicaid, the cost is probably excessive.

RECAP AND POLICY IMPLICATIONS

This has been a relatively extensive discussion of the features of the U.S. health care system that may produce too much health care. Thus, we pause for a brief recap before plunging into some of the policy implications.

RECAP

Two of the features we have evaluated seem to stand out above the rest as potential sources of excess spending: partial-cost payments and the federal tax exemption for employer-provided health insurance. Partial-cost payments lower the price at the point of purchase so much that they provide a powerful incentive for consumers to overconsume health care, whether the care is paid for by private insurance companies, Medicare, or Medicaid.[24] Partial-cost payments produce excess spending equal to at least 10 percent of personal health care expenditures. The federal tax exemption for employer-provided health insurance dramatically reduces the net cost of private health insurance; so much, in fact, that it may stimulate extra spending of 10 percent or more.

We find the case for the other suspected causes of excess spending less convincing. There is compelling evidence of significant spending on ineffective or inappropriate care, but it probably cannot be attributed to physician-induced demand.

---

[24]Actually, this is also the case for CHAMPUS, the health insurance policy provided to the nation's military personnel.

In fact, the evidence for physician-induced demand seems too weak to ascribe it much policy importance.

The fear of malpractice lawsuits induces doctors to practice defensive medicine. The evidence indicates, however, that defensive medicine creates excess spending no larger than 1 percent of personal health care expenditures.

Technological change is a favorite cause of overspending for many observers of the U.S. health care system. We believe, however, that much of it reflects consumers' preferences and willingness to pay. In any event, there is no compelling evidence that suggests much of the technological change that has occurred represents wasted resources.

Experience rating may produce significant costs associated with insurance administration, discrimination, and job lock. The latter two effects suggest that the opportunity cost of health care could be reduced by moving in the direction of more community rating, but much of the cost saving from doing so would show up in the form of higher national output, rather than in the form of lower health care expenditures.

Finally, there is some scope for health care savings with reformulated Medicare and Medicaid benefit packages that provide less coverage for routine care and more coverage for catastrophic care, coupled with realistic caps on total outlays by the insuree. We do not know, however, how large the savings might be.

POLICY IMPLICATIONS

The bottom-line conclusion from this evaluation is that if we follow the economist's exacting prescription to "cut costs only if the costs saved exceed the benefits given up," only a few prospects may be worth pursuing vigorously through public policy. The most promising targets appear to be partial-cost payments, ineffective and inappropriate procedures, and the federal tax exemption of health insurance premiums. At first blush, the policy actions seem obvious: raise partial-cost payments, reduce the frequency of ineffective and inappropriate procedures, and eliminate the tax exemption. In reality, however, the details of how these actions are to be taken and how far we can or should go in each instance are highly uncertain.

INCREASED PARTIAL-COST PAYMENTS
In appraising the prospects for increased partial-cost payments, it is essential to recognize that not all of the difference between the full cost of a unit of health care and the partial-cost payment is policy relevant. That is, there is an economic upper limit to the partial-cost payment as a share of total cost. Beyond some point, the benefits of insurance will be reduced enough by the partial-cost payment that large numbers of people will quit buying insurance.

We are not certain where this limit is, but it is safe to conclude that the partial-cost payment share for both privately insured hospital care and Medicaid of around 3 percent and zero, respectively, are well below the limit. The 15 percent cost share for Medicare Part A probably leaves some room for increasing the partial-cost payment share for this program as well. Evidence from the RAND HIS study indicates that a 10 percentage point increase in the partial-cost payment share would reduce health care expenditures by 1 to 2 percent.[25] If the payment shares for privately insured hospital care, Medicaid, and Medicare Part A were raised to 25 percent (the level suggested as appropriate by the RAND HIS study), the maximum cost savings would be $18 billion to $36 billion.

Actually, this is probably an optimistic cost-saving scenario. An increase in the partial-cost payment for Medicaid would probably be ruled out on the obvious grounds that recipients could not afford it; after all, Medicaid is aimed at people who can't afford adequate health care. Thus, the upper limit on cost savings from increasing the partial-cost payment share is probably more like $15 billion to $30 billion.

VOUCHERS One possible way to reduce overspending for Medicaid (and Medicare) without denying medical benefits to program recipients would be to replace the current system of reimbursement with a system of vouchers. **Vouchers** are coupons that the recipient can use to pay for something, in this case health care at hospitals or doctors' offices chosen by the recipient. Alternatively, the individual could be required to use the voucher to purchase a conventional health insurance policy or to participate in a lower-cost managed care system (explained in the next section of this chapter). In fact, the voucher program could be tailored to encourage Medicaid/Medicare recipients to choose managed care by providing a slightly larger voucher for those who do.

The government would save costs by issuing vouchers for a smaller amount than it currently spends. Economists argue that this could be done without materially reducing beneficial health care to the recipients because they would be faced with a greater share of the costs of their own care and make better health care choices. Proponents of vouchers also stress that their use would enhance the competition by health care providers for Medicaid/Medicare patients with good—that is, cost-saving—results.

Critics of vouchers stress that vouchers may not work as intended because there is a risk that recipients will make poor choices of health insurers. Some proponents answer that, if this were a problem, the government could provide accurate information about the merits of alternative insurance policies (a similar role for government was cast in the ill-fated Clinton health care reform proposal).

MANAGED CARE Whatever the merits of vouchers, they are unlikely to significantly reduce excessive spending as long as the recipients have only traditional private insurance plans from which to choose. Significant cost saving may be possible only with the availability of organizations that help to control costs at the source—that is, on the supply side of the market.

Organizations established principally for the purpose of reducing health care costs are commonly referred to as **managed care organizations.** The three

Vouchers
Coupons that can be used by the recipient to pay for something.

Managed Care Organizations
Organizations established principally for the purpose of reducing health care costs.

---

[25]Phelps, *Health Economics*, 303.

principal types of managed care organizations are health maintenance organizations (HMOs), independent practice associations (IPAs), and preferred provider organizations (PPOs).

The HMO is the oldest of the three types and probably the one best known to the public. The idea behind the HMO is simple: the insurance coverage and delivery of medicine are integrated into a single organization. The insurance plan hires doctors, or contracts with a group of doctors to provide care, and either builds or contracts for the services of a hospital. The money to pay for this comes from the premiums of the insured. The doctors and hospital agree to provide all of the medical care required by the insurees for the fixed amount paid by the insurer.

The HMO budget constraint creates a need to restrict the amount of medical care provided, as opposed to traditional fee-for-service medicine, in which the incentive is to increase the amount of care provided. Doctors are given a further incentive to cut costs through their right to a share of the profits generated by keeping costs lower than revenues from premiums. Not surprisingly, the primary cost savings in an HMO come from reduced hospitalization, the one very costly activity over which doctors can exercise the most control. For example, HMO hospital costs were 28 percent lower than fee-for-service hospital costs in the RAND HIS study.[26] HMOs should have a lower incidence of ineffective and inappropriate surgical and diagnostic procedures as well. In fact, since the hospital is often the site of extensive surgery and expensive diagnostic equipment, lower hospital costs reflect savings in these areas.

IPAs are sometimes referred to as a halfway house between the HMO and the fee-for-service system. In this model the doctors who are members of the IPA maintain their own practices but agree as a group to provide all the physician care, as well as hospital admissions, needed by a certain group of insurees for a total negotiated sum. The IPA will commonly withhold a portion of the fees due doctors as a reserve against high costs, and this reserve will be paid to the doctors if costs are kept sufficiently low overall. Since the fee-for-service feature is not entirely absent from IPAs, however, they do not experience the cost savings of HMOs.

PPOs are even closer to traditional fee-for-service medicine. Basically, the PPO strikes a deal with doctors and hospitals for the fees they will charge patients whose firms or organizations are members of the PPO. The PPO agrees to bring patients to the providers for the reduced price. Since the doctor is still rewarded for more services in the PPO arrangement, even if at a reduced fee per service, there is an incentive to provide more services. Thus, the PPO is expected to experience smaller cost savings than the HMO or IPA.

These types of plans have not yet captured the majority of the privately insured population, but they are growing fast, especially on the West Coast and in the upper Midwest. Increasingly, insurance companies will, in effect, do the

---

[26]W. G. Manning, J. P. Newhouse, N. Duan, et al., "Health Insurance and the Demand for Medical Care: Evidence from a Randomized Experiment," *American Economic Review,* 77, no. 3 (1987), 251–77. This is an example of the kind of evidence that relates to cost-minimization, or attaining the lowest possible cost of achieving something (for a fuller explanation of this concept, see Chapter 2).

health care price shopping for consumers by striking agreements with providers for lower prices. In turn, these plans will attract more enrollees from increasingly cost-conscious employers. Where the use of these plans will eventually lead is not known for certain, but it raises the possibility that the industry will go a long way in reforming itself, thereby reducing the need for government reform of the system. In fact, the recent highly visible attempts to change the system through government action may actually prove to be the catalyst that the industry needed to move further and faster along the road to greater cost-consciousness.

Nor have the lessons of managed care been ignored by government health care officials. At the state level, in particular, there is an earnest search for ways to cut down on the cost of Medicaid (remember, Medicaid is a federal-state program), with some states offering incentives or requiring Medicaid enrollees to use HMOs or other types of managed care. Oklahoma provides an example of the innovation in this area. In 1996 the state health care authority solicited bids for the care of the Medicaid population for a fixed fee per capita. Only HMOs were eligible to bid.

ELIMINATING THE TAX EXEMPTION FOR HEALTH INSURANCE   We come finally to the last, and possibly the biggest, "big ticket" item: elimination of the federal tax exemption for health insurance. We are not the first to suggest this course; elimination of this exemption has been proposed to Congress many times, most recently as part of President Clinton's health care reform package, but Congress refuses to change it.

The exemption was granted initially to encourage employer-provided insurance as a means of helping workers secure the lower premiums that come with group purchases of insurance. Many in Congress may believe that the elimination of the exemption would undo this advantage. However, the exemption tends to be enjoyed primarily by workers in larger firms, and they would be able to secure favorable premiums, anyway, because of their numbers. In fact, it is doubtful that the exemption has had anything to do with the development of the employer-provided insurance market; that can be attributed largely to the competition among insurers for clients that looked more profitable based on their experience rating. Take the exemption away, and they would still have looked like the most profitable risk pools.

Thus, there are two problems with the exemption: (1) it leads to excessive health care spending, and (2) it is unnecessary as a means of increasing the availability of low-cost insurance. But that's not all. Because its value to workers rises with the marginal tax rate, it provides a greater subsidy to higher-income workers than to lower-income workers. This pattern violates most notions of equity. In addition, the subsidy contributes to the federal deficit as much as would direct federal expenditure of a like amount. How much is this? The exemption was worth more than $36 billion in 1991.[27]

This is a formidable array of problems. Why, then, does the exemption persist? Probably because it provides a subsidy to the purchase of health care from

---

[27]Henry J. Aaron, *Serious and Unstable Condition* (Washington, DC: Brookings Institution, 1991), 67.

THE MEDICALLY UNINSURED

Given the high costs of health care and the likelihood that most families and individuals need at least some health care, it has become crucial for all individuals to have access to health insurance. For those who are not eligible for government health care programs, health care insurance in the United States has become closely linked to the workplace. Eighty-five percent of the population under age 65 has some type of health insurance, 82 percent of which is employment-based, and only 8 percent of which is private insurance that is not employment-based. The 15 percent who have no insurance translates into 34 million people.

It is common, but inaccurate, to attribute people's lack of insurance to their having no attachment to the work force. Over 80 percent of the 34 million, however, have some connection to the work force, either as workers or as dependents of workers. The key to lack of work-force coverage seems to be the size of the employees' firm. The likelihood that a worker will not be covered is inversely related to the size of the firm (that is, the smaller the firm, the greater the probability of no insurance). The problem is not lack of availability of health insurance to small firms, but the fact that the cost of health insurance per employee is much higher for small firms than for large firms. The higher costs are due to significantly higher insurance administration costs per employee, and the higher risk of loss associated with small pools of employees.

Some groups have advocated that either the federal or state governments mandate employer-provided health insurance. Unfortunately, this would increase the cost of insurance coverage for small firms as insurers take on the greater administrative burden of additional small groups and the higher risks associated with small groups of employees. The increase in costs to employers would result in some rise in unemployment, especially among low-wage workers. In this sense, mandated health care insurance would have effects similar to the minimum wage, discussed in Chapter 12.

Should a program of mandated insurance be adopted, it may have to be supplemented with a program of subsidies to those firms that truly cannot afford it without firing employees or going out of business. This may greatly reduce the political prospects for mandated insurance, including the so-called play-or-pay schemes that would require employers either to "play" by providing insurance or to "pay" by remitting a tax, the proceeds from which would be used to provide government-financed insurance coverage.

which thousands of insurance companies, thousands of hospitals, hundreds of thousands of doctors, millions of businesses, and scores of millions of workers benefit. Together they form an almost irresistible force against significant political change. Given the rapidly rising concern about the level of health care spending, we may be closer than ever to the time when economics will triumph over politics on this issue, but we would not bet on it.

SUMMARY

The fundamental premise of health care reformers is that we are spending too much for health care in the United States. One important dimension of "too much" health care from an economic perspective is that we are consuming health care that yields marginal benefits less than marginal costs. The following features of the health care system are the most probable sources of excessive spending of this kind:

1. Payment by the patient of only part of the cost of health care at the point of purchase induces them to consume too much health care. This partial-cost payment feature characterizes all types of health care and both the private and public health care sectors. It is a significant source of excessive spending.

2. There is a suspicion that physicians have been able to induce patients to overconsume health care. Although we find little evidence of this, there is evidence of ineffective and inappropriate care.

3. Physicians purportedly prescribe unnecessary procedures as a defensive measure against possible malpractice lawsuits. The costs associated with this practice, however, probably do not exceed 1 percent of health care costs.

4. Technological change is often viewed as an important cause of too much health care spending. We conclude, however, that consumers probably have been willing to pay for most of the technological change that has occurred and that there is little evidence of pure waste from this source.

5. Most private insurance is experience-rated. Experience rating has produced lower health insurance premiums for many Americans, but in exchange for higher costs of insurance administration, discrimination, and "job lock."

6. Employer-provided health insurance enjoys a substantial subsidy in the form of a federal tax exemption of health insurance premiums. This exemption stimulates the purchase of more insurance and indirectly induces consumers to buy excessive amounts of health care. The effect of this exemption on health care purchases rivals that of partial-cost payments.

7. There are significant incentives for overspending in the public sector of the health care industry. Both Medicare and Medicaid have low partial-cost payment rates. Medicare is structured to provide excessive coverage for routine, inexpensive care and deficient coverage for expensive long-term care. Medicaid covers long-term care, but only after recipients meet excessively stringent asset criteria.

The policy implications of these findings seem relatively clear: the most promising policy options are (1) increasing partial-cost payments, (2) reducing ineffective and inappropriate care, and (3) eliminating the federal tax exemption for health insurance. Partial-cost payments can be increased somewhat for private insurance and Medicare, but not for Medicaid. Managed care organizations can realize cost savings from reducing ineffective and inappropriate care, and their growth may significantly reduce the need for radical health care reform. Vouchers may be an attractive substitute for increasing the partial-cost payment of Medicaid recipients. Finally, there are several reasons for eliminating the federal tax exemption for health insurance, but such a move faces formidable political opposition.

KEY TERMS

Third-party payment	Defensive medicine	Vouchers
Partial-cost payment	Experience-rated	Managed-care
Physician-induced demand	insurance	organizations

REVIEW QUESTIONS

1. What is meant by "too much" health care? Illustrate and explain briefly how partial-cost payments for hospital care cause too much hospital care to be produced.
2. Carefully define physician-induced demand. Can it explain the large amount of ineffective and inappropriate care? Why or why not?
3. "Defensive medicine is one of the primary causes of excessive health care spending." Is this statement true or false? Justify your answer.
4. "Technological change can explain a lot of the growth in health care costs, but little of the excessive spending that takes place." Do you agree? Why? Why not?
5. Explain the practice of experience rating of insurance policies. What are some of the benefits and costs of this procedure?
6. How can the federal tax exemption for health insurance make the net cost of an insurance policy negative?
7. Which of the two government programs, Medicare or Medicaid, has the best prospects for cutting costs? Defend your choice.
8. Based on your reading of this chapter, how much government action do you think is necessary to achieve health care reform? Justify your answer.
9. Based on your reading of this chapter, what do think is the most promising way to reduce excessive health care spending? Explain why.

SUGGESTIONS FOR FURTHER READING

Aaron, Henry J. ed., *The Problem That Won't Go Away*. Washington, DC: The Brookings Institution, 1996. The authors of this book recount the history of the ill-fated Clinton health plan, present alternative strategies the administration might have pursued, and propose several incremental reforms that seem possible in the future.

Congress of the United States, Congressional Budget Office. *Rising Health Care Costs: Causes, Implications, and Strategies*. Washington, DC: Government Printing Office, 1991. A report on trends in health care costs, including an evaluation of past attempts to control costs in the United States. Also contains a discussion of strategies used in Canada, Great Britain, France, and the former West Germany to contain health care costs.

Folland, Sherman, Allen C. Goodman, and Miron Stano. *The Economics of Health and Health Care*. New York: Macmillan, 1993. An excellent guide to the field of health economics. It is useful for reference even if some of the analysis is too advanced for novices in economics.

Newhouse, Joseph P. "Medical Care Costs: How Much Welfare Loss?" *Journal of Economic Perspectives* 6, no. 3 (Summer 1992), 3–21. Newhouse poses the same question as we do: "Are we spending too much for health care?" He argues that the case is not as clear-cut as the recent flurry of political proposals would lead one to believe.

Phelps, Charles E. *Health Economics.* New York: HarperCollins, 1993. A very good but somewhat advanced reference book. An especially good source for summaries of empirical studies.

6

CRIME AND DRUGS

A Modern Dilemma

TERMS YOU SHOULD KNOW

Marginal social benefit (Chapter 2)

Marginal social cost (Chapter 2)

Opportunity cost (Chapter 1)

Demand (Chapter 1)

Supply (Chapter 1)

About three-fourths of U.S. citizens, according to opinion polls, believe that federal, state, and local governments do not spend enough fighting crime. More people believe that the United States spends too little on crime control than believe it spends too little on dealing with drug addiction or with improving education. The reason for the concern about crime is evident in other polls, which find that almost one-half of the population fears walking at night in some areas within a mile of their home.[1] This percentage increased from 40 percent in 1989 to 47 percent in 1994.

Such feelings of insecurity have fueled a massive increase in government crime control. For instance, state expenditures (in inflation-adjusted dollars) on prisons have grown at over 8 percent a year since the beginning of the 1980s. This almost triples expenditures in 13 years. Federal expenditures on prisons are much smaller, but they have grown even faster. The growth in expenditures accompanies a similar growth in the number of state and federal prisoners. More than three times as many people are in state and federal prisons now than at the beginning of the 1980s. State expenditures on police protection have also grown, but at less than half the rate of prison expenditures. Total expenditures on police and prisons have increased substantially in response to the fear of crime. Why have they not affected peoples' feelings of safety?

It is not because crime rates are rising. The best evidence is that crime rates have fallen since 1980. Victimization surveys, which ask people if they have been victims of crimes, probably provide the best evidence about crime rates over time.[2] They report that from 1980 to 1994 the violent crime rate (rape, robbery, and assault) fell from 116 to 94 per 100,000 people—a 21 percent decrease. The rate of burglary, larceny, and motor vehicle theft fell even more. Perhaps peoples' fears about crime have not eased because the most widely reported crime, homicide, has not followed the pattern. The 1980 homicide rate of about 10 per 100,000 people fell in the early 1980s and climbed back to about 10 in 1991. It has since fallen to under 9 (1995).

Homicide and other crime rates are much higher in metropolitan areas than in smaller cities and in rural areas. The homicide rate, for instance, is more than twice as high—11 versus 5 per 100,000 people—in metropolitan areas than in other cities or rural areas. Homicide rates in the large central cities are much higher than in the rest of the country. In 1994 New Orleans led the nation with more than 85 homicides per 100,000 people. In 1993 Washington, D.C., had 78 homicides per 100,000 people, and cities such as Atlanta, Baltimore, Birmingham, Detroit, Oakland, and St. Louis had rates over 40 per 100,000 people.

---

[1] The introduction is based on data from U.S. Bureau of the Census, *Statistical Abstract of the United States* (Washington, DC: Government Printing Office), and Kathleen Maguire and Ann L. Pastore, eds., *Sourcebook of Criminal Justice Statistics—1993* (Washington, DC: U.S. Department of Justice, Bureau of Justice Statistics, 1995).

[2] Crime rates based on police reports have the disadvantage that not all crimes are reported to the police. Moreover, in some years a higher percentage of crimes are reported than in others. Except for homicides, victimization surveys provide more accurate information about crime over time than do crimes reported to the police.

One reason that cities have such high rates of homicide (and other crimes) is that they attract a large amount of illegal drug activity. Although the casual use of illegal drugs—as well as alcohol and nicotine—has declined from its peak in the 1970s, the use of marijuana, cocaine, and increasingly heroin by frequent users continues to create profitable, but illegal, markets. Violence is endemic on the supply side of these markets. Property crime, with associated violence, on the demand side allows heavy users of illegal drugs to afford their habits.

Government attempts to prevent the manufacture, sale, and use of marijuana, cocaine, and heroin—the War on Drugs—account for much of the increased activity against crime. Drug arrests increased by almost 50 percent from 1985 to 1994. In 1982 more than half of these arrests were for possession of marijuana and fewer than 1 in 10 were for possession of cocaine or heroin. By 1994 about 30 percent of the arrests were for marijuana possession and about 30 percent were for possession of cocaine or heroin. Arrests for sale and or manufacture of illegal drugs went from about 2 to 3 in 10 of total drug arrests. The War on Drugs has resulted in a massive increase in police activity. Arrests on drug charges have exploded. Moreover, the arrest pattern has shifted toward more arrests for sale and manufacture and fewer for possession. Arrests for possession have shifted sharply from those for marijuana possession to those for cocaine or heroin possession.

This chapter explores government's role in crime and drug control. First, it discusses crimes in which one person uses force to violate another person's rights. Second, it discusses crimes in which the government prohibits two people from voluntarily agreeing to a transaction, for instance, exchanging money for illegal drugs. In both cases, the rationale for government action is discussed. The chapter then discusses drug policy.

PUBLIC GOODS

Understanding the concept of a **public good** is important to an understanding of the role of government in crime and drug control. Public goods provide a rationale for government's role in the economy. A public good is a good with two characteristics. One characteristic is that it is difficult to prevent or exclude people from consuming the good. For instance, if a strong police effort makes streets safe, it is difficult to restrict the feeling of security to people who voluntarily pay for the police effort. In contrast, it is easy to restrict the use of a private good, such as a candy bar, to people who pay for it. So a public good is a **nonexcludable good** and a private good is an excludable good.

The other characteristic is that an individual can consume a public good without reducing the amount available to other people. To continue the example, if the streets are safe, the fact that one person is enjoying the safety does not reduce the feeling of security available to anyone else. Again, in contrast, if one person consumes a unit of a private good—eats a candy bar—other people are not able to consume it. So a public good is a **nonrival good** and a private good is a rival good. In short, a public good is nonexcludable and nonrival; a private good is excludable and rival.

Public Good
A good that is nonexcludable and nonrival.

Nonexcludable Good
A good that is impossible or extremely difficult to exclude nonpayers from consuming.

Nonrival Good
A good that one person can consume without reducing the amount available for other people to consume, such as a feeling of security in a safe city.

The government may be able to provide a public good more effectively than the private market for at least three reasons. First, it is costly to exclude people from the benefits of a public good. In the secure street example, a private supplier would have to identify when people are enjoying the secure streets and bill them for the security in much the same way that an electric utility sends a monthly utility bill. It would be more costly, however, to monitor people's street use than their electricity use. Furthermore, people can conceal their enjoyment of security, making it difficult, if not impossible, for a private supplier to bill them. Government provision of secure streets, on the other hand, does not require that citizens pay voluntarily for the feeling of security. They pay through taxes. But this payment does not vary with enjoyment, so the government does not have to measure it.

Second, in addition to the opportunity costs of the resources used for measuring street use, there may be privacy costs in monitoring the use of some public goods. Many people do not want a private firm or government to have a record of where they are or who they visit.

Third, private provision of a public good, like security, would create economic inefficiency. The opportunity cost of providing security to one more person is zero; the good is nonrival. Nevertheless, a private firm would charge an additional user a price greater than its zero marginal cost. The demand price would be greater than its zero supply price. Therefore, too little of the good would be used. If the government finances the public good through taxation, the price to an additional person of consuming security is zero. No one is excluded from the public good by its price. Because the marginal cost of providing the good is also zero, the zero price leads to efficient use of the public good. People consume it up to the point where marginal benefit equals the zero marginal cost.

GOVERNMENT ENFORCEMENT OF PROPERTY RIGHTS

A decentralized market economy requires a government to establish and enforce property rights. To have a property right in a good means that an individual has an exclusive right to use or sell the good within certain constraints. The existence of property rights allows the voluntary transactions of a market system to work well. Dave would not buy a car from Joanna if he did not have a reasonable hope that it would not be taken by the government or stolen.

Imagine an economy in which the government does not establish and protect property rights. Individuals would have to protect their own property. With no government protection of property, more theft would occur. To counter the theft, individuals would use resources to protect their property.

In this imaginary economy, if Hugh is skilled in protecting his property, he makes it easier for other people to protect theirs. To see how this might happen, suppose people in a neighborhood get a reputation for protecting their property well. Some people in the neighborhood could take advantage of that reputation. For instance, imagine that Hugh and a few other people organize a Neighborhood Watch. Missy, who lives in the neighborhood, could receive some benefit from the watch without participating in the program. If she acts in this way, she is a **free rider.** A free rider is someone who uses goods or services provided by others without paying for them.

Hugh and his colleagues may not be able to collect any fees or volunteer work from some of the people whose property rights they are inadvertently defending. People have a tendency to be free riders. Free riders will reason that the Neighborhood Watch is going to exist and provide protection whether they contribute or not, so why contribute?

Hugh and his colleagues will try to prevent free riding by concentrating on protecting their own property. For instance, they will put security locks on their doors but not on the free riders' doors. They may have security patrols only on their own property. But security patrols in the neighborhood will, by their mere presence, provide some protection to the free riders' property as well, even though the level of protection will be less than the efficient level. The marginal social benefit of the protection equals the marginal private benefit to Hugh (and his colleagues) plus the marginal benefit to the free riders. Hugh and his colleagues, who pay all of the cost, will expand protection to the point where their marginal private benefit equals marginal cost. But marginal social benefit is greater than their marginal private benefit. Therefore, Hugh will not expand protection to the efficient level (marginal social benefit equal to marginal cost). If the free riders were willing to share the cost, Hugh would be willing to supply more protection, but the essence of free riding is to avoid paying.

It is cheaper to have a single agency provide security for a town instead of having several types of Neighborhood Watches. Rather than having security patrols concentrate on particular pieces of property, it is probably cheaper and as effective to have people provide security for the entire town. In other words, monopoly provision of property rights protection may be cheaper than the alternative of individuals providing their own protection.

Another point is involved. Property rights protection requires use of force: coercion. Rather than allowing individuals to decide what type of coercion to use, many people believe that coercive powers should be reserved for representative government.

Finally, because it does not cost anything to provide property rights protection to one more person, it is not efficient to charge for it. One more person can consume property rights without reducing their availability to everyone else. In other words, the establishment and enforcement of property rights is a public good. Exclusion is difficult. The good is nonrival.

Free Rider
An individual who uses goods or services provided by others without paying for them.

CRIME

Given that property rights protection is a public good, it can be efficient for the government to provide it. Crime control is one part of property rights protection. Government, through the political process, is responsible for determining how much crime control to provide. Everyone benefits from crime control. But because it is a public good, few people would be willing to pay full value for it. As free riders, people reason that they will get the crime control because other people will pay for it. But if everyone reasons this way, too little crime control will be provided.

To overcome this free-rider problem, people agree to let the government tax them and to use the resources gained from taxation to provide the crime control.

If government can, in fact, control crime, then the amount of crime that we have is a political decision. Why do we decide to have so much crime? Figure 6.1 shows the marginal social benefit of reducing the crime rate through crime control. As the amount of resources used for crime control increases, the number of crimes and therefore the probability of being a victim decrease. The marginal social benefit of reducing crime and the probability of being a victim decrease as the crime rate decreases. The feeling of security increases as the probability of being a crime victim decreases from 50 percent to 49 percent for a particular time period. The feeling of security also increases as that probability decreases from 3 percent to 2 percent. Yet people probably would not be willing to pay as much for the decrease from 3 to 2 percent as for the decrease from 50 to 49 percent. If the chances of being a victim are already low, a given reduction in the probability of being victimized would not be worth as much.

The marginal social cost of reducing the probability of being a victim increases as the amount of crime control increases, as shown in Figure 6.1. The

THE EFFICIENT LEVEL OF CRIME CONTROL

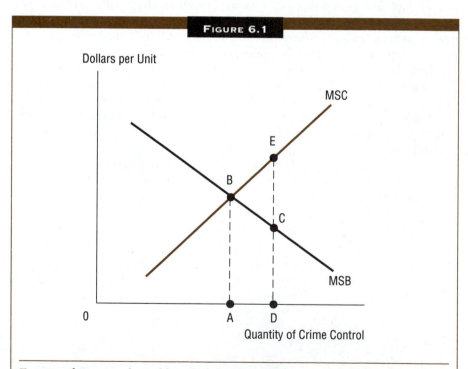

FIGURE 6.1

Equating the marginal social benefit and cost of crime control gives the efficient level. Because the marginal social benefit is positive at that level, the efficient level of crime control does not result in the elimination of crime—additional benefit results from additional crime reduction. But the additional benefit is less than the additional cost.

marginal social cost increases for three reasons. First, to reduce crime, more resources must be devoted to crime control. As more resources are devoted to crime control, their opportunity cost increases. These resources must be pulled from other government programs, such as defense, AIDS research, and aid for the homeless—or from taxpayers' pockets.

Second, it takes more resources to reduce crime by a given amount if the crime rate is already very low than to reduce it by the same amount if the crime rate is very high. The first stage of crime reduction is easy—catch the incompetent criminals. As the crime rate decreases, however, only the most talented or the luckiest criminals will be in business. It will be more difficult to deter their criminal activity.

Third, as the amount of crime falls, reducing it further requires an assault on our freedom. By and large, U.S. citizens and their representatives prefer one type of mistake in our judicial system to the other. Specifically, we believe punishing the innocent is a worse mistake than not punishing the guilty. Our unwillingness to accept confessions that police obtain by trickery or threat might be interpreted as a way of protecting the innocent. If we had less respect for civil rights, the conviction rate for crimes could be increased. The crime rate might be lower, but many people believe that the cost would be too high.

The intersection of the marginal social benefit and marginal social cost curves in Figure 6.1 gives the efficient level of crime control and, implicitly, the efficient level of crime. An increase in crime control from A to D reduces everone's chance of being a crime victim. At D the marginal social benefit is DC, which is the value that people would place on the increased security and reduced crime rates. The extra cost of an increase in crime control (of a lower crime rate) is DE. This marginal social cost includes the opportunity cost of using more resources for crime control, including the value of lost freedom, if any. Given the circumstances, the crime rate associated with D is too low. It costs more to increase crime control from A to D than is gained.

This analysis suggests that the reason that we have so much crime is that it is very costly to control it. Crime control may be costly because many people are willing to be criminals. Or it may be costly because of the problems, such as poor economic prospects, that have developed in inner cities. Another possibility is that increased drug use has increased the cost of crime control.

DRUG LEGALIZATION: COMPETING VIEWS

In any year, over 10 percent of all arrests reported to the FBI are for prostitution, drug abuse, gambling, and drunkenness (not including driving while intoxicated). These arrests are for voluntary transactions between buyer and seller that have little direct effect on anyone outside the transaction. Why do we make voluntary transactions crimes? In particular, why do we expend so much of our crime fighting resources in combating the drug trade?

POLICE, GUNS, AND CRIME

An economic approach to crime control implies that government can control crime, particularly property crime, because it can create conditions in which crime does *not* pay. According to this approach, crime decreases if potential criminals think that their chances of getting away with, say, a bank robbery, have decreased. They will hesitate if they think that, upon getting caught, the chances have increased that they will be subjected to a speedy trial and, upon conviction, a harsh punishment. Besides making crime less profitable, government can reduce crime by jailing criminals. First, imprisonment raises the cost of crime, making the choice less attractive. Second, it reduces the supply of criminals because potential offenders are locked up. This works because (1) offenders tend repeat their criminal activity, (2) an imprisoned criminal is not immediately replaced by a new offender, and (3) imprisonment does not increase after-prison criminal activity.

Recent information suggests that the economic approach may be valid. New York City, which suffered more than 2,000 murders in 1990, may have only half that many in 1996. Crime rates of all kinds in New York City have plummeted over the last few years. Associated with this decrease in crime in New York has been (1) an increase of 7,000 police officers (2) a doubling of the New York prison population, (3) a focus on efficient management of the NYPD, and (4) an aggressive use of police power to arrest people for minor violations that had in the past been overlooked. For instance, someone drinking in public or writing graffiti is now more likely to be arrested and required to produce identification, which allows the officer to check for other violations. In short, New York City provides an example of more, and more aggressive, police activity, possibly lending to reduced crime rates.

A statistical study of crime across the United States also supports the economic approach. Two economists writing in the *Journal of Legal Studies* report statistical evidence that violent crime rates decrease in states that permit their residents to carry concealed handguns. If potential victims might be armed, the expected cost of crimes against people goes up. In turn, criminals may switch to crimes where they are less likely to meet armed resistance. Their study also finds that counties with higher arrest rates per violation have lower crime rates. In response to the possibility that an armed citizenry might lead to more accidental deaths, the study finds that states that introduce concealed handgun laws do not have an increase in accidental deaths.

Although these examples are not conclusive, they are consistent with an economic approach to crime. Moreover, they provide an excellent example of the rising cost of crime control. For example, living in a city that investigates people for minor violations can be unpleasant. Encouraging the police to be more aggressive may lead to more incidents of police brutality and to actual or perceived discrimination. A well-dressed jaywalker is likely to escape police attention, whereas a less well-groomed young man is likely to be hassled. Similarly, even if we believe that allowing people to carry concealed handguns reduces the violent crime rate, we also may believe that a society that cannot control crime in other ways is not the ideal society. In short, increased crime control runs into increasing marginal social cost.

Sources: John J. DiIulio, Jr., "Arresting Ideas: Tougher Law Enforcement Is Driving Down Urban Crime," *Policy Review* 74 (Fall 1995) and John R. Lott, Jr., and David B. Mustard, "Crime Deterrence, and Right to Carry Concealed Handguns," *Journal of Legal Studies* 26 (January 1997).

LIBERTY: AN ARGUMENT FOR LEGALIZATION

Some people argue that illegal drugs should be legalized. They argue that each responsible individual should have the freedom to engage in any voluntary transaction, as long as it does not impose substantial, involuntary harm on a third party. To John Stuart Mill, the 19th-century economist who made this argument, individual liberty was an extremely important value. Similarly, Milton Friedman says, "I believe that adults—by this I mean people whom we regard as responsible, and as a practical matter this means people who are neither insane nor below a certain age—should be responsible for their own lives. . . . People's freedom to make their own decisions is my fundamental objective."[3]

The argument that people should be allowed to make their own decisions is subject to two qualifications. One qualification is that children should not have this freedom. If, say, cocaine were legal, the argument requires that children not be allowed to use it until they reach a certain age. Indeed, it may require strong policies to ensure that children do not use it.

The second qualification is that people should not be allowed to sell themselves into slavery. If you sell yourself into slavery, you are giving up your freedom to make your own decisions. The question then arises of whether dependence on drugs—alcohol, cocaine, or what have you—implies that drug users are selling themselves into slavery. The evidence shows that drug dependence is a very powerful force that ruins many lives. Nevertheless, the evidence also suggests that the ideas that most drug users become addicts or even that all addicts remain addicts until they die are wrong. An unqualified acceptance of the liberty argument implies the legalization of such drugs as cocaine, heroin, and marijuana.

PATERNALISM: AN ARGUMENT AGAINST LEGALIZATION

John Kaplan rejects the absolutist principle that would allow people to engage in self-destructive activity if there is no involuntary harm. He argues that people can through government "morally attempt to keep others from likely harm even though they themselves are foolish enough to take the risk. After all, Mill's view that all adults must be assumed to know their own best interest is certainly contrary to fact, as most of us see it."[4]

Furthermore, the U.S. public does not accept the argument that all drugs should be made legal. Polls indicate only small percentages of the population— usually less than 5 percent—favor legalizing all drugs. Furthermore, these polls indicate that only small percentages—less than 20 percent—agree that people should be allowed to use any drug as long as no one else is hurt. It is ironic that this large majority in favor of the prohibition of such illegal drugs as cocaine and

---

[3]Milton Friedman, "Stop Taxing Non-Addicts," *Reason* (October 1988), 24.
[4]John Kaplan, *The Hardest Drug: Heroin and Public Policy* (Chicago: The University of Chicago Press, 1983), 104. See this book for an excellent discussion of these issues.

heroin does not also favor the prohibition of alcohol and nicotine. We know that alcohol and nicotine are responsible for more deaths and illnesses and that alcohol is related to more crime than all of the prohibited drugs combined. Of course, if we legalized the prohibited drugs, they might generate more problems than alcohol and nicotine.

MORALITY: AN ARGUMENT FOR PROHIBITION

William J. Bennett, Irving Kristol, and James Q. Wilson, along with many other social scientists, argue that government has a responsibility for prohibiting the use of mind-altering drugs, regardless of (1) whether such drug users are fully responsible and (2) the absence of involuntary harm to others. Wilson flatly states that "Drug use is wrong because it is immoral and it is immoral because it enslaves the mind and destroys the soul."[5] In this view, the possibility that marijuana or any other drug may not be very dangerous to health is irrelevant. The immorality of drug use is due to its purpose, which, in this interpretation, is to withdraw from society and civilization.

The immorality implicit in the use of mind-altering drugs resolves the seeming contradiction in the failure to prohibit nicotine. Although the use of tobacco is arguably as dangerous medically as the use of various controlled substances, it does not debase life; it only shortens it. According to Wilson, drug users lack such virtues as self-control, sobriety, and the ability to delay gratification. The immorality lies in the effects of drug use on the moral character and on the subsequent harmful effects on society.

THE FINAL ANALYSIS

The inconsistent treatment of alcohol (a mind-altering drug), nicotine and cocaine suggests that our drug laws do not follow from either Friedman's liberty argument, Kaplan's paternalism argument, or Wilson's morality argument. Kaplan tempers his position by stating that the general argument that government should not interfere in basically private behavior is sound practical advice. He simply concludes that the cost of legalization is greater to society than the cost of prohibition. Similarly, Friedman makes his case more persuasive by arguing that drug prohibition causes more harm than good. In short, both Kaplan and Friedman take a positive approach to drug policy. Wilson's position, however, does not leave room for a positive analysis.

A positive approach analyzes the consequences of a particular action, say, drug prohibition, without judging whether the action is desirable or undesirable. The next section turns to a positive analysis of drug policy.

---

[5]As quoted by "Reclaiming the War on Drugs," Empower America Brochure, October 1996. See also James Q. Wilson, "Against the Legalization of Drugs," *Commentary* (February 1990), 23–28.

A POSITIVE ANALYSIS OF DRUG PROHIBITION

To analyze the effects of the prohibition of a drug like cocaine, an alternative is necessary. For simplicity, suppose that cocaine is available on demand from government-owned stores. The price paid includes a substantial government tax. Thus, the alternative is similar to the legal situation for liquor in some states. Assume that the supply curve is flat, S_0 in Figure 6.2. This supply curve is the market marginal cost of cocaine. Including a heavy rate of taxation, this marginal cost might be on the order of $20 per gram. Initial users might get 50 doses per gram. Therefore, the cost per dose could be as low as 40 cents.[6] The demand curve, D_0 in Figure 6.2, as usual holds a number of things constant: the price of other drugs, income, the method of distribution, laws, and consumer preferences.

Now suppose new laws make cocaine and other drugs—except alcohol and nicotine—illegal. Assume that possession and use of the illegal substances would be a felony. Furthermore, selling these substances would be an even more serious felony.

In the new situation, assume the method of distribution matches the one observed in the United States today. A cartel buys cocaine in other countries and exports it to the United States. Presumably, this cartel chooses an output that maximizes profit. After the cocaine arrives in the United States, the cartel distributes it to wholesalers throughout the country. These wholesalers distribute it to city wholesalers, who, in turn, may distribute it to another level of wholesalers, and so on until it reaches local retailers. The several layers of distribution protect the importers and large wholesalers from detection by the authorities. The large difference between the price they pay for their raw material—coca leaves—and the price they receive for their product—cocaine—is partly due to monopoly restriction of output. The price differential is also partly due to the extra compensation that smugglers require to cover the cost, including the risk of punishment, of evading the drug laws.

Each level of distribution includes compensation for the risk of supplying an illegal product. Additional risks exist for distributors closer to the street. Retail distributors trying to claim a particular neighborhood market sometimes kill other distributors and bystanders.

As the transactions get further away from the well-organized deals between large wholesalers, the system of property rights established by organized crime disintegrates. Organized crime imposes stiff penalties for stealing rather than buying a major shipment of drugs from a large wholesaler. The penalty—death—is more severe than the penalty imposed by law for, say, hijacking a truckload of whiskey. But the retailer and the wholesalers close to the retailer cannot call on a large organization to enforce their property rights. Deals at this level are made through openings in bulletproof doors. Thus, two factors cause the large increase in cost and therefore large decrease in supply of cocaine in the United States. One factor includes the cartelization of the smuggling of

---

[6]See John Kaplan, "Taking Drugs Seriously," *The Public Interest* (Summer 1988), 41.

THE EFFECT OF
DRUG PROHIBITION
ON DRUG USE

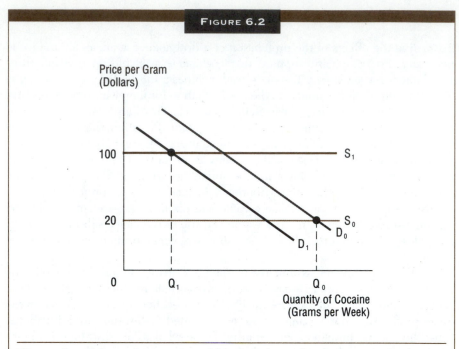

FIGURE 6.2

The supply and demand curves, S_0 and D_0, show the market for cocaine when cocaine is legal. Prohibition causes supply to decrease to S_1 and demand to decrease to D_1. Price goes from \$20 to \$100 per gram, and quantity exchanged falls from Q_0 to Q_1.

cocaine into the United States. The other factor is the risk of punishment for distributing an illegal product and the risk associated with a lack of government-enforced property rights. As a result, if cocaine becomes illegal, the supply curve in Figure 6.2 shifts to S_1.

The demand curve also shifts—from D_0 to D_1—when the product becomes illegal. First, it may decrease because many people do not want to engage in illegal activities. This effect may be offset, however, by other people who get a kick out of violating the law. Second, it will decrease because the deterioration of property rights under the illegal system raises the nonprice costs of buying the good. It is now more difficult to find a supplier of the good. To buy the good, you now have to deal with people who may murder you if you fail to pay. If you develop a reliable connection at the street level, your connection may be arrested and out of circulation at any time. Then you have to go through the dangerous process of finding another supplier. Third, it will decrease because of the legal penalties associated with possession and use. Fourth, it will decrease because of the risk of buying a product in an irregular market. The customer has little recourse if the product purchased is not what it is supposed to be. (This point is comically illustrated by the recent arrest of a cocaine buyer. The buyer reported to the police that he had been sold fake cocaine. The police investigated and found that the substance contained only a small amount of cocaine. Nevertheless, the cheated buyer was arrested for possession.) It may be contaminated because toxic substances have been used to dilute it. It may be a cocaine look-alike. The percentage of the product that is pure cocaine may not be known or accurately described. Many heroin overdoses, including those resulting in death, occur because the substance taken was of inferior quality or unknown purity; it is likely that the same is true of cocaine overdoses.

The effects of the changes in supply and demand are easy to see. The price increases from \$20 to \$100 per gram, and the quantity exchanged decreases from Q_0 to Q_1.

The experience of people who have tried to reduce their use of cocaine supplements the economic analysis. People who have requested treatment for cocaine dependence either through hot lines or clinics have reported spending, on average, from \$450 to \$800 per week on cocaine. Extremely heavy users have spent as much as \$2,000 to \$3,000 per week. According to one survey, almost 50 percent of the people who called a cocaine hot line said they had sold cocaine to finance their habit. About 25 percent of them stole at work and about 35 percent stole from families and friends. About 15 percent had lost their jobs because of cocaine, and about 30 percent had lost their spouses. The *illegal* use of cocaine clearly involves substantial cost to other people in the economy. In particular, cocaine abusers are similar to heroin abusers in how they finance their habit. If they are unable to support their habit legally, they often resort to crime to support it.[7]

It seems clear that drug prohibition reduces drug use and drug abuse. Demand is less when the drug is illegal. A major exception might arise if drug pushing is an important route to drug dependence. The drug pusher supposedly entices people—sometimes young people in the schoolyard—into drug abuse. This is similar to the approach that tobacco companies used when they distributed free cigarettes on college campuses: Hook a customer, and you may have one for life, albeit a shortened one. This may have been a good strategy for a tobacco company because it expected to remain in business for a long time. But it does not seem to be a good strategy for drug dealers. It takes more than a couple of doses of heroin or cocaine to create drug dependence. Giving drugs away means less for the dealer-user with no certainty of a future payoff. Furthermore, the target customer might be an undercover drug agent. Even if the pusher creates a dependent customer, either the pusher or the new user might be arrested before the pusher profits on the initial investment. Drug pushing seems to be an investment with little payoff because buyer-seller relationships are so unstable.

---

[7]See Mark S. Gold, Andrew M. Washton, and Charles A. Dackis, "Cocaine Abuse: Neurochemistry, Phenomenology, and Treatment," 142–143, and Sidney H. Schnoll et al., "Characteristics of Cocaine Abusers Presenting for Treatment," 173–176 in *Cocaine Use in America: Epidemiologic and Clinical Perspectives,* eds., Nicholas J. Kozel and Edgar H. Adams, National Institute on Drug Abuse, Research Monograph 61, U.S. Department of Health and Human Services (Washington DC: Government Printing Office, 1985).

In fact, heroin and cocaine use spread like an epidemic. Availability is the key. If people have access to and use heroin, they share their knowledge and their drugs with their friends. Heroin use begins much like a venereal disease: A friend infects you; with some promiscuity, the disease soon spreads through a social network.[8]

Cocaine use apparently is similar. One study, for example, found that almost 90 percent of the initial use of cocaine took place at a party or other informal social event. About 70 percent of new users obtained it from friends or relatives. Only 5 percent of the new users obtained it from dealers.[9] Kaplan concludes that the drug pusher is a myth. If this is correct, making drugs illegal does not result in dealers pushing drugs on nonusers. Instead, making drugs illegal reduces their general availability and reduces young people's exposure to them.

DOES INCREASED ENFORCEMENT WORK?

The laws against selling and possessing certain drugs reduce their use by reducing supply and demand. The relatively larger reduction in supply leads to an increase in price. The law of demand then implies that the quantity of drugs purchased decreases further along the new demand curve. Some economists argue, however, that increased enforcement will not work. They say that the quantity demanded of illegal drugs is not very responsive to price; therefore, an increase in price caused by increased enforcement leads to only a small decrease in quantity. Total expenditure for drugs could increase. Drug dealers would be better off—except, of course, for the ones who get caught.

THE EFFECTS OF POLICIES TO REDUCE SUPPLY   If the drug is sold in a market with significant monopoly power, increased enforcement will reduce cartel profits. The cartel will have pushed price up until it would no longer be profitable to push it any higher. Because of the monopoly, any increase in cost caused by greater enforcement will reduce the cartel profits.

Different customers, however, may have different responses to a price increase. Over any significant period of time, say, six months, almost every user will decrease cocaine consumption. Figure 6.3 shows the demand curve, D_c, for a casual user of cocaine. If price goes from P_0 to P_1, the quantity demanded falls from Q_0 to Q_c. The percentage reduction in quantity is greater than the percentage reduction in price; quantity demanded is very responsive to the price change. As the figure shows, the casual user spends less; the shaded area labeled A measures the reduction in expenditure because quantity demanded is less. The increase in price leads to an offsetting increase in expenditure measured by the shaded area labeled B. Because the area of A is greater than the area of B, the net effect is for the casual user to spend less when price goes up. Given that the objective of the law is to reduce cocaine use, the increased enforcement works. The user, of course, may substitute other substances for cocaine: alcohol, heroin, or marijuana, for instance.

---

[8]See Kaplan, *The Hardest Drug.*
[9]Dale D. Chitwood, "Patterns and Consequences of Cocaine Use," in *Cocaine Use in America,* eds., Kozel and Adams. 114–115.

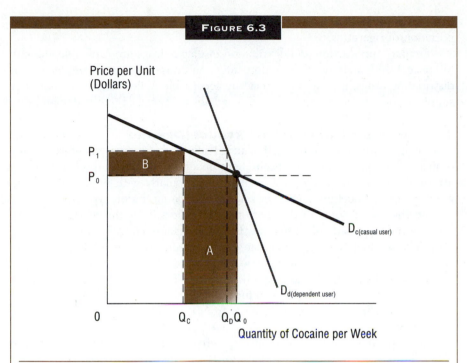

FIGURE 6.3

Price per Unit
(Dollars)

P_1

B

P_0

A

$D_{c(casual\ user)}$

$D_{d(dependent\ user)}$

0   Q_c Q_DQ_0

Quantity of Cocaine per Week

If the price of cocaine goes from P_0 to P_1, the casual cocaine user reduces quantity demanded from Q_0 to Q_c. The percentage reduction in quantity demanded is greater than the percentage increase in price. The casual user reduces expenditures on cocaine by the amount represented by shaded area A (due to lower quantity demanded). The casual user increases expenditures by the shaded area B (due to higher price). By inspection, it is clear that the net effect is a reduction in expenditure. The dependent user, on the other hand, reduces quantity demanded from Q_0 only to Q_d and, by inspection, increases expenditure.

Figure 6.3 also shows the demand curve, D_d, for a dependent user of cocaine. If price goes from P_0 to P_1, the quantity demanded falls from Q_0 to Q_d. But this user is dependent. The higher price reduces quantity demanded only slightly. Here, the percentage decrease in quantity is smaller than the percentage increase in price. The dependent user buys slightly less cocaine if price increases, but spends more. (Using the steeper demand curve, can you identify the areas that represent the expenditure reduction because less is bought and the increase because the price is higher?)

Many people would attack drug use and abuse in this country by going after the foreign sources. But the cultivation of coca or opium poppies is possible and profitable over a large part of the world. Coca and opium poppies are traditional crops in many countries. It is unlikely that the U.S. government can convince or afford to bribe farmers in all parts of the world to grow other crops. The implicit position of these farmers is that if U.S. consumers do not want the product, they do not have to buy it. This, by the way, is the same position that the U.S. government and U.S. tobacco companies take with regard to U.S. exportation of cigarettes.

Similarly, production and distribution of illegal drugs are profitable and easy to conceal. Although increased enforcement can raise the cost of producing and distributing drugs, it is not clear that any acceptable policies can eliminate their supply. If there is an answer to drug use and abuse, it may lie on the demand side.

THE EFFECTS OF POLICIES TO REDUCE DEMAND   The second way that the laws work is by reducing demand. The effect of increased enforcement is to make the buyer-seller relationship more uncertain. Buyers and sellers both get arrested. New connections must be made. Particularly with increased enforcement, a new connection—buyer or seller—may be an undercover officer. Given the increased risk, some of the more reliable sellers leave the market. Also because of the increased risk, it may pay to deal in a more concentrated form of the drug. The product changes with greater enforcement. It probably becomes more variable in purity and more likely to be adulterated with toxic substances, leading to more overdoses, deaths, and serious illnesses. These effects will decrease the demand of users and potential users for the drug. But it is a very harsh way to reduce demand. It brings to mind a quote from the Vietnam War: "We had to destroy the village to save it."

Many people argue that a better way to reduce demand is through education about the dangers of drug use and abuse. We certainly agree that young people should get accurate information about all drugs—legal and illegal. If the opportunity cost of enforcement is a reduction in benefits from education about drugs, then a careful study of alternatives would be important.

Social conditions also may be important determinants of drug use and abuse. Some drug use, no doubt, stems from the tendency of young people to take risks. Another part stems from the boredom and alienation experienced by suburban youth. The poverty, despair, and chaos of inner cities also contribute to drug use. A society without inner-city poverty, suburban alienation, and risk-taking youth probably would have a lower demand for drugs. Do we know how to change such social conditions sufficiently to have a large and timely effect on drug use? The economic analysis of the effect of drug prohibition, on the other hand, suggests that it works. It reduces use, and increased enforcement of the laws reduces use even more.

UNINTENDED BUT INEVITABLE CONSEQUENCES OF DRUG PROHIBITION

Many people argue that drug laws and their increased enforcement have important undesirable and inevitable consequences. First, drug prohibition creates criminals where there were none before. Ten percent of the population above the age of 11—more than 20 million people per year—commit crimes simply by using illegal drugs. Almost 1 million people are arrested for drug use each year. The law, intended to protect potential users by keeping them away from drugs, makes criminals out of more than 10 percent of the adult population.

Furthermore, the drug user consumes products that are unsafe because they are exchanged in illegal markets and because our government at times sprays the raw material with toxic substances. Of course, the illegal drugs also are unsafe because of their chemical properties. It is an open question, however, whether the more common illegal drugs would be more dangerous, if legal, than alcohol or nicotine. A significant part of the health problems related to drug use is a result of the drug laws.

Another undesirable consequence is that some users commit numerous property crimes in order to get money to buy drugs. In fact, as discussed earlier, increased enforcement—which causes a price increase—may lead to increased crime because dependent users spend more for illegal drugs at higher prices. Many drug users commit crimes. About 80 percent of all people arrested in New York City in 1992 and 1993 for serious nondrug-related crimes tested positive for hard drug use. This figure ranged from 50 to 80 percent for such cities as Birmingham, Chicago, Kansas City, Missouri, San Diego, and San Jose.[10] Many of these drug users have committed numerous felonies. It is not correct, however, to assume that these people would not commit felonies if they were sober. Many drug-using criminals were criminals before they were drug users.

In addition, prohibition has created opportunities for many people to earn large incomes as drug dealers. For youth—especially those in the poor areas of large cities—the quickest way to a BMW is through dealing illegal drugs. This opportunity would decrease if drugs were legal. At the wholesale and import level, drug prohibition is a bonanza for organized crime. The profit from drug dealing is enormous. And almost all of it is available because of drug prohibition.

Large profits in illegal drugs also lead to corruption of public officials. Police officers realize that their salaries are low relative to the earnings of some drug dealers. Moreover, the police know that many citizens see nothing wrong with drug use. In such circumstances, bribes may entice some police officers, judges, procurators, prison guards, and other public officials into corruption. The drug war, as presently prosecuted, may lead to police corruption in other ways. The police have the right to confiscate any assets they think are linked to drug dealing. These assets can include your money, your house, and your car. Suppose you get stopped for a traffic violation. If there is the slightest evidence of an illegal substance in your car, the police can confiscate it. If your assets are confiscated, to get them back you have to prove that they were not somehow obtained from or involved in illegal drug transactions. It is sometimes difficult to prove a negative. Moreover, in some instances, the police get to keep the assets or a portion of the assets for use of the police department. This creates an obvious incentive for improper police behavior. Although the courts have not ruled such action unconstitutional, many people believe that it diminishes our constitutional liberties. Finally, if any of us condone illegal drug activity, respect for the law diminishes.

In short, drug prohibition causes a link between drug use and crime. If drugs were available legally, the number of crimes caused by drug use would be much

---

[10]*Statistical Abstract of the United States, 1994,* 206.

smaller than it is now. Our experience with outlawing products and establishing price controls has taught us that such laws will be broken. Thus, this link between drug prohibition and crime is undesirable but inevitable.

Unintended but Perhaps Avoidable Consequences of Drug Prohibition

There are several unintended but perhaps avoidable consequences of the drug laws in this country. One may be an increased use of cocaine at the expense of marijuana. Cocaine is an inherently more dangerous drug than marijuana. Periods of extensive cocaine use lead to depression, sexual problems, convulsions, unconsciousness, and death.[11] Babies with low birth weights, brain damage, and malformations are a tragic consequence of crack cocaine use by pregnant women.

Ironically, increased enforcement of drug laws may have increased the attraction of cocaine relative to marijuana. The price of cocaine per gram is much higher than the price of marijuana. It is much easier to smuggle a million dollars worth of cocaine than to smuggle a million dollars worth of marijuana. The greater weight and bulk of marijuana make it easier to detect in transit than cocaine. The penalties for smuggling or wholesaling cocaine were, at times, not much greater than for smuggling or wholesaling marijuana. Therefore, the laws and more aggressive enforcement of the laws have caused the supply of marijuana to decrease more than the supply of cocaine.

Changes in the retail prices of cocaine and marijuana support this analysis. During the 1980s, the street price of cocaine fell until 1988, and then it began to rise. The price of marijuana increased throughout the 1980s, reaching a historically high level. Furthermore, the purity of street cocaine increased. Consquently, the relative price of marijuana may have doubled, increasing the attraction of cocaine.

Another unintended and related consequence of increased enforcement of the drug laws may have been the development and widespread use of crack cocaine. The crack epidemic is related to the increased purity of street cocaine. One reason for this increased purity is that the penalty for dealing cocaine is similar whether the cocaine is 35 percent pure or 70 percent pure, making it relatively more profitable to deal in the purer or more concentrated product. Whatever the dangers of cocaine and whatever its addictive properties, it is clear that the more concentrated the product, the greater these dangers. Moreover, crack cocaine is smoked, which means that its effects are almost immediate compared to the slower effects of inhaled cocaine. The immediate reinforcement obtained from smoking crack is one of the reasons for its greater addictive properties.

Yet another unintended consequence of the increased enforcement of the drug laws is the recruitment of teenagers and preteenagers into the retailing of

---

[11]Chitwood, "Patterns and Consequences of Cocaine Use," 121–124.

drugs. These children are lured by the fame and fortune of the successful drug dealers. The drug dealers use these children for street activities with a high risk of arrest. This keeps the dealers out of jail, while the children arrested from these high-risk activities receive mild treatment from the courts. Thus, tragically, children become valuable gang members. It is ironic that current drug enforcement is leading young people into drug dealing, when everyone agrees that one goal of drug policy should be to keep young people away from drugs.

Another consequence of current drug policy is the siphoning of resources from the control of nondrug-related crime. Almost everyone would agree that a basic premise of crime control is to protect people from involuntary harm. Our drug control policies run counter to this premise. First, as we have seen, drug prohibition creates numerous crimes that result in involuntary harm to innocent bystanders. Second, using so many resources for drug control almost inevitably drains resources from crime control. Effective deterrence requires a high probability of being caught combined with a quick trial and sure punishment if convicted. Clogging the courts and prisons with drug offenders reduces the probability of being caught, swiftly convicted (if guilty), and surely punished for nondrug crimes. In short, the opportunity cost of drug prohibition is very high.

UNINTENDED CONSEQUENCES OF DRUG LEGALIZATION

Many people argue that significant third-party effects of drug use exist. If prohibition reduced alcohol consumption, then it is clear that the legalization of alcohol has had significant third-party effects. The legalization of cocaine and other illegal drugs presumably would have similar effects.

First, the abuse of alcohol by pregnant women has caused many children to suffer from fetal alcohol syndrome. Certainly, this effect of alcohol use is an unintended consequence. If the elimination of prohibition leads to increased use of drugs by pregnant women, then an increased incidence of birth problems is an unintended consequence.

Second, drug (alcohol) abuse has led to the breakup of many families and to serious problems for many families that do not break up. This is another unintended consequence of drug legalization. Some people might argue that these first two unintended consequences are confined to the family unit and thus are not third-party effects. But the effect on children must be of concern to the rest of society, and specifically to government.

Third, drug (alcohol) abuse has been responsible for the deaths of many innocent individuals in automobile accidents. Here is a clear third-party effect that requires government action. For instance, scarce police resources must be used to try to keep drunken drivers off the highways.

Fourth, drug (alcohol) abuse means that we have more automobile accidents and higher automobile insurance rates for everybody. We also have more illness and higher medical insurance rates for everybody. Presumably, the legalization of illegal drugs would have similar unintended consequences.

EVALUATION: HAWKS, DOVES, AND OWLS

This analysis of the relationship between crime control and drug control could lead to a pessimistic conclusion. If we continue to follow the current policy, drug-related crime levels will remain high. Drug users, drug dealers, and some public officials will engage in criminal acts. On the other hand, if we legalize drugs, many more people—including young people—will become drug users and abusers. Is there a middle ground?

COMPETING VIEWS IN PRACTICE

Peter Reuter stereotypes the debate between the advocates of strict prohibition, such as William Bennett, and those of legalization, such as Milton Friedman, as one between hawks and doves. According to him, hawks perceive the drug problem as one of values—users and sellers do not care about right and wrong. Drug use, according to hawks, implies a concentration on short-term benefits and a lack of concern for others. Hawks believe drug use to be an evil that requires tough enforcement of prohibition as a means of restoring fundamental values. Reuter points out that, in addition to the crime and violence inherently associated with prohibition, hawkish policies may threaten constitutional guarantees. For instance, surveys show that a majority of adults agree that searches of a known drug dealer's house should not require court-approved search warrants.

Doves, according to Reuter, believe that the greatest drug problems are those associated with prohibition, not use. They are particularly concerned about the violence inflicted on third parties and about the threat to constitutional guarantees of freedom. Doves believe that if adults have appropriate information they will make informed choices about drugs and that government and society should not interfere. Reuter fears, however, that dovish policies risk a large increase in drug use and abuse.

According to Reuter, owls—Kaplan seems to fit—believe that the drug problem is one of drug abuse, addiction, and associated disease. In their view, drug use and abuse results from bad social conditions. Although owls would retain prohibition, bold, demand-side intervention is the core of their policy. Rather than minimizing drug use or minimizing enforcement costs, owls want

> *the lowest level of enforcement compatible with keeping initiation down and encouraging the dependent to seek treatment. Drug control is also not the only goal, and higher drug use may be accepted in return for better performance with respect to some other social goal, such as reduced spread of HIV infection.*[12]

---

[12]Reuter, "Hawks Ascendant," 19. Reuter, a self-proclaimed owl, denies that the imagery is loaded. Based on his reading of Winnie-the-Pooh, Owl is "learned (he can misspell long words) but unrealistic and self-deluded," fn. 8, p. 48.

CURRENT POLICY

Hawks, doves, and owls agree that an important goal is to keep young people away from drugs. Marijuana use by young people peaked about 1980 with a somewhat later peak for older people. Recent surveys indicate that marijuana and other illicit drug use is increasing, but it remains below the peaks of the late 1970s.[13]

Hawks presumably would argue that punitive drug policy is responsible for reducing drug use. As discussed in the introduction to this chapter, governments have funneled more resources into enforcing prohibition. This policy has made it risky to use and to sell illegal drugs. One estimate is that marijuana users face a 2 percent chance per year of being arrested. A 10-year user, then, would face a 20 percent chance of being arrested. As may be appropriate for a more dangerous drug, the annual arrest risk for a cocaine user is 6 percent, or 60 percent over a 10-year period. Similarly, cocaine dealers have a four times greater chance of being arrested in a year of dealing—40 percent—than do marijuana dealers.

The greater enforcement effort directed at cocaine reflects a perhaps owlish conclusion that cocaine is more dangerous than marijuana. It is owlish because the danger of concern is the risk to the mental and physical health of the user; recall that hawks perceive the danger as the risk to society of a collapse of values due to narcissistic drug use.

Economists often analyze a program's effectiveness assuming that it has a fixed budget. Suppose that a drug program were given $28 billion, the combined drug-control budget for all levels of government in 1990. Is this the efficient amount; the amount where marginal social benefit equals marginal social cost? We don't know; furthermore, it is extremely difficult to find out.

Consequently, the policy question often becomes whether the amount allocated is used most effectively. For instance, is the split between marijuana and cocaine control appropriate? The answer depends on whether the equimarginal principle is satisfied. The *equimarginal principle* requires that in the allocation of a fixed budget the last dollar spent on one activity should yield the same marginal benefit as the last dollar spent on any other activity. For instance, if the last dollar spent on marijuana enforcement yields a marginal benefit of $3 and the last dollar spent on cocaine enforcement yields a marginal benefit of $8, too much is being spent on the former. A dollar taken away from marijuana enforcement causes benefits to fall by $3. Switching this dollar to cocaine enforcement yields a benefit of $8 for a net gain of $5. As this switching continues, marginal benefit will fall for cocaine enforcement and rise for marijuana enforcement until the marginal benefits are equalized.

OWLISH CRITICISM

Owls argue that the enforcement is still too concentrated on marijuana. They believe that marijuana is less dangerous to the individual than cocaine. Hawks

---

[13]Monitoring the Future Study, University of Michigan, 1996, www.isr.umich.edu.src.

DUTCH DRUG POLICY

Drug policy in the Netherlands differs from that of the United States in significant ways. The Dutch drug policy emphasizes risk reduction for individual drug users, their neighborhoods, and the general society. Possession, distribution, production, advertising, and international trade of all drugs, except for medicinal or scientific purposes, are illegal. So far, this sounds like U.S. drug policy, but the application is different. Dutch law explicitly distinguishes between soft drugs, such as marijuana, and hard drugs, such as cocaine and heroin. Although federal and most state law enforcement agencies may make this distinction in practice, it is not formal policy in the United States. The recent successful referenda in Arizona and California that exempted possession, cultivation, and use of marijuana for medicinal purposes upon a doctor's recommendation are exceptions. In response, however, the Clinton administration has said that it would strip doctors who made such recommendations of their right to prescribe pharmaceuticals, which would probably destroy their medical practices.

Dutch law permits nonenforcement if to do so is in the public interest. Using this expediency principle, regulations have stated that the possession of small amounts of soft or hard drugs for personal use will not be prosecuted. These regulations permit the establishment of coffeehouses and other retail sites for the sale of marijuana for personal use. Coffeehouses are strictly regulated, with advertising, hard drugs, nuisances, sales to persons younger than 18 years of age, and large quantities sold per transactions strictly prohibited. With wholesale drug dealing prohibited, the retailers must obtain their inventory from illegal sources, presumably just as it is obtained by the recently (January 1997) reopened San Francisco Cannabis Cultivators' Club.

The Dutch rationale for the decriminalization of the retail sale and use of marijuana is straightforward. The government argues that marijuana, unlike heroin and other hard drugs, does not create an unacceptable risk for users. Moreover, the government rejects the gateway hypothesis, by which the use of marijuana for physiological or psychological reasons leads to hard drug use. The Dutch position is that it is all but impossible to prevent people, including young people, from obtaining marijuana. Consequently, obtaining and using it in a legal, controlled environment is better for them than obtaining and using it in an illegal, uncontrolled environment where, Dutch authorities believe, young people are much more likely to be introduced to hard drugs. This argument implies that if marijuana is a gateway drug in the United States, the gateway is through illegal purchase rather than use.

---

might respond that marijuana is as dangerous to social values as other illegal drugs and that the danger to the individual is less significant for social policy. Owls and hawks, therefore, disagree about the allocation of the enforcement budget because of different objectives. Owls emphasize harm minimization to individuals, whereas hawks emphasize minimization of illegal drug use.

Reuter argues that the hawks are ascendant. First, he cites increased enforcement budgets, increased severity of laws, and increased punishment for drug possession and sale. As further evidence, he cites the unwillingness of the U.S. government to allow the therapeutic prescription of marijuana to people with AIDS, cancer, and glaucoma. Reuter suggests that the main reason for this prohibition, and the prohibition of heroin's use for pain relief for the terminally ill, is to signal that these drugs have no redeeming social value.

Similarly, HIV infection spreads partly because drug addicts share needles. To combat its spread, several European countries, including Britain, the Netherlands,

The effect of Dutch policy on drug use and abuse is not easily determined. Many factors other than its legal status affect the demand for drugs. The Monitoring the Future Study of the University of Michigan reports that in 1990 14 percent of high school seniors had used marijuana in the 30 days before the survey was taken, and 8 percent had used other illicit drugs. By 1996 these percentages had risen to 22 and 10 percent. According to a 1990 survey, 6 percent of the population above age 12 in Amsterdam had used marijuana in the previous 30 days, and a 1992 survey reported that about 10 percent of 18-year-old Dutch youths had used marijuana recently. At worst, marijuana consumption among Dutch young people would appear to be no higher than among U.S. young people. Perhaps this is not surprising; repeated surveys show that from 80 to 90 percent of U.S. high school seniors believe that marijuana is fairly or very easy to obtain.

Furthermore, the incidence of hard drug addiction in the Netherlands is no higher than in other European countries and in the United States. Dutch tolerance of marijuana does not obviously increase the demand for hard drugs. The Dutch also follow a harm-minimization policy in the treatment of hard drug users. Needle exchanges are available, and methadone, a heroin substitute, is freely available to addicts on a maintenance basis. Although addicts are encouraged to reduce methadone use, it is not required. Moreover, methadone clients may use alcohol and other drugs in moderation. This program is designed to inhibit the addicts' health deterioration and perhaps to allow them to function in society. With this approach, only about 12 percent of the diagnosed Dutch AIDS patients were intravenous drug users, compared to about 24 percent in the United States and 38 percent in Europe. Again, little, if any, evidence exists that this non-punitive approach has caused any substantial increase in addiction.

The Netherlands' more lenient drug policy is something for citizens and policy makers to consider. One pertinent question is whether soft and hard drug use is greater in the Netherlands than it would be under alternative policies. It apparently is not greater than it is in the United States. Other things being equal, however, what might be the effect of changing U.S. drug policy? This is a question to be answered by positive analysis. Another pertinent question is, what should be the objective of U.S. drug policy? This normative issue turns on one's ideas about liberty, pragmatics, and morality.

Sources: *Drug Policy in the Netherlands: Continuity and Change*, Ministry of Health, Welfare, and Sport, Ultrecht, The Netherlands, www.minvws.nl and *Dutch Cannabis Policy*, Fact Sheet 1, Netherlands Institute for Alcohol and Drugs, Ultrecht, The Netherlands, www.niad.nl.

and parts of Switzerland, have syringe-exchange programs. Syringe exchange is almost taboo in the United States, perhaps because it would imply that the HIV-costs of needle sharing are greater than the costs of a recognition that there are evils worse than heroin use.

If hawkish drug policy were necessary in the successful termination of the drug epidemic of the last decade or in the reduction of drug use by youth, owls might believe that the hawkish policy is appropriate. But was it necessary? If so, why does the epidemic show signs of a recurrence?

Education, a demand-side policy, may have contributed to the declining use of drugs by young people in the 1980s. Figure 6.4 shows large changes in attitudes regarding the legalization of marijuana. In 1980 between 40 and 45 percent of the people age 18 to 29 favored the legalization of marijuana. By 1990 this dropped, with only about one-fourth of this age group favoring it. Why the change? Part of it may be attributable to the unrelenting war on drugs. But certainly another part may

PERCENT THAT
AGREES MARIJUANA
SHOULD BE
LEGALIZED

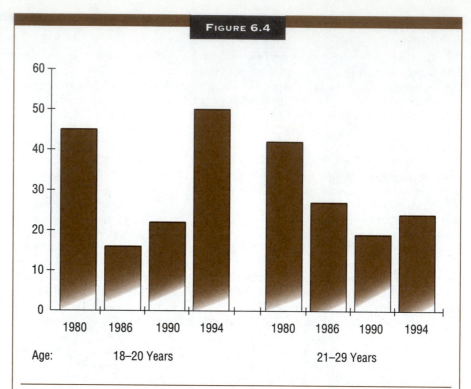

FIGURE 6.4

This figure shows that in the 1980s young people became less willing to legalize marijuana use, but in the 1990s they are becoming more willing.

Source: Maguire and Pastore, *Sourcebook of Criminal Justice Statistics*, 1996.

have been attributable to drug education in homes, churches, and schools (DARE programs, for instance); to a greater concern for health; and to public service announcements in the mass media ("Just Say No"). By 1994, however, the percentage of 18 to 20 year olds favoring legalization had climbed back to 50 percent.

Similarly, from 1981 to 1991, marijuana use by high school seniors fell, along with the use of other illicit drugs and cigarettes (Figure 6.5). Cigarette use declined for demand-side reasons that were more likely related to educational programs than to the war on drugs. Presumably, marijuana and other illicit drug use declined, in part, for the same reasons as cigarette use. As with young peoples' attitudes about legalization, larger percentages of high school seniors in the 1990s are using marijuana, other illicit drugs, and cigarettes. The resurgence of drug use by high school students suggests that neither education nor a harsh war on drugs is sufficient to restrain it. There has been little change in either policy in the 1990s, yet drug use has increased.

Nevertheless, hawks argue for a continuation of current punitive drug policies. Without it, they believe that drug use would be even higher. Owls oppose

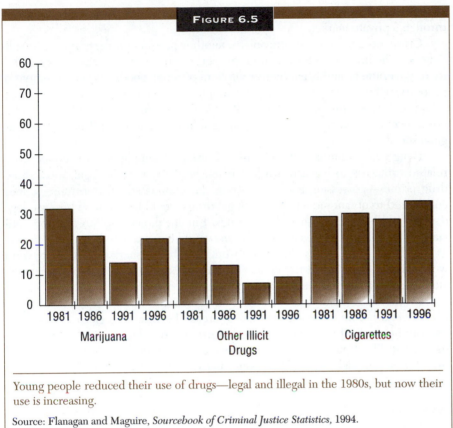

FIGURE 6.5

PERCENT OF HIGH
SCHOOL SENIORS
WHO USED MARI-
JUANA, OTHER
ILLICIT DRUGS OR
CIGARETTES IN THE
30 DAYS BEFORE
THE SURVEY

Young people reduced their use of drugs—legal and illegal in the 1980s, but now their use is increasing.

Source: Flanagan and Maguire, *Sourcebook of Criminal Justice Statistics,* 1994.

legalization, but they would reduce the punitiveness of current policy and reorient it toward education and treatment. They also would make greater distinctions between types of drugs and enforcement measures. They believe that the current level of expenditures would yield greater benfits if they were reallocated. Neither hawks nor owls have convincing explanations for the recent upsurge in drug use.

SUMMARY

Free riders can consume public goods without paying for them because it is difficult to prevent people from using public goods. Furthermore, it is inefficient to exclude people from using public goods because the marginal cost of one more user is zero. The existence of public goods provides a rationale for government action in the economy because it is often inefficient for the private market to supply public goods. Imagine the results if national defense were provided through a private market.

Crime occurs if one person violates another person's property rights, broadly defined. The provision of a system of property rights is an important responsibility of government and is another example of a public good. The enforcement of property rights—crime control is an example—is also a public good. Therefore, crime control is an important responsibility of government. The efficient level of crime occurs when the marginal social benefit of crime control equals its marginal social cost.

Drug prohibition is a major cause of crime. A simple way to reduce drug-related crimes is to legalize drugs. Obviously, if drugs were legal, most direct drug crimes—possession and sale—would be eliminated. Furthermore, crimes committed to obtain money to buy illegal drugs would be reduced because legal drugs could be cheaper than illegal drugs. Finally, the corruption of public officials that accompanies illegal drug markets would be eliminated.

With the huge profits eliminated from illegal drug markets, inner-city youth would have less incentive to become criminals. Gang activity and indiscriminate violence would decrease in the inner city.

On the other hand, drug legalization will increase the supply of such drugs as cocaine and heroin. Demand will also increase because of legalization, so drug use will increase. If it is true that cocaine use is more dangerous than marijuana use, a possible strategy is to relax marijuana prohibition and strengthen cocaine prohibition. The debate over drug policy in the United States will continue.

KEY TERMS

Public good	Nonrival good
Nonexcludable good	Free rider

REVIEW QUESTIONS

1. Which of the following would be classified as a public good and why?
   a. Clean air
   b. Universities
   c. National defense
   d. A loaf of bread
2. Why are public goods generally provided by the government rather than by private firms?
3. Have you ever had a free-rider problem in a group project? How did you resolve it?
4. Because of high crime rates, crime prevention is often a political issue. Do these high rates imply that government should increase crime prevention activities? Defend your answer.
5. Analyze the theory of crime as presented in the box titled "Police, Guns, and Crime." Is this theory useful for short-term crime control? For long-term control? Discuss.

6. Some people argue that marijuana and other illegal drugs should be legalized, because people should have the freedom to do as they please. They also argue that counterfeiting compact discs should be illegal. Are they being inconsistent?

7. Government restrictions on drug use seem inconsistent with the way alcohol and nicotine (both drugs themselves) are treated. Why do you believe we see this inconsistency?

8. How might the legalization of cocaine affect its market price and quantity? Use graphical analysis to aid in your answer.

9. Why is the cost of drugs likely to increase and the demand for drugs likely to decrease in the face of prohibition?

10. "Making drugs illegal results in dealers pushing drugs on nonusers." Is this statement true or false? Defend your answer.

11. What are the pros and cons of drug laws and their increased enforcement?

12. People can come to different conclusions about the desirability of "Dutch Drug Policy." How can people look at the same situation and come to different conclusions?

13. The chapter argues that present drug laws ensure that drug-related crimes will continue. On the other hand, legalization would ensure increased drug use and abuse. Could any actions be undertaken to improve the situation?

SUGGESTIONS FOR FURTHER READING

DiIulio, John J., Jr. "A Limited War on Crime That We Can Win." *The Brookings Review* (Fall 1992), 6–12. This article summarizes DiIulio's longer position on federal crime policy cited in the text. It includes a discussion of the benefits of drug treatment for prisoners. The *Review* is a good source for policy studies.

———. "The Next War on Drugs." *The Brookings Review* (Summer 1993), 28–33. This article presents a spirited defense of government demand and supply (prohibition) policies to reduce drug use and abuse. DiIulio is particularly concerned about the effect of drug legalization on the inner city.

Duke, Steven B., and Albert C. Gross. *America's Longest War: Rethinking Our Tragic Crusade Against Drugs.* New York: Putnam's Sons, 1993. This book, which powerfully attacks the War on Drugs, argues that the war has increased crime in many ways and has weakened the constitutional protection of our civil rights.

Kaplan, John. *The Hardest Drug: Heroin and Public Policy.* Chicago: The University of Chicago Press, 1983. This book presents a balanced discussion of public policy and heroin. Kaplan, a lawyer, develops the economics of drug policy in an insightful way. The book provides background for some of the discussion in this chapter.

———. "Taking Drugs Seriously." *The Public Interest* (Summer 1988), 32–50. In this article, Kaplan discusses public policy and cocaine. The article is a source for some of the policy discussion in this chapter.

Maguire, Kathleen, and Ann L. Pastore, eds. *Sourcebook of Criminal Justice.* Washington, D.C. U.S. Department of Justice, various years. This source provides fascinating information about the U.S. criminal justice system. It contains much of the information about crime and drugs that is in the *Statistical Abstract of the United States* and much more.

Monitoring the Future Study. University of Michigan, 1996, www.isr.umich.edu.src. This annual survey tracks drug use among young people.

Morley, Jefferson. "The New Politics of the Drug War." *Slate* (December 13, 1996). *Slate* is a magazine published on the World Wide Web. It has numerous articles about economics and politics. Its address is www.Slate.com.

Nadelmann, Ethan A. "The Case for Legalization." *The Public Interest* (Summer 1988), 3–31. Nadelmann provides a persuasive analysis of the failures of current drug policy and argues that legalization is a preferred alternative. The article is a source for some of the policy discussion in this chapter.

———. "Thinking Seriously about Alternatives to Drug Prohibition." *Daedalus* 121 (Summer 1992), 85–132. This article updates the case for drug legalization.

Reuter, Peter. "Hawks Ascendant: The Punitive Trend of American Drug Policy." *Daedalus* 121 (Summer 1992), 15–52. This article introduces the hawks, doves, and owls approach to looking at drug policy.

Wilson, James Q. "Against the Legalization of Drugs." *Commentary* (February 1990), 23–28. The title of this article, by a well-known student of crime and other urban problems, is self-explanatory.

7

AIR POLLUTION: BALANCING BENEFITS AND COSTS

TERMS YOU SHOULD KNOW

Marginal cost (Chapter 3)

Marginal external cost (Chapter 2)

Marginal benefit (Chapter 3)

Marginal private cost (Chapter 2)

Marginal social cost (Chapter 2)

Marginal social benefit (Chapter 2)

We live on a small planet with a thin, life-sustaining mantle of air, the quality of which is constantly threatened by economic activities. Millions of urban dwellers are plagued by smog created by factories, power plants, and automobile engines. Lakes and forests in the eastern United States and Canada suffer from acid rain produced by electricity-generating plants in the Midwest. Scientists argue that the Earth will get warmer if we don't control our consumption of fossil fuels. Others fear that the Earth is losing its ozone shield, which protects the planet from harmful ultraviolet rays.

To counter threats such as these, federal and state governments have adopted an imposing array of laws and regulations. Our focus in this chapter is the federal Clean Air Act. We examine some of the ways in which it has shaped environmental regulation and assess whether it has resulted in improved air quality. We also outline estimates of the benefits and costs of air quality regulation and conclude with a look at some ways to reduce the costs of cleaner air.

THE PRINCIPAL AIR POLLUTION PROBLEMS

The air pollution problem has several aspects. The most important of these are (1) poor-quality air in urban areas, (2) acid rain, (3) global warming, (4) ozone depletion, and (5) hazardous air pollutants.

URBAN AIR QUALITY

Urban air quality is measured in terms of atmospheric (ambient) concentrations of six common air pollutants: total suspended particulates, sulfur dioxide, carbon monoxide, nitrogen dioxide, ozone, and lead. Particulate matter consists primarily of chemically stable substances such as dust, soot, ash, and smoke. This was the most common air pollutant when coal was used extensively for home heating and industrial processes.

Sulfur dioxide is a pungent, toxic gas with several beneficial uses: as sulfuric acid, as a bleaching agent, as a compound in preservatives, and as a refrigerant. It becomes an air pollutant, however, when excessive amounts are emitted as a by-product of economic activity, chiefly by electricity-generating plants that burn coal and oil.

Carbon monoxide is a colorless, odorless, toxic gas produced by the incomplete combustion of fossil fuels. It can be a silent killer when an automobile exhaust system is not ventilated properly and a chronic—but less lethal—problem when autos vent their exhaust gases into urban airsheds.

Nitrogen dioxide emissions are also caused by the incomplete combustion of fossil fuels, primarily by electric utilities and cars. Urbanites see the results of this process when nitrogen dioxide combines with other elements, such as ozone, to form smog.

Ozone is a form of oxygen with a pungent odor; it is formed naturally in the upper levels of the atmosphere (the stratosphere) by a photochemical reaction with ultraviolet radiation from the sun. In fact, stratospheric ozone shields the Earth from the sun's harmful rays. Ozone is produced commercially and used in disinfectants, deodorizers, oxidizers, and bleaches. It is also produced when volatile organic compounds (chemically unstable hydrocarbons) are emitted from sources such as oil refineries and motor vehicles. This ground-level ozone is a primary ingredient in smog.

Lead is a mineral with many beneficial uses, but it is toxic when inhaled or ingested, even in tiny doses. It is transported by the atmosphere following emission from gasoline engines, nonferrous smelters, and battery plants.

Concern about urban air quality stems largely from the adverse effects air pollution has on human health, crops and plants, property, safety, and visibility. Research shows that poor air quality is a factor in bronchitis, asthma, lung cancer, emphysema, and in general mortality and morbidity rates. Evidence suggests that crop damage from air pollution can be extreme.

Air pollutants may cause extensive damage to property. Particulates soil clothes, autos, homes, and other structures. Sulfur dioxide and ozone corrode and weaken many materials.

Particulates and smog reduce visibility and the amenities associated with a clear vista. High levels of some pollutants, such as carbon monoxide, impair judgment and motor skills, increasing the risk of injury.

ACID RAIN

Acid rain occurs when airborne sulfur dioxide, emitted largely from electricity-generating plants, is chemically transformed into a weak sulfuric acid solution that falls to the Earth as part of natural precipitation. Sulfur dioxide emissions are transported long distances by the wind currents that flow from west to east in the Northern Hemisphere. Thus, the acid rain that falls in the eastern United States and Canada comes partly from emissions that originate in the midwestern United States.

Some lakes and streams have apparently become highly acidified, impairing their ability to sustain life. Acid rain may cause forests in the eastern United States and Canada to experience retarded growth and increased mortality. It may also corrode materials, erode and discolor paint, and deteriorate structures.

GLOBAL WARMING

As fossil fuels are burned, carbon dioxide is released into the atmosphere. The clearing of land (especially heavily forested land) reduces the Earth's capacity to absorb released carbon. The cumulative effect of burning and clearing has been a 22 to 33 percent increase in the level of atmospheric carbon dioxide since the mid-1800s.

Carbon dioxide is a *greenhouse gas*—a gas that helps the Earth retain heat from the sun. Rays from the sun that reach the Earth are partly absorbed and partly reflected into space. Some of the reflected energy is redirected toward the

Earth by greenhouse gases, further warming the planet. Without these gases, the Earth would be too cold for habitation. If greenhouse gases continue to accumulate, however, the warming they will cause could have serious consequences.

Carbon dioxide is not the only greenhouse gas, but it is far more important than the others—chlorofluorocarbons, methane, and nitrous oxides—as a source of global warming.

There has been a slight warming of the Northern Hemisphere over the past century. If the industrial nations continue to emit greenhouse gases at current rates and today's Third World countries industrialize, the atmosphere will get warmer. William Cline estimates, in fact, that greenhouse gases are likely to raise the global mean temperature for as long as 300 years, eventually by as much as 18 degrees Fahrenheit.[1] Scientists have constructed climatic models that predict an increase in the level of the oceans as the polar ice caps melt, putting the lives and fortunes of millions of people living in coastal areas in jeopardy. In addition, global warming could create significant changes in weather patterns, altering the present distribution of precipitation and changing the location of the world's crop lands and forests.

STRATOSPHERIC OZONE DEPLETION

As indicated above, ozone is both a beneficial and a harmful gas. It is harmful when high concentrations are present in the lower atmosphere, but it is beneficial when present in the Earth's stratosphere. Ozone in the stratosphere prevents harmful solar ultraviolet radiation from reaching the Earth's surface. A reduction in the protection it provides would increase the incidence of skin cancer and possibly trigger genetic mutations.

When chlorofluorocarbons enter the stratosphere, they trigger a chemical reaction that destroys ozone. Chlorofluorocarbons are used primarily as aerosol propellants, refrigerants, foam-blowing agents, and cleaning solvents. Other gases, principally carbon dioxide and methane, increase the atmospheric concentration of ozone. The effect of these conflicting forces on ozone levels is not known with certainty. Measurements taken to date, however, indicate that significant decreases have occurred periodically in the ozone layer over Antarctica. Moreover, some computer models indicate a significant decrease in stratospheric ozone with continued growth in the use of chlorofluorocarbons.

HAZARDOUS AIR POLLUTANTS

The air also serves as a transport medium for thousands of chemicals, many of which may be hazardous to humans, animals, and plants, even if inhaled or ingested in small doses. The Environmental Protection Agency (EPA) targeted 189

---

[1]William R. Cline, *The Economics of Global Warming* (Washington, DC: Institute for International Economics, 1992).

of these chemicals for regulation in the Clean Air Act of 1990. The primary impetus for these regulations is evidence that they impair human health, especially in the form of central nervous system damage and cancer.

THE ECONOMIST'S PERSPECTIVE

Economists view pollutants as by-products of economic activity. Figure 7.1 shows how pollution relates to the ordinary economic activities of energy production, industrial production, and household consumption. The process begins with inputs of natural resources, such as oil and coal. Some resources are converted to useful energy, such as electricity and gasoline; some are used in industrial production. Some of the useful energy is used, in turn, in industrial production; some of it

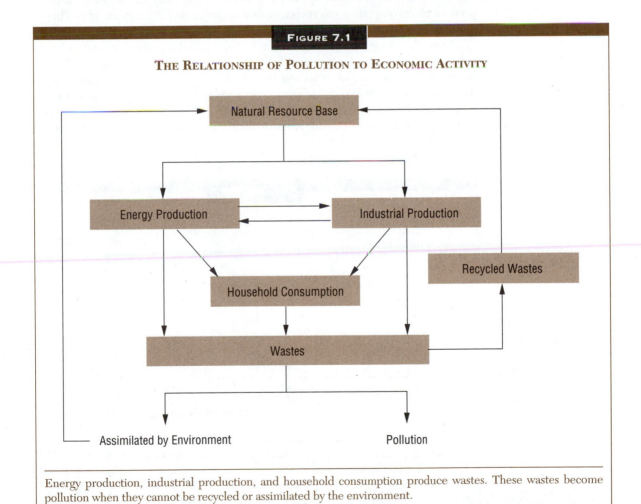

FIGURE 7.1

THE RELATIONSHIP OF POLLUTION TO ECONOMIC ACTIVITY

Energy production, industrial production, and household consumption produce wastes. These wastes become pollution when they cannot be recycled or assimilated by the environment.

goes directly to households. Goods produced through industrial production are sold partly to energy producers but primarily to households. Energy production, industrial production, and household consumption all generate wastes, the amount of which grows as the economy grows.

Waste, however, is not necessarily pollution. Some waste is assimilated without harm by the natural environment, and some of it is recycled. The waste that is neither assimilated nor recycled constitutes *pollution*—residual wastes that are harmful to humans, animals, plants, and structures.

Pollution is inevitable in a market economy. The amount produced, however, is likely to be excessively large because polluters normally are not required to pay the costs of damages inflicted by the pollution they produce. These points are illustrated in Figures 7.2 to 7.5.

Figure 7.2 illustrates a case in which pollutants are a by-product of oil refining. For a given refining technology, a direct relationship exists between emissions of airborne pollutants, such as sulfur dioxide, and refinery output. That is, pollution increases when production increases.

Over the range from 0 to 3 million barrels, pollutants are assimilated by the natural environment. Beyond 3 million barrels, pollutants damage human health, plants, and property. The costs associated with these damages, such as working time lost due to illness or reduced crop production, are called external costs: costs attributable to production that are not paid by the producers or the buyers of the product. The external costs of each additional unit of production are

MARGINAL EXTERNAL COST OF OIL REFINING

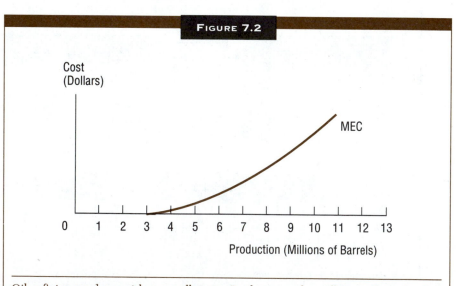

FIGURE 7.2

Oil refining produces airborne pollutants. In this example, pollutants from the first 3 million barrels are assimilated by the environment, and no external costs occur. Beyond 3 million barrels, the pollutant load is too heavy to be naturally assimilated and marginal external costs appear, growing as the pollutant load grows.

known as marginal external costs (MEC). Here they are assumed to rise at an increasing rate as total emissions of pollutants increase. This happens, for example, when the number of people adversely affected per barrel grows or more serious illnesses are triggered for the people who are affected.

The producers of refined oil products buy crude oil, labor, capital equipment, chemicals, and other inputs to make refined products. The cost of inputs such as these required to produce an additional unit of product is the marginal private cost (MPC) of that unit. The MPC curve in Figure 7.3 reflects the assumption that the refining industry eventually will encounter rising marginal private cost. The MEC curve of Figure 7.2 is added vertically to the MPC curve (starting at 3 million barrels) to obtain the marginal social cost (MSC) curve in Figure 7.3.

The quantity of refined products and the level of pollutants that will be produced depend on costs and on the demand for refined products. The refining industry faces a downward-sloping demand curve, as in Figure 7.4. The demand curve is also a marginal benefit curve in the sense that the vertical distance at each unit represents the amount that people are willing to pay for that unit, and the amount they are willing to pay reflects the benefits they derive from each unit. If the consumers of refined products are the only ones deriving such benefits, the demand curve is a marginal social benefit (MSB) curve.

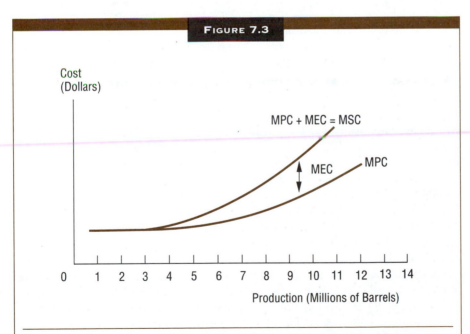

FIGURE 7.3

Cost (Dollars)

MPC + MEC = MSC

MEC   MPC

Production (Millions of Barrels)

MARGINAL EXTERNAL, MARGINAL PRIVATE, AND MARGINAL SOCIAL COSTS OF OIL REFINING

The marginal private cost (MPC) of oil refining is constant per barrel between zero and 3 million barrels, beyond which MPC increases. Marginal social cost (MSC) is also constant per barrel between zero and 3 million barrels. MSC starts to increase beyond 3 million barrels because both MPC and marginal external costs (MEC) rise.

FIGURE 7.4

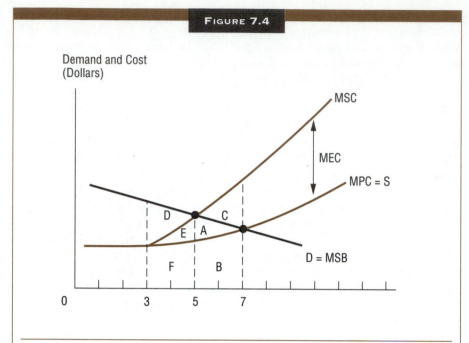

The equilibrium level of production is 7 million barrels, where MPC = MSB, or S = D. The efficient level is 5 million barrels, where MSC = MSB. Area C is the net social loss from exceeding the efficient level, which is the difference between increased social costs (areas A, B, and C) and increased social benefits (areas A and B).

In a competitive industry, the amount produced is that at which demand equals supply. The MPC curve is the supply curve; because producers are liable only for MPC, they govern the supply decision. Producers (and consumers) ignore marginal external costs, and the industry produces 7 million barrels, where supply and demand are equal.

The efficient output in Figure 7.4 is 5 million barrels, where MSB equals MSC. Thus, the market-determined output of 7 million barrels exceeds the efficient output by 2 million barrels. Because producers ignore the marginal external costs of production, they refine too much oil from society's perspective. They also produce too much pollution—namely, the amount associated with the last 2 million barrels. The cost of the pollution associated with the first 5 million barrels (area E) is covered fully, along with production costs, by the amount consumers are willing to pay for refined products. Therefore, the efficient level of pollution is *not zero;* rather, it is the amount associated with production of the first 5 million barrels.

The last 2 million barrels produced provide social benefits equal to the area under the demand curve from 5 million to 7 million barrels, or A plus B, but social costs over this range equal areas A plus B plus C. Thus, production at 7 million

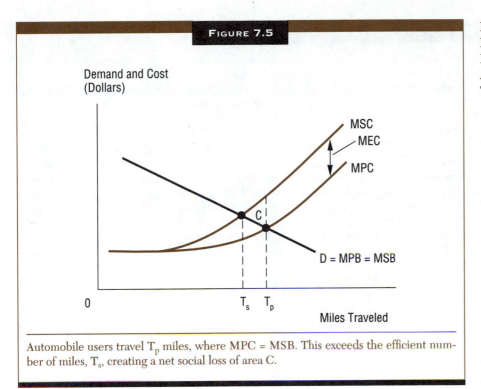

FIGURE 7.5

EFFICIENT AND INEFFICIENT LEVELS OF AUTOMOBILE TRAVEL

Automobile users travel T_p miles, where MPC = MSB. This exceeds the efficient number of miles, T_s, creating a net social loss of area C.

barrels results in a **net social loss** equal to area C—the excess of social cost over social benefit on the last 2 million barrels.

Similar logic applies to pollutants associated with consumption, such as those generated by household use of the automobile. This case is outlined in Figure 7.5, which depicts the relationships that determine the number of automobile miles traveled, benefits, and costs. Each auto owner compares the marginal private benefit (MPB) from travel with the marginal private cost (MPC) of travel and travels an extra mile only if MPB exceeds MPC. The marginal private benefit falls as the number of miles traveled increases and less valuable trips are taken. This relationship is illustrated by the MSB curve (we assume that MPB = MSB). Figure 7.5 assumes that MPC eventually increases: beyond some point, for example, owners incur higher maintenance costs per mile. As in the oil refinery example, there is a wedge between MPC and MSC equal to the MEC attributable to emissions of pollutants.

Under these conditions, private owners will travel T_p miles, where MPB (= MSB) equals MPC. The efficient level is only T_s miles, where MSB equals MSC. At T_p, there is too much travel (T_p minus T_s miles), too many pollutants, and a net social loss (area C).

These cases illustrate that economists view pollution problems in terms of both costs and benefits. Some pollution is appropriate, provided that the costs associated with it are less than the benefits associated with it. This perception

Net Social Loss
The excess of social cost over social benefit over some range of production (also called deadweight loss).

INTERNATIONAL PERSPECTIVE

> ### THE TOTAL SOCIAL COST OF THE AUTOMOBILE: POLLUTION AND MUCH MORE

It is widely acknowledged that the privately owned, gasoline-powered automobile is a major source of air pollution throughout the world. The financial consequences of air pollution, however, amount to just one of several external costs for which the auto is responsible. Others are the costs due to congestion, noise, accidents, increased vulnerability to recession, and oil-related national security expenditures. All of the world's major oil-consuming nations experience the costs of congestion, noise, accidents, and pollution. All of the major oil-importing countries—such as the United States, Japan, Germany, Italy, France, and the United Kingdom—are susceptible to the costs associated with increased vulnerability to recession. These countries and others devote part of their national security expenditures to assuring the continued flow of oil from unstable sources of supply.

Anyone who drives in a major urban area of the United States knows firsthand of the congestion that normally occurs during the morning and evening rush hours. It has been estimated that these urban drivers annually waste between 1 and 2 billion hours stuck in traffic, and that the delayed delivery of goods and lost employee time amounts to a cost of $100 billion per year. But such costs are not confined to the United States. Bangkok, Thailand's workforce loses an average of 44 days in traffic each year, costing the country several percentage points in potential gross domestic product (GDP), and *each* driver in central London during peak traffic hours costs *all other* drivers on the highway about 80 cents per mile in wasted time.°

Consider also the economic costs to the oil-importing nations when they suffer an unanticipated oil cutoff. Oil prices suddenly increase, causing recessions. In fact, the largest decline in U.S. real GDP during the post-World War II era was 4.1 percent in 1974–1975, which was initiated by a reduction in oil exports from the Middle East. The impact of this action was felt far beyond the United States as total world GDP dipped about 6 percent below its trend value. Such outcomes can be blamed only in part on the world's love affair with the automobile—imported oil is used for many purposes other than the self-transport of people—however, the world's appetite for gasoline heightens its vulnerability to oil supply disruptions.

And the world *is* vulnerable to oil supply disruptions. The politically volatile countries of the Persian Gulf produce about one-fourth of the world's oil and sit atop two-thirds of the world's known oil reserves. The U.S.–Iraq War and its aftermath provides vivid evidence of the need for the United States and its allies to spend money to protect their interests in secure oil supplies from this region. The bill for this war—paid partly by the United States and partly by

contrasts sharply with that of some environmentalists, who emphasize the costs produced by pollution and ignore the benefits forgone by reducing pollution.

MARKET FAILURE: IS GOVERNMENT ACTION NECESSARY?

The cases just examined are examples of market failure—situations in which private decisions coordinated through the market produce inefficiency. Many economists believe that government action, such as regulation, is necessary to correct market failures. Other economists question, however, whether government regulation is necessary to achieve a cleaner environment. They argue that the only its allies—came to more than $50 billion, and it appears that billions more will be required each year to maintain readiness for future action.

The difficulty with these costs is that, because they are external costs, the consumers of gasoline and other oil products ignore them. The challenge to policy makers, then, is to find ways to impose these costs on consumers. Economists have suggested a variety of ways to do this. Here we look briefly at three of them: (1) congestion pricing, (2) parking cashouts, and (3) higher gasoline taxes.

Congestion pricing involves imposing a fee on vehicles that use the central city. Singapore has used a congestion pricing scheme since 1975, and officials are either planning or considering such schemes in Chile, France, Norway, the United Kingdom, the United States, and several other countries.[†]

One of the principal reasons that congestion is so pronounced in central cities is the prevalence of solo commuters. Solo commuting is greatly facilitated when employers provide free parking for their employees. U.S. employers offer free parking because the Internal Revenue Code allows them to deduct any costs of employer-provided parking as a business expense and lets workers deduct the benefits from their taxable income, up to $155 per month. As a result, 95 percent of automobile commuters receive free or subsidized parking. *Parking cashouts* require employers who provide free parking to offer a travel allowance worth the value of the parking space as an alternative. Employees who choose the less expensive options of carpooling or public transit can pocket most of the alloted amount. Los Angeles County substituted travel allowances for free parking in 1990 and experienced a 40 percent decrease in the demand for parking.[‡] The Internal Revenue Code could be modified to require all employers who currently provide free or subsidized employee parking to offer such a substitution.

Gasoline taxes in the United States average about 40 cents per gallon. They average $1.68 per gallon in Japan, $2.35 in the United Kingdom, $2.66 in Germany, $2.86 in France, and an astounding (to Americans) $3.64 per gallon in Italy. Although American travelers to these countries are puzzled by this practice, there really is no mystery about why this occurs: officials in these countries have acted aggressively to reduce their dependence on imported oil by allowing *higher gasoline taxes*. As a by-product, they have also reduced the air pollution attributable to automobiles. So they have, in effect, charged automobile users more fully for the social costs of the automobile by shifting the costs from those who are not responsible to those who are.

---

[*]The data in this paragraph come from Marcia D. Lowe, "Reinventing Transport," in Lester D. Brown et al., *State of the World, 1994* (New York: W. W. Norton, 1994), 80–98.

[†] Kenneth A. Small, "Urban Traffic Congestion: A New Approach to the Gordian Knot," *The Brookings Review*, Spring 1993.

[‡]Lowe, "Reinventing Transport," 96.

---

thing government needs to do is to establish and enforce property rights to the natural environment.

Proponents of this view argue that the atmosphere is used excessively for waste disposal because polluters do not have to pay a price to use it in this fashion. Normally, a market price for a particular use of a resource can be established only if there is a clear **property right**—a legally defined and enforceable right to use property in a specific way. A market for alternative uses of the atmosphere has never developed as have markets for other natural resources because the atmosphere is a **common property resource**—a resource that is the property of all. In the absence of the right to use property exclusively, no market in particular uses of the resource is possible.

Property Rights
The legally allowable uses of property.

Common Property Resource
A resource that belongs to all.

Ronald Coase, a winner of the Nobel Prize for Economics, recognized this aspect of the pollution problem and argued that a market in the right to pollute—to use the environment for waste disposal—would be established if the right to exclusive use (including the right to transfer that privilege to others) was given to some private party. He demonstrated that such a policy would yield the efficient level of pollution regardless of whether the use right was assigned to a polluter or to an environmentalist.[2]

Consider the following possibilities. First, if polluters have the property rights to the environment (as they do implicitly in the oil refining case discussed earlier), there will be too much pollution. In this case, individuals who suffer damages will have an incentive to pay polluters to reduce pollution. Alternatively, if environmentalists have the property rights, there will be too little pollution (and production). In this case, producers have an incentive to pay environmentalists for the right to increase production (and pollution). In either case, the levels of production and pollution will tend toward the efficient levels if such payments are made.

If the world worked this smoothly, the government would be needed only to assign and enforce property rights. Alas, it probably works this way only if the number of producers and environmentalists is relatively small; smallness in numbers facilitates the bargaining necessary for the affected parties to negotiate a mutually satisfactory payment arrangement. Real-world cases of air pollution most often involve too many affected parties for Coase's solution to work. Thus, some kind of government regulatory activity appears to be necessary as a means of achieving a cleaner environment.

AIR POLLUTION REGULATION: THE CLEAN AIR ACT

The Environmental Protection Agency (EPA) has regulated air pollution in the United States since 1970. Although a small agency, its authority extends not only over air pollution, but also over water and noise pollution, pesticides, ocean dumping, solid wastes, toxic chemicals, resource recovery, and land use. The exercise of this authority has given the EPA an impact on the economy much greater than its size would suggest.

The mandate for the EPA in the realm of air pollution comes from the Clean Air Act of 1963, as amended in 1965, 1970, 1977, and 1990. It is impossible to summarize neatly all the important features of the Clean Air Act; it is too long and too complicated and has been greatly expanded by administrative directives. We will focus instead on the principal regulatory tools or concepts that the EPA relies upon to carry out its regulatory responsibilities.

---

[2]Ronald Coase, "The Problem of Social Cost," *Journal of Law and Economics* 3, no. 2 (October 1960), 1–44.

NATIONAL AMBIENT AIR QUALITY STANDARDS (NAAQS)   The NAAQS are the upper limits permitted for concentrations of the six common air pollutants described earlier: particulates, sulfur dioxide, carbon monoxide, nitrogen dioxide, ozone, and lead. The limits have both a physical and a time dimension. For example, the standard for ozone is violated when the average hourly concentration is 0.12 parts per million or more for one or more days per year.

The NAAQS represent threshold concentrations above which the EPA believes the pollutant poses a significant risk to health. The law requires that these standards be set, and that they be achieved, without consideration of costs. The law also requires that they be applied uniformly across the country.

EMISSIONS LIMITS   The NAAQS govern concentrations in the atmosphere after pollutants have been released or emitted. The law also fixes limits on the amounts of certain pollutants that may be emitted into the atmosphere. Strict limits have been placed on carbon monoxide (CO) and hydrocarbon (HC) emissions from automobiles since 1968. The 1970 amendments to the Clean Air Act added emissions limits for nitrogen dioxide and reduced the limits on CO and HC emissions. Reductions in all three pollutants were prescribed in both the 1977 and 1990 amendments to the Clean Air Act. The 1990 amendments also require the EPA to establish limits on emissions of 189 toxic chemicals equal to those of the cleanest 12 percent of existing sources and to limit emissions of sulfur dioxide and nitrogen oxides from electricity-generating plants as a means of reducing acid rain.

RESTRICTED TECHNOLOGY   The Clean Air Act not only requires that certain standards be attained, but it also places restrictions on the technologies that may be used to achieve them. For example, it requires automobile manufacturers to install catalytic converters with a minimum life of 100,000 miles. Gasoline-vapor-recycling equipment must be installed on new cars, and gasoline stations in areas where NAAQS for ozone are exceeded must install vapor-recovery devices on fuel-dispensing hoses. New stationary sources of pollution in these areas must use technologies that produce the Lowest Achievable Emissions Rate (LAER). Existing stationary sources in ozone nonattainment areas must install Reasonably Available Control Technology (RACT). The new air toxics regulations require use of Maximum Achievable Control Technology (MACT)—except for small sources that must use Generally Available Control Technology (GACT). This patchwork of permissible technologies is a source of great uncertainty to manufacturers, a major administrative burden for the EPA, and as noted later in this chapter, a source of excessive costs of air pollution regulation.

NEW SOURCE PERFORMANCE STANDARDS   Although the exact dimensions of the permissible technologies are difficult to determine, the state-of-the-art technologies for new sources of emissions (LAER and MACT) are undoubtedly more expensive than the technologies required for existing sources (RACT and GACT). These more exacting New Source Performance Standards are a powerful incentive to keep older and more costly plants in operation longer.

PRESCRIBED FUELS   The Clean Air Act also prescribes certain fuel requirements for mobile sources of pollution. Gasoline stations in nonattainment carbon monoxide areas must sell oxygenated gasoline, and the areas that violate the ozone standards most frequently must increase their reliance on alternative fuels, such as methanol, compressed natural gas, liquid petroleum gas, and electricity.

OFFSET REQUIREMENTS   Areas that fail to meet the ozone and carbon monoxide standards can permit new major sources of pollution, such as new factories, but only if ways are found to **offset** the increased pollution by reducing pollutants from existing sources. In fact, the offset must exceed the addition. In the areas just above the NAAQS, the offset is 1.1 units for each new source unit. This ratio grows to 1.5 to 1.0 for areas with serious air quality problems like Los Angeles.

Offset
The reduction in emissions achieved by an existing source that permits the introduction of a new pollution source in areas not meeting air pollution standards.

EMISSIONS TRADING   The offset policy has provided the impetus for the development of markets in **emissions reduction credits.** Should a producer control any emission source to a higher degree than legally required, it can receive an emissions reduction credit. For example, suppose that an electricity-generating plant is required to reduce its emissions of sulfur dioxide by 100 tons per year (to reduce acid rain) and that it can reduce its emissions by 200 tons at reasonable cost. If it does so, it would receive an emissions reduction credit for 100 tons of sulfur dioxide.

Emissions Reduction Credit
The right to produce additional emissions, earned by reducing emissions below a level specified by regulators.

Credits can be earned for excess reductions of each of the pollutants subject to the NAAQS. They can then be sold to firms seeking an offset for new sources. They can also be used in the context of the EPA's netting, bubble, and banking programs.

Netting allows a firm to add a new source of emissions in a plant if it can reduce emissions by as much, or more, from other sources in the plant. That is, net emissions cannot increase.

Netting
A regulation that allows a firm to add a new source of pollutant emissions to a plant if it can reduce emissions from other sources.

The **bubble** program allows several sources to be grouped together and treated as a unit—as if they were enclosed by a bubble. The regulatory objective is to limit total emissions from the bubble. Thus, some sources within the bubble can increase emissions as long as other sources reduce emissions by an equivalent or greater amount.

Bubble
A regulatory unit, containing several sources of pollution, that is evaluated according to the total emissions it produces rather than the emissions produced by each source.

The banking program allows firms to save emissions reduction credits for subsequent use in the offset, netting, or bubble programs. Firms may bank them for their own use at a later date or for later sale to another firm seeking to change or expand operations.

Accurate data on the level of emissions trading do not exist because so many of the trades are conducted at the local level, and uniform reporting is not required. Some observers estimate that as many as 7,000 to 12,000 transactions have taken place. Most of these have been used for netting or offsets.

PREVENTION OF SIGNIFICANT DETERIORATION   Areas that were cleaner than the NAAQS when the Clean Air Act was enacted or amended are not exempt from regulation. To prevent air quality from deteriorating, the Clean

Air Act establishes limits on the permissible reductions in air quality in these areas. In fact, the limits on additional pollution are stricter for the areas that started with better air quality.

STATE IMPLEMENTATION PLAN (SIP)   The responsibility for ensuring that the NAAQS are met (and for facilitating sales of emissions credits) falls on state pollution-control agencies. The means by which they intend to meet the standards are spelled out in the SIP, which must be approved by the EPA. The typical SIP identifies a state's significant emissions sources and, through the use of mathematical modeling, determines the emissions reductions needed from each source and the measures necessary to achieve them.

SIPs have grown over time to be very detailed, complicated, and difficult to access and to change. To ease this problem, the Clean Air Act now requires the states to establish a pollution permit system. Under this system, permits will be issued for all major air pollution sources, covering all provisions of the Clean Air Act that apply to that source. If they work well, permits will resolve uncertainties regarding the regulations that apply to each source. They will also promote a clearer understanding of clean air requirements at the operating level and facilitate monitoring and compliance by state authorities.

EFFECTS OF THE CLEAN AIR ACT ON AIR QUALITY

The goal of the Clean Air Act is to improve air quality. A two-step process is required to determine if it has done so. First, changes in air quality must be measured. Second, the effects of the Clean Air Act on these measures must be separated from all the other factors that could account for the measured changes in air quality, such as economic growth or the weather. Unfortunately, the available evidence reflects only the first step in this process.

At first glance the national trends for ambient air concentrations are encouraging. According to the EPA, the annual average concentration of particulates fell 24 percent between 1975 and 1991. Over the same period, concentrations of sulfur dioxide, carbon monoxide, nitrogen dioxide, and ozone fell by 50, 53, 24, and 25 percent, respectively. Concentrations of lead fell nearly 95 percent.

By 1991, the *average* nationwide concentrations of all the common pollutants were below the relevant NAAQS. Unfortunately, however, the average varied significantly and many areas still exceeded the standards. The ozone standard was exceeded most often. In 1991, nearly 70 million people lived in counties that were out of compliance with the ozone standards. The record was better for the other common pollutants, but another 16 million people lived in counties where pollution levels in 1991 exceeded at least one of the other national air quality standards. Thus, it seems clear that even though the trends may be encouraging, the common pollutants still constitute a significant problem in some parts of the country.

The historical record is not at all encouraging where hazardous air pollutants are concerned. During its first 20 years, the EPA issued standards for only nine

ADDITIONAL INSIGHT

CARBON TAXES

As noted in the text, the United States has taken no action to deal with the threat of global warming. If it does, however, many economists would urge that we adopt a carbon tax—a tax on different fuels based on the amount of carbon they contain.

A carbon tax is advocated as a cost-effective means of dealing with the problem of global warming. Such a tax would directly raise the price of fossil fuels—especially oil, natural gas, and coal—and the products derived directly from them, such as gasoline and electricity. This increase would encourage energy conservation and the use of relatively cleaner energy sources, such as solar and wind energy. The net result would be less carbon dioxide emitted to the atmosphere.

Economists have estimated the carbon taxes required to reduce carbon dioxide emissions to various target levels. Generally, they fall in the $100 to $400 per ton range. Manne and Richels estimate, for example, that a $250 tax per ton of carbon will be required to reduce long-run U.S. carbon emissions by 20 percent below their present level.[*]

The Congressional Budget Office calculates that a tax of $100 per ton of carbon amounts to $60 per ton of coal, $1.63 per thousand cubic feet of natural gas, $13 per barrel of oil, and 30 cents per gallon of gasoline.[**] Compared to projected year-2000 prices, a $100 carbon tax would be 256 percent of the price of coal, 53 percent of the price of natural gas, and 40 percent of the price of oil.

Carbon taxes in the $100 to $400 range would raise enormous amounts of revenue. A tax of $100 per ton, for example, would raise about $130 billion per year in the United States—about 2 percent of gross domestic product. This obviously makes the carbon tax an inviting prospect for government officials who want to reduce the budget deficit.

Governments could choose to levy a carbon tax but offset the revenues raised by lowering other taxes, such as personal or corporate income taxes. Although this would not ease the deficit problem, economists generally agree that even a revenue-neutral carbon tax would have beneficial effects. Not only would the carbon tax reduce the distortion created by people's failures to consider the external costs associated with fossil fuel use, but reducing income taxes would reduce the adverse effects these taxes have on incentives to work and invest.

Carbon taxes also appeal to government officials who want to reduce the nation's trade deficit. As the carbon tax raises the price of oil, American consumers and producers would reduce the quantity they buy—from both domestic and foreign producers.

This lineup of forces favoring a carbon tax would not necessarily ensure passage of authorizing legislation. Forces opposing the tax are bound to be powerful, as it would have an adverse impact on the coal, oil, gas, and automobile industries. Higher energy prices could also trigger falling GDP and rising unemployment. Consumer groups could join the opposition out of concern that the tax would be passed on to them in the form of higher prices. We probably are going to witness a spirited and protracted debate whenever the carbon tax rises to the top of the policy agenda.

---

[*]Alan S. Manne and Richard G. Richels, "CO$_2$ Emissions Limits: An Economic Cost Analysis for the USA." *The Energy Journal* 11, no. 2 (1990), 51–74.
[**]Congressional Budget Office, *Carbon Charges as a Response to Global Warming: The Effects of Taxing Fossil Fuels* (Washington, DC: Congressional Budget Office, 1990), iv.

---

such pollutants. The 1990 amendments to the Clean Air Act promise to change this record, however; the EPA is required to issue standards for 189 toxic chemicals by the year 2000. Architects of this legislation are hopeful that these standards will eventually reduce total emissions of toxic chemicals by 90 percent. There is no way to tell at this time if this is a realistic goal.

The situation regarding acid rain seems somewhat more certain. The 1990 Clean Air Act amendments require the nation's electricity-generating plants to reduce sulfur dioxide and nitrogen oxide emissions by several million tons. Reductions in acid deposition should follow.

It also appears that the United States is well on its way toward solving the stratospheric ozone depletion problem. The EPA used its authority under the Toxic Substances Control Act several years ago to ban the use of chlorofluorocarbons (CFCs) as aerosol propellants because of their potential for ozone depletion. The Clean Air Act requires that production and sale of several CFCs and other related chemicals be phased out, and recent international agreements offer real hope that this problem will disappear in the next decade or two.

The Clean Air Act is not aimed, however, at solving the problem of global warming. The pollutant of most concern, carbon dioxide, is targeted for reduction in western Europe, but not in the United States, where there is greater skepticism about the threat of global warming. If it does become a target in the United States, economists hope that it will be reduced in the least costly way. One way to do this is to levy a carbon tax, as outlined in the Additional Insight, "Carbon Taxes."

THE ECONOMICS OF THE CLEAN AIR ACT: HAVE WE GONE TOO FAR?

Has the Clean Air Act gone too far? At first glance it may seem like the obvious answer is no. After all, the record we just reviewed shows that we are far from eliminating air pollution in the United States. Adoption of the economic perspective, however, indicates that the answer may be yes for some of the provisions of the Clean Air Act.

What is this economic perspective? Simply stated, it is the notion that a government regulation is appropriate as long as the benefits from the regulation exceed the costs. It is, in fact, the same kind of test we imposed earlier when we argued that the efficient level of pollution may be greater than zero because the marginal benefits of reducing pollution to zero may be less than the marginal costs of doing so.

Economists have long been concerned that the Clean Air Act imposes costs on society that are greater than the benefits received. Their concern stems from the fact that virtually all of the regulations based on the Clean Air Act can be established and implemented without any consideration of the effects on costs and benefits. Their concern has been reinforced by the results of studies aimed at measuring and comparing benefits and costs of environmental regulation. A good example is a recent study by Alan J. Krupnick and Paul R. Portney.[3]

In this study, the authors estimated the benefits and costs likely to be associated with the controls prescribed in the 1990 Clean Air Act amendments for meeting the standards on ground-level ozone, the most troublesome of the six

---

[3]"Controlling Urban Air Quality: A Benefit-Cost Assessment," *Science* 252 (1991), 522–28.

common pollutants. They aimed their analysis at the measures required to reduce volatile organic compounds (VOCs), one of the two primary ingredients for producing smog (the other is nitrogen dioxide). These measures require significant investment in pollution control equipment by thousands of stationary sources of VOCs, hazardous waste facilities, and applicators of surface coatings. They also require expensive refueling controls on autos and gas pumps, costly vehicle inspection and maintenance programs, stringent emissions controls for motor vehicles, more expensive reformulated gasoline, and retrofitting of fleet vehicles in selected cities so that they may use methanol and other alternative fuels. According to Krupnick and Portney, these control measures would reduce emissions of VOCs by 35 percent between 1994 and 2004 at an annualized cost of $8.8 billion to $20.8 billion.

The predicted air quality improvement from adopting these measures would mean fewer asthma attacks, reduced incidence of coughing and chest discomfort, and fewer days of restricted activity for the affected populace. Additional positive effects may result in the form of increased visibility and reduced damages to materials, crops, and other vegetation.

These improvements in physical health, reduced damages, and increased visibility are the sources of the benefits produced by the control measures. The ideal measure of benefits is the amount that individuals would be willing to pay for these effects. Drawing upon a number of studies in which these values had been determined, Krupnick and Portney estimated that the health benefits from the new VOC control measures would be in the range of $250 million to $800 million per year. They estimated that reduced damages to crops and other vegetation could add more than $1 billion dollars to benefits.

The authors did not estimate the benefits from increased visibility. Studies of visibility improvements in eastern U.S. cities and in San Francisco, however, indicate an average annual willingness to pay $26–$101 annually per household for a 10 percent improvement in visibility.[4] If we assume the control measures would yield a 10 percent improvement in visibility and if we apply the high estimate of $101 to each of the 22 million households living in ozone nonattainment counties in 1989, the improved visibility benefits would be a little more than $2.2 billion.

With this addition, total benefits would range from $4 billion to $4.5 billion. This is not a trivial sum, but it does fall far short of even the low estimate of $8.8 billion for the costs of the new ozone control measures. Thus, these measures fail the economist's benefit-cost test; they overallocate resources to pollution control.

Economists will not be surprised by this result. The ozone control measures specified in the Clean Air Act amendments of 1990 contain a large dose of technology-forcing; that is, they require decision makers to choose from a relatively narrow range of pollution control technologies. They also require that these technologies be applied uniformly to air pollution sources that may differ greatly

---

[4]These findings are reported in Maureen L. Cropper and Wallace E. Oates, "Environmental Economics: A Survey," *Journal of Economic Literature* 30 (June 1992), 719.

in the cost with which they can achieve additional reductions in emissions. There is, in fact, considerable evidence that command-and-control measures such as these are very expensive means of controlling air pollution.[5]

COST-REDUCING MEASURES

Economists have identified several ways to reduce the costs of environmental regulation without reducing environmental quality. The two that have received the most attention are (1) the use of emissions taxes and (2) the use of marketable emissions permits.

EMISSIONS TAX

One of the economist's favorite solutions to pollution is an excise tax on emissions of pollutants, commonly called a Pigovian tax after its originator, the late British economist A. C. Pigou. An **emissions tax** regulates the level of pollution by establishing a price that emitters must pay per unit of emissions.

Emissions Tax
A tax levied on emissions; also called a Pigovian tax.

To show how an emissions tax works and how it can lower the costs of achieving a cleaner environment, we have constructed a simple example. Suppose that there are six coal-fired electric generating plants that are initially unregulated. Each plant emits two tons of sulfur per year. Each of the plants could eliminate its sulfur emissions, but at widely varying costs per ton, as indicated in Table 7.1. The variation in cost per ton reflects factors such as differences in the plants' ages and their access to low-sulfur coal.

In an effort to reduce acid rain, the government could require that each plant reduce its emissions, by half—from two tons to one ton per year. Such an approach would be quite consistent with the government's tendency to specify targets and expect everyone to achieve them. Given the costs per ton as listed in Table 7.1, the total cost of eliminating half of the sulfur emissions of the group, or six tons, would be $2,100 − the sum of $100 + 200 + 300 + 400 + 500 + 600.

Alternatively, the government could set a tax that achieved the same goal of cutting group emissions in half. A tax of $350 per ton of emissions would work, for the following reasons. If the tax were $350 per ton of emissions, plants A, B and C would eliminate two tons of sulfur each because, according to the data in Table 7.1, it is cheaper for them to eliminate sulfur than to pay the tax. Plants D, E and F would continue to emit two tons each, however, because it would be cheaper for them to emit sulfur and pay the tax than to eliminate sulfur. With the tax in place, six tons of sulfur would be eliminated, just as in the case of the regulation requiring each to eliminate one ton. The total cost of eliminating the six tons is

[5]A good summary of this evidence appears in Tom Tietenberg, *Environmental and Natural Resource Economics,* 3rd ed. (New York: HarperCollins, 1992), 402–5.

COST PER TON OF
ELIMINATING
SULFUR IN SIX
ELECTRIC
GENERATING
PLANTS

TABLE 7.1

Plant	Cost per Ton
A	$100
B	200
C	300
D	400
E	500
F	600

much less with the tax in place, however—only $1,200, or (2) $100 + (2) $200 + (2) $300.

When plants have the option of emitting sulfur and paying the tax or eliminating sulfur and not paying the tax, the task of eliminating sulfur will be assumed by the plants with the lowest cost means of eliminating sulfur. This produces not only the desired level of emissions, but it saves scarce resources at the same time.

MARKETABLE POLLUTION PERMITS

As noted earlier, the Clean Air Act often requires all air emission sources to achieve the same emission standard regardless of circumstances. This requirement ignores the variation among sources in the cost of achieving the standard and leads to excessive costs of eliminating pollution. Costs of eliminating pollution can be reduced by allocating a larger share of the burden to sources with lower costs and a smaller share of the burden to sources with higher costs. Pigovian taxes can be used to achieve such an allocation, but they have not been used for this purpose to date. Legislators and regulators appear, instead, to be leaning toward marketable pollution permits as a means of reducing the costs of eliminating pollution.

A pollution permit specifies the amount of a pollutant that the source may emit during a given time period. The EPA has issued air pollution permits for sulfur dioxide to about 100 electricity-generating plants in the first phase of a program to reduce acid rain. Permits will be issued to additional plants in subsequent phases of the program. When the program is fully phased in, the permits issued will allow electricity-generating plants in the aggregate to emit only one-half of the sulfur dioxide they were emitting before the program was initiated.

These permits are marketable; that is, they may be sold to the highest bidder. They are similar in this respect to the emission reduction credits used in the offset program discussed earlier in this chapter. It is the marketability feature of both programs that gives them the potential to reduce costs.

An example can help to explain how permit trading can reduce the cost of eliminating pollution. Suppose that two coal-fired electricity-generating plants in Indiana emit four tons each of sulfur dioxide every day, which eventually falls as

	Cost per Ton of Eliminating Emissions	
Tons per Day	**Plant A**	**Plant B**
First	$100	$300
Second	200	600
Third	300	900
Fourth	400	1,200

TABLE 7.2

COSTS PER TON OF ELIMINATING EMISSIONS FROM ELECTRIC GENERATING PLANTS

Plants A and B differ in terms of their costs of eliminating sulfur dioxide. Each plant initially eliminates the first and second tons of sulfur dioxide and has a permit allowing the emission of the third and fourth tons. Both plants would gain if plant A sold the permit for its third ton to plant B (which would use it to emit its second ton).

acid rain in the Adirondack Mountains of New York. The EPA wants to reduce total emissions to four tons, and it is considering two ways of doing so: (1) requiring each plant to eliminate two tons and issuing two one-ton emissions permits to each plant or (2) doing the same as (1) but allowing the plants to sell their permits.

The two plants experience increasing cost per ton of eliminating emissions. Plant A has lower costs of eliminating sulfur dioxide than Plant B, by virtue of its age and location. The cost data for each plant are displayed in Table 7.2.

If the EPA adopts the first plan, both plants will emit two tons and eliminate (not emit) two tons. Plant A will spend $300 on eliminating emissions (for the first two tons) and Plant B will spend $900 (for the first two tons), for a total of $1,200 per day. Both plants will emit two tons, as allowed by their permits.

If the EPA adopts the second plan, one permit would be marketed. Plant B would buy a permit to emit its second ton if it could pay something less than $600, the cost of eliminating this unit itself. Plant A would sell a permit it is currently using for its third ton if it could receive something more than $300, the cost of eliminating this unit if it no longer had a permit to emit it. The two plants could strike a bargain for one permit, somewhere between $300 and $600.

Suppose that they negotiate a sale at $450. Both plants are better off by $150: Plant A receives $450 and increases its costs of eliminating emissions by only $300, and Plant B pays $450 and reduces its costs by $600. Total costs of eliminating emissions fall from $1,200 to $900: Plant A now eliminates three tons at a cost of $600, and Plant B eliminates one ton at a cost of $300.

This simple example is a small indication of the cost savings possible through permit trading. Tietenberg estimates that trades of emission reduction credits to date have saved more than $10 billion in capital costs, alone.[6] The EPA estimates

---

[6]Tom Tietenberg, *Environmental and Natural Resource Economics,* 3rd ed. (New York: HarperCollins, 1992), 410.

that trading of sulfur dioxide permits will save $1 billion in costs (out of $5 billion) of complying with the acid rain provisions of the Clean Air Act. Economists have hinted, also, at large potential savings from using transferable permits for emissions of carbon dioxide and toxic chemicals.

SUMMARY

Five important air pollution problems exist: (1) poor air quality in urban areas, (2) acid rain, (3) global warming, (4) ozone depletion, and (5) hazardous air pollutants.

Air pollution is a source of concern primarily because of its harmful effects on human health. It also damages plants and property, and it impairs visibility.

Air pollution is an inevitable by-product of energy production, industrial production, and household consumption, and it cannot be eliminated short of reducing these activities to very low levels. In fact, from the economic perspective, it would be unwise in many cases to eliminate pollution because the costs of doing so would exceed the benefits. Such a conclusion follows directly from application of the rule for achieving efficiency in resource allocation: Expand each economic activity to the level where marginal social benefit equals marginal social cost—including the cost attributable to pollution.

Private-sector decision makers often expand these activities to the point where marginal social cost exceeds marginal social benefit because they ignore the marginal external cost of pollution. This behavior produces excessive pollution.

The Clean Air Act establishes ambient air quality standards, emissions limits, restrictions on pollution abatement technology, constraints on motor fuel sales in certain areas, procedures for the trading of emissions credits and pollution permits, and an extensive federal-state partnership for implementing the act.

The Clean Air Act appears to have improved urban air quality. It has not materially reduced either acid rain or hazardous air pollutants, but it should do so in the next decade. Considerable progress has been made in combating stratospheric ozone depletion. Global warming has not been addressed by the Clean Air Act.

Although the Clean Air Act has reduced air pollution, the latest amendments may increase the costs of regulation more than benefits. This is apparently true, for example, of the new provision to further reduce ground-level ozone.

Economists have suggested several alternatives to the regulatory approach that they believe would be a less costly means of reducing pollution. We examined two of these: (1) adoption of emissions taxes and (2) use of marketable pollution permits. Both the emissions tax and marketable permits show promise as means of achieving cleaner air at lower cost.

KEY TERMS

Net social loss

Property rights

Common property resource

Offset

Emissions reduction credit

Netting

Bubble

Emissions tax

REVIEW QUESTIONS

1. According to this chapter, what are the five most important air pollution problems? Briefly discuss them.
2. Explain the following concepts. Use specific examples, if needed.
    a. Marginal private cost
    b. Marginal social cost
    c. Marginal external cost
    d. Marginal social benefit
3. "Generally, we would not expect the efficient level of pollution to be zero." Using graphical analysis, explain why this statement is true.
4. Use the following graph to answer questions a through e.
    a. In the absence of government regulation, how many tons of paper will be produced?
    b. What is the efficient level of production?
    c. What area depicts the benefits from production in excess of the efficient level?

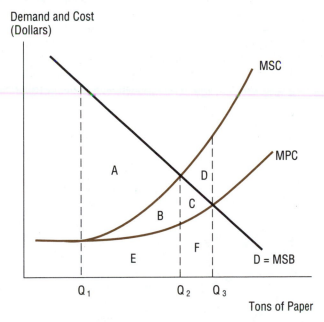

d. What area depicts the costs of production in excess of the efficient level?
e. What area depicts the external cost of production?

5. What are the principal features of the Clean Air Act?
6. Has the Clean Air Act improved air quality? Why is it difficult to determine if it has?
7. Describe a case in which the Clean Air Act overallocates resources to regulation. Why does this happen?
8. Briefly describe the features of an emissions tax. Carefully explain how such a tax can reduce costs of eliminating pollutants.
9. How do marketable pollution permits work to abate pollution and reduce costs of eliminating pollutants?

SUGGESTIONS FOR FURTHER READING

Cline, William. *The Economics of Global Warming.* Washington, DC: Institute for International Economics, 1993. A thorough analysis of the global warming issue, containing several estimates of the benefits and costs of public policy. Cline argues that a very long-run perspective leads to the conclusion that measures to curb global warming are likely to produce benefits greater than costs.

Council on Environmental Quality. *Environmental Quality,* Annual. Washington, DC: Government Printing Office. These annual reports contain up-to-date discussions of the major pollution problems, provide data on primary pollutants, and examine policy issues.

Portney, Paul, ed. *Public Policies for Environmental Protection.* Washington, DC: Resources for the Future, 1990. An informative and accessible examination of the nation's principal policies to achieve a cleaner environment. Chapter 3 deals with air pollution policy. Other chapters cover water pollution, hazardous wastes, toxic substances, and problems of monitoring and compliance.

Tietenberg, Thomas H. *Environmental and Natural Resource Economics.* 3rd ed. New York: HarperCollins, 1992. A leading intermediate-level text. In the last half of this book, the author examines all the principal pollution problems and policies, including their effects on output, employment, inflation, and the distribution of economic welfare.

8

COLLEGE EDUCATION

Is It Worth the Cost?

A college education has long been viewed as a ticket to a better life in America. It is not, however, an inexpensive ticket. In 1995, a year of college cost an estimated $20,000 for the typical full-time student. Around $5,000 of this amount went for tuition, books, and supplies; the remainder is the money the person could earn at a full-time job if not attending college.[1]

Tuition paid by students is not enough, however, to cover the cost of running the nation's colleges and universities. For example, tuition covers only about a third of the cost of educating a student in public institutions. State legislatures appropriated over $5,000 per student in 1995 to bridge the gap between operating costs and tuition.

A college education is expensive, then, for both college students and taxpayers. For the typical full-time student who spends four years earning a bachelor's degree, the total cost is around $80,000—roughly the price of the typical home. The typical bachelor's degree also costs taxpayers around $20,000. Given these amounts, it is easy to understand why students, parents, and taxpayers want to know if a college degree is worth the cost. Much of this chapter addresses this issue.

Taxpayers also expect the opportunity for a college education to be available to students with limited income. In fact, state appropriations to higher education are often justified on the grounds that they reduce the cost of college to students who are less able to pay tuition. Financial help provided to students in the form of government grants and government-subsidized loans is justified on the same basis. In the last part of this chapter we ask whether appropriations, grants, and subsidies actually make college more accessible to low-income students.

THE SIMPLE ANALYTICS OF THE INVESTMENT DECISION

As noted, the typical college student (and his or her family!) invests a lot of money in acquiring a college education. We are interested in determining whether this is a wise investment. Properly done, however, the decision to invest in a college education is relatively complex. Thus, we begin with a simplified example that illustrates how investment decisions, in general, are made, and then in the next section we apply this process to a college education.

For this illustration, imagine that your friend, Tom, offers you the opportunity to invest in his new enterprise, Tom's Tops, a business that will make and sell customized T-shirts, sweatshirts, tank tops, and so on. Tom asks you to invest $1,000 today and another $1,000 one year from today. In return, he promises to pay you $700 two years from today, $950 three years from today, and $902 four years from today. You are certain that Tom will pay you these amounts on these dates, but you are uncertain whether this is a wise investment.

---

[1]*The Almanac of Higher Education,* 1993. The Editions of the Chronicle of Higher Education.

To make your determination you must do the following: (1) estimate all of the costs (C) you expect to pay and all of the benefits (B) you expect to receive, including when these events will occur, (2) adjust your estimates of C and B for the number of years you will be able to wait before making a payment and the number of years you will have to wait before realizing a benefit, and (3) compare the adjusted Cs and Bs, using an investment decision rule.

All of the elements of the first step are displayed in Table 8.1, which lists each of the expected costs and benefits according to the time (t) at which they will be made or realized. The present date, or "today," is designated by $t = 0$. One year from today is designated by $t = 1$, two years from today by $t = 2$, and so on. The investment decision itself is to be made at $t = 0$, or today.

Given the elements in Table 8.1, a little addition quickly indicates that expected benefits are greater than expected costs. Before you jump to conclude from this, however, that you should invest in Tom's Tops, you must adjust each of the benefits and costs for time of occurrence.

To understand why this step is necessary, consider the following example. Suppose that you were offered the choice between receiving $1,000 today or $1,000 one year from today. Which would you choose? Unless you were quite unusual, you would choose $1,000 today because you could invest the money today and end up with more than $1,000 tomorrow. How much more would depend upon your investment alternative. Suppose that your alternative is to put the money into a savings account that pays an interest rate (i) of 5 percent. If you did that, you would have $1,050 a year from now. Thus, $1,000 today has the same value to you as $1,050 one year from today, or, what is the same thing, $1,050 one year from today is worth only $1,000 to you today.

What is true in this example is true, in general: the present value (PV) of a sum of money is less than the future value (FV) of that sum. Formally,

$$(1)\ FV_t = PV_t = (1 + i)^t.$$

Alternatively,

$$(2)\ PV_t = FV_t (1 + i)^t.$$

TABLE 8.1		
t	B	C
0	0	$1,000
1	0	$1,000
2	$700	0
3	$950	0
4	$902	0
	$2,552	$2,000

BENEFITS FROM, AND COSTS OF, INVESTING IN TOM'S TOPS

TABLE 8.2

t	B	$(1 + i)^t$	PVB_t	C	PVC_t
0	$ 0	1.000	$ 0	$1,000	$1,000
1	0	1.050	0	1,000	952
2	700	1.103	635	0	0
3	950	1.158	820	0	0
4	902	1.216	742	0	0
			$2,197		$1,952

Applied to the current example,

$$(1)'\ \$1,050 = \$1,000\ (1.05)^1\ \text{or}\ (2)'\ \$1,000 = \$1,050/(1.05)^1,$$

where the $1,050 is a future value at t = 1, and the $1,000 is its present value at t = 0.

Stated simply, equations (2) and (2)' indicate that each future value of a sum of money must be "discounted" by the factor $(1 + i)^t$ to determine what that future sum is worth to the investor today, the time the investment decision is made. Table 8.2 shows the results of applying equation (2) to the data in Table 8.1. Columns 1, 2 and 5 in Table 8.2 are the same as the three columns of Table 8.1. Column 3 in Table 8.2 depicts the value of the discount factor for each value of t from 0 to 4 when the value for i is 0.05. Column 4 contains the present values of the benefits (hence, PVB) listed in column 2. For example, PVB_t for t = 2 is $700/(1.05)^2$ or $700/1.103$. Column 6 contains the present values of the costs (hence, PVC) listed in column 5.

The first two steps in the investment evaluation are now complete; that is, you have all of the relevant data, properly adjusted for time of occurrence. The final step is to decide if the investment is worthwhile. One way to do this is to simply add all of the PVBs and the PVCs and compare them. If the sum of the PVBs exceeds the sum of the PVCs, as they do in this example ($2,197 versus $1,952), the investment is worthwhile.

Rate of return
The discount rate that makes the sum of the present value of benefits equal to the present value of costs.

Alternatively, you could calculate the **rate of return.** The rate of return (r) is the discount rate (the interest rate in the discount factor) at which the *sum* of the PVBs is equal to the *sum* of the PVCs. That is, you must solve the following equation for the value of r:

$$(3)\quad \$1,000/(1 + r)^0 + \$1,000/(1 + r)^1 = \$700/(1 + r)^2 + \$950/(1 + r)^3 + \$902/(1 + r)^4$$

If several time periods are involved, as in this investment, the value of r can be determined fastest by using a financial calculator or a computer program that calculates rates of return. We have relieved you of this task and already determined that the solution value for r in equation (3) is 0.10, or 10 percent. This solution is confirmed by the data in Table 8.3, where the sums of the PVBs and PVCs are

t	B	$(1 + r)^t$	PVB_t	C	PVC_t
		TABLE 8.3			
0	$ 0	1.000	$ 0	$1,000	$1,000
1	0	1.100	0	1,000	909
2	700	1.210	579	0	
3	950	1.331	714	0	
4	902	1.464	616	0	
			$1,909		$1,909

CONFIRMATION OF A 10 PERCENT RATE OF RETURN FROM INVESTING IN TOM'S TOPS

determined using r = 0.10 in the discount factor in column 3. Note that at this discount rate, the sums of both the PVBs and the PVCs are $1,909. If this rate exceeds the rate you could earn on your best alternative, then this investment is worthwhile. In our example, you should make the investment in Tom's Tops if the savings account is your best alternative, because you would earn 10 percent on your investment and only 5 percent on the savings account.

INVESTING IN COLLEGE: A STUDENT'S PERSPECTIVE

In this section, we suggest how the analytics of the investment decision can be applied to the typical investment in a college education. We begin with costs and benefits easily valued in dollars.

COSTS AND BENEFITS EASILY VALUED IN DOLLARS

We have already mentioned the principal costs to the student: tuition, books, supplies, and income forgone. Other costs may exist that cannot be easily measured in dollars. We will discuss these later.

The principal benefit to the student that can be measured in dollars is the increase in lifetime income that will be received as a result of having completed a college degree. In 1995, for example, the typical worker with a bachelor's degree earned approximately $14,000 more each year than the typical worker with only a high school diploma. Other benefits may exist that cannot be easily measured in dollars. We will discuss these later along with the costs that are difficult to measure in dollars.

The costs and benefits that can be easily measured in dollars can be visualized with the help of Figure 8.1. This figure depicts the case of the student who enters college at age 18, graduates with a bachelor's degree at age 22, and works uninterrupted until age 65.

The costs of tuition, books, and supplies for this student are represented by area T. The line HH′ represents the student's expected lifetime earnings profile—the

EFFECTS OF
A COLLEGE
EDUCATION

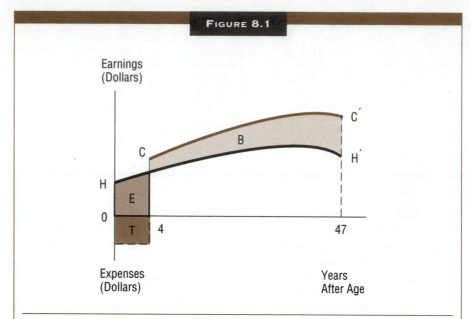

FIGURE 8.1

This figure illustrates the principal items used in evaluating an investment in a college education from the student's perspective. CC′ and HH′ are lifetime earnings profiles for college graduates and high school graduates, respectively. Area B is the difference in lifetime earnings between a college graduate and a high school graduate. Area E represents earnings a college student forgoes while in school, and area T represents the cost of tuition, fees, books, and supplies. The investment is worthwhile if B exceeds E plus T by enough to yield a rate of return at least as large as the student's best alternative investment.

expected annual earnings associated with all of the years worked—with only a high school diploma. Earnings forgone by attending college are represented by area E, the expected earnings associated with a high school diploma during the first four years after high school. Thus, the student's costs are represented by area E plus area T.

The line CC′ represents the lifetime earnings profile for the same individual, but with a bachelor's degree. The difference between CC′ and HH′, area B, represents the increase in lifetime earnings attributable to the bachelor's degree—the principal benefit from earning the degree. The shapes of the earnings profiles reflect the typical lifetime earnings patterns for high school and college graduates in which annual earnings increase over most of the working lifetime.

The areas in Figure 8.1 represent specific dollar amounts. Suppose, as noted earlier, that the typical student pays $5,000 per year for tuition, books, and supplies, gives up a job that would have paid $15,000 per year, and earns $14,000 more each year after graduating from college. In this instance, area T has a value of $20,000 (4 years at $5,000 per year), area E has a value of $60,000 (4 years at $15,000 per year), and area B has a value of $602,000 (43 years at $14,000).

Based on this information alone, a college degree seems to be worth it: benefits are $602,000 and costs are only $80,000. Such a simple comparison is

	TABLE 8.4		ESTIMATED RATES OF RETURN FROM A BACHELORS DEGREE
Year	**Rate of Return (in Percent)**	**Number of Studies**
1939	15.0	3
1949	11.6	5
1959	12.3	12
1969	13.0	10
1973	11.7	6
1980	16.5	1

Source: Larry L. Leslie and Paul T. Brinkman, *The Economic Value of Higher Education* (New York Macmillan, 1988), 47, 73.

misleading, however, because the benefits and costs have not been adjusted for time of occurrence.

As you know, one way to do this is to divide each annual benefit and cost by the appropriate discount factor to determine its present value, sum the present values and compare the sums. We have done this, using an assumed best alternative rate of interest, i, of 5 percent. Given this value for i, the sum of the PVBs is $201,332 and the sum of the PVCs is $70,920.

The other way to account for time of occurrence is to compute the rate of return, r — the interest rate at which the sums of the PVBs and PVCs are equal. We have also done this, and determined a value for r of 14.1 percent.

Given these results, investing in a college degree appears to be a very good decision. This is just a hypothetical example, however, that only very roughly conforms to the model outlined in Figure 8.1. Is this example representative? Is the rate of return on a college education typically this high? The answer is an emphatic yes, as indicated by the summary in Table 8.4 of rates of return reported in the economics literature.

COSTS AND BENEFITS NOT EASILY VALUED IN DOLLARS

Up to now we have emphasized the benefits and costs that can be readily valued in dollars, but there are benefits and costs associated with a college education that are difficult or impossible to value in dollars that may be relevant to the individual investment decision.

Benefits of this type have been analyzed and summarized in a 1984 study by Robert Haveman and Barbara Wolfe.[2] They compiled a list of 20 such effects of education. Although they did not state whether these effects applied to college education, many would appear to.

---

[2]Robert H. Haveman and Barbara L. Wolfe, "School and Economic Well-Being: The Role of Nonmarket Effects," *Journal of Human Resources* 19, No. 3 (1984), 382.

ADDITIONAL INSIGHT

THE DEMAND FOR EDUCATION

The fact that a college education represents a sound investment for individuals does not necessarily mean that students base the decision to attend college solely, or even primarily, on estimated rates of return. In fact, the evidence indicates that they are strongly influenced by the same factors—such as the price of the good or service itself, consumer income, and the prices of related goods and services—that determine their demand for other goods and services, like food, housing, and health care.

Higher education is subject to the law of demand; that is, a higher price, in terms of tuition and fees (after a deduction for grants) is associated with a smaller number of students enrolled. In fact, Leslie and Brinkman found this relationship confirmed in 25 studies of the demand for higher education.* According to their calculations, enrollment in U.S. higher education in 1982 could be expected to drop about 2.1 percent for each $100 increase in tuition.

The demand for higher education is also affected by the income of students and their families. For example, in their seminal study of the demand for education in the United States, Campbell and Siegel found that the influence over time of tuition on enrollment was apparent only after controlling for changes in income.[†] Their findings have been confirmed repeatedly, most recently by economists studying the determinants of enrollment in public colleges in New York, New Jersey, and Pennsylvania who determined that a 1 percent increase in income in these states increases the demand for public higher education by 1.67 percent.[‡] These economists also found a relationship between the demand for public education and the price of private higher education. A 10 percent increase in the price of private colleges increases the demand for public higher education by 2.8 percent in the three states.

Information such as this on the determinants of the demand for higher education should be of great interest to officials of both public and private colleges who are responsible for determining tuition and financial aid policy. Proper application of this kind of information would enable them to predict the effects of policy changes on enrollment and institutional revenues more accurately.

---

*Larry L. Leslie and Paul T. Brinkman, "Student Price Response in Higher Education," *The Journal of Higher Education* 58, no. 2 (1987), 181–204.
[†]Robert Campbell and Barry Siegel, "The Demand for Higher Education in the United States 1919–1964," *American Economic Review* 57 (1967), 482–94.
[‡]Cindy Kelly and Suzanne Tregarthen, "Price Plays Key Role in College Selection," *The Margin* (Fall 1991), 60.

Education enhances the value of leisure. Better-educated parents improve their children's health, intellectual development, occupational status, and future earnings. Schooling produces improved health. Education enables people to make better choices among consumer goods, locations, jobs, and prospective mates. Schooling also increases the returns people realize from saving, and the schooling experience per se is a source of satisfaction to many students.

Haveman and Wolfe's discussion of these effects strongly suggests that education yields many economic benefits not reflected in estimates of rates of return based primarily on earnings differences. But they found few estimates of the value of these benefits. They did develop a new estimating procedure, however, and used it to calculate the value of four nonearnings effects.

They found that parents place a value of $300 to $1,800 per year on the contribution that an additional year of their own schooling makes to the intellectual

ADDITIONAL INSIGHT

DOES WHERE YOU GO TO SCHOOL MATTER?

The results of the rate of return studies reported in Table 8.1 should be very encouraging to high school graduates who are trying to decide whether to invest their time and money in a college education. But prospective students have to decide where, as well as whether, to go to college. Among the many things they may want to know before they decide where to go is whether a degree from an elite college is worth more than a degree from a less prestigious one.

Given the voluminous literature on the rates of return from investing in a college education, it is surprising how little work has been done on this question. It is difficult, however, to get the kind of detailed individual and institutional information needed to find an answer.

Fortunately, this situation is about to change as more data become available from the *National Longitudinal Study of the High School Class of 1972*. In fact, the results of a recent study based on these data provide an interesting answer to the question of whether college reputation makes a difference in terms of post-college earnings. James and colleagues found that the choice of school can provide a slight advantage in later earnings, but only if one is fortunate enough to graduate from a selective private Eastern institution.* They found a much larger earnings advantage, however, associated with a student's choices and achievements while in college, regardless of the institution. The choice of major is important, with higher earnings advantages to engineering majors and to business majors who function as managers after college, as opposed, for example, to education majors, especially if they function as teachers after college. There is a significant payoff to taking lots of math regardless of major. The biggest payoff of all, however, is for a high grade-point average. Apparently, what matters most is not which college or university you attend but what you do while you are there.

---

*Estelle James, Nabeel Alsalam, Joseph C. Conaty, and Duc-Le To, "College Quality and Future Earnings: Where Should You Send Your Child to College?" *American Economic Review* 79 (May 1989), 247–52.

---

development of one of their children. They also estimate that parents are willing to pay $360 annually per additional year of schooling for its effect on their own attainment of desired family size and child spacing through the use of contraceptives. They calculate that an additional year of education is worth $100 per year in terms of its effects on improved consumer decisions. Haveman and Wolfe's largest estimate, however, is the value of improved health that an additional year of education produces. They place an upper limit on this effect of $3,000 per year. The lower rate of smoking among college graduates is an example of the behavior that leads to better health.

Haveman and Wolfe do not claim these findings are definitive, but they do suggest that effects such as these might be as valuable as those due to earnings alone. These four effects, alone, appear to increase the benefits from a college education by as much as 25 percent.

Not all of the effects that are hard to value in dollars, however, are benefits. Especially troublesome to some observers is the possibility of overeducation.

ADDITIONAL INSIGHT

EDUCATION AND ECONOMIC GROWTH

This chapter indicates that a college education is a major contributor to the income of individual graduates. Estimates made by economists indicate that education has been a major contributor, also, to the growth in national income. Studies based on "growth accounting" indicate that investment in education at all levels tends to explain directly about 15 to 20 percent of recorded growth in U.S. national income, and that higher education accounts for about one-fourth of this effect.* Another 20 to 40 percent of income growth generally is attributed to growth in knowledge and its application, and higher education is believed to contribute importantly to this process.

---

*The leading developer of the art of growth accounting was Edward F. Denison, who produced several estimates of the contribution of education to economic growth. For a good review of his work, see "Accounting for Slower Growth: An Update," in J. Kendrick, ed., *International Comparisons of Productivity and Causes of Slowdowns* (Cambridge, MA: Ballinger, 1984).

Overeducation occurs whenever college graduates believe they are overqualified for their jobs. Basically, those who suffer from overeducation expect their college degree to be the ticket to more challenging and interesting work than the labor market provides.

Tsang and Levin argue that overeducation may lead to job dissatisfaction, adverse workplace behavior, and deteriorating health. They find evidence that overeducation reduces labor productivity.[3] The lost productivity and increased health care costs should both be counted as part of the costs of college education. If they were, rates of return on educational investment would fall, although most likely not by enough to reduce them to questionable levels.

INVESTING IN COLLEGE: A SOCIAL PERSPECTIVE

The fact that investing in a college education yields such high rates of return to students raises the question of the appropriateness of government support for higher education. If students are going to be so richly rewarded for a college degree, they will make the financial commitment necessary to achieve the degree and there is no need for governmental support—or so the argument goes.

Government financial support of higher education is normally justified in three ways. In the absence of government support (1) the benefits that a college education confers on individuals other than students would be undersupplied, (2) students would be unable to borrow as much to finance a college education as they can reasonably be expected to repay, and (3) the number of students

---

[3]Mun S. Tsang and Henry M. Levin, "The Economics of Overeducation," *Economics of Education Review* 4, no. 2 (1985), 93–104.

attending college from lower-income families would be far less than the number intellectually capable of earning a college degree.

EXTERNAL BENEFITS

The benefits from a college education realized by individuals other than college students are the **external benefits of a college education.** The external benefits normally claimed for college education are (1) reduced criminal activity, (2) increased social cohesion, and (3) increased knowledge through research.

External Benefits of a College Education Benefits from a college education realized by individuals other than college students.

There is a negative correlation between years of schooling completed and incidence of crimes committed. Given the social background of college students and their personal motivation to succeed as indicated by their perseverance, especially in the case of less affluent students, the expected proportion of potential criminals among college students is quite small, however. Thus, college attendance per se probably has little independent influence on criminal activity.

Education may enhance social cohesion by transmitting essential social values from one generation to another, by instructing students on the rights and responsibilities of citizenship, by increasing effective participation in public affairs, and by preparing students to participate cooperatively in an economy characterized by a high degree of competition and specialization of labor. Few people doubt that education has such effects and that much of their benefit is external to the individuals educated. Yet most economists who write on this subject believe that the bulk of this socialization function of schooling is completed by the time a student graduates from high school. Thus, the external benefits from college education due to enhanced social cohesion are likely to be small.

The nation's colleges and universities are major producers of research, the benefits from which are often widely diffused among the populace. Most of these benefits are produced as a by-product of graduate education, however, or as a separately contracted activity. Thus, the external benefits from research produced solely as a consequence of an undergraduate education—the primary focus of this chapter—are not likely to be significant.

The bottom line is that it is difficult to justify taxpayer support for the nation's public college students and institutions on the basis of the external benefits they generate from activities associated with the typical bachelors degree program.

CAPITAL MARKET FAILURES

Students are turning increasingly to borrowing as a means of financing college education. To help them do this, both the federal and state governments have established direct and guaranteed loan programs. In the direct loan programs students borrow directly from a government agency. In the guaranteed loan programs students borrow from private lenders, such as banks, and the government guarantees payment to the lender in the event of default on the part of the student borrower.

RATES OF RETURN AROUND THE WORLD

It is almost universally accepted that investment in education is worthwhile. It is worthwhile for individuals because it allows them to earn higher incomes and make better choices about health care, consumption, and mate selection. It is also worthwhile for society because it promotes upward mobility, improves the quality of citizen participation in civic affairs, reduces crime, and increases the availability of a scarce resource—human capital—that promotes economic growth and improves the standard of living. In fact, the value of investing in education has been confirmed by studies of rates of return around the world. The following table summarizes the social rates of return estimated in many of these studies, arranged by region and level of education.

The social rate of return is determined by comparing the social costs and benefits of education, rather than the private costs and benefits. The primary difference on the cost side is that private costs consist only of the costs borne by the student and his or her family, whereas social costs include both private costs and all tax funds used to pay for education. The primary difference on the benefit side is that private benefits consist largely of the extra income earned as a consequence of securing the education, while social benefits include both this income and external benefits such as the values of literacy, lower

crime rates, and improved public health and sanitation. In many instances, the difference between social and private costs exceeds the difference between social and private benefits; thus, social rates of return are often less than private rates of return. This is especially true when applied to college education, where the external benefits are small, at best.

The table depicts rates of return on investment in primary, secondary, and tertiary education. Tertiary education is advanced, or post-secondary, education, including college education.

The estimates reported in this table indicate that investment in education is a productive use of society's resources throughout the world. It promises relatively higher rates of return, however, in lesser-developed countries and at lower levels of education. The higher rates in lesser-developed countries reflect the relatively greater shortage of educated people at all levels in these countries. The decline in the rate of return as the level of education increases reflects two primary factors: (1) costs per student increase as the level of education increases and (2) the external benefits of education are associated mostly with primary education, less with secondary education, and minimally with tertiary education.

The rates in this table are probably high enough to justify investment in education at all levels throughout the world, but they do indicate that the less-developed countries should give a high priority to achieving universal primary and secondary education before they build college systems that rival those in

These programs typically provide three types of subsidies to students: (1) the use of money for some period of time before interest is charged, (2) interest rates below those charged on comparable loans to other individuals, and (3) government reimbursement to private lenders for defaulted loans. These subsidies together probably amount to as much as 25 percent of the value of loans issued to college students each year. Given the current rate of lending of this type, the total subsidy is close to $500 per student per year. Can such a subsidy be justified when a college education yields the high rates of return to individual borrowers that we have previously identified?

Loan subsidies are normally justified either as a corrective for capital market failures or as a means of making college more affordable for the borrower. Here our attention is focused on the former justification.

the developed countries. It probably makes more sense for most of these countries to send their high school graduates to the developed countries for higher education than to build their own colleges and universities themselves, at least in the earlier stages of development.

It is worth noting, finally, that the rate of return on tertiary education in the developed countries is quite low compared to the private rates of return cited elsewhere in this chapter for college education in the United States. This could be due to lower rates of return in other countries in the developed countries group than those in the United States, but it probably reflects the fact that social rates of return on college education are less than private rates of return.

AVERAGE SOCIAL RATE OF RETURN ON INVESTMENT IN EDUCATION BY GEOGRAPHICAL REGION AND LEVEL OF EDUCATION (PERCENTAGES)

	Level of Education		
Region	**Primary**	**Secondary**	**Tertiary**
Africa	26	17	13
Asia	27	15	13
Latin America	26	18	16
Developed countries	NA	11	9

Notes: African countries included are Ghana, Kenya, Uganda, and Nigeria. Asian countries included are India and the Philippines. Latin American countries included are Mexico, Colombia, Venezuela, Chile, and Brazil. Developed countries included are the United States, the United Kingdom, Canada, the Netherlands, and Belgium. Information on the rate of return to investment in primary education in the developed countries was not available because there was no group of illiterates to serve as a control group.

Source: George Psacharopoulos, "Returns to Education: A Further International Update and Implications," *Journal of Human Resources* 20 (April 1985): 583–604.

College students, as a group, constitute a very attractive pool of borrowers. Lenders are well aware of the facts that typical college graduates will realize a higher lifetime income than typical nongraduates and have a lower rate of unemployment throughout their working lifetimes. But lenders do not deal with the group; they deal with specific individuals, and they know that there is a greater risk of individual financial difficulty than of group financial difficulty.

The same problem arises, however, for many groups of individuals with which lenders do business. Lenders normally protect themselves in these instances by requiring collateral for a loan; for example, the lender owns the car or the house until the loan is repaid. This protection is not available for student loans; that is, students cannot serve as collateral. This makes a loan to a specific individual relatively risky and requires the lender to charge a relatively high rate of interest to cover this risk.

There is a conflict, then, between individual and group risk in the market for college student loans: group risk is small but individual risk is high. In this instance, the government guarantee against default makes good sense. The guarantee provides the necessary collateral and the government assumes the relatively low risk associated with lending to college students as a group. Defaults will occur, but that is to be expected, and they could not be eliminated under any conceivable financing arrangement.

What is true of the government guarantee against default, however, is not necessarily true of the other types of government subsidies to student borrowers. Given government guarantees, the market for student loans would function quite well in meeting demand without the provision of interest-free periods or below-market interest rates. These two provisions can probably be justified only as means of making college more affordable or accessible to certain groups of students.

MAKING COLLEGE MORE ACCESSIBLE

Suppose we accept the argument that government subsidies to college students are justified as a means of ensuring greater access to low-income students. This section examines existing subsidies to determine how well they have accomplished this objective.

PELL GRANTS   The largest federal government subsidy to higher education is the Pell grant. Pell grants provide cash assistance directly to students enrolled in college, based on their own and their parents' income and assets.

The Pell grant is an income-tested transfer payment—one in which the payment falls as income rises. Pell grants are not confined, however, to students from low-income families. First, students from families with middle-class incomes are eligible for a grant. Second, the grant award tends to be larger for students attending more expensive schools, and attendees at these institutions are more likely to come from higher income families. Third, some of the students from higher income families establish independent status so that they can qualify for a Pell grant on the basis of their income instead of their parents' income. In spite of these factors, however, overall the proportion of students receiving Pell grants declines as family income rises.

The Pell grant lowers the net cost, or price, of a college education. The law of demand (see Chapter 3) predicts that this will result in an increase in enrollment. The earliest empirical studies of the relationship between grants and enrollment seemed to indicate that federal grants did little, if anything, to increase enrollment of students from low-income families.[4] More recent studies, however,

---

[4]See W. Lee Hansen, "Impact of Student Financial Aid on Access," in *The Crisis in Higher Education*, ed. Joseph Froomkin (New York: Academy of Political Science, 1983), 84–96.

provide strong evidence of a positive effect of Pell grants on college enrollment by low-income students. According to Manski and Wise,[5] the Pell grant program, as it existed in 1979–1980, increased enrollments among low-income students by 4.9 percent for each $100 in grant funds. According to McPherson and Schapiro, each $100 in grant funds increased enrollment by low-income students by about 1.6 percent over the 1974–1984 period.[6] Results such as these have led many observers to conclude that the Pell grant program, and others that are targeted primarily to lower-income students, are at least moderately successful in increasing the number of lower-income students who attend college.

TUITION SUBSIDIES   The largest source of subsidies to college students is the money appropriated by state legislatures for higher education: $35.3 billion in 1990–1991. If this money had not been available to institutions of higher learning, they would have had to increase tuition by this much to provide the same level of services. Thus, state appropriations provide a large **tuition subsidy.**

Tuition Subsidy
State appropriations used to subsidize tuition at institutions of higher education.

The concern here is with the distribution across income classes of this subsidy. It seems likely that, in many states, a large part of the tuition subsidy is received by upper-middle-income and high-income families. This pattern follows from the structure of higher education. Public institutions of higher learning are arranged according to a three-tiered structure in many states: junior colleges, four-year colleges, and comprehensive universities. It is likely that educational costs increase more than tuition in moving from the junior colleges to the comprehensive universities; thus, the tuition subsidy is greater the more comprehensive the institution. It is also likely that students from lower-income and lower-middle-income families are over-represented in less comprehensive institutions and underrepresented in more comprehensive institutions. Thus, tuition subsidies are directly related to family income.

State-provided tuition subsidies are similar to Pell grants, then, in the sense that part of the money provided in this fashion—perhaps a large part in the case of tuition subsidies—has little to do with increasing access to higher education by students from lower-income families. We are aware of no studies that have examined the effect of tuition subsidies on lower-income students per se, but the small share that they do receive may raise the enrollment rate of such students—also in a fashion similar to the Pell grants.

In both cases, the subsidy turns out to be very inefficient in achieving the objective of increasing access by lower-income students. In fact, this objective could be achieved at lower total cost by more precisely targeting a smaller sum of money. The fact that governments have not embraced this tactic, even in times of relatively great fiscal stress, suggests to us that governments are trying to appeal to a much broader constituency than lower-income families when they provide support to colleges and college students. The politics of higher education finance,

---

[5]Charles F. Manski and David A. Wise, *College Choice in America* (Cambridge, MA.: Harvard University Press, 1983).

[6]Michael S. McPherson and Morton Owen Schapiro, "Does Student Aid Affect College Enrollment?" *American Economic Review* 81, no. 1 (1991), 309–18.

that is, may only vaguely resemble the economics of higher education finance. In the state where the authors live, for example, the legislature has turned down more than one requested tuition increase on the grounds that it would reduce the enrollment of middle-income students.

SUMMARY

A college education is a large investment for students. Governments also invest heavily in this endeavor by subsidizing student and institutional expenditures. In this chapter, we explain how economists evaluate college education as an investment—from both the student's and society's perspective.

The soundness of an investment is determined by comparing its benefits and costs. We distinguish between two types of benefits and costs: those easy to value in dollars and those not easy to value this way. The primary source of benefits in dollars to college graduates is the increase they realize in lifetime earnings. The principal costs in dollars to students are tuition, books, and supplies, the earnings they forgo, and the income they forgo on alternative investments.

We illustrate how benefits and costs are measured and compared, using an example for a hypothetical college student. Actual data show that the typical four-year college degree yields real rates of return greater than 11 percent.

Governments provide financial support to college students and their host institutions through loan subsidies and appropriations. This support is justified, arguably, as a means of financing external benefits, correcting capital market failure, and enhancing accessibility.

There appears to be little need for the financing of external benefits. Government loan guarantees appear to be justified, but interest-free loan periods and below-market rates of interest are not necessary to make the market for student loans function properly.

We examined the Pell grant program to determine whether it is likely to increase access to higher education. The Pell grant is not structured to provide aid solely to lower-income students; recent empirical evidence, however, indicates that Pell-type grants have improved access to higher education for lower-income students.

Tuition subsidies in the form of state appropriations are also evaluated. The typical pattern of tuition subsidies may help to improve access to a college education for lower-income students, but they are an inefficient method for doing so. This may not be their intended purpose, however.

KEY TERMS

Rate of return   External benefits of education   Tuition subsidy

REVIEW QUESTIONS

1. Using the following data and an interest rate of 5 percent (.05), calculate the sums of the PVBs and the PVCs. Also determine the rate of return:

t	B	C
0	$ 0	$3,000
1	1,100	0
2	1,210	0
3	1,331	0

2. Using graphical analysis, explain how expected lifetime earnings profiles and various costs relate to an individual's decision to invest in a college education.
3. Explain why benefits and costs must be adjusted for time of occurrence.
4. Explain the costs and benefits of a college education that are not easy to value in dollars. Do they appear to be a source of a higher or a lower rate of return to a bachelors degree? Explain.
5. Some estimates show that rates of return on investment in a college education are highest for black females. Explain why, using the effects identified in this chapter.
6. Discuss the three external benefits claimed for education. Do they justify government support of college education?
7. "Government subsidies have substantially increased the access of low-income students to higher education." Is this statement true or false? Defend your answer.
8. Evaluate government loan programs as a means of providing financial support to college students.

SUGGESTIONS FOR FURTHER READING

Fischer, Frederick. "State Financing of Higher Education: A New Look at an Old Problem" *Change* (January/February 1990), 42–56. A review and critical evaluation of the current system used by the state and federal governments to finance higher education, followed by a proposal for reform of the federal government's programs of student aid.

Halstead, Kent. *State Profiles: Financing Public Higher Education—1978–1992.* Washington, DC: Research Associates of Washington, 1992. A compendium of data on higher education finances, compiled by state. Contains estimates of who pays for higher education from a lifetime perspective.

Hansen, W. Lee, and Robert J. Lampman. "Basic Opportunity Grants for Higher Education: Good Intentions and Mixed Results." In *Public Expenditure and Policy Analysis,* 2nd ed., ed. by Robert Haveman and Julius Margolis, 493–512. Boston: Houghton-Mifflin, 1983. An evaluation of the features of what is now the Pell grant program and an assessment of its probable effect on college enrollment by lower-income students.

Hauptman, Arthur. *The Tuition Dilemma.* Washington, DC: The Brookings Institution, 1990. A guide through the maze of college financing that explains the pressures leading to the development of new financing plans and examines the various options that are being discussed.

Leslie, Larry L., and Paul T. Brinkman. "Student Price Response in Higher Education." *Journal of Higher Education* 58, no. 2 (1987), 181–204. An extensive review of the literature on student demand for a college education, including summary tables that indicate the percentage change in enrollment per $100 increase in price. Beginning students will have some difficulty in understanding the authors' comparative method, but they should benefit from the authors' perspective on college education as an economic choice.

McPherson, Michael S., and Morton Owen Schapiro. *Keeping College Affordable.* Washington, DC: The Brookings Institution, 1991. This book evaluates the role of federal and state legislatures in subsidizing higher education and keeping college affordable for all prospective students. Contains projections of trends in college affordability.

9

SOCIAL SECURITY

Where Are We? Where Are We Going?

TERMS YOU SHOULD KNOW

Present value (Chapter 8)

Rate of return (Chapter 8)

During much of U.S. history, the elderly have been plagued by economic insecurity. Growing old has often meant the loss of the breadwinner's job and a drastic reduction in family income. During the worst years of the Great Depression of the 1930s, many older people were literally penniless. The "poorhouses" and other public and private relief efforts of the time could meet only part of the needs of the elderly poor.

Acting on his belief that the federal government had an obligation to these people, President Franklin D. Roosevelt appointed the Committee on Economic Security to study the problem and make recommendations to Congress. The committee's recommendations were embodied in the Social Security Act of 1935. This law provided, among other things, for a federal system of old-age benefits for retired workers who had been employed in industry and commerce.

Since then, Social Security has grown to be the largest income-maintenance program in the United States. Social Security still provides money for its original purpose: to replace, in part, the income lost when a worker retires. Benefits are also paid to workers who become severely disabled, to the survivors of workers who die, and to the elderly for medical care (Medicare).

In 1994, nearly 139 million people were engaged in work covered by Social Security and more than 42 million people were receiving cash benefits.

These benefits have helped greatly to improve the economic status of the elderly. But the Social Security program has problems, including low rates of return to taxpayers, adverse effects on investment and the labor supply, and a prospective long-run deficit. These are issues of individual and social importance. In this chapter, we provide the basic information and principles essential for understanding them.

SOCIAL SECURITY: HOW IT WORKS

Social Security
All social insurance programs established by the Social Security Act or, as used in this chapter, the Old-Age and Survivors' Insurance (OASI) Program alone.

Social Security in the broadest sense includes all the social insurance programs established by the Social Security Act. But the term is often used, as it is in this chapter, to refer to the Old-Age and Survivors' Insurance (OASI) Program.

Benefits paid by OASI were more than $284 billion in 1994. They were financed largely by a tax levied on the wages and salaries of covered employees, on employers' payrolls, and on the income of self-employed individuals. In 1995, employers and employees each paid 5.6 percent, for a combined rate of 11.2 percent on maximum taxable earnings up to $61,200.

The Social Security payroll tax is the second largest source of federal government revenue, exceeded only by the individual income tax. Revenues from the payroll tax are deposited in the OASI Trust Fund. Table 9.1 shows the status of this fund for 1994. OASI revenues came largely (93 percent) from payroll tax collections, but the OASI Trust Fund also received revenues from interest earnings on assets and from federal income taxes levied on Social Security benefits of higher-income retirees. Over 99 percent of expenditures were paid as benefits to retirees; administrative costs account for the rest. Assets were the funds on hand at the end of 1994.

TABLE 9.1		
Revenues	Expenditures	Assets
$328.3	$284.1	$413.5

The OASI Trust Fund receives a continuous flow of revenues from the Social Security payroll tax, the federal individual income tax, and interest earned on trust fund assets, and it makes monthly payments to Social Security beneficiaries. Trust fund assets accumulate whenever annual revenues exceed annual expenditures.

Source: *The 1995 Annual Report of the Board of Trustees of the Federal Old-Age and Survivors Insurance and the Federal Disability Insurance Trust Funds.* Washington, DC: Government Printing Office, 1995.

OASI TRUST FUND, 1994 (BILLIONS OF DOLLARS)

Social Security is *social* retirement insurance. As such, it differs in some important respects from *private* retirement insurance. Failure to appreciate these differences has caused misunderstanding about the nature of Social Security. Table 9.2 lists the basic ways in which Social Security, as an example of social insurance, differs from private retirement insurance.

First, individuals are free to purchase the amount of private insurance they want, but Social Security taxes are compulsory for all persons in covered employment (over 95 percent of the labor force).

Second, until recently Social Security has been primarily financed on a pay-as-you-go basis. Private insurance is financed on a fully-funded basis. In a **pay-as-you-go insurance plan,** annual revenues are not much larger than annual expenditures. This was the case for Social Security until recently. Now annual revenues exceed annual expenditures by enough that the OASI Trust Fund grows by a significant amount each year ($44.1 billion in 1994). Social Security is still a long way, however, from being fully funded. In a **fully-funded insurance plan,** annual expenditures can be funded largely by interest income; annual revenues are not normally used to fund annual expenditures.

Third, because Social Security has traditionally operated on a pay-as-you-go basis, the OASI Trust Fund has been largely a **buffer fund**—a fund large enough to cover only unexpected short-run changes in revenues or expenditures. Private insurance trust funds are large enough to cover both unexpected short-run contingencies and all long-run obligations. The OASI Trust Fund will accumulate a large enough asset balance in the next 20 years that it will be sufficient to pay for several years' obligations. Yet it is not projected to become large enough to fund all future obligations fully.

Fourth, both private retirement insurance and Social Security provide periodic benefit payments to retirees. There are differences, however, in how these benefits are determined.

For private insurance, the periodic benefit reflects the **principle of individual contribution.** The simplest version of this principle is that the size of the

Pay-as-You-Go Insurance Plan
A plan in which annual expenditures are primarily financed by current annual revenues.

Fully-Funded Insurance Plan
A plan in which annual expenditures are funded by income earned on assets.

Buffer Fund
An insurance reserve fund composed of assets intended to cover unexpected short-run declines in revenues or increases in expenditures.

Principle of Individual Contribution
Individuals' insurance benefits are directly related to their contributions and the conditions under which these contributions are invested.

SOCIAL VERSUS PRIVATE RETIREMENT INSURANCE: DIFFERENCES IN KEY FEATURES

	TABLE 9.2	
	Key Features	
Source of Difference	**Private Insurance**	**Social Insurance**
Nature of participation	Voluntary	Compulsory
Method of financing	Fully funded	Pay as you go
Role of trust funds	Insurance reserve	Buffer
Determinants of benefits	Individual contribution	Individual contribution and equity considerations

Social Security is a social retirement insurance program. Social retirement insurance can differ in several ways from private retirement insurance, as illustrated.

benefit payment is in direct proportion to the amount contributed by the beneficiary. More generally, benefits vary directly with the size of the preretirement contribution, the length of time contributions are invested in income-earning assets, the average annual rate of return on investment, and the age at retirement. Later retirement results in higher benefits because it lengthens the time over which investment earnings accumulate and shortens the benefit pay-out period.

Social Security is similar to private retirement insurance in that payments are directly related to contributions (in the form of payroll taxes) and to age at retirement. Social Security payments are more generous, however, for retirees with lower preretirement earnings. They are also more generous for retirees with spouses and dependents than for retirees who are single and without dependents.

Table 9.3 shows the relationship between the annual Social Security benefit in the first year of retirement and wages in the preceding year before taxes (gross wages) for three typical workers retiring in 1995 at age 65. The average-wage worker earned $23,708 in 1994 and received Social Security benefits of $9,744 in 1995. For this worker, Social Security benefits replaced 41.1 percent of 1994 earnings—a **gross replacement rate** of .411.

Table 9.3 shows that Social Security benefits increase as wages increase but not as rapidly as wages increase. Thus, the gross replacement rate is larger for low-wage workers than for average-wage or high-wage workers. This is a clear indication that Social Security is more generous to retirees with lower preretirement wages.

The benefits noted are for single workers who retire at age 65. These amounts are reduced for persons who retire between age 62 (the earliest age at which Social Security benefits can be received) and age 65 and increased for persons who retire between age 65 and age 70. These benefits are increased by 50 percent for a retiree with a spouse, provided that the spouse does not qualify for a larger payment on the basis of his or her own earnings record. Retirees also receive additional benefits for dependents. Private insurers do not pay more to retirees for their spouses and dependents, but they do provide larger payments to those who retire later and penalize those who retire earlier.

Gross Replacement Rate
The ratio of the retirement benefit in the first year to before-tax wages in the year before retirement.

TABLE 9.3			
	Low-Wage Worker	**Average-Wage Worker**	**High-Wage Worker**
Benefits in 1995	$5,904	$9,744	$13,599
1994 before-tax wages	$10,657	$23,708	$57,868
Gross replacement rate	.554	.411	.235

Social Security benefits replace over 55 percent of preretirement before-tax earnings for low-wage workers. The replacement percentage falls, however, as wages increase.

Source: C. Eugene Steuerle and Jon M. Bakija, *Retooling Social Security for the 21st Century*, Washington, DC: The Urban Institute Press (1994), 260–61.

DETERMINATION OF THE GROSS REPLACEMENT RATE FOR LOW-, AVERAGE-, AND HIGH-WAGE WORKERS RETIRING IN 1995 AT AGE 65

Social Security benefits received after retirement increase each year at the same rate as the Consumer Price Index (CPI), unlike private retirement insurance benefits, which are not indexed for price increases.

Social Security benefits will be paid to insured retirees, *provided* that their earnings after retirement stay below a certain level. In 1995, retirees who were 65 to 70 years old could earn up to $11,280 per year without any decrease in benefits. Retirees 62 to 64 could earn up to $8,160 without penalty. These amounts are scheduled to increase each year at the same rate as the national average wage.

For earnings above the penalty-free levels, benefits are reduced by an **earnings penalty** of $1 for each $3 earned. Such a penalty is unheard of for private retirement insurance.

Workers who do not retire at age 65 receive extra Social Security benefits when they do retire. Their basic benefit is increased by a delayed retirement credit of 4 percent for each year retirement is delayed up to age 70. This credit is scheduled to increase gradually to 8 percent per year by 2009.

Finally, income from Social Security is treated more favorably in the federal tax code than is income from private retirement insurance. The latter is fully subject to taxation. Only part of Social Security benefits are subject to the federal income tax, however.

Earnings Penalty
A reduction in Social Security benefits because postretirement earnings exceed a certain level.

SOCIAL SECURITY INCOME

The average monthly benefit from Social Security in 1994 was $697. Column 2 in Table 9.4 shows how the average monthly benefit paid to individual retirees has grown since the first Social Security checks were issued in 1940. Column 3 provides data on the price index for personal consumption expenditures for comparison. Consumer prices were about 9 times larger in 1994 than in 1940, while the average monthly benefit check from Social Security in 1994 was over 30 times larger than in 1940. Clearly, Social Security benefits have increased significantly in terms of purchasing power over the last half-century.

	TABLE 9.4	
Year	**Average Monthly Benefit**	**Index of Consumer Prices (1987 = 100)**
1940	$23	14.7
1950	44	24.2
1960	74	30.8
1970	118	37.9
1980	341	72.6
1994	697	131.3

Monthly Social Security benefits are more than 29 times larger than they were 54 years ago. Moreover, they have grown faster than the CPI.

Source: Social Security Administration, Office of Information Systems, *Executive Handbook of Selected Data,* May 1987; *Social Security Bulletin, Annual Statistical Supplement, 1994;* U.S. Department of Commerce, *Survey of Current Business,* September 1994. All are published by the Government Printing Office, Washington, DC.

Social Security benefits are an important source of income to the elderly. In 1992, Social Security provided 50 percent or more of family income to 63 percent of the elderly.

These data suggest that there would be a relatively high incidence of poverty among the elderly in the absence of Social Security. In fact, the average poverty rate for the elderly was less than the poverty rate for the population as a whole, 12.2 versus 13.5 percent, in 1990. This would not have been true without Social Security. Social Security benefits were high enough to keep 38 percent of the elderly out of poverty in 1992.

SOCIAL SECURITY AS AN INVESTMENT

Social Security benefits, like most good things in life, are not free. The typical retiree pays Social Security taxes over a working lifetime of 40 to 50 years and receives 15 to 20 years of retirement benefits. There is considerable interest among taxpayers, then, as to whether the benefits they are likely to receive constitute an adequate pay-off for the investment they are likely to make in terms of Social Security taxes.

Suppose that the individual in question is a male born in 1975 who enters the labor force for the first time in 1996, after earning a bachelors degree. His starting salary is $30,000, about one-half of the maximum taxable Social Security wage. His salary will grow rapidly during the first stage of his career and by the time our subject is 40 he will have achieved a salary equal to the maximum taxable Social Security wage at that time. His salary stays above the maximum taxable

Social Security wage for the remainder of his career. He retires at the normal retirement age (then) of 67, never having married. Assuming an annual rate of growth in real (inflation-adjusted) wages of 1.2 percent (the rate assumed by Social Security planners), this individual can expect to pay more than $380,000 in real Social Security taxes, including the contributions that both he and his employer will make.

Is his first year of retirement (2043), our subject will receive approximately $24,000 in real benefits from Social Security (a little more than one-fourth of his real earnings in 2042). His annual benefit increases each year through an inflation adjustment, but this is just enough, of course, to keep his real benefits constant. Thus, he expects to receive $24,000 each year until he dies. If he is typical of males at that time, he should receive this amount for 15 years, or total Social Security benefits of $360,000.

Is his investment in Social Security sound from a financial perspective? It certainly does not appear to be, in as much as the sum of expected benefits is less than the sum of expected costs. But this is not an appropriate test (as explained in Chapter 8) because neither the benefits nor the costs have been adjusted for time of occurrence. One way to do this is to calculate the present value of each benefit and cost, sum the present values of the benefits (PVBs) and the costs (PVCs), and compare them; if the sum of the PVBs exceeds the sum of the PVCs, the investment is financially sound. The other way to adjust for time of occurrence is to calculate the rate of return, or the interest rate at which the sums of the PVBs and PVCs are equal. If the rate of return is more than the investor can earn on his best alternative, the investment is financially sound.

We have calculated the present values of the benefits and costs and summed them, using an interest rate of 2 percent. This is the same rate Social Security planners use to represent the real rate of interest earned historically on safe, long-term securities. The sums of the present values of benefits and costs are approximately $129,000 and $254,000, respectively. Thus, Social Security is not a wise investment for this individual if he can earn 2 percent or more on his money. Note that the sum of the PVCs exceeds the sum of the PVBs by more ($125,000) than the unadjusted costs exceed the unadjusted benefits ($20,000). This happens because the benefits occur later than the costs; consequently, the discounting or adjustment procedure reduces the value of the benefits more than the value of the costs.

We have also calculated the rate of return as −0.15 percent. This seemingly peculiar result follows from the fact that the unadjusted sum of the costs exceeds the unadjusted sum of the benefits. What it means is that the lender (taxpayer) is actually paying the borrower (Social Security) a small premium of 0.15 percent per year. It is equivalent to putting $1,000 in the bank and having a balance of only $985 at the end of the year, because the bank paid no interest, but charged a $15 fee, instead.

Although this is an assumed case, the numbers we have used are similar to those used by other economists to determine the real rate of return to the typical single male born in 1975 who can expect to earn a high wage throughout his working lifetime. Steuerle and Bakija's estimate for such a person is a real rate of return of −0.13 percent, as noted in Table 9.5. Actually, this table contains estimates of the real rate of return on taxes invested in Social Security for representative household units of four types of Social Security retirees: males and females who remain single all their working lives, husbands with wives who never work, and husbands with wives who always work but receive a lower wage than the husband. Each of the four types is assumed to have three possible preretirement wage histories—low, average, and high—or the combinations for two-earner couples indicated in the notes to Table 9.5. The retiree unit is assumed to pay *all* of the Social Security taxes that are collected on preretirement wages; that is, employers are assumed successful in shifting their half of Social Security taxes to workers by reducing their wages. All of the individuals in this illustration are assumed born in 1975 (around the year of birth of many of our readers) and assumed to retire in 2040 at age 65 (two years earlier than the normal retirement age at that time). Each individual is assumed to work without interruption from age 21 to age 65, and the estimates reflect adjustments for the probability of death in each year after age 21.

Estimates of real rates of return are available for individuals born in other years, but the 1975 age group shows levels and patterns of rates that will be typical of those earned by both their parents and their children. Four patterns are obvious.

First, real rates of return decrease as preretirement wages increase. This reflects a Social Security benefit formula that favors lower-wage retirees, the same formula that produces gross replacement rates that are also more generous for lower-wage retirees.

Second, real rates of return are higher for females than for males. This result can be attributed to the fact that females are expected to live longer than males; thus, they will receive benefits for a longer period of time.

Third, married couples receive higher real rates of return from investing in Social Security than unmarried individuals. This occurs because Social Security benefits are paid to all wives who do not work, based on their husbands' wage

REAL RATES OF RETURN FROM TAXES INVESTED IN SOCIAL SECURITY BY INDIVIDUALS BORN IN 1975

TABLE 9.5

Household Unit	Low Wage	Average Wage	High Wage
Single Male	1.98	1.12	−0.13
Single Female	2.70	1.97	0.71
One-Earner Couple	4.25	3.41	2.20
Two-Earner Couple	2.65[a]	2.34[b]	1.18[c]

[a]Low-wage man married to a low-wage woman
[b]Average-wage man married to a low-wage woman
[c]High-wage man married to an average-wage woman

Source: C. Eugene Steuerle and Jon M. Bakija, *Retooling Social Security for the 21st Century* (Washington, DC: The Urban Institute Press, 1994), 282.

history. Social Security benefits are also assumed to be paid to lower-wage working wives on the basis of the earnings of higher-wage husbands.

Fourth, married one-earner couples receive higher real rates of return than married two-earner couples. The basic reason this occurs is that, for couples in which the husbands have the same wage histories, one-earner couples pay less in Social Security taxes than two-earner couples.

We view the one-earner couple as a rapidly vanishing breed and the two-earner couple as the most likely case. Thus, we expect that the typical reader of this text (who we assume will be in the average or high wage category) will receive a 1 to 2 percent real rate of return on Social Security.

This will seem to many readers like a very low rate of return compared to other investments. Is it? Real rates of return on several important alternatives available to private investors have been within this range. Long-term U.S. government bonds earned a 1.7 percent average real rate of return from 1926 to 1994, and corporate bonds generated a 2.3 percent real rate of return. Common stocks have done much better, however, earning a real rate of return of 7.7 percent before taxes between 1926 and 1994, and the before-tax real rate of return on private corporate investment has averaged about 10 percent since World War II.

The prospect of higher returns on stocks and corporate investment leads many to believe that they would be better off if they could opt out of Social Security and invest their payroll tax dollars in the private sector. There is more involved in this choice, however, than simple comparisons of rates of return.

First, although rates of return in the private sector are higher on average, they are subject to considerable variation. For example, there is a one-third chance that rates of return on stocks could be as much as 21 percentage points lower than 6 percent, and a one-third chance that they could be as much as 21 percentage points higher. Thus, significantly greater risk is associated with private investment. In fact, much of the differential between private rates of return and returns on government securities reflects a premium necessary to compensate investors for the extra risk involved in private investment; that is, the risk premium merely compensates for the costs associated with uncertainty. Thus a private alternative paying 6 percent with a risk premium of 4 percent is equivalent to a risk-free Social Security fund paying 2 percent.

Second, private investments are not indexed for inflation, whereas Social Security benefits are indexed to keep pace with inflation. Thus, income from private investment is at greater risk of purchasing power erosion due to inflation. Risk-averse individuals should be willing to accept a lower rate of return on Social Security because of the inflation protection it provides.

Third, for people who end up with low lifetime income, Social Security provides a safety net in the form of benefits that are disproportionately large relative to taxes paid. Private securities do not offer this kind of protection; thus they expose individuals to greater risk of poverty than does Social Security. Risk-averse individuals should be willing to accept a lower rate of return on Social Security for the poverty protection it provides.

In summary, it is quite possible that the benefits offered by Social Security in the form of reduced risk, inflation indexing of retirement benefits, and insurance against old-age poverty may be enough to make up the difference between rates of return on private securities and Social Security.

EFFECTS ON SAVINGS

The fact that many of the elderly depend so heavily on Social Security as a source of income suggests to some economists that the prospect of Social Security benefits induces people to save less of their preretirement income. If people do save less, then private investment will be less, resulting ultimately in a smaller GDP.

Social Security can reduce aggregate saving as follows. Workers assume that Social Security will provide them with a guaranteed annual retirement income. This prospect frees up some of their preretirement income, allowing them to increase their consumption each year prior to retirement; that is, to save less. Social Security is said to have a **wealth substitution effect** if it induces workers to substitute Social Security wealth (the present value of the benefits expected from Social Security) for other types of wealth, such as private pensions.

It is not obvious, however, that the only effect of Social Security is an inducement to save less. The availability of Social Security benefits may induce people to retire earlier, which will increase their need to save more for retirement. In fact, as will be shown later in this chapter, there is some evidence of such an **induced retirement effect** of Social Security.

Another possibility is that working people realize that their children will have to pay the Social Security taxes that will support them in their retirement. This may induce workers to increase their saving so as to increase the bequests they leave to their children. A few economists believe that this **bequest effect** of Social Security is important.

Finally, suppose that without Social Security, children normally would bear the burden of supporting their aging parents out of their current earnings; that is, that parents normally would save little for their own retirement. Under these circumstances, Social Security would not affect private saving; direct support of aging parents by children would merely be replaced by payroll tax support.

Given this variety of possibilities, the relationship between Social Security and saving must be determined by empirical analysis.

Martin Feldstein is well known for his studies of this relationship. In the latest of several studies, Feldstein analyzed annual U.S. data from 1929 to 1976.[1] He found that, over this period, an increase of $1 in Social Security wealth was associated with a decrease in saving of $.018. He interpreted this result as evidence that the wealth substitution effect outweighs the other effects of Social Security.

How significant is this relationship between Social Security wealth and saving? Social Security wealth was more than $5,000 billion in 1990. An amount this large reduced saving by at least $90 billion (= .018 × $5,000 billion).

Wealth Substitution Effect
An effect that induces workers to substitute one type of wealth (Social Security) for other types that could be financed by saving.

Induced Retirement Effect
The tendency of Social Security benefits to encourage people to retire earlier than they would in their absence.

Bequest Effect
The tendency of Social Security to induce working people to increase their saving so as to increase the bequests they leave their children.

---

[1]Martin Feldstein, "Social Security and Private Savings: Reply," *Journal of Political Economy* 90 (June 1982), 630–42.

If Feldstein's estimate is correct, Social Security has had an important negative impact on the capital stock and consequently on productivity and GDP. There is considerable dispute among economists, however, about the accuracy and significance of his findings. In fact, other studies have produced significantly different results. Munnell found a negative, but smaller, effect of Social Security on saving—only about one-fourth of the impact that Feldstein estimated.[2] Leimer and Lesnoy found that Social Security wealth could actually increase saving, depending on how Social Security wealth was estimated.[3] More recently, Bernheim and Levin, using new measures of expected Social Security benefits, found that expected Social Security wealth reduced the savings of single individuals by $1.21 for each dollar of Social Security wealth, but that it had no effect on the saving behavior of couples.[4]

Given the mixed results of the empirical research, we cannot say for certain how much Social Security affects private saving. It would seem premature, however, to rule out the possibility of some negative impact.

EFFECTS ON WORK DECISIONS

Economists also are interested in whether Social Security induces people to change their work plans.

Social Security may affect three basic work decisions: the number of hours worked by preretirees, the number of hours worked by retirees, and the age of retirement from full-time employment. In all cases, Social Security may have a negative impact.

First, because the payroll tax reduces the hourly reward from working, workers may work fewer hours. Second, as noted earlier, retirees are penalized by a reduction in their Social Security benefits when their postretirement earnings exceed a certain level. This earnings penalty is similar to a payroll tax on labor income, so it may also cause workers to work fewer hours. Third, the expectation of Social Security benefits may induce people to retire earlier than they would otherwise.

THE PAYROLL TAX EFFECT

Two general models of the work decision may be used to examine the effect of the payroll tax on hours worked; they are the current-period and the life-cycle models. In the current-period model, workers perceive no link between payroll taxes and future Social Security benefits. In the life-cycle model, workers perceive the tax as a means of acquiring retirement benefits.

[2]Alicia H. Munnell, *The Future of Social Security* (Washington, DC: The Brookings Institution, 1977).
[3]Dean R. Leimer and Selig D. Lesnoy, "Social Security and Private Saving: New Time Series Evidence," *Journal of Political Economy* 90 (June 1982), 606–29.
[4]B. Douglas Bernheim and Lawrence Levin, "Social Security and Personal Saving: An Analysis of Expectations," *American Economic Review* 79 (May 1989), 97–102.

The current-period model can be summarized in the form of a supply-demand diagram for the labor market. Figure 9.1 contains two diagrams that illustrate the range of opinion regarding the effect of payroll taxes.

Figure 9.1a depicts the view that the tax reduces hours worked. In the absence of the payroll tax, the market is in equilibrium at wage W_1 and hours H_1. The employers' tax share, T_e, reduces the wage they are willing to pay by 5.6 percent at each wage level. This effect is illustrated by the downward shift in demand to $D - T_e$. The workers' tax share, T_w, is also remitted by the employer to the government. Thus, employers' willingness to pay for labor is reduced by a further 5.6 percent at each wage level. This effect is shown by the further downward shift in demand to $D - T_e - T_w$. The two effects together produce a lower equilibrium wage, W_2, and fewer hours worked, H_2.

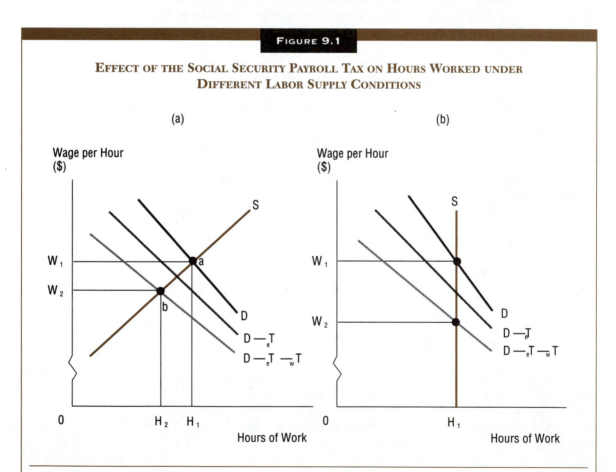

FIGURE 9.1

EFFECT OF THE SOCIAL SECURITY PAYROLL TAX ON HOURS WORKED UNDER DIFFERENT LABOR SUPPLY CONDITIONS

The payroll tax consists of the employer's share, T_e, and the worker's share, T_w. Because both shares are remitted by the employer to the tax authority, employers reduce the wage they are willing to pay by the full amount of the tax, reducing the demand for labor from D to $D - T_e - T_w$. If the labor supply curve is upward sloping, hours of work fall from H_1 to H_2. There is no reduction in hours worked with a vertical labor supply curve, as in (b).

Figure 9.1b illustrates the case in which the payroll tax has no effect on hours worked. The tax has the same effects on the demand side of the labor market as in Figure 9.1a. In this case, however, the labor supply curve is vertical.

If the labor supply curve is vertical, the payroll tax will lower the equilibrium after-tax wage to W_2. The tax, however, will not change the hours worked. In this case, workers pay the entire payroll tax; wages would be W_1 in the absence of the tax.

These examples clearly show that the key to whether the payroll tax reduces hours worked is the slope of the labor supply curve. In general, the steeper the slope, the smaller the reduction in hours worked.

What is the evidence on the slope of the labor supply curve? Brittain found evidence suggesting a vertical supply curve.[5] Beach and Balfour, however, found evidence for Great Britain that suggests an upward-sloping supply curve for female workers.[6] This result implies a negative effect on hours worked, but not necessarily for the United States.

What if individuals base their work decision on life-cycle considerations instead of the current-period wage? Within this context, workers would perceive that taxes "buy" future benefits. The largest adverse effect on work effort would occur if workers assigned a value of zero to future benefits, acting as they do in the current-period model. If they calculate that the present value of benefits from Social Security is at least as great as the present value of the taxes they pay, then hours worked will not be affected. Some workers making this calculation could even decide to increase their work hours to qualify for greater future benefits. Thus, if labor supply decisions are based on the life-cycle model, it is more likely that the effect of the payroll tax on hours worked will be insignificant.

THE EFFECT OF THE EARNINGS PENALTY

Elderly persons may be discouraged from working by the Social Security earnings penalty. As noted earlier, Social Security benefits are reduced by $1 for each $3 earned above certain penalty-free amounts; it is equivalent, in effect, to a 33 percent marginal income tax rate.

At first glance, the effect of the earnings penalty on the work decision appears to be clear-cut. Because the penalty lowers the financial reward for each hour worked when earnings exceed the penalty-free amount, it is equivalent to a tax on work and would seem, therefore, to reduce the number of hours worked. There is, however, an effect that works in the opposite direction. Although the penalty reduces a worker's wage, it also reduces a worker's income. Some workers respond to this threat to their income by working more hours, rather than fewer.

---

[5]John R. Brittain, *The Payroll Tax for Social Security* (Washington, DC: The Brookings Institution, 1972).

[6]Charles M. Beach and Frederick S. Balfour, "Estimated Payroll Tax Incidence and Aggregate Demand for Labour in the United Kingdom," *Economica* 50 (January 1983), 35–48.

The existence of opposing effects actually suggests that the earnings penalty may have little net effect on the number of hours that retirees are willing to work. This is what Leonesio concludes after reviewing the available evidence on the earnings penalty.[7] His conclusion is consistent, moreover, with the general literature in public finance, which indicates that a marginal tax rate of 33 percent is not large enough to significantly reduce work effort.[8]

THE EFFECT ON RETIREMENT

Labor Force Participation Rate
The percentage of a certain population in the labor force.

There is a strong historical trend toward reduced labor force participation by older people. Between 1950 and 1984, for example, the **labor force participation rate** (the percentage of a certain population in the labor force) for men age 65 and older fell from 41.4 percent to 16.3 percent. A number of factors have probably contributed to this trend: rising income, the growth in private pensions, the increased availability of government transfers, and changing lifestyles, to name a few. Social Security may also be a major contributor.

This trend can be viewed as a laudable achievement, but it also has some adverse consequences. Reduced labor force participation by older workers reduces the nation's pool of experienced workers and potential national output. Retirement for a significant segment of the older work force also reduces Social Security revenues and increases Social Security expenditures.

These effects elicited little concern by policy makers for many years. In fact, one of the original purposes of Social Security was to provide older workers with enough income to leave the labor force and make way for younger workers who were having great difficulty finding work during the Great Depression. Today, however, Social Security is faced with the prospect of a long-run deficit (examined in the next section). In this context, early retirement is a problem instead of an opportunity.

Actually, the most disturbing aspect of the trend in reduced labor force participation of older workers is the large number of workers who retire early; nearly a third of Social Security beneficiaries leave the work force before age 65. Many of these workers are near the peak of their productivity and will live to receive Social Security benefits for much longer than people their age three decades ago when Social Security first allowed early retirement.

The prospect of Social Security benefits works in the direction of encouraging retirement, of course. However, other features of Social Security tend to discourage retirement. First, extra years of work may increase a worker's Social Security benefits if the wages earned during these years exceed wages earned during earlier years in the individual's work history. Second, Social Security benefits are increased by a Delayed Retirement Credit (noted earlier) for each extra year worked up to age 70. Third, there is a penalty (described earlier) for early retirement.

---

[7]Michael V. Leonesio, "Social Security and Older Workers," *Social Security Bulletin* 56 (Summer 1993), 47–57.

[8]For a brief summary of the evidence, see David N. Hyman, *Public Finance* (Hinsdale, IL: The Dryden Press, 1990), 471–72.

In spite of these incentives to keep working, Social Security appears, on balance, to contribute to its own problems through the strong incentive it provides for workers to retire earlier. This has led policy makers to seriously consider alternatives that might encourage older workers to delay retirement. Among these are accelerating the timing of the scheduled increase in the Delayed Retirement Credit, further increasing the normal retirement age and/or the early retirement age, changing the benefit computation rules to give more weight to wages earned in the years closer to retirement, eliminating the payroll tax for workers aged 65 and older, and increasing the income threshold at which Social Security benefits are subject to the federal income tax. These alternatives are too uncertain to warrant more discussion; however, we predict that interest in them will grow as Congress begins to take a serious look at the problem of the long-run deficit.

THE LONG-RUN DEFICIT

The question that appears to be raised most often about Social Security is whether it will be able to provide future generations with the same cushion against economic insecurity that it provides to today's retirees. Many younger people believe that Social Security will not be able to pay them *any* benefits when they retire. Are they right? To find out, we turn to the 1995 projections of the Social Security trustees.

In assessing long-run prospects for Social Security, the trustees rely on 75-year projections of income and expenditures prepared by Social Security actuaries.[9] Because the future cannot be predicted with certainty, three projections are reported: Alternatives I, II, and III. Each alternative is based on assumptions about economic growth, wage growth, inflation, unemployment, fertility, immigration, and mortality. The assumptions underlying Alternative I produce the most optimistic projection of trust fund surpluses; those underlying Alternative III produce the most pessimistic projection. Congress currently relies on Alternative II, a "best estimate" projection, as the guide for long-run planning.

According to the Alternative II projections in the 1995 Annual Report of the Trustees, the future for Social Security looks both promising and bleak. The promising aspect is that the OASI Trust Fund will grow rapidly during the next 16 years. Starting in 2013, however, annual expenditures will begin to exceed annual receipts and the Trust Fund will begin to shrink. The assets in the Trust Fund in 2013 combined with the annual receipts after 2013 will be sufficient to pay annual expenditures, but Trust Fund balances at the end of each year will become progressively smaller. Finally, in 2031, annual expenditures will have grown so much relative to annual receipts that the small remaining balance in the Trust Fund will be used to pay benefits that year. In other words, the OASI Trust Fund will be exhausted in 2031.

---

[9]These projections are reported each year in the *Annual Report of the Board of Trustees of the Federal Old-Age and Survivors Insurance and Disability Insurance Trust Funds* (Washington, DC: Government Printing Office).

INTERNATIONAL PERSPECTIVE

> ### PUBLIC PENSION PLANS IN TROUBLE: THE U.S. IS NOT UNIQUE

The combination of an aging population and a maturing pension scheme spell long-run difficulty for the U.S. Social Security system. The United States has lots of company, however, and in some ways is even better off than other developed countries, at least according to the numbers in the following table.

In 1990, the present value of the pension promises of Social Security in the United States amounted to about 90 percent of GDP, or nearly $5 trillion. As you know from reading the text, receipts from the payroll tax and other sources will not accumulate fast enough at currently legislated rates to pay all of these obligations. Other countries seem to be in worse shape, however; Canada, Germany, Japan, and the United Kingdom owed more than 100 percent of GDP in 1990 to current and future retirees, and in France and Italy the obligation exceeded 200 percent.

In order to meet these obligations in the future, each of these countries will have to find additional revenues, reduce benefits, or both. One revenue possibility is the adoption of a once-and-for-all increase in taxes. Had these countries done this in 1990, the increase required to avoid a long-run deficit would have ranged from 1.1 percent of GDP in the United States to 5.3 percent of GDP in Italy. One benefit-reduction possibility would be to adopt an increase in the normal retirement age. Had these countries used this policy in 1990, the increase required to avoid a long-run deficit would have ranged from 4 years in the United States to a whopping 16 years in Canada.

These options do not exhaust the possibilities for these countries to deal with the long-run deficit in public pension plans, of course, but they do illustrate some of the tough choices that will have to be made. Americans who lament this fact may feel fortunate to know that it is not going to be as tough for the United States as it is going to be for other countries.

MEANS OF FINANCING PENSION LIABILITIES		
Country	Tax Increase as % GDP	Increase in Retirement Age (Years)
Canada	4.4	16
France	4.0	8
Germany	3.6	11
Italy	5.3	10
Japan	4.3	9
United Kingdom	3.5	12
United States	1.1	4

Source: World Bank, *Averting the Old Age Crisis,* New York: Oxford University Press, 1994, 159.

ADDITIONAL INSIGHT

IS PRIVATIZATION IN SOCIAL SECURITY'S FUTURE?

Every four years the President appoints an advisory council to review the long-range forecasts made for the Social Security trustees and to comment on relevant policy issues. In the past, some of these panels have had important impacts on Social Security policy. The latest advisory council was formed in 1994, and after two years it has produced recommendations that may trigger the most fundamental changes in Social Security since its inception.

As the council members see it, their recommendations must address two principal problems: (1) a prospective long-run deficit in Social Security and (2) an unacceptably low rate of return for future generations of Social Security retirees. To deal with these problems they have debated three approaches.*

The first approach would make a larger share of Social Security benefits subject to the income tax, and require that 40 percent of the assets of the OASI Trust Fund be invested in equities (stocks of private corporations). The extra tax revenues would help to avoid the expected long-run deficit. The investment of part of the system's assets in equities would raise Social Security's overall rate of return, provided the stock market continues to outperform the bond market in the future as it has in the past.

The second approach would scale back benefits to eliminate the long-term deficit, principally by increasing the retirement age and reducing the replacement rate for high-income retirees. It would increase the rate of return on Social Security by establishing mandatory individual savings accounts, financed by a 1.6 percent increase in the payroll tax. The benefits produced by these accounts would be in addition to the scaled-back benefits the system otherwise promised. The Social Security system would hold these accounts, but individuals would be free to choose among investments in bond or stock index funds. The rate of return would probably increase, but not by as much as it would under the first approach because this approach requires a smaller amount of equity investment.

The third approach would require individuals to invest half of the funds collected for Old-Age Insurance through private registered investment companies. Social Security would invest the other half in government securities and use it to finance a flat benefit equal to two-thirds of the poverty line. After the funds committed to private investment were set aside, there would not be enough money in the trust fund to pay benefits promised during the transition to this system. Thus, it would be necessary to effect a tax increase of around 1.5 percent of taxable payroll.

Each of the three approaches advocates investing some of the money collected each year by Social Security taxes in the stock market. Such a privatization of Social Security would add an element of financial risk not now present in the system, but it may be necessary to head off a taxpayer revolt led by those who are fully aware of the superior investment returns realized by the stock market over time.

---

*See Edward M. Gramlich, "Different Approaches for Dealing with Social Security," *Journal of Economic Perspectives,* 10, no. 10 (Summer 1996), 55–66.

The rapid buildup in the Trust Fund is expected because of a combination of favorable demographic circumstances and reforms adopted in 1983. On the demographic side, the labor force has been swelled by record numbers of *baby boomers,* persons born during the years 1945 to 1965. The sheer size of the baby boom generation relative to the number of retirees will keep the ratio of workers to Social Security beneficiaries roughly constant until about 2010, when large numbers of baby boomers begin to retire from the work force.

Reforms of Social Security in 1983 contained several features deliberately designed to create a Trust Fund surplus in anticipation of the problems likely to arise after the baby boomers retire. Scheduled tax rate increases were advanced, self-employment tax rates were increased, benefits to upper-income beneficiaries were made partly taxable, and coverage was expanded to include federal civilian employees hired after December 31, 1983, and all employees of nonprofit organizations. Congress also approved a gradual increase in the age of eligibility for full benefits from age 65 to age 66 by 2009 and to age 67 by 2027.

Unfortunately, as the baby boomers retire, they will be replaced by fewer workers—a consequence of the decline in the fertility rate (the number of children ever born to the average woman) between 1965 and 1988. This will slow down Social Security tax collections just when benefits paid are rising rapidly.

The date of exhaustion of the Trust Fund is so far in the future that it is difficult to get Congress to focus its attention on the problem. The Trust Fund trustees argue, however, that the changes that will be required in Social Security can be relatively small and gradual if they are begun soon.[10]

What changes should be made? The trustees aren't saying, but they urge careful study of the options. Such studies are currently underway both within and outside the Social Security Administration. Many of the relevant options for dealing with the long-run deficit in Social Security have been addressed in a recent study published by The Urban Institute.[11]

The authors of that study, Eugene Steuerle and Jon Bakija, examine several options for either reducing the future level of Social Security benefits or increasing the future receipts of the Social Security Trust Fund—the two general ways to avoid Trust Fund exhaustion. They come to some conclusions about the "right ways" to proceed in addressing the long-run deficit in Social Security. Although they will certainly not have the last word on this matter, some of their suggestions are bound to be on the policy agenda of the future.

Among the options they highlight are an increase in the retirement age for OASI, an increase in the penalty for early retirement, and an increase in the tax base for the Social Security payroll tax. Regarding the increase in the retirement age and penalty for early retirement, they argue that not only do the young-elderly still have much to contribute to the economy, but that they are better off financially than the old-elderly and many younger families and, therefore, less deserving of public support.

Steuerle and Bakija argue that the Social Security tax base should be increased by including various forms of worker compensation that are currently excluded, especially employer contributions to fringe benefits such as health insurance, life insurance, and employee pensions. This, they claim, would not

---

[10]This view is expressed in a summary of the 1994 Trustees Annual Report: "Actuarial Status of the Social Security and Medicare Programs," *Social Security Bulletin* 57 (Spring 1994), 53–59.

[11]C. Eugene Steuerle and Jon M. Bakija, *Retooling Social Security for the 21st Century* (Washington, DC: The Urban Institute Press, 1994).

only increase Social Security revenues, but also improve equity by treating all forms of compensation the same and by increasing the relative share of taxes paid by higher-income taxpayers who tend to receive a higher share of their income in the form of fringe benefits. Increasing the tax base in a manner such as this is preferred by Steuerle and Bakija to further increases in the payroll tax rate.

Stay tuned to Congress for a discussion of these and other options in the next few years. Surely it has not escaped the attention of most of the readers of this text that it is their Social Security future that is at stake.

THE LOOMING SURPLUS

Social Security will enjoy a growing surplus, however, for the next 16 years. The surplus provides a means of meeting the system's obligations after revenue growth slows relative to expenditure growth, as noted previously. How the surplus is used until then is also an important matter. If the surplus is managed so that it increases national savings, national output will get a long-run boost and Social Security will benefit from a bigger tax base as well.

The size of the country's capital stock depends critically on the nation's savings rate. If the savings rate is high, the capital stock grows rapidly and the country experiences rapid growth in potential output. A low savings rate ultimately confines the nation to a lower growth path and slower increases in the Social Security tax base.

In the last 20 years, the net national savings rate (gross national savings minus depreciation, divided by net domestic product) in the United States has fallen from 10 percent to around 2 percent, one of the lowest in the industrialized world. Many economists are studying this phenomenon, but there is no consensus regarding why this has happened. There is considerable agreement, however, that this savings rate is too low to deliver the increases in the standard of living that the American people expect.

Viewed in this context, the Social Security program is both a potential problem and a potential opportunity. We already discussed the potential problem, namely, the possibility that the growth of Social Security wealth is responsible for some reduction in U.S. savings. Here we focus on the potential opportunity.

A surplus in the Social Security trust fund occurs whenever Social Security taxes (and other receipts of lesser importance) exceed Social Security benefits. Because Social Security taxes are paid by workers in the form of wages forgone (see Figure 9.1b), they are equivalent to household income that otherwise would have been partly spent on consumer goods and partly saved. Because households normally spend 95 percent or more of their income, it is reasonable to assume that the primary source of Social Security taxes is reduced private consumption, not saving and investment.

Taxes provide government with the means, however, to increase national investment. Whether this is done or not depends on how the government reacts to the money piling up in the Social Security Trust Fund.

There is no mystery regarding what the trustees do with the surplus; they use it to buy, or invest in, U.S. Treasury securities. If there is a deficit in the federal budget, the money Social Security pays for these bonds will be used by the Treasury to finance the deficit. If there is no budget deficit, the money would presumably be used to buy back, or retire, outstanding Treasury securities—that is, to reduce the national debt.

In the deficit-finance case, the Social Security surplus provides funds for government programs that otherwise would have been borrowed from private investors. In this, the more likely case, the surplus frees up private funds that can then be used to produce private capital. The effect on private investment is equivalent to what would happen if there were an increase in private savings and these savings were lent through financial intermediaries to private purchasers of capital goods. In this instance, an increase in the Social Security surplus is equivalent to an increase in national savings.

So far, so good, from the perspective of economic growth. This scenario will unfold, however, only if the prospect of Social Security surpluses does not induce Congress to increase the federal budget deficit. If it does, then the funds that would have been released for private investment will be used, instead, to finance current government expenditures. If these are expenditures for consumption-type goods and services, the Social Security surplus will have been used, in effect, to increase national consumption, rather than national savings, and the nation will have squandered an opportunity to achieve a higher rate of economic growth and a larger Social Security tax base.

How likely is this reaction? Very likely in the view of some economists. According to them,[12] Congress will not be able to resist the temptation to use the surplus in the Social Security trust fund to finance a larger deficit in the rest of the federal budget.

Does it matter whether they are right or wrong about the reactions of Congress to the Social Security surplus? Yes, for at least two reasons. First, this reaction to the surplus is equivalent to substituting more regressive (Social Security) taxes for more progressive (income) taxes as a means of financing government expenditures. Senator Daniel Patrick Moynihan of New York has objected to the rising Social Security surplus for precisely this reason.

The second significant consequence is a lower rate of economic growth. According to a study by Henry Aaron, Barry Bosworth, and Gary Burtless,[13] if Congress could exercise enough fiscal discipline to reduce the federal budget deficit (in programs other than Social Security) to 1.5 percent of GDP and keep it at that level as the Social Security surpluses are realized, the surpluses would increase national savings and the borrowing of these savings for private investment would yield significant growth dividends. Among the dividends would be an

[12]Carolyn L. Weaver (Ed., *Social Security's Looming Surpluses* (Washington, DC: American Enterprise Institute, 1990).

[13]Henry Aaron, Barry Bosworth, and Gary Burtless, *Can America Afford to Grow Old?* (Washington, DC: The Brookings Institution, 1990).

increase of 23.6 percent in the capital stock by 2020. This, in turn, would produce a 4.2 percent annual increase in Net National Product (NNP). In terms of today's NNP of approximately $6 trillion, this amounts to $252 billion, or about $1,000 for every man, woman, and child in the United States. Such a dividend would go a long way toward providing the means to finance the annual deficits in Social Security that will occur after the baby boom generation begins to retire.

If it does matter, as it seems, that Congress is likely to use the Social Security surplus as a means of financing a larger deficit in the non-Social Security portion of the federal budget, how can this outcome be avoided? Some economists suggest that this can be done by precluding Congress from including Social Security in the budget that must be balanced. This was not done when Congress made its futile attempt to balance the budget under the provisions of the Gramm-Rudman-Hollings Act.

The inclusion of the Social Security surplus made the budget appear to be closer to a balanced state than it really was, but the inclusion of the Social Security surplus does not deserve much credit for the failure of this attempt to balance the budget. Apparently, Congress did not have the political will to either reduce expenditures or increase taxes enough to reach the Gramm-Rudman-Hollings targets. In fact, some economists argue that Congress will always lack such political will. Consequently, they view a balanced budget amendment to the U.S. Constitution as the only way to achieve a balanced budget, and, by inference, the increase in national savings that could accompany the looming Social Security surplus.

Summary

Social Security is the commonly used label for the programs of Old-Age and Survivors' Insurance established by the Social Security Act. These programs provide benefits to retired workers and to their survivors in the event of their death.

Social Security as a form of social retirement insurance differs from private retirement insurance in four important ways. Social Security is (1) compulsory, rather than voluntary, (2) financed as a pay-as-you-go basis, rather than a fully-funded basis, (3) secured by a trust fund that is a buffer fund, rather than an insurance reserve fund, and (4) characterized by benefits based on individual contributions and equity considerations, rather than on individual contributions alone.

Social Security retirement benefits are based on an individual's preretirement wages, age at retirement, family status, postretirement earnings, and the annual rate of inflation. Benefits are inversely related to preretirement earnings.

Social Security is an important source of income for the elderly, and it has been a primary factor in reducing poverty among the aged.

Viewed as an investment of tax dollars in an individual retirement insurance policy, Social Security exhibits great variation in individual rates of return. The rate of return is generally larger for (1) married couples, (2) workers with lower average earnings, and (3) females. The average real rate of return for the student reading this book will probably be 1 to 2 percent.

Social Security may have reduced aggregate saving, thereby producing less investment, a smaller capital stock, and a lower level of national output. Empirical evidence of this effect, however, is inconclusive.

Social Security may reduce hours worked via the payroll tax levied on workers and employers, the penalty applied to excess postretirement earnings, and the level of support provided to early retirees. Economic theory and available evidence suggest that these effects are likely to be small.

Social Security faces both a looming surplus in the next 16 years and a long-run deficit after 2031. The long-run deficit may call for immediate action, however, to raise future revenues or to reduce future expenditures. Under the current law, the surpluses will be used to finance annual deficits in the federal budget. If the deficit is cut, the surplus can be used to increase investment and enhance the nation's ability to support future retirees.

KEY TERMS

Social Security
Pay-as-you-go insurance
    plan
Fully-funded insurance
    plan
Buffer fund

Principle of individual
    contribution
Gross replacement rate
Earnings penalty
Wealth substitution
    effect

Induced retirement effect
Bequest effect
Labor force participation
    rate

REVIEW QUESTIONS

1. Briefly discuss the differences between Social Security and private retirement insurance.

2. Explain how Social Security benefits some groups in society more than other groups. Be certain to examine this phenomenon in terms of gross replacement rates and rates of return.

3. "Social Security pays only a 1 to 2 percent real rate of return. This return is so low that individuals would be better off if they were allowed to take the money invested in Social Security and invest it in other assets." Is this statement true or false? Defend your answer.

4. Are the elderly better off because of the payment of Social Security benefits? Why or why not?

5. Economists assume that individuals maximize their utility, or satisfaction. The consumption of goods and services is a major source of this satisfaction. If Social Security enables individuals to devote more of their income to consumption and less to savings, individuals are presumably better off. Why, then, are economists concerned that the payment of Social Security benefits may cause a decrease in savings?

6. "Because Social Security is a source of wealth to the elderly, it has induced people to save less of their income for retirement." Evaluate this statement.

7. Suppose the supply curve of labor is vertical (as in Figure 9.1b). What is the effect of a payroll tax on work? How does this result change if the supply of labor varies directly with the wage rate?

8. You are a research analyst for a member of Congress. She asks you to determine the impact on the work decision of an increase in Social Security benefits that is to be funded by increasing the payroll tax. What are the basic results of your analysis?

9. "It is likely that the increase in the proportion of the population that is aged will lead to a deficit in the OASI Trust Fund by the year 2050." Is this statement true or false? Defend your answer.

10. Explain how the Social Security surplus can be used to increase investment in the U.S. economy.

SUGGESTIONS FOR FURTHER READING

Aaron, Henry J., Barry P. Bosworth, and Gary Burtless. *Can America Afford to Grow Old?* Washington, DC: The Brookings Institution, 1989. The authors answer yes to the question posed in the book's title, but only if the deficit is reduced and the growing Social Security surplus ultimately increases saving. This book is not light reading, and two or three of the chapters are too advanced for beginning students, but its major message is discernible with a little effort.

Diamond, Peter A., David C. Lindeman, and Howard Young, eds. *Social Security: What Role for the Future?* Washington, DC: National Academy of Social Insurance, 1996. An up-to-date discussion by experts of the prospects for Social Security, both in the United States and other countries.

Feldstein, Martin S. "Facing the Social Security Crisis." *The Public Interest* 47 (Summer 1977), 88–100. The seminal discussion of the effect of Social Security on saving contains a proposal for phasing out, or privatizing, Social Security.

Garner, Alan C. "The Social Security Surplus—A Solution to the Federal Budget Deficit?" *Economic Review*. Federal Reserve Bank of Kansas City (May 1989), 25–39. An evaluation of the effects of staying on course and using the Social Security surplus to finance annual deficits in the federal budget.

Steuerle, C. Eugene, and Jon M. Bakija. *Retooling Social Security for the 21st Century*. Washington, DC: The Urban Institute, 1994. The most comprehensive analysis available of the long-range financing problems confronting Social Security.

World Bank. *Averting the Old Age Crisis*. New York: Oxford University Press, 1994. A review and evaluation of the means used around the world to pay for the post-retirement needs of the elderly.

10

POVERTY AND DISCRIMINATION

In 1962, Michael Harrington wrote *The Other America*. The "other Americans" were the poor who lived in a land of plenty, primarily out of sight and out of mind. Harrington's work stirred the conscience of many Americans, including President John F. Kennedy, who directed his Council of Economic Advisers to study the problem. After Kennedy's assassination, President Lyndon Johnson embraced the issue and, in his State of the Union address in 1964, declared war on poverty.

In the next decade, the federal government introduced new antipoverty programs and expanded the old ones. It became fashionable in Washington to ask, "What does it do for poverty?" whenever budget priorities were discussed. In fact, according to the federal government's official measure, the United States made substantial progress toward eliminating poverty between 1964 and 1973, and government initiatives have often been credited with much of this success.

In 1974, however, the number of persons living in poverty started to grow, and it has generally trended upward since then, reaching a high of nearly 37 million people in 1992 and hovering around that level through 1995.

Some economists interpret this as a sign that we are losing the War on Poverty, although they do not necessarily agree on the causes of our failure. Some attribute it to cutbacks in government assistance to the poor. Others argue that this assistance is the wrong kind or is focused on the wrong people. Still others contend that government assistance actually increases the poverty rate by inducing recipients to work less or by increasing the size of the population at risk of being poor. Other economists claim that the official poverty data overstate the poverty problem, however, and that more accurate measures actually show that we have come closer to winning the war than is commonly acknowledged.

There is, in short, no universal agreement among economists about the extent or causes of poverty in the United States. Not surprisingly, economists also disagree about what, if anything, should be done to reduce poverty further. This chapter will not settle these issues, but it is intended to clarify them. It begins by addressing the question of how much poverty we have. Then it examines the long-run poverty trend and reviews the arguments (and evidence) that government assistance causes poverty and/or misses the appropriate target groups. Policy alternatives are considered in the final section.

HOW MANY PEOPLE ARE POOR?

Official Poverty Measure
A measure that counts a family as poor if its income is below the official poverty threshold.

Official Poverty Threshold
The annual cost of a nutritionally adequate diet multiplied by three.

Individuals are poor whenever their resources are not sufficient to provide what society considers an acceptable minimum standard of living. There are many possible measures, however, of both resources and an appropriate minimum standard of living. Thus, many possible measures of poverty exist. The one referred to most often is the **official poverty measure.** According to this measure, a person is poor who lives in a family with an annual income below the **official poverty threshold.** The official poverty threshold is the annual cost of a nutritionally adequate diet multiplied by three. This multiplier is based on the idea that the poor should not have to spend more than one-third of their income for food.

The government adjusts the poverty threshold each year for price changes. The poverty threshold also increases (though not uniformly) as family size increases. In 1959, the official poverty threshold for a family of four was $2,973. To compensate for price increases between 1959 and 1996, the government increased this poverty threshold from $2,973 to $15,719. In 1996, the poverty threshold ranged from $7,763 for a single individual to $33,752 for a family of 9 or more.

The other half of the official measure of poverty—resources available—is the **money income** reported to the Census Bureau in its surveys of income. Money income includes earnings before taxes plus private and government cash transfers, such as alimony and child support payments, Social Security benefits, unemployment checks, and payments from the Aid to Families with Dependent Children program. If a family's money income is less than its relevant poverty threshold, all members of that family are counted as poor. In 1995, 36.4 million people, or 13.8 percent of the population, lived in poverty.

Money Income
Earnings before taxes, plus private and government cash transfers.

Many economists are not satisfied with the official poverty measure, however, on the grounds that money income fails to (1) include relevant, and important, sources of income, and (2) adjust for the effect of taxes on income. Accordingly, the Census Bureau has produced time series for 15 different definitions of income as a means of determining how sensitive the measure of poverty is to the various types of income and taxes not included in money income.

Income definition 14 (ID 14) is of special interest. In addition to money income, ID 14 includes income from **capital gains,** health insurance supplements to wages and salaries, the value of Medicare and Medicaid and other **in-kind transfers** such as food and housing, and the value of the Earned Income Tax Credit. ID 14 also subtracts Social Security payroll taxes and Federal and State income taxes from money income.

Capital Gains
The increased value of assets, such as stocks and houses.

In-kind Transfers
Payments for specific goods and services such as food, housing, and medical care.

According to ID 14, the poverty rate was 2.5 to 3.0 percentage points lower each year from 1979 to 1994 than the official poverty rate.[1] The trend in the poverty rate was quite similar over this time period, however, for both the official measure and ID 14; that is, poverty generally increased according to both measures.

THE LONG-RUN TREND

Estimates of the official poverty rate and poverty population for selected years are displayed in Table 10.1. Comparable series for adjusted rates and populations do not exist. These data show that poverty declined significantly from 1959 to 1973 and that it has generally increased since 1973 (although there was significant improvement between 1983 and 1989).

The reduction in the official poverty rate from 1959 to 1973 is commonly attributed to the combined effect of rapid growth in the economy and large

---

[1]Committee on Ways and Means, U.S. House of Representatives, *1996 Green Book* (Washington, DC: Government Printing Office, 1994), 1231.

TABLE 10.1

Year	Poverty Rate	Number of Poor (Millions)
1959	22.4	39.5
1965	17.3	33.2
1967	14.2	27.8
1973	11.1	23.0
1979	11.7	26.0
1983	15.2	35.3
1989	12.8	31.5
1992	14.5	36.9
1995	13.8	36.4

According to the official poverty measure, the U.S. poverty rate and the number of poor decreased between 1959 and 1973, increased between 1973 and 1983, fell again between 1983 and 1989, and then rose from 1989 to 1992.

Source: Committee on Ways and Means, U.S. House of Representatives, *1994 Green Book* (Washington, DC: Government Printing Office, 1994), 1158; Bureau of Labor Statistics and Census Bureau, *Annual Demographic Survey, March Supplement, 1995* (Washington, DC: Government Printing Office, 1996).

increases in government cash transfers. The effect of a growing economy was especially pronounced during the 1960s, when the unemployment rate fell from 6.7 percent to 3.5 percent, creating millions of jobs for all segments of the population, including the poor. This impulse abated somewhat during the first part of the 1970s, but government cash transfers were growing fast enough to maintain the downward trend in the poverty rate.

The principal government cash transfer programs are Social Security, Supplemental Security Income, Public Employee Retirement, Aid to Families with Dependent Children, unemployment insurance, and workers' compensation. The first three programs provide money directly to the elderly. Although only one of these, Supplemental Security Income, is commonly viewed as an antipoverty program, the benefits from all three programs help to keep elderly families from falling into poverty. Aid to Families with Dependent Children is the program most people identify with "welfare" payments. Unemployment insurance and workers' compensation provide benefits to people who are unemployed or suffer from work-related injuries or illnesses, but many of these people would be poor if it were not for these benefits. The benefits provided by all of these cash transfer programs increased by $135 billion between 1959 and 1975, after adjustment for inflation. Without this money, the poverty rate would have been 7.8 percentage points higher in 1975.

Government cash transfers increased another $138 billion between 1975 and 1992, after adjustment for inflation. Without this additional money, the poverty rate would have been 8.2 percentage points higher in 1992. Thus, the upward drift in the poverty rate occurred in the face of a continued commitment to provide significant cash transfers.

What distinguishes the second half of the 1959–1992 period from the first half is the increase in the pretransfer poverty rate. The pretransfer poverty rate is the estimated poverty rate in the absence of all government cash transfers. This rate increased by 3 percentage points between 1975 and 1992.

The increase in the pretransfer poverty rate has not been fully explained in the literature, but four factors are normally given the most credit: (1) the increasing incidence of unemployment, (2) the changing composition of the poverty population, (3) discrimination, and (4) the effects of government transfers on work incentives and family formation.

INCREASING INCIDENCE OF UNEMPLOYMENT

High unemployment rates are bad news for the poor. As a group, they lack the skills and patterns of workforce attachment that are in great demand in the labor market. Thus, they tend to be hit harder than other groups when the economy slumps. Blank and Blinder estimate that a 2 percentage point rise in the unemployment rate of prime-age men sustained for two years adds about 0.9 percentage point to the poverty rate.[2]

During the 1960–1974 period, the unemployment rate averaged a little under 5 percent. Between 1975 and 1992, it averaged a little over 7 percent. Blank and Blinders' findings suggest that this upward drift of 2 percent in the unemployment rate may explain nearly one-third (0.9 of 3.0 percentage points) of the increase in the pretransfer poverty rate.

CHANGING COMPOSITION OF THE POVERTY POPULATION

Among the factors that increase poverty, probably the most important in the last two decades has been the change in the demographic makeup of the poverty population. Poverty is not spread evenly across the population; some groups are more poverty-prone than others. Table 10.2 shows the incidence of poverty in different groups for 1995.

While 13.8 percent of the total population fell below the official poverty threshold, the rate among blacks was nearly three times higher than that among whites. The poverty rate for Hispanics exceeded that of blacks. The highest incidence of poverty was recorded in the families headed by women.

These three groups have become relatively more important contributors to the overall poverty population. In 1959, 25 percent of the poor were black and

[2]Rebecca Blank and Alan Blinder, "Macroeconomics, Income Distribution, and Poverty," in *Fighting Poverty, What Works and What Doesn't*, Sheldon H. Danziger and Daniel Weinberg, eds. (Cambridge: Harvard University Press, 1986), 180–208.

THE TIDE HAS NOT BEEN RISING, BUT SOME BOATS HAVE BEEN

When the War on Poverty began in the mid-1960s, the dominant view among economists was that the U.S. economy was poised for a prolonged period of growth and that this growth would be a strong force in reducing poverty. (To describe it metaphorically, they thought the tide would rise and lift all boats when it did.) Events of the following decade seemed to confirm this expectation—economic growth was associated with reduced poverty. Since the early 1970s, however, real economic growth has faltered—the tide has not been rising—and poverty has risen. Moreover, during this period families and households at the upper end of the income distribution have experienced gains in real income—some boats have risen even though the tide has not. Thus, we have had a relatively stagnant average standard of living coupled with growing income inequality.

One way to measure the tide is the level of real mean income. In 1973 real mean income per household in the United States was $30,341 (in 1989 dollars); in 1990 it stood at only $31,346, an increase of only 3.3 percent. Between these two years, the average family cash income of the lowest 20 percent of households fell 14 percent, while the average family cash income of the highest 20 percent of households grew nearly 14 percent. The dismal growth record of the economy is explored in detail in Chapter 16. Here we take a brief look at the factors that lie behind growing income inequality.

A flurry of research in recent years has focused on the subject of growing income inequality. Much of it concerns the nation's labor markets and the distribution of wages. According to this research, real earnings growth did indeed slow down in the 1970s and the 1980s relative to earlier decades, and earnings became more unequally distributed.°

One of the factors that appears to be responsible for this trend is the shift in economic activities from goods production to services production. Industries involved in the production of services typically have paid lower wages and exhibited more variation in their wage structures than industries involved in the production of goods. Increased wage inequality has also marked the goods-producing industries, however, so other explanations must be sought.

One of the more popular explanations focuses on the growing gap in the earnings of well-educated and poorly educated workers, presumably due to the faster growing demand for workers with more skills. The nation's trade deficit also may have added to the problem because a greater proportion of unskilled labor is used to produce this country's imports than its exports. Many of these imports could have been made by low-skilled workers in this country but were made abroad, reducing the demand for unskilled domestic workers.

The declining influence of unions on wage-setting practices also may have played a role because less-skilled workers have typically received significant wage benefits from union membership. The maturing of the baby-boom generation (individuals born in large numbers between 1945 and 1965) probably had some effect, as it flooded the labor market with record numbers of younger entrants, driving down their wages relative to those of older workers.

Finally, some of the growth in family income inequality is undoubtedly due to changes that occurred in family composition. Between 1969 and 1989, married-couple households as a proportion of all households fell by 20 percent. They were replaced by single-parent family households and nonfamily households, groups that have traditionally exhibited greater inequality of income than married-couple households.

Economists are carefully examining these and many other possible explanations of the growing inequality in the distribution of income. What they find may matter a great deal in the design of future social and economic policy.

°Gary Burtless, "Earnings Inequality over the Business and Demographic Cycles," in Gary Burtless, ed., *A Future of Lousy Jobs?* (Washington, DC: The Brookings Institution, 1990), 77–117.

TABLE 10.2	
Group	**Poverty Rate (Percent)**
All persons	13.8
Female-headed families	36.5
Blacks	29.3
Hispanics	30.3
Whites	11.2

Poverty in the United States is not distributed evenly. The poverty rate is especially high among female-headed families, blacks, and Hispanics.

Source: U.S. Bureau of Labor Statistics and Bureau of the Census, *Annual Demographic Survey, March Supplement, 1996* (Washington, DC: U.S. Government Printing Office).

POVERTY RATES FOR INDIVIDUALS IN SELECTED DEMOGRAPHIC GROUPS, 1995

26 percent lived in families headed by women. In 1995, blacks and individuals in female-headed families accounted for 27 percent and 38 percent of the poor, respectively. Hispanics constituted 10 percent of the poor in 1972, but 24 percent in 1995. Thus there has been a **feminization of poverty**—an increase in the portion of the poor who live in families headed by women—and a greater concentration of poverty among minorities.

Feminization of Poverty
The growth in the percentage of poor families headed by women.

THE FEMINIZATION OF POVERTY   The feminization of poverty has occurred because more people live in female-headed families today than 30 years ago—not because the poverty rate of this group has risen. In 1965, less than 9 percent of all families were headed by women. They were 18 percent of all families in 1995. The poverty rate for this group fell from 49 percent in 1959 to 37.5 percent in 1973 and has remained close to this level since then.

The growth in female-headed families is due to rising divorce rates, declining remarriage rates, declining marriage rates, and an increase in out-of-wedlock childbearing. The percentage of families headed by women with children who had never married increased from 26 percent in 1979 to 41 percent in 1992.

Why has poverty been so persistent in this group? First, divorce has a devastating effect on family income. The father's paycheck is lost, and often very little of it is replaced by alimony and child support payments.

It is even harder for female heads of families who have never been married to collect child support payments from fathers. Members of this group are also likely to have completed less schooling and to have less labor market experience, making it more likely that they will command a wage too small to escape poverty by working. Child care responsibilities further weaken their job prospects.

Those who do work face higher-than-average unemployment rates. Table 10.3 shows clearly that the unemployment rates of women who maintain families are consistently higher than the overall rate.

SELECTED
UNEMPLOYMENT
RATES, 1976–1995

TABLE 10.3

Year	Overall	White	Black	Female Heads of Households
1976	7.7	7.0	14.0	10.1
1978	6.1	5.2	12.8	8.5
1980	7.1	6.3	14.3	9.2
1982	9.7	8.6	18.9	11.7
1984	7.5	6.5	15.9	10.3
1986	7.0	6.0	14.5	9.8
1988	5.5	4.7	11.7	8.1
1990	5.5	4.7	11.3	8.2
1992	7.4	6.5	14.1	9.9
1996	5.2	4.5	10.5	8.5

Unemployment rates vary among selected groups. They tend to be less than average among whites and greater than average among blacks and female heads of households.

Sources: Committee on Ways and Means, U.S. House of Representatives, *The 1994 Green Book* (Washington, DC: Government Printing Office, 1994), 1096; U.S. Bureau of Labor Statistics and Bureau of the Census, *Annual Demographic Survey, 1996* (Washington, DC: U.S. Government Printing Office).

GREATER CONCENTRATION OF POVERTY AMONG MINORITIES   The populations of both blacks and Hispanics have grown faster than the population as a whole in the past two decades. On this basis alone, they would probably constitute a growing portion of the poverty population. This effect is reinforced by an increase in the poverty rate among Hispanics from 22 percent in 1972 to 30.3 percent in 1995. The poverty rate among blacks has remained relatively constant (at about one-third of the black population) since 1968, although the rate declined from 33.3 percent in 1992 to 29.3 percent in 1995.

Table 10.3 indicates that unemployment plays an important role in maintaining a high poverty rate among blacks. The black unemployment rate has consistently been roughly twice the overall rate, and anywhere from two to three times higher than that for whites. The average duration of a spell of unemployment also has been longer for blacks than for whites.

DISCRIMINATION

As noted, the data in Table 10.2 indicate much higher rates of poverty for individuals living in female-headed families, for blacks, and for Hispanics, than for whites. The following data also indicate lower earnings for females relative to males and for black and Hispanic males relative to white males. Such differences

TABLE 10.4	
Group	**Ratio**
White women	.73
Black men	.70
Black women	.63
Hispanic men	.62
Hispanic women	.53

Source: U.S. Department of Labor, Bureau of Labor Statistics, "Usual Weekly Earnings of Wage and Salary Workers: Third Quarter of 1996" (obtained via the Internet).

RATIO OF AVERAGE EARNINGS OF FULL-TIME WORKERS IN SELECTED GROUPS TO AVERAGE EARNINGS OF FULL-TIME WHITE MALE WORKERS, THIRD QUARTER, 1996

raise the specter of discrimination and suggest that poverty may be, at least to some extent, caused by discrimination.

The purpose of this section is to explore the relationship between poverty and discrimination. We begin by examining the extent of labor market discrimination. We then look more closely at the means by which labor market discrimination and poverty may be linked and briefly examine some of the implications of those linkages for public policy toward poverty.

HOW MUCH LABOR MARKET DISCRIMINATION IS THERE? Table 10.4 contains data for full-time wage and salary workers in the third quarter of 1996, as compiled by the Bureau of Labor Statistics. The data are reported as earnings ratios—in this case, the ratio of the average earnings by individuals in a selected group to the average earnings of white males. They indicate, for example, that the average white female had earnings that were 73 percent of the earnings of the average white male, the average black male had earnings that were 70 percent of the average white male, and so on.

Although these data represent only one recent period, the general pattern displayed here has persisted for as long as reliable data have been collected; that is, white males have always outearned the other groups represented in Table 10.4. As a general rule, differences in earnings reflect a host of factors that distinguish one worker, or group of workers, from another. Discrimination is one of these factors, but the list also includes education, training, work experience, occupation, location, hours worked, work effort, industry, marital status, verbal skills, intelligence, and others. The trick is to separate the effect of discrimination from the effects of all of the other factors that could explain differences in earnings.

Many economists have attempted to do this, using various kinds of empirical or statistical techniques. There is no reliable measure, however, of discrimination. Thus, using these approaches economists have determined only the share of observed earnings differentials that can be attributed to factors other than discrimination. The portion that is not explained by factors other than discrimination can then be attributed either to discrimination or to factors omitted from the analysis.

According to the data in Table 10.4, black males appear to pay a 30 percent penalty in earnings for being black. Empirical studies indicate, however, that possibly as much as half of this penalty can be attributed to differences in experience, education, location, veteran and marital status, number of children, and hours worked.[3] Thus, the earnings differential between black and white males produced by discrimination is probably no larger than around 15 percent of white male earnings and possibly less (some of the differential may be due to other omitted factors).

According to the data in Table 10.4, white females appear to pay a 27 percent earnings penalty for being female. Womens' careers are interrupted more often and for longer periods of time than mens', however, primarily for child rearing. This puts them at a disadvantage in the labor market in terms of work experience. In fact, the evidence suggests that perhaps half of the observed pay difference between white women and men can be explained by differences in experience.[4]

Another 5 to 6 percent of the 27 percent differential can probably be attributed to occupational segregation.[5] Simply put, women are overrepresented in relatively lower-paying clerical and service occupations and underrepresented in relatively higher-paying precision production, crafts, and repair occupations, and also among operators, fabricators, and laborers. Several studies have shown, however, that at least half of the occupational wage differential is eliminated when job characteristics are held constant; that is, higher pay by occupation in part reflects compensation for less attractive working conditions.[6]

As was the case for black-white earnings differentials, we do not know for certain how much of the differential in male and female earnings is due to labor market discrimination. Differences in work experience and working conditions, however, appear to account for more than half of the observed earnings differential. Some of the unexplained variation, moreover, can be attributed to prelabor market discrimination—that is, to gender differences in socialization. Overall, it seems reasonable to infer that labor market discrimination produces no more, and possibly less, than a 10 percent difference in male and female earnings.

The data in Table 10.4 also suggest substantial earnings penalties for Hispanic males and females. The evidence indicates, however, that the wages of Mexican-Americans, Cuban-Americans and Puerto Ricans living in the United States are only slightly below (5 percent at most) those of non-Hispanic whites after adjusting for differences in education, age, hours worked, marital status, region, fluency in English, and place of birth.[7] Fluency in English has been an

[3]Francine Blau and Andrea Beller, "Black-White Earnings over the 1980s: Gender Differences in Trends," *Review of Economics and Statistics* 74 (1992), 276–86.

[4]Mary Corcoran, "The Structure of Female Wages," American Economic Association, *Papers and Proceedings* 68 (1978), 165–70.

[5]Erica Groshen, "The Structure of the Female/Male Wage Differential," *Journal of Human Resources* 26 (1991), 457–72.

[6]See, for example, David Macpherson and Barry Hirsch, "Wages and Gender Composition: Why Do Women's Jobs Pay Less?" *Journal of Labor Economics* 13 (1995), 426–71.

[7]Leonard Carlson and Caroline Swartz, "The Earnings of Women and Ethnic Minorities, 1959–1979," *Industrial and Labor Relations Review* 41 (1988), 530–46.

especially important factor keeping Hispanics out of higher-paying professional and managerial occupations.

This quick review of the evidence indicates, then, that unexplained differences in pay do exist between apparently identical white and black workers, between male and female workers, and between Hispanic and non-Hispanic white workers. Based on the evidence we have reported, however, the unexplained pay differences appear to be no larger than the 15 percent penalty paid by blacks and they are probably less for both females and Hispanics. These differences should be viewed, moreover, as the upper limits; they may represent the effects of discrimination, but they may also result from unmeasured differences in productivity.

These results are not really very surprising when viewed in the context of economic theory. Wage discrimination can arise from the unwillingness of employers, consumers, or fellow employees to hire, buy from, or work with persons of a certain race, ethnic group, or gender. Such choices, however, inevitably require firms to pass up more productive employees in favor of less productive employees. This will elevate costs of production above the level achievable in the absence of discrimination and eventually drive discriminating firms from the market. Thus, economic theory suggests that normal market forces will tend to moderate the extent of labor market discrimination.

How Much Does Labor Market Discrimination Contribute to Poverty?

We turn now from the general issue of the overall extent of labor market discrimination to the question of whether discrimination has much to do with poverty. Frankly, we doubt that it does, for several reasons.

First, although poverty rates are higher among blacks, Hispanics, and female-headed families, 48 percent of the poor live in families headed by white males. Thus at the very least, nearly half of the poor are not subjected to labor market discrimination.

Second, there is some evidence that indicates that the earnings differential between white males and others is smaller for lower-paying occupations than it is for higher-paying occupations.[8] This is a significant fact because the poor will be working, if at all, in the lower-paid occupations. In fact, evidence of discrimination against the so-called average worker is irrelevant in determining the contribution of discrimination to poverty in the United States.

Third, evidence suggests that the earnings differential between white males and others is smaller among individuals with less education—that is, among individuals more likely to be poor. For example, in 1993, the black-white earnings ratio for full-time male workers with less than a high school education was 0.97.[9] Discrimination seems to be more effective in creating wage differences among

---

[8]For example, women's wages were 88 percent of men's in service occupations (except private household and protective) in the third quarter of 1996, according to the data in U.S. Bureau of Labor Statistics, *Usual Weekly Earnings of Wage and Salary Workers: Third Quarter of 1996* (obtained from the Internet).

[9]R. K. Filer, D. S. Hammermesh, and A. S. Rees, *The Economics of Work and Pay*, 6th ed., (New York: HarperCollins, 1996), 552.

more educated workers competing for higher-paying jobs than among less educated workers competing for lower-paying jobs.

Fourth, poverty rates have persisted even though earnings differentials have narrowed over time. We have already presented evidence of the failure of the poverty rate to fall appreciably since 1975. During the same period, however, female-male earnings ratios (white female/white male, black female/black male, Hispanic female/Hispanic male) in the United States rose from 0.58 to 0.73 for whites, from 0.75 to 0.89 for blacks, and from 0.68 to 0.88 for Hispanics.[10]

Fifth, the earnings penalty imposed by discrimination would not be large enough in many cases to cause poverty—that is, to lower a family's income from above the poverty threshold to below the poverty threshold. Alternatively, if the income lost because of discrimination were somehow restored to the victims of discrimination, it would not be enough in most cases to raise their income above the poverty threshold.

Whether such a restoration would be sufficient to raise a family's income above the poverty threshold depends on how close the family's income is to the poverty threshold, how much of that income is derived from wages, and how large the restoration would be (or the size of the discrimination penalty). It is impossible to apply a combination of all of these factors to the poverty data short of a lengthy study, but we can suggest an upper limit by using some general characteristics of the poverty population.

The typical poverty family in the United States has between three and four people. The poverty thresholds in 1996 for families of three and four were $11,921 and $15,719, respectively. Assuming a discrimination penalty of 15 percent, the largest possible penalty would be 2,357.85 (0.15 × $15,719). But this is the penalty for a worker whose entire income is from wages, and whose wages are just equal to the poverty threshold. Most poor families do not receive this large a percentage of their income from work, and they are not this close to the poverty threshold. This is a penalty based, moreover, on a penalty percentage that our previous discussion suggests is too high. Let us assume, however, that every female-headed, black, and Hispanic family with an income below the poverty threshold suffers from a discrimination penalty of $2,000. If even this much income were given to each family in these three categories, only about 17 percent of the families would be elevated above the poverty threshold.

POLICY IMPLICATIONS   Much of the above discussion suggests that labor market discrimination is not a significant source of poverty in the United States. Thus, even if policies aimed at reducing labor market discrimination, such as affirmative action, were successful in reducing discrimination, they would have little effect on the poverty rate. There is probably a stronger link between poverty and occupational segregation, and some hope that reducing the latter will also lower the poverty rate. So far, however, we have not devised an effective way to do this through public policy. The one approach that has been suggested most often is paying workers according to pay scales based on comparable worth, or in-

[10]Ibid., 556, 568.

herent job requirements. This approach has failed, however, to generate much political support in the United States.

EFFECTS OF GOVERNMENT TRANSFERS ON WORK INCENTIVES AND FAMILY FORMATION

Government transfers have been an important source of poverty reduction by directly boosting the income of the poor. Unfortunately, transfers may also indirectly reduce the income of the poor by (1) inducing transfer recipients to work less, and (2) promoting the formation of female-headed families.

The primary suspects in this regard are the major public assistance programs: Medicaid, food stamps, Supplemental Security Income, Aid to Families with Dependent Children, and housing subsidies. The amounts spent on these programs in 1992 are indicated in Table 10.5.

FOOD STAMPS   Under the food stamp program, households are given food coupons that are accepted by grocery stores as payment for food purchases. The program is paid for largely by the federal government and administered through local welfare offices. To be eligible, gross household income cannot exceed 130 percent of the relevant poverty line for the particular household.

The food stamp program is an **income-tested transfer** program—one in which the amount of the transfer tapers off as the recipient's net income rises. Net income is equal to gross income minus allowances for housing, child care, and other expenses of working. Gross income is income from before-tax earnings and non-income-tested transfers.

Table 10.6 illustrates how the amount given monthly in food stamps varies inversely with net income. Table 10.6 also illustrates three features common to

Income-Tested Transfer
A government program in which the amount transferred falls as the recipient's net income rises.

TABLE 10.5	
Program	**Expenditures**
Medicaid	118.1
Food stamps	24.9
Supplemental Security Income	22.2
AFDC	22.2
Housing assistance	18.2
	205.6

GOVERNMENT ASSISTANCE PROGRAMS, 1992 (BILLIONS OF DOLLARS)

The federal and state governments spent $205.6 billion on public assistance in 1992, more than half of which was for medical care.

Source: Calculated from data in Committee on Ways and Means, U.S. House of Representatives, *The 1994 Green Book* (Washington, DC: Government Printing Office, 1994).

FOOD STAMP
BENEFITS FOR A
TYPICAL FAMILY
OF THREE IN 1996

TABLE 10.6

Monthly Net Income	Food Stamps ($)	Transfer Reduction Rate
$0	$310	—
100	280	.30
200	250	.30
300	220	.30
400	190	.30
500	160	.30
600	130	.30
700	100	.30
800	70	.30
900	40	.30
1,000	10	.30
1,033	0	.30

The dollar value of food stamps falls as monthly net income rises. In this illustration, the amount transferred falls by $30 for every $100 increase in monthly net income, for a transfer reduction rate of 0.30.

Source: Committee on Ways and Means, U.S. House of Representatives, *The 1996 Green Book* (Washington, DC: Government Printing Office, 1996), 438.

Basic Transfer
The amount transferred in an income-tested transfer program when net income is zero.

Break-Even Net Income
The net income in an income-tested transfer program at which the amount transferred becomes zero.

Transfer Reduction Rate
The decrease in the amount transferred in an income-tested transfer program when net income increases.

most income-tested transfers. One is the **basic transfer**—the transfer when net income is zero. In this case it is $310, the median U.S. amount for a family of 3 in 1996. The basic food stamp transfer increases with increases in family size and in the consumer price index. Another important feature is the **break-even net income**—the net income at which the transfer becomes zero. This occurs at $1,033 in Table 10.6. The third feature is the **transfer reduction rate**—the decrease in the transfer divided by the increase in net income. In Table 10.6, the transfer reduction rate is 0.3; for example, when net income increases by $100 (from 0 to $100), the transfer decreases by $30 (from $310 to $280). Technically, the transfer reduction rate has a negative value because the change in net income and the change in the transfer have opposite signs. Normally, however, the negative sign is ignored.

The transfer (T) at each net income (NI) can be determined by solving the transfer equation

$$T = BT - TRR\,(NI), \tag{10.1}$$

where BT is the basic transfer and TRR is the transfer reduction rate. For example, when BT = $310, TRR = 0.3, and NI = 0, the transfer (T) = $310. When BT = $310, TRR = 0.3, and NI = $100, then T = $280.

The break-even net income (BENI) can be determined by substituting BENI for NI and solving Equation 10.1 when T = 0. That is, Equation 10.1

becomes: $0 = BT - TRR$ (BENI). Solving this equation for BENI yields

$$BENI = \frac{BT}{TRR}.$$ (10.2)

Using Equation 10.2, BENI = \$1,033.33 when BT = \$310 and TRR = 0.3.

The break-even net income is an indicator of the **target efficiency** of a transfer program: the degree to which program benefits are confined to the poor. In general, the lower the break-even net income relative to the poverty threshold, the greater the target efficiency. In this case, the monthly break-even net income of \$1,033 is 84 percent of the 1996 monthly poverty threshold of \$1,226 (for a family of 3), and it is likely that most food stamp coupons are provided to the poor.

Target Efficiency
The degree to which transfer program benefits are confined to the poor.

SUPPLEMENTAL SECURITY INCOME (SSI)

SSI provides payments to the aged (those 65 or older), blind, and disabled. The federal government finances the program, although some states supplement the federal payment.

SSI is an income-tested transfer program in which the transfer varies inversely with net income. Each \$1 increase in net income results in a reduction in the SSI payment of 50 cents. The basic transfer in 1996 was \$470 per month for a person living alone and \$705 for a couple living in their own household. As in the food stamp program, the basic transfer is adjusted for price increases, providing protection against inflation. The monthly break-even net income is \$940 for a single-person household and \$1,410 for a two-person household.

AID TO FAMILIES WITH DEPENDENT CHILDREN (AFDC)

AFDC is the public assistance program that most people have traditionally thought of as "welfare." This program provided monthly income to needy families with dependent children. More than half of the states and the District of Columbia provided AFDC payments if two parents were present in the household, provided one was unemployed. In the remaining states, one parent had to be absent or no benefits were provided.

The states set their own benefit levels, established income and resource limits for eligibility (within federal guidelines), and administered the program. In 1994, the basic transfer for a one-parent family of three persons (the typical AFDC family) ranged from \$120 per month in Mississippi to \$923 in Alaska. The median basic transfer was \$366 per month—about 36 percent of the 1994 poverty line for a family of three.

AFDC is another program in which the transfer received varied inversely with the recipient's net income. During the first four months of participation, one-third of gross earnings was omitted from net income. This means that AFDC benefits were reduced by two-thirds of each dollar of net income, for a transfer reduction rate of 0.67. After four months, benefits were reduced by a dollar for each dollar of net income, for a transfer reduction rate of 1.0. The break-even net income for the median transfer family of three was \$546 during the first four months and \$366 after that. These values were far below the monthly poverty threshold, making it likely that AFDC was very target efficient.

WELFARE REFORM 1996 STYLE

In 1996, President Clinton signed a Republican-sponsored bill, The Personal Responsibility and Work Opportunity Reconciliation Act, that many observers have called "historic" welfare reform legislation. Politics often makes strange bedfellows, but in this case there was bipartisan frustration over the nation's long record of failure to reduce either its welfare rolls or the federal deficit, and proponents argued that the approach this bill required could do both. Whether it will or not remains to be seen.

With the stroke of Clinton's pen, the federal government reduced its planned financial commitment to the poor and apparently bowed out of an active role in solving the nation's poverty problem. Planned federal expenditures for various poverty programs were reduced by $56 billion over the next six years. To ensure that this expenditure reduction target is met, the federal programs for Aid to Families with Dependent Children (AFDC) and Job Opportunities and Basic Skills (JOBS) were changed from entitlements to block grants to the states. In the future, each state will receive a fixed sum of money each year from the federal government. The amount given initially to each state will reflect its historic allocation, but it will not necessarily vary (as is the era of entitlements) with the size and composition of the poverty population.

In order to continue to receive federal support, each family head on welfare must find work within two years or face the loss of benefits. A lifetime limit of five years was also imposed on all recipients of welfare benefits.

Each state is also subject to new federal regulations as a condition of the federal block grant it receives. Within a year, at least 25 percent of the welfare recipients in each state must be working at least 20 hours per week. Within five years, at least 50 percent of a state's welfare recipients must be working at least 30 hours per week. To appreciate the magnitude of this task, consider that in 1995 only 3.7 percent of the women on AFDC worked full time. In fact, to hit the federal target, the states will have to find jobs for more than 2 million people.

By some estimates, up to one quarter of the nation's welfare recipients are virtually unemployable due to factors such as unwillingness to work, difficulty in retaining jobs, chronic mental or physical prob-

---

The basic AFDC transfer increased with family size, at about $70 per person on average. Unlike food stamps and SSI, AFDC payments were not automatically adjusted for price increases. The lack of this feature resulted in a 47 percent decrease in the purchasing power of AFDC payments between 1970 and 1993.

In 1997, this program was replaced by a new federal program, Temporary Assistance for Needy Families (TANF). The essence of TANF is explained in the Additional Insight box titled "Welfare Reform—1996 style."

HOUSING ASSISTANCE   The federal government has two principal programs aimed at providing housing assistance to the poor: public housing and the Housing Assistance Payments (Section 8) Program. In the public housing program, the government subsidizes the construction and operation of housing units owned and operated by local public housing authorities. The local authorities offer the units at below-market rents—typically, at one-third to one-half less than the market rate on comparable units. The federal government reimburses the authorities for this difference in rents.

lems, lack of basic skills, and serious language deficiencies. The average recipient has the reading and math skills of a typical eighth grader and 30 percent have basic skills that are below the minimum of all women in the lowest-skill occupation (household workers).°

In spite of these difficulties, Wisconsin, which has cut its welfare case load by 44 percent since 1987, shows that the targets can probably be met. But the Wisconsin secret has been to spend more, not less, on the poor, investing millions in job training, health benefits, child care, and other support. The Wisconsin experience indicates, moreover, that it usually takes about 18 months of support to prepare a person to leave the dole for good—only then do the savings begin. Robert Haveman claims, in fact, that no inexpensive way exists to do the task right. For those who might think otherwise, he asks them to consider all the support that nonpoor families give their children before they finish their education and are launched on the path to a meaningful career.†

Not all states will want to, or could afford to, take the Wisconsin route. The federal grants will provide a spending cushion initially, but the cushion will disappear quickly in the face of a recession. When it does give out, the states hardest hit will be those with relatively high unemployment, few welfare recipients currently working, and large immigrant populations. Many state officials will have an irresistible urge to simply deny welfare benefits in order to keep from cutting other state programs to find the money for job programs.

Howard Chernick and Andrew Reschovsky estimate that, over the course of several years, states will respond to the imposition of block grants for welfare by reducing benefit levels by about 20 percent.‡ They expect total welfare spending to decline by more than this as more stringent eligibility constraints and lower benefits reduce the number of beneficiaries. Increased job training for the poor is likely to be financed, then, by ever more meager support for those who are poor.

°Robert Haveman, "From Welfare to Work: Problems and Pitfalls," *Focus* 18 (1), Special Issue (1996), 21–24.
†*Ibid*
‡Howard Chernick and Andrew Reschovsky, "State Responses to Block Grants: Will the Social Safety Net Survive?" *Focus* 18 (1), Special Issue (1996), 25–29.

Tenants are required to contribute from 15 to 30 percent of their net income to rent payments. This requirement causes the government transfer to fall as net income increases. To illustrate, assume a unit could earn $200 per month if rented on the open market. An eligible household with a monthly net income of $400 occupies the unit and pays rent of $120 (30 percent of $400) per month, and the government makes a transfer of $80 (the difference between the market rent and the payment by the renter) to the unit's owner. If the renter's monthly net income rises to $500, the rent payment increases to $150 (30 percent of $500) and the government transfer falls to $50.

Thus, the housing assistance programs are income-tested programs like food stamps, SSI, and AFDC. The transfer provided through housing assistance varies inversely with net income. The transfer reduction rate is a maximum of 0.30 (it ranges from 0.15 to 0.30 within the various housing programs). The basic transfer increases with family size in the sense that a larger unit is subsidized for a larger family. The basic transfer also increases as rents increase; thus, it provides some protection against inflation.

MEDICAID   Medicaid is the largest of the public assistance programs. It is financed by both the federal and state governments. The program covers all persons receiving AFDC and SSI payments plus persons designated "medically needy" by some of the states. Medicaid covers the cost of most medical care for participants, including the cost of nursing home care for poor elderly persons.

Medicaid is an income-tested program in the sense that people with incomes below the maximums prescribed for AFDC and SSI eligibility are also eligible for Medicaid. Unlike these public assistance programs, however, the Medicaid transfer does not taper off as the participant's net income rises. Medicaid pays for all covered medical expenses as long as a person remains eligible for coverage. When net income rises to the level where a family is no longer eligible, Medicaid payments drop to zero.

EFFECT OF TRANSFERS ON WORK EFFORT

Three features of income-tested transfers may influence a recipient's willingness to work: the transfer reduction rate, the basic transfer, and allowances. The transfer reduction rate is often equated to a marginal tax on earned income. The two are not equivalent, however, in terms of their effect on work effort. A tax on earned income reduces the hourly reward from working. This induces workers to work fewer hours. At the same time, however, the tax reduces a worker's income, an effect that may encourage the worker to work more hours in order to maintain a desired standard of living. Thus, the net effect of a tax on earned income is ambiguous; the tax may either decrease or increase hours worked.

An income-tested transfer reduces work effort in two ways. First, an individual finds that more earnings from work cause the transfer to fall due to the effect of the transfer reduction rate. This should have a negative effect, like that of a tax, on the amount an individual is willing to work. Second, the individual's transfer increases when fewer hours are worked. Thus, there is no incentive to work more to maintain one's income as there is in the case of a tax on income from work.

The size of the basic transfer may influence the decision to work or not to work (with a larger basic transfer making work less likely), but it will have no effect on the decision of someone already working to work more or fewer hours. This follows from the fact that the basic transfer does not change the hourly reward from working. Income allowances also may influence the decision to work or not to work, with larger allowances for child care and transportation making work more likely.

Based solely on a comparison of transfer reduction rates, the AFDC program provided the greatest work disincentive of the income-tested transfers. This was likely to be the case when the transfer reduction rate equaled 0.67 during the first four months of participation; it was even more likely when the transfer reduction rate switched to 1.0 after four months.

The transfer reduction rate for AFDC should have been high enough, by itself, to affect work effort. This also may be true for SSI, but it seems unlikely for food stamps and housing assistance. Many families receive transfers, however, from two or more of these programs simultaneously. Those who do are subject to the sum of the combined transfer reduction rates. In these cases, the relatively low transfer reduction rates associated with food stamps and housing assistance may be large enough to tip the scales in favor of less work. To illustrate, many AFDC families also received food stamps. If they did, each extra dollar they earned during their first four months on AFDC resulted in a loss of 97 cents in transfers: 67 cents in AFDC and 30 cents in food stamps.

The available evidence indicates that income-tested transfers have caused welfare recipients to work about five fewer hours per week. The income loss this created increased the poverty rate by about 1.2 percent and the number of people in poverty by about 3 million.[11]

EFFECT OF TRANSFERS ON FAMILY COMPOSITION

Earlier we documented the dramatic increase in families headed by women, arguing that this change has increased the overall poverty rate. Public assistance could be responsible for some of this trend, for three reasons.

First, AFDC payments were denied to households with both parents present in many states. Thus, otherwise intact couples may have separated so that the custodial parent could receive AFDC payments. Second, public assistance may have simply provided unhappy couples with the means to establish separate households. Third, the prospect of public assistance may have increased out-of-wedlock childbearing.

The evidence indicates, however, that public assistance was not a major cause of the growth of female-headed families; the percentage of all households headed by females grew dramatically in the 1970s and 1980s in spite of a 42 percent drop in the real value of public assistance. Garfinkel and McLanahan estimate that public assistance accounted for only 5 to 14 percent of the growth of female-headed households that occurred from 1960 to 1975.[12] If these findings are extrapolated to the period since 1975, the family composition effect of income-tested transfers accounts for only 0.2 to 0.3 percent of the poverty rate.

POLICY CHOICES

Some traditionally poor groups—especially the elderly—have made significant economic gains over the past quarter century. Some traditionally poor groups have made little, if any, progress. This is especially true of the working poor:

---

[11]Isabel V. Sawhill, "Poverty in the U.S.: Why Is It So Persistent?" *Journal of Economic Literature* 26 (September 1988), 1110–11.

[12]Irwin Garfinkel and Sara McLanahan, *Single Mothers and Their Children: A New American Dilemma* (Washington, DC: Urban Institute Press, 1986).

families headed by people who work, but earn less than the poverty threshold. Some traditionally poor groups—most notably, female-headed families—have become a larger part of the poverty problem.

The relatively larger gains of the elderly are due primarily to the benefits they get from Social Security. The working poor suffer more than other groups from unemployment and from technological change, and they also fare poorly in terms of transfers received. The system of public assistance treats female-headed families more generously, but there is growing dissatisfaction with this group's poor work record and rising concern that transfers breed long-term dependence on public support.

This section reviews some suggestions for policies to deal with the poverty experienced by the working poor and female-headed families. It also examines an alternative that has been on the policy agenda for nearly three decades: a negative income tax.

POLICIES FOR THE WORKING POOR

Over 6 million workers head families with incomes below the poverty line. What explains their poverty? There are three principal factors: inadequate public assistance, low pay, and lack of jobs. As already noted, only a small number of working poor receive assistance from government transfer programs. Families headed by someone who works full- or nearly full-time are eligible only for food stamps and housing subsidies and, if they have children, the Earned Income Tax Credit (discussed later). The significance of low pay can be understood by realizing that many heads of working poor households earn no more than the minimum wage, and even full-time work at the minimum wage by the household head would have left a family of four nearly $7,000 short of the poverty threshold in 1996. In a 1984 survey of two-parent poor families, 35 percent of husbands and 10 percent of wives claimed they were seeking work and unable to find it.

A number of proposed policies might reduce the poverty of the working poor. Among these are (1) medical protection, (2) earnings supplements, (3) child care assistance, (4) employment and training assistance, and (5) stabilization policy.

MEDICAL PROTECTION   Many of the working poor have no medical insurance. As already noted, Medicaid covers only one-fourth of this group. Low-wage jobs often provide no medical insurance, and when those who work at the few jobs that do provide medical insurance become unemployed, they can rarely afford to pay for the insurance they had while working.

Greater medical protection could be provided to the working poor. One way would be to extend Medicaid to everyone in families whose incomes are below some designated level, such as the official poverty threshold—that is, to make Medicaid truly income-tested, like the food stamp program.

Medicaid is not provided solely on an income-tested basis; it is provided to individuals receiving federally supported public assistance payments but also to the "medically needy." Coverage for the "medically needy" is determined and financed by the states, however, and only about half of the states provide this coverage.

Extending Medicaid to all of the poor would significantly expand Medicaid coverage and increase the tax cost of Medicaid. Whether it would significantly increase the opportunity cost of medical care is less certain. Many of the poor not currently covered by insurance receive medical services anyway. If they cannot pay for them, the cost is shifted to other patients. Thus, some part of any increase in Medicaid outlays would represent cost shifting (from nonpoor patients to the general taxpayer) rather than an increase in the opportunity cost of medical care. It is likely, however, that some of the poor not currently covered by insurance go without needed medical care, and that they would obtain some of this care if Medicaid paid the bill. Thus, the opportunity cost of medical care would somewhat increase.

Medicaid also has a potential, but unknown, effect on work effort. Individuals earning more than the Medicaid maximum income may reduce their work effort to become eligible for Medicaid. An extension of Medicaid to all of the poor would tempt more individuals with incomes above the Medicaid maximum to work less in order to establish eligibility.

A second way to provide medical insurance for the poor is to require employers to provide it as a fringe benefit. Although this plan is well-intentioned, it could be counterproductive. Employers could reduce the amount they are willing to pay in wages by the amount of the fringe benefit, or reduce the number they employ. Wage reductions and job losses are the last things the working poor need.

A third alternative is a government-supported residual insurance plan. Under this proposal, people who do not receive adequate insurance from employers or private insurance companies would be required to buy government medical insurance. Such a plan could be financed in a variety of ways; for example, the poor could be required to pay some percentage of their income as a "premium," or the plan could be wholly subsidized by the general taxpayer. The first of these financing arrangements could have some adverse effect on the work effort of the poor, while the latter may affect the work effort of the nonpoor.

In the larger sense, a no-cost alternative does not exist. Much more research remains to be done, however, before we fully understand how large the costs of full medical protection would be and who would bear them.

EARNINGS SUPPLEMENTS   As already noted, the working poor are poor partly because their wages are so low. There is considerable interest, then, in policies that increase the rewards that workers realize from their efforts. The three most-discussed policies are (1) raising the minimum wage, (2) providing wage subsidies, and (3) expanding the earned-income tax credit.

RAISING THE MINIMUM WAGE   The federal minimum wage is currently $5.15 per hour. Even full-time work at this wage cannot eliminate poverty. Thus, even though Congress increased the minimum wage in 1996, political pressure for further increases cannot be ruled out.

Although few people—economists included—question the motive for raising the minimum wage, economists note that a higher minimum wage generates unemployment (see Chapter 12). Empirical studies show that the minimum wage increases unemployment primarily in low-wage industries and among teenagers. Apparently, no studies have discovered a significant effect on the full-time working poor. Nevertheless, their employment prospects may be adversely affected because the working poor are concentrated in low-wage industries.

A further difficulty with a higher minimum wage is its target inefficiency. A policy is target inefficient when a large share of the benefits it provides is distributed to individuals other than those the policy is designed to assist. Of the 3.9 million workers who earned the minimum wage when it was $3.35 per hour, less than 10 percent were household heads of poor families. A further increase in the minimum wage would probably go largely to nonpoor individuals as well.

PROVIDING WAGE SUBSIDIES   In a program of wage subsidies, low-wage workers would receive a subsidy for each hour worked. The **wage subsidy** would equal some percentage of the difference between a designated maximum wage and the worker's wage. To illustrate, suppose that the designated maximum wage is $8 per hour and the subsidy percentage is 50 percent. Someone earning a wage of $5.15 per hour would receive a wage subsidy of $1.43 per hour [$0.5 \times (8 - 5.15)$], thus increasing the effective wage to $6.58 per hour. If a person were earning $6 per hour, the wage subsidy would be $1, and the effective wage would be $7.

Wage Subsidy
A payment to a low-wage worker for each hour worked, equal to a percentage of the difference between a maximum wage and the worker's wage.

A wage subsidy can be more effectively targeted to the poor than can the minimum wage, provided it is restricted to principal family workers. A wage subsidy probably would not reduce employment. It does not require employers to pay workers more than they are worth as employees, as does the minimum wage. The prospect of the government picking up part of the tab for labor costs, however, may provide employers with an incentive to reduce the wage they are willing to pay.

Paradoxically, a wage subsidy does not guarantee increased work effort, as one would expect a higher effective wage to do. On the one hand, the higher wage increases the opportunity cost of leisure, inducing people to work more. On the other hand, a higher wage enables an individual to maintain a given standard of living by working less. The net effect is uncertain.

EXPANDING THE EARNED INCOME TAX CREDIT (EITC)   The federal tax code has provided an earned income tax credit since 1975. As the label implies, this is a credit against income tax liability. To be eligible, the taxpayer must have dependents and a relatively low adjusted gross income (income from all sources less adjustments to income, such as excess employee business expenses and contributions to Individual Retirement Accounts). The credit is refundable; taxpayers may claim the full credit even if their tax liability is less than the credit.

Generally, the credit equals a specified percentage of wages up to a maximum dollar amount. The maximum amount applies over a certain range of adjusted gross income and then diminishes to zero over a specified phaseout range.

For a family with two children in 1996, the credit rate was 40 percent. The maximum credit was $3,560, reached when adjusted gross income was $8,900. The phaseout rate was 21.06 percent, which began when adjusted gross income exceeded $11,620. Given these parameters, the credit was zero when adjusted gross income reached $28,524.

In 1996, the EITC program was expected to provide over $25 billion in tax credits and refunds to nearly 18.7 million families. Although it is obvious from the relatively wide phaseout range that the program would provide benefits to many families that were not poor, about $6.5 billion of the benefits would go to families with incomes below the poverty line. This amount would have been sufficient to raise the incomes of more than 1 million families to a level above the poverty line.[13]

CHILD CARE ASSISTANCE   The lack of affordable child care can significantly hinder the labor market participation of adults in poor families. Child care in organized facilities is expensive—roughly $2,500 to $3,000 per child per year. Consequently, relatives are the primary source of child care for low-income working mothers with children.

The federal government currently has 22 separate programs that provide some form of child care assistance. The largest of these is the child and dependent care tax credit feature of the federal individual income tax.

The child and dependent care tax credit provides a credit against federal income tax liability equal to 30 percent of employment-related child care expenses for taxpayers with adjusted gross incomes (AGI) up to $10,000. The credit is reduced for taxpayers with AGI greater than $10,000 until it reaches a minimum of 20 percent at an income of $28,000 or more. Eligible expenses are limited to $2,400 per child under age 13 for the first two children. Thus, the maximum credit is $1,440 (= $4,800 × 0.3). The credit can be claimed by working heads of one-person families or by families with children in which both parents are working.

This credit provides virtually no benefits to the poor; less than 1 percent of the total credit goes to families with adjusted gross incomes less than $10,000. It is doubtful that the working poor can afford child care in the first place. Moreover, in many poor two-parent families, only one parent works (probably because of high child care expenses in many cases!), making the family not eligible for the credit.

What can be done? Simply expanding the percentage of child care expenses covered by the credit, as is often suggested, would largely help the nonpoor and significantly increase program cost. It would be more target efficient to provide vouchers for child care services to the poor.

EMPLOYMENT AND TRAINING ASSISTANCE   The working poor are more likely to be unemployed, to be working part time rather than full time, and

---

[13]Robert H. Haveman and John Karl Scholz, "The Clinton Welfare Reform Plan: Will It End Poverty As We Know It?" *Focus* 16, no. 2 (Winter 1994–1995), 6.

to be employed at such low wages that even full-time employment does not raise their family income above the poverty line. A wide array of government programs is aimed at increasing the employability and employment of workers, including vocational education, adult education, job training, employment services, and vocational rehabilitation. Two of these programs, the Job Training and Partnership Act program and Job Corps, are targeted exclusively at the poor. The federal government also requires that a small percentage of federal grants to the states for vocational education be spent on disadvantaged youth.

The Job Corps provides intensive vocational training and basic education to youths from 14 to 21 years old who are poor, out of school, and out of work. It is largely a residential program that operates on the premise that the most seriously disadvantaged youths can only be rehabilitated away from their normal environment. It is not designed to meet the job training needs of family heads.

Most of the responsibility for training and retraining adults rests currently with the Job Training Partnership Act (JTPA) program. The federal government spent $1 billion on this program in 1996 in the form of block grants to the states. Measured in dollars of constant purchasing power, this was less than 20 percent of the amount put into the program at its peak in 1981.

This money is targeted efficiently, going primarily to AFDC participants and disadvantaged youth. The restriction of funds to these individuals, however, effectively precludes the provision of services to most of the working poor. Restrictions on the use of funds for living expenses also makes the program inaccessible to the working poor. There may be some merit, then, in removing restrictions that bias the use of funds against the working poor, and in expanding such a reformed program.

STABILIZATION POLICY   Macroeconomic policies to reduce unemployment are not normally thought of as an antipoverty tool. Yet they may be vital in any effort to make lasting progress against the poverty of the working poor. Relatively full employment is a precondition for the success of job training; it does little good to make a person more productive unless a reasonable prospect of employment exists. Also, as noted earlier, a significant part of the poverty of the working poor is associated with increases in unemployment. Thus, elimination of this problem would make an important contribution to the War on Poverty.

POLICIES FOR FEMALE-HEADED FAMILIES

The increase in the percentage of families headed by women and the high incidence of poverty among them have focused increasing attention on this group. While this cohort has been growing, income transfers have come under attack for reducing work effort and making the recipients dependent on the transfer system. This linkage of transfers and work effort has resulted in renewed interest in ways to get more single parents into the work force. The alternative most often discussed is **workfare:** work for welfare.

The increase in female-headed families has also focused attention on the poor record of absent parents in supporting the children they leave behind, and

Workfare
Government programs that require recipients of public assistance to enhance their employment prospects in exchange for such assistance.

there is a growing interest in government playing a major role in collecting child support payments. Although other policy initiatives may be helpful to female-headed families, such as the programs just outlined for the working poor, workfare and the improved collection of child support payments are aimed primarily at this group.

WORKFARE The first AFDC work program, the Work Incentive program, was established in 1967 to provide job skills evaluation, job training, and job placement for AFDC recipients. Recipients over 16 with children under 6 years of age were required to register for the program, but funding limitations restricted the availability of the necessary services and training.

In 1981, the federal government gave the states the option of establishing other work programs for AFDC recipients. The best known of these is the Community Work Experience program, which required adult AFDC recipients to perform community work in exchange for benefits. The 1981 act also permitted states to operate work supplementation programs, in which federal funds were used to subsidize jobs for AFDC recipients.

In 1988, Congress required all states to establish and operate a Job Opportunities and Basic Skills (JOBS) program. Under JOBS, states provided job search aid, work experience, work supplementation, and on-the-job training. Individuals required to participate in JOBS who failed to do so lost AFDC benefits. To get states to participate, the federal government paid a large share of program costs.

The JOBS program was eliminated as part of the 1996 welfare reform bill passed by Congress. Federal money for workfare will still be given to the states, but it will be included as part of the block grant that replaces AFDC. The states have full responsibility for making workfare work.

All of the states have a work experience program, although most have been severely underfunded. In an earlier evaluation of some of these programs, the Manpower Development and Research Corporation found that workfare resulted in smaller welfare outlays and reduced use of welfare services for both single parents and unemployed heads of intact families.[14] In addition, single parents were more likely to be employed and to experience earnings gains. Whether these experiences portend success for recent welfare reform measures remains to be seen.

CHILD SUPPORT ASSURANCE Even if welfare mothers were fully employed, many of them could earn no more than their annual welfare grant. It seems unreasonable in view of this fact to expect these women to be totally self-supporting. One way to reduce poverty without creating total dependency is to supplement, rather than replace, the earnings of single parents who have custody of minor children. Some of this supplement must come from public assistance, but some can (and should) come from private child support.

Nearly one of every two children born today will become eligible for child support by an absent parent at some point before reaching age 18. Currently, however, courts award child support to only 58 percent of eligible mothers. The

---

[14]Judith M. Gueron, *Reforming Welfare with Work* (New York: Ford Foundation, 1987).

process of setting the award is expensive and contentious. The size of the award as a percentage of the noncustodial parent's income varies greatly. Awards are extremely difficult to collect; fewer than 30 percent of awardees receive the full amount awarded on a regular basis.

A more adequate child support system is possible. The first step in this direction was the establishment by Congress of the Child Support Enforcement program, which created a bureaucracy to enforce private child support obligations for all AFDC recipients and for others on request.

Legislation passed in 1984 required the states to adopt expedited procedures for obtaining child support orders from the courts, to establish child support guidelines to be used by the courts, and to initiate automatic withholding from paychecks for child support beginning one month after failure to pay.

The Family Support Act of 1988 stiffened federal resolve on this issue. As of November 1990, states have been required to provide for immediate wage withholding for all cases handled by the Office of Child Support Enforcement. Starting in 1994, withholding was required for all support orders.

The nation's child support program collected nearly $11 billion in 1995. Some scholars believe, however, that potential collections are much greater, perhaps as much as an additional $34 billion.[15] Prospects like this induced Congress to include new provisions for strengthening the child support collection system in the 1996 welfare reform legislation.

Wisconsin has implemented a child support assurance system that may become a model for the nation in the long run. Under Wisconsin's system, all noncustodial parents are required to share income with their children, at a rate specified by law. The share is collected through payroll withholding. Children are entitled to benefits equal to a government-financed minimum benefit or to the share awarded by the courts, whichever is higher. This part of the design has not been fully realized, however, due to state budget constraints.

The Wisconsin program is not just for the poor; it serves children of all income classes. This is a feature that may be vital for long-term political support. Moreover, the benefits do not decrease as income increases, so it should not have a negative effect on work effort. Evaluation of the Wisconsin experiment indicates that it reduced the AFDC caseload and significantly increased hours worked. Although this experiment needs to be replicated on a larger scale, the Wisconsin results are encouraging to those who want to reduce dependence on welfare and increase self-sufficiency among females who head families.

A NEGATIVE INCOME TAX

The final alternative we examine is a negative income tax (NIT). This alternative used to command the most attention by economists, but it has been superceded in recent years by the new wave of proposals aimed at the working poor and

---

[15]E. Sorenen, *The Benefits of Increased Child Support Enforcement* (Welfare Reform Briefs, no. 2) (Washington, DC: The Urban Institute, April 1995).

female-headed families. There is still enough interest in an NIT, however, to warrant a brief examination.

Economists use the term *negative tax* as a synonym for *transfer*. Thus, a negative income tax is really an income transfer program. It does have certain characteristics, however, that distinguish it from other transfers.

A **negative income tax** is normally envisioned as a federally funded, income-tested transfer, in which the amount transferred varies inversely with income. Federal funding would ensure uniform payments to people at the same income level, regardless of where they live. The transfer would be income-tested only. A person would not have to fit into a particular category with respect to age, sex, marital status, parental status, or employment status to receive transfer payments. The payments could be administered at relatively low cost by the Internal Revenue Service; no social case workers would be used, as in the AFDC program.

A negative income tax has some of the same elements as existing income-tested transfers: a basic transfer, a transfer reduction rate, and a break-even net income. That is, the transfer equation for an NIT has the same structure as the one used for food stamps: $T = BT - TRR(NI)$. Thus, the transfer tapers off just as in existing income-tested programs, and the transfer reduction rate is a potential deterrent to work effort.

The same amount of money currently transferred to the poor by existing public assistance programs could be transferred at lower cost through a negative income tax. This program therefore would have a smaller transfer reduction rate than the ones applicable to many poor families, especially those currently receiving transfers from more than one program. It would not be possible, however, to eliminate the transfer reduction rate and confine benefits of a negative income tax primarily to the poor.

Perhaps the real difficulty with the negative income tax is that it has never captured the fancy of politicians for any extended period of time. The Nixon administration came close to pushing a modest program through Congress in 1971, but no attempt to do so since then has gone very far.

Negative Income Tax
A federally funded, income-tested transfer program, often proposed as a substitute for existing income-tested transfer programs.

SUMMARY

The extent of poverty is normally determined by comparing a family's resources with resources required to achieve an acceptable minimum standard of living. The most widely used comparison is the official poverty measure, according to which a person is poor who lives in a family whose money income is below the poverty threshold. Many economists prefer adjusted official poverty measures, which include additional resources and produce lower estimates of the poverty rate and poverty population than does the official poverty measure. The official poverty rate in 1995 was much smaller than it was in 1959 but higher than it was in 1973.

Vigorous economic growth and large increases in cash transfers reduced the poverty rate continuously from 1960 to 1974. Pretransfer poverty has risen since then as a result of increasing unemployment, demographic changes, and the effects of government transfers on work effort and family formation.

Poverty is higher in black and Hispanic families and in families headed by females. Blacks, Hispanics, and women also suffer from labor market discrimination. It is unlikely, however, that labor market discrimination is a significant cause of poverty, or that policies aimed at reducing labor market discrimination will have much effect on the poverty rate.

The transfer programs examined in this chapter are Medicaid, food stamps, Supplemental Security Income, AFDC, and housing subsidies. Each of these programs is an income-tested transfer. Except for Medicaid, these transfers can be characterized in terms of the size of the basic transfer, the transfer reduction rate, the break-even net income, and income allowances.

Higher transfer reduction rates cause recipients to reduce hours worked. Higher basic transfers adversely influence the decision to work. Income allowances positively influence the decision to work. Empirical evidence indicates a small adverse effect of these factors on work effort.

Government transfers also are expected to increase the number of female-headed households. Empirical evidence confirms a small impact of this type.

Recent discussions of public policy have focused on programs designed to aid the working poor and poor families headed by women. Poverty among the working poor could be reduced by providing (1) more adequate protection against medical expenses, (2) more generous earnings supplements, (3) more effective child care assistance, (4) better-funded employment and training assistance, and (5) effective policies against rising unemployment. Female-headed families could benefit from these policies, also, as well as from better-funded workfare programs and more effective systems of assuring child support payments by absent fathers.

The final alternative considered is a negative income tax. Similar in structure to existing income-tested transfers, it may be a lower-cost substitute with a smaller impact on work effort.

KEY TERMS

Official poverty measure	Feminization of poverty	Target efficiency
Official poverty threshold	Income-tested transfers	Wage subsidy
Money income	Basic transfer	Workfare
Capital gains	Break-even net income	Negative income tax
In-kind transfers	Transfer reduction rate	

REVIEW QUESTIONS

1. Currently, in-kind transfers are not included in the official measure of resources that individuals have available to meet their basic needs. Do you believe these transfers should be included? Defend your answer.

2. "Instead of enacting new transfer programs to eliminate poverty, we should concentrate on policies that would reduce unemployment." Do you agree or disagree with this statement? Defend your answer.

3. In addition to lowering unemployment, what other factor decreased poverty significantly from 1960 to 1974? Briefly explain why.

4. The average female earned 73 percent as much as the average male in 1996. Explain why this comparison overstates the degree of labor market discrimination against females.

5. There is evidence of labor market discrimination against blacks, Hispanics and females, but such discrimination has little to do with poverty. Explain why.

6. Congressperson Smith argues that government transfers have worked to alleviate poverty. Congressperson Jones argues that these transfers have worked to increase poverty. Who is correct? Defend your answer.

7. Using the transfer equation, solve each of the following:
   a. Suppose the basic transfer is $500 per month and the break-even net income is $2,000 per month. What is the transfer reduction rate?
   b. Suppose the basic transfer is $200 per month, the transfer reduction rate is 0.5, and net income is $100 per month. What is the amount of the transfer received by the individual?
   c. What is the break-even net income when the transfer reduction rate is 0.3 and the basic transfer is $360 per month?

8. "One of the major disadvantages of transfer programs is the fact that they can lead to the dissolution of the family unit, thereby resulting in increased numbers of households headed by females." Is this statement true or false? Defend your answer.

9. List and briefly discuss the five major public assistance programs currently in place.

10. "Extending Medicaid to cover all of the working poor would significantly increase the opportunity cost of medical care." Is this statement true or false? Defend your answer.

11. Increasingly, poverty has become a problem faced disproportionately by females. Briefly discuss the various policies that have been suggested to deal with the feminization of poverty.

12. Congress is currently debating the pros and cons of the various methods of increasing the earnings of the poor (increasing the minimum wage, expanding the earned income tax credit, and granting wage subsidies). You are called before the House to testify. Briefly outline your views on these various programs.

13. What are the advantages and disadvantages associated with a negative income tax?

SUGGESTIONS FOR FURTHER READING

Burtless, Gary T., and Robert H. Haveman. "Taxes and Transfers: How Much Economic Loss?" *Challenge* (March/April 1987), 45–51. An examination of the view that the U.S. tax and transfer system has eroded the work ethic. The authors argue that little evidence supports calls for slashing taxes and welfare programs.

Committee on Ways and Means, U.S. House of Representatives. *The Green Book*. Washington, DC: Government Printing Office. This is an annual compilation of information and data on poverty and income redistribution programs. The 1996 issue also contains an extensive summary of 1996 welfare reform legislation.

Danziger, Sheldon H., Gary D. Sandefur, and Daniel H. Weinberg, eds., *Confronting Poverty: Prescriptions for Change*. Cambridge, MA: Harvard University Press, 1995. Papers from a 1992 conference, reflecting some of the latest knowledge on a number of poverty-related issues. Most of the book is understandable by nonspecialists.

Ellwood, David T. *Poor Support: Poverty in the American Family*. New York: Basic Books, 1988. A review of data, trends, and abiding values with respect to the poor. Contains an outline of many alternatives aimed at the working poor and female-headed households.

Focus 18 (Special Issue 1996). This publication from the Institute for Research on Poverty (University of Wisconsin, Madison) contains a review of many of the issues raised by recent congressional action, which places the primary responsibility for solving the poverty problem at the state level.

Haveman, Robert. "Who Are the Nation's 'Truly Poor'?" *The Brookings Review* (Winter 1993), 24–27. Haveman reviews the problems with the official measure of poverty and the pitfalls inherent in designing an improved measure. Contains an easy-to-understand discussion of earnings capacity poverty—a type of measure that may be recommended by a panel of experts convened by the National Academy of Sciences to review measures of poverty in the United States.

Levy, Frank, and Richard C. Michel. *The Future of American Families*. (Washington, DC: The Urban Institute Press, 1991). This book documents and explains the growing inequality in the distribution of income in the United States, and discusses some of the implications of this trend for the country's future—including its probable effect on the poverty problem.

Sawhill, Isabel V. "Poverty in the U.S.: Why Is It So Persistent?" *Journal of Economic Literature* 26 (September 1988), 1073–119. A more advanced treatment of many of the issues and programs reviewed in this chapter.

11

TRACKING THE
MACROECONOMY

TERMS YOU SHOULD KNOW

Demand curve (Chapter 1)

Supply curve (Chapter 1)

Equilibrium (Chapter 1)

This chapter introduces many of the concepts used to measure the economy's performance. As measures of the economy's performance, they provide helpful information to households, firms, and policymakers, which is why the news media bombard us with data based on these concepts.

Information on the performance of the economy can improve decision making for households, firms, and policymakers. With regard to households, suppose a person is considering quitting his job to search for a better one. If the economy is performing well, his chances of success are better than if the economy is performing poorly. Similarly, suppose a graduating college senior is considering attending graduate school to obtain her master's degree. If the economy is performing well, good jobs are relatively plentiful, and she may wish to postpone her graduate education. On the other hand, if it is performing poorly, good jobs are relatively scarce, and she may wish to continue her education.

With regard to firms, suppose you wish to start your own firm. If the economy is performing well, you have a better chance of succeeding than if it is performing poorly. Similarly, suppose a firm is considering increasing its output and employment. If the economy is performing well, this may be a wise decision. If it is performing poorly, however, increasing output and employment may be unwise.

Finally, information on the performance of the economy is important to policymakers, who compare the nation's economic performance with both its past performance and that of other countries. If the economy is performing poorly, policymakers can try to enact policies to improve its performance. If the economy is performing well, no policy action is necessary. Instead, policymakers can concentrate on taking credit, whether it is deserved or not.

The performance of the economy is always an important issue at election time. Indeed, it can be decisive in presidential elections. Most experts believe that President Bush lost his bid for reelection in 1992 primarily because of the economy's mediocre performance. They also believe that President Clinton's bid for reelection in 1996 was successful partly because of the economy's strength.

In addition to discussing various concepts used to measure the economy's performance, this chapter introduces aggregate demand–aggregate supply analysis. As we shall see, aggregate demand and aggregate supply determine the nation's output and price level. Because aggregate demand and supply change over time, output and the price level level also change.

Because they determine output and the price level, aggregate demand and supply are important in determining the nation's unemployment and inflation rates. We consider unemployment in Chapter 12 and inflation in Chapter 13. Aggregate demand and supply also help to determine the nation's budget and balance of payments deficits. We cover the federal government's budget deficit in Chapter 14 and the nation's balance of payments deficit in Chapter 15. Finally, aggregate demand and supply determine the nation's output growth rate. We examine economic growth in Chapter 16.

GROSS DOMESTIC PRODUCT (GDP)

In judging the nation's economic performance, measuring the nation's output is clearly important. Various measures of output exist, but the one most frequently cited is gross domestic product. **Gross domestic product (GDP)** is the market value of all final goods and services produced in the economy over the relevant time span, usually a year.

Only final goods and services are counted in GDP. **Final goods** are goods purchased (or available to be purchased) for final use. By definition, final goods are not used to produce other goods. In contrast, **intermediate goods** are goods purchased for resale or for use in producing other goods. Automobiles and bread are final goods because they are typically purchased for final use. Steel and flour are intermediate goods because they are used in the production of other goods.

If all goods—intermediate and final—were counted as part of GDP, part of the nation's output would be counted twice. To illustrate, part of the steel industry's output is used in the production of automobiles. If the outputs of both the steel and automobile industries were included in GDP, the part of the steel industry's output that is used in the production of automobiles would be counted twice, first as part of the steel industry's output and second as part of the automobile industry's output. The same thing would happen if the outputs of both the flour and bread industries were included in GDP. To prevent multiple counting of the nation's output, only final goods and services are included in GDP.

GDP is an estimate of the market value of all final goods and services. It is the sum of the market value of each final good or service. The sum must be in value, or dollar, terms because it is not meaningful to add the physical units of the various goods and services. In estimating the nation's output, it would, for example, make no sense to add together the numbers of automobiles and toothbrushes produced because automobiles are worth much more than toothbrushes.

The GDP summation must be in value, or dollar, terms, but it need not be in terms of market prices. Any set of prices could be used. The market price of each good or service is used, however, because it represents the value that people place on that good or service. As a result, market prices are less arbitrary than any other set of prices. Even so, the use of market prices makes it difficult to compare the nation's output in different time periods.

Finally, GDP is a measure of production, not sales. Goods produced during the year are counted as part of GDP regardless of whether they are sold or added to business inventories. Suppose firms produced $100 billion worth of automobiles in 1997, but they sold only $90 billion worth. The automobile industry's contribution to GDP in 1997 would be $100 billion, not $90 billion.

As defined, GDP excludes many transactions. It excludes purchases of used or secondhand goods because these goods were counted when they were produced. It also excludes financial transactions such as the purchase of stocks or bonds because they involve an exchange of assets, not production.

Gross Domestic Product (GDP)
The market value of all final goods and services produced in the economy over the relevant time span, usually one year.

Final Goods
Goods purchased (or available to be purchased) for final use.

Intermediate Goods
Goods purchased for resale or for use in producing other goods.

GDP's COMPONENTS

GDP has four parts: personal consumption expenditures, gross private domestic investment, government purchases of goods and services, and net exports of goods and services.

CONSUMPTION

Personal Consumption Expenditures
Household purchases of durable and nondurable goods and services.

Personal consumption expenditures (consumption) consist of household purchases of durable goods (such as automobiles, appliances, and furniture), nondurable goods (such as food, clothing, and cigarettes), and services (such as medical and dental care, legal advice, and hairstyling). Of these expenditures, most are for nondurable goods and services. The distinguishing characteristic of these goods and services is that they last only a short period of time. Durable goods, on the other hand, last much longer; even so, their contribution to GDP is recorded when they are produced rather than over their life span.

As shown in Table 11.1, personal consumption expenditures account for about two-thirds of GDP. Thus, they make up the largest part of GDP by a wide margin. As a percentage of GDP, these expenditures do not vary much from year to year; they are a relatively stable component of GDP.

GROSS INVESTMENT

Gross Private Domestic Investment
Firms' purchases of new equipment, purchases of all newly produced structures, and changes in business inventories.

Gross private domestic investment (gross investment) is (1) the purchases of new equipment by firms, (2) the purchases of all newly produced structures, and (3) changes in business inventories. Thus, a firm's purchase of a new lathe or drill press is treated as investment. The construction of a factory is also classified as investment. The construction of residential housing, including apartment houses and homes, is treated as investment. Finally, changes in business inventories are included in investment because GDP is a measure of production, not sales. As discussed earlier, suppose that firms produced $100 billion worth of automobiles in 1997 but sold only $90 billion worth in that year. If the automobiles were sold to households, the $90 billion would be counted as consumption and included in GDP. Because $10 billion worth of automobiles were not sold, business inventories increased by that amount. This $10 billion increase in inventories is investment and is part of GDP. If it were not included, the contribution of the automobile industry to GDP in 1997 would be underestimated by $10 billion.

So far, we have discussed gross private domestic investment, or gross investment. Part of gross investment merely replaces structures and equipment that have worn out or been destroyed during the period. To determine the part of gross investment that adds to the existing stock of structures and equipment, we subtract consumption of fixed capital from gross investment to obtain

GROSS DOMESTIC PRODUCT AND ITS COMPONENTS, 1995 (BILLIONS OF CURRENT DOLLARS)

TABLE 11.1		
Gross domestic product		7,253.8
Personal consumption expenditures		4,924.9
Gross private domestic investment		1,065.3
Government purchases of goods and services		1,358.3
Net exports of goods and services		–94.7
Exports of goods and services	807.4	
Imports of goods and services	902.0	

GDP has four components: personal consumption expenditures, gross private domestic investment, government purchases of goods and services, and net exports of goods and services. The largest component by a wide margin is personal consumption expenditures.

Source: U.S. Department of Commerce, Bureau of Economic Analysis, *Survey of Current Business* 76 (Washington, DC: Government Printing Office, August 1996), 8.

net private domestic investment, or net investment. **Consumption of fixed capital** consists of depreciation, an estimate of the deterioration of the nation's structures and equipment, and an allowance for accidental damage to them. To illustrate, gross investment was $1,065.3 billion in 1995. Of this amount, $825.9 billion was used to replace structures and equipment that had deteriorated or been destroyed during the year. As a result, net investment was only $239.4 billion, obtained by subtracting consumption of fixed capital from gross investment.

Net investment is a very important concept because it implies a change in the nation's capital stock. The nation's **capital stock** is its accumulated stock of structures, producers' durable equipment, and business inventories. Gross investment is the amount of newly produced structures and producers' durable equipment plus changes in business inventories. Because part of gross investment simply replaces structures and equipment that wear out or are destroyed during the period, only net investment adds to the nation's capital stock.

The capital stock is important because it is a major determinant of the nation's productive capacity. All other things equal, an increase in the nation's capital stock (positive net investment) implies an increase in the nation's productive capacity. With the increase, the economy will be capable of producing more goods and services.

In 1995, gross investment accounted for approximately 15 percent of GDP. In contrast, net investment was only about 3 percent. In addition to constituting a smaller proportion of GDP than consumption, investment also exhibits greater instability from year to year.

Net Private Domestic Investment
Refers to the portion of investment that adds to the existing stock of structures and equipment.

Consumption of Fixed Capital
Allowances for depreciation of the nation's structures and equipment and for accidental damage to them.

Capital Stock
The nation's accumulated stock of structures, producers' durable equipment, and business inventories.

GOVERNMENT PURCHASES

Government
Purchases of Goods
and Services
The purchases of
federal, state, and
local governments.

Government purchases of goods and services are simply the purchases of federal, state, and local governments.[1] These purchases include the procurement of military hardware; the construction of dams, highways, and schools; and payment for the services of accountants, teachers, and other government employees. State and local governments account for most governmental purchases.

In 1995, government purchases accounted for approximately 19 percent of GDP—a surprisingly low percentage. The primary reason for the low percentage is that **government transfer payments** are excluded from GDP.

Government Transfer
Payments
Payments made to
individuals or institutions
by government that
involve no production
and exchange of goods
and services.

Government transfer payments include Social Security benefits, Medicare and Medicaid payments, and unemployment compensation. Like purchases of goods and services, transfer payments involve payments by government; unlike them, the government receives no goods or services in return. Because transfer payments do not involve the production of goods and services, they are excluded from GDP. Although excluded, these payments are obviously very important.

NET EXPORTS

Net Exports of Goods
and Services
The amount by which
foreign spending on
domestically produced
goods and services is
greater (less) than
domestic spending on
goods and services
produced abroad.

Net exports of goods and services is the difference between exports of goods and services and imports of goods and services. **Exports** are produced in this country and purchased by foreigners. **Imports** are produced abroad and purchased by persons in this country. Because GDP is a measure of domestic production, exports are included in GDP. Consequently, exports are added to consumption, gross investment, and government purchases to arrive at GDP. Because imports are produced abroad, they are excluded from GDP. They are subtracted from consumption, gross investment, and government purchases because those components include the purchases of goods produced both here and abroad. Suppose a household purchases a new car that was made in Japan. The purchase is counted as consumption. Similarly, suppose a firm purchases machine tools made in Sweden. The purchase is included in gross investment. Because the various components of GDP include both domestic and foreign production, imports must be subtracted from those components to guarantee that only domestic production is included in GDP. If the subtraction were not made, the nation's output of goods and services would be greatly overstated.

Exports
Goods and services
produced in this
country and purchased
by foreigners.

Imports
Goods and services
produced abroad and
bought by persons
in this country.

Rather than treating exports and imports separately, we take the difference between them to arrive at net exports. This concept may be interpreted as the amount by which foreign spending on domestically produced goods and services is greater (less) than domestic spending on goods and services produced abroad. This difference may be either positive or negative. In recent years, imports have exceeded exports. The difference, therefore, has been negative.

---

[1]With regard to government purchases, the U.S. Department of Commerce now distinguishes between government consumption and investment. For convenience, however, we shall refer to government purchases rather than government consumption expenditures and gross investment.

MEASURED GDP AND THE UNDERGROUND ECONOMY

Over the years, many economists have become concerned that measured GDP may drastically underestimate the nation's level of economic activity because of the existence of an underground economy. The *underground economy* consists of economic activity that avoids official detection and measurement. The activities are either inherently illegal or not reported to avoid taxes, detection by the Immigration and Naturalization Service (INS), or for other reasons. Examples of the former include illegal drug trafficking, bookmaking, and prostitution. Examples of the latter include the nondeclaration of receipts by owners or managers of restaurants, bars, and various retail establishments and the failure to report income from tips and casual or part-time work. Although an underground economy has always existed, many believe that it is larger now than in the past because of the increased tax burden, greater government regulation, and widespread dissatisfaction with government. In this regard, marginal tax rates are important, but people's perceptions of the fairness of the tax system and the extent to which they believe that others are complying with the system are also important.

How large is the underground economy? No one knows for sure. In one of the first studies of the underground economy, Peter M. Gutmann estimated that economic activity in the underground economy equaled about 10 percent of the nation's measured output.° Since Gutmann's study, many others have been conducted. Some of the estimates are lower than Gutmann's, but most are higher. Because of the nature of the problem, it is impossible to obtain a precise estimate. Even so, we can conclude that the underground economy is large.

Although the existence of the underground economy casts doubt on the accuracy of reported GDP, the data remain useful, particularly if the official and underground economies are growing at the same rate. Suppose, however, that measured GDP is growing more slowly than in the past. Policymakers may react by implementing more expansionary monetary and fiscal policies. If economic activity is expanding at the same rate as in the past, but with relatively more of it occurring in the underground economy, the added expansionary policies will result in inflation, not increased economic activity.

The existence of a large underground economy has other implications. It implies that a disproportionate share of the tax burden is carried by those who are not participating in the underground economy. If those who participate in the underground economy paid taxes, tax rates could be reduced significantly without loss of tax revenue. In addition, the underground economy may be less efficient. The various activities must be carried out covertly, which often precludes the most efficient means of production and distribution. Also, most or all transactions must be conducted with cash, which is disadvantageous in many instances. These factors, however, are offset to some degree by the lack of government regulation and by the greater flexibility, including part-time and at-home work, in the underground economy.

Various suggestions have been made to reduce the size of the underground economy. These include reducing tax rates, making the tax system more equitable, devoting more resources to law enforcement, and increasing the penalties for participating in the underground economy. It must be recognized, however, that with existing tax rates (or even lower ones) a stong economic incentive exists for people to participate in the underground economy. Moreover, given its shadowy nature, one cannot be optimistic about reducing its size by devoting more resources to law enforcement. For these reasons, a large underground economy is likely to persist for the foreseeable future.

°Peter M. Gutmann, "The Subterranean Economy," *Financial Analysts Journal* 33 (November/December 1977), 26–27 and 34.

In 1995, exports of goods and services totaled $807.4 billion, approximately 11 percent of GDP. Imports of goods and services were $902.0 billion, about 12 percent of GDP. Net exports of goods and services equaled a minus $94.7 billion, obtained by subtracting $902.0 billion from $807.4 billion.

NOMINAL GDP, REAL GDP, AND THE GDP DEFLATOR

GDP is calculated by adding the market values of various goods and services. Unfortunately, quantities *and* prices change over time. Because GDP reflects changes in both quantities and prices, a person can be easily mislead when comparing the output of goods and services in different years.

To illustrate the problem and to show how it is resolved, consider the following example. We will assume, for simplicity, only one good (good A) and two years (1997 and 1998). The relevant quantities and prices are shown in Table 11.2.

As indicated in the table, 6 million units of good A were produced in 1997. The price per unit was $1,000. With only one good, the nation's GDP in 1997 was $6 billion, obtained by multiplying 6 million (the number of units produced) by $1,000 (the price per unit). In contrast, 6.3 million units were produced in 1998 at a price per unit of $1,100. GDP in 1998 is therefore $6.93 billion, obtained by multiplying 6.3 million by $1,100.

A GDP of $6 billion in 1997 and $6.93 billion in 1998 seems to indicate that the nation's output of goods and services increased by about 15 percent. Thus, a person might conclude that 15 percent more goods and services were available to members of society in 1998 than in 1997. This conclusion is incorrect. As indicated in Table 11.2, the number of units produced increased from 6 million to 6.3 million; thus, only 5 percent more units of good A were available in 1998.

Why does GDP overstate the increase in output? The answer is that most of the increase is due merely to the increase in good A's price. In 1997, the price was $1,000. In 1998, it was $1,100. This 10 percent increase in price, along with the 5 percent increase in quantity, is reflected in the increase in GDP.

This example illustrates the nature of the problem. To show how it is resolved, we first construct a price index and then divide, or deflate, GDP by the appropriate price index number. The division is necessary to compensate for the change in the price level that has occurred.

QUANTITIES, PRICES, AND GDP: A SIMPLE EXAMPLE

TABLE 11.2			
Year	Number of Units Produced	Price per Unit	GDP
1997	6 million	$1,000	$ 6 billion
1998	6.3 million	1,100	6.93 billion

This table shows that output increased by 5 percent and price increased by 10 percent from 1997 to 1998. Consequently, GDP increased by about 15 percent.

A **price index** measures the price level for a given period relative to the base period. The first step is to select a base period. In our example, let's select 1997 as the base period, and specify the price level in that year as 100. We are now in a position to compare the price level in other periods with the base period, and we do so according to the formula

$$\text{Price index} = \frac{\text{Price for period in question}}{\text{Price in base period}} \times 100.$$

Price Index
A measure of the price level for a given period relative to the base period.

Note that, after dividing the price for the period in question by the price in the base period, we multiply by 100. We do so to express the price index as a percentage. To illustrate, the price of good A was $1,100 in 1998 and $1,000 in 1997 (the base period), so we have

$$\text{Price index} = \frac{\$1,100}{\$1,000} \times 100 = 1.1 \times 100 = 110.$$

Thus, the price index number for 1998 is 110, indicating that the price level in 1998 is 110 percent of the price level in 1997 (the base period).

The price index numbers for 1997 and 1998, along with the data from Table 11.2, are shown in Table 11.3. Note that GDP from column 4 of Table 11.2 now appears as nominal GDP in column 5 of Table 11.3. **Nominal GDP** is GDP measured on the basis of current, or nominal, prices. In this example, nominal GDP in 1997 is calculated using 1997 prices, while nominal GDP in 1998 is calculated using 1998 prices.

Nominal GDP
GDP measured on the basis of current, or nominal, prices.

As we have seen, prices may change. If they do, nominal GDP gives a false impression of the nation's output of goods and services. To correct for price changes, we can divide, or deflate, nominal GDP by the price index. The result is real GDP. In equation form, the relationship is

$$\text{Real GDP} = \frac{\text{Nominal GDP}}{\text{Price index (in decimal form)}}.$$

DEFLATING GDP

TABLE 11.3					
Year	Number of Units Produced	Price per Unit	Price Index	Nominal GDP	Real GDP
1997	6 million	$1,000	100	$ 6 billion	$ 6 billion
1998	6.3 million	1,100	110	6.93 billion	6.3 billion

By deflating, or dividing, nominal GDP by the price index, we obtain real GDP. Adjusting for the price change indicates that output increased by 5 percent from 1997 to 1998.

Note that we divide nominal GDP by a price index written as a decimal rather than as a percentage. Conversion from percentage to decimal form requires moving the decimal point two places to the left or, what amounts to the same thing, dividing by 100.

Real GDP
GDP measured on the basis of constant prices; reflects only changes in quantities.

Real GDP is GDP measured on the basis of constant prices. To calculate real GDP in 1997, we divide nominal GDP in 1997 ($6 billion) by the price index number for that year (100). Before making the calculation, however, we convert the 100 (percentage form) to 1.00 (decimal form). Thus,

$$\text{Real GDP} = \frac{\$6 \text{ billion}}{1.00} = \$6 \text{ billion.}$$

Real GDP in 1997 is $6 billion, the same as nominal GDP. This is not surprising because we are, in effect, using 1997 prices to calculate GDP in that year.

To calculate real GDP in 1998, we repeat the procedure. We divide nominal GDP in 1998 ($6.93 billion) by the price index number, in decimal form, for that year (1.10). Thus,

$$\text{Real GDP} = \frac{\$6.93 \text{ billion}}{1.10} = \$6.3 \text{ billion.}$$

Real GDP in 1998 is $6.3 billion, which is less than nominal GDP in that year. This occurs because by dividing nominal GDP in 1998 by the price index for that year, we have eliminated the effect of higher prices on GDP. Recall that the price of good A increased from $1,000 in 1997 to $1,100 in 1998, a 10 percent increase. By dividing nominal GDP in 1998 by 1.10—the price index (in decimal form) in 1998—we have calculated GDP *as if* prices had not changed.

By adjusting nominal GDP in this manner, we obtain real GDP, a measure of the nation's output that reflects only changes in quantities. (Nominal GDP reflects changes in both quantities and prices.) Because real GDP reflects only changes in quantities, real GDP is a better measure of the nation's output of goods and services than is nominal GDP.

In our example, we assumed only one good.[2] To deflate nominal GDP, a price index for *all* final goods and services must be used. This index is called the implicit price deflator for GDP, or the GDP deflator. The relationship between nominal GDP, real GDP, and the GDP deflator is

$$\text{Real GDP} = \frac{\text{Nominal GDP}}{\text{GDP deflator}}.$$

---

[2]With many goods and services, it becomes more difficult to calculate real GDP and the GDP deflator. For a discussion of the U.S. Department of Commerce's procedures, see J. Steven Landefeld, Robert P. Parker, and Jack E. Triplett, "Preview of the Comprehensive Revision of the National Income and Product Accounts: BEA's New Featured Measures of Output and Prices," *Survey of Current Business* 75 (July 1995), 31–38.

NOMINAL GDP, REAL GDP, AND THE GDP DEFLATOR: 1979–1995

	TABLE 11.4		
Year	Nominal GDP (Billions of Current Dollars)	Real GDP (Billions of 1992 Dollars)	GDP Deflator
1979	2,557.5	4,624.0	55.3
1980	2,784.2	4,611.9	60.4
1981	3,115.9	4,724.9	65.9
1982	3,242.1	4,623.6	70.1
1983	3,514.5	4,810.0	73.1
1984	3,902.4	5,138.2	75.9
1985	4,180.7	5,329.5	78.4
1986	4,422.2	5,489.9	80.6
1987	4,692.3	5,648.4	83.1
1988	5,049.6	5,862.9	86.1
1989	5,438.7	6,060.4	89.7
1990	5,743.8	6,138.7	93.6
1991	5,916.7	6,079.0	97.3
1992	6,244.4	6,244.4	100.0
1993	6,553.0	6,386.4	102.6
1994	6,935.7	6,608.7	104.9
1995	7,253.8	6,742.9	107.6

Nominal GDP and the GDP deflator increased annually from 1979 to 1995. Except for decreases in 1980, 1982, and 1991, real GDP also increased. Real GDP may be obtained by dividing nominal GDP by the GDP deflator.

Source: *Economic Report of the President* (Washington, DC: Government Printing Office, 1996), 280, 282, and 284.

The **GDP deflator** is a weighted average of the prices of all final goods and services produced in the economy. It is a weighted average because the various goods and services are not of equal importance. At present, the GDP deflator has 1992 as its base.

Nominal GDP, real GDP, and the GDP deflator for the 1979–1995 period are shown in Table 11.4.

GDP Deflator
A weighted average of the prices of all final goods and services produced in the economy.

THE NATION'S ECONOMIC PERFORMANCE

Over the years, the U.S. economy has performed well. From 1929 to 1995, the nation's output of goods and services increased at an average annual rate of 3 percent. At first glance, a 3 percent growth rate appears modest. A 3 percent growth rate implies, however, that output doubles every 24 years.

Despite its upward trend, output, as illustrated in Figure 11.1, did not grow steadily. During some periods, output grew relatively rapidly, while in others, it

**REAL GDP:
1960–1995**

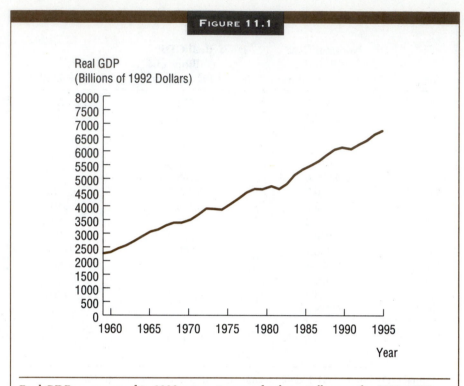

FIGURE 11.1

Real GDP
(Billions of 1992 Dollars)

Real GDP, as measured in 1992 prices, increased substantially over the 1960–1995 period. It did not, however, increase steadily. Real GDP increased more rapidly in some years than in others. In fact, it declined in 1970, 1974, 1975, 1980, 1982, and 1991.

Business Cycles
Recurring fluctuations in the general level of economic activity.

Expansion Phase
The phase of the business cycle during which real GDP, employment, productive capacity use, and profits increase while unemployment falls.

Peak
The highest point in the business cycle, during which real GDP is at a maximum and employment, profits, and productive capacity use are high.

grew less rapidly or even declined. Real GDP grew at a 1 percent rate from 1988 to 1991. In contrast, it grew at a 4 percent rate from 1982 to 1988 and at a 3 percent rate from 1991 to 1995. The experience of the 1930s is more dramatic. With the advent of the Great Depression, U.S. output decreased at a 7 percent rate from 1929 to 1933. As the nation recovered from the depression, it increased at a 10 percent rate from 1933 to 1941.

As measured by real GDP, the nation's level of economic activity has fluctuated throughout its history. The recurring fluctuations in the level of economic activity are **business cycles.**

As shown in Figure 11.2, a business cycle has four phases: expansion, peak, contraction, and trough. During the **expansion phase,** real GDP increases relatively rapidly. As it does, employment increases and the unemployment rate decreases. Also, a higher percentage of the nation's productive capacity is used and profits increase. As the unemployment rate falls and a higher percentage of productive capacity is used, however, wages and prices start increasing or increase more rapidly.

Eventually, a **peak** is reached. At the peak, real GDP is at a maximum. Employment, capacity use, and profits are high; the unemployment rate is low. With

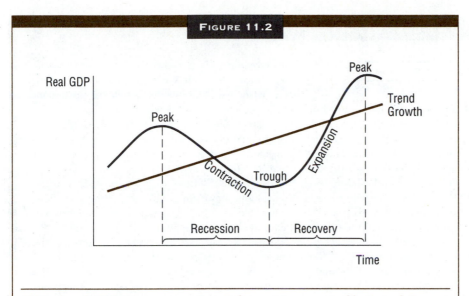

FIGURE 11.2

THE PHASES OF
THE BUSINESS
CYCLE

Real GDP

Peak

Peak

Trend
Growth

Contraction

Trough

Expansion

Recession

Recovery

Time

Although real GDP increases over time, it does not increase steadily. Instead, it grows rapidly, reaches a peak, falls, reaches a trough, and then repeats the cycle. This figure shows the four phases of the business cycle: expansion, peak, contraction, and trough.

unemployment low and capacity use high, wages and prices will increase more rapidly, and inflation may become a problem.

After the peak, the economy enters the **contraction phase.** During the contraction, real GDP decreases. With the decline, employment decreases and the unemployment rate rises. The percentage of the nation's productive capacity used falls. Profits also fall. With the increase in the unemployment rate and reduction in capacity use, wages and prices increase less rapidly or fall.

Eventually, a **trough** will be reached. At the trough, GDP is at its low point. Employment, capacity use, and profits are low. The unemployment rate, however, is high. With the high unemployment rate and low capacity use rate, there is little or no upward pressure on wages and prices. Indeed, wages and prices may fall.

The expansion phase is sometimes called a *recovery*. The contraction phase is often referred to as a *recession*. When a recession is particularly severe and prolonged, it is called a *depression*. The Great Depression of the 1930s is an example of the latter. Although we have had a number of recessions since the 1930s, none is in the same class as the Great Depression, when output decreased by about 30 percent from 1929 (peak) to 1933 (trough) and the unemployment rate increased from 3.2 percent to 24.9 percent.

Although each business cycle (as measured from peak to peak or trough to trough) has the same four phases, it must be emphasized that cycles differ in duration and intensity. Historically, contractions have averaged 18 months in length. The longest contraction lasted 65 months, while the shortest lasted only 6

Contraction Phase
The phase of the business cycle during which real GDP, employment, productive capacity use, and profits decrease while unemployment rises.

Trough
The lowest point of the business cycle, during which real GDP is at a minimum and employment, profits, and productive capacity use are low.

ADDITIONAL INSIGHT

WHITHER THE ECONOMY?

Real GDP data are very helpful in determining the current level of economic activity. But to deal with questions like those posed in the introduction (such as whether to quit a job in order to search for a better one), it is important to know not only the current level of economic activity, but the future level as well.

No shortage of economic forecasts exists. The federal government's forecasts are reported in the *Economic Report of the President* and elsewhere. Various individuals and firms make forecasts. These are often reported in newsletters and summarized in *The Wall Street Journal* and in other publications.

Given the large number of forecasts, the question is which to use. These forecasts usually differ and, unfortunately, no single forecast is consistently better than the others.

Rather than relying on forecasts, you could use leading indicators to predict future business conditions. A *leading indicator* is a variable that, based on past experience, usually turns down prior to recessions and turns up prior to recoveries. One such leading indicator is stock market prices. Stock prices typically go down several months before downturns in industrial production. It is not clear why this happens but the relationship has been consistent over time—the only requirement of a leading indicator.

In the past, a single leading indicator has proved somewhat unreliable in forecasting cyclical movements in the economy. To overcome this problem, the Conference Board, a private nonprofit organization, publishes the *composite index of leading indicators,* which is a weighted index of 11 leading indicators.* This composite index is much more reliable than any single leading indicator.

Except for the 1990–1991 recession, the composite index successfully forecast our last seven recessions. (The rule of thumb is that three consecutive months of decline in the index means a recession is likely three to six months later.) At the same time, however, it forecast several recessions (most recently in 1995) that never materialized. Thus, the index is capable of giving false signals. In addition, the time span between downturns in the index and recessions is often too short to be of much help to policymakers. Finally, although the composite index is useful in forecasting recessions and recoveries, it is not of much help in forecasting their intensity.

Changes in the composite index of leading indicators are announced each month by the Conference Board. These changes are widely reported in the news media. Because the index is somewhat volatile, it is unwise to rely too heavily on the reported change for a single month.

---

*The 11 leading indicators that form the basis for the composite index of leading indicators are average manufacturing workweek, average weekly initial claims for state unemployment insurance, manufacturers' new orders for consumer goods and materials, stock prices, orders for plant and equipment, housing starts, vendor performance, index of consumer expectations, change in manufacturers' unfilled orders, change in sensitive materials prices, and money supply.

months. Expansions have averaged 35 months, with the longest lasting 106 months and the shortest, 10 months. The most recent contraction, or recession, began in July 1990 and ended in March 1991. At 8 months, it was shorter than average; it was also milder than most. Indeed, the distinguishing feature of this recession was neither its length nor its severity: it was the slow recovery that followed. With the economy growing relatively slowly, the unemployment rate continued to rise.

Like the long-run trend, cyclical movements in real GDP have important implications for the economy. These cyclical movements in GDP represent fluctuations in the nation's output. They are also important because of their implications for unemployment and inflation. As the economy enters the contraction phase, unemployment increases and becomes a major problem at or near the trough. As the economy recovers, unemployment decreases. As the recovery continues, however, the price level may rise. Indeed, as the economy approaches the peak, inflation may become a major problem.

Both the long-run trend and cyclical movements of real GDP are determined by aggregate demand and aggregate supply. Because of their importance, we shall devote the rest of this chapter to a careful development of these concepts.

DETERMINING THE NATION'S OUTPUT AND PRICE LEVEL

Over time, the nation's output increases, but not steadily. It increases more rapidly in some years than in others. Similarly, the price level increases, but not steadily. As we shall see, aggregate demand and aggregate supply determine the nation's output and price level. By determining output and the price level, aggregate demand and supply also help to determine the nation's unemployment, inflation, and output growth rates. Finally, aggregate demand and supply help to determine the nation's budget and balance of payments deficits. Because aggregate demand and supply are extremely important in determining the nation's economic performance, we must master those concepts.

AGGREGATE DEMAND

An **aggregate demand curve** shows the total amount of final goods and services (real GDP) that will be purchased at each price level (the GDP deflator). As discussed earlier, the total amount of final goods and services purchased can be divided into the amounts spent for consumption, investment, government purchases, and net exports.

Aggregate Demand Curve
A curve showing the total amount of final goods and services (real GDP) that will be purchased at each price level (GDP deflator).

MOVEMENTS ALONG AN AGGREGATE DEMAND CURVE   Aggregate demand curve AD is depicted in Figure 11.3. Like the demand curve for a single product, the aggregate demand curve slopes downward and to the right. As the price level (as measured by the GDP deflator) decreases, the total amount of final goods and services purchased (as measured by real GDP) increases.

Both the demand curve for a single product and the aggregate demand curve are negatively sloped, but for different reasons. As you may recall from Chapter 1, nominal income and the prices of other goods and services are assumed constant in deriving the demand curve for a single product. As the price of the product falls, the product becomes less expensive relative to other goods and services. Consequently, individuals buy more of it.

THE AGGREGATE
DEMAND CURVE

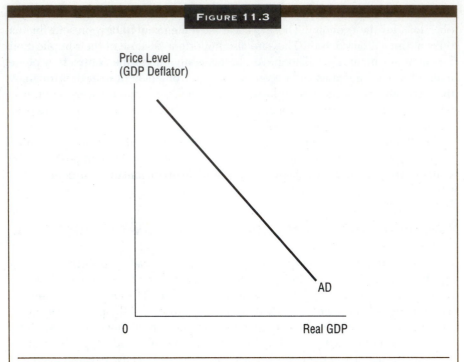

FIGURE 11.3

An aggregate demand curve shows the total amount of final goods and services (real GDP) that will be purchased at each price level (the GDP deflator). The aggregate demand curve is negatively sloped.

This explanation is *not* appropriate for the derivation of the aggregate demand curve. When the price level falls in that context, the prices of *all* final goods and services fall. Consequently, we cannot argue that more will be purchased because one product is becoming less expensive relative to other goods and services.

The aggregate demand curve owes its negative slope primarily to three effects: (1) the effect of the price level on real balances and hence consumption, (2) the effect of the price level on interest rates and hence investment and consumption, and (3) the effect of the price level on exports and imports.

The first effect has to do with the impact of the price level on financial assets that have fixed dollar values. These assets include currency and checking account balances. As the price level rises, their purchasing power declines. As the real value of these assets erodes, households can be expected to reduce the real amount that they spend on consumption. To illustrate, suppose you have a balance of $1,000 in currency and in your checking account. If the price level is 1, the real value of these money balances is $1,000. If the price level were to double (to 2), their real value would be only $500. If your real money balances decline in this way, you are very likely to reduce the real amount that you spend on consumption. We call the effect of changes in real balances on consumption the **real balance effect.**

As we have just seen, an increase in the price level tends to reduce consumption—one component of aggregate demand—through its impact on real balances. The increase in the price level and decrease in real balances also have an impact on aggregate demand through the interest rate. When a reduction in real money balances occurs, households and firms may attempt to maintain their spending by borrowing more. As they borrow more, interest rates rise. The increase in interest rates causes the cost of borrowing to rise. As a result, firms will invest less in new plant and equipment. Higher interest rates also discourage the construction of housing and the purchase of new automobiles and other consumer durables. Thus, an increase in the price level tends to reduce investment and consumption—two components of aggregate demand—through its impact on interest rates.

The third and final effect of the price level on aggregate demand is through exports and imports. As discussed earlier, exports and imports are important to the U.S. economy. The amounts that the United States exports and imports depend, in part, on the price level in the United States relative to the price level abroad. Suppose the price level in the United States rises while the price level abroad is constant. U.S. exports will be less competitive in world markets and will therefore decline. Similarly, as the price level rises in the United States relative to the price level abroad, households and firms will buy fewer goods produced in this country and more goods produced abroad because goods produced here are now relatively more expensive. Like the reduction in exports, this increase in imports reduces net exports and, therefore, aggregate demand. We can conclude that an increase in the U.S. price level tends to reduce net exports, a component of aggregate demand.

SHIFTS IN THE AGGREGATE DEMAND CURVE   We have just explained why the aggregate demand curve is negatively sloped. We now consider the causes of shifts in the aggregate demand curve. One factor is changes in the degree of optimism (or pessimism) among households and firms. Suppose households were to become more optimistic about the future state of the economy. They may, as a result, spend more of their incomes on consumption. If they do, consumption will increase, and because consumption is a component of aggregate demand, aggregate demand will increase. This increase in aggregate demand is shown in Figure 11.4 as a shift in the aggregate demand curve from AD_0 to AD_1. With the shift, aggregate demand is now greater at each price level. A similar shift occurs if firms become more optimistic about the future state of the economy. The only difference is that if firms become more optimistic, investment increases.

The aggregate demand curve will shift for other reasons. For our purposes, the most important shifts are caused by changes in the nation's fiscal and monetary policies. **Fiscal policy** is the use of government purchases and taxes to achieve full employment and other economic goals. Government purchases are one component of aggregate demand. If government purchases increase, the aggregate demand for goods and services increases and the aggregate demand curve, as shown in Figure 11.4, shifts to the right. If taxes are reduced, house-

Real Balance Effect
The change in consumption caused by a change in the real value of financial assets that have fixed dollar values.

Fiscal Policy
Use of government purchases and taxes to achieve full employment and other economic goals.

A SHIFT IN THE AGGREGATE DEMAND CURVE

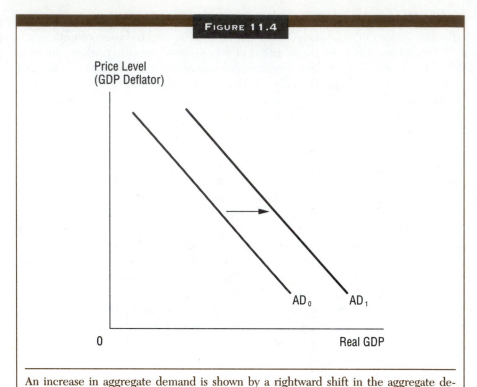

FIGURE 11.4

An increase in aggregate demand is shown by a rightward shift in the aggregate demand curve. The aggregate demand curve may shift to the right because policymakers are pursuing an expansionary fiscal policy.

Disposable Income
Household income less taxes; spendable income.

Expansionary Fiscal Policy
An increase in aggregate demand brought about by an increase in government purchases, a decrease in taxes, or both.

Contractionary Fiscal Policy
A decrease in aggregate demand brought about by a decrease in government purchases, an increase in taxes, or both.

Money Supply
Currency (including coins), checkable deposits, and travelers' checks.

holds find that their after-tax income, or **disposable income,** is higher. Because of the increase in their disposable income, households will increase their consumption. Because consumption is one component of aggregate demand, the aggregate demand for goods and services rises and the aggregate demand curve shifts to the right.

As just demonstrated, both an increase in government purchases and a decrease in taxes cause aggregate demand to increase. Thus we define an **expansionary fiscal policy** as an increase in aggregate demand brought about by an increase in government purchases, a decrease in taxes, or some combination of the two.

A decrease in government purchases or an increase in taxes has the opposite effect on aggregate demand. Both reduce aggregate demand, thereby causing the aggregate demand curve to shift to the left. Thus we define **contractionary fiscal policy** as a decrease in aggregate demand brought about by a decrease in government purchases, an increase in taxes, or some combination.

A change in the money supply also affects the aggregate demand for goods and services. For the purposes of this chapter, we define the nation's **money supply** as its currency (including coins), checkable deposits, and travelers' checks.

These items are considered money because they are generally accepted as payment for goods and services.

If the nation's money supply increases, the aggregate demand for goods and services increases and the aggregate demand curve shifts to the right. The increase in aggregate demand occurs for at least two reasons. First, the increase in the money supply increases real balances. As a result, households increase their consumption. Second, the increase in the money supply reduces interest rates. Lower interest rates mean firms will invest more in new plant and equipment. Lower interest rates also encourage the construction of housing and the purchase of new automobiles and other consumer durables. The increase in real balances and the decrease in interest rates cause consumption and investment to increase. Because consumption and investment are components of aggregate demand, aggregate demand increases and the aggregate demand curve shifts to the right.

The nation's money supply can be altered by the Federal Reserve, an independent agency of the federal government that is discussed at length in Chapter 13. The Federal Reserve conducts U.S. monetary policy. **Monetary policy** is the use of the money supply to achieve full employment and other economic goals.

As just shown, an increase in the money supply causes aggregate demand to increase. Thus, we define **expansionary monetary policy** as an action by the Federal Reserve to increase the money supply. In contrast, we define **contractionary monetary policy** as an action by the Federal Reserve to decrease the money supply. A decrease in the money supply causes aggregate demand to decrease.

AGGREGATE SUPPLY

An **aggregate supply curve** shows the total output of final goods and services (real GDP) that will be produced at each price level (the GDP deflator). Aggregate supply curve AS is depicted in Figure 11.5.

MOVEMENTS ALONG AN AGGREGATE SUPPLY CURVE   The aggregate supply curve in Figure 11.5 has two segments: a positively sloped segment up to price level P_1 and a vertical segment from P_1 up. The positively sloped segment of AS is like the supply curve for a single product. As the price level (as measured by the GDP deflator) increases, the total quantity of goods and services (as measured by real GDP) supplied increases. In deriving the positively sloped segment of the aggregate supply curve, it is assumed that wage rates and other input prices (as well as the labor supply, capital stock, and technology) are constant. Consequently, when the price level rises from, say, P_0 in Figure 11.5 to P_1, firms find it profitable to increase production and output increases from GDP_0 to GDP_{FE}. As firms expand production, they hire more workers. The rise in employment causes the unemployment rate to fall.

Once price level P_1 is reached, the aggregate supply curve becomes vertical at output GDP_{FE}, the full employment output level. Suppose the price level rises

Monetary Policy
Use of the money supply to achieve full employment and other economic goals.

Expansionary Monetary Policy
An action by the Federal Reserve to increase the money supply.

Contractionary Monetary Policy
An action by the Federal Reserve to decrease the money supply.

Aggregate Supply Curve
A curve showing the total output of final goods and services (real GDP) that will be produced at each price level (the GDP deflator).

THE AGGREGATE
SUPPLY CURVE

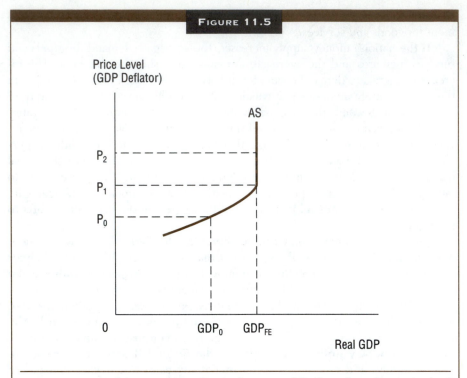

FIGURE 11.5

An aggregate supply curve shows the total output of final goods and services (real GDP) that will be produced at each price level (the GDP deflator). The aggregate supply curve is positively sloped until the full employment level of output, GDP_{FE}, is reached. It then becomes vertical.

from P_1 to P_2. Wage rates and other input prices can no longer be assumed constant. With the economy at full employment, individual firms may increase output by offering higher wage rates to attract workers from other firms. These increases in output are offset by the decreases in output experienced by firms that lose workers. Thus, despite the increase in the price level and wage rates, total output is unchanged.

SHIFTS IN THE AGGREGATE SUPPLY CURVE   We turn now to the causes of shifts in the aggregate supply curve. As just discussed, the positively sloped segment of the aggregate supply curve is derived assuming that wage rates and other input prices are constant. For most firms, wages and salaries are the largest expense, typically accounting for 70 to 75 percent of all expenses. Consequently, wage and salary increases cause a major cost increase. This cost increase means firms must receive higher prices to continue producing the same amounts. Thus a wage increase causes the aggregate supply curve to shift from AS_0 to AS_1 in Figure 11.6. An increase in the prices of other inputs will shift the aggregate supply curve in the same manner.

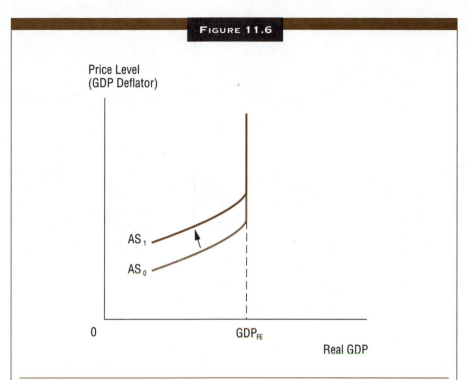

FIGURE 11.6

THE IMPACT OF
AN INCREASE IN
WAGE RATES ON
THE AGGREGATE
SUPPLY CURVE

The positive slope of a portion of the aggregate supply curve is due to the assumption that wage rates and other input prices are constant. If wage rates rise, the relevant portion of the aggregate supply curve shifts to the left.

In deriving the aggregate supply curve, the nation's labor supply, capital stock, and technology are assumed constant. If the labor supply or the capital stock increases, the aggregate supply curve shifts to the right. Similarly, if technological progress occurs, the aggregate supply curve shifts to the right. One such shift is shown in Figure 11.7. Note that, with the shift, the full employment level of output increases from GDP_{FE} to GDP'_{FE}. This is because increases in the labor supply and capital stock and technological progress increase the nation's productive capacity. If wage rates or other input prices rise, however, the full employment level of output (see Figure 11.6) does not change, because the nation's productive capacity is unaltered.

AGGREGATE DEMAND AND SUPPLY INTERACTION

In Chapter 1, you saw that the demand for and supply of a particular good determine its equilibrium output and price. Similarly, aggregate demand and supply determine the equilibrium levels of real GDP and the GDP deflator. In Figure 11.8, the aggregate demand curve is AD_0 and the aggregate supply curve is AS_0. The

THE IMPACT OF
AN INCREASE IN
THE CAPITAL
STOCK ON THE
AGGREGATE SUPPLY
CURVE

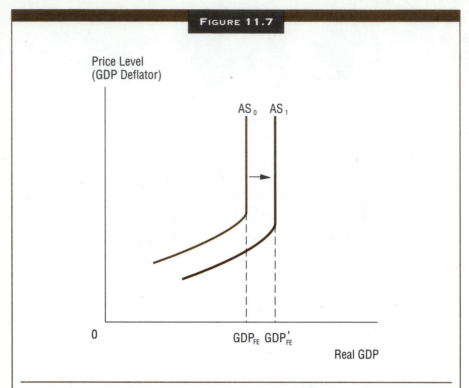

FIGURE 11.7

The aggregate supply curve is drawn on the assumption that the economy's labor supply, capital stock, and technology are constant. If the capital stock increases, the aggregate supply curve shifts to the right.

equilibrium levels of real GDP and the GDP deflator are GDP_0 and P_0, respectively, given by the intersection of these aggregate demand and supply curves.

To show that GDP_0 and P_0 must be the equilibrium combination of real GDP and the GDP deflator, consider alternative price levels. Suppose that the price level is P_1, which is less than the equilibrium price level. At P_1, the aggregate quantity demanded exceeds the aggregate quantity supplied, implying that purchasers would like to buy more goods and services than firms are willing to produce. This excess demand for goods and services puts upward pressure on prices. Consequently, the price level rises. It will continue to rise until it reaches P_0, the equilibrium price level. At P_0, purchasers buy the quantity of goods and services that firms produce. Consequently, neither purchasers nor firms have an incentive to alter their behavior.

Suppose that the price level is P_2, which is above the equilibrium price level. At P_2, the aggregate quantity supplied exceeds the aggregate quantity demanded, implying that purchasers are unwilling to buy as many goods and services as firms are willing to produce. This excess supply of goods and services places downward pressure on prices. As a result, the price level falls until the equilibrium price level, P_0, is reached.

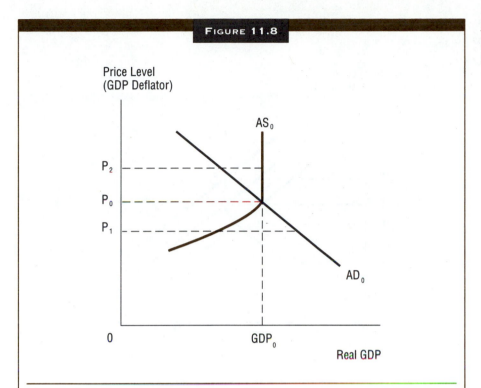

FIGURE 11.8

AGGREGATE
DEMAND AND
SUPPLY

The equilibrium combination of output (real GDP) and the price level (GDP deflator) is given by the intersection of the aggregate demand and supply curves. In this case, the equilibrium level of output is GDP_0 and the equilibrium price level is P_0.

In this example, P_0 is the equilibrium price level because it is the only price level at which purchasers are willing to buy the quantity of goods and services that firms are willing to produce. At any other price level, either excess aggregate demand or excess aggregate supply exists, and the price level changes until the equilibrium price level is restored.

In Figure 11.8, the equilibrium level of real GDP is GDP_0, the full employment level of output. We know that GDP_0 is the full employment level of output because the aggregate supply curve becomes vertical at that output level, indicating that the nation's productive capacity is fully utilized. There is no guarantee, however, that GDP will be at its full employment level. Suppose that, in Figure 11.9, aggregate demand falls from AD_0 to AD_1. With aggregate demand AD_0, real GDP was GDP_0—the full employment level of output. With the reduction in aggregate demand, purchasers now buy less at each price level. As a result, both real GDP and the GDP deflator fall. As real GDP decreases, firms reduce employment and the unemployment rate rises. With wage rates and other input prices constant (or slow to adjust), the unemployment rate may be above the full employment rate of unemployment for a substantial period of time.

CHANGES IN
AGGREGATE
DEMAND AND
THEIR IMPACT ON
REAL GDP AND
THE PRICE LEVEL

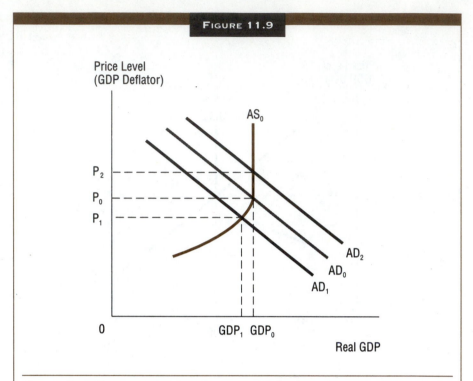

FIGURE 11.9

The initial equilibrium combination of output and the price level is GDP_0, P_0. If aggregate demand decreases (to AD_1) with wage rates and other input prices constant, output and the price level fall. If aggregate demand increases (to AD_2), the price level rises. Output, however, remains constant because the economy is already operating at full employment.

Just as aggregate demand may fall from AD_0 to AD_1, it could increase from AD_0 to AD_2. When aggregate demand increases to AD_2, purchasers buy more at each price level. This increase in aggregate demand causes the price level to rise to P_2. It does not, however, alter real GDP. With the economy already producing at the full employment level of output, GDP_0, the increase in aggregate demand results in higher output and input prices, but not higher output.

SUMMARY

Gross domestic product (GDP) is the market value of all final goods and services produced in the economy over the relevant time span, usually a year. GDP, the most frequently cited measure of the nation's output, is divided into four components: consumption, gross investment, government purchases, and net exports.

In compiling GDP, market prices are used. This makes it difficult to measure the nation's output because both quantities and prices change over time. To overcome this problem, we must first construct a price index and then divide, or deflate, GDP by this price index.

A price index measures the price level for a given period relative to the base period. Once the price index—called the GDP deflator in this context—is constructed, we divide, or deflate, nominal GDP by the GDP deflator to obtain real GDP. Thus, the relationship between real GDP, nominal GDP, and the GDP deflator is

$$\text{Real GDP} = \frac{\text{Nominal GDP}}{\text{GDP deflator}}.$$

Nominal GDP reflects both quantity and price changes. In contrast, real GDP reflects only quantity changes. Because real GDP reflects only quantity changes, it is a better measure of the nation's output.

The GDP deflator is a weighted average of the prices of all final goods and services produced in the economy. It is the most comprehensive measure of the nation's price level.

Historically, the economy has performed well. Since 1929, output has increased at an average annual rate of about 3 percent. It has not, however, increased steadily. Periods of rapidly increasing real GDP have been followed by periods of slowly rising or even falling real GDP. These fluctuations in the level of economic activity are called business cycles.

An aggregate demand curve shows the total amount of final goods and services that will be purchased at each price level. Similarly, an aggregate supply curve shows the total output of final goods and services that will be produced at each price level.

The nation's equilibrium output and price level are given by intersection of the aggregate demand and supply curves. Because aggregate demand and supply change over time, output and the price level also change over time.

Fiscal policy is the use of government purchases and taxes to achieve full employment and other economic goals. Similarly, monetary policy is the use of the money supply to achieve those same goals. Through the use of fiscal and monetary policy, policymakers can alter aggregate demand and, hence, the nation's output and price level.

KEY TERMS

Gross domestic product (GDP)
Final goods
Intermediate goods
Personal consumption expenditures
Gross private domestic investment

Net private domestic investment
Consumption of fixed capital
Capital stock
Government purchases of goods and services

Government transfer payments
Net exports of goods and services
Exports
Imports
Price index
Nominal GDP

Real GDP
GDP deflator
Business cycles
Expansion phase
Peak
Contraction phase
Trough

Aggregate demand curve
Real balance effect
Fiscal policy
Disposable income
Expansionary fiscal policy
Contractionary fiscal
   policy

Money supply
Monetary policy
Expansionary monetary
   policy
Contractionary monetary
   policy
Aggregate supply curve

REVIEW QUESTIONS

1. Define GDP. Why are only final goods and services included? Why are changes in business inventories included?
2. List and briefly describe GDP's major components.
3. Describe the effects of each of the following on U.S. GDP:
   a. A flood that destroys 1,500 homes along the Mississippi River
   b. A ban on U.S. imports from Japan
   c. The legalization of marijuana
   d. U.S. involvement in a war in Central America
4. What is the underground economy? Why do people participate in the underground economy? How might its size be reduced?
5. What is the difference between nominal and real GDP?
6. "An increase in nominal GDP means that more goods and services are available to society." Using a specific example, explain why this statement is true or false.
7. Fill in the blanks in the following table:

Year	Nominal GDP (Billions of Current Dollars)	Real GDP (Billions of 1992 Dollars)	GDP Deflator
1996	———	4,800.0	120.0
1997	6,500.0	5,000.0	———
1998	9,000.0	———	150.0

8. Discuss the business cycle and its phases. What are the short- and long-run implications of the business cycle for the growth of real GDP?
9. Explain the following statement: "The composite index of leading indicators has forecast ten of our last seven recessions."
10. What is the aggregate demand curve? Why is it negatively sloped?
11. What factors may cause the aggregate demand curve to shift? Graphically, illustrate both an increase and a decrease in aggregate demand.
12. Carefully explain why the aggregate supply curve has two segments: a positively sloped segment and a vertical segment.
13. What factors will cause the aggregate supply curve to shift? How will these factors affect the two segments of the curve?
14. Using graphical analysis, explain why the equilibrium levels of GDP and the GDP deflator are determined by the intersection of the aggregate demand and supply curves.

15. In 1973–1974 and again in 1979–1980, actions by foreign oil suppliers greatly increased crude oil prices in the United States. What effect did this have on real GDP and the GDP deflator? Defend your answer.

SUGGESTIONS FOR FURTHER READING

Economic Indicators. Prepared for the Joint Economic Committee of Congress by the Council of Economic Advisers. Washington, DC: Government Printing Office, published monthly. Contains current data on the economy's performance.

Economic Report of the President. Washington, DC: Government Printing Office, published annually. Contains an evaluation of the economy's performance supported by an extensive collection of data.

Pozo, Susan, ed. *Exploring the Underground Economy: Studies of Illegal and Unreported Activity.* Kalamazoo, MI: W. E. Upjohn Institute for Employment Research, 1996. A collection of studies relating to the underground economy.

Sommers, Albert T., with Lucie R. Blau. *The U.S. Economy Demystified.* 3rd ed. New York: Lexington Books, 1993. Contains an extensive discussion of the concepts presented in this chapter.

U.S. Department of Commerce, Bureau of Economic Analysis. *Survey of Current Business.* Washington, DC: Government Printing Office, published monthly. Contains current data on the economy's performance.

Welch, Patrick J., and Gerry F. Welch. *Economics: Theory and Practice.* 6th ed. Fort Worth: The Dryden Press, 1998. Discusses various concepts used to measure the economy's performance. Develops aggregate demand and supply curves and explains how they determine the nation's output and price level.

12

Unemployment: A Recurring Problem

Unemployment is often a problem in our society. Most college seniors, for example, do not have jobs at graduation time. Fortunately, almost all of them find jobs within a few months. This type of unemployment is not a serious problem for either the individual or society. Unfortunately, most unemployment is different. Some people have difficulty finding jobs during economic expansions. More people have difficulty during recessions. During much of the 1981–1982 recession, the U.S. unemployment rate was about 10 percent, implying that one person in every ten who wanted a job was unable to find one. Matters were worse during the Great Depression of the 1930s. In 1933, the unemployment rate averaged about 25 percent, implying that one person in every four was unable to find a job. The hardships and miseries of the unemployed characterize that period.

In this chapter, we take up unemployment and related issues. Among other things, we consider its costs to the individual and to society, the various types of unemployment, and policies to reduce it. Although the chapter emphasizes unemployment in the United States, it also considers unemployment in Europe.

COSTS OF UNEMPLOYMENT

Both economic and noneconomic costs are associated with unemployment. Moreover, these costs differ for the individual and for society.

ECONOMIC COSTS

For the individual, the most obvious economic cost of unemployment is the income that the person would have received if employed. This lost income may be partially offset by unemployment compensation, food stamps, or other government transfer payments. In general, however, these benefits are less than the income lost. As a result, the individual's economic position deteriorates.

So long as the period of unemployment is short, the impact on the individual is not severe. The individual and family may be able to maintain their standard of living by spending from savings. As time passes, however, the family may be forced to alter its lifestyle by spending less for food, clothing, and entertainment. More drastic changes might include moving to less expensive housing and selling assets. Ultimately, the individual and family may be impoverished.

For society, the cost of unemployment is the goods and services that could have been produced by the unemployed. To illustrate, the U.S. unemployment rate increased from 3.2 percent in 1929 to 24.9 percent in 1933. As a result, the nation's output of goods and services fell by about 30 percent, a tremendous decline.

NONECONOMIC COSTS

In addition to economic costs, individuals experiencing prolonged unemployment are subject to other costs. Many unemployed persons experience anxiety, stress, loss of self-confidence and self-esteem, and depression. It is, after all, frustrating and depressing to apply for job after job and be unsuccessful. It is also frustrating to be unable to buy things that you and your family want and not to know when you will be able to buy them.

Various studies suggest that high unemployment rates are associated with a higher incidence of alcoholism and drug abuse as well as higher crime and suicide rates. Other studies indicate that prolonged unemployment has an adverse effect on physical and mental health. Prolonged unemployment also has an adverse effect on families, which tend to break apart. Studies suggest that high unemployment rates are associated with higher divorce rates, a higher incidence of child abuse, and increased infant mortality.

Compared to the economic costs of unemployment, these noneconomic costs are very difficult or impossible to quantify. They are, however, no less real and should be taken into account when discussing the costs of unemployment.

COUNTING THE UNEMPLOYED

More attention is paid to the unemployment rate than to any other economic statistic. Given the costs associated with unemployment, this is not surprising. The **unemployment rate** is the percentage of the **civilian labor force** that is unemployed. Briefly, the civilian labor force is the number of persons working plus the number of persons not working but looking for work.

The unemployment rate is calculated monthly on the basis of household interviews. Each month, interviewers visit nearly 60,000 households scattered throughout the United States and ask questions about the employment status of each member of the household 16 years of age and older. The answers to the questions allow the government to classify each member of the household as employed, unemployed, or not in the civilian labor force.

People are employed if they worked as paid employees (either full or part time) or worked 15 hours or more as unpaid employees in a family business. People also are employed if they have jobs but did not work because of illness, bad weather, vacation, labor management disputes, or personal reasons.

People are unemployed if they did not have jobs, were available for work, and had actively looked for work during the past four weeks. Also counted as unemployed are persons who are waiting to start new jobs within 30 days or waiting to be recalled to jobs from which they had been laid off.

After counting the number of persons employed and unemployed, we can calculate the number of persons in the civilian labor force. It is the number of persons employed plus the number of persons unemployed. Suppose the number of employed persons is 114 million and the number of unemployed persons is 6 million. The civilian labor force is then 120 million.

Persons 16 years of age and older who are neither employed nor unemployed are not in the civilian labor force.[1] College students who do not have jobs (and

Unemployment Rate
The percentage of the civilian labor force that is unemployed.

Civilian Labor Force
The number of persons employed plus the number of persons unemployed.

---

[1]Also excluded from the civilian labor force are members of the armed forces and persons institutionalized in mental and correctional facilities.

are not looking for jobs) are not in the civilian labor force. Because they are not actively looking for jobs, homemakers and retired persons are not in the labor force. Persons without jobs who have become discouraged and stopped actively looking for jobs also are not in the civilian labor force.

In calculating the unemployment rate, only people in the civilian labor force are counted. Suppose once more that 6 million persons are unemployed and the civilian labor force is 120 million. We may use the following equation to determine the unemployment rate:

$$\text{Unemployment rate} = \frac{\text{Number of persons unemployed}}{\text{Civilian labor force}} \times 100.$$

In the equation, the ratio of the number of persons unemployed to the civilian labor force is multiplied by 100 to express the unemployment rate as a percentage. With 6 million persons unemployed and a civilian labor force of 120 million, we have the following:

$$\text{Unemployment rate} = \frac{6}{120} \times 100 = 0.05 \times 100 = 5.0 \text{ percent}.$$

Thus, the unemployment rate is 5 percent.

The unemployment rate is reported monthly.[2] Although very important, it conceals many differences among demographic groups. Many of these differences are illustrated in Table 12.1. Note that the overall unemployment rate for 1995 is 5.6 percent. Several of the other rates are significantly higher than this rate. First, the unemployment rate for teenagers (persons ages 16 to 19) is approximately three times the overall rate. The teenage unemployment rate is always much higher than the overall rate. Second, the unemployment rate for females is the same as that for males. This has not always been the case. In the 1960s and 1970s, the unemployment rate was significantly higher for females than for males. Third, the unemployment rate for blacks is more than twice that of whites. This differential has been relatively constant over the years. The unemployment rate for persons of Hispanic origin is usually between that for whites and blacks. Finally, although not shown in Table 12.1, lower unemployment rates are associated with higher levels of educational attainment. This tendency suggests that while graduating from college does not guarantee that a person will never be unemployed, it does reduce the probability.

These differences in unemployment rates have two important implications. First, they suggest that an increase in the overall unemployment rate is not shared equally. Suppose the unemployment rate increases by 1 percentage point. Because the unemployment rates for teenagers and blacks are about three and

---

[2]The monthly rates are adjusted to eliminate the effects of holidays and other seasonal influences.

TABLE 12.1

Demographic Group	Unemployment Rate (Percent)
Overall	5.6
Age	
16–19	17.3
20 and over, males	4.8
20 and over, females	4.9
Sex	
Males	5.6
Females	5.6
Race	
White	4.9
Black	10.4

Although the overall unemployment rate in the United States was 5.6 percent in 1995, the rate was much higher for some demographic groups, particularly, teenagers and blacks. The unemployment rate for females was the same as for males.

Source: *Economic Report of the President* (Washington, DC: Government Printing Office, February 1996), 324.

two times the overall rate, respectively, the increase implies that the teenage unemployment rate will rise about 3 percentage points and the black unemployment rate, about 2 percentage points. Second, the different unemployment rates among demographic groups suggest that different policies may be necessary to reduce the unemployment rates of the various groups. We shall return to this implication later in the chapter.

TYPES OF UNEMPLOYMENT

Economists commonly distinguish among three types of unemployment: frictional, structural, and cyclical. Each type has different policy implications. In this section, we consider each type. In later sections, we discuss policies to alleviate each type of unemployment.

FRICTIONAL UNEMPLOYMENT

Frictional unemployment is temporary unemployment arising from the normal job-search process. It includes persons who are entering the job market for the first time (or reentering after an absence). It also includes persons who have quit jobs to search for better ones. Finally, it includes persons who have been

Frictional Unemployment Temporary unemployment arising from the normal job-search process.

ADDITIONAL INSIGHT

JOB OPPORTUNITIES AND DISCRIMINATION

The unemployment rate for blacks is about double that for whites and has been for years. Is this differential in unemployment rates due to discrimination? Before answering, we must analyze the situation.

Employers consider workers' productivity in their hiring decisions. At a given wage, hiring the most productive workers minimizes the firm's costs and maximizes its profits. Unfortunately, blacks typically receive less education and on-the-job training than whites. Moreover, the education that blacks do receive is often inferior to that of whites. With less education and on-the-job training, some blacks are less productive and are denied employment because of their low productivity. In fact, much, perhaps most, of the differential in unemployment rates is due, not to job discrimination, but to differences in productivity, which, in turn, is related to discrimination in the amount and quality of education that blacks receive.

Given that the unemployment rate for blacks is relatively high, the way to reduce it is to eliminate the cause. The productivity of blacks would be enhanced by more and better—that is, equal—education. Improving access to better schools and ensuring that persons from disadvantaged homes have the financial resources through student loan and other programs would go far to eliminate the differential in unemployment rates between blacks and whites.

Affirmative action programs to provide blacks with greater educational and job opportunities are desirable. Quotas, however, are probably undesirable because they contribute to racial tensions and can result in reverse discrimination.

To the extent that blacks are the last to be hired and the first to be fired, stabilizing output and employment at their full employment levels is another way of reducing the differential in unemployment rates. With stability of employment, blacks will gain valuable experience and on-the-job training. Also, with full employment, employers are less able to discriminate because of the limited number of prospective employees. With less than full employment, employers are better able to discriminate because they can choose from a large number of unemployed workers, both black and white.

laid off or fired. While some people find jobs almost immediately, many others take several months. Consider the case of a young man who does not have a job when he graduates from college. He must first identify available jobs and apply for them. Then he must wait for prospective employers to examine his credentials, check his references, interview candidates, and decide whom to hire. Even after he receives a job offer, the effective date of employment may be some time in the future. All in all, the job search process is time consuming, which is one reason why college students are urged to start interviewing early in their senior years.

Because of the time involved in finding a job, some frictional unemployment is inevitable. This unemployment may not be pleasant, but it is temporary. Moreover, it helps the economy to function more efficiently. It enables people to search for higher-paying jobs. Those who are successful receive higher incomes. To the extent that workers move to higher-productivity jobs, the nation's output of goods and services increases. Because frictional unemployment is temporary and serves some useful social functions, it is not a major policy concern.

STRUCTURAL UNEMPLOYMENT

A second type of unemployment is structural unemployment. **Structural unemployment** arises when jobs are eliminated by changes in the structure of the economy. These changes occur because of technological progress and shifts in the demand for goods and services. Technological progress creates new jobs and eliminates old ones. The production process in many industries, for example, is becoming increasingly computerized. As a result, some production-line workers are losing their jobs. At the same time, new jobs such as computer repair technician and software engineer are appearing. Even so, there is no guarantee that the displaced production-line workers will have the skills necessary to fill these new jobs. Similarly, the demand for some goods and services declines over time, while the demand for others rises. Again, there is no guarantee that workers who lose their jobs in the declining industries will have the skills needed in the expanding industries.

As with frictional unemployment, the problem is not caused by a lack of jobs. Jobs are available. With structural unemployment, the problem is caused by a mismatch between the skills of prospective workers and the skills needed in the vacant jobs. Michigan may have unemployed automobile workers and unfilled computer science jobs. Similarly, Oklahoma may have a surplus of oil field workers and a shortage of airplane mechanics.

Although structural unemployment is like frictional unemployment in that the problem is not caused by a lack of jobs, it is different in two important (and related) respects. First, a person who is frictionally unemployed has marketable job skills. A person who is structurally unemployed does not. Indeed, that person may need substantial retraining or additional education to become employable. Second, a frictionally unemployed person can look forward to obtaining a job soon. A structurally unemployed person—without new training or additional education—faces a bleak future of long-term unemployment broken, perhaps, by sporadic employment spells. Because it is long term, policymakers regard structural unemployment as a more serious problem than frictional unemployment.

Structural Unemployment Unemployment caused by structural changes in the economy that eliminate certain jobs.

CYCLICAL UNEMPLOYMENT

The third and final type of unemployment is cyclical unemployment. **Cyclical unemployment** occurs when the level of economic activity falls. As firms reduce output, they also lay off or discharge workers, causing the unemployment rate to rise. (Unlike frictional and structural unemployment, cyclical unemployment is characterized by a job shortage.) The unemployment rate continues to increase during the contraction phase of the business cycle and reaches a maximum at or near the trough. As the economy enters the expansion phase of the business cycle, firms increase output and employment, and the unemployment rate falls. The unemployment rate continues to decrease during the expansion phase and reaches a minimum at or near the peak. At the peak of the business cycle, cyclical unemployment is negligible.

Cyclical Unemployment Unemployment caused by the drop in economic activity that occurs during the contraction phase of the business cycle.

The U.S. unemployment rate for 1960 through 1995 is plotted in Figure 12.1. The unemployment rate has varied appreciably over this time span, mostly due to cyclical unemployment. As a result, policymakers are very concerned with cyclical unemployment.

FULL EMPLOYMENT

Full Employment Rate of Unemployment
The frictional rate of unemployment plus the structural rate of unemployment; the lowest unemployment rate consistent with a nonaccelerating inflation rate.

Full employment is defined in terms of frictional and structural unemployment. The **full employment rate of unemployment** is the frictional rate of unemployment plus the structural rate of unemployment. To put it differently, it is the lowest unemployment rate consistent with a nonaccelerating inflation rate. If aggregate economic policies force the unemployment rate below the full employment rate, the price level will rise more and more rapidly. During the 1980s and 1990s, economists estimated the full employment rate of unemployment to be about 5.5 percent.

THE U.S. UNEMPLOYMENT RATE: 1960–1995

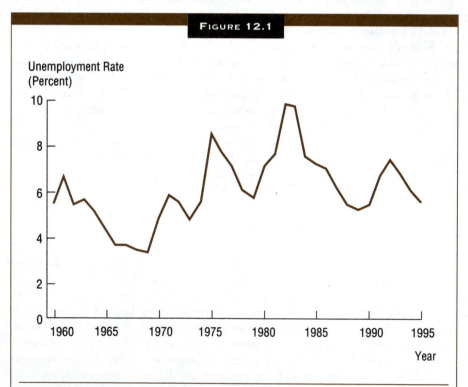

FIGURE 12.1

Unemployment Rate (Percent)

Year

The U.S. unemployment rate varied appreciably over the 1960–1995 period. It ranged from 3.5 percent in 1969 to 9.7 percent in 1982.

Most economists refer to the full employment rate of unemployment as the **natural rate of unemployment.** This choice of terminology is unfortunate because "natural" implies to some people that the rate of unemployment is constant or unchanging. The natural rate of unemployment does change slowly over time because of changes in the composition of the labor force and other factors. In the 1960s, the natural unemployment rate was widely regarded to be 4 percent. During that period, however, teenagers started entering the labor force in record numbers. Given their significantly higher unemployment rate, they drove up the natural unemployment rate. Women also began entering the labor force in record numbers. At that time, the unemployment rate for females was significantly higher than the rate for males. Because of their higher unemployment rate, women also caused the natural unemployment rate to rise.

The natural rate increased in the 1960s and 1970s in part because of changes in the composition of the labor force. Most economists believe, however, that the natural rate has peaked and is now declining. Ironically, some of the factors that led to its increase are now leading to its decline.[3] The baby bust has resulted in fewer teenagers entering the labor force. As a result, teenagers now account for a smaller part of the labor force. Even though the teenage unemployment rate remains high, the natural unemployment rate is lower because they are a smaller part of the labor force. Women continue to participate in the labor force in record numbers. Fortunately, however, the unemployment rate for females is no longer higher than the rate for males. This too has reduced the natural unemployment rate.

Natural Rate of Unemployment
The full employment rate of unemployment.

POLICIES TO REDUCE UNEMPLOYMENT

We now turn to policies to reduce unemployment. Because most of the variation in the unemployment rate is due to variations in cyclical unemployment, we start with policies to reduce cyclical unemployment.

REDUCING CYCLICAL UNEMPLOYMENT

Most economists believe that changes in the unemployment rate over the business cycle are caused by changes in aggregate demand.[4] During the expansion phase of the business cycle, aggregate demand increases, thereby increasing output and employment and decreasing the unemployment rate. During the contraction phase, aggregate demand decreases, thereby decreasing output and employment and increasing the unemployment rate.

---

[3]For a contrary view, see Stuart E. Weiner, "New Estimates of the Natural Rate of Unemployment," Federal Reserve Bank of Kansas City, *Economic Review* 78 (Fourth Quarter 1993), 53–69.

[4]Proponents of the real business cycle theory do not share this view. For an introduction to this theory, see Charles I. Plosser, "Understanding Real Business Cycles," *Journal of Economic Perspectives* 3 (Summer 1989), 51–77.

In Figure 12.2, we consider the impact of a decrease in aggregate demand. Suppose initially that aggregate demand is AD_0 and aggregate supply is AS_0, so that the price level is P_0 and real GDP is GDP_0, the full employment level. Next, suppose that aggregate demand falls to AD_1. With wage rates and other input prices constant, the price level falls to P_1 while real GDP falls to GDP_1. The reduction in aggregate demand also causes employment to fall and unemployment to rise.

As just demonstrated, a reduction in aggregate demand can cause unemployment. Whether it persists depends, in part, on the flexibility of wage rates and other input prices. If wage rates fall in response to the increase in unemployment, aggregate supply increases and output and employment return to their full employment levels. In Figure 12.2, falling wage rates cause the aggregate supply curve to shift from AS_0 to, say, AS_2, and ultimately to AS_3.

THE IMPACT OF A DECREASE IN AGGREGATE DEMAND ON THE UNEMPLOYMENT RATE

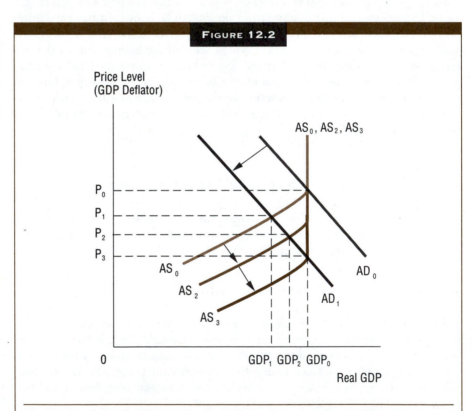

FIGURE 12.2

If aggregate demand is AD_0 and aggregate supply is AS_0, the equilibrium price and output levels are P_0 and GDP_0, respectively. If aggregate demand falls to AD_1, the price level falls to P_1 and output falls to GDP_1, assuming wages and other input prices remain constant. As the price level and output fall, employment also falls and the unemployment rate rises.

Most economists believe that wage rates are "sticky"; that is, they respond slowly to change in labor market conditions. One reason why they are sticky is that the wage rates of many workers are determined by long-term contracts.[5] Most labor union contracts, for example, are for three years. Even in industries where wage rates are not set by contract, they usually are adjusted only once a year. Most workers receive wage rates well above the legal minimum wage. But some workers receive only the minimum wage, which cannot legally be reduced. For these and other reasons, wage rates are sticky—especially downward. Because wage rates are slow to respond to an increase in unemployment, economists believe that unemployment caused by a reduction in aggregate demand may persist for two or three years.

Rather than letting the adjustment process run its course, policymakers can implement expansionary fiscal or monetary policies to reduce or eliminate the unemployment. If expansionary fiscal policy is used, either government purchases increase or taxes are reduced (or some combination of the two). Because government purchases are a component of aggregate demand, an increase in government purchases results in an increase in aggregate demand. A tax cut, on the other hand, increases disposable income, causing households to increase their consumption. Because consumption is a component of aggregate demand, aggregate demand increases. Consequently, expansionary fiscal policy acts to increase aggregate demand. The increase in aggregate demand in turn causes output and employment to rise and the unemployment rate to fall. If aggregate demand increases from AD_1 to AD_0 (or some higher level), full employment is restored. If aggregate demand increases by a smaller amount, output and employment still increase, but by smaller amounts. Consequently, some cyclical unemployment will remain.

Now suppose instead that expansionary monetary policy is applied. An increase in the money supply results in increased investment and consumption. Because investment and consumption are components of aggregate demand, aggregate demand increases, thereby increasing output and employment and reducing the unemployment rate. If aggregate demand increases to AD_0 (or some higher level), full employment will be restored. If it increases by a smaller amount, some unemployment will remain.

In conclusion, unemployment due to inadequate aggregate demand can be alleviated by expansionary fiscal or monetary policies. If pursued vigorously, either of these two policies can increase aggregate demand enough to restore full employment.

In the foregoing analysis, the price level increased from P_1 to P_0 with the increase in aggregate demand from AD_1 to AD_0. Although the price increase may be undesirable, most economists believe that the benefits of reducing the unemployment rate are well worth the costs associated with the price increase. If the economy is at full employment, however, the situation is different. Suppose aggregate

---

[5]Other input prices may be fixed by long-term contracts. Examples include the prices paid for raw materials and rental prices of buildings and machinery.

demand in Figure 11.9 is initially AD_0 and that it increases to AD_2. This increase in aggregate demand causes the price level to rise to P_2, but output, employment, and the unemployment rate are unaltered. At first glance, the increase in aggregate demand appears to do no harm; the price level is higher, but the other variables are unchanged. As we shall see in the next chapter, however, an increase in the price level imposes costs on society. For that reason, it is important that aggregate demand be stabilized at AD_0. To keep aggregate demand from rising, either contractionary fiscal or monetary policy can be applied.

Stabilization Policies
Government policies (generally fiscal or monetary) undertaken to maintain full employment and a reasonably stable price level.

To prevent or reduce cyclical unemployment while maintaining a reasonably stable price level, policymakers can pursue stabilization policy. **Stabilization policies** are government policies—usually fiscal and monetary policies—intended to maintain full employment and a reasonably stable price level. Indeed, policymakers in the United States have actively pursued stabilization policy since 1946. Many economists believe that it has reduced the instability of the economy in the post–World War II period. At the same time, we still observe cyclical movements in the economy and fluctuations in output and employment. These fluctuations occur for at least two reasons.

First, policymakers are uncertain as to the magnitude of the changes in government purchases, taxes, and the money supply necessary to restore or maintain full employment. Is a $20 billion increase in government purchases sufficient to restore full employment, or is a larger increase necessary? Even if policymakers accurately estimate the necessary increase, political and other considerations may prevent adoption of the appropriate policy. Members of Congress, for example, are often reluctant to reduce government spending or raise taxes in an election year.

Second, for stabilization policy to reduce the instability of the economy, it must be timely. Suppose the unemployment rate rises. If policymakers act in a timely manner, they can use expansionary fiscal and monetary policies to reduce the unemployment rate. Suppose, however, that they are slow to act. By the time they agree on a new set of policies to reduce the unemployment rate and these policies have an impact, the economy may once again be at full employment. If it is, these new policies will result in a higher price level rather than higher levels of output and employment.

Most economists believe that stabilization policy plays a valuable role in reducing the economy's instability. They concede that policymakers have made mistakes in the past, but, on balance, are optimistic that policymakers can do better in the future. Some economists believe, however, that stabilization policy actually increases the economy's instability and that policymakers should abandon its use.

REDUCING STRUCTURAL UNEMPLOYMENT

In the late 1950s and early 1960s, the U.S. unemployment rate increased. Most economists believed that the increase was due to inadequate aggregate demand. But some argued that rapid structural change was causing structural unemployment to rise.

A Tale of Two Recessions

Since 1980, the United States has had two recessions. The first started in July 1981 and ended in November 1982. Although about average in length (16 months), it was one of the most severe of the post–World War II period. The second started in July 1990 and ended in March 1991. This recession was relatively short (8 months) and mild.

In the late 1970s and 1980, prices were rising rapidly. To reduce inflation, the Federal Reserve pursued a contractionary monetary policy. As a result, the inflation rate dropped. At the same time, however, the nation's output and employment fell, and the unemployment rate increased. Real GDP fell by 2.2 percent in 1982, a large decrease by historical standards. The unemployment rate increased steadily, reaching a high of 10.8 percent in November 1982 (the trough).

Following 1982, the nation's output and employment grew rapidly and the unemployment rate dropped sharply. Both monetary and fiscal policy contributed to the strong recovery. Starting in December 1982, the nation's money supply grew much more rapidly. Also, government spending grew rapidly. Finally, federal personal income tax rates were reduced by 5 percent on October 1, 1981, by 10 percent on July 1, 1982, and by another 10 percent on July 1, 1983.

The economic expansion that followed the November 1982 trough was the nation's longest peacetime expansion, almost eight years. During the expansion, the unemployment rate fell steadily, reaching 5.3 percent in 1989. With the economy at or near full employment, the price level started rising more rapidly. As a result, the Federal Reserve reduced the growth rate of the money supply. Although this policy was successful in reducing the inflation rate, it had adverse effects on the economy. Indeed, it was one of the factors causing the recession of 1990–1991. Other factors include

(1) increases in debt—household, business, and government—which contributed to cutbacks in spending, (2) cuts in defense and in state and local spending, and (3) the impact of the savings and loan crisis on households and firms.

As previously stated, the 1990–1991 recession was both short and mild. Real GDP increased in 1990 and fell by only 0.7 percent in 1991. Similarly, the unemployment rate in March 1991 (the trough) was only 6.8 percent, 4 percentage points less than it was in November 1982.

Why did the public view this short and mild recession so negatively? One reason may have been that it followed a very long and vigorous expansion. Another reason may have been the slow recovery that followed. Real GDP grew very slowly during the last three quarters of 1991 and the first two quarters of 1992. As a result, the unemployment rate continued its rise, reaching a high of 7.8 percent in May 1992. Starting in the third quarter of that year, the economy began to grow more rapidly and the unemployment rate finally started dropping.

The recovery that followed the 1981–1982 recession was very strong. In contrast, the recovery that followed the 1990–1991 recession was weak. Why the difference? Unlike the recession of 1981–1982, neither expansionary fiscal nor expansionary monetary policy was applied. Very little was done to increase government spending or cut taxes to curb the rising unemployment rate. In fact, the administration and Congress agreed in 1990 to raise taxes with most of the tax increases taking effect on January 1, 1991. (Presumably, the tax hike was motivated by a desire to reduce the huge deficit in the federal government's budget.) Similarly, the money supply continued to grow at a moderate rate. (One reason for the moderate growth rate was the Federal Reserve's concern about inflation.) Finally, many of the factors that caused the 1990–1991 recession continued to plague the economy. Given these factors and the absence of aggressive fiscal and monetary policies, it is not surprising that the recovery was weak.

With structural unemployment, the problem is not caused by a lack of jobs. As old jobs are destroyed, new ones are created. Instead, the problem is that the displaced workers do not meet the skill and educational requirements of the new jobs. In this situation, expansionary fiscal and monetary policies are ineffective because the jobs created are like those already available.

In retrospect, it is clear that the increased unemployment of the late 1950s and early 1960s was cyclical rather than structural. Even so, there is little doubt that mismatches between the skill and educational levels of unemployed workers and those of existing job vacancies are a problem. To put it differently, even if no cyclical unemployment exists, the nation's unemployment rate will still be about 5.5 percent. Most economists think this is too high. What can be done to reduce the full employment rate of unemployment?

Expansionary fiscal and monetary policies cannot help. As we observed earlier, if aggregate demand increases when the economy is operating at full employment, only prices and wage rates rise. Output and employment are unchanged.

Instead of stabilization policy, other policies must be used. One possibility is government programs to retrain displaced workers. With new job skills, these workers should be able to compete successfully in the job market. Another possibility is to provide subsidies to firms that will employ these workers and train them on the job. Still another possibility is to help workers relocate to areas where jobs exist. Without assistance, prospective workers may be reluctant or unable to relocate. Alternatively, firms may be given favorable tax or other treatment to induce them to build or expand plants in areas with labor surpluses. Finally, prospective workers might be induced to continue or resume their educations. Without more education, many of them will have great difficulty in finding jobs–or at least good jobs–in a technologically advanced society.

Starting in the 1960s, the federal government has sponsored various job training programs. Unfortunately, the results have been mixed.[6] In some programs, many of the enrollees failed to complete their training. In others, the enrollees were trained for jobs that were virtually nonexistent. In still others, the enrollees were trained with obsolete equipment. Finally, the placement record of many of these programs is disappointing.

Despite the mixed results to date, job training programs are probably necessary to reduce structural unemployment. Because we live in a dynamic society, some structural unemployment will always be present. Even so, many economists believe we can reduce it and thus reduce the full employment rate of unemployment.

---

[6]For discussions of the impact of training programs, see Robert J. LaLonde, "The Promise of Public Sector-Sponsored Training Programs," *Journal of Economic Perspectives* 9 (Spring 1995), 149–68; Duane E. Leigh, *Does Training Work for Displaced Workers?* (Kalamazoo, MI: W.E. Upjohn Institute for Employment Research, 1990); and Duane E. Leigh, *Assisting Workers Displaced by Structural Change* (Kalamazoo, MI: W.E. Upjohn Institute for Employment Research, 1995).

REDUCING FRICTIONAL UNEMPLOYMENT

For the most part, frictional unemployment exists because searching for a job is time consuming. Job seekers have imperfect information about vacancies, salaries, retirement and fringe benefits, and working conditions. Similarly, prospective employers have imperfect information about job seekers and their qualifications. With imperfect information, job seekers and prospective employers must search for the best matches of jobs and job seekers' qualifications.

To reduce frictional unemployment, job seekers and prospective employers must be given better information about job vacancies and job seekers' qualifications. One way to do this is to establish a computerized national job bank. With an easy-to-access job list, job seekers should be able to reduce the time they spend searching for jobs. As of September 1996, the United States was well on its way to establishing a national job bank. At that time, more than 500,000 jobs were listed on the Internet. (Many resumes are also listed.) Indeed, some firms advertise job openings only on the Internet. To assist prospective workers who do not have easy access to the computerized job listings, the U.S. Department of Labor is funding "Internet Access Zones" at colleges and universities and at state employment service offices. It is also possible to access these listings at many public libraries.

Although providing job seekers and prospective employers with more information is desirable, it may have the unintended effect of increasing worker turnover. If it is easier to find another job, workers are more likely to quit their present jobs. If it is easier for employers to find new workers, they are more likely to fire present employees. The increases in the number of people who quit jobs and in the number of firings result in a higher turnover rate. The effects of the higher turnover rate, in turn, tend to offset the effects of the faster placement of job seekers.

Another approach to reducing frictional unemployment is to implement apprenticeship programs similar to those in Austria and Germany. These programs ease the transition from high school to full-time employment and provide some on-the-job training. The apprenticeship programs in those countries, however, have existed for many years. It may prove difficult, therefore, to adopt them in the United States, at least on a large-scale basis.

In conclusion, reducing frictional unemployment will not be easy. Fortunately, frictional unemployment is not a major problem, because it is temporary and serves some useful social functions.

UNEMPLOYMENT AND THE MINIMUM WAGE

Earlier, we observed that one of the reasons for a high full employment rate of unemployment is that some prospective workers lack the skills necessary to fill the existing job vacancies. The imposition of a minimum wage makes this problem worse. A minimum wage discourages firms from hiring persons with minimal skills.

A federal minimum wage—25 cents per hour—was first imposed in 1938. Over the years, the minimum wage has been increased and the covered number of workers expanded. It was $3.35 per hour from January 1, 1981, to April 1, 1990. It increased to $3.80 on April 1, 1990, and to $4.25 on April 1, 1991. More recently, the minimum wage increased to $4.75 on October 1, 1996, and to $5.15 on September 1, 1997. Over 80 percent of the nonagricultural labor force is now covered. In addition to the federal legislation, many states have passed minimum wage legislation. In some states, the state-imposed minimum wage exceeds the federal minimum wage.

The expressed intent of increasing the minimum wage is to help the working poor. It is possible for a family headed by a person working full time at the minimum wage to have an income below the poverty line. By raising the minimum wage, it is argued, the worker's income will be increased and the family's standard of living improved. To politicians, increasing the minimum wage is a particularly attractive way to alleviate poverty because it does not require an increase in transfer payments and accompanying tax hike.

Although advocates of a high minimum wage have the best of intentions, the outcome is likely to be different than they expect. In Figure 12.3, we plot the de-

THE DEMAND FOR AND SUPPLY OF LOW-SKILL WORKERS

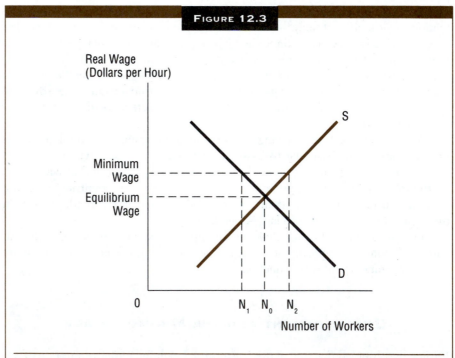

FIGURE 12.3

The demand for and supply of low-skill workers determine the equilibrium wage for low-skill workers. If minimum wage legislation results in the establishment of a wage higher than the equilibrium wage, fewer low-skill workers will be employed. In this case, employment is reduced from N_0 to N_1.

mand for and supply of low-skill workers. We focus on low-skill workers because the equilibrium wage rate for high-skill workers is likely to be well above the minimum wage. Consequently, the minimum wage will have no direct effect on them. Suppose a minimum wage higher than the equilibrium wage is imposed. The increase in the wage causes the quantity of labor demanded in Figure 12.3 to fall from N_0 to N_1 while the quantity of labor supplied increases to N_2. Because firms cannot pay less than the minimum wage, they will hire only N_1 workers. As a result, unemployment increases.[7]

The imposition of the minimum wage causes firms to discharge or decline to hire workers with minimal skills and experience. Many teenagers fall into this category, so it is not surprising that they are among those most adversely affected by the minimum wage. It is believed that a 10 percent increase in the minimum wage reduces teenage employment by 1 to 3 percent.[8]

The impact of the minimum wage on teenagers is unfortunate. Many teenagers lack work experience and have few skills. Consequently, they have difficulty getting jobs. But without jobs, they cannot get experience and upgrade their skills—a vicious circle. Because the minimum wage can make it prohibitively expensive for firms to hire teenagers, many economists believe that the minimum wage should not apply to them or that they should receive a lower minimum wage. To this end, current federal legislation allows employers to pay a training wage of $4.25 an hour for employees younger than 20 during their first 90 days on the job.

In addition to teenagers, structurally unemployed persons may be adversely affected. A minimum wage reduces firms' incentive to offer on-the-job training, making it more difficult for structurally unemployed persons to find jobs. To ease this problem, some economists have recommended that the long-term unemployed either be exempt from the legislation or face a lower minimum wage.

Another problem has to do with the excess supply of labor generated by the imposition of the minimum wage. At the minimum wage, firms wish to hire only N_1 workers (refer to Figure 12.3). On the other hand, N_2 prospective workers are seeking jobs. This excess supply of workers, $N_2 - N_1$, provides employers with the opportunity to choose among the job seekers. As a result, they are in a position to discriminate—if they desire to do so—against blacks and others. If the wage rate is the equilibrium rate, the quantity of labor demanded equals the quantity supplied, and employers are not in a position to choose among applicants.

---

[7]The imposition of—or a significant increase in—the minimum wage has other adverse effects. The minimum wage raises the costs of producing goods and services. In general, some of this increase in costs will be passed on to purchasers in the form of higher prices. At the same time, firms may reduce fringe benefits and allow working conditions to deteriorate to offset, or partially offset, the costs imposed on them by the minimum wage.

[8]Young adults (persons ages 20 to 24) are adversely affected, but to a lesser extent. Women and blacks are also adversely affected. See Charles Brown, Curtis Gilroy, and Andrew Kohen, "The Effect of the Minimum Wage on Employment and Unemployment," *Journal of Economic Literature* 20 (June 1982), 487–528.

Those workers who remain employed after the imposition of a higher minimum wage have higher incomes. But does this mean that the lot of the working poor has improved? Unfortunately, the increase in the minimum wage is less beneficial to the working poor than supposed. Over half of the low-wage workers in the United States are members of households with *above average* family incomes. These workers include high school and college students with part-time jobs and spouses with low-wage jobs. Consequently, only part of the increase in incomes accrues to the working poor.

If the goal is to help the working poor, the earned income tax credit approach is a better solution. As discussed in Chapter 10, working families with low incomes are permitted to deduct the credit from the taxes that they owe. For families with very low incomes, the credit will exceed the tax liability. Consequently, they will receive a payment from the federal government. Because the earned income tax credit does not raise labor costs to firms, it does not reduce the quantity of labor demand and, hence, employment. On the other hand, the tax credit does reduce tax revenue.

UNEMPLOYMENT IN EUROPE

Although unemployment is a problem in the United States, it is an even greater problem in Europe. As shown in Table 12.2, the unemployment rate for most European countries is significantly higher than for the United States. This has not always been the case. As late as the early 1970s, the unemployment rate for most European countries was significantly lower than for the United States. Since

STANDARDIZED UNEMPLOYMENT RATES FOR SELECTED COUNTRIES: 1995

TABLE 12.2			
Country	**Unemployment Rate (Percent)**	**Country**	**Unemployment Rate (Percent)**
Switzerland	3.6°	Sweden	9.2
Norway	4.9	Belgium	9.4
United States	5.5	France	11.6
Netherlands	6.5	Italy	12.2
Portugal	7.1	Ireland	12.9
Germany	8.2	Finland	17.1
United Kingdom	8.7	Spain	22.7

°For 1994.

The unemployment rate for most European countries is higher than for the United States. For some countries, it is much higher.

Source: Federal Reserve Bank of St. Louis, *International Economic Trends* (July 1996), 19.

then, unemployment rates in Europe have increased while the unemployment rate in the United States has fluctuated, but with little or no upward trend.

In addition to higher unemployment rates, long-term unemployment is a greater problem in most European countries. In many of those countries, over half of the persons classified as unemployed have been unemployed for one year or more. In the United States, only about 10 percent of those classified as unemployed have been unemployed for a year or more.

To reduce the unemployment rate, European policymakers could implement expansionary monetary and fiscal policies. Most economists, however, believe that such policies would have little or no effect on unemployment rates. Instead, these policies would cause prices to rise more rapidly.

Most economists believe that unemployment rates are high in many European countries because of structural impediments that discourage employment. For convenience, we divide these impediments into two categories: (1) those that discourage firms from hiring more workers and (2) those that discourage unemployed persons from accepting jobs.

IMPEDIMENTS TO HIRING

As in the United States, European governments have set minimum wages that employers must pay. These minimum wages are higher in France and most European countries than they are in the United States. As previously discussed, a minimum wage discourages firms from hiring persons with minimal job skills and experience.

Labor unions in most European countries are more powerful than those in the United States. Through the collective bargaining process, these unions have been able to achieve high wages for their members. Unfortunately, the effect is to reduce the number of workers that firms hire.

In addition to the effects of minimum wage legislation and labor unions on wages, European firms must pay relatively high social security, unemployment compensation, and other payroll taxes. Also, government regulations often mandate numerous vacation days and other paid leaves. These taxes and paid leaves add greatly to the cost of employing workers. As a result, they discourage hiring.

In many European countries, it is both costly and time consuming to discharge workers. Often, firms must make large severance payments. In the United States, the typical discharged worker gets a week's severance pay for each year of service. In Germany, the average worker gets four times as much—one month's pay for each year of service. In addition, notification must be given well in advance. In the United States, a discharged worker usually gets a one-month notice, whereas in Germany, the worker gets almost a seven-month notice. In some countries, firms must get outside approval to discharge workers.

At first glance, it appears that these requirements regarding dismissal increase employment. As employees retire or quit, however, firms are reluctant to replace them because it is so costly to discharge workers.

Finally, in many European countries, government regulations and controls make it difficult for entrepreneurs to start new firms or expand existing ones. In the German state of North Rhine-Westphalia, a firm must get permission from almost 90 different federal, state, and local government offices to open a new plant. In the United States, firms are subject to fewer regulations. As a result, new firms and the growth of small firms have made an important contribution to the increase in employment in the United States.

IMPEDIMENTS TO ACCEPTING EMPLOYMENT

In both the United States and Europe, unemployed persons can draw unemployment benefits. Although these benefits serve a useful social purpose, they reduce the incentive to work. The problem is more acute in Europe than it is in the United States because (1) benefits abroad are relatively higher and (2) unemployed persons can draw benefits for a longer period. (Normally, unemployed persons in the United States can draw unemployment benefits for only six months.)

In addition, tax rates are relatively high in European countries. High tax rates, combined with loss of unemployment and other benefits, sharply reduce the incentive for unemployed persons to take jobs. Finally, unemployed persons in Europe have little or no incentive to work to obtain health insurance and other benefits because they are usually provided by the state.

CONCLUSION

For various reasons, unemployment rates in most European countries are higher than in the United States. To reduce those rates, European policymakers must reduce or eliminate the impediments that discourage firms from hiring and unemployed persons from accepting jobs. Because the causes of the high unemployment rates vary from country to country, one should not expect the same set of policies to be successful in all countries.

SUMMARY

Unemployment is very costly both to the individual and to society. To society, the cost of unemployment is the goods and services that could have been produced by the unemployed.

The unemployment rate is the percentage of the civilian labor force that is unemployed. Unemployment rates vary among demographic groups. Teenage and black unemployment rates are well above the overall rate.

Economists distinguish three types of unemployment: frictional, structural, and cyclical. Because of its temporary nature, frictional unemployment is not a major policy concern. In contrast, the structurally unemployed face long-term unemployment unless they retrain or obtain additional education. Structural unemployment is, therefore, a serious problem. In recessions and early stages of recoveries, cyclical unemployment is also a serious problem.

The full employment, or natural, rate of unemployment is the frictional rate of unemployment plus the structural rate of unemployment. It is the lowest unemployment rate consistent with a nonaccelerating inflation rate. Currently, this rate is estimated to be about 5.5 percent.

Aggregate demand and supply determine the equilibrium combination of real GDP and the GDP deflator. If the aggregate demand curve cuts the aggregate supply curve at the full employment level of output, cyclical unemployment is zero. If aggregate demand falls, real GDP decreases. As firms reduce output, they also reduce employment, and the unemployment rate rises. Policymakers may use either expansionary fiscal or monetary policy to increase aggregate demand, thereby causing output and employment to rise and the unemployment rate to fall.

Most economists believe that stabilization policy may be used to maintain full employment and a reasonably stable price level. Stabilization policy can do little, however, to reduce structural unemployment. Other government programs may be needed here, such as retraining workers, subsidizing firms to hire structurally unemployed workers and train them on the job, and helping workers relocate to areas where jobs exist.

By forcing the wage rate above the equilibrium wage rate, the minimum wage causes unemployment—particularly among those with minimal job skills and experience.

Unemployment rates in most European countries are higher than those in the United States. These higher unemployment rates are due to structural impediments that reduce the incentives for firms to hire and for unemployed persons to take jobs. These impediments include high minimum wages, high tax rates, high unemployment benefits, and excessive government regulation.

KEY TERMS

Unemployment rate	Cyclical unemployment	Natural rate of unemployment
Civilian labor force	Full employment rate of unemployment	ment
Frictional unemployment		Stabilization policies
Structural unemployment		

REVIEW QUESTIONS

1. Briefly discuss both the economic and noneconomic costs of unemployment to the individual and society.

2. Suppose you are given the following information about the simplistic economy:

Persons over 65 years not actively seeking employment	20,000
Persons over 65 years actively seeking employment	4,000
Homemakers	40,000
School-age children under 16 years	60,000
Military personnel	15,000
Persons 16 years and older working	85,000
Persons 16 years and older not working because of illness, labor disputes, vacation, bad weather, or personal reasons	5,000
Persons between 16 and 65 years actively seeking employment	6,000

   a. Calculate the number of persons in the civilian labor force.
   b. Calculate the number of persons who are unemployed.
   c. Calculate the simplistic economy's unemployment rate.

3. "A decrease in the unemployment rate will benefit society; however, these benefits will not be shared equally by all groups in society." Explain why this statement is true.

4. List and briefly discuss the different types of unemployment. Should policymakers regard each type as equally detrimental to society?

5. "Full employment means that everyone who wants a job is able to find one." Is this statement true or false? Defend your answer.

6. Why isn't the natural rate of unemployment constant over time? Is this rate likely to increase or decrease over time? Defend your answer.

7. "So long as the economy tends to move toward the equilibrium level of GDP, there is no need to be concerned about unemployment." Is this statement true or false? Defend your answer.

8. Should government undertake stabilization policies if wage rates and other input prices are flexible? Suppose wage rates and other input prices are "sticky." What policy should government pursue in the face of unemployment caused by a drop in aggregate demand?

9. "If pursued vigorously, expansionary fiscal or monetary policies can be used to reduce unemployment caused by inadequate aggregate demand." If this statement is true, why do we still experience periods of cyclical unemployment?

10. Can stabilization policy be used to deal with structural unemployment? Why or why not? If we cannot use stabilization policy, what—if anything—can policymakers do to reduce structural unemployment?

11. Suppose the economy is experiencing full employment. In response to political pressure, Congress reduces taxes. What are the effects of this tax cut on GDP, the GDP deflator, and employment? Defend your answer.

12. Discuss the impact of an increase in the minimum wage on the market for low-skill workers. Use graphical analysis to assist you.

13. "Even though some low-skill workers are laid off as the minimum wage increases, the economic situation of the working poor is improved because those low-skill workers who retain their jobs are receiving a higher wage." Is this statement true or false? Defend your answer.

14. Compare and contrast unemployment in the United States and Europe. If unemployment in Europe is caused by structural factors, what will be the effect of an increase in aggregate demand?

15. Based on the European experience, list and briefly discuss the factors that discourage
    a. firms from hiring and
    b. unemployed persons from accepting jobs.
    How might these factors be altered to reduce unemployment?

SUGGESTIONS FOR FURTHER READING

Bean, Charles R. "European Unemployment: A Survey." *Journal of Economic Literature* 32 (June 1994), 573–619. A survey article evaluating alternative explanations of unemployment in Europe.

Cain, Glen. "The Economic Analysis of Labor Market Discrimination: A Survey." In *Handbook of Labor Economics,* edited by Orley Ashenfelter and Richard Layard, vol. 1, 693–785. Amsterdam: North-Holland, 1986. Reviews alternative theories of discrimination and the relevant empirical evidence.

Kaufman, Bruce. *The Economics of Labor Markets.* 4th ed. Fort Worth: The Dryden Press, 1994. Presents detailed discussions of many of the issues treated in this chapter.

Layard, Richard, Stephen Nickell, and Richard Jackman. *The Unemployment Crises.* Oxford: Oxford University Press, 1994. Short book discussing unemployment in the United States and other countries.

Leigh, Duane E. *Assisting Workers Displaced by Structural Change.* Kalamazoo, MI: W.E. Upjohn Institute for Employment Research, 1995. An up-to-date discussion of job training programs in the United States and other countries.

Organization for Economic Cooperation and Development. *The OECD Jobs Study.* Paris: Organization for Economic Cooperation and Development, 1994. A study of unemployment in countries that belong to the Organization for Economic Cooperation and Development, with emphasis on West European countries.

Reducing Unemployment: Current Issues and Policy Options. Kansas City: Federal Reserve Bank of Kansas City, 1994. Proceedings of a symposium sponsored by the Federal Reserve Bank of Kansas City and held August 25–27, 1994, at Jackson Hole, Wyoming. A collection of papers discussing unemployment in the United States and other countries.

U.S. Department of Labor, Bureau of Labor Statistics. *Employment and Earnings.* Washington DC: Government Printing Office, monthly. Contains data relating to the job market, including unemployment rates.

———, *Monthly Labor Review.* Washington DC: Government Printing Office, monthly. Contains articles and data relating to the job market, including unemployment rates.

13

INFLATION: A MONETARY PHENOMENON

During the last decade, prices in the United States have increased by about 3.2 percent per year. Some prices, including college tuition, have increased at a higher rate; others have increased at a lower rate or even fallen. Although prices have been increasing, they have been rising at a much lower rate than during the preceding 10 or 15 years. They have also been increasing at a more moderate rate than in most countries.

With prices rising, the costs to society seem obvious. Rising prices erode the purchasing power of people's wages, salaries, and pensions. It is not this simple because, as prices rise more rapidly, wages and salaries also rise more rapidly.

In this chapter, we show that inflation helps some individuals and harms others. Among those who benefit are persons whose incomes rise more rapidly than prices. Those who are harmed include persons whose incomes rise less rapidly than prices. Although some people benefit from inflation, inflation—like unemployment—is costly to society. For that reason, policies to reduce or eliminate it are important. To find such policies, we must determine the causes of inflation.

DEFINING INFLATION

Inflation is commonly defined as any increase in the price level. This definition is not useful because it includes both once-and-for-all increases in the price level and continuing increases. It is better to refer to a once-and-for-all increase in the price level as a *rise* in the price level (or a similar term) and to refer to a continu-

Inflation
A continuing rise in the price level.

ing rise in the price level as **inflation.**

The distinction is important because once-and-for-all increases in the price level do not require policy action, but inflation does. Suppose, for instance, that part of the nation's capital stock is destroyed by an earthquake. The decrease in the capital stock reduces the aggregate supply of goods and services. As the aggregate supply curve shifts to the left, the price level rises. Once the economy adjusts to the lower capital stock, however, the price level stops rising. Consequently, policies to keep the price level from rising are unnecessary. On the other hand, if inflation occurs, the price level continues to rise until action is taken to stop it.

Deflation
A continuing fall in the price level.

Deflation, the opposite of inflation, is a continuing fall in the price level. Deflations—usually associated with depressions—are rare. The last deflation in the United States occurred during the Great Depression of the 1930s.

MEASURING INFLATION

This section discusses two price indexes used to measure inflation.[1] They are (1) the implicit price deflator for GDP (the GDP deflator) and (2) the consumer price index (CPI).

---

[1]In this context, the producer price indexes should be mentioned. These indexes measure the prices received by domestic producers of commodities at various stages of production (finished goods, intermediate goods, and crude materials). These indexes are important because movements in them usually foreshadow movements in the CPI. For that reason, the indexes receive widespread attention when they are released each month.

THE GDP DEFLATOR

As defined in Chapter 11, the GDP deflator is a weighted average of the prices of all final goods and services produced in the economy. It is, therefore, the broadest-based measure of the nation's price level. Price deflators are also available for the various components of GDP, such as consumption and investment. Like the GDP deflator, these deflators are available quarterly. Because of its comprehensiveness, most economists consider the GDP deflator to be the best measure of a nation's inflation rate.

THE CONSUMER PRICE INDEX

The **consumer price index** (CPI) is a weighted average of the prices of goods and services purchased by a typical urban household. It includes the prices of food, clothing, housing, transportation, medical care, and entertainment. The current market basket of goods and services was determined by a survey of urban household purchases conducted during the 1982–1984 period. In addition to the CPI, subindexes for such specific goods as food and energy are also compiled. Like the CPI, these subindexes are available monthly.

Consumer Price Index (CPI)
A weighted average of the prices of goods and services purchased by a typical urban household.

Although the GDP deflator provides the best overall measure of inflation, the CPI is the most widely cited measure of inflation in the United States. The main reason for its popularity is that the CPI focuses on the prices of goods and services purchased by households. The GDP deflator, in contrast, focuses on the prices of *all* final goods and services produced in the economy, including those purchased by firms and government.

Because it is based on the prices of goods and services purchased by households, the CPI is widely regarded as a cost-of-living index. As a measure of the cost of living, however, the CPI has several shortcomings. First, it is an index for the *typical* urban household. Consequently, we would not expect it to be accurate for the atypical household. To illustrate, the typical urban household allocates 42.6 percent of its expenditures to housing. If the price of housing were to rise relatively rapidly, households allocating more than 42.6 percent of their expenditures to housing would find their cost of living rising more rapidly than the CPI. By the same token, households allocating less than 42.6 percent to housing would find their cost of living rising less rapidly.

Second, the CPI overstates the increase in the cost of living because it is based on a fixed market basket of goods and services. In actuality, when households find that some prices rise more rapidly than others, they substitute goods and services that have risen less in price for those that have risen more. The CPI doesn't take this substitution into account, and so it overstates the increase in the cost of living.

Third, the CPI also overstates the increase in the cost of living because it doesn't fully account for changes in quality. The quality of many goods and services (such as televisions, personal computers, and medical care) has improved over the years. If it took these changes into account, the CPI would increase less rapidly.

Despite its shortcomings as a measure of the cost of living, the CPI plays an important role in our economy. As the most common measure of inflation, it is often a basis for policymaking. As a measure of the cost of living, it is a basis for labor

Cost-of-Living Adjustment (COLA) Clause
A clause in a labor contract that allows wage rates to increase automatically as the CPI rises.

negotiations. In addition, millions of workers have **cost-of-living adjustment (COLA) clauses** in their contracts. Under these clauses, wage rates increase automatically as the CPI rises. Similarly, tens of millions of retirees find that their social security benefits increase automatically as the CPI rises. Finally, the CPI is used to adjust the federal personal income tax system to eliminate the effects of inflation.

CALCULATING THE INFLATION RATE

To determine the inflation rate (the percentage rate of increase in the price level) from one period to the next period, we apply the following formula:

$$\text{Inflation rate} = \frac{\text{Current period's price level} - \text{Previous period's price level}}{\text{Previous period's price level}} \times 100. \qquad (13.1)$$

We first subtract the previous period's price level from the current period's price level to obtain the change in the price level from one period to the next. Then we divide the change in the price level by the previous period's price level and multiply the result by 100. (Multiplying by 100 expresses the inflation rate as a percentage.)

THE GDP DEFLATOR: 1960–1995

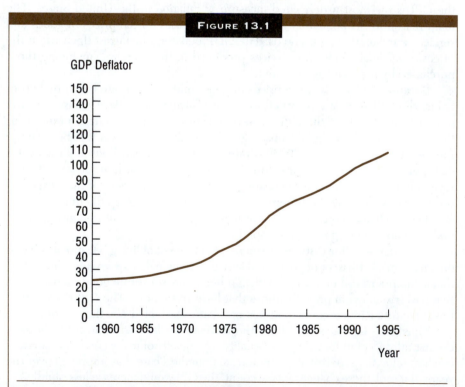

FIGURE 13.1

The price level, as measured by the GDP deflator, increased substantially over the 1960–1995 period. It increased more rapidly in the 1970s and 1980s than in the 1960s.

To illustrate, we can find the inflation rate for 1995. In 1994, the GDP deflator was 104.9; in 1995, 107.6. Applying the formula, we have

$$\text{Inflation rate} = \frac{107.6 - 104.9}{104.9} \times 100 = \frac{2.7}{104.9} \times 100$$

$$= 0.026 \times 100 = 2.6 \text{ percent.}$$

We conclude, therefore, that the inflation rate was 2.6 percent in 1995.

RECENT EXPERIENCE

Inflation is a relatively new phenomenon in the United States. During most of the nation's history, increases in the price level have been followed by falling prices. Since 1940, however, the price level has more or less increased steadily. The price level rose during World War II and the immediate postwar period. It rose again during the Korean War. From 1953 to 1965, the price level increased at a moderate rate. Starting in 1966, it increased more rapidly (see Figure 13.1). Inflation was high, by U.S. standards, throughout the 1970s (see Figure 13.2). The inflation

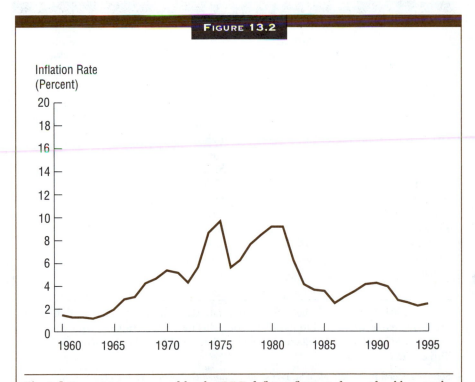

FIGURE 13.2

THE INFLATION RATE: 1960–1995

The inflation rate, as measured by the GDP deflator, fluctuated considerably over the 1960–1995 period. It peaked at 9.6 percent in 1975.

rate, as measured by the GDP deflator, peaked in 1975 at 9.6 percent. In the early 1980s, the inflation rate decreased. In the late 1980s, it increased once more, peaking at 4.3 percent in 1990. Since the early 1990s, the inflation rate has been relatively low. In 1994, it was only 2.3 percent, the lowest rate since 1965.

Although the inflation rate in the United States averaged 3.3 percent for the 1983–1995 period, the United States experienced less inflation than most countries over that time span. As shown in Table 13.1, some countries—Portugal, Greece, Chile, Venezuela, Mexico, and Turkey—had double-digit inflation. Whether here or abroad, inflation always has adverse effects.

EFFECTS OF INFLATION

Unanticipated Inflation
Inflation that is unexpected or higher than expected.

Anticipated Inflation
Inflation that is expected.

The effects of inflation depend largely on whether it is unanticipated or anticipated. **Unanticipated inflation** is inflation that is unexpected or higher than expected. For example, people might expect no inflation and instead experience an actual inflation rate of 5 percent. **Anticipated inflation** is inflation that is expected. For instance, people might expect inflation to occur at a 5 percent rate and the price level might, in fact, rise at that rate.

INFLATION RATES FOR SELECTED COUNTRIES: 1983–1995

TABLE 13.1

Country	Inflation Rate (Percent)	Country	Inflation Rate (Percent)
Japan	1.4	Australia	4.6
Netherlands	1.5	United Kingdom	4.7
Malaysia	2.4	Sweden	5.6
Canada	2.7	South Korea	6.1
Switzerland	3.1	Italy	6.6
Denmark	3.2	New Zealand	6.6
Ireland	3.2	Spain	6.9
Austria	3.3	China	9.2
Norway	3.3	Portugal	13.2
United States	3.3	Greece	15.8
France	3.4	Chile	19.7
Belgium	3.5	Venezuela	35.8
Thailand	4.2	Mexico	47.7
Finland	4.4	Turkey	62.7

For the 1983–1995 period, the U.S. inflation rate (as measured by the GDP deflator) was 3.3 percent. Compared to most countries, this rate is low. In fact, many countries experienced double-digit inflation, including Venezuela (35.8), Mexico (47.7), and Turkey (62.7).

Source: Federal Reserve Bank of St. Louis, *International Economic Trends* (July 1996), 8.

THE REDISTRIBUTION OF INCOME AND WEALTH

One of the effects of inflation is a redistribution of income and wealth—a substantial redistribution if the inflation is unanticipated. Some individuals gain because their wages and salaries rise more rapidly than the price level. Others lose because their wages, salaries, and pensions rise less rapidly than the price level. In this sense, real income is redistributed from some individuals to others. To illustrate, suppose workers in a particular industry, expecting no inflation, agree to a long-term contract calling for annual 4 percent wage increases. By most standards, 4 percent wage increases are very satisfactory *if* no inflation is occurring. Suppose, however, inflation occurs at an 8 percent rate. With wage rates rising less rapidly than prices, income is redistributed—in this case, from the workers to the owners of the firms in the industry.

In the preceding illustration, the workers received 4 percent wage increases that partially offset the 8 percent price increases. Inflation is a more serious problem for those living on fixed incomes. Suppose you had retired in 1979 on a fixed income. From 1979 to 1995, the CPI more than doubled, implying that your fixed income bought less than half as much in 1995 as it did in 1979.

High inflation rates can have a disastrous impact on persons living on fixed incomes. Fortunately, most retirees do not live on fixed incomes. Social Security benefits constitute the bulk of the typical retiree's income, and these benefits are **indexed.** That is, they are linked to the CPI so that they increase automatically as the CPI rises. If the CPI rises by, say, 5 percent, Social Security benefits increase by 5 percent. Consequently, the effects of inflation on retired persons are not as disastrous as one might think.

Indexing
The linking of benefits to the CPI so that they increase automatically as the CPI rises.

Just as income is redistributed with inflation, wealth is also redistributed. Inflation causes many asset prices to rise, some more than the price level and others less. People whose assets appreciate more in price gain from the inflation; those whose assets appreciate less lose.

One important type of redistribution is that from creditors to debtors. A **creditor** is a person to whom money is owed. A **debtor** is a person who owes money. Suppose you borrow at a fixed interest rate to buy a home and that your monthly payment on the principal and interest is $800. Then, over time, the price level doubles. The prices of the goods and services that you typically buy double, but, with the inflation, so does your income. Consequently, you can continue to buy the same amount of food, clothing, and so on. What about your mortgage payment? It will remain the same. Because your income has doubled, this $800 payment is much less burdensome than before. To put it differently, the inflation means you are able to repay the loan in dollars with substantially less purchasing power than those that you borrowed. You benefit from the inflation.

Creditor
A person to whom money is owed.

Debtor
A person who owes money.

Just as debtors gain from inflation, creditors lose. They are repaid with dollars that have less purchasing power than the dollars that they lent. In the example, the institution from which you borrowed finds that the $800 monthly payment will buy only half as much as before because the price level has doubled.

Unanticipated inflation causes a substantial redistribution of income and wealth. With anticipated inflation, however, the redistribution is much less dramatic. When people anticipate inflation, they can take action to protect themselves. Consider once more the workers who agreed to a contract calling for 4 percent wage increases and then experienced 8 percent inflation. If the 8 percent inflation continues, these workers will expect the inflation rate to be 8 percent, and the inflation will become anticipated inflation. At the expiration of their contract, the workers will bargain for wage increases that take the anticipated inflation into account.

With anticipated inflation, the redistribution of wealth from creditors to debtors is also less dramatic. When they expect no inflation, creditors are willing to lend money at relatively low interest rates. A lender might be willing to lend $100 for a year at a 4 percent interest rate, which means that the borrower must pay the lender $104 at the end of the year. If the price level rises by 8 percent during the year, the $104 that the lender receives at the end of the year will buy less than the $100 would have at the start of the year. Under these circumstances, the lender will no longer agree to lend at a 4 percent rate. Instead, the lender will insist on a rate that will compensate for the expected deterioration in the purchasing power of money. If the inflation rate is anticipated to be 8 percent, the lender will insist on a 12 percent rate. The additional 8 percent is to compensate for the anticipated inflation.

It is easy to see why the lender will insist on a higher interest rate when the anticipated inflation rate rises. It is perhaps less easy to see why borrowers will agree to it. To the typical borrower, however, a 12 percent interest rate with 8 percent inflation is no more burdensome than a 4 percent rate with no inflation. This is because, with 8 percent inflation, the typical wage earner can expect his or her income to rise 8 percent faster. Of course, not all wage earners will find their incomes rising 8 percent faster.

Thus, the switch from unanticipated to anticipated inflation causes interest rates to rise. The rise in interest rates protects lenders so that no redistribution of wealth occurs between lenders and borrowers. (People who borrowed at relatively low interest rates before the increase in the inflation rate still benefit.)

Even with anticipated inflation, some redistribution of income and wealth occurs. Persons who retired on fixed incomes and those who lent money at a low interest rate can do little or nothing when they realize that the inflation rate has increased. Consequently, they are adversely affected by inflation. Others, however, gain at their expense, so that society as a whole is unaffected.

In one important case, society is adversely affected by an increase in the inflation rate. Inflation hurts people who hold money because it erodes its purchasing power. Consequently, as the inflation rates rise, people attempt to reduce the amount of money that they hold. To the extent that they devote more time and effort to reducing their holdings of money, fewer resources are devoted to the production of goods and services. The reduced production represents a cost to society. Studies suggest that this cost is small at low inflation rates but increases as the inflation rate rises.

INFLATION AND GOVERNMENT

Inflation affects government in two important ways. First, the federal government is a huge debtor, owing more than *$4 trillion*. As a debtor, the federal government gains from inflation. Creditors, on the other hand, lose.

Second, under inflation the federal government gains additional real tax revenue at the expense of taxpayers because part of our nation's tax system is based on nominal income rather than real income. Let us first examine the pre-1985 federal personal income tax system. That system had many tax brackets (for example, $20,000–$22,000). Moreover, the tax rate increased as the taxpayer's income bracket increased. As we have seen, inflation results in higher incomes. If the price level doubles over some time span, the income of a typical household also doubles. Even though the typical household may not experience an increase in real income because of the increase in the price level, under the pre-1985 personal income tax system, it would have experienced an increase in its real tax liability. This occurred because the increase in *nominal* income moved the household into a higher tax bracket, with its higher tax rate.

Under these circumstances, real income was redistributed from taxpayers to government and, ultimately, to those who benefited from government spending. This redistribution may or may not have been desirable. It must be recognized, however, that it took place without congressional action to raise taxes. Consequently, it was not possible for voters to properly "reward" those in Congress responsible for higher taxes. Moreover, because inflation increases real tax revenue, Congress may have had less of an incentive to pursue anti-inflationary policies than it would otherwise have had.

To prevent the redistribution of income through the personal income tax system, Congress passed and President Reagan signed legislation in 1981 to index the personal income tax system, starting in 1985. The system is now adjusted each year to eliminate the effects of inflation on real tax revenue.

Unfortunately, while the federal personal income tax system is now indexed, the rest of the federal tax system is not. This is particularly unfortunate with regard to the federal corporate income tax system. When inflation occurs, corporations find that their real tax liability increases. The reduction in real after-tax profits makes it less profitable for them to invest in new plant and equipment. As a result, they reduce investment. Less investment means the nation's capital stock increases less rapidly, which in turn means the nation's output and standard of living also increase less rapidly.

INFLATION AND NET EXPORTS

Inflation also can affect exports and imports. Suppose the United States is experiencing more inflation than the rest of the world. All other things equal, U.S. exports will become less competitive in world markets. Consequently, the United States will export less. This will have an adverse impact on output and employment in the economy's export-producing sector (such as the agricultural and airplane industries).

With prices rising more rapidly in the United States, imports become relatively less expensive. As a result, purchasers will buy fewer domestically produced goods and services and more imports. The increase in imports has an adverse impact on output and employment in the economy's import-competing sector (such as the automobile and steel industries).

We find that a higher inflation rate in the United States than in the rest of the world decreases U.S. exports and increases U.S. imports. (A lower inflation rate would have the opposite effect.) Over time, the dollar will depreciate (decrease) in value in terms of foreign currencies. The depreciation in the dollar will compensate for the higher inflation rate in the United States, although it may take a number of years. In the interim, both the export-producing and import-competing sectors of the U.S. economy will endure economic hardship.

OTHER EFFECTS

As the inflation rate rises, it becomes more variable, making it more difficult to plan for the future. Under these circumstances, more resources will be devoted to predicting the inflation rate. Similarly, people will devote more resources to devising ways to protect their real income and wealth. To the extent that fewer resources are allocated to the production of goods and services, the nation's output of goods and services will be reduced.

A high and variable inflation rate also may lead to speculation in real estate, gold, antiques, and art. During periods of rising prices, these assets often appreciate significantly in value. While buying these assets may prove profitable, it does not increase the nation's capital stock. Indeed, to the extent that resources are diverted from investment in plant and equipment, the nation's capital stock will grow less rapidly. As a result, the GDP growth rate will be reduced and the nation's standard of living will improve less rapidly.

Finally, when the inflation rate becomes very high, a nation's monetary system may disintegrate. When prices rise very rapidly, the purchasing power of money deteriorates sharply. As a result, people will hold little or no money. They also will insist on being paid often so that they can buy goods before they increase further in price. At some point, money will become worthless and people will exchange goods and services only for other goods and services. Such an arrangement is extremely inefficient because it takes much time and effort to find people who both have what you want and are willing to trade for what you have. The nation's output of goods and services will decline, and the economy may collapse.

History has provided many examples. The most famous involves Germany after World War I. In 1922, its inflation rate was over 5,000 percent. Prices increased almost continuously. Diners at restaurants found, for example, that they had to pay more for their meals than was listed on the menu when they ordered. Prices became astronomical, with meat and butter costing millions of marks per pound. Money became worthless or virtually worthless. It was used as kindling to start fires.

Hyperinflation
Extremely high inflation rates.

Although many examples of **hyperinflation**—extremely high inflation rates—exist, inflation need not and typically does not reach such high proportions.

The hyperinflation in post–World War I Germany was caused by the government's printing huge amounts of money. Most governments are much more prudent.

MONEY AND THE MONEY SUPPLY

As just discussed, hyperinflations are caused by huge increases in the money supply. What about more moderate inflation rates? Are they caused by increases in the money supply? This is a very important question. Before answering it, however, we must consider money, its functions, and the money supply.

MONEY'S FUNCTIONS

Money has three functions. Money serves as (1) a unit of account, (2) a medium of exchange, and (3) a store of value. With regard to money's unit of account function, we keep track of the value of things in terms of money. A pizza costs $5.00, a hamburger $2.50, a hot dog $1.00, and so on. By using a common measure, we can compare relative costs very easily. A pizza costs twice as much as a hamburger and five times as much as a hot dog. This ease of comparison greatly aids decision making.

Money's medium of exchange function is extremely important. A **medium of exchange** is something that can be used to purchase goods and services and pay debts. In ancient times, households were largely self-sufficient. They grew and cooked their own food, made their own clothes, built their own dwellings, and so on. Because of this self-sufficiency, very few goods and services were exchanged. Little need existed, therefore, for a medium of exchange. As time passed, however, households found it in their interest to specialize in a relatively small number of activities and trade or barter the goods that they produced for other goods and services. As a result, a need for a medium of exchange developed. Money is that medium of exchange, greatly aiding in the exchange of goods and services. It would be almost impossible for a modern economy to function without a medium of exchange, because the alternative—barter—is extremely inefficient.

With regard to its store of value function, money is a way for households to hold their savings. They may hold their savings in other forms, including bonds, common stock, and real estate. Money, therefore, is not unique as a store of value. Moreover, during periods of inflation, money is an unsatisfactory store of value because rising prices erode its purchasing power. For this reason, households and firms seek to reduce their holdings of money during periods of inflation.

THE MONEY SUPPLY

Money usually is defined in terms of its medium of exchange function. **Money** is anything generally accepted as final payment for goods, services, and debt. **Currency (cash)**—paper money and coins—is money because currency is generally accepted as payment for goods, services, and debt. Similarly, **demand deposits**—checking

Medium of Exchange
Anything used to purchase goods and services and pay debts.

Money
Anything generally accepted as final payment for goods, services, and debt.

Currency (cash)
Paper money and coins.

Demand Deposits
Checking accounts at commercial banks.

accounts at commercial banks—are money because they are generally accepted as payment for goods, services, and debt. The same is true of other checkable deposits, including those at savings and loan associations and credit unions. Based on this definition, however, savings and time deposits are not money because we cannot use them as final payment for goods, services, and debt. We must first convert them to currency or some other form of money. The same is true of other assets such as bonds and stocks. Those assets are not generally accepted as final payment for goods, services, and debt.

Given the definition of money, we are now in a position to define the nation's money supply. The **money supply** is defined as currency, travelers' checks, demand deposits, and other checkable deposits. Like the other components of the money supply, travelers' checks are included in the money supply because they are generally accepted as final payment for goods, services, and debt. As shown in Table 13.2, travelers' checks account for less than 1 percent of the nation's money supply. Currency accounts for 34.0 percent of the money supply, while demand and other checkable deposits account for the remaining 65.2 percent.

The money supply, as defined here, corresponds to one of the monetary aggregates published by the Federal Reserve. This aggregate is referred to as M1. The other aggregates—M2, M3, and L—are defined more broadly.

M2 includes the various components of M1. It also includes savings and (small-denomination) time deposits, money market deposit accounts, and money market mutual funds. Savings and time deposits are included because they are easily converted to cash or checkable deposits. Persons with money market deposit accounts can, within certain limits, write checks on these accounts. Persons participating in money market mutual funds also have that privilege. M2 is of importance because, from time to time, the Federal Reserve has emphasized M2 in conducting monetary policy.

Money Supply
Currency, travelers' checks, demand deposits, and other checkable deposits.

THE MONEY SUPPLY AND ITS COMPONENTS: JUNE 1996

TABLE 13.2

Component	Amount (Billions of Dollars[a])	Relative Importance (Percent)
Currency	379.4	34.0
Travelers' checks	8.6	0.8
Demand deposits	413.6	37.0
Other checkable deposits	315.6	28.2
Totals	1,117.2	100.0

The nation's money supply (M1) was $1,117.2 billion in June 1996. Demand and other checkable deposits accounted for 65.2 percent of the total. Currency accounted for almost all (34.0 percent) of the remainder.

[a]Average of daily figures (seasonally adjusted).

Source: Board of Governors of the Federal Reserve System, *Federal Reserve Bulletin* 82 (September 1996), A13.

M3 and L are defined even more broadly. Many of their components, however, are not easily convertible to cash or checkable deposits. Consequently, they are not important for our purposes. In addition, the Federal Reserve places more emphasis on M1 and M2 than on M3 and L in conducting monetary policy.

THE FEDERAL RESERVE

The Federal Reserve, an independent agency of the federal government, is the United States' central bank. By **central bank,** we mean a government-established agency that controls the nation's money supply, conducts monetary policy, and, in general, supervises the nation's monetary system. Because these functions are so important, countries typically have central banks. In England the central bank is the Bank of England, in Germany it is the Bundesbank, and so on.

The Federal Reserve controls the nation's money supply. If policymakers at the Federal Reserve believe that the money supply should increase more rapidly, they can take the appropriate action to increase it more rapidly. Conversely, if they believe that it should increase less rapidly, they can take the appropriate action to increase it less rapidly. The Federal Reserve and the nation's monetary system are discussed in greater detail in the appendix to this chapter.

Central Bank
A government-established agency that controls the nation's money supply, conducts monetary policy, and supervises the monetary system.

THE CAUSES OF INFLATION

After defining and discussing the nation's money supply, we now turn to the causes of inflation. Inflation is a continuing rise in the price level. In the absence of policies to reduce or eliminate it, inflation will continue indefinitely. Inflation, therefore, is a long-run phenomenon.

THE QUANTITY THEORY OF MONEY

Inflation can best be explained in terms of the **quantity theory of money.** This theory emphasizes that the money supply is the principal determinant of nominal GDP. The quantity theory of money, in turn, can be explained with reference to the equation of exchange. The **equation of exchange** shows the relationship among the money supply (M), the income velocity of money (V), the GDP deflator (P), and real GDP. It is

$$M \times V = P \times GDP. \tag{13.2}$$

(The money supply was defined earlier in this chapter; the GDP deflator and real GDP were defined in Chapter 11.) The **income velocity of money** is the number of times the money supply is used to purchase final goods and services during a year. It is calculated by dividing nominal GDP (P × GDP) by the money supply (M). Suppose that nominal GDP is $1 trillion and that the money supply is $100

Quantity Theory of Money
A theory emphasizing that the money supply is the principal determinant of nominal GDP.

Equation of Exchange
An equation showing the relationships among the money supply, the income velocity of money, the GDP deflator, and real GDP (M × V = P × GDP).

Income Velocity of Money
The number of times the money supply is used to purchase final goods and services during a year.

ADDITIONAL INSIGHT

CURRENCY HOLDINGS AND THE UNDERGROUND ECONOMY

Although currency is convenient for small transactions, checkable deposits have many advantages as a medium of exchange. Currency can be lost, destroyed, or stolen. For large transactions, it is bulky. Checks can be made for any amount, large or small. They also provide a record of the transactions. Finally, checkable deposits are typically insured.

With these advantages, it is not surprising that checkable deposits account for most of the nation's money supply. Even so, both on a per capita basis and as a percentage of the money supply, currency is more important now than it was in 1960. Indeed, there is more than $1,400 in cash in circulation for every man, woman, and child in the United States. For those of us who rarely have more than $20 or $30 in cash, this statistic is astounding.

What accounts for this increase in cash balances? Is it because we have more coin-operated machines and the like? Most experts believe that this explanation can account for only a small part of the increase in cash balances. One reason for the increase, they believe, is the growth of the underground economy, especially the part that deals with illegal drugs.

When people participate in the underground economy, they do not want to leave records of their transactions. After all, records can be used to identify them and as evidence in a court of law. Also, while there may be honor among thieves, there is unlikely to be trust. People engaged in illegal activities usually insist on payment in cash.

The large influx of immigrants—particularly those from Mexico and Vietnam—may have contributed to the increase in cash balances. For various reasons, many immigrants prefer to hold cash rather than open checking accounts at banks.

Finally, much U.S. currency is held abroad. Individuals in foreign countries often prefer to hold dollars because they distrust their own currency. Large amounts of U.S. currency are held in Central and South America, Eastern Europe (particularly Russia), and the Middle and Far East. Although some U.S. currency has always been held abroad, the trend toward foreign ownership has become more pronounced in recent years.

---

billion. The income velocity of money is 10, obtained by dividing $1 trillion by $100 billion.

As the equation stands, it is a tautology—something that is true by definition. This is so because the velocity of money is defined in terms of the other variables (V = Nominal GDP/M). In the example, the money supply is $100 billion. If that much money is used to purchase $1 trillion worth of goods and services, it must be used 10 times. Another way to view it is to note that the left-hand side of the equation of exchange ($M \times V$) represents the amount spent on final goods and services, and the right-hand side ($P \times GDP$) represents the amount received for those final goods and services. These two amounts must be equal.

The quantity theory of money assumes that the velocity of money is constant or approximately so. Although velocity varies to some extent from year to year, it shows greater stability in the long run. Because inflation is a long-run phenomenon, we shall assume initially that it is constant.

Chapter 11 shows that an increase in the money supply, through its impact on aggregate demand, results in an increase in nominal GDP. The same is true in the quantity theory. Moreover, the increase in nominal GDP is proportional to the increase in the money supply, provided that the velocity of money is constant. Suppose the money supply increases from $100 billion to $200 billion. With the velocity of money constant, nominal GDP must increase from $1 trillion to $2 trillion. If unemployment existed initially, both the GDP deflator and real GDP will rise. If full employment prevailed, only the GDP deflator will rise.

To determine the impact of an increase in the money supply on the inflation rate, it is convenient to rewrite Equation 13.2 to obtain

$$\frac{\Delta M}{M} + \frac{\Delta V}{V} = \frac{\Delta P}{P} + \frac{\Delta GDP}{GDP}.$$

In the equation, $\Delta M/M$, the change in the money supply (ΔM) divided by the money supply, is the growth rate of the money supply; $\Delta V/V$, the change in velocity (ΔV) divided by velocity, is the growth rate of velocity; $\Delta P/P$, the change in the GDP deflator (ΔP) divided by the GDP deflator, is the inflation rate; and $\Delta GDP/GDP$, the change in real GDP (ΔGDP) divided by real GDP, is the output growth rate. If the velocity of money is constant, ΔV and therefore $\Delta V/V$ equal zero. Consequently, we have

$$\frac{\Delta M}{M} = \frac{\Delta P}{P} + \frac{\Delta GDP}{GDP}. \tag{13.3}$$

Equation 13.3 states that the growth rate of the money supply equals the inflation rate plus the output growth rate. Rearranging terms gives

$$\frac{\Delta P}{P} = \frac{\Delta M}{M} - \frac{\Delta GDP}{GDP}. \tag{13.4}$$

Equation 13.4 states that the inflation rate equals the growth rate of the money supply less the output growth rate.

The growth rate of the money supply is determined by the Federal Reserve. In the long run, the growth rate of output is determined by the growth rates of the nation's resources and by the rate of technological progress. Over the business cycle, the growth rate of real GDP varies. In the long run, however, aggregate supply and real GDP increase by about 3 percent per year.

The growth rate of the money supply that is consistent with a stable price level, or a zero inflation rate, can now be determined. To do so, substitute zero for the inflation rate and 3 percent for the output growth rate in Equation 13.4, and then solve for $\Delta M/M$. The solution is 3 percent, implying that the money supply can grow at a 3 percent rate and the price level will still remain constant.

The aggregate supply–aggregate demand framework can illustrate this result. Suppose that, in Figure 13.3, aggregate demand is AD_1 and aggregate supply is AS_1. (For convenience, the aggregate demand and supply curves are assumed to be linear.) The price level, given by the intersection of AD_1 and AS_1, is P_1. As the nation's capital stock and labor supply increase and technological progress occurs, aggregate supply

AGGREGATE DE-
MAND, AGGREGATE
SUPPLY, AND THE
PRICE LEVEL

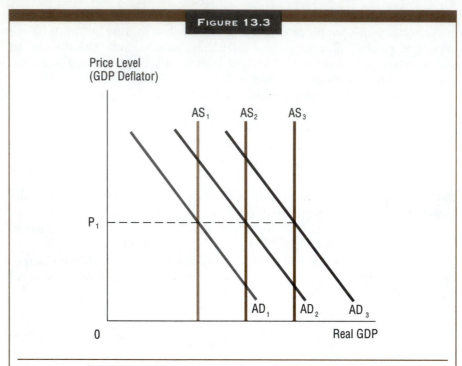

FIGURE 13.3

The price level is determined by aggregate demand and supply. The initial price level is P_1, given by the intersection of the initial aggregate demand curve AD_1 and aggregate supply curve AS_1. If aggregate demand and supply grow at the same rate, the price level remains constant.

increases. Suppose the new aggregate supply curve is AS_2. If aggregate demand increases at the same rate, the price level will be constant. In this case, suppose aggregate demand increases to AD_2. The price level, given by the intersection of AD_2 and AS_2, will be P_1, the same as the original price level. Should aggregate demand and supply continue to grow at the same rate, the price level will remain constant.

In the example, the money supply can grow at a 3 percent rate without causing inflation. Suppose the money supply were to grow at, say, an 8 percent rate. What will be the impact of the increased growth rate of the money supply on the inflation rate? Equation 13.4 gives the answer. With an 8 percent growth rate in the money supply and a 3 percent output growth rate, the inflation rate is 5 percent (8 percent − 3 percent).

Once again, the aggregate supply–aggregate demand framework can demonstrate this result. Suppose that, in Figure 13.4, aggregate demand is AD_1 and aggregate supply is AS_1. The price level, given by the intersection of AD_1 and AS_1, is P_1. As the nation's capital stock and labor supply increase and technological progress occurs, aggregate supply increases. As a result, the new aggregate supply curve is AS_2. Previously, aggregate demand increased at the same rate as

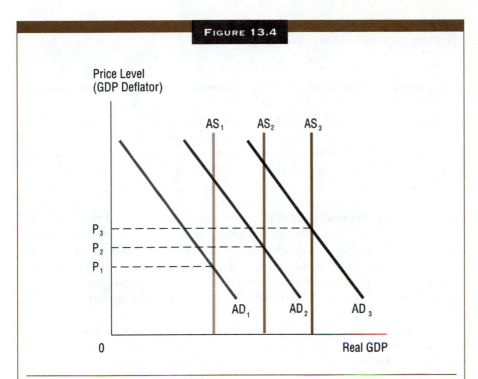

FIGURE 13.4

The price level is determined by aggregate demand and supply. The initial price level is P_1, given by the intersection of the initial aggregate demand curve AD_1 and aggregate supply curve AS_1. If aggregate demand grows more rapidly than aggregate supply, the price level rises.

aggregate supply and the price level was constant. The money supply, however, is now increasing at an 8 percent rate rather than a 3 percent rate. With the velocity of money constant, aggregate demand also grows at an 8 percent rate. If the new aggregate demand curve is AD_2, the new price level is P_2, given by the intersection of AD_2 and AS_2. This price level is higher than the original price level, P_1.

With aggregate demand growing more rapidly than aggregate supply, the price level will continue to rise. With aggregate demand growing at an 8 percent rate and aggregate supply at a 3 percent rate, the price level will rise at a 5 percent rate.

INFLATION IS A MONETARY PHENOMENON

The inflation rate rises from 0 percent to 5 percent when the growth rate of the money supply rises from 3 percent to 8 percent. This demonstrates a very important proposition: the higher the growth rate of the money supply, the higher the inflation rate. Excessive rates of growth of the money supply cause inflation;

therefore, inflation is a monetary phenomenon. Before examining the policy implications, we consider two qualifications.

INFLATION AS A MONETARY PHENOMENON: TWO QUALIFICATIONS

Based on Equation 13.4, an increase in the growth rate of the money supply causes the inflation rate to rise. This conclusion assumes that (1) the output growth rate is constant and (2) the velocity of money is constant. If these assumptions are relaxed, the relationship between the growth rate of the money supply and the inflation rate is not as strong.

THE OUTPUT GROWTH RATE

Previously, we assumed that real GDP grew at a 3 percent rate. Although the output growth rate has averaged about 3 percent since 1929, the growth rate varies over the business cycle. Typically, it exceeds 3 percent during expansions (particularly during the early stages) and is less than 3 percent during contractions. Given this variation in growth rates, the inflation rate will vary over the business cycle even if the growth rate of the money supply is constant.

Suppose the economy is beginning to recover from a recession. During a recession, unemployment is high and firms have excess capacity. Because they have idle equipment and easily can hire more workers, firms can increase output relatively rapidly. Suppose the money supply is growing at an 8 percent rate. If output grows at a 3 percent rate (the long-run average), the inflation rate will be 5 percent. With excess capacity and high unemployment, output may grow at a higher rate, say, 5 percent. With the money supply growing at an 8 percent rate and output growing at a 5 percent rate, the inflation rate is only 3 percent.

Output cannot grow at a 5 percent rate indefinitely. Sooner or later, full employment will be achieved and output will grow less rapidly. If the money supply continues to grow at an 8 percent rate and the output growth rate falls, the inflation rate will rise.

With variable output growth, the inflation rate varies even if the growth rate of the money supply is constant. Because the output growth rate varies in the short run, we find that the relationship between the growth rate of the money supply and the inflation rate is not as strong as originally stated. Even so, the growth rate of output is 3 percent in the long run. Because inflation is a long-run phenomenon, it is appropriate to use the long-run output growth rate—3 percent—in analyzing inflation. Thus, the short-run variation in the output growth rate does not modify the conclusion that inflation is a monetary phenomenon. Instead, it merely obscures the relationship between the growth rate of the money supply and the inflation rate.

THE VELOCITY OF MONEY

Just as the output growth rate varies in the short run, the velocity of money varies. Suppose the growth rate of the money supply increases. With velocity and the output growth rate constant, the inflation rate rises. If the velocity of money falls at the same time the growth rate of the money supply increases, the inflation rate will rise but by a smaller amount. In both situations, the increase in growth rate of the money supply is the same. In the second situation, the money supply circulates less rapidly. It, therefore, has less of an impact on the inflation rate.

In the short run, the velocity of money may fall in response to an increase in the growth rate of the money supply. In the long run, however, the velocity of money is relatively constant. Consequently, the short-run variation in velocity does not alter the conclusion that inflation is a monetary phenomenon. Like the short-run variation in the output growth rate, it merely obscures the relationship between the growth rate of the money supply and the inflation rate.

Similarly, suppose government purchases increase while the money supply is constant. With the increase in government purchases, aggregate demand increases and the price level rises. With the money supply constant, the increase in the price level must be due to an increase in the velocity of money caused by the increase in government purchases.

Although factors other than the money supply (in this case, government purchases) affect the price level through variations in the velocity of money in the short run, these factors are much less important in the long run because of the relative constancy of the velocity of money in the long run. If the velocity of money is constant (or approximately so), it is the growth rate of the money supply that determines the growth rate of aggregate demand and, with a constant growth rate of aggregate supply, the inflation rate. Inflation is a monetary phenomenon.

LABOR UNIONS, MONOPOLIES, AND INFLATION

Economists generally agree that inflation is a monetary phenomenon. Some economists, however, argue that inflation is due to the exercise of monopoly power by labor unions and firms.

LABOR UNIONS   According to the argument, labor unions—through the collective bargaining process—force up wages more rapidly than they would otherwise increase. Firms, in turn, pass their higher labor costs on to their customers in the form of higher prices. In terms of the aggregate demand–aggregate supply model, a general increase in wage rates causes the aggregate supply curve to shift to the left, at least over part of its range (see Figure 11.6). With a reduction in aggregate supply and with aggregate demand constant, the price level rises. In this situation, labor unions cause the price level to rise.

But is this a likely occurrence? Most economists think not. First, many labor unions lack significant bargaining power and therefore cannot force up the wages of their members more rapidly than they would otherwise increase. Second, even if labor unions can force up union wages, it is unlikely that they will alter wages in general. Only about 15 percent of nonagricultural workers belong to unions. Consequently, the overwhelming majority of workers are not covered by union contracts. In addition, unions can force up wages only by limiting employment opportunities in the unionized sector of the economy. Those unable to find employment in the unionized sector will turn to the nonunionized sector, thereby depressing wages there. Consequently, even if unions can force up union wages, average wages are unlikely to be altered significantly. Labor unions, therefore, are an unlikely cause of inflation.

FIRMS   Like labor unions, firms often are accused of causing inflation by exercising monopoly power. That is, firms are accused of raising prices even in the absence of increased demand or rising costs.

This could not happen in a purely competitive economy. In a purely competitive economy, there are many sellers of each product. Because there are many sellers, a single seller would be unable to raise prices above the market price and retain its customers. Moreover, because many sellers exist, it is impossible for them to collude. Thus, the argument that firms cause inflation cannot hold in a purely competitive economy.

Although part of the U.S. economy is purely competitive, part of it is not. In industries characterized by imperfect competition, firms have discretion regarding the prices of their products. Even so, inflation is not inevitable. Indeed, economic theory suggests that a monopolist (to take the simplest case) will set a price that maximizes profits. Once the monopolist sets the profit-maximizing price, however, management has no incentive to raise price further. (As explained in Chapter 4, a higher price would reduce profits.)

In conclusion, monopolists are interested in charging "high" prices. Inflation, however, is not about high prices; it is about rising prices. Consequently, while we would expect prices to be higher under monopoly than under pure competition, we would *not* expect price to rise indefinitely under imperfect competition. Thus we would not expect inflation to be a greater problem under imperfect competition than under pure competition.

INFLATION AND POLICY

The appropriate cure for inflation depends upon its cause. Monetary policy, fiscal policy, supply-side policies, and incomes policy are proposed cures. Monetary and fiscal policies are government actions designed to control aggregate demand. **Supply-side policies** are government actions aimed at increasing aggregate supply. **Incomes policy** is government action, other than monetary and fiscal policies, to restrain or control wages, prices, and other forms of income.

Supply-Side Policies Government actions aimed at increasing aggregate supply.

Incomes Policy Government action, other than monetary and fiscal policies, to restrain or control wages, prices, and other forms of income.

MONETARY POLICY

Earlier, we concluded that inflation is a monetary phenomenon; that is, it is caused by excessive rates of growth of the money supply. To reduce the inflation rate, the growth rate of the money supply must therefore be reduced. Reducing the growth rate of the money supply will cause aggregate demand to grow less rapidly. With aggregate supply growing at a constant rate in the long run, slower growth in aggregate demand will lower the inflation rate. We found earlier that a growth rate in the money supply of 8 percent implies an inflation rate of 5 percent. If the growth rate of the money supply were reduced to 5 percent, the inflation rate would drop to 2 percent (see Equation 13.4).

Reducing the growth rate of the money supply reduces the inflation rate. Because the Federal Reserve controls the money supply, this would seem to be an easy matter. Unfortunately, two problems exist. One is that an unexpected reduction in the inflation rate causes a redistribution of income and wealth in much the same manner as an unexpected increase in the inflation rate. Firms that agreed to large wage increases in anticipation of continued inflation will find that the prices of their products increase less rapidly if the inflation rate falls, making it more difficult for them to fulfill their contractual obligations. People who borrowed at high interest rates in anticipation of continued inflation also will find themselves worse off if the inflation rate falls. Because some firms and households will be adversely affected, they will resist policies aimed at reducing inflation.

Another problem is that the reduction in the inflation rate is likely to be accompanied by an increase in the unemployment rate in the short run. This is especially true if the inflation has been occurring for some time. One reason for the increase in unemployment is the contractual obligations of firms to pay higher wages. These contracts were presumably signed when it appeared that the inflation would continue. The reduction in the inflation rate means that firms will see the prices of their products increase less rapidly or not at all. Consequently, they may be forced to discharge workers in order to meet their contractual obligations to the remaining employees. Such reductions in employment cause the unemployment rate to rise.

Historically, reductions in inflation are often accompanied by increases in unemployment. This happened, for example, in the early 1980s. During President Carter's administration, the price level increased more rapidly each year. In 1979 and 1980, inflation (as measured by the CPI) reached double-digit levels. To reduce the inflation rate, the Federal Reserve sharply reduced the growth rate of the money supply in 1981. The inflation rate fell dramatically in 1982 and 1983. At the same time, the unemployment rate increased dramatically. As time passed, the unemployment rate returned to its full employment level.

During the transition period from a high inflation rate to a lower one, the unemployment rate tends to be above its full employment level. This increased unemployment with its attendant hardships is perhaps the most important reason why the Federal Reserve often does not take action to reduce the growth rate of the money supply to a level consistent with price stability.

FISCAL POLICY

Because fiscal policy can alter aggregate demand, it is appropriate to examine its role in reducing inflation. In the short run, contractionary fiscal policy can hold

ADDITIONAL INSIGHT

THE FED AS INFLATION FIGHTER

As discussed, the Federal Reserve, or Fed, has primary responsibility for achieving and maintaining a low inflation rate. To this end, the Fed significantly reduced the growth rate of the money supply (M1) and raised short-term interest rates during 1994. By reducing the growth rate of the money supply and raising interest rates, the Fed hoped to reduce the growth rate of aggregate demand, thereby reducing the upward pressure on the price level.

Except for the discount rate, the Federal Reserve does not have direct control over interest rates.* The Fed, however, can alter the federal funds rate. Federal funds are loans between banks of their deposits at the Federal Reserve. The interest rate on these loans is called the federal funds rate. By increasing or decreasing bank reserves, the Fed can lower or raise the federal funds rate.

During 1994, the Fed raised the federal funds rate on six occasions for a total increase in the rate of 2.5 percentage points. On each occasion, other short-term interest rates increased.

Critics of the Federal Reserve's actions note that the inflation rate did not rise in 1994. This, however, does not necessarily imply that the Fed's actions were unwarranted. Like an ocean liner, the U.S. economy has considerable momentum. If an ocean liner is headed toward a reef, the helmsman cannot wait until the last moment to turn the rudder. Because of the ship's momentum, the rudder must be turned well in advance. The same is true for the economy. If the Federal Reserve is to avoid a significant increase in the inflation rate, it must act before the inflation rate rises. Moreover, once the inflation rate rises, it is extraordinarily difficult to reduce it without causing a recession.

Should the economy grow rapidly in the future and inflation threaten, we can expect the Federal Reserve to reduce the growth rate of the money supply and raise interest rates.

---

*The discount rate is the interest rate at which banks and other depository institutions borrow from the Federal Reserve. It is discussed in the appendix to this chapter.

the price level in check. As before, suppose the money supply and, hence, aggregate demand are growing at an 8 percent rate. With aggregate supply growing at a 3 percent rate, the inflation rate is 5 percent. To slow the rate of increase in aggregate demand, government spending may be reduced or taxes increased. If policymakers enact a contractionary fiscal policy, the effect of the growth of the money supply on aggregate demand will be at least partially offset. As a result, the price level will rise less rapidly. Unfortunately, so long as the money supply continues to grow, policymakers must continue to reduce government spending or raise taxes. Most government spending is for social security, national defense, interest on the national debt, and various programs to assist the poor. These programs cannot be cut indefinitely. Similarly, taxes cannot be raised indefinitely.

Thus, although contractionary fiscal policy may achieve temporary relief from increases in the price level, it cannot be used indefinitely to offset the effects of the growth in the money supply on aggregate demand. Consequently, fiscal policy cannot be regarded as a serious alternative to monetary policy in fighting inflation. In the long run, contractionary monetary policy must be applied.

SUPPLY-SIDE POLICIES

A potential cure of inflation is an increase in the growth rate of aggregate supply. If aggregate supply were to grow more rapidly, the inflation rate would fall. As before, suppose the money supply and aggregate demand are growing at an 8 percent rate. If aggregate supply is growing at a 3 percent rate, the inflation rate is 5 percent. Suppose the growth rate of aggregate supply could be increased to 6 percent. The inflation rate would then fall to 2 percent.

Are policies to increase the growth rate of aggregate supply—supply-side policies—effective? Unfortunately, no. It is very difficult to increase the growth rate of aggregate supply, which depends on the growth rate of the labor supply, the rate of capital accumulation, and the rate of technological progress. The growth rate of the labor supply depends, ultimately, on the growth rate of the population. Barring changes in immigration laws, little can be done, at least in the short run, to change the population growth rate. The nation's tax laws could be altered to favor investment in plant and equipment. Even if politically feasible, such a change might have a small impact on investment. Similarly, the tax laws could be altered to encourage firms to devote more resources to research and development. This might increase the rate of technological progress; however, the impact could be small.

In view of the U.S. experience, most economists believe that an increase in the growth rate of aggregate supply from 3 to 4 percent (a 33 ⅓ percent increase) would be a tremendous achievement. If the growth rate of aggregate supply were to increase by 1 percentage point, the inflation rate would fall by 1 percentage point. If the inflation rate is low (say, 2 or 3 percent), the increase in the growth rate of aggregate supply would significantly reduce the inflation rate. If the inflation rate is higher, the reduction would be much less significant.

Suppose the money supply and aggregate demand are growing at a 13 percent rate and aggregate supply at a 3 percent rate. The inflation rate is 10 percent. Now suppose the growth rate of aggregate supply increases from 3 percent to 4 percent. If the money supply and aggregate demand continue to grow at the 13 percent rate, the inflation rate falls—but only to 9 percent. Thus, despite the tremendous achievement (by historical standards) of increasing the growth rate of aggregate supply by 33 ⅓ percent (from 3 to 4 percent), the inflation rate falls by only 10 percent (from 10 to 9 percent). Given its variation over time, a reduction in the inflation rate from 10 to 9 percent is barely noticeable.

It is apparent that increasing the growth rate of aggregate supply is unlikely to reduce the inflation rate significantly. If policymakers are serious about reducing inflation, they must focus on reducing the growth rate of aggregate demand. In particular, they must concentrate on reducing the growth rate of the money supply.

Although increasing the growth rate of aggregate supply is unlikely to have a major impact on the inflation rate, it is nevertheless extremely important. The growth rate of aggregate supply determines the nation's output growth rate and hence the standard of living. If the growth rate of aggregate supply could be increased from 3 to 4 percent, the nation's output of goods and services would increase 33 ⅓ percent more rapidly, and living standards would improve much more rapidly than at present.

INCOMES POLICY

Incomes policy is governmental action, other than fiscal and monetary policy, aimed at influencing or controlling the rate of increase of prices, wages, and other forms of income. Although incomes policy takes various forms, the most common are wage-price guidelines and controls.

Either explicitly or implicitly, advocates of incomes policy usually believe that inflation is caused by the exercise of monopoly power by labor unions and firms. Although most economists do not share this view, it is important to become familiar with incomes policies and their effects.

The U.S. economy has been subjected to wage-price guidelines and controls during part of its history, most recently in 1979–1980. During the Carter administration, the price level increased more rapidly each year. To restrain inflation, President Carter announced a set of voluntary pay and price standards. Under these standards, firms and workers were to slow the rate at which prices and wages increased.

These standards proved ineffective. In fact, prices and wages increased even more rapidly after their imposition. Some economists claimed that inflation would have been even worse in the absence of the standards. Yet it was generally agreed that the program was not working, and it was dropped.

The Kennedy and Johnson administrations also subjected the U.S. economy to wage-price guidelines, starting in 1962. These guidelines suffered the same fate as the Carter pay and price standards. When inflationary pressure became intense, they became ineffective and were abandoned. For all practical purposes, they ended in 1966.

Because guidelines are voluntary, some people advocate the use of wage-price controls. With controls, firms cannot legally raise prices or wages more than the maximum permissible amount. The U.S. economy was subjected to wage and price controls during World War II and again during the 1970s. In August 1971, President Nixon imposed a 90-day freeze on prices and wages. The freeze was the first phase of a wage and price controls program that ended in 1974. This program, like the others, ended in failure.

Economists oppose wage and price controls for at least four reasons. First, they tend to be ineffective. Second, to the extent that they are effective, controls distort the allocation of resources. Third, they are costly to administer. Finally, they are likely to cause inequities.

Controls often prove ineffective. Unless the growth rate of the money supply is reduced, strong upward pressure on prices and wages exists. In response, firms may reduce the size of their products or allow the quality of their products to deteriorate. Both actions are price hikes in disguise. With regard to wage hikes, firms usually are permitted to give wage increases to workers who are promoted. If a firm wishes to give a worker a raise, it can create a position and then "promote" the person.

To the extent that price controls are effective, they are likely to lead to a misallocation of resources. Consider the demand, D_0, and supply, S_0, curves for product A in Figure 13.5. The equilibrium price is P_0, while the equilibrium quantity is Q_0. Next, suppose the demand for product A increases. In the absence

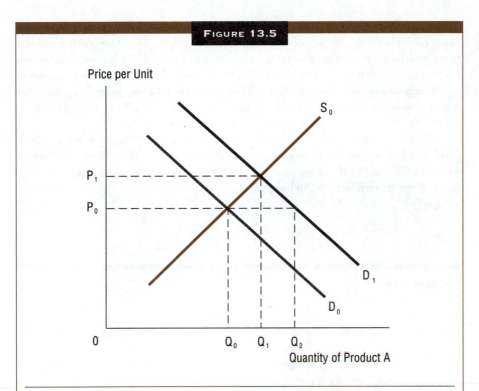

FIGURE 13.5

Price per Unit

S_0

P_1

P_0

D_1

D_0

0   Q_0 Q_1 Q_2

Quantity of Product A

In the absence of price controls, an increase in the demand for good A results in a higher price, P_1. The increase in price induces firms to produce more of good A. With price controls, however, the price remains P_0. Firms have no incentive, therefore, to increase production. Consequently, too few resources will be devoted to the production of good A and, by implication, too many resources will be devoted to the production of other goods and services.

of price controls, the equilibrium price rises to P_1, giving firms an incentive to increase production. They will buy more raw materials, hire more workers, and so on. As they do so, production increases to Q_1.

Suppose, however, that price controls fix the price of the product at P_0. As a result, firms have no incentive to expand production. Indeed, output will remain at Q_0. A misallocation of resources occurs. Consumers would like to buy more of the product and are willing to pay a higher price. Legally, however, they cannot.[2] From society's standpoint, too few resources are devoted to the production of product A and, by implication, too many resources are devoted to the production of other goods.

[2]After the increase in demand, a shortage, $Q_2 - Q_0$, exists at price P_0. The limited supply, Q_0, must be allocated in some way. During World War II, rationing was used. Despite widespread support of the war effort, black markets developed. In these markets, products were exchanged at prices well above the official price. For other ways to allocate a limited supply, see the discussion of rent controls in Chapter 1.

Controls are costly to administer. During World War II, a large government bureaucracy administered the program. The Nixon controls were less costly to administer, both because existing government employees were primarily used and because the program was viewed as temporary. Even so, the controls were costly to taxpayers.

Controls are also costly to firms. They must keep better records so that they are available for scrutiny. Controls do have one beneficial effect: They greatly increase the demand for accountants, lawyers, and economists!

Finally, controls are likely to be inequitable. Firms and labor unions in high-profile industries are likely to be scrutinized more closely than those in other industries. Because of the huge numbers of firms, controls often apply only to large firms. Both tendencies lead to inequities.

SUMMARY

Inflation is a continuing rise in the price level, which means that it is a long-run phenomenon.

Although the GDP deflator is the most comprehensive of the various price indexes, the CPI usually receives more attention.

Unanticipated inflation causes a substantial redistribution of income and wealth. With anticipated inflation, the redistribution is less dramatic because people take action to protect themselves.

Inflation is costly to society because it results in fewer resources being devoted to the production of goods and services and reduces investment in new plant and equipment.

The nation's money supply—currency, travelers' checks, and checkable deposits—is controlled by the Federal Reserve.

With a constant income velocity of money, the inflation rate equals the growth rate of the money supply less the output growth rate. With the velocity of money and the output growth rate constant, the growth rate of the money supply determines the inflation rate. Inflation, therefore, is a monetary phenomenon.

In the short run, the velocity of money and the output growth rate vary, implying that the short-run relationship between the growth rate of the money supply and the inflation rate is not as strong as the long-run relationship.

To reduce the inflation rate, the growth rate of the money supply must be reduced. Reduced inflation is likely to be accompanied by increased unemployment in the short run.

Reducing government spending or raising taxes can keep the price level from rising in the short run. Because government spending cannot be cut or taxes raised indefinitely, fiscal policy cannot be regarded as a serious alternative to monetary policy in reducing inflation.

Because it is very difficult to increase the growth rate of aggregate supply, supply-side policies are unlikely to reduce inflation significantly.

The U.S. economy was subjected to wage-price guidelines under the Carter and Kennedy-Johnson administrations and wage-price controls under the Nixon administration. These programs were unsuccessful.

Economists generally oppose controls because they are ineffective, distort the allocation of resources, are costly to administer, and result in inequities.

KEY TERMS

Inflation	Indexing	Money supply
Deflation	Creditor	Central bank
Consumer price index (CPI)	Debtor	Quantity theory of money
	Hyperinflation	Equation of exchange
Cost-of-living adjustment (COLA) clause	Medium of exchange	Income velocity of money
	Money	Supply-side policies
Unanticipated inflation	Currency (cash)	Incomes policy
Anticipated inflation	Demand deposits	

REVIEW QUESTIONS

1. What is the difference between an increase in the general price level and inflation? Why is it necessary to make this distinction?
2. Why is the CPI the most widely cited measure of inflation in the United States? Why is this index an imprecise measure of the cost of living?
3. "Inflation will always cause some economic agents to gain and others to lose." Is this statement true or false? Defend your answer.
4. How might unanticipated inflation result in a redistribution of income and wealth?
5. Inflation can be detrimental to the economy. Therefore, the proper role of government is to enact policies to deal with inflation. Why might government be reluctant to undertake anti-inflationary policies?
6. Aside from its effects on income, wealth, and the government, in what other ways might inflation affect the economy?
7. What is money? What basic functions does it perform?
8. "Inflation is a long-term phenomenon caused by a too-rapid growth in the money supply." Is this statement true or false? Use the quantity theory of money in defense of your answer.
9. Use the aggregate demand–aggregate supply framework to demonstrate how increases in the money supply can result in inflation.
10. "If the growth rate of the money supply is constant, there will be no inflation." Is this statement true or false? Defend your answer.
11. Using the aggregate demand–aggregate supply model, explain how labor unions can cause inflation. Is such a scenario likely? Why or why not?
12. "A monopolist charges higher prices for its products than does a pure competitor; hence, an economy characterized by a large number of monopolies is more likely to experience inflation than an economy characterized by a large number of competitive firms." Is this statement true or false? Defend your answer.

13. Explain and graphically show how monetary policy may be used to reduce inflation. Are there any problems associated with the use of this policy?
14. In the long term, why can't fiscal policy be used to reduce the inflation rate?
15. Show and explain how supply-side policies could be used to lessen inflation. Are such policies a viable alternative for policymakers? Why or why not?
16. What is an incomes policy? Why have such policies generally been unsuccessful in dealing with inflation?

SUGGESTIONS FOR FURTHER READING

Achieving Price Stability. Kansas City: Federal Reserve Bank of Kansas City, 1996. Proceedings of a symposium sponsored by the Federal Reserve Bank of Kansas City and held August 29–31, 1996 at Jackson Hole, Wyoming. A collection of papers discussing inflation in the United States and other countries.

Economic Report of the President. Washington, DC: Government Printing Office, published annually. Contains data on the GDP deflator, consumer price index, producer price indexes, and the money supply

Edgmand, Michael R. *Macroeconomics: Theory and Policy*. 3rd ed. Englewood Cliffs, NJ: Prentice Hall, 1987. Chapter 20 discusses various incomes policies and the U.S. experience with wage-price guidelines and controls.

Friedman, Milton. "Quantity Theory of Money." In *The New Palgrave: Money*, edited by John Eatwell, Murray Milgate, and Peter Newman. New York: Norton, 1989, 1–40. Discusses the quantity theory of money.

Hess, Gregory D., and Charles S. Morris. "The Long-Run Costs of Moderate Inflation." Federal Reserve Bank of Kansas City, *Economic Review* 81 (Second Quarter 1996), 71–88. Examines the long-run costs of moderate inflation and concludes that even moderate inflation is harmful.

U.S. Department of Labor, Bureau of Labor Statistics. *CPI Detailed Report*. Washington, DC: Government Printing Office, monthly. Contains data on consumer prices.

Wynne, Mark A., and Fiona D. Sigalla. "The Consumer Price Index." Federal Reserve Bank of Dallas, *Economic Review* (Second Quarter 1994), 1–22. Discusses the consumer price index and concludes that it has an upward bias. The authors, however, believe that the bias is less than 1 percentage point.

Appendix to Chapter 13

MONEY CREATION AND MONETARY POLICY

This appendix first examines the money creation process and then considers the various ways in which the Federal Reserve can alter the money supply.

THE MONEY CREATION PROCESS

In the money creation process, the actions of depository institutions and the Federal Reserve are very important. This section discusses both.

DEPOSITORY INSTITUTIONS

By **depository institutions,** we mean financial institutions that accept checkable and savings deposits. Commercial banks, savings and loan associations, mutual savings banks, and credit unions are depository institutions.

Depository Institutions
Financial institutions that accept checkable and savings deposits.

COMMERCIAL BANKS   Of these institutions, commercial banks are the second most numerous (after credit unions) and account for most of the deposits. There are about 10,000 commercial banks in the United States. Each bank is organized as a corporation and has a charter authorizing it to engage in banking. Banks offer a variety of services. Among other things, they accept demand and time deposits, make business and consumer loans, and finance home mortgages. A commercial bank is either a national or a state bank. **National banks** are banks chartered by the federal government. **State banks** are those chartered by state governments. State banks outnumber national banks almost two to one, but national banks are typically larger.

National Banks
Banks chartered by the federal government.

State Banks
Banks chartered by state governments.

By law, national banks must belong to the Federal Reserve System. State banks may join if they desire to do so and if they meet the requirements. Most have elected not to do so. In fact, fewer than half of the nation's commercial banks are members of the Federal Reserve System. But these banks, called **member banks,** account for well over half of total deposits.

Member Banks
Banks that are members of the Federal Reserve System.

Member banks are subject to the rules and regulations of the Federal Reserve System, including its reserve requirements. Member banks must hold a percentage of their deposits as cash and deposits at Federal Reserve Banks. Prior to the passage of the Depository Institutions Deregulation and Monetary Control Act of 1980, nonmember banks were required by state law to hold reserves, but the requirements were usually less restrictive than those of the Federal Reserve. Today, both member and nonmember banks are subject to the same reserve requirements.

OTHER DEPOSITORY INSTITUTIONS   Although commercial banks account for most deposits, the other depository institutions—savings and loan associations, mutual savings banks, and credit unions—are important. Savings and loan associations accept both checkable and savings deposits. Historically, they specialized in home mortgage lending, but they now make other types of loans as well. Like other depository institutions, mutual savings banks accept checkable and savings deposits and make loans. Geographically, they are concentrated in New York and New England. Credit unions differ from other depository institutions in that their depositors typically have the same employer or belong to the same labor union. Credit unions make loans, mostly consumer, but only to their depositors.

Since the 1970s, many of the distinctions among commercial banks, savings and loan associations, mutual savings banks, and credit unions have become blurred. Also, since the implementation of the Depository Institutions Deregulation and Monetary Control Act of 1980, the reserve requirements are the same for all depository institutions.

THE FEDERAL RESERVE

After a long history of monetary crises in the United States, Congress created the Federal Reserve in 1913. Among other things, the Federal Reserve is responsible for controlling the nation's money supply and conducting monetary policy.

A seven-person Board of Governors oversees the Federal Reserve. Members are appointed by the president (with Senate confirmation) to 14-year terms. The appointments are staggered so that one member is appointed every two years. The president also appoints a chairman of the board to a four-year term. Historically, that person has commonly been referred to as the second most powerful person in the nation. Currently, Alan Greenspan is chairman of the Board of Governors. He succeeded Paul Volcker in 1987.

Rather than having a single Federal Reserve, or central, bank, as is common in other countries, the United States is divided into 12 Federal Reserve Districts, each with its own Federal Reserve Bank. Each of these district banks has its own board of directors. The district banks are located in Atlanta, Boston, Chicago, Cleveland, Dallas, Kansas City, Minneapolis, New York, Philadelphia, Richmond, St. Louis, and San Francisco. Some of these district banks have branch banks. The Federal Reserve Bank of Chicago, for example, has a branch bank in Detroit. For the most part, these Federal Reserve Banks (and their branch banks) do not deal directly with the general public. Instead, they provide services to commercial banks and other financial institutions.

Primary authority over control of the money supply rests with the Federal Open Market Committee (FOMC). The FOMC has twelve members. Each of the seven members of the Federal Reserve Board of Governors is a member of the FOMC. The other five members of the FOMC are presidents of Federal Reserve Banks. Because New York City is the nation's financial center, the president of the Federal Reserve Bank of New York is a permanent member. The presidents of the 11 other Federal Reserve Banks rotate.

In addition to controlling the money supply and conducting monetary policy, the Federal Reserve (1) assists in the check-clearing process, (2) supervises the operations of member banks, and (3) acts as the federal government's fiscal agent. Although these three functions are important, the role of the Federal Reserve as manager of the nation's money supply is crucial if the nation is to achieve its economic goals.

THE FEDERAL RESERVE AND THE MONEY SUPPLY

This section examines how actions of the Federal Reserve affect the nation's money supply (M1). As discussed previously, depository institutions must hold reserves against their deposits. Member banks, for example, hold their reserves in cash and deposits at their Federal Reserve Banks. (Cash held by banks and other depository institutions is usually referred to as **vault cash.** Because it is not actively circulating, vault cash is *not* counted as part of the nation's money supply.) **Required reserves** are reserves that depository institutions are required to hold. **Excess reserves** are reserves over and above those that are required. The **reserve requirement** is the ratio of required reserves to deposits.

Suppose Sunshine National Bank has demand deposits of $5 million. If the reserve requirement is 20 percent, its required reserves are $1 million ($5 million × 20 percent). If its actual reserves against demand deposits are $1.2 million,

Vault Cash
Cash held by banks and other depository institutions.

Required Reserves
Reserves that depository institutions are required to hold.

Excess Reserves
Reserves over and above required reserves.

Reserve Requirement
The ratio of required reserves to deposits.

Sunshine Bank has required reserves of $1 million and excess reserves of $0.2 million ($1.2 million − $1.0 million). Because reserves do not earn interest, depository institutions have a strong economic incentive to lend their excess reserves. (Like other firms, depository institutions are in business to make profits.)

Open Market Operations
The purchase or sale of U.S. Treasury securities by the Federal Reserve.

Although the Federal Reserve can alter the money supply in several ways, it almost always uses open market operations to do so. **Open market operations** are the purchase or sale of U.S. Treasury securities. When the U.S. Treasury borrows, it issues Treasury securities. These securities are in effect IOUs indicating, among other things, when the Treasury will repay the loan. The Treasury issues three types of securities: bills, notes, and bonds. Treasury bills mature in one year or less. Notes mature in two to ten years. Bonds mature in ten or more years.

THE CREATION OF MONEY   We now consider the purchase of a U.S. Treasury security by the Federal Reserve and its impact on the money supply. In doing so, we have two purposes in mind. The first is to show that an open market purchase of Treasury securities results in an increase in the money supply. The second is to show that the purchase results in the creation of money by commercial banks or, more generally, depository institutions.[1] This money creation process results in an increase in the money supply that exceeds the initial increase.

Suppose the Federal Reserve buys a U.S. Treasury security from Melanie for $10,000. It will pay for the security with a check drawn on a Federal Reserve Bank. If Melanie deposits this $10,000 check in her checking account at Sunshine National Bank, Sunshine Bank's demand deposits increase by $10,000. This increase in demand deposits constitutes an increase in the nation's money supply. (Recall that demand deposits are one component of the money supply.) This increase in the money supply, however, is only the beginning of the money creation process.

As the check that Melanie deposited at Sunshine Bank clears, the Federal Reserve credits Sunshine Bank's deposits at its Federal Reserve Bank. Consequently, Sunshine Bank's reserves increase by $10,000. With an increase in demand deposits of $10,000 and a reserve requirement of 20 percent, Sunshine Bank's required reserves increase by $2,000 ($10,000 × 0.20). Its excess reserves increase by $8,000 ($10,000 − $2,000).

Sunshine Bank has excess reserves of $8,000. Because reserves earn no interest, it has a strong incentive to lend these excess reserves. Suppose Sunshine Bank lends Joe the $8,000 to pay for a car. If Joe's check is deposited in the car dealership's checking account at Moonbeam National Bank, Moonbeam Bank's demand deposits increase by $8,000.

---

[1] In describing the money creation process, we focus on the behavior of commercial banks because most people are more familiar with banks than with other types of depository institutions. Because all depository institutions are subject to the same reserve requirements, we would arrive at the same conclusions if both banks and other depository institutions were taken into account. Similarly, we focus on demand deposits. Because other checkable deposits are subject to the same reserve requirement as demand deposits, we would reach the same conclusions if both demand and other checkable deposits were considered.

This increase in demand deposits at Moonbeam Bank represents an increase in the money supply. With an increase in demand deposits of $10,000 at Sunshine Bank and $8,000 at Moonbeam Bank, the total increase in the money supply is now $18,000 ($10,000 + $8,000). The money supply will continue to increase because, in addition to the increase in demand deposits, Moonbeam Bank experiences an increase in excess reserves. Sunshine Bank no longer has excess reserves. (It lent them to Joe.) Moonbeam Bank, however, has excess reserves. As the check that the car dealership deposited at Moonbeam Bank clears, the Federal Reserve credits Moonbeam Bank's deposits at its Federal Reserve Bank. With an $8,000 increase in both demand deposits and reserves and a reserve requirement of 20 percent, Moonbeam Bank's required reserves increase by $1,600 ($8,000 × 0.20) and its excess reserves increase by $6,400 ($8,000 − $1,600). Because reserves earn no interest, Moonbeam Bank has a strong incentive to lend these excess reserves.

Suppose Moonbeam Bank lends the $6,400 to Andrea and Greg to pay for the remodeling of their home. If Andrea and Greg's check is deposited in the builder's checking account at Starlight National Bank, Starlight Bank's demand deposits increase by $6,400.

This increase in demand deposits at Starlight Bank constitutes an increase in the money supply. With increases in demand deposits of $10,000 at Sunshine Bank, $8,000 at Moonbeam Bank, and $6,400 at Starlight Bank, the total increase in the money supply is now $24,400 ($10,000 + $8,000 + $6,400). The money supply will continue to increase, however, because in addition to the increase in demand deposits, Starlight Bank experiences an increase in excess reserves.

Although Sunshine and Moonbeam Banks no longer have excess reserves, Starlight Bank does. As the check that the builder deposited at Starlight Bank clears, the Federal Reserve credits Starlight Bank's deposits at its Federal Reserve Bank. With a $6,400 increase in both demand deposits and reserves and a reserve requirement of 20 percent, Starlight Bank's required reserves increase by $1,280 ($6,400 × 0.20) and its excess reserves increase by $5,120 ($6,400 − $1,280). Starlight Bank has a strong incentive to lend these excess reserves. And so it goes.

THE CHANGE IN THE MONEY SUPPLY   Instead of following the money creation process indefinitely, we can derive an equation to determine the total increase in demand deposits and, hence, the money supply. Two simplifying assumptions are made. First, depository institutions do not hold excess reserves. Second, the public does not add to its holdings of cash.

In the illustration, demand deposits and reserves first increased by $10,000. This increase in demand deposits was followed by successive increases of $8,000 and $6,400. As demand deposits increased, more and more of the initial $10,000 increase in reserves was used as required reserves. Sunshine Bank's required reserves increased by $2,000 to support its $10,000 increase in demand deposits. Moonbeam Bank's required reserves increased by $1,600, and Starlight Bank's by $1,280. Given the assumptions, depository institutions will continue to make loans until all of the initial increase in reserves becomes required reserves. Thus, the initial change in reserves, denoted as ΔR, ultimately becomes a change in required reserves, denoted as ΔRR. In equation form,

$$\Delta R = \Delta RR.$$

The change in required reserves, in turn, equals the ratio of required reserves to demand deposits (the reserve requirement) multiplied by the total change in demand deposits. If the ratio of required reserves to demand deposits is denoted as r and the total change in demand deposits as ΔDD, we have

$$\Delta R = \Delta RR = r\Delta DD.$$

Dividing both sides of the equation by r and rearranging terms yields

$$\Delta DD = \frac{\Delta R}{r}.$$

This equation indicates that the total change in demand deposits equals the initial change in reserves divided by the reserve requirement. In the illustration, the initial change in reserves is $10,000 and the reserve requirement is 20 percent. Consequently, the total change in demand deposits is calculated by dividing $10,000 by 0.20. Thus, the total change in demand deposits is $50,000. We know that this must be the case because with an initial increase in reserves of $10,000 and a 20 percent reserve requirement, demand deposits must ultimately increase by $50,000 for all of the increase in reserves to become required reserves.

The foregoing analysis indicates that the initial increase in reserves of $10,000 results in an increase in demand deposits of $50,000. Because demand deposits are a component of the nation's money supply, we find that the money supply also increases by $50,000. If the change in the money supply is denoted by ΔM, the relationship between the change in the money supply and the change in reserves is

$$\Delta M = \frac{\Delta R}{r}. \tag{13A.1}$$

Equation 13A.1 indicates that a change in reserves, ΔR, results in a change in the money supply, ΔM, equal to the change in reserves divided by the reserve requirement, r.

Equation 13A.1 holds for both increases and decreases in the money supply. In our illustration, we showed that an open market purchase of U.S. Treasury securities by the Federal Reserve increases the money supply. Equation 13A.1 indicates that the total increase in the money supply is equal to the increase in reserves divided by the reserve requirement. By the same token, an open market sale of U.S. Treasury securities by the Federal Reserve decreases the money supply.

To illustrate, suppose the Federal Reserve sells a U.S. Treasury security to Tiffany for $10,000. Tiffany pays for the security with a check drawn on Boomtown National Bank. Boomtown Bank's demand deposits decrease by $10,000. As the check clears, Boomtown Bank's reserves also decrease by $10,000. The decrease in reserves will force Boomtown Bank to curtail its loans. This loss of reserves and curtailment of loans will lead to successive decreases in demand deposits and the money supply just as an increase in reserves leads to successive increases in demand deposits and the money supply (see review question 3 following this appendix). Equation 13A.1 indicates that the total decrease in the money supply equals the decrease in reserves divided by the reserve requirement.

THE CHANGE IN THE MONEY SUPPLY: TWO QUALIFICATIONS   The change in the money supply indicated by Equation 13A.1 is the maximum possible change. Again, the equation assumes that (1) depository institutions do not hold excess reserves, and (2) the public does not add to its holdings of cash. If these assumptions are met, the money supply will change by the amount indicated by Equation 13A.1. If the assumptions are not met, the change in the money supply will be less than the amount indicated by the equation.

To demonstrate that the change in the money supply indicated by Equation 13A.1 represents the maximum possible change, we now relax each of the assumptions. Previously, we assumed that depository institutions hold no excess reserves. Based on this assumption, institutions with excess reserves will lend them and the money creation process will be as described earlier. Suppose depository institutions lend only part of their excess reserves. If so, the corresponding increases in demand deposits will be smaller. As a result, the total increase in demand deposits and hence the money supply will be smaller, too.

Thus, if depository institutions hold excess reserves, the money supply increases in response to the purchase of U.S. Treasury securities by the Federal Reserve, but not by the maximum possible amount. The same is true if the public adds to its holdings of cash during the money creation process. If the public adds to its holdings of cash, depository institutions lose some of their reserves and so will not be able to increase their loans by as much as before. The corresponding increases in demand deposits will be smaller. As a result, the total increase in demand deposits and hence the money supply will be smaller.

In conclusion, we find that the money supply increases in response to an open market purchase. If the simplifying assumptions are met, the money supply increases by the maximum possible amount; if they are not met, the money supply increases by a smaller amount. We could develop an equation to determine the increase in the money supply when the assumptions are not met, but this is unnecessary for our purposes and beyond the scope of this text.

THE FEDERAL RESERVE AND CONTROL OF THE MONEY SUPPLY

The Federal Reserve can alter the money supply by (1) conducting open market operations, (2) changing reserve requirements, and (3) changing the discount rate.

OPEN MARKET OPERATIONS

As defined earlier, open market operations are the purchase or sale of U.S. Treasury securities. Suppose the Federal Reserve decides to increase the money supply by purchasing U.S. Treasury securities. It pays for these securities with checks drawn on Federal Reserve Banks. These checks will be deposited at various depository institutions. The Federal Reserve will credit these institutions' deposits at Federal Reserve Banks, and these increased deposits will constitute an increase in reserves. Banks and other depository institutions will respond by making new loans, and the money creation process will begin.

Just as the Federal Reserve increases the money supply by purchasing U.S. Treasury securities, it can reduce the money supply by selling Treasury securities. Those buying the securities pay for them with checks drawn on various depository institutions. During the check-clearing process, the Federal Reserve will reduce those institutions' deposits at Federal Reserve Banks. Banks and other depository institutions will respond to the decrease in reserves by curtailing their loans. Fewer loans will cause demand and other checkable deposits to decline. Because these deposits are part of the money supply, the nation's money supply will fall.

The ultimate authority regarding the conduct of open market operations rests with the Federal Open Market Committee. Once the committee decides on the appropriate course of action, it issues a directive to the appropriate person at the Federal Reserve Bank of New York. This person actually supervises the purchase and sale of the Treasury securities. The Federal Reserve almost *always* uses open market operations to control the nation's money supply.

RESERVE REQUIREMENTS

The Federal Reserve can also alter the money supply by changing the reserve requirements for depository institutions. If the Federal Reserve wants to increase the money supply, it can reduce reserve requirements, thereby creating excess reserves in the monetary system. As a result, depository institutions will make new loans, resulting in the creation of demand and other checkable deposits. The increase in these deposits constitutes an increase in the money supply.

In the illustration, it was assumed that depository institutions were required to have reserves equal to 20 percent of their deposits. Suppose that Sunshine Bank initially had $1 million in reserves and $5 million in deposits. As a result, it was not in a position to make new loans. Now suppose the reserve requirement were reduced to 10 percent. Sunshine Bank would be required to hold only $500,000 in reserves. It would be free to lend up to $500,000 (its excess reserves), and the money creation process would begin.

Just as the Federal Reserve can increase the money supply by reducing reserve requirements, it can decrease the money supply by raising reserve requirements. By raising requirements, it can make depository institutions hold more reserves, forcing them to curtail loans. As fewer loans are made, demand deposits and therefore the nation's money supply fall. In the illustration, suppose the reserve requirement were raised from 20 to 30 percent. Sunshine Bank's required reserves would now be $1.5 million. With reserves of only $1 million, Sunshine Bank would have to curtail its loans. Fewer loans lead to fewer demand and other checkable deposits and therefore a smaller money supply.

Although changes in reserve requirements are a powerful means to alter the money supply, they are rarely used. For one thing, changing reserve requirements is a very blunt way to alter the nation's money supply. Even small changes in reserve requirements cause large changes in required reserves and the money supply. For another, changes in reserve requirements are not easily reversed. Suppose reserve requirements are lowered in order to increase the money supply. Should the increase in the money supply prove too large, the Federal Reserve could raise reserve requirements to reduce the money supply. But these new reserve requirements would be disruptive, especially for depository institutions not sufficiently liquid to meet them.

THE DISCOUNT RATE

In addition to using open market operations and altering reserve requirements, the Federal Reserve may alter the money supply by changing the discount rate. The **discount rate** is the interest rate at which depository institutions can borrow from Federal Reserve Banks. Each Federal Reserve Bank's rate is determined by that bank's board of directors. The rate must be approved, however, by the Federal Reserve's Board of Governors.

Discount Rate
The interest rate at which depository institutions can borrow from Federal Reserve Banks.

If the Federal Reserve wishes to increase the money supply, it could reduce the discount rate, thus giving depository institutions a greater incentive to borrow. If the Federal Reserve does increase the money supply, their reserves increase, permitting an expansion in the money supply. If the Federal Reserve wishes to reduce the money supply, it could raise the discount rate, thereby discouraging depository institutions from borrowing. If they borrow less, the Federal Reserve's reserves decrease and the money supply falls.

Although changing the discount rate is a means to alter the money supply, it is rarely altered for that purpose. Depository institutions are discouraged from borrowing from their Federal Reserve Banks except as a last resort. Consequently, the discount rate may change significantly without altering depository institution borrowing from the Federal Reserve.

Unlike reserve requirements, the discount rate is altered frequently. On most occasions, the intent is to bring it into line with other interest rates, not to alter the money supply. Consequently, when the discount rate is changed, we cannot be sure that the Federal Reserve is altering its monetary policy.

SUMMARY

Depository institutions—financial institutions that accept checkable and savings deposits—include commercial banks, savings and loan associations, mutual savings banks, and credit unions. All depository institutions are subject to the same reserve requirements.

The Federal Reserve, an independent government agency, is the United States' central bank. It controls the nation's money supply, conducts monetary policy, and, in general, supervises the nation's monetary system.

A Board of Governors oversees the Federal Reserve. The Federal Open Market Committee, which includes the Board of Governors as members, has primary responsibility for the conduct of monetary policy.

Open market operations are the purchase or sale of U.S. Treasury securities by the Federal Reserve. If the Federal Reserve wishes to increase (decrease) the nation's money supply, it can do so by buying selling U.S. Treasury securities. By buying (selling) U.S. Treasury securities, the Federal Reserve adds to the reserves of the monetary system. The increase in reserves causes depository institutions to make new loans, resulting in increases in the nation's money supply.

The money creation process results in an increase in the money supply greater than the initial increase in reserves. The maximum possible increase in the money supply equals the initial increase in reserves divided by the reserve requirement.

The Federal Reserve can also alter the money supply by changing reserve requirements. If it wishes to increase (decrease) the money supply, it can lower (raise) the reserve requirement. Finally, the Federal Reserve can alter the money supply by changing the discount rate—the interest rate at which depository institutions can borrow from Federal Reserve Banks. If it wishes to increase (decrease) the money supply, it can lower (raise) the discount rate.

KEY TERMS

Depository institutions	Vault cash	Reserve requirement
National banks	Required reserves	Open market operations
State banks	Excess reserves	Discount rate
Member banks		

REVIEW QUESTIONS

1. Briefly discuss the structure of the Federal Reserve.
2. Suppose the required reserve ratio is 10 percent. Assume that the banking system has $20 million in deposits and $5 million in reserves. Find the required reserves, excess reserves, and the maximum amount by which demand deposits could expand.

3. Suppose the required reserve ratio is 25 percent. Assume that banks lend all of their excess reserves and the public does not add to its cash holdings. Briefly explain how the Federal Reserve's purchase of a $1,000 U.S. Treasury security will affect the money supply. Suppose the Federal Reserve had instead sold a $1,000 security. How would this action affect the money supply?

4. What factors could cause the increase in the money supply to be less than the maximum possible increase?

5. What actions can the Federal Reserve undertake if it wishes to increase the money supply?

6. "An increase in the discount rate means that the Federal Reserve is attempting to decrease the money supply." Is this statement true or false? Defend your answer.

SUGGESTIONS FOR FURTHER READING

Dolan, Edwin G., and David E. Lindsey. *Economics.* 7th ed. Fort Worth: The Dryden Press, 1994. Contains discussions of the nation's monetary system, money supply, and monetary policy.

Federal Reserve Bulletin. Washington, DC: Board of Governors of the Federal Reserve System, monthly. A Federal Reserve publication containing money supply and other data.

Welch, Patrick J., and Gerry F. Welch. *Economics: Theory and Practice.* 6th ed. Fort Worth: The Dryden Press, 1998. Contains elementary discussions of the nation's monetary system, money supply, and monetary policy.

14

DEFICITS AND DEBT:
WHAT LEGACY?

TERMS YOU SHOULD KNOW

Aggregate demand curve (Chapter 11)

Aggregate supply curve (Chapter 11)

Unemployment rate (Chapter 12)

Recession (Chapter 11)

Inflation (Chapter 13)

Capital stock (Chapter 11)

Fiscal policy (Chapter 11)

Personal consumption expenditures (Chapter 11)

Gross private domestic investment (Chapter 11)

Exports (Chapter 11)

Imports (Chapter 11)

Budget deficits and the national debt receive widespread attention. Much of this attention is due, no doubt, to their harmful effects. Most economists, for example, believe that budget deficits cause interest rates to be higher than they would otherwise be. Higher interest rates make it more costly for households and firms to borrow. A higher interest rate can increase a household's mortgage payments by thousands of dollars over the life of the mortgage. Higher interest rates also greatly add to the cost of financing automobiles and other consumer durables. Finally, higher interest rates make it more costly for firms to invest in new plant and equipment. To the extent that higher interest rates discourage investment, capital accumulation is slowed and the nation's growth rate is reduced. A lower growth rate implies that our standard of living will improve less rapidly over time.

In this chapter, we deal with a number of issues relating to budget deficits and the national debt. How do we define these concepts? How large are the deficits and debt? What impact do they have on the economy? Should they be reduced? And what is the best way or ways to reduce them?

BUDGET DEFICITS

Budget Deficit
The amount by which government expenditures exceed government revenue over the relevant time span.

Budget Surplus
The amount by which government revenue exceeds government expenditures over the relevant time span.

Structural Deficit
The deficit that would occur if the economy were at full employment.

Actual Deficit
The amount by which actual government expenditures exceed actual government revenue over the relevant time span.

A **budget deficit** occurs when government expenditures exceed revenue over the relevant time span, usually a year.[1] For instance, the expenditures of the federal government totaled $1,560 billion in fiscal 1996, receipts, only $1,453 billion. As a result the federal government had a budget deficit of $107 billion. A **budget surplus**, on the other hand, occurs when government revenue exceeds expenditures. Surpluses in the federal government's budget are rare. The only federal government budget surplus since 1960 was in 1969.

Economists discuss two types of deficit. The first is the structural, or full employment, deficit. The **structural deficit** is the deficit that would occur if the economy were at full employment. To calculate the structural deficit, economists estimate the government's expenditures and revenues as if full employment prevailed. The second is the **actual deficit**, the difference between the government's actual expenditures and revenue. At full employment, the structural and actual deficits are equal; if a recession occurs, however, the actual deficit will be greater than the structural deficit because a recession triggers automatic government expenditure increases and tax revenue decreases. Government expenditures increase as unemployment increases, because the government pays more in unemployment compensation and for other transfer payment programs. Tax revenue decreases because those who become unemployed pay less taxes. Those who remain employed but experience declining incomes also pay less in taxes. Firms pay less in taxes because profits fall during recessions.

---

[1]The federal government operates on a fiscal-year basis, with the fiscal year running from October 1 through September 30. To illustrate, fiscal 1999 runs from October 1, 1998 through September 30, 1999.

From our perspective, the structural deficit is more important than the actual deficit for two reasons. First, the automatic changes in government expenditures and revenue that occur when the economy enters a recession help to stabilize the economy. The increase in expenditures and decrease in tax revenue provide households with more disposable income, thereby maintaining consumption at a higher level than it would be otherwise. As a result, the recession is less severe.

Second, the portion of a deficit resulting from a depressed economy is of little concern because it will become smaller as the economy recovers and disappear completely when the economy reaches full employment. On the other hand, the structural portion of a deficit will remain even after the economy reaches full employment. To illustrate, huge government deficits developed in the early 1980s. Much of the deficit was due to the depressed state of the economy—particularly during 1981 and 1982, when the United States experienced a severe recession. Economists were not particularly concerned with this portion because they realized that it would disappear when full employment was restored. They were, however, concerned with the large structural portion because it would remain even after full employment was restored.

THE SIZE OF THE FEDERAL BUDGET DEFICIT

One reason for the increasing concern about budget deficits in the early 1980s was that huge deficits (by historical standards) were occurring. The absolute and relative magnitudes of these deficits are shown in Table 14.1.

In 1929, the federal government had a small surplus, but with the advent of the Great Depression, it soon became a deficit. During World War II, the government ran huge deficits. For the 1941–1945 period, the deficit averaged 20.8 percent of GDP. These deficits financed the extraordinary level of government expenditures needed to fight the war. In the 15-year span following World War II, the deficits and surpluses were small. The government, in effect, balanced its budget. In the 1960s, deficits were common, but they averaged less than 1.0 percent of GDP. In the 1970s, deficits became the rule. They averaged 1.9 percent of GDP over the 1971–1975 period and 2.8 percent over the 1976–1980 span.

Starting in 1982, the deficit became much larger—both absolutely and relative to GDP. In absolute terms, the deficit peaked at $290.4 billion in 1992. Since then it has declined, reaching $107.3 billion in 1996. Beginning in 1997, however, the deficit is expected to rise steadily, largely due to higher spending for Medicare and Social Security.

Although the United States experienced large budget deficits in the 1980s and 1990s, its deficit relative to GNP is small compared to that of many countries. (GNP, gross national product, is a measure of output similar to GDP.) In 1994, the U.S. budget deficit was equal to 3.0 percent of its GNP (see Table 14.2). Most countries had larger deficits relative to GNP and some countries—Italy, Sweden, and Finland—had deficits that exceeded 10 percent of their GNP.

TABLE 14.1

Fiscal Year	Deficit (−) or Surplus (+) (Billions of Current Dollars)	Deficit (−) or Surplus (+) as a Percentage of GDP
1977	−53.7	−2.8
1978	−59.2	−2.7
1979	−40.7	−1.7
1980	−73.8	−2.8
1981	−79.0	−2.7
1982	−128.0	−4.1
1983	−207.8	−6.3
1984	−185.4	−5.0
1985	−212.3	−5.4
1986	−221.2	−5.2
1987	−149.8	−3.4
1988	−155.2	−3.2
1989	−152.5	−2.9
1990	−221.4	−4.0
1991	−269.2	−4.7
1992	−290.4	−4.9
1993	−255.1	−4.1
1994	−203.2	−3.1
1995	−163.8	−2.3

The United States had budget deficits during the 1977–1995 period. Starting in the early 1980s, the deficits became very large. Since 1992, they have declined.

Source: *Economic Report of the President* (Washington, DC: Government Printing Office, February 1996), 367, 368.

DIFFERENT VIEWS OF DEFICITS

Over the years, attitudes toward budget deficits have changed. Prior to the 1930s, most people believed that the government's budget should be balanced annually–that government expenditures should equal tax revenue regardless of the state of the economy. With the advent of the Great Depression and the publication of John M. Keynes's *The General Theory of Employment, Interest, and Money* in 1936, this view faded.[2]

According to Keynesian economics, deficits are desirable during recessions. We already know that government expenditures increase and tax revenues decrease automatically as the economy enters a recession. Despite their impact

---

[2]John M. Keynes, *The General Theory of Employment, Interest, and Money* (New York: Harcourt, Brace and Company, 1936).

	TABLE 14.2		
Country	Surplus (+) or Deficit (−) as a Percentage of GNP°	Country	Surplus (+) or Deficit (−) as a Percentage of GNP°
New Zealand	+0.8	France	−5.5
Netherlands	−0.5	Denmark	−5.7
Japan	−1.6	Belgium	−6.1
Germany	−2.5	United Kingdom	−6.6
Australia	−2.9	Norway	−7.5
United States	−3.0	Italy	−10.6
Canada	−4.5	Sweden	−13.4
Austria	−5.1	Finland	−14.1

Like the United States, most countries have budget deficits. Indeed, most have deficits that relative to their GNP are larger. Some countries—Italy, Sweden, and Finland—have deficits that exceed 10 percent of their GNP.

°GNP, gross national product, is a measure of output similar to GDP.

Source: The International Bank for Reconstruction and Development/The World Bank, *World Development Report: 1996* (New York: Oxford University Press, 1996), 215.

THE RELATIVE IMPORTANCE OF BUDGET DEFICITS AND SURPLUSES FOR SELECTED COUNTRIES: 1994

on the budget, these changes provide households with additional disposable income, thus maintaining consumption at a higher level than it would be otherwise. Because these automatic changes moderate the recession, government should not act to offset them by reducing expenditures or increasing taxes to maintain a balanced budget. In fact, Keynesian economics suggest that the appropriate fiscal policy during a recession is to increase expenditures, reduce taxes, or do both. These changes cause aggregate demand to increase, thereby increasing the nation's output and employment. The increase in government expenditures or decrease in tax revenue helps to restore prosperity despite the growing budget deficit.

The spread of Keynesian economics gave birth to a new philosophy: Run deficits during recessions to stimulate the economy, and run surpluses during periods of inflation to restrain the economy. This view is in sharp contrast to the earlier view that the government's budget should be balanced regardless of the state of the economy.

The new view reached its heyday in the 1960s and continued into the 1970s in a somewhat weaker form. In the late 1970s and early 1980s, more and more people began to question the desirability of running large deficits. Congress and the president apparently agreed because, in 1985, Congress passed and President Reagan signed the Gramm-Rudman-Hollings Act, which dictated that the budget deficit be reduced by at least $36 billion each fiscal year so that it would be eliminated by the 1991 fiscal year.

EFFECTS OF DEFICITS

In the early 1980s, more and more people became convinced that the large budget deficits should be reduced or eliminated because of their adverse impact on the economy. Many people feared that deficits (1) cause inflation, (2) reduce the nation's growth rate because they raise interest rates and therefore lower investment, and (3) increase the balance-of-payments deficit by altering the value of the dollar. We shall be concerned primarily with the first two effects in this chapter; the last effect is discussed in greater detail in Chapter 15.

When discussing the effects of a budget deficit, we must distinguish between two methods of financing: issuing Treasury bonds and issuing money. The U.S. Treasury must borrow to finance a federal deficit. It does so by selling U.S. Treasury securities. These securities may be purchased by households and firms, including commercial banks and other financial institutions. If they are, the nation's money supply is unaltered, because the money that is borrowed by the Treasury is soon spent by the various agencies of the federal government.

The Treasury securities offered for sale may, however, be purchased by the Federal Reserve. If they are, the nation's money supply increases. As discussed in the Appendix to Chapter 13, the purchase of Treasury securities by the Federal Reserve increases the reserves of the banking system. As the system's reserves increase, the nation's money supply increases. Indeed, the sale of Treasury securities to the Federal Reserve has the same impact on the money supply as if the Treasury simply printed the money.

In short, the method of financing a deficit determines whether the money supply is altered. If the Treasury sells securities to the private sector, the money supply is unaffected. If the Treasury sells securities to the Federal Reserve, the money supply increases. For brevity, we shall refer to the first method of financing as issuing Treasury bonds; the second as issuing or printing money.

Suppose that government purchases increase or taxes are cut and, as a result, the federal government has a deficit. The increase in government purchases increases aggregate demand and, assuming less than full employment, the nation's output and employment. The *level* of economic activity increases regardless of the method of financing. The *degree* to which it increases, however, depends on the method of financing.

THE ISSUANCE OF TREASURY BONDS

Loanable Funds
Funds—including those supplied by households and firms—available for borrowing by other households and firms and by government.

Suppose the deficit is financed by issuing bonds (selling U.S. Treasury securities to the private sector). The effect is expansionary but less so than you might think, because this method of financing causes higher interest rates. Interest rates increase because the government must compete with the private sector for loanable funds and, all other things equal, an increased demand for loanable funds causes the interest rate to rise (see Figure 14.1).

Loanable funds are funds—including those supplied by households and firms—that are available for borrowing by other households and firms and by

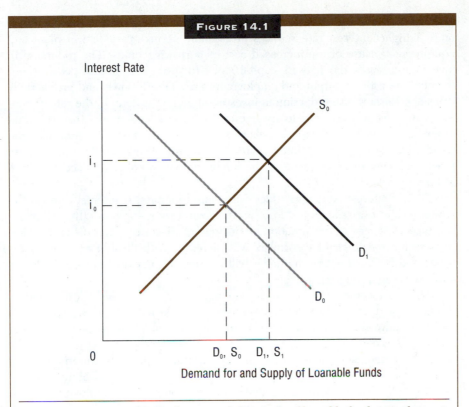

THE IMPACT OF AN
INCREASE IN
THE DEMAND
FOR LOANABLE
FUNDS ON THE
INTEREST RATE

FIGURE 14.1

Interest Rate

S_0

i_1

i_0

D_1

D_0

0

D_0, S_0 D_1, S_1

Demand for and Supply of Loanable Funds

If the demand for loanable funds is D_0 and the supply of loanable funds is S_0, the equilibrium interest rate is i_0. If the federal government develops a deficit and finances it by borrowing from the public, the demand for loanable funds increases to D_1. As a result, the equilibrium interest rate increases to i_1.

government. In Figure 14.1, the D_0 curve represents the demand for loanable funds. It is negatively sloped because, as the interest rate falls, firms and households wish to borrow more funds. Firms may desire more funds to finance an increase in their productive capacity. Similarly, households may wish to borrow to buy new homes or automobiles. The S_0 curve represents the supply of loanable funds. It is positively sloped because, as the interest rate rises, households and firms are more willing to lend funds. Given the demand for and supply of loanable funds, the initial equilibrium interest rate is i_0.

Suppose that a deficit develops in the federal government's budget. Because we are assuming that the federal government finances this deficit by borrowing from the private sector, the demand for loanable funds increases. This increase is depicted in Figure 14.1 by the shift in the demand curve from D_0 to D_1. The increase in demand causes the interest rate to increase from i_0 to i_1. Thus, if the federal government finances the deficit by borrowing from the private sector, the interest rate will be higher than it would be otherwise.

The increase in the interest rate has important implications for the economy. A higher interest rate reduces investment. Firms invest less in plant and equipment because of the increased cost of borrowing funds. The reduction in investment causes the nation's capital stock to grow less rapidly. As a consequence, the nation's output and employment grows more slowly and productivity gains lag. In short, the reduction in investment and, therefore, in the rate of capital accumulation mean our living standard improves less rapidly than it would otherwise. Indeed, many people believe that one very important reason why the standard of living in the United States has improved less rapidly than that in Japan and some other countries is the relatively low rate of capital accumulation in this country.

Higher interest rates also affect exports and imports. If interest rates in the United States rise relative to those in other countries, people in other countries will take advantage of the situation by buying U.S. Treasury and other securities. As a result, the demand for dollars will increase. With flexible exchange rates (discussed in Chapter 15), the dollar will appreciate (increase) in value in terms of one or more foreign currencies.

The appreciation of the dollar will make U.S. goods more expensive to foreigners and, as a result, less competitive in world markets. U.S. exports will decrease, adversely affecting output and employment in the export-producing sector of the economy.

The appreciation of the dollar has the opposite effect on imports, causing foreign goods to become less expensive to people in the United States. Consequently, U.S. imports increase, adversely affecting output and employment in the import-competing sector of the economy.

This problem was particularly acute in the early 1980s. Interest rates increased in the United States relative to other countries—largely due to the big budget deficits of that period. These higher interest rates increased the demand for dollars, and the dollar appreciated significantly over the 1981–1985 period. As a result, exports decreased and imports increased, causing economic hardship in the export-producing and import-competing sectors of the U.S. economy.

As we have observed, a government deficit financed by issuing bonds raises interest rates, which discourages investment and reduces the nation's growth rate. At the same time, output and employment *do* increase, provided the economy is at less than full employment. Moreover, if the economy is operating at less than full capacity, the increase in interest rates may be small. With excess capacity, firms have less incentive to borrow in order to invest in new plant and equipment and they may reduce their demand for loanable funds. With this reduction in demand, the increase in interest rates resulting from the federal government's increase in demand for loanable funds may be small.

Given the increases in output and employment and provided that the increase in interest rates is small, budget deficits may be justified when the economy is at less than full employment. If the economy is at full employment, however, they are not. In this situation, the growth in government purchases and subsequently in aggregate demand increases the price level, not output and employment. As a result, no increase in the level of economic activity occurs. Moreover, interest rates increase by a larger amount at full employment. With little or no excess capacity, firms have a greater incentive to borrow in order to invest in new plant and equipment. They may, therefore, increase their demand for loanable funds. This increase, along with the federal government's increase in demand for loanable funds, results in a larger increase in interest rates. These higher interest rates curtail investment. Consequently, the rate of capital accumulation slows, reducing the growth rate and retarding improvement in the standard of living.

THE ISSUANCE OF MONEY

Instead of financing the deficit by issuing Treasury bonds, suppose the government finances it by issuing money (selling U.S. Treasury securities to the Federal Reserve). The effect is more expansionary than if the deficit had been financed by issuing Treasury bonds. The reason is that the increase in the money supply is, in itself, expansionary, thereby reinforcing the effect of the increase in government purchases.

The change in the government's budget and increase in the money supply cause aggregate demand to increase. If the economy is experiencing unemployment, output and employment increase. Moreover, the increase in economic activity is unlikely to be accompanied by significantly higher interest rates. An increase in government purchases tends to increase interest rates. An increase in the money supply, on the other hand, has the opposite effect, provided that the economy is at less than full employment. The net result will be little or no change in interest rates and, therefore, little or no change in investment and the value of the dollar.

Thus, given less than full employment, an increase in government purchases has no harmful effects on the economy, provided that the deficit is financed by issuing money. Indeed, it has a positive effect by increasing output and employment. (The same effect could have been achieved with lower interest rates by merely increasing the money supply.) When the economy is at full employment, this justification for deficits disappears. Under full employment, the increase in aggregate demand causes the price level—not output and employment—to increase because the economy is already fully using its productive capacity. Moreover, if the deficit persists and the Federal Reserve continues to buy U.S. Treasury securities, the inflation rate will rise. With no increase in output and employment and with rising inflation, the deficit—even if financed by issuing money—is clearly undesirable.

Before proceeding, we note that the Federal Reserve—an independent agency of the federal government—is not compelled to buy the securities issued by the Treasury. If it declines (and it often does), the deficit must be financed by borrowing from the private sector.

REDUCING THE DEFICIT

Over the years, Congress and the various administrations have had great difficulty balancing the budget. With a view to balancing the budget, Congress passed and President Reagan signed the Gramm-Rudman-Hollings Act in 1985. In 1990, Congress approved and President Bush signed a deficit reduction program. In 1993, Congress passed and President Clinton signed another deficit reduction program.

Despite these efforts, the deficit remains high and is projected to rise steadily starting in 1997. As a result, much support exists for the passage of an amendment to the U.S. Constitution that would force the federal government to balance its budget annually.

THE GRAMM-RUDMAN-HOLLINGS ACT

To reduce the deficit and ultimately balance the budget, Congress passed and President Reagan signed the Balanced Budget and Emergency Deficit Control Act of 1985, better known as the Gramm-Rudman-Hollings (or Gramm-Rudman) Act for the act's chief sponsors. Under this act, the budget deficit was to be reduced by at least $36 billion each fiscal year so that the budget would be balanced by fiscal 1991. (As amended in 1987, the act required that the budget be balanced by fiscal 1993.) If Congress and the president could not agree on a budget with a sufficiently small deficit, the act required across-the-board cuts in government spending (after excluding certain programs).

As Table 14.3 shows, the federal budget experience under the Gramm-Rudman-Hollings Act was mixed. In 1986, the actual deficit of $221.2 billion was far in excess of the Gramm-Rudman target of $172 billion. Over the 1987–1989 span, the actual deficit exceeded the Gramm-Rudman target, but by smaller amounts. Of course, one reason for the smaller discrepancies was the revision of the Gramm-Rudman targets in 1987—the more modest targets were easier to meet. Another reason was the nation's economic performance, as the economy continued to expand relatively rapidly over the period. This expansion helped to reduce the deficit. Finally, the existence of the Gramm-Rudman targets discouraged the creation of new federal expenditure programs and the expansion of existing programs.

After three years of lower budget deficits, the deficit soared to a record $221.4 billion in fiscal 1990. This deficit was almost $70 billion more than that of the preceding year and more than double the $100 billion Gramm-Rudman target for 1990. This huge deficit marked the end of the Gramm-Rudman-Hollings approach to balancing the federal government's budget.

PRESIDENT BUSH'S DEFICIT REDUCTION PLAN

With the huge increase in the budget deficit and with the anticipation of large deficits in the future, President Bush presented a plan aimed at reducing the

Fiscal Year	Original Gramm-Rudman Target	Revised Gramm-Rudman Target	Actual Deficit
1986	172.0	—	221.2
1987	144.0	—	149.8
1988	108.0	144.0	155.2
1989	72.0	136.0	152.5
1990	36.0	100.0	221.4
1991	0.0	64.0	269.2
1992	—	28.0	290.4
1993	—	0.0	255.1

TABLE 14.3

DEFICIT REDUCTION UNDER THE GRAMM-RUDMAN-HOLLINGS ACT (BILLIONS OF CURRENT DOLLARS)

Although the budget deficit declined after fiscal 1986, it remained above both the original and revised Gramm-Rudman targets. In fiscal 1990, the deficit increased sharply, marking the end of the Gramm-Rudman approach to reducing the budget deficit.

Source: *Economic Report of the President* (Washington, DC: Government Printing Office, February 1995), 365.

projected deficits by almost $500 billion over five years starting with fiscal 1991. After months of tough negotiations and often heated debates, Congress approved the plan in October 1990.

Most of the deficit reduction was to come from cuts in government spending. Spending for defense, Medicare, farm subsidies, and various other programs was to be cut relative to their projected increases.

The remainder of the deficit reduction was to come from tax increases, most of which were effective on January 1, 1991. The marginal tax rate for couples with relatively high incomes was raised to 31 percent from 28 percent. The base on which the Medicare payroll tax (2.9 percent) is calculated was increased to $135,000 from $51,300. Employees typically pay half of this tax.

The gasoline tax was raised by 5 cents a gallon. Taxes on cigarettes and alcoholic beverages were also increased. The tax on airline tickets went from 8 percent to 10 percent. The telephone tax, scheduled to expire, was extended. A luxury tax was imposed: 10 percent of the price above $30,000 for cars, $100,000 for boats, $5,000 for jewelry, $10,000 for furs, and $250,000 for planes, except for those used by business.

The budget agreement eliminated the annual Gramm-Rudman deficit targets. In addition, it mandated a pay-as-you-go approach for increases in spending or decreases in taxes. If a program is initiated or expanded, the cost must be offset by equal cuts in spending on other programs or by tax hikes. Similarly, if some taxes are reduced, others must be raised to offset the revenue loss or spending must be reduced by the same amount.

Despite the best intentions of Bush and Congress, the deficit increased in 1991 and 1992 largely because of the economy's lackluster performance. As a result, one of Clinton's first acts as president was to propose a new plan to reduce the budget deficit.

PRESIDENT CLINTON'S DEFICIT REDUCTION PLAN

After much debate over his plan, Congress passed and President Clinton signed legislation in August 1993 to reduce the federal government's budget deficit. According to official projections, the combination of tax hikes and spending cuts will reduce the estimated budget deficits by $496 billion over five years. Also according to official projections, the tax hikes ($241 billion) and spending cuts ($255 billion) are approximately equal.

The legislation resulted in significant tax hikes for people with relatively high incomes. The marginal tax rate for couples with taxable income of more than $140,000 ($115,000 for individuals) was raised from 31 percent to 36 percent. Also, couples and individuals with incomes of more than $250,000 must pay a 10 percent surcharge, effectively raising their marginal tax rate to 39.6 percent.

People receiving Social Security benefits may also be subject to higher taxes. Previously, couples with a joint income that exceeded $32,000 ($25,000 for individuals) had to pay taxes on 50 percent of their Social Security benefits. Under the plan, couples with a joint income of more than $44,000 ($34,000 for individuals) must pay taxes on 85 percent of their benefits. The plan also eliminated the base for the 2.9 percent Medicare payroll tax. Prior to the change, the tax did not apply to income over $135,000.

Under the legislation, the top corporate income tax rate was raised from 34 percent to 35 percent. The legislation also imposed a 4.3 cent per gallon tax on gasoline and other fuels. Finally, the legislation repealed the luxury taxes (except on cars) imposed during the Bush administration.

In addition to tax hikes, the deficit reduction plan included various spending cuts. Defense spending was to be cut sharply. Medicare and Medicaid spending was also to be cut. Other spending cuts included a delay of cost-of-living adjustments for government retirees, reform of student loan programs, and cuts in various agricultural and veterans' programs.

In conclusion, the budget deficit declined steadily from 1992 to 1996. The Bush and Clinton deficit reduction plans were partly responsible for these lower deficits (see the "Why Has the Budget Deficit Decreased Recently?" box). The deficit, however, is projected to rise starting in fiscal 1997. Given this dismal outlook, much support exists for a balanced budget amendment to the U.S. Constitution.

THE BALANCED BUDGET AMENDMENT

Support for a constitutional amendment requiring that the federal government's budget be balanced each year dates back to at least the 1970s. Congress has

WHY HAS THE BUDGET DEFICIT DECREASED RECENTLY?

After peaking in 1992 ($290.4 billion), the federal government's budget deficit decreased in 1993 ($255.1 billion), 1994 ($203.2 billion), and 1995 ($163.8 billion). After rising steadily from 1989 to 1992, what reversed the trend? The answer is straightforward. Government spending grew less rapidly and receipts grew more rapidly in 1992–1995 than in 1989–1992.

On a fiscal-year basis, receipts grew at an 8.0 percent rate from 1992 to 1995, compared to a 3.4 percent rate from 1989 to 1992. The higher growth rate of receipts is due partly to the tax increases that occurred during the Bush and Clinton administrations and partly to the increase in the nation's growth rate that occurred in the later period.

Government spending grew less rapidly in 1992–1995, 3.2 percent, than in 1989–1992, 6.9 percent. Expenditures for national defense decreased during both periods with a larger decrease during the later period (−0.6 versus −2.9 percent). Expenditures for the other major categories increased with some rising at a lower rate and others at a higher rate. Spending for Social Security grew less rapidly (6.4 percent versus 5.6 percent); spending for Medicare (9.5 percent versus 11.5 percent) and net interest (5.0 percent versus 5.5 percent) grew more rapidly.

The lower growth rate in spending is due mostly to decisions by Congress and Presidents Bush and Clinton to reduce spending. (When the president and members of Congress refer to spending cuts, they usually have reductions in the rate of increase in mind.) It is also due partly to the increase in the nation's growth rate and the corresponding reduction in the unemployment rate.

voted on a balanced budget amendment on several occasions, most recently in 1995 and 1996. The House of Representatives passed it by a wide margin, but it failed in the Senate by a very narrow margin. (Passage requires a two-thirds majority in each house.) Even if both houses had passed the amendment, three-fourths of the states would have to ratify the amendment before it becomes law. (see "The Balanced Budget Amendment" box).

Proponents of the amendment want to both eliminate the adverse effects of structural deficits and limit the size of government. Without the budget balancing amendment, they believe that members of Congress and the president have a strong political incentive to increase spending without increasing taxes, leading to both large structural deficits and more rapid government growth than would otherwise occur. By forcing Congress and the president to raise taxes (which is politically unpopular) to finance an increase in government expenditures, they believe they can slow the growth of the government sector. (Whether the government sector is growing "too" fast is, of course, an open question.)

Despite popular support for the amendment, many, perhaps most, economists do not support it. Economists who oppose the amendment concede the desirability of eliminating structural deficits. At the same time, they believe that balancing the budget each year will cause greater instability in the economy. Suppose the economy experiences a recession and, as a result, government expenditures increase and tax revenues decrease. In the absence of a budget

ADDITIONAL INSIGHT

THE BALANCED BUDGET AMENDMENT

Proposals for a balanced budget amendment to the Constitution vary slightly. This version was passed by the House of Representatives on January 26, 1995.

SECTION 1. Total outlays for any fiscal year shall not exceed total receipts for that fiscal year, unless three-fifths of the whole number of each House of Congress shall provide by law for a specific excess of outlays over receipts by a rollcall vote.

SECTION 2. The limit on the debt of the United States held by the public shall not be increased, unless three-fifths of the whole number of each House shall provide by law for such an increase by a rollcall vote.

SECTION 3. Prior to each fiscal year, the President shall transmit to the Congress a proposed budget for the United States Government for that fiscal year in which total outlays do not exceed total receipts.

SECTION 4. No bill to increase revenue shall become law unless approved by a majority of the whole number of each House by a rollcall vote.

SECTION 5. The Congress may waive the provisions of this article for any fiscal year in which a declaration of war is in effect. The provisions of this article may be waived for any fiscal year in which the United States is engaged in military conflict which causes an imminent and serious military threat to national security and is so declared by a joint resolution, adopted by a majority of the whole number of each House, which becomes law.

SECTION 6. The Congress shall enforce and implement this article by appropriate legislation, which may rely on estimates of outlays and receipts.

SECTION 7. Total receipts shall include all receipts of the United States Government except those derived from borrowing. Total outlays shall include all outlays of the United States Government except for those for repayment of debt principal.

SECTION 8. This article shall take effect beginning with fiscal year 2002 or with the second fiscal year beginning after its ratification, whichever is later. °

If both houses of Congress pass the proposed amendment by a two-thirds majority, the amendment will then go to the states for ratification. (With regard to constitutional amendments, the president has no veto power.) For it to become an amendment to the Constitution, three-fourths of the states must ratify it. Thirty-two state legislatures have approved similar proposals in recent years. Consequently, it has a good chance for ratification.

———————

°House Joint Resolution 1, 104th Congress, 1st Session, 1995.

balancing amendment, these automatic changes in government expenditures and taxes reduce the severity of the recession. With a budget balancing amendment in effect, however, government expenditures must be reduced and/or taxes increased in order to maintain a balanced budget. The effects of reduced expenditures and/or higher taxes will offset the effects of the automatic changes in those variables, making the recession more severe.

Proponents of the amendment contend that this objection is not as serious as it first appears because (1) more reliance can be placed on monetary policy and (2) under the amendment the federal government can run deficits during recessions, provided that three-fifths of the members of each house approve.

Opponents of the amendment note that Congress and the president can, if they desire, balance the budget. They believe that it is best to leave decisions regarding budget priorities and the balance between the government and private sectors to our elected representatives. Opponents also note that forcing balanced budgets may not effectively limit the growth of the federal government. Congress can always raise both expenditures *and* taxes. Indeed, the experiences at the state and local levels are not encouraging. Although most state and local governments must balance their budgets, spending by those governments has increased more rapidly than spending by the federal government.

Balancing the budget annually would lead to several practical problems. Government expenditures and revenues for the budget year in question must be forecast. These forecasts are often inaccurate because of changing business conditions. Consequently, even when all parties have the best of intentions, the budget may prove to be in deficit. When the parties do not have the best of intentions, they may adopt the most optimistic expenditure and revenue forecasts, thus thwarting the intent of the amendment.

Another consequence might be to force the private sector to bear the cost of new programs whether it is appropriate or not. Instead of increasing taxes to finance the programs, as would be required by a balanced budget amendment, Congress and the president might mandate that the private sector pay the cost directly.

Although many arguments are posed against a balanced budget amendment, the fact remains that the federal government has balanced its budget only once (1969) since 1960. Given (1) the failure of the Gramm-Rudman approach and (2) the inability of Congress and various administrations to balance the budget, support for a balanced budget amendment is likely to grow.

THE NATIONAL DEBT

The national, or public, debt is closely related to budget deficits. In fact, the **national debt** is defined as the accumulated total of the federal government's deficits and surpluses that have occurred over time. To illustrate, a $200 billion budget deficit implies an increase in the national debt of that amount. In contrast, a $100 billion budget surplus implies a decrease in the national debt of that amount.

National Debt
The aggregate of the federal budget deficits and surpluses that have accumulated over time.

The national debt is composed of various financial instruments: U.S. Treasury bills, notes, and bonds; U.S. government savings bonds; and the like. Most of the debt is marketable; that is, it can be bought and sold. Some of it (such as government savings bonds) is not.

The national debt is huge. On March 31, 1996, the gross national debt was more than $5.1 *trillion*—about $20,000 for every man, woman, and child in the United States. U.S. government agencies and trust funds hold about 27 percent and the Federal Reserve holds about 8 percent of this debt. Private investors (including individuals, commercial banks, and other financial institutions) and state and local governments hold the remainder. Of the amount owned by private investors, foreign investors hold about 28 percent. Over the years, both the amount and percentage held by foreign investors have increased.

Over time, the national debt has grown tremendously. In 1929, it was negligible. By 1940, the debt reached $50.7 billion due to the budget deficits of the 1930s (see Table 14.4). The debt at this time was 53.1 percent of GDP. The large budget deficits used to finance the war effort caused the debt to grow enormously during World War II. It increased fivefold from 1940 to 1945, reaching 122.7 percent of GDP in 1945 (see Table 14.4 and Figure 14.2).

After World War II, the national debt grew much less rapidly, reaching $994.8 billion in 1981. More important, the debt grew less rapidly than GDP. The national debt peaked at 127.5 percent of GDP in 1946. By 1981, it had fallen to just 33.6 percent of GDP. The declining percentage indicates that the national debt was becoming relatively less important over time.

GROSS NATIONAL DEBT OF THE UNITED STATES: SELECTED YEARS

TABLE 14.4		
Year	Gross National Debt (Billions of Current Dollars)	Gross National Debt as a Percentage of GDP
1940	50.7	53.1
1945	260.1	122.7
1950	256.9	96.6
1955	274.4	71.3
1960	290.5	57.6
1965	322.3	48.0
1970	380.9	38.7
1975	541.9	35.9
1980	909.1	34.4
1981	994.8	33.6
1982	1,137.3	36.4
1983	1,371.7	41.4
1984	1,564.7	42.3
1985	1,817.5	45.8
1986	2,120.6	50.3
1987	2,346.1	52.7
1988	2,601.3	54.1
1989	2,868.0	55.4
1990	3,206.6	58.5
1991	3,598.5	63.4
1992	4,002.1	67.6
1993	4,351.4	69.5
1994	4,643.7	70.0
1995	4,921.0	70.3

The U.S. debt grew rapidly during World War II. Following years of slow growth, the debt again grew rapidly in the 1980s and 1990s. Debt as a percentage of GDP reached a low point in 1981 and has increased each year since.

Source: *Economic Report of the President* (Washington, DC: Government Printing Office, February 1996), 367, 368.

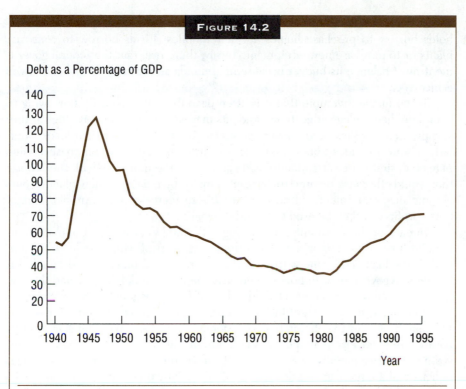

FIGURE 14.2

GROSS NATIONAL DEBT AS A PERCENTAGE OF GDP: 1940–1995

Debt as a Percentage of GDP

Year

The national debt, as a percentage of GDP, increased sharply during World War II. It peaked in 1946 and declined more or less steadily until 1981. Following 1981, the percentage increased.

After 1981, the situation changed dramatically. In 1981, the debt was slightly less than $1 trillion. In 1996, it was more than $5.1 trillion. In a 15-year span, the debt increased fivefold. To put its growth into perspective, the debt increased far more during that 15-year span than during the entire history of the United States to 1981. As previously discussed, some of the increase in the debt was due to the depressed state of the economy, particularly during 1981–1982 and 1990–1991. Even so, the poor performance of the economy cannot account for all of the increase in the debt because much of the deficit was (and is) structural in nature. The large deficits after 1982 caused the debt as a percentage of GDP to increase.

THE BURDEN OF THE DEBT

Given its magnitude, many people are concerned about the debt. They are particularly vocal about their concern when the government deficit is large. Often, people assert that the federal government should balance its budget on an annual basis because households and firms must balance their budgets. This analogy is inappropriate. Households and firms often do not balance their budgets on an annual basis. Students borrow to help finance their college educations. Households borrow to purchase homes and automobiles. Firms borrow to construct plants or to purchase new equipment. To say, therefore, that the federal government must balance its budget because households and firms must balance theirs is incorrect.

To go further, we note that it is often desirable to borrow. By borrowing to complete their college educations, students may significantly increase their future earnings. Part of these additional earnings can be used to repay their loans. Similarly, a home provides a flow of services over time. Borrowing to purchase a home may be desirable because a household can pay off the mortgage with the income that would otherwise be used to pay rent. Finally, by building a new plant or purchasing new equipment, a firm may be able to increase future profits. Part of these profits can then be used to pay off the loan.

In each of these examples, borrowing is desirable because it results in an increased flow of income or services in the future, part of which could be used to pay off the loan. The same is true for the federal government. It is desirable for the federal government to borrow (increase the national debt), provided that the money is spent on projects that yield a flow of future benefits sufficient to repay the loan. Such projects might include dams, irrigation projects, and schools. Unfortunately, the overwhelming bulk of federal government spending is *not* of this nature. Most government spending is more analogous to consumption than investment. Consequently, we cannot rationalize the existence of large budget deficits and a large national debt by arguing that borrowed funds have generally been used to increase the nation's capital stock.

Similarly, it is sometimes asserted that national debt, like private debt, ultimately must be repaid. This is true in the sense that part of the debt falls due each year. The Treasury, however, typically borrows to pay the holders of the securities as they mature. Thus, the national debt need not be repaid in the sense of ultimately being reduced to zero. In fact, most economists concede that the debt never will be reduced to zero. They note, however, that if the deficit is reduced to zero, the debt will stop growing. Because GDP will continue to grow, the debt will become relatively less important over time.

Many people also claim that the national debt imposes a burden on present and future generations. Yet the national debt is largely owed to ourselves. As just shown, most of the debt is held internally—by federal agencies and trust funds, the Federal Reserve, and private investors in this country. This portion of the debt represents a liability to taxpayers and an asset to national debt holders in the United States. Interest payments on the debt redistribute income from taxpayers to debt holders. Because taxpayers generally have lower incomes than persons who hold the national debt, the transfer of income from taxpayers to the debt holders may result in a more unequal distribution of income. But this redistribution does not *directly* reduce the nation's productive capacity, output, or available goods and services. Consequently, it doesn't represent on this account a burden to either present or future generations.

As indicated previously, part of the national debt is held by foreigners. We do not, therefore, owe the entire debt to ourselves. Interest payments and repayment of principal to foreign investors involve more than a transfer of dollars. These dollars represent a potential claim against goods and services produced in the United States. If foreigners use them to buy goods and services produced in this country, the amount of goods and services available to U.S. citizens decreases. This reduction in goods and services represents a burden to both present and future generations.

Perhaps the most serious concern about the burden of the debt has to do with its impact on the nation's capital stock. Earlier we found that budget deficits—if financed by issuing Treasury bonds—cause interest rates to rise. Higher interest rates reduce investment, thereby slowing the rate of capital accumulation. As a result, future generations will inherit a smaller capital stock and have lower output and therefore a lower standard of living.

Even if the budget deficit were eliminated, a substantial burden would remain because of the interest that must be paid on the debt. As matters now stand, interest on the national debt is the third largest single item in the federal budget after defense and Social Security. To pay this interest, tax rates must be higher than otherwise. High marginal tax rates may dampen incentives to work, save, invest, and innovate. High marginal tax rates reduce the after-tax rate of return to work, thereby reducing the supply of labor. They also reduce the after-tax rate of return to saving, which discourages saving. If saving falls, interest rates rise. The higher interest rates—combined with a reduced after-tax rate of return to investment due to higher marginal tax rates—reduce investment and, therefore, the rate of capital accumulation. Finally, high marginal tax rates reduce the after-tax rate of return to innovation which, in turn, reduces the nation's growth rate.

If the tax rates necessary to finance the interest on the national debt (and various government programs) are high enough to reduce the incentives to work, save, invest, and innovate, the nation's productive capacity and output will be lower than otherwise. Smaller output represents a burden to the present generation. A reduction in productive capacity means that output will be less in the future, representing a burden to future generations.

This analysis doesn't imply that everybody will be harmed by deficits and debt. In fact, those over age 30 may actually benefit.[3] Deficits cause interest rates to rise and investment to fall. Consequently, the rate of capital accumulation is lower. The existing capital stock is huge, however, so the lower rate of capital accumulation will not have much effect on the nation's capital stock and therefore its output for years. Moreover, the decline in investment causes consumption to increase in the short run, presumably benefiting people of all ages. Because they have fewer years to live, older people will be less affected by the lower rate of capital accumulation. Younger people (and those not yet born) will be more affected; for those under 30, the effect on consumption of a lower rate of capital accumulation will be greater than the effect of the initial reduction in investment. Young people and future generations, therefore, have a greater stake in reducing or eliminating budget deficits than older people.

---

[3]Paul N. Courant and Edward M. Gramlich, *Federal Budget Deficits: America's Great Consumption Binge* (Englewood Cliffs, NJ: Prentice Hall, 1986), 25–26.

In conclusion, grounds do exist for concern about the size of the national debt. Even so, few economists believe that the federal government should run budget surpluses so as to reduce the debt. Instead, they favor reducing or eliminating the budget deficit so that the debt grows slowly, if at all. Economic growth would cause debt as a percentage of GDP to decline as it did during most of the post–World War II period, making the national debt less of a problem over time.

SUMMARY

A budget deficit occurs when government expenditures exceed revenue. Prior to the 1930s, most people believed that the government's budget should be balanced annually. With the spread of Keynesian economics, a new view developed—namely, to run deficits during recessions to stimulate the economy and surpluses during periods of inflation to restrain it.

In the early 1980s, the federal government started running huge deficits. In light of these deficits and their impact on the national debt, even Keynesians began to question the desirability of deficits.

Although expansionary, deficits have adverse effects on the economy. These effects depend, in part, on how the deficit is financed. If the deficit is financed by borrowing from the private sector, it causes higher interest rates. If the deficit is financed by borrowing from the Federal Reserve, the nation's money supply increases so that the net effect on interest rates may be negligible.

If the economy is at less than full employment, the deficit results in higher output and employment regardless of the method of financing. Thus, at less than full employment, some justification for running deficits exists. With full employment, the deficit results in higher prices, but not higher output and employment. At full employment, no justification exists.

Congress passed and President Reagan signed the Gramm-Rudman-Hollings Act in 1985. Under this act (as amended), the federal government's budget deficit was to be reduced each year so that the budget would be balanced by fiscal 1993. With the huge increase in the fiscal 1990 deficit, the Gramm-Rudman-Hollings approach to deficit reduction died.

Presidents Bush and Clinton introduced deficit reduction programs. Due in part to these programs, the budget deficit declined steadily from 1992 to 1996. It, however, is projected to rise starting in 1997. As a result, much support exists for a balanced budget amendment.

The national debt is huge, and interest on the debt is now the third largest item in the federal budget after national defense and Social Security.

If high marginal tax rates are necessary to pay the interest on the national debt, the incentives to work, save, invest, and innovate will be reduced. As a result, the nation's output will decrease. This reduction in output makes the national debt a burden to the present generation. Less investment means the nation's capital stock will grow less rapidly and output will be smaller in the future. Consequently, the debt also constitutes a burden to future generations.

Although the national debt is a burden to both present and future generations, most economists do not favor running budget surpluses to reduce it. Instead, they favor reducing or eliminating the deficit. With a small or nonexistent deficit and economic growth, debt as a percentage of GDP would decline, and the national debt would become less of a problem.

KEY TERMS

Budget deficit	Structural deficit	Loanable funds
Budget surplus	Actual deficit	National debt

REVIEW QUESTIONS

1. When are the structural and actual deficits the same? How do these deficits differ if the economy is experiencing a recession? Suppose the economy is temporarily producing beyond its full employment capacity. How will these deficits differ?

2. According to the authors, why should a person be more concerned with the structural deficit?

3. Is it possible for budget deficits and surpluses to stabilize the economy? On the basis of your response, evaluate the argument for an annually balanced federal budget.

4. Discuss the differences between financing a deficit by issuing Treasury bonds and money.

5. Suppose the economy is currently at full employment and the federal government's budget is showing a surplus. How would balancing the budget (eliminating the surplus) affect the economy?

6. Why is it undesirable for the federal government to run a deficit with the economy at full employment?

7. Evaluate the following statement: "Forcing the federal government to annually balance its budget would work to limit its size."

8. Briefly discuss the Gramm-Rudman-Hollings Act and its effects on the deficit.

9. Briefly discuss the national debt, who holds this debt, and its growth over time.

10. Evaluate the following statement: "No burden is associated with a national debt that is primarily held by U.S. citizens."

11. During the 1980s and 1990s, there was an increase in the proportion of the national debt held by foreigners. How is this likely to affect the burden of the debt?

12. Is it likely that any U.S. citizen will benefit from the increase in the national debt?

13. Do you favor running government surpluses in order to reduce the national debt? Defend your answer.

14. The federal government has two important advantages over households and firms when it comes to reducing or financing deficits. What are these advantages? With these advantages in mind, evaluate the following statement: "Like households that go too deeply in debt, the federal government with its large deficits may be forced into bankruptcy."

SUGGESTIONS FOR FURTHER READING

Budget Deficits and Debt: Issues and Options. Kansas City: Federal Reserve Bank of Kansas City, 1995. Proceedings of a symposium sponsored by the Federal Reserve Bank of Kansas City and held August 31–September 2, 1995, at Jackson Hole, Wyoming. A collection of papers discussing budget deficits and national debt in the United States and abroad.

Chrystal, K. Alec, and Daniel L. Thornton. "The Macroeconomic Effects of Deficit Spending: A Review." Federal Reserve Bank of St. Louis, *Review*, 70 (November/December 1988), 48–60. An article discussing the effects of budget deficits.

Collender, Stanley E. *The Guide to the Federal Budget.* Lanham, MD: Rowman and Littlefield, published annually. Contains much information regarding the federal government's budget and budgetary processes.

Courant, Paul N., and Edward M. Gramlich. *Federal Budget Deficits: America's Great Consumption Binge.* Englewood Cliffs, NJ: Prentice Hall, 1986. A short book dealing with budget deficits, their impact on the economy, and ways to reduce or eliminate them.

Heilbroner, Robert, and Peter Bernstein. *The Debt and the Deficit.* New York: Norton, 1989. A short, nontechnical book dealing with various aspects of the national debt and budget deficits.

Moore, W.S., and Rudolph G. Penner, eds. *The Constitution and the Budget.* Washington DC: American Enterprise Institute, 1980. A collection of articles presenting alternative views regarding the desirability of amending the U.S. Constitution to require balanced budgets.

Office of Management and Budget, *Budget of the United States Government.* Washington, DC: Government Printing Office, published annually. Contains the federal government's budget and underlying assumptions.

"Symposium." *Journal of Economic Perspectives* 3 (Spring 1989), 17–93. A collection of articles presenting alternative views regarding budget deficits.

15

THE UNITED STATES AND THE WORLD ECONOMY

The U.S. economy is becoming increasingly internationalized. Exports and imports are rising relative to GDP. Travel to and from the United States is commonplace. U.S. and foreign investors participate in domestic and international financial markets by purchasing each others' stocks and bonds. To the dismay of some U.S. citizens, foreign investors are active in U.S. real estate markets.

International trade touches us all. Many of the foods that we eat, many of the clothes that we wear, and many of the cars that we drive come from foreign countries. International trade also affects our incomes. The incomes and even the jobs of many workers in manufacturing and agriculture depend crucially on the ability to compete in world markets.

In this chapter, we consider U.S. participation in the world economy. We shall examine some arguments in favor of greater participation as well as some for more limited participation. In addition, we shall examine the U.S. balance of payments and the effects of balance-of-payments deficits. Finally, we shall consider some policies to reduce or eliminate deficits.

U.S. PARTICIPATION IN WORLD TRADE

U.S. exports and imports have increased significantly over the last few decades. As shown in Figure 15.1, exports rose from $86.8 billion in 1960 to $775.4 billion in 1995, a ninefold increase. Imports rose from $108.1 billion to $883.0 billion, an eightfold increase. In 1960, exports were 3.8 percent of GDP; in 1995, they were 11.5 percent. Similarly, imports were 4.8 percent of GDP in 1960 and 13.1 percent in 1995.

Although exports and imports are very important to the United States, they are even more important—relative to GDP—in many other countries, including Canada, France, Japan, the United Kingdom, and Germany. The reason is *not* that the United States exports and imports less than other countries; in fact, the United States exports and imports more than any country in the world. But the U.S. economy is huge, highly diversified, and rich in natural resources, so its exports and imports are small relative to its GDP.

The United States exports a variety of goods, including commercial aircraft, computers, scientific equipment, machinery, chemicals, and grain. It also imports a variety of goods, including automobiles, steel, clothing, footwear, various foodstuffs (such as coffee, bananas, cocoa, and tea), crude oil, and various raw materials (such as bauxite and natural rubber). The United States' main trading partner is Canada, followed by Japan and Mexico. Germany, the United Kingdom, France, and Italy are also important trading partners.

Comparative Advantage
The advantage a country has if it can produce a good or service at a lower opportunity cost than its trading partner.

Comparative Disadvantage
The disadvantage a country has if it produces a good or service at a higher opportunity cost than its trading partner.

COMPARATIVE ADVANTAGE AND INTERNATIONAL TRADE

Trade among nations is based on comparative advantage. A country has a **comparative advantage** (or a **comparative disadvantage**) in a good or service if it can produce the good or service at a lower (higher) opportunity cost than its trad-

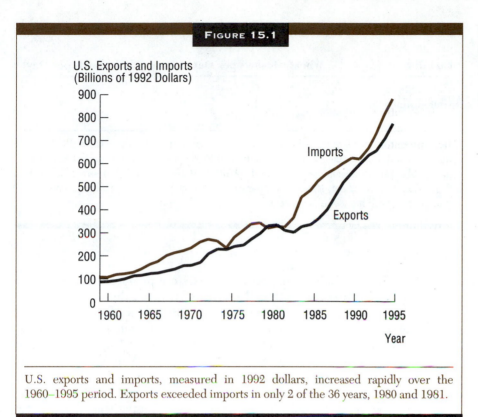

FIGURE 15.1

U.S. Exports and Imports
(Billions of 1992 Dollars)

Imports

Exports

Year

U.S. exports and imports, measured in 1992 dollars, increased rapidly over the 1960–1995 period. Exports exceeded imports in only 2 of the 36 years, 1980 and 1981.

U.S. EXPORTS AND IMPORTS: 1960–1995

ing partner. Countries gain by producing goods and services for which they have a comparative advantage and exchanging them for goods and services for which they have a comparative disadvantage.

The principle of comparative advantage was developed early in the nineteenth century by David Ricardo, a famous English economist. Following Ricardo, we assume only two countries, the United States and the United Kingdom, and two goods, wheat and cloth. In addition, we assume only one factor of production, labor, and no transportation costs.

Table 15.1 assumes that a U.S. worker can produce either 6 bushels of wheat or 6 yards of cloth per day. In contrast, a U.K. worker can produce either 1 bushel of wheat or 3 yards of cloth. Because the output of both goods is higher in the United States, it has an **absolute advantage** in the production of both wheat and cloth. Correspondingly, the United Kingdom has an **absolute disadvantage** in the production of both goods.

It may appear that no basis for mutually advantageous trade exists. After all, output per worker is higher in the United States for both goods. Nevertheless, a basis for trade exists because the United States is relatively more efficient in the production of wheat, and the United Kingdom is relatively more efficient in the

Absolute Advantage
The advantage a country has if it can produce a good or service at a lower cost than its trading partner.

Absolute Disadvantage
The disadvantage a country has if it produces a good or service at a higher cost than its trading partner.

TABLE 15.1

Country	Wheat (Bushels per Day)	Cloth (Yards per Day)
United States	6	6
United Kingdom	1	3

Because output per worker is higher for both wheat and cloth in the United States, it has an absolute advantage in the production of those goods and the United Kingdom has an absolute disadvantage. Because the United States is relatively more efficient in the production of wheat, it has a comparative advantage in wheat production and the United Kingdom has a comparative advantage in cloth production.

production of cloth. A worker in the United States can produce 6 times as much wheat per day as a worker in the United Kingdom, but only 2 times as much cloth.

Because the United States is relatively more efficient in producing wheat, it can specialize in wheat production, export wheat to the United Kingdom in exchange for cloth, and be better off. Similarly, because the United Kingdom is relatively more efficient in producing cloth, it can specialize in cloth production, export cloth to the United States in exchange for wheat, and be better off.

To demonstrate that both countries will be better off, we first note that the opportunity cost of 1 bushel of wheat is 1 yard of cloth in the United States. (In the U.S. economy, it is necessary to give up 1 bushel of wheat to obtain an additional yard of cloth.) In contrast, the opportunity cost of 1 bushel of wheat is 3 yards of cloth in the United Kingdom.

Although we cannot say exactly what the terms of trade will be, trade will be mutually advantageous if the United States can get more than 1 yard of cloth in exchange for 1 bushel of wheat and the United Kingdom can get 1 bushel of wheat for less than 3 yards of cloth. Suppose the international exchange ratio is 1 bushel of wheat for 2 yards of cloth. The United States is better off because it can now get 2 yards of cloth from the United Kingdom by giving up 1 bushel of wheat. Domestically, it can get only 1 yard of cloth by giving up 1 bushel of wheat. The United Kingdom is also better off because it can now get 1 bushel of wheat by giving up 2 yards of cloth. Domestically, it must give up 3 yards of cloth to get 1 bushel of wheat.

The example shows that both countries gain from international trade by producing goods in which they have a comparative advantage and exchanging them for goods in which they have a comparative disadvantage. We can demonstrate this result in a slightly different manner, one that shows that specialization with international trade results in a higher level of consumption for both countries.

With full employment, the United States can, by assumption, produce 600 bushels of wheat (and no cloth), 600 yards of cloth (and no wheat), or some combination of wheat and cloth (see Table 15.2). Suppose, in the absence of

TABLE 15.2	United States	United Kingdom
Production at full employment	600 bushels of wheat or 600 yards of cloth (or some combination)	600 yards of cloth or 200 bushels of wheat (or some combination)
Consumption before international trade	400 bushels of wheat and 200 yards of cloth	300 yards of cloth and 100 bushels of wheat
Consumption after international trade[a]	475 bushels of wheat and 250 yards of cloth	350 yards of cloth and 125 bushels of wheat

Before the introduction of international trade, the United States produced and consumed 400 bushels of wheat and 200 yards of cloth, while the United Kingdom produced and consumed 300 yards of cloth and 100 bushels of wheat. After the introduction of international trade, the United States specializes in wheat production and exports wheat to the United Kingdom in exchange for cloth. The United Kingdom specializes in cloth production and exports cloth to the United States in exchange for wheat. With specialization and international trade, both countries consume more wheat and cloth.

[a]Assumes an international exchange ratio of 1 bushel of wheat for 2 yards of cloth.

international trade, it produces and consumes 400 bushels of wheat and 200 yards of cloth.

With full employment, the United Kingdom can, by assumption, produce 600 yards of cloth (and no wheat), 200 bushels of wheat (and no cloth), or some combination. Suppose, in the absence of international trade, the United Kingdom produces and consumes 300 yards of cloth and 100 bushels of wheat.

Next, suppose that trade opens up between the United States and the United Kingdom. Because of its comparative advantage in wheat production, the United States will specialize in wheat production and export wheat to the United Kingdom in exchange for cloth. Similarly, the United Kingdom has a comparative advantage in cloth production. It will specialize in cloth production and export cloth to the United States in exchange for wheat. As before, assume that 1 bushel of wheat exchanges for 2 yards of cloth.

After the introduction of international trade, the United States will produce 600 bushels of wheat (and no cloth) and export, say, 125 bushels to the United Kingdom in exchange for 250 yards of cloth. As a result, consumption in the United States will be 475 bushels of wheat and 250 yards of cloth. Thus, after the trade, the United States will consume more wheat and more cloth.

The United Kingdom will produce 600 yards of cloth (and no wheat) and export 250 yards to the United States in exchange for 125 bushels of wheat. Consequently, consumption in the United Kingdom will be 350 yards of cloth and 125 bushels of wheat. After trade, the United Kingdom also will consume more wheat and more cloth.

In this example and in general, international trade is advantageous. It allows countries to specialize in the production of goods in which they have a comparative advantage and then exchange those goods for goods in which they have a comparative disadvantage. In this way, countries are able to achieve higher levels of consumption.

BARRIERS TO INTERNATIONAL TRADE

The principle of comparative advantage makes a strong case for unrestricted, or free, international trade. Free international trade, however, is not the rule. Most countries, including the United States, restrict trade by imposing barriers such as tariffs, quotas, and voluntary export restraints.

TARIFFS

Tariff
A tax levied on a good when it crosses a nation's border.

A **tariff** is a tax levied on a good when it crosses a nation's border. The United States has tariffs on many imported goods, including textiles, apparel, and footwear. Historically, the United States has had high tariffs. With the passage of the Smoot-Hawley Act in 1930, the average tariff on imported goods reached 60 percent. Since then, tariffs have been reduced. Today, the average tariff on imports into the United States is about 5 percent. Some goods, however, are subject to much higher tariffs.

The imposition of a tariff causes the domestic price of the good to rise. Consumers buy less of the product and imports fall. Domestic producers, not subject to the tariff, receive a higher price for the good. As a result, they expand production, implying that more domestic resources are devoted to the production of the good.

When it imposes a tariff, the federal government experiences an increase in tax revenue (unless the tariff is so high that no imports enter the country). Indeed, for much of our nation's history, tariffs were an important source of federal tax revenue. Today, tariff revenue is only a small part of total tax revenue, and few tariffs are levied for that purpose.

The imposition of a tariff makes consumers worse off because they must pay a higher price for the product. Domestic producers, however, are better off. They receive a higher price for their product; they are also able to increase production. (Foreign producers are, of course, worse off.) Because domestic producers are better off, it is not surprising that many domestic firms favor tariffs or other trade restrictions and lobby strongly for such measures.

Because consumers are worse off and domestic producers are better off, what can be said for society as a whole? Society is worse off. The imposition of tariffs causes resources to flow to industries that have a comparative disadvantage. Some of these resources come from industries that have a comparative advantage. When more resources are engaged in less efficient productive activities and fewer resources in more efficient productive activities, people experience a lower standard of living.

QUOTAS

An import **quota** specifies the maximum amount of a good that may be imported during any time period. Although tariffs are more common than quotas, the United States has set quotas for various goods, including steel, textiles, sugar, and beef.

By limiting the amount that can be imported, a quota—like a tariff—results in a higher price for the product. Indeed, the price may be higher with a quota than with a tariff. With a tariff, imports can increase in response to an increase in demand. The increase in imports limits the rise in price. But with a quota, it is not possible to import more.

Because of the increase in price, domestic producers increase their output. As a result, more domestic resources are used to produce this good, implying that fewer resources are available to produce other goods.

So far, the effects of tariffs and quotas are similar. They both raise prices, thus hurting consumers and helping domestic producers. Yet they do differ in one important respect. Tariffs usually generate revenue for the federal government; quotas do not.

Although domestic producers benefit from quotas, society as a whole is worse off. Like tariffs, quotas shift resources from industries that have a comparative advantage to those that have a comparative disadvantage. The result is a reduction in people's standard of living.

Quota
An upper limit on the amount of goods that may be imported during any time period.

VOLUNTARY EXPORT RESTRAINTS

Voluntary export restraints (VERs) are agreements whereby exporting nations agree to limit the amounts of goods that they ship to importing nations. The United States negotiated a VER with Japan on automobiles in the early 1980s. Under this agreement, the Japanese "volunteered" to limit the number of automobiles that they ship to the United States. (As with most VERs, the Japanese agreed because they feared that even more stringent import restrictions might be imposed.) The United States has negotiated VERs on steel, machine tools, televisions, VCRs, and lumber, thus limiting U.S. imports of those products.

VERs reduce imports, thereby raising the prices of goods subject to VERs. Consumers are, of course, worse off. Domestic producers, however, are better off because they can charge higher prices for their products. They also benefit from increased production.

Although domestic producers benefit from VERs, society as a whole is worse off. Like tariffs and quotas, VERs shift resources from industries that have a comparative advantage to those that have a comparative disadvantage. The result is a reduction in the nation's standard of living.

Voluntary Export Restraints (VERs)
Agreement whereby exporting nations limit the amounts of goods that they ship to importing nations.

THE CASE FOR FREE TRADE

The case for free trade based on the principle of comparative advantage is strong. When other factors are taken into account, the case is even stronger.

DECREASING COSTS

In many industries, the average cost of production decreases as output increases. Large-scale production may, for example, make for more efficient use of machinery. In industries with decreasing costs, a higher volume of output enables firms to sell their products at lower prices.

In the absence of international trade, an industry's market may be too small for firms to achieve the lowest possible average cost. With international trade, these firms may be able to increase production and sell the extra output abroad, resulting in lower average costs and price. Both producers and consumers benefit from the increased production and lower price.

Although markets in the United States are typically large, international markets enable some industries to produce more, thus lowering average costs and prices. The commercial aircraft industry is an example. If that industry's sales were confined to the United States, the average cost and price of aircraft would be higher than they are today.

In conclusion, the possibility of increasing output and selling the extra output abroad is important, even for a large country like the United States. It is even more important for smaller countries with limited domestic markets.

INCREASED COMPETITION

As discussed in Chapter 4, competition among firms results in higher output and lower prices. The same analysis applies to competition between domestic and foreign firms.

Domestically, one or a few firms may dominate an industry. A case in point is the automobile industry in the United States. For all practical purposes, the domestic industry consists of only three firms. If foreign competition did not exist, these firms would be likely to restrict output and raise prices.

Domestic producers, however, are subject to considerable competition from foreign automobile manufacturers, particularly in Japan and Western Europe. This competition forces domestic producers to charge lower prices. It also forces them to compete in terms of quality, gas mileage, and other dimensions that are important to consumers.

In conclusion, free trade is desirable because competition from foreign firms is often the only way to keep markets from being dominated by one or a few domestic firms.

DIVERSITY OF PRODUCTS

Another argument for free trade is that it increases the diversity of products available to consumers. With trade, consumers in the United States can buy many goods that might not otherwise be available, such as coffee, tea, cocoa, bananas, spices, and silk.

Trade also enhances choice among competing models of the same good. With trade, consumers can choose among many types of automobiles. Besides domestically produced automobiles, consumers in the United States can choose among various foreign automobiles, including very expensive models from Japan and Germany and inexpensive models from South Korea.

THE CASE FOR PROTECTION

Despite the strength of the arguments for free trade, some people argue that government should act to protect domestic industries by imposing tariffs, quotas, or similar measures. Indeed, many arguments have been advanced to restrict international trade. We shall consider some of the most common.

INFANT INDUSTRY

Some people argue that new, or infant, industries should be protected. They claim that these industries, after they are established, will have a comparative advantage. Initially, however, they will be unable to compete with industries already established in other countries. According to this argument, protection would only be temporary. It would be eliminated as the industry becomes competitive in world markets.

Although this view may have some relevance for less-developed countries, it is not particularly relevant for mature industrial economies like the United States. In the United States, it is mature industries (such as the steel and automobile industries) that typically request protection. These industries often claim that they need time to modernize in order to become more competitive, and that protection will provide them that time. Once the modernization is complete, they claim, the protection can be removed.

Industries may use that time to modernize. On the other hand, protection reduces or eliminates the incentive to modernize. Indeed, experience suggests that little modernization occurs unless competition forces it.

Even if we concede that new industries need help in establishing themselves, tariffs and quotas are not the best means to that end. Economists agree that direct government subsidies would be a better approach. With subsidies, the price will remain low to consumers. Subsidies also make it clear which industries are being helped and to what extent. Finally, it may be easier to eliminate a subsidy than it is to remove a tariff or quota.

NATIONAL DEFENSE

Some people argue that industries producing goods important to national security should be protected. They claim, for example, that steel, petroleum, and military hardware are crucial for national defense and so should be protected. Proponents of this argument recognize that protectionist measures will raise the prices of these products. They believe, however, that the benefits of increased military preparedness outweigh the costs associated with the higher prices.

Even if we concede the validity of this argument, protectionist measures are not the best means by which to strengthen the industries in question. If increased national security is a benefit, it is shared by society as a whole—not just the persons who buy the industries' goods. Consequently, government should assist the industries by providing direct subsidies. Because subsidies are financed from tax revenue, the costs of the subsidization (as well as its benefits) would be shared by society as a whole.

SAVE AMERICAN JOBS

Another argument for protection has to do with jobs. It is claimed that foreign competition can reduce output and employment in import-competing industries. Consequently, some form of protection is necessary to maintain employment in those industries.

There is little doubt that imports can cause unemployment in import-competing industries. Over time, some industries lose their comparative advantage and become vulnerable to foreign competition. To maintain full employment, however, the solution is not the imposition of tariffs and quotas. Instead, it is to use monetary and fiscal policy (see Chapter 12). Because some workers who lose their jobs may not have the skills and education necessary to fill the jobs that are available, government may need to assist them in upgrading their skills and relocating.

In conclusion, the best way to protect American jobs is to pursue monetary and fiscal policies that provide for full employment and, at the same time, pursue policies to help the structurally unemployed. With this approach, resources will flow from industries that have lost their comparative advantage to those that have gained a comparative advantage. The imposition of protectionist measures to preserve the old and now inefficient allocation of resources would result in a lower standard of living.

CHEAP FOREIGN LABOR

Still another argument for protection has to do with the importation of goods from countries with low wages. It is claimed that many U.S. industries cannot compete because wages are much higher in the United States than in foreign countries. Therefore, tariffs or quotas—so the argument goes—must be imposed to protect those industries.

It must be understood at the outset that high wages do not necessarily imply high costs. Wages in the United States are high because labor productivity is very high. Workers in the United States are well trained and work with relatively large amounts of capital. It is not surprising, therefore, that they are very productive and earn high wages. Because of their high productivity, their high wages don't necessarily mean that the United States is a high-cost producer.

THE COST OF SAVING U.S. JOBS

Often, people argue that the United States should impose tariffs or quotas to save jobs. As argued elsewhere, trade restrictions are not the best way to achieve or maintain full employment.

In addition, saving jobs by imposing trade restrictions is costly. Trade restrictions raise prices, costing consumers billions of dollars. The U.S. International Trade Commission has estimated the cost to consumers of saving a job in various industries. The commission found, for example, that it costs $63,500 to save a job in the U.S. bicycle industry (see table). This cost is well above the typical worker's salary in the bicycle industry, making it costly to society to save a worker's job through trade restrictions. To put it differently, consumers could pay a former bicycle worker $40,000 a year to do nothing, and still be $23,500 better off than if the government had restored the worker's job in the bicycle industry through trade restrictions.

The cost of saving jobs through trade restrictions is even higher in other industries. In the cera-

THE COST OF SAVING A JOB: SELECTED INDUSTRIES

Industry	Consumer Cost per Job
Ceramic tiles	$225,000
Earthenware	173,500
Rubber footwear	113,400
Luggage	103,500
Women's footwear	92,900
Costume jewelry	86,700
Women's purses	84,000
Canned tuna	76,600
Chinaware	73,000
Bicycles	63,500
Leather gloves	46,800

Source: U.S. International Trade Commission, *The Economic Effects of Significant U.S. Import Restraints, Phase I: Manufacturing* (Washington, DC: Government Printing Office, October 1989), x.

mic tile industry, the cost to consumers of saving a job is $225,000; in the earthenware industry, $173,500; and so on.

Suppose it were true that high wages gave the United States an absolute disadvantage in all industries. Would it be advantageous to the United States to trade with other nations? Of course. Trade among nations is based on comparative advantage, not absolute advantage. It is desirable for the United States to concentrate on goods it produces more efficiently and export those goods in exchange for goods that it produces less efficiently.

REDUCING TRADE BARRIERS

Since World War II, barriers to international trade have been reduced significantly. In reducing these barriers, countries have taken two approaches: (1) trade negotiations on a global basis and (2) formation of regional trading blocs.

THE GLOBAL APPROACH

In the post–World War II period, there have been eight rounds of international trade negotiations conducted under the auspices of the General Agreement on

Tariffs and Trade (GATT), an international organization.[1] Each of these rounds resulted in reductions in tariff rates.

The Uruguay Round, called that because the initial discussions were held in Punta del Este, is the most recent round of GATT negotiations. The negotiations were both long and difficult. They began in 1986, and agreement was not reached until December 1993.

The agreement is more comprehensive than past agreements. It covers trade in services as well as trade in goods. It also covers trade-related intellectual property rights (such as patents and copyrights) and trade-related investment. Finally, it created the World Trade Organization (WTO), which will monitor trade among the more than 120 countries that signed the agreement.

Under the agreement, many tariffs and nontariff barriers (quotas, VERs, and so forth) will be reduced or eliminated. Although the agreement took effect on January 1, 1995, these reductions in trade barriers will occur over a number of years. They are expected to greatly stimulate international trade and to increase world welfare.

The Regional Approach

Rather than relying entirely on the global approach, many countries have formed regional trading blocs. That is, they have agreed to reduce or eliminate trade barriers among themselves while maintaining barriers against countries outside the bloc.

The North American Free Trade Area

In 1988, the United States and Canada ratified an agreement to gradually eliminate trade barriers between the two countries beginning January 1, 1989.

Following the agreement between the United States and Canada, the two countries began talks with Mexico regarding the formation of a free-trade area to include Mexico. President Bush announced in August 1992 that the leaders of the three nations had reached an agreement—the North American Free Trade Agreement (NAFTA). The agreement was later approved by Congress and the other countries' legislative bodies and took effect January 1, 1994. As of that date, the free-trade area encompassed 362 million people and had a combined GDP that was 25 percent greater than that of the European Union.

The agreement eliminates tariffs over a 15-year span, although many tariffs will be eliminated over a much shorter span. It also eliminates quotas and other trade barriers. While eliminating trade barriers within the free-trade area, each country is free to maintain trade barriers against nonmember countries. Finally, the agreement calls for opening investment opportunities within each country to member countries.

---

[1]GATT, founded in 1947, has more than 115 members. In addition to GATT's status as an international organization, it is also an agreement detailing the rules of conduct for international trade.

THE EUROPEAN UNION   The European Union (EU) is another important trading bloc. It was founded in 1957 with six members: Belgium, France, Italy, Luxembourg, the Netherlands, and West Germany. Nine other countries—Austria, Denmark, Finland, Greece, Ireland, Portugal, Spain, Sweden, and the United Kingdom—joined later. The EU has eliminated most trade barriers between member countries. As a result, trade within the EU has increased tremendously. The EU, however, still maintains trade barriers against nonmember nations.

THE BALANCE OF PAYMENTS

In recent years, the United States has had large balance-of-payments deficits. The **balance of payments** is a summary of all economic transactions between the residents of one country and those of all other countries during a given period of time. These transactions include exports, imports, and various capital flows. Table 15.3 summarizes the U.S. balance of payments in 1995.

The transactions in Table 15.3 are divided into two categories: those that give rise to dollar inpayments and those resulting in dollar outpayments. Inpayments

Balance of Payments
A summary of all economic transactions between the residents of one country and those of all other countries during a given period of time.

TABLE 15.3		
Current Account		
1. Exports of goods and services	+965.0	
2. Imports of goods and services	−1,087.8	
3. Unilateral transfers, net	−30.1	
4. Balance on current account (1 + 2 + 3)		−152.9
Capital Account		
5. Private capital flows, net	+45.5	
6. Official capital flows, net	+100.7	
7. Statistical discrepancy	+6.7	
8. Balance on capital account (5 + 6 + 7)		+152.9
9. Overall Balance (4 + 8)		0.0

U.S. BALANCE OF PAYMENTS: 1995 (BILLIONS OF DOLLARS)

In 1995, the United States' current account deficit was $152.9 billion. This deficit, due primarily to an excess of imports over exports, was offset by a capital account surplus of $152.9 billion. The overall balance, therefore, was 0.0. (The overall balance is *always* zero.)

Source: U.S. Department of Commerce, Bureau of Economic Analysis, *Survey of Current Business* 76 (April 1996), 45.

are recorded as plus (credit) items; outpayments as minus (debit) items. Exports of goods and services (line 1) are recorded as a plus item because they require dollar inpayments; imports of goods and services (line 2) are entered as a minus item because they require dollar outpayments.

In 1995, exports were $965.0 billion and imports were $1,087.8 billion. Imports, therefore, exceeded exports by $122.8 billion. Unilateral transfers (line 3) include foreign aid as well as private monetary gifts to residents of foreign countries. In 1995, net unilateral transfers were −$30.1 billion.

The balance on current account (line 4) is obtained by adding exports (line 1), imports (line 2), and net unilateral transfers (line 3). In 1995, this balance was −$152.9 billion.

We now turn from the current account (lines 1 through 4) to the capital account (lines 5 through 8). Private capital flows are summarized in line 5. They include direct private investment abroad by U.S. corporations (such as the establishment of foreign subsidiaries) and purchases of foreign securities (such as stocks and bonds) by U.S. citizens. They also include direct private investment in the United States by foreign corporations and purchases of U.S. securities by foreigners. In 1995, these private capital flows totaled +$45.5 billion, indicating that relatively more capital was flowing to the United States.

Official capital flows are summarized in line 6. These flows include the purchase and sale of dollars, dollar-denominated assets (such as U.S. Treasury securities), and foreign currencies by the U.S. and foreign governments. In 1995, these flows totaled +$100.7 billion.

The statistical discrepancy is recorded in line 7. It is very difficult to maintain accurate records of the nation's exports, imports, and capital flows. In some cases, the data are inaccurate; in other cases, they are not available. The statistical discrepancy adjusts for these errors and omissions. Because most of the errors and omissions relate to capital flows, the statistical discrepancy is included in the capital account.

The balance on capital account, shown in line 8, is obtained by summing lines 5 through 7. For 1995, this balance was $152.9 billion.

Finally, the overall balance is given in line 9. It is obtained by summing lines 4 and 8. Note that this balance is 0.0. It is *always* zero because the balance of payments must always balance. All international transactions must be financed in some way. In 1995, the United States imported $122.8 billion more than it exported. This excess of imports over exports must have been financed in some manner for it to have occurred. The other entries in Table 15.3 indicate how it was financed.

Because the overall balance must be zero, a country cannot have an overall deficit or surplus. It can, however, have a deficit or surplus in various portions of its balance of payments. In 1995, the United States had a deficit of $152.9 billion in its current account (line 4) and a surplus of $152.9 billion in its capital account (line 8).

Since the early 1980s, the United States has had deficits in its current account (see Figure 15.2). In 1982, the deficit started to rise. In 1987, it peaked at

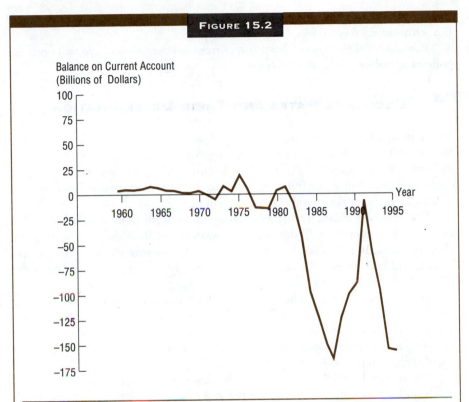

FIGURE 15.2

U.S. BALANCE
ON CURRENT
ACCOUNT:
1960–1995

For most of the 1960–1995 period, the United States had small surpluses and deficits in its balance on current account. Starting in 1983, it began running large deficits. The deficit reached $166.3 billion in 1987 and then declined. It is now rising.

$166.3 billion. After decreasing from 1987 to 1991, the deficit increased.[2] Throughout the period, most of the deficit occurred because the United States imports more than it exports.

Much concern exists about the magnitude and duration of this deficit. Most of the deficit is financed by foreign investment in the United States. So long as this foreign investment continues, more and more of the nation's assets will become the property of foreigners. The increase in foreign ownership means that

[2] The current account deficit was very small, $7.4 billion, in 1991. The main reason was that a number of countries—including Kuwait and Japan—reimbursed the United States for expenses incurred during Operation Desert Storm.

foreigners will receive more income and interest from the United States, and U.S. citizens will receive less.

Because of the concern about the current account deficit, we will consider policies to reduce it later in the chapter.

EXCHANGE RATES AND THEIR DETERMINATION

Exchange Rate
The number of units of one currency exchangeable for one unit of another.

An **exchange rate** is the number of units of one currency that can be exchanged for one unit of another. Suppose the exchange rate between the French franc and the dollar is 10 francs for $1. A tourist from the United States visiting France could exchange dollars for francs at that rate. If the tourist spends 100 francs for a Paris lunch, he or she spends the equivalent of $10.

Flexible (Floating) Exchange Rates
Exchange rates determined by demand and supply.

For most of our nation's history, exchange rates were fixed, implying that they were constant over time. Today, we have a system of **flexible** (or **floating**) **exchange rates.** In a flexible exchange rate system, exchange rates are determined by demand and supply.[3] Should demand or supply change, exchange rates also change.

We can show how exchange rates are determined in this context. For simplicity, we will consider only two countries—the United States and France. The demand and supply curves for dollars are shown in Figure 15.3. The exchange rate, francs per dollar, is plotted on the vertical axis and the demand for and supply of dollars on the horizontal axis.

The demand for dollars is based on the desire of the French to purchase U.S. goods and services, invest in this country, and so on. As the price of the dollar in terms of francs falls, the quantity of dollars demanded by the French increases. At an exchange rate of 15 francs per dollar, the quantity demanded is $10 billion. If the exchange rate falls to 10 francs per dollar, the quantity demanded increases to $20 billion. The increase in quantity demanded occurs because dollars are now less costly to the French. Previously, it cost the French 15 francs to purchase a dollar. Now, it costs only 10 francs. Consequently, U.S. goods and services are less costly to the French. The decline in the exchange rate means the French can buy a dollar's worth of U.S. goods for only 10 francs. Previously, the same dollar's worth of goods cost them 15 francs.

The supply of dollars is based on the desire of U.S. citizens to purchase French goods and services, invest in France, and so on. As the price of the dollar rises in terms of francs, the quantity of dollars supplied by Americans rises. At an exchange rate of 10 francs per dollar, the quantity supplied to the French is $20 billion. If the exchange rate rises to 15 francs per dollar, the quantity supplied increases to $30 billion. The increase in quantity supplied occurs because francs are now less costly to Americans. Previously, they could obtain only 10 francs for a dollar. Now, they can obtain 15 francs for a dollar. Consequently, French goods and services are less costly to Americans. The rise in the exchange

---

[3]Strictly speaking, we have a system of managed flexible exchange rates. With a managed system, central banks frequently buy and sell foreign currencies to moderate fluctuations in exchange rates.

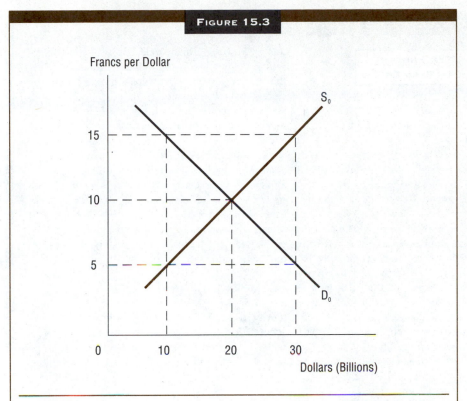

FIGURE 15.3

In a flexible exchange rate system, exchange rates are determined by demand and supply. In this figure, the equilibrium exchange rate—given by the intersection of the demand and supply curves—is 10 francs per dollar.

rate means Americans can buy 15 francs' worth of French goods for a dollar. Previously, they could buy only 10 francs' worth of French goods for a dollar.

Given the demand and supply curves, the equilibrium exchange rate is 10 francs per dollar. At that rate, the quantity of dollars demanded equals the quantity supplied. As a result, there is no tendency for the rate to change.

Suppose the exchange rate were 15 francs per dollar. The quantity of dollars supplied would exceed the quantity demanded, and the exchange rate would fall. With flexible exchange rates, a fall in the exchange rate (a fall in the value of one currency relative to another) is called a **depreciation** of the currency. If the exchange rate falls from 15 francs per dollar to 10 francs per dollar, the dollar is said to depreciate.

Similarly, suppose the exchange rate were 5 francs per dollar. At that rate, the quantity of dollars demanded exceeds the quantity supplied, and the exchange rate would rise. A rise in the exchange rate (a rise in the value of one currency relative to another) is called an **appreciation** of the currency. If the exchange rate rises from 5 to 10 francs per dollar, the dollar is said to appreciate.

Depreciation
Under a flexible exchange rate system, a fall in the value of one currency relative to another.

Appreciation
Under a flexible exchange rate system, a rise in the value of one currency relative to another.

NAFTA AND THE MEXICAN PESO CRISIS

When the North American Free Trade Agreement (NAFTA) went into effect on January 1, 1994, it was widely anticipated that trade between the United States and Mexico would grow rapidly. In 1994, trade did grow rapidly. In December 1994, however, the peso depreciated vis-à-vis the dollar, depressing U.S. exports to Mexico and stimulating U.S. imports from Mexico.

In 1994, Mexican authorities were maintaining an approximately constant exchange rate between the peso and dollar by buying and selling pesos in foreign exchange markets. At the same time, Mexico was experiencing a current account deficit that was largely financed by foreign investment. As time passed, the deficit became larger. Moreover, events within Mexico—including a rebellion in Chiapas province and the assassination of the ruling party's presidential candidate, Luis Donaldo Colosio—caused concern abroad. As a result, the peso began to depreciate. To keep the peso from depreciating further, Mexican authorities used their international reserves (including dollars) to buy pesos in foreign exchange markets. By December 1994, Mexico's holdings of international reserves were low.

On December 20, the Mexican peso was devalued by 20 percent. This devaluation proved insufficient and by December 27 the exchange rate was 5.7 pesos per dollar, a decline of nearly 40 percent since just before the initial devaluation. With the assistance of a direct-loan package that included $20 billion from the United States, the situation eventually stabilized, but not before interest rates soared and the Mexican economy experienced a severe recession.

The depreciation of the peso made Mexican goods and services much cheaper to Americans. It also made American goods and service much more expensive to Mexicans. Consequently, U.S. imports from Mexico increased in 1995 while its exports to Mexico decreased. In addition to the depreciation of the peso, the recession in Mexico contributed to the decrease in imports from the United States.

For the United States, the net effect of these changes was to go from a trade surplus with Mexico, averaging about $4 billion from 1991 through the third quarter of 1994, to a trade deficit of about $15 billion. Even so, output in the United States continued to rise while the unemployment rate continued to fall. In 1994, the U.S. unemployment rate was 6.1 percent. In 1995, it was only 5.6 percent.

With the Mexican economy now expanding, U.S. exports to Mexico are at record levels and are expected to grow in the future. Indeed, in the absence of another peso crisis, the growth in trade between the United States and Mexico that was anticipated with the signing of the North American Free Trade Agreement is likely to occur.

Movements in exchange rates are very important because they alter the international prices of goods and services. Suppose the dollar depreciates from 15 francs per dollar to 10 francs per dollar. The depreciation makes U.S. goods and services less costly to the French. Because U.S. goods are now less costly, the French will import more from the United States, and U.S. exports will rise.

In contrast, French goods and services will be more costly to Americans. Previously, Americans could buy 15 francs' worth of French goods for a dollar. Now, they can buy only 10 francs' worth for a dollar. Because French goods are now more costly, Americans will buy less from France, and U.S. imports will fall.

Depreciation of a nation's currency increases its exports and reduces its imports. Appreciation of a currency has the opposite effect. Suppose the dollar appreciates from 5 francs per dollar to 10 francs. The appreciation makes French goods and services less costly to Americans, and the United States will import more from France. U.S. goods are now more costly to the French, and the United States will export less to France.

Because movements in exchange rates affect a nation's exports and imports, it is important to identify the factors that determine those movements. Exchange rates are determined by supply and demand. Consequently, any factor that can cause a change in supply or demand can alter the exchange rate. We consider three of these factors: real GDP, the inflation rate, and the interest rate.

REAL GDP

As a nation's real GDP rises, its imports also rise. With a higher GDP, the nation will import more intermediate goods and raw materials. It will also import more final goods and services.

Suppose real GDP in the United States rises while real GDP in France remains constant. The United States will import more from France, and the dollar will depreciate. These changes are shown in Figure 15.4.

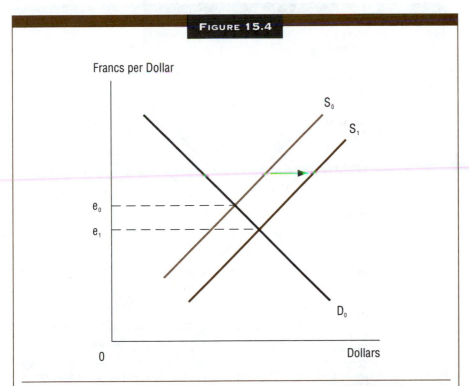

FIGURE 15.4

Francs per Dollar

S_0

S_1

e_0

e_1

D_0

0   Dollars

EFFECT OF AN INCREASE IN REAL GDP ON THE EXCHANGE RATE

An increase in real GDP causes the United States to import more from France. As a result, France's supply of dollars increases. The shift in the supply curve from S_0 to S_1 causes the exchange rate to fall from e_0 to e_1.

Suppose that, in Figure 15.4, the demand for dollars is D_0 and the supply of dollars is S_0. As a result, the exchange rate is e_0. The increase in U.S. GDP means that the United States will import more. Consequently, the supply of dollars to the French will increase. The shift in the supply curve from S_0 to S_1 causes the exchange rate to fall from e_0 to e_1, and the dollar depreciates.

INFLATION RATES

If a nation's inflation rate rises relative to that of other nations, its exports will become less competitive in world markets and will decline. Similarly, as a nation's prices rise relative to prices in other countries, foreign goods become more attractive and so imports rise.

Suppose the inflation rate in the United States rises relative to that in France. Because U.S. goods are becoming relatively more expensive, the United States will export less to France. Because French goods are becoming relatively less expensive, the United States will import more from France. These changes, shown in Figure 15.5, cause the dollar to depreciate.

EFFECT OF A HIGHER INFLATION RATE ON THE EXCHANGE RATE

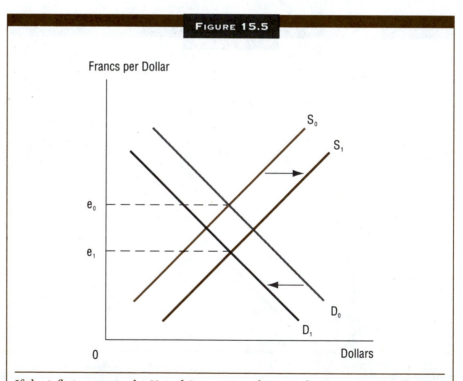

FIGURE 15.5

If the inflation rate in the United States rises relative to that in France, it will export less to France and import more. Consequently, the French demand for dollars will decrease, and the supply of dollars to France will increase. The shifts in the demand and supply curves to D_1 and S_1, respectively, cause the exchange rate to fall from e_0 to e_1.

In Figure 15.5, the demand for dollars is D_0 and the supply of dollars is S_0 so that the exchange rate is e_0. If the U.S. inflation rate rises, the United States will import more from France, causing the supply of dollars to increase from S_0 to S_1. At the same time, the United States will export less to France, causing the demand for dollars to decrease from D_0 to D_1. These shifts cause the exchange rate to fall to e_1, so that the dollar depreciates.

INTEREST RATES

Suppose U.S. interest rates rise relative to interest rates abroad. With its higher rate of return, the United States would attract more funds from abroad.[4] Because other countries now have relatively lower interest rates, they will attract fewer funds from the United States. With more funds flowing to the United States and fewer funds flowing from the United States, the dollar will appreciate.

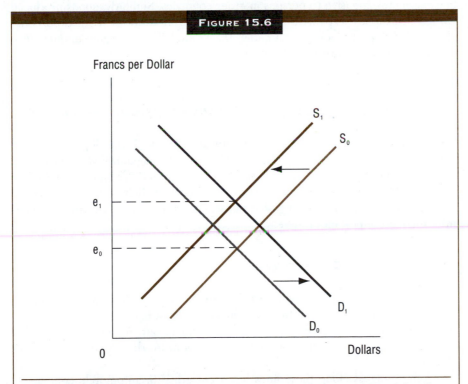

FIGURE 15.6

Francs per Dollar

S_1

S_0

e_1

e_0

D_1

D_0

0

Dollars

EFFECT OF A HIGHER INTEREST RATE ON THE EXCHANGE RATE

If interest rates in the United States rise relative to those in France, the French will invest more heavily in the United States and Americans will invest less heavily in France. Consequently, the French demand for dollars will increase, and the supply of dollars to France will decrease. The shifts in the demand and supply curves to D_1 and S_1, respectively, cause the exchange rate to rise from e_0 to e_1.

[4]Strictly speaking, it is the real interest rate—the actual rate adjusted for inflation—that is relevant.

These changes are shown in Figure 15.6. With higher interest rates in the United States than in France, the French will find it desirable to invest more in the United States, and the demand for dollars will increase from D_0 to D_1. At the same time, Americans will find it less desirable to invest in France, and the supply of dollars will decrease from S_0 to S_1. Consequently, the exchange rate will rise from e_0 to e_1.

From 1980 to 1985, the dollar appreciated by 50 percent or more relative to most major currencies. The main reason for the appreciation was the increase in interest rates that occurred in the United States. The rise in interest rates, in turn, was due to the expansionary fiscal policy (and resulting budget deficits) pursued during that period (see Chapter 14). The higher interest rates in this country caused the demand for dollars to increase, which in turn caused the dollar to appreciate.

The appreciation of the dollar made it increasingly difficult for U.S. goods and services to compete in world markets. Goods produced in the United States became more expensive to persons in other countries. Similarly, goods produced abroad became less expensive to persons in the United States. With exports declining and imports increasing rapidly, the United States began running huge deficits in its balance on current account.

POLICIES TO REDUCE THE CURRENT ACCOUNT DEFICIT

Starting in 1985, the dollar began to depreciate. Although the depreciation did not have an immediate impact on the deficit on current account (which peaked in 1987), it ultimately reduced it. Even so, the deficit was $152.9 billion in 1995 and is expected to be higher in the future. Many economists believe that it should be reduced or eliminated and suggest various policies to accomplish this. We consider the most important of these.

INCREASED U.S. COMPETITIVENESS

If U.S. firms could reduce their costs of production and therefore their prices and improve the quality of their products, American goods would be more competitive in world markets. The result would be an increase in exports, a decrease in imports, and therefore a reduction in the deficit on current account.

Some progress along these lines has occurred. U.S. automobile companies, for example, have reduced their costs. They have also improved the quality and reliability of their cars.

Despite this progress, it is not clear to what extent American manufacturers will become more competitive through cost cutting. Also, if foreign firms are equally successful, U.S. firms will be unable to achieve a competitive edge. Such efforts may be necessary just for the United States to maintain its current position.

CONTRACTIONARY MONETARY AND FISCAL POLICY

Contractionary monetary and fiscal policy could reduce the current account deficit. To illustrate, the U.S. inflation rate has been about 3 percent in recent years. If the inflation rate could be reduced by cutting the growth rate of the money supply, American goods and services would be more competitive in world markets.

In applying contractionary monetary and fiscal policies, care must be taken to maintain output and employment at their full employment levels. If contractionary monetary and fiscal policies are applied and real GDP falls, imports and hence the current account deficit will decline. While a reduced deficit may be desirable, the decreases in output and employment are clearly undesirable. Indeed, most economists believe that the costs associated with reducing the deficit in this manner outweigh the benefits.

As an alternative, many economists favor combining a contractionary fiscal policy with an expansionary monetary policy. The combination of policies would presumably maintain aggregate demand at its full employment level while reducing interest rates. Interest rates would fall, in part, because of the decrease in government purchases and/or increase in taxes and the accompanying reduction in the federal government's budget deficit. They would also fall because of the increase in the money supply.

Lower interest rates in the United States would reduce the demand for dollars, and the dollar would depreciate. As a result, U.S. products would become more competitive in world markets. U.S. exports would increase, imports decrease, and the current account deficit decrease.

Finally, representatives of the U.S. government could urge their counterparts in other countries to pursue more expansionary monetary and fiscal policies. Much of the increase in the U.S. current account deficit that occurred during the 1992–1995 period was due to the rapid growth of the U.S. economy. With U.S. GDP rising relatively rapidly, U.S. imports also increased relatively rapidly. If policymakers abroad were to implement more expansionary monetary and fiscal policies, foreign GDP would rise more rapidly which would have a favorable effect on U.S. exports.

During the early 1990s, representatives of the U.S. government did urge the representatives of other governments—including Germany and Japan—to enact more expansionary policies, but they had little or no success. It is not clear whether U.S. representatives will be more successful in the future.

IMPOSITION OF TRADE RESTRICTIONS

Still another way to reduce the deficit on current account is to impose tariffs, quotas, or other trade restrictions. This approach is clearly undesirable. By reducing imports in this manner, the nation would forgo some of the advantages of specialization and suffer a lower standard of living as a result. In addition, the imposition of trade restrictions may provoke retaliation on the part of other countries. If those countries respond by imposing their own trade restrictions, U.S. exports will fall. The decline in imports may be offset by the drop in exports, thus keeping the deficit at a high level. Finally, the imposition of trade restrictions will do little to make U.S. goods more competitive in world markets. In fact, imposing trade restrictions removes much of the incentive for firms to modernize their productive facilities and to make other changes that would make them more competitive.

Much of the United States' deficit on current account is with Japan. From time to time, it is suggested that the United States bargain with Japan to open the Japanese market to U.S. exports. It is also suggested that if Japan doesn't respond favorably, the United States should impose trade restrictions on Japanese exports.

Negotiations with the Japanese are desirable. At the same time, imposing trade restrictions on U.S. imports from Japan is foolhardy. While it may harm the Japanese, it would also hurt American consumers and reduce the standard of living in the United States. It amounts to shooting oneself in the foot.

DEPRECIATION OF THE DOLLAR

Under a flexible exchange rate system, exchange rates are determined by demand and supply. Under the present system, however, central banks do intervene to prevent wide swings in exchange rates.

Some economists argue that this intervention has kept the dollar from depreciating as much as it should. Others argue that central banks should intervene to force a depreciation of the dollar.

There is little doubt that exports and imports respond (with a lag) to changes in exchange rates. Consequently, depreciation of the dollar can be expected to reduce the deficit on current account. On the other hand, the dollar may have depreciated sufficiently from its 1985 level to significantly reduce or eliminate the deficit. We know that the full effects of a depreciation do not take place until well after the depreciation.

Alternatively, suppose the dollar needs to depreciate even more. If central bank intervention has kept the dollar from falling, it can be argued strongly that the intervention should cease. If it is necessary for central banks to intervene to drive the dollar lower, it is still not clear how much lower the dollar should go. In the absence of such information and given the delayed impact on exports and imports, central banks should proceed very slowly, if at all.

SUMMARY

U.S. participation in world trade has been increasing. Although the United States is not as dependent on international trade as some countries, it exports and imports more than any other country in the world.

Trade among nations is based on the principle of comparative advantage, whereby countries produce and export goods and services in which they have a comparative advantage and import goods and services in which they have a comparative disadvantage.

Despite the strong arguments for free trade, most countries—including the United States—restrict trade in various ways. Among other measures, they impose tariffs, quotas, and voluntary export restraints.

These protectionist measures raise domestic prices by restricting imports. As a result, consumers are worse off. Domestic producers, however, receive higher prices and are better off. Society as a whole is worse off because trade restrictions shift resources from industries with a comparative advantage to those with a comparative disadvantage. As a result, the nation's standard of living is reduced.

The case for free trade is based primarily on the principle of comparative advantage. Some other arguments are that (1) specialization allows firms to produce higher levels of output, enabling them to produce at lower average cost; (2) free trade increases competition; and (3) international trade increases the diversity of goods and services available to consumers.

Despite the strong case for free trade, many people argue that domestic industries should be protected. The most common arguments stress that (1) new industries should be protected until they can become competitive, (2) industries essential for national defense should be protected, (3) protection is necessary to save jobs, and (4) American workers must be protected from cheap foreign labor. To the extent that these arguments are valid, the goals can best be accomplished in ways other than trade restrictions.

Since World War II, countries have significantly reduced barriers to international trade. In reducing these barriers, countries have followed both global and regional approaches.

The United States has had large current account deficits since the early 1980s. For the most part, the deficit is financed by foreign investment in this country. If the deficit continues, more and more of the nation's assets will become the property of foreigners. Consequently, foreigners will receive more income and interest from the United States, and U.S. citizens will receive less.

In a flexible exchange rate system, exchange rates are determined by supply and demand. The dollar appreciated significantly over the 1980–1985 period. Until recently, it has depreciated.

Various policies have been recommended to reduce or eliminate the large and persistent current account deficits. They include increased U.S. competitiveness, contractionary monetary and fiscal policies, imposition of trade restrictions, and allowing, or forcing, the dollar to depreciate.

KEY TERMS

Comparative advantage	Voluntary export	Depreciation
Comparative disadvantage	restraints (VERs)	Appreciation
Absolute advantage	Balance of payments	
Absolute disadvantage	Exchange rate	
Tariff	Flexible (floating)	
Quota	exchange rates	

REVIEW QUESTIONS

1. Distinguish between absolute and comparative advantage.
2. Suppose that a worker in the United States is able to produce more beef and more steel than a worker in Japan. Does this mean that Japan will be unable to trade with the United States? Defend your answer.
3. Use the information in the table to answer parts a, b, and c.

Country	Car Production per Day	Wine Production per Day
United States	6	2
France	1	1

   a. Which country has the absolute advantage in cars? In wine?
   b. Which country has the comparative advantage in cars? In wine?
   c. Is there a basis for trade between the two countries? Explain in detail why or why not.
4. Compare and contrast the different restrictions that the United States might place on steel imports.
5. "If we allow free trade in the automobile industry, some automobile workers will lose their jobs. This unemployment will make society worse off." What advantages of free trade does this argument overlook? How might the unemployment be alleviated?
6. Despite the fact that society is generally better off with free trade, governments often impose trade barriers. Why might a government take such action?
7. Compare and contrast the global and regional approaches to reducing barriers to international trade.
8. Even though the United States has a large current account deficit, it has an overall balance of zero. Why, then, is there such concern about the large current account deficit?
9. Carefully explain how exchange rates are determined in a system of flexible exchange rates.
10. Suppose the U.S. dollar appreciates relative to the Japanese yen. How will the exports and imports of the two countries be affected?
11. How will each of the following domestic factors affect the exchange rate?
   a. An increase in real GDP.
   b. A decrease in the inflation rate.
   c. An increase in the interest rate.
12. Discuss the various policies that might be used to reduce the current account deficit.

SUGGESTIONS FOR FURTHER READING

Fieleke, Norman S. "The Uruguay Round of Trade Negotiations: Industrial and Geographic Effects in the United States." Federal Reserve Bank of Boston, *New England Economic Review,* (July/August 1995), 3–11. Discusses the effects of the Uruguay Round agreement on world trade with emphasis on the United States.

_____. "The Uruguay Round of Trade Negotiations: An Overview." Federal Reserve Bank of Boston, *New England Economic Review,* (May/June 1995), 3–14. Summarizes in nontechnical language the main aspects of the Uruguay Round agreement.

Hakkio, Craig S. "The U.S. Current Account: The Other Deficit." Federal Reserve Bank of Kansas City, *Economic Review* 80 (Third Quarter 1995), 11–24. Discusses the U.S. current account deficit and its implications.

Hufbauer, Gary Clyde, and Jeffrey J. Schott. *NAFTA: An Assessment*. Washington, DC: Institute for International Economics, 1993. An analysis of the impact of the North American Free Trade Agreement on the United States, Canada, and Mexico.

King, Philip, ed. *International Economics and International Economic Policy: A Reader.* 2nd ed. New York: McGraw-Hill, 1995. A collection of articles dealing with many of the topics covered in this chapter.

Kreinin, Mordechai E. *International Economics: A Policy Approach*. 8th ed. Fort Worth: The Dryden Press, 1998. A comprehensive, although somewhat advanced, treatment of international economics.

Welch, Patrick J., and Gerry F. Welch. *Economics: Theory and Policy*. 6th ed. Fort Worth: The Dryden Press, 1998. Chapters 16 and 17 contain very readable discussions of international trade and finance.

Whitt, Joseph A., Jr. "The Mexican Peso Crisis." Federal Reserve Bank of Atlanta, *Economic Review* 81 (January/February 1996), 1–20. Examines the collapse of the Mexican peso, its implications for the Mexican and U.S. economics, and efforts to deal with the crisis.

16

ECONOMIC GROWTH: POVERTY REDUCTION PAR EXCELLENCE

D

Economic growth has transformed the material basis of society in industrialized countries. The material standard living in the United States is incomprehensibly higher for the average citizen now than it was in 1776. Measures of health, education, longevity, and material goods show vast improvement. The biggest improvement is in the standard of living of the average person. The material life of the rich and famous two hundred years ago was vastly superior to that of the average person in most dimensions—health, diet, entertainment, housing, education, and so on. Abraham Lincoln's early childhood in a small, windowless cabin with a few books and little time for schooling contrasted sharply with the luxurious lifestyle enjoyed by Thomas Jefferson's children at Monticello. The difference between the material quality of life—food, shelter, education, convenience, health, and so on—available to the rich and the middle class is large today, but arguably not as large as then. Although economic growth has improved the living standards of the rich, the greatest improvement has been for members of the lower and middle class.

The ability of compound growth to raise living standards is immense. Since 1820, GDP per capita in the United States has increased more than 15 times. In effect, average income has gone from $1,000 per person to $15,000, although the growth rate was only 1.6 percent per year. The growth rate in Japan over this period was higher, 1.9 percent per year, but this seemingly small difference was big enough to increase GDP per capita in Japan 25 times. In 1820 GDP per capita was 100 percent greater in the United States than in Japan; in 1992 it was only 16 percent greater. Big oaks grow from small acorns.

Understanding the sources of persistent economic growth is crucial. Why does one country grow at 1.5 to 2 percent a year over long periods while another country grows at less than 0.5 percent a year? The first country becomes prosperous and the second country remains a low-income country. Since 1820, Japan has gone from low-income status—with GDP per capita 1.2 times that of India—to advanced status with per capita output 15 times greater than India's. One country converges on the high-income country, the United States, and the other country diverges.[1]

In this chapter we develop the fundamentals of economic growth analysis. We look at several countries' recent economic growth—1952 to 1992—emphasizing three points. First, growth slowed after 1972. Second, GDP per capita in some countries is catching up to that in the United States. Third, some countries have escaped low-income status since 1952; others remained mired at absolute low levels. We will discuss the sources of growth in the U.S. context and examine why U.S. growth has slowed. Then we will examine why some other countries are converging on the United States. Finally, we will consider the problems that some countries face escaping poverty.

---

[1]Computed from data in Angus Maddison, "Explaining the Economic Performance of Nations," in William J. Baumol, Richard R. Nelson, and Edward N. Wolff, eds., *Convergence of Productivity: Cross-National Studies and Historical Evidence* (New York: Oxford University Press, 1994), 20–61.

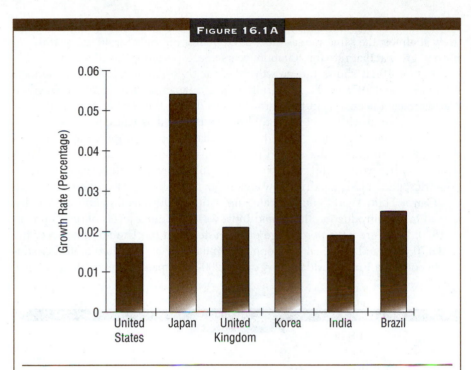

FIGURE 16.1A

GROWTH RATES OF GDP PER CAPITA 1952–1992

Since 1952, GDP per capita in Japan and South Korea has grown much faster than in the United States, the United Kingdom, India, and Brazil.

Source: Computed from Penn World Table 5.6. For a description, see Alan Heston and Robert Summers, "International Price and Quantity Comparisons," *American Economic Review* 86 (May 1996).

RECENT GROWTH EXPERIENCES

As seen in Figure 16.1A the United States has had a lower growth rate than an assortment of other countries since 1952.[2] Its 1.6 percent growth rate, however, is the same as its growth rate since 1820, a rate that propelled its citizens to their current living standards. The 5+ percent growth rates in Japan and the Republic of Korea show that higher growth rates are possible. Such growth rates double GDP per capita in 14 years compared with a 40-year doubling time for the U.S. growth rate.[3] If output per person doubles every 14 years in Japan and every 40

---

[2]These countries were selected to provide a variety of experiences to compare with that of the United States and among themselves.

[3]A useful rule of arithmetic is that the doubling time for something growing at a compound rate can be approximated by dividing the rate into 72. So if you have an investment that is earning compound interest of 8 percent, it will double in nine years.

years in the United States, Japan quickly pulls ahead. India, on the other hand, grew at almost the same rate as the United States, but only for 40 years. It would have to grow at that rate for 100 more years to escape Third World status.

Figure 16.1B shows the growth rates for these countries for two periods: 1952–1972 and 1972–1992. The United States, Japan, and the United Kingdom had significant decreases in their growth rates during the second period. This experience, shared with most industrialized countries, has caused much concern about economic stagnation. Note, however, that the growth rates for Korea and India increased during the second period. Several other countries in Southeast Asia and other parts of the world, including China, saw growth accelerate. Other countries, particularly in Africa, saw almost no growth in the latter period.

Can a Third World country catch up with the advanced countries? As discussed in the introduction, Japan and India were at similar levels of development in 1820. Japan grew 0.3 percentage points faster than the United States over the next 170 years and achieved development similar to that of United States. Gradually becoming a First World country over a 200-year span, however, does not give

GROWTH RATES 1952–1972 VERSUS 1972–1992

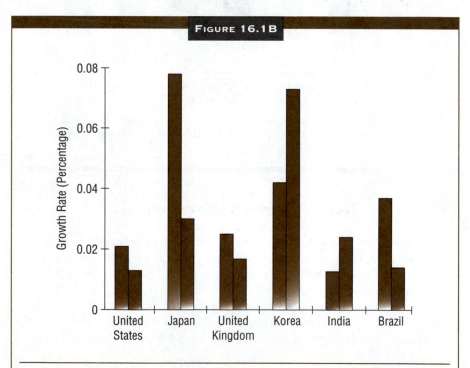

After 1972, growth rates of GDP per capita slowed in the United States, Japan, the United Kingdom, and Brazil, but they increased in South Korea and India.

Source: Computed from Penn World Table 5.6. For a description, see Alan Hestor and Robert Summers, "International Price and Quantity Comparisons," *American Economic Review* 86 (May 1996).

much hope for current generations. As the Japanese experience, and now the experience of other countries in Asia, shows, it does not necessarily take 200 years. In fact, partly because of World War II, average income in the United States gained on Japan until about 1950. In 1820, U.S. per capita GDP was twice that of Japan's; by 1950 it was five times greater. Then, as Figure 16.2A shows, Japan's GDP per capita began to converge on that of the United States. With a growth rate of more than 5 percent, Japan all but caught the United States in 40 years. Perhaps the Japanese experience was an exception—Japan was a previously industrialized country whose economy was devastated in World War II. Korea, however, provides another example. As Figure 16.2A shows, Korea started to close the relative gap with the United States in the 1960s. In 1962, Korea's per capita GDP was about one-eleventh that of the United States; by 1992 it was one-half. Moreover, by 1982 the absolute gap between the two countries began to fall from about $12,000 to about $10,000 in 1992. Inspection of the figure shows that Korea is gaining rapidly.

Unfortunately, not all countries have been as successful at economic growth as Japan and Korea. Figure 16.2B shows GDP per capita for the United States, Korea, Brazil, and India over this period. Although each country has closed a

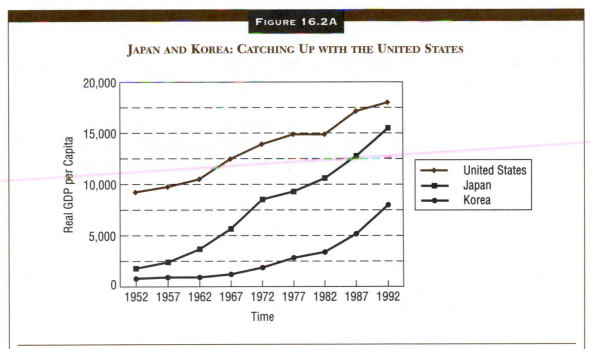

FIGURE 16.2A

JAPAN AND KOREA: CATCHING UP WITH THE UNITED STATES

GDP per capita in Japan and Korea is catching up with that of the United States.

Source: Computed from Penn World Table 5.6. For a description, see Alan Hestor and Robert Summers, "International Price and Quantity Comparisons," *American Economic Review* 86 (May 1996).

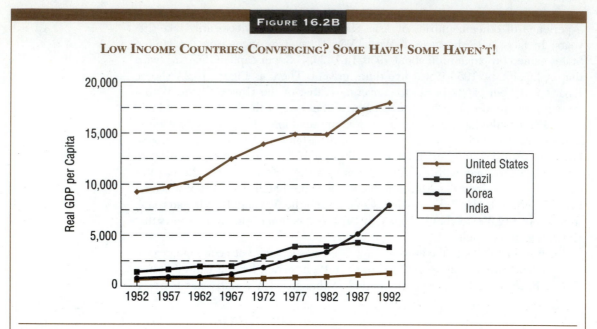

FIGURE 16.2B

LOW INCOME COUNTRIES CONVERGING? SOME HAVE! SOME HAVEN'T!

Although Korea is catching up with the United States, Brazil and India are not. After 1972, growth rates of GDP per capita slowed in the United States, Japan, the United Kingdom, and Brazil, but they increased in South Korea and India.

small part of its relative gap with the United States, the absolute differences between Brazil (India) and the United States continue to grow. India's per capita production has doubled over the 40-year period and Brazil's has tripled. Although this is encouraging, it is quite slow compared with countries like Korea, which were at a similar level of development in 1952.

In this overview of recent growth in selected countries, at least three questions arise: What are the sources of economic growth and why has it slowed in the United States? What aspects of the economies or policies of countries like Japan and Korea are responsible for their success? What aspects of the economies or policies of countries like Brazil and India have hindered their attempts to grow? These are big questions, and we can only touch on some of the factors involved. In the next section, we turn to the sources of growth and the growth slowdown.[4]

---

[4]Answers to these questions are controversial. See the suggested readings at the end of the chapter for some of the relevant literature.

SOURCES OF ECONOMIC GROWTH AND THE GROWTH SLOWDOWN

An understanding of economic growth requires consideration of society's production possibilities. Economic growth occurs when an economy can produce more goods and services, a greater GDP. This section first develops the production possibilities curve, and then applies it to economic growth.

PRODUCTION POSSIBILITIES FOR THE ECONOMY

An axiom of economics is that the resources required to produce goods and services are scarce relative to peoples' aggregate wants for goods and services. There are three primary resources: **land, labor,** and **capital.** Land includes all natural resources and raw materials. Labor includes all the physical and mental abilities of the population. Capital consists of durable produced goods, such as factories, industrial equipment, highways, and airports. Technology is how the resources are combined to produce output.

In a world of scarcity, choices must be made among alternative uses of resources. As discussed in Chapter 1, every economic system must choose what goods and services will be produced, how these goods and services will be produced, and to whom they will be distributed. Its choices help to determine the growth rate of GDP per capita.

People require food. Consequently, scarce resources are used to produce food. Because resources can be used to produce other desirable goods and services, the cost of food production is the value of the highest-valued other goods *not* produced. Thus, people must choose between food and other goods and services.

Suppose, for simplicity that the choice is between only two alternatives: food and cars. Figure 16.3 illustrates the important dimensions of this choice. The horizontal axis measures cars: thousands of cars per year. The vertical axis measures food production in millions of baskets per year. Point A shows the maximum amount of food that can be produced per year—100 million baskets—if all resources are used for food production and the best methods of producing food are used.

An increase in car production requires a reduction in food production because resources must be transferred from food to car production. Starting at point A, with no cars and 100 million baskets of food, an increase to 100,000 cars causes a reduction in food production from 100 million baskets to 95 million baskets. The value of the 5 million baskets of food given up is the opportunity cost of the additional cars.

Increasing car production from 100,000 to 200,000 requires that food production drop to 85 million baskets; that is, that people give up 10 million more baskets of food. The intervals on the horizontal axis associated with successive moves down the curve from A to B, C, D, and E correspond to equal increases in car production: each interval equals 100,000 cars. The corresponding vertical

Land
Resources found in nature, such as land, water, forests, mineral deposits and air.

Labor
All physical and mental abilities used by people in production.

Capital
Man-made, durable items used in the production process, such as factories, equipment, dams, and transportation systems.

THE PRODUCTION
POSSIBILITIES
CURVE APPLIED
TO THE CHOICE
BETWEEN FOOD
AND CARS

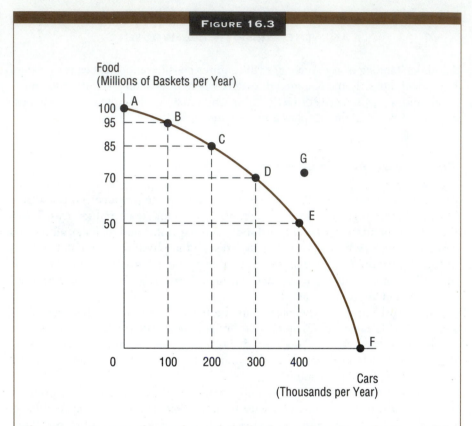

FIGURE 16.3

The economy is assumed to produce only food and cars. Along the production possibilities curve, marked by points A to F, resources are used fully and the best technology is applied. The combinations of food and cars, A to F, are the largest possible combinations. Starting at point A, it is necessary to reduce the production of food by 5 million baskets (from 100 million to 95 million) to produce the first 100,000 cars. Production of the next 100,000 cars requires that 10 million more baskets of food be given up. The amount of food given up with each move down the curve is the marginal cost of cars, which increases with each successive increase in car production.

Production Possibilities Curve
A curve showing the maximum combinations of two goods or services that can be produced by an economy when resources are fully used and the best technology is applied.

intervals measure the reduction in food production for each increase in car production. As Figure 16.3 shows, each successive increase in car production requires that more food be given up; the marginal cost of a car increases as more cars are produced.

The curved line in Figure 16.3 is a **production possibilities curve.** It shows the maximum combinations of two goods or services that can be produced using available resources. A maximum combination is the largest quantity that can be produced of one good for a given quantity of the other good. Each combination on AF assumes full employment of labor, capital, and land and the use of the **best technology**—the technology that requires the fewest resources to produce a given combination of goods and services—in this case, cars and food.

Best Technology
The technology that requires the fewest resources to produce a given combination of goods and services.

Costs increase as resources are transferred out of food production and into the production of cars because resources that are especially well-suited to food production must be converted to a greater and greater degree to a use for which they are less well-suited. Initial expansion of car production is supported by using land, labor, and capital that are actually better suited to car than to food production. Thus, relatively little food production is sacrificed. Eventually, however, car production can be expanded only by taking more fertile cropland, more skilled farm labor, farmers who are especially good at farming, factories that are better suited for making farm implements than cars, scientists who are better at creating fertilizers and pesticides than at developing new methods of combustion, and engineers and construction workers who are better at designing and building farm structures than designing cars. Thus, expansion of car production requires ever-increasing sacrifices in food production.

In Figure 16.3, point G is a combination of 400,000 cars and 70 million bushels of food. It cannot be obtained with available resources and technology; the curve shows that the maximum amount of food possible, given that 400,000 cars are produced, is 50 million bushels. To reach point G, technology must improve or the economy must have more resources—land, labor, and capital. The land and labor available to an economy are not influenced much by day-to-day economic decisions. Thus economic decisions that influence growth are those that increase capital and improve technology. To examine these decisions, we first expand on the production possibilities analysis.

THE BEST COMBINATION OF GOODS AND SERVICES: CONSUMPTION VERSUS GROWTH

The best combination of goods and services is the one that fulfills wants as completely as possible. Figure 16.4, which assumes that the economy produces consumption goods (popcorn) and capital goods (tractors), helps clarify what this requires. In the figure, a move down the curve results in an increase in the number of tractors (capital goods) produced at the expense of a reduction in the amount of popcorn (consumption goods) produced. The opportunity cost of the tractors is the value of the popcorn that is not produced. For instance, suppose at A it is necessary to sacrifice 1,000 bushels of popcorn to produce another tractor. The marginal cost of the tractor is the value of 1,000 bushels of popcorn. What is the marginal benefit? In this example, the marginal benefit of the tractor is the value of the increased popcorn that can be produced in the future because more capital equipment—tractors—will be available in the future.

It pays to move down the production possibilities curve from A to B and so on—producing more capital goods by sacrificing the production of consumption goods this year—so long as the marginal benefit of increased consumption goods in the future is greater than the marginal cost of a reduction in consumption goods today. Marginal cost increases and marginal benefit decreases as we move

PRODUCTION
POSSIBILITIES AND
ECONOMIC
GROWTH

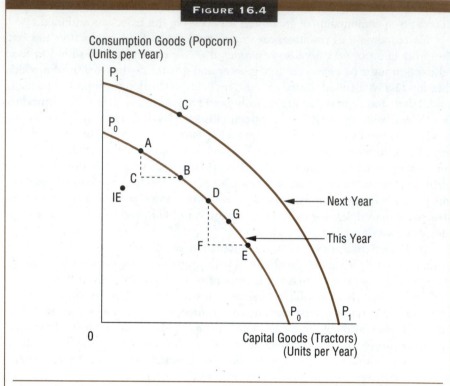

FIGURE 16.4

Economic growth increases the economy's capacity to produce, as illustrated by a rightward shift in the production possibilities curve. It can be caused by resource accumulation or technological improvement. Efficiency improvement, a movement from IE to P_0P_0 can also result in economic growth.

down the curve. The move from A to B and the move from D to E increase tractor production by the same amount. Inspection of the figure shows, however, that the sacrifice of popcorn production is greater with the second move. As discussed, some resources are more suited to the production of one type of good; other resources are more suited to another type. As land, labor, and capital are transferred from the production of consumption goods to capital goods, the first increments transferred will be those with the greatest advantage in producing capital goods. As the process continues, the resources will have smaller and smaller advantages in producing capital goods. Because it takes more resources to produce another unit of the capital good, greater amounts of the consumption good are sacrificed to increase capital good production. Marginal cost also increases because of the reduction in the quantity of consumption goods; with fewer consumption goods, the law of demand implies that the demand price goes up. As capital good production increases, more units of the consumption good are sacrificed and the value of the consumption good increases.

As more capital goods are produced, the marginal benefit associated with another unit of capital goods decreases. The increment in the future production of consumption goods—the marginal benefit of the capital good—falls because of declining *marginal productivity* of capital. The marginal productivity of capital is the increase in the production of consumption goods that will occur when more units of capital are added to the fixed amount of labor and land that will be available in the future. At first, as more capital is available in the future, the extra output of the consumption good will be large because it allows better use of labor. But as more and more tractors are added to a fixed labor force and a fixed amount of land, the increases in popcorn production will get smaller. There may be no one to drive the new tractor, or there may be no land to plow. Besides the declining marginal productivity of capital, the value of increments in consumption goods—the future demand price—falls as more goods become available.

This analysis identifies the best combination of consumption and capital goods to produce. So long as the marginal benefit of additional capital goods is greater than the marginal cost, it increases satisfaction to produce more capital goods. The value of future consumption gained is greater than the value of the present consumption lost. These values depend both on the amounts sacrificed and gained and on the values that individuals place on present and future consumption. At some combination, marginal benefit just equals marginal cost; this is the best combination. This analysis shows why more growth is not always better because more growth implies a reduction in present consumption.

RESOURCE ACCUMULATION, TECHNOLOGICAL IMPROVEMENT, AND EFFICIENCY IMPROVEMENT

Long-term economic growth occurs when an economy develops and realizes the capacity to expand its GDP—its production possibilities. An economy's production possibilities expand if its resources—land, labor, and capital—expand. Labor and capital have greater potential for expansion than land, so we will restrict attention to labor and capital growth. Production possibilities also expand if the best technology improves. **Technological improvement** means that the same amount of goods and services can be produced with less labor and capital or equivalently that more goods and services can be produced with the same quantity of labor and capital. Finally, long-term growth occurs if an economy moves from using less than the best technology to using the best technology. This process, called **efficiency improvement,** also allows more output to be produced with a given amount of resources.

Figure 16.4 explains the three sources of economic growth in terms of production possibilities curves. In this analysis the economy produces two goods, consumption goods and capital goods, with two resources, labor and capital. This year's production possibilities curve, P_0P_0, shows the combinations of consumption and capital goods that can be produced if the economy has full employment of its labor and capital and uses the best technology. For instance, it could produce a combination represented by A, which emphasizes the production of consumption

Technological Improvement
An improvement in best technology that allows more output to be produced with a given amount of resources.

Efficiency Improvement
A change from the use of less than the best to the best technology. It allows more output to be produced with the same resources.

goods relative to capital goods. The only ways that this economy could grow, so that it has the potential to produce more of both goods in the next year, would be for it to have more labor and capital resources or for it to experience technological improvement. Thus, resource accumulation or technological improvement could cause the production possibilities curve to shift to P_1P_1 next year.

RESOURCE ACCUMULATION   Resource accumulation consists of increases in the labor force or in the stock of capital available to the economy. Population growth is the major source of labor-force growth. If the individual standard of living is to grow, GDP has to grow faster than population or the labor force. Just as with the marginal product of capital, the marginal product of labor decreases as more labor is added to a fixed amount of capital. Therefore, population (labor force) growth, with capital and technology fixed, will result in successively smaller increases in GDP. Although labor-force growth causes GDP to grow, it will not cause GDP to grow fast enough to increase living standards.

Capital accumulation, on the other hand, can increase living standards, because the use of more capital permits an increase in GDP without any increase in the use of labor. Capital accumulation may consist of producing more capital equipment (physical capital) or increasing education and training levels (human capital).

Unfortunately, investment in physical and human capital is not free. Suppose that this year the economy is producing at A in Figure 16.4. For a given rate of technological improvement and labor-force growth, assume that capital good production at A, added to this year's capital stock, is just enough to push next year's production possibility curve to P_1P_1. Now suppose that people believe that this growth is too slow. The only way to have more growth in this circumstance is to increase the production of physical and human capital—to move from A to a point like B. To have more growth, more consumption in the future, it is necessary to sacrifice consumption goods today. Greater economic growth is not necessarily desirable; it may mean sacrificing the present for the future.

TECHNOLOGICAL IMPROVEMENT AND EFFICIENCY IMPROVEMENT
Another source of economic growth is technological improvement. Improvements in the best technology could also shift the next year's production possibilities curve to P_1P_1 in Figure 16.4. It simply means that more of both goods can be produced with the same amount of resources. A movement from A to C could occur because of scientific and engineering advances.

Examples of advances in science that have expanded production possibilities are numerous. The basic discoveries related to DNA have resulted in improved plant varieties and new drugs. The discovery of the transistor revolutionized communications. The introduction of the videocassette recorder and player (VCR) transformed the entertainment industry.

New economic institutions are another source of technological improvement. The rapid introduction and widespread acceptance of the self-serve gasoline station is an example. Someone who drives 10,000 miles a year and averages 20 miles per gallon uses 500 gallons of gasoline per year. If full-service gasoline costs

30¢ more per gallon, the person who opts for self-service saves $150 per year. Self-service saves time as well as money. If Tom averages 12 gallons per fill-up, he makes 42 stops for gasoline per year. Self-service is usually faster. Suppose Tom saves 10 minutes per stop. He thus would save 420 minutes, or 7 hours, per year. The value of the time saved may be greater than the money saved.

Efficiency improvements are another source of economic growth and, in some ways, are similar to technological improvements. Improvements in efficiency lead to greater output from a given amount of inputs, but they do not shift the production possibilities curve. For instance, an economy may be operating inside its production possibilities curve, P_0P_0, at a point such as IE in Figure 16.4. It may be because farm programs have resulted in inefficiency. Perhaps some land is not being used at all. Or, it may be operating inside the curve because of monopoly or price controls. Failure to use the best available technology is another source of technical inefficiency. Elimination of such inefficiencies allows the economy to move closer to the production possibilities curve. Such a change means that greater output is obtained from a given amount of resources. (Remember that the production possibilities curve assumes that the amounts of labor and capital are fixed.)

Growth based on technological or efficiency improvements can be much less costly than growth based on capital accumulation. Technological improvements can occur as a by-product of investment in human and physical capital. A higher level of education or greater use of capital equipment can lead to scientific discoveries, to discoveries of new ways of doing old tasks, and to new ways of organizing economic activity (for example, modern retailing). As discussed in Chapter 1, such discoveries can result from division and specialization of labor. Similarly, as educational levels increase, and as firms compete more with firms from other parts of the country and of the world, we may learn about and borrow state-of-the-art production techniques; efficiency will improve. Growth caused by such factors might not require much sacrifice of present consumption. Although not free, sometimes such growth can be close to it. By its nature, achieving growth through technical progress is uncertain, and it can be very costly because efforts to generate technical progress may fail.

THE IMPORTANCE OF PRODUCTIVITY GROWTH

Growth in productivity—output per hour—is important because it limits how fast compensation per hour can grow. Real output per hour, as Figure 16.5 shows, grew about 2.5 percent per year from 1960 to 1973.[5] From 1973 to 1993, it grew by less than 1 percent a year, much less than the previous growth rate. (Although these differences in percentages may seem small, they compound rapidly over a

---

[5] To analyze long-run productivity growth, it is necessary to study long time periods that span similar points in the business cycle. For instance, a comparison of a peak-to-trough period to a trough-to-peak period could be misleading. Therefore, rather than examining decades, we examine 1960–1973 and 1973–1993, which roughly fit this requirement.

GROWTH IN
PRODUCTIVITY AND
HOURLY
COMPENSATION IN
THE PRIVATE
NONFARM
BUSINESS SECTOR

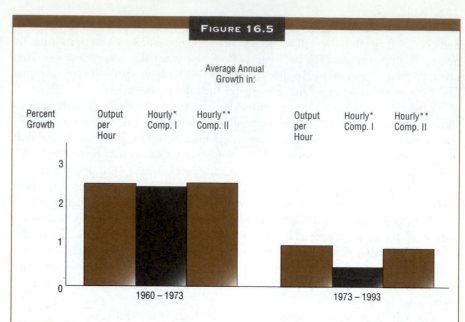

FIGURE 16.5

Labor producitivity—output per hour—grew at close to 2.6 percent a year from 1960 to 1973, but at less than 1 percent from 1973 to 1993. Hourly compensation followed output per hour closely.

*Hourly Comp. I is compensation (wages plus benefits) per hour deflated by the Consumer Price Index.

**Hourly Comp. II is compensation per hour deflated by the relevant Implicit Price Deflator. For this second period, the Consumer Price Index gives misleading information.

Source: Computed from U.S. Department of Labor, *Monthly Labor Review,* selected issues.

short time period.) Compensation per hour grew at about the same rate as output per hour—productivity—in both periods, illustrating the close dependence of compensation or wages on productivity. From 1960 to 1973, real compensation per hour in private business grew at an annual rate of 2.5 percent. At this rate, it doubles about every 28 years. Labor productivity growth and compensation growth (by the more accurate measure) collapsed to 0.9 and 0.8 percent per year from 1973 to 1993—about one-third the previous rate—increasing the doubling time to 90 years.

Nevertheless, from 1973 to 1993, disposable personal income per capita adjusted for inflation grew by about 30 percent, or by 1.3 percent per year. This growth is about 62 percent faster than that of real compensation.[6] Real disposable

[6]Computed from "Selected per Capita Income and Product Items" in U.S. Bureau of the Census, Statistical Abstract of the United States (Washington, DC: Government Printing Office, 1994), 451.

income per capita has grown about 62 percent faster than real compensation. Have we found a contradiction? Not at all. More people are working. The percentage of the working-age population employed increased in the 1970s and again in the 1980s.[7] The increased participation of women in the labor force was a major factor. In 1970, 76.2 percent of males and 40.8 percent of females were employed. Twenty years later, the percentage of males employed fell to 71.9. In contrast, for females, it rose to 54.3.

An important part of this increased relative employment of women is the participation in the labor force of married women with children. In 1970, less than one-half of all married women with children and less than one-third of married women with children under age 6 were in the labor force. Now, however, two-thirds of married women with children and three-fifths of married women with children under age 6 are in the labor force.

One reason for this increased employment of married women with children is that many families found that they needed two wage earners to improve their standard of living. With earnings adjusted for inflation growing slowly at best, increases in real income for many families require increases in hours worked and second workers in the household. The possibility of increased real income through higher labor force participation rates, however, diminishes as higher and higher percentages of women become employed.

In the final analysis, continued increases in real income per family or per capita require increases in labor productivity. To understand whether and how the United States can return to a period of faster productivity growth, it is important to understand what caused the slowdown in productivity growth.

CAUSES OF THE SLOWDOWN IN PRODUCTIVITY GROWTH

To understand what has happened to productivity growth, we must understand its components. The growth of labor productivity can be divided into the part caused by the growth of capital relative to labor and the part caused by technological and efficiency improvements. (From here on, the two concepts together are called technical change.) **Technical change** contributed 2.1, 0.3, and 0.4 percentage points to the 2.9, 1.0, and 1.1 annual percent growth of labor productivity in the private business sector over the periods 1948–1973, 1973–1979, and 1979–1993, respectively. Growth in capital relative to labor—the capital-labor ratio—contributed the remainder—0.9, 0.7, and 0.7 percentage points respectively.[8] (The output per hour bars in Figure 16.6 give a visual description of the growth rate of

Technical Change
Technological and efficiency improvements combined.

---

[7]"Employment Status of Civilian Noninstitutional Population," in U.S. Bureau of the Census, *Statistical Abstract of the United States* (Washington, DC: Government Printing Office, 1994), 396.
[8]See "Annual Indexes of Multifactor Productivity and Related Measures, Selected Years," *Monthly Labor Review* (various issues) for the raw data from which the numbers in the text were computed.

ADDITIONAL INSIGHT

WERE THE GOOD OLD DAYS REALLY BETTER?

In the early 1970s bookkeepers in most small businesses collected and paid bills using manual calculators, typewriters, and ledger sheets. Letters were typed with electric typewriters, some of which had built-in corrections devices. Medical procedures such as cataract removal required long hospitalizations and recovery. Cars and televisions required frequent repair. Today, most businesses process information with computers. Laser and other new surgical techniques have reduced recovery time from many surgeries, converting what might have required a week in a hospital to a one-day procedure. Cars, televisions, and many other goods require much less maintenance and repair.

Individual and family consumption of goods and services has increased substantially since 1970. The average family has more living space with more conveniences—air conditioning, dishwashers, home entertainment systems, and so on. International travel, attendance at cultural events, eating out, and visits to national parks have all mushroomed. A Rip Van Winkle who fell asleep in 1972 would be amazed at the changed production techniques, the greater productivity of labor in the service sector, and the increased consumption of goods and services today.*

Imagine his surprise if you told him that real earnings per hour had fallen by 13 percent since 1973

and that technological improvement in the service sector had stopped after 1980. He might question your accuracy or your veracity. Yet the most frequently quoted government statistics on these issues suggest exactly that. What is wrong with this story? As implied in Chapter 13, the problem may be with the way inflation is measured. In December 1996, the Advisory Commission to Study the Consumer Price Index (the Boskin Commission) in a report to the Senate Finance Committee claimed that changes in the Consumer Price Index (CPI) overstate changes in the cost of living by 1.1 percent per year.[†] If earnings adjusted by the CPI fell by 13 percent after 1973, this bias in the CPI implies that real earnings actually grew by 13 percent. Moreover, instead of falling by 4 percent, real median family income grew by 24 percent. As we discuss in Chapter 13, the CPI is not a good cost-of-living index because it ignores the substitution of one good for another when relative prices change and because it does not handle quality changes and new products well. The Boskin Commission gives many examples of how the CPI is biased as a cost-of-living index.

The substitution bias results because the CPI measures the price changes for a fixed commodity bundle. Suppose a Florida freeze drives up the price of citrus fruit by 50 percent. Many consumers would substitute other fruits for oranges and grapefruits. These consumers will not be as well off as they were before the price increase. Imagine a consumer who spends $10 a month on oranges. The CPI would show

labor productivity. The shaded bars within the output-per-hour bars give the contribution of technical change.) Thus, the contribution to growth from the growth of capital relative to labor declined after 1973. But the biggest change after 1973 is in the contribution of technical change, which dropped to less than one-fifth of its level during the 1948–1973 "Golden Age." Both contributions remain depressed today.

The pattern in the manufacturing sector of the economy, which produces about 20 percent of privately produced GDP, is important in understanding productivity change in the private business sector. Labor productivity in manufacturing is currently growing about 2.8 percent a year, which is about the same rate that overall labor productivity grew in the Golden Age. From 1973 to 1979 labor productivity growth in manufacturing slowed to a crawl. The part of the growth a $5 per month increase in her cost of living. If she substitutes other fruits for oranges, she must think she is better off than spending the extra $5 a month on oranges. She is not as well off as she was before the freeze, but she is not $5 a month worse off.

Other biases exist in practice. For instance, if a consumer switches from buying at a department store to buying at Wal-Mart, he will pay lower prices. Even if the service at Wal-Mart is not up to that of the department store, the consumer is better off. He must be or he would revert to the department store. The CPI does not treat lower prices that result from switching to a discount store as a price decrease. It ignored the lower gasoline prices associated with the shift to self-service gasoline, and it is ignoring the lower prices associated with the continuing shifts to discount retailers.

The tremendous increase in the number of new and improved products also causes the CPI trouble. The goods in the current index were chosen in early 1980s. New products enter the index every 10 or 15 years, depending on the frequency of revision. Microwave ovens and VCRs were commonly used for ten years before they became part of the index. During that ten years, quality improved and prices fell by almost 100 percent. These prices decreases never caused the CPI to fall because they occurred before the goods were part of the index. Similarly, quality improvements are not fully accounted for, although the government tries.

As discussed later in this chapter, measuring the output of many industries, particularly service industries, is difficult. Rather than measuring the output of the medical industry, for instance, the costs of the inputs are measured. This means that surgery performed by new, less-invasive techniques is considered the same as surgery performed by older techniques that resulted in recovery periods measured in weeks rather than days. Because input prices have gone up rapidly, and the improved outcome (greater output) is not measured; no productivity increase appears. Yet the productivity increase has in fact been substantial. These measurement difficulties probably cause an underestimate of productivity growth in many service industries; the other side of the coin is that they cause an overestimate of price increases.

According to the Boskin Commission, we can add 1 percent per year to wages, earnings, or income, if it has been adjusted by the CPI. U.S. living standards have improved more than the statistics show.

---

[*]See Michael J. Boskin, "Prisoner of Faulty Statistics," *The Wall Street Journal* (December 5, 1996), and W. Michael Cox and Richard Alm, "The Good Old Days Are Now," *Reason* (December 1995).
[†]Advisory Commission to Study the Consumer Price Index, "Toward a More Accurate Measure of the Cost of Living," Report to the Senate Finance Committee, December 1996.

---

caused by technical change collapsed to zero. All of the private business sector's annual growth due to technical change in that period occurred in nonmanufacturing industries. Since 1979, however, productivity growth caused by technical change in manufacturing has recovered to Golden Age rates. Indeed, the situation has reversed. Now manufacturing accounts for all of the technical change part of productivity growth in the private business sector. Nonmanufacturing industries contribute nothing.[9]

---

[9]William Gullickson, "Multifactor Productivity in Manufacturing Industries," *Monthly Labor Review* 115 (October 1992), 20–32.

THE CONTRIBUTION OF GROWTH IN THE CAPITAL-LABOR RATIO

As Figure 16.6 shows, the labor input grew more rapidly after 1973 than before. The acceleration in the growth of labor combined with a reduction in the growth of the capital input after 1979 caused the growth in the capital-labor ratio, in *capital intensity,* to slow after 1973 and again after 1979. This reduced growth rate of capital equipment available per worker has resulted in a reduction of about 20 percent in the contribution of the growth of capital intensity to labor productivity growth. Before 1973, growth in the capital intensity contributed about 0.9 percent per year to labor productivity growth. After 1973, it contributed about 0.7 percent per year.

This slower growth in capital intensity from 1973–1979 was due entirely to the more rapid growth of the labor input. Since 1979, however, there has been a

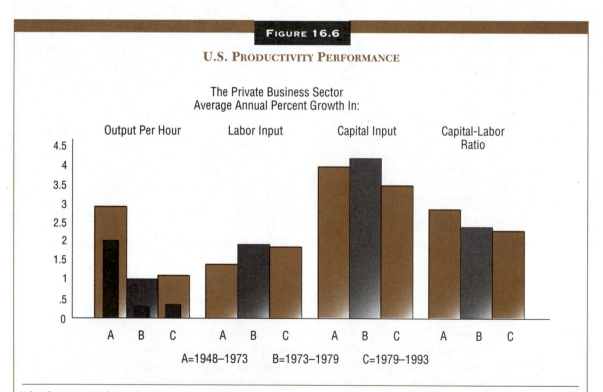

FIGURE 16.6

U.S. PRODUCTIVITY PERFORMANCE

The Private Business Sector
Average Annual Percent Growth In:

A=1948–1973   B=1973–1979   C=1979–1993

The figure provides information about the private business sector. A comparison of the height of the first three bars shows the pattern of growth of output per hour—labor productivity—since 1948. The shaded part of these bars gives growth due to technical change. The chart illustrates the decline of labor productivity growth and technical change. The increased growth of the labor input, the reduced growth of the capital input, and the reduced growth of the capital-labor ratio are also presented.

marked decrease in the growth rate of capital. It is probably no coincidence that the slower growth of private capital occurred during the same period that the federal budget deficit became so large. As discussed in Chapter 14, if the federal government is borrowing substantial sums to finance its activities, it becomes more difficult for the private sector to invest in new capital equipment.

THE CONTRIBUTION OF TECHNICAL CHANGE

Productivity growth is the sum of the contribution of growth in the capital-labor ratio and the contribution of technical change (technological efficiency improvements). From 1973 to 1979, the contribution of technical change to productivity growth dropped to zero in the manufacturing sector, but it recovered completely in the 1980s. The contribution of technical change in the private business sector also dropped substantially from 1973 to 1979, but it did not recover. In fact, after 1979 it fell to zero in the nonmanufacturing sector.

It is ironic that during a period of rapid scientific change, technical change in the U.S. economy all but disappeared. Remember, however, that technical change is more than scientific and engineering advances; technical change is anything that results in getting more output from a fixed amount of resources. It might be caused by a higher quality of labor because of more education and experience, by improved or new products that result from research and development, by greater efficiency in the economy, or by improved management techniques.

A small part of the collapse in technical change in the 1970s was caused by a slowdown in the increase in labor quality as measured by education and experience. Another small part of this collapse was due to an error in the measurement of hours worked.[10] Much of the collapse was unexplained.

As you might expect, the mystery surrounding the disappearance of technical change in the 1970s generated a lot of suspects including research and development (R&D). This suspect has been cleared. Careful studies show that there has been no slowdown in R&D activity that could account for the collapse of technical change. Furthermore, there is no evidence that R&D has become less effective.

Two important differences between the 1973 to 1979 period and later might account for the death and resurrection of technical change in manufacturing in the 1970s and 1980s. First, the world economy experienced huge increases in the price of crude petroleum in 1973 and 1979. Due to price controls on gasoline and other energy sources, these petroleum price increases led to excess demand for gasoline and other fuels. Some economists argue that huge price increases and price controls for a basic resource like petroleum could cause the economy to operate inefficiently, thereby stifling technical change. Such price increases for basic resources have not happened since 1980.

---

[10]Edward Dean and Kent Kunze, "Recent Changes in the Growth of U.S. Multifactor Productivity," *Monthly Labor Review* 111 (May 1988), 14–21.

Second, unlike later, the 1970s were a period of rapid and variable inflation. With government intervention in the economy causing excess demand for fuels and the money supply growing at a rapid rate, it was not surprising that managers concentrated on present profits rather than on long-term investments. After the government brought inflation under control in the 1980s, managers could again concentrate on the long term. Thus, the poor performance of technical change in the 1970s almost certainly was due in part to U.S. government mismanagement, and its turnaround was due in part to improved government performance.

Another suspect in the slowdown of technical change was the U.S. management style. The press bombards us with stories about takeovers and mergers in the U.S. corporate world. According to the popular wisdom, such activity makes managers fear that they must show profits every quarter. Thus, they ignore long-term investment opportunities such as R&D because their payoff lies in the distant future. Rather, they pursue short-term investments that pay well immediately but do not have good long-term prospects. This may have been true in the 1970s; if so, however, it may have been an appropriate response to the uncertainty created by high and variable inflation and erratic government energy policies.

This picture of the corporate manager with limited vision does not square well with the rapid technical change in the manufacturing sector since 1980. The manufacturing sector has almost the same productivity growth now that it had from 1950 to 1973. If corporate managers in the manufacturing sector are avoiding the lures of short-term decision making, we presume that managers in other sectors of the economy also are doing so.

Manufacturing productivity growth has recovered, but productivity in other sectors of the economy is growing slowly. The difference lies in the contribution of technical change rather than in the contribution of the capital-labor ratio. This raises a crucial question: Why has the contribution of technical change to productivity growth returned to its previously high rate in manufacturing but not in other sectors of the economy?

Some people argue that slow productivity growth is a mirage, a result of measurement error. The major problem is how to measure the output and prices of service industries. To measure productivity, economists start with output measured in current dollars. They deflate this nominal output by an appropriate price index to get real output. Then they divide real output by a measure of labor input to get output per unit of labor—labor productivity. The problem is how to devise an appropriate price index. Although prices are economists' bread and butter, good price information often does not exist. One reason is that the announced price is not always the price paid. Another reason is that the quality of the product might change.

Some examples might clarify the problems. For instance, the official measure of labor productivity in air transportation fell from 1972 to 1986. At the same time, passenger miles per employee—a direct measure of labor productivity—increased substantially. The explanation for differences in these two measures of productivity in air transportation is simple—the official productivity statistics ignore discounted airfares. (The announced price is not the price paid.) Thus, the growth in the price index is overstated, and the growth in real output is understated. Consequently, the growth in productivity is understated.

Another reason for errors in productivity measurement is the difficulty of controlling product quality. For instance, price indexes for construction assume that the quality of construction has changed but little since 1929. In other words, they ignore air conditioning, better insulation, built-in dishwashers, faster elevators, and so on. By assuming that the quality of construction has not changed, these price indexes overstate price increases and thus understate productivity growth.

In some industries—finance, retailing, wholesaling—it is difficult to define the product and thus to adjust for quality change. Improvements in economic institutions, which are part of technical change, get little attention in the official productivity statistics. For instance, automatic tellers, convenience stores, automatic bill paying, and laser scanners in supermarkets do not have the appropriate effect on measured productivity.[11]

The *Economist* magazine reviewed another hypothesis regarding productivity growth differences between manufacturing and services.[12] It notes that the U.S. manufacturing sector faced severe foreign competition in the 1980s. This competition forced manufacturing firms to become more efficient. Firms in the service sector did not face the same competition. Thus, they doubled the amount of technology per worker—due to a greater use of computers and so on—but they apparently did not increase productivity. But competition, including foreign competition, has increased in services. And stories about white-collar unemployment were common during the latest recession, suggesting that employment restructuring was occurring. Perhaps service firms, like manufacturing firms, will experience accelerated productivity growth. Indeed, the *Economist* notes that labor productivity in services has begun to grow much faster.

CATCHING UP: EXAMINING THE PROGRESS OF GERMANY AND JAPAN AFTER WORLD WAR II HELPS TO EXPLAIN HOW COUNTRIES CATCH UP WITH THE LEADER

Angus Maddison has provided important insights into productivity in his comparative study of capitalistic development in the advanced industrial nations.[13] He shows both that the U.S. economy is the lead economy operating at the technological frontier and that the follower countries are converging on the U.S. position. Our discussion will compare the U.S. with the two largest follower

---

[11]William E. Cullison, "The U.S. Productivity Slowdown: What the Experts Say," *Federal Reserve Bank of Richmond Economic Review* (July/August 1989), 10–21. This article provides an excellent review of these issues.

[12]"America the Super-Fit," *The Economist,* February 13, 1993, 67.

[13]Angus Maddison, *Dynamic Forces in Capitalistic Development: A Long-Run Comparative View* (New York: Oxford University Press, 1991).

economies, Germany and Japan. After examining the basis for the convergence of the follower countries, we will consider policies that they followed.

THE CONTRIBUTION OF GROWTH IN THE CAPITAL-LABOR RATIO

In 1992, GDP per capita in the United States—in U.S. dollars appropriately adjusted for differences in purchasing power of different national currencies—was about 16 percent higher than in West Germany and Japan. Productivity (GDP per hour), a slightly different measure, was 40 percent less in Japan and 20 percent less in Germany in 1987 than in the United States. Although German and Japanese productivity approaches or exceeds U.S. levels in some manufacturing industries, productivity in other sectors is much lower. For instance, retailing in Japan is notoriously obsolete.

With hourly productivity so much lower, why is Japanese per capita GDP equal to Germany's and close to that of the United States? The answer is simple. The average hours worked per worker is much greater in Japan. In addition, labor force participation is much greater in Japan than in Germany.

The follower countries are converging rapidly on the leader. Since 1950 productivity growth has been more than 3.5 times faster in Japan and more than 2.5 times faster in Germany than in the United States. Why? Over one-half of the convergence since 1973 results from a more rapid growth of the capital-labor ratio. Although capital stock per person employed has grown faster in Germany and Japan, employment has grown faster in the United States. Consequently, the capital-labor ratio has increased much faster in Germany and Japan. Indeed, it has increased more than four times faster in Japan and close to three times faster in Germany. Little wonder that their productivity has grown faster.

We have seen that part of the productivity growth slowdown in the United States is because of a slower growth in the capital-labor ratio. Now, we have also seen that a major part of the faster productivity growth in Germany and Japan is because of a faster growth of the capital-labor ratio. Relatively faster capital accumulation is one road to faster growth. If U.S. citizens wish to maintain a rising standard of living and their leading position in productivity, more rapid investment is one key. Increases in the private investment rate can only come through production of more investment goods, fewer consumption goods, and fewer government goods. In other words, saving rates must increase and government spending must be controlled.

THE CONTRIBUTION OF TECHNICAL CHANGE

Germany and Japan also get a greater boost to labor productivity growth from technical change—in particular, efficiency improvement—than does the United States. Maddison identifies three major sources that contribute: the structural effect, the technological diffusion effect, and the foreign trade effect.

Both Germany and Japan had much larger shifts out of agriculture—structural effects—over this period than did the United States. Shifts out of agriculture tend to raise overall productivity. Shifts into the service sector did not cause a relative disadvantage for the United States because Germany and Japan were becoming service economies even faster.

Technological diffusion is simply a result of technology transfer. In 1950, output per hour in the United States was over twice the output per hour in other industrial countries. Part, but only part, of this difference was due to the devastation of World War II in the other countries. Since that time, other countries have adopted some U.S. technology and production methods; to a lesser extent, the United States has adopted technology and production methods from other countries.

Technology and production techniques are easily transferred to a country that has an educated labor force and an economy that provides incentives for entrepreneurial activity. Productivity in such a country is not likely to lag behind the leader for long. The United States is the leader. Other countries are catching up. It is unfortunate, however, that only a few other countries have provided an economic and political environment that allows them to catch up.

The result of foreign trade is Maddison's final important effect. Freer trade after World War II gave an advantage to follower countries. This advantage, however, was not at the expense of the United States. It arose because freer trade, through the European Common Market, for example, increased competition in smaller economies. Small economies, like small towns, are fertile ground for monopolies. Monopolies sheltered by trade barriers lack incentive to become more efficient. In addition, in a small economy a firm may not be able to grow large enough to realize the advantages of a large size. With its larger economy, the United States already had the advantage of a large internal market. But with freer trade, firms in these smaller economies became more like U.S. firms; they were forced by carrots and sticks to become more effective. Carrots are the profits to be earned in other markets. Sticks are the foreign competitors, not unlike a Wal-Mart coming into a small town.

GERMANY AND JAPAN AFTER WORLD WAR II

Germany, Japan, and other industrialized countries have spent most of the last half-century catching up with the United States. As we have seen, the faster economic growth of West Germany and Japan was based on faster accumulation of capital and more rapid technical change. These countries were in position to benefit from these developments because they had previously experienced many decades of economic development, during which they accumulated human capital by investing in education, knowledge, health, and on-the-job-training. Although much of their physical capital was destroyed in the war, their surviving citizens were well endowed with human capital. Other countries, such as Czechoslovakia, Hungary, and in particular East Germany, shared this starting point. The

INTERNATIONAL PERSPECTIVE

ECONOMIC FREEDOM AND ECONOMIC GROWTH IN DEVELOPING COUNTRIES

In this chapter and in the first chapter, we have argued that the level and growth of living standards are likely to be higher in a market economy than in a centrally planned economy. We have argued that market incentives encourage people to make wealth-creating decisions, and we have discussed the efficiency advantages (and disadvantages) of a market economy. In this and other chapters we have noted several countries that have both economic freedom and stronger economies. At least two criticisms of our position must be considered. One is that we were selective in the examples chosen, but this box overcomes that criticism. The other criticism is more challenging. One can argue that economic and political freedoms are luxuries that only prosperous economies can afford. In short, that prosperity causes economic and political freedom, rather than the other way around. We consider this criticism, but it is more difficult to dismiss.

Several studies have computed indexes of freedom for most of the countries of the world. For example, the Heritage Foundation and *The Wall Street Journal* recently published the "1997 Index of Economic Freedom." Similarly, James D. Gwartney, Robert A. Lawson, and Walter E. Block have written *Economic Freedom of the World: 1975–1995*, published by the Cato Institute and other free-market-oriented institutes around the world. These and other studies show a strong correlation between economic freedom and prosperity. According to the Executive Summary of the former, "The study demonstrates unequivocally that countries with the highest levels of economic freedom also have the highest living standards. Similarly, countries with the lowest levels of economic freedom also have the lowest living standards."[*] The study by Gwartney and colleagues reaches the same conclusion. These correlations, however, do not imply that economic freedom causes prosperity.

To understand what causes what, Gwartney and Lawson, in *Economic Reform Today,* examined their index for developing or low-income countries and identified the 12 (top 10 with ties) countries that had the greatest increase in economic freedom from 1975 to 1990, according to the index. They were Chile, Jamaica, Malaysia, Turkey, Pakistan, Egypt, Portugal, Mauritius, Singapore, Costa Rica, Indonesia, and Thailand. They also identified those developing countries with the greatest decrease in economic

contradictory growth experiences of West and East Germany show that having a labor force endowed with much human capital helps, but it does not ensure that a follower country will catch a leader country. The two countries had similar starting points, but only West Germany succeeded economically.

We believe that a large part of the explanation for the difference is that West Germany, Japan, and other successful countries had well-functioning market systems. As we discussed in Chapter 1, to work well a market economy must have (1) reasonably stable prices, (2) private property rights, (3) appropriate incentives for individual decision makers, (4) markets that allow prices to fluctuate, and (5) a legal system that is obeyed and that generates trust. Satisfying these conditions for a market economy led to the German and Japanese success in accumulating capital and in generating technical change (particularly efficiency improvements).

Today, the rapid growth of Hong Kong, Singapore, South Korea, and Taiwan is the Asian (economic) miracle, but West Germany experienced an earlier freedom: Panama, Morocco, Algeria, Tanzania, Zambia, Congo, Venezuela, Honduras, Iran, Somalia, and Nicaragua. If economic freedom promotes prosperity, one can reasonably expect developing countries with increases in freedom to experience more growth in a later period than developing countries with decreases in freedom. Consequently, Gwartney and colleagues examined growth rates of these same countries in a later period (1985–1994). In the countries with the biggest increases in economic freedom, real per capita GDP grew an average of 4 percent a year. In the countries with the biggest decreases, it fell at 1.2 percent per year. Thus, increases in economic freedom were followed by higher growth rates in a later period. Although other explanations are possible, this relationship between growth of economic freedom and growth of per capita GDP is consistent with the proposition that well-functioning market economies promote economic growth.

Greater appreciation for the results requires some understanding of the index. Gwartney and colleagues argue that low taxes, secure property rights, free domestic and international exchange, and price and monetary stability promote growth. To measure the last factor, for instance, the index uses money supply growth, the variability of inflation, and whether citizens have the right to have foreign currency in domestic and foreign accounts. By holding one's assets in a stable foreign currency, one can protect against domestic inflation. The 12 countries that achieved the faster growth rate had several things in common. They improved their inflation performance, and 11 of the 12 now allow their citizens to hold foreign-currency accounts, making the domestic inflation less harmful.[†] International trade became more important, with its importance (approximately) doubling for countries like Malaysia, Turkey, and Thailand. Finally 11 of the 12 countries reduced their highest marginal income tax rates from above to below 50 percent. For instance, the highest marginal taxes rate from 82 percent to 40 percent for Portugal and from 50 percent to 34 percent for Malaysia. Gwartney and colleagues concluded that the economic success of Hong Kong and other countries that have well-functioning market economies is "powerful evidence concerning the potency of economic freedom and a market economy as an engine of growth and development."[‡]

---

[*]Kim R. Holmes, Bryan T. Johnson, and Melanie Kirkpatrick, "1997 Index of Economic Freedom: Executive Summary," *The Wall Street Journal*, December 16, 1996.
[†]James Gwartney and Robert Lawson, "Economic Freedom and the Growth of Emerging Markets," *Economic Reform Today* 2 (1996) online at www.cipe.org.
[‡]Ibid.

economic miracle. Soon after World War II, West German political leaders shocked the economy by eliminating price controls while gaining control over inflation. With flexible relative prices and a stable price level, markets allocated resources in response to individual preferences. With prices providing appropriate information about scarcity, German consumers, entrepreneurs, managers, and workers began the hard task of economic reconstruction. Those who made profitable decisions kept much of the wealth that they created, but the decisions also generated wealth for other people. That is why they were profitable. Before the Nazis, the German people had lived in an economic and political system that protected property rights and generated trust. Perhaps this background made the reconstruction of the German economy easier.

Both West Germany and Japan strived for price stability and encouraged their citizens to save by allowing savers to earn positive rates of return. Each country encouraged saving in different ways. Moreover, they encouraged investors to seek ideas from other countries, particularly the United States. Each country provided special incentives to some industries or sectors of the economy. Nevertheless, the role of government was restricted compared with countries under Russian influence and the other countries that adopted elements of central planning. The Japanese government, in particular, engaged in significant interventions, but unlike many governments, it allowed subsidized projects to fail. Just as some European countries were successful after World War II and others were not, some developing countries have had rapid economic growth and others have not.

DEVELOPING COUNTRIES AFTER 1950

From 1950 to 1973, GDP per capita grew faster in selected Asian countries than in selected Latin American countries, which in turn grew faster than selected African countries.[14] (The growth experiences of these selected countries are typical of many but not all countries in each region.) Growth accelerated in these Asian countries after 1973, but it declined in Latin American and ceased in Africa. As in any economy, growth in GDP per capita in developing economies requires either (1) that labor grow faster than population, (2) that capital grow faster than labor, or (3) technical change. Compared with the past, developing countries may have a disadvantage because improved health care has increased life expectancy and accelerated population growth. More rapid population growth may make it difficult for labor to grow faster than population or for capital to grow faster than labor. Although it may be more difficult for developing countries to grow based on labor and capital accumulation, they also have an advantage compared with countries that grew in the 19th century. The advantage is in catching up with technology. Their technical change can be due to efficiency improvement rather than technological improvement because the more advanced technology already exists. Their problem is to adapt it to their economies, rather than develop it from scratch. Although this is probably easier than developing new technology, taking ideas and processes that work in one economy and adapting them to another can be difficult. Planners cannot simply take a process that works in one country and use it in another country without any changes.

In 1950 Korea and Taiwan had incomes comparable to that of Ghana and Nigeria and below that of Argentina and Brazil. By 1989 they had moved well ahead of these countries. One factor that stands out in economies of Korea, Taiwan, and other East Asian countries that have experienced rapid growth is the emphasis on primary and later secondary education for boys and girls. As these economies developed, birthrates and population growth rates declined more

---

[14]The Asian countries are Bangladesh, China, India, Indonesia, Japan, Korea, Pakistan, Taiwan, and Thailand; the Latin American countries are Argentina, Brazil, Chile, Colombia, Mexico, and Peru; and the African countries are Cote d'Ivoire, Ghana, Kenya, Morocco, Nigeria, South Africa, and Tanzania. Angus Maddison, "Explaining the Economic Performance of Nations," in William J. Baumol, Richard R. Nelson, and Edward N. Wolff, eds., *Convergence of Productivity: Cross-National Studies and Historical Evidence* (New York: Oxford University Press, 1994), 20–61.

rapidly than in the comparison countries of Latin America and Africa. With development, the opportunity cost of children increases because of increased opportunities for adults in the labor force. As parental income and education increase, parents invest more in children rather than increasing the number of children that they have. The resulting reduction in the population growth rate, combined with increased labor force participation, leads to the labor force growing faster than population. According to Maddison, the successful countries in Asia had several other attributes: (1) their policies encouraged the establishment of a private business sector and established secure property rights; (2) they encouraged domestic saving and investment; (3) they invested heavily in education. In short, they accumulated capital—human and physical—rapidly. Moreover, they were open to foreign influences; this openness was expressed in various ways. Asian students studied abroad, foreign ideas and investments were imported into Asia, and Asian firms competed in international markets. This openness to foreign influence made efficiency improvements easier, permitting these countries to move toward the technological frontier. Combining this openness with individual incentives encouraged appropriate adaption of foreign technology to each country's individual situation. Finally, the successful countries followed prudent monetary and fiscal policies avoiding extreme inflation, while individual product and labor markets were allowed to adjust to changing demand and supply conditions.

The Latin American countries, particularly after 1973, had lower growth rates. Maddison says that their slower growth can be attributed to failures in government policy. These countries have used significant barriers to international trade to protect their domestic industries. Because the firms had protected home markets and were not expected to export, they became inefficient. Additional problems arose because government monetary and fiscal policies caused extremely rapid inflation. Governments dealt with this inflation with price indexing, price controls, and many regulations instead of halting the inflation. Attempting to deal with the inflation caused additional inefficiencies in resource allocation.

Developing countries that are closing the gap with high-income countries are the ones that have satisfied the requirements for a market system. As for government intervention, these economies range from those like Hong Kong with limited government intervention to Singapore with its stringent regulations requiring that people save substantial amounts of their income. Nevertheless, successful countries permit wide scope for individual initiative and do not develop detailed central plans.

SUMMARY

Economic growth has raised citizens of the United States, Canada, Japan, and other countries of Western Europe to living standards unimaginable just 100 years ago. Per capita income continues to grow in these economies, although at a slower rate than in the period just after World War II. Several other countries, particularly in East Asia, have experienced rapid growth beginning in the 1960 and 1970s that has transformed their economies and their living standards. Countries in other parts of the world have had mixed experiences.

The development of the production possibilities curve for an economy helps to explain the sources of economic growth. The curve shows that for a fixed amount of resources and a given technology, an economy has a menu of efficient combinations of output. In particular, it can produce more consumption goods and less capital goods or the reverse. If more rapid growth is wanted, an economy can increase the production of capital goods at the expense of consumption goods. It can sacrifice present consumption for the increased future consumption that increased investment in capital goods allows. It can also grow through technical progress: technological and efficiency improvements.

There is some evidence that U.S. economic growth might pick up. The slowdown in productivity growth has reversed in the manufacturing sector. Slower labor force growth means that, with current investment and saving rates, the capital-labor ratio will increase faster. Even if technical progress outside of manufacturing does not recover completely, increases in the capital-labor ratio will result in increases in labor productivity and the real wage. New products and processes continue to emerge.

Higher-income countries that have closed the gap with the United States have effective market economies: private property rights, flexible prices, a stable price level, appropriate incentives, and a stable legal system. Lower-income countries that are growing rapidly share these characteristics. Nevertheless, a great variety of economic policies have been followed by countries that have had sustained economic growth. In addition to promoting education and developing appropriate infrastructure, some countries have used tariffs and other subsidies for some of their industries. Other countries have taken more of a hands-off approach. Few, if any, of the countries that have sustained economic growth for long periods have used a comprehensive central plan.

KEY TERMS

Land	Best technology	Technical change
Technological improvement	Capital	Labor
Production possibilities curve	Efficiency improvement	

REVIEW QUESTIONS

1. Compare the economic growth of Japan, Korea, and the United States since 1952.
2. Define the following terms:
   a. production possibilities curve

b. technological improvement
c. efficiency improvement
3. Is a faster rate of economic growth always desirable? Explain carefully using the production possibilities curve.
4. Use the accompanying graph to answer questions a through d.
    a. What point would represent a combination of goods and services that cannot be produced with the economy's given resources and technology?
    b. What point would represent a combination of goods and services that might be produced if the economy were experiencing unemployment? What else could cause the economy to be at that point?
    c. Suppose the economy is currently producing at point C and would like to have the consumption goods represented by point D. What must be given up to obtain the increased consumption goods?
    d. Suppose the economy is at point D. What might be done to increase the chances of being at B next year? What are other ways to get to B?

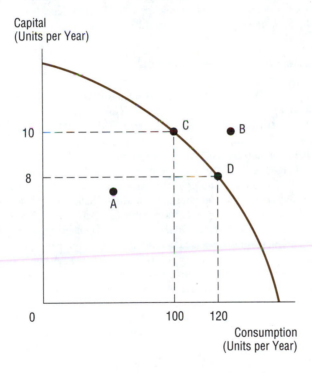

5. Why did compensation per hour not increase as fast after 1973 as it did from 1960 to 1973?
6. Explain why income per family (or income per person) has increased faster than compensation per hour since 1973.
7. According to the box titled "Were the Good Old Days Really Better?," the growth in the American standard of living since the early 1970s has been greater than suggested by government statistics that use the CPI to adjust for inflation. Explain.

8. What caused the slowdown in labor productivity growth in the United States after 1973? How has the growth of technical change differed in the manufacturing sector and the nonmanufacturing sector?

9. "Productivity growth in Japan is greater than productivity growth in the United States because its workers are more productive." Is this statement true or false? Defend your answer.

10. What factors explain why labor productivity in Japan and Germany has grown faster than in the United States?

11. According to the box titled "Economic Freedom and Economic Growth in Developing Countries," countries with more economic freedom have higher levels of per capita income. Does this prove that economic freedom causes prosperity? Defend your answer. The box also states that countries with increased economic freedom subsequently experience faster economic growth. Does this give you any more information about economic freedom and economic growth? Explain.

12. Discuss one advantage and one disadvantage that developing countries have as they try to encourage economic growth. What policies have proven successful in promoting economic growth?

SUGGESTIONS FOR FURTHER READING

Cullison, William E. "The U.S. Productivity Slowdown: What the Experts Say." *Federal Reserve Bank of Richmond Economic Review* (July/August 1989), 10–21. This article reviews the explanations of the productivity slowdown. The Federal Reserve Bank journals are excellent sources of articles for reports and term papers.

International Bank for Reconstruction and Development/The World Bank. *The World Development Report,* annual. Recent volumes have had themes such as from plan to market, workers in an integrating world, infrastructure for development, investing in health; development and the environment, and the challenge of development.

International Monetary Fund and International Bank for Reconstruction and Development/The World Bank. *Finance and Development,* quarterly. A journal containing articles on various aspects of economic growth and development.

Maddison, Angus. *Dynamic Forces in Capitalistic Development: A Long-Run Comparative View.* New York: Oxford University Press, 1991. An analysis of the economic growth of developed countries. An advanced treatment, but accessible to the determined student.

Meier, Gerald M. *Leading Issues in Economic Development* (6th ed.). Oxford: Oxford University Press, 1995. Covers the main issues relating to economic development from several perspectives.

Page, John, et al. *The East Asian Miracle: Economic Growth and Public Policy.* Oxford: Oxford University Press, 1994. This study discusses the rapid economic growth of several countries in East Asia and examines policies followed by different countries to promote growth.

Rosenberg, Nathan, and L. E. Birdzell, Jr. *How the West Grew Rich: The Economic Transformation of the Western World.* New York: Basic Books, 1985. An economic history of the western world since the Middle Ages that emphasizes economic growth. Technology and institutions are important along with political and economic factors.

Stein, Herbert, and Murray Foss. *The New Illustrated Guide to the American Economy.* 2nd ed. Washington, DC: The AEI Press, 1995. A fascinating presentation of data and a discussion of important topics about the American economy.

GLOSSARY

Absolute advantage The advantage a country has if it can produce a good or service at a lower cost than its trading partner.

Absolute disadvantage The disadvantage a country has if it produces a good or service at a higher cost than its trading partner.

Actual deficit The amount by which actual government expenditures exceed actual government revenue over the relevant time span.

Aggregate demand curve A curve showing the total amount of final goods and services (real GDP) that will be purchased at each price level (GDP deflator).

Aggregate supply curve A curve showing the total output of final goods and services (real GDP) that will be produced at each price level (the GDP deflator).

Allocative efficiency A state in which the economy achieves the largest possible output of goods and services from existing resources, technologies, and organizations.

Anticipated inflation Inflation that is expected.

Antitrust laws Laws prohibiting price fixing and other explicit cartel or monopoly behavior.

Appreciation Under a flexible exchange-rate system, a rise in the value of one currency relative to another.

Balance of payments A summary of all economic transactions between the residents of one country and those of all other countries during a given period of time.

Barrier to entry Any condition that prevents new firms from entering an industry with the same or lower cost conditions than existing firms.

Basic transfer The amount transferred in an income-tested transfer program when net income is zero.

Bequest effect The tendency of social security to induce working people to increase their saving so as to increase the bequests they leave their children.

Best technology The technology that requires the fewest resources to produce a given combination of goods and services.

Break-even net income The net income in an income-tested transfer program at which the amount transferred becomes zero.

Bubble A regulatory unit containing several sources of pollution that is evaluated according to the total emissions produced by the unit rather than according to the emission produced by each source.

Budget deficit The amount by which government expenditures exceed government revenue over the relevant time span.

Budget surplus The amount by which government revenue exceeds government expenditures over the relevant time span.

Buffer fund An insurance reserve fund composed of assets that are intended to cover unexpected short-run declines in revenues or increases in expenditures.

Business cycles Recurring fluctuations in the general level of economic activity.

Capital Man-made, durable items used in the production process, such as factories, equipment, dams, and transportation systems.

Capital-labor ratio The ratio of the amount of capital input to the amount of labor input.

Capital stock The nation's accumulated stock of structures, producers' durable equipment, and business inventories.

Cartel An organized group of producers who manage their output and pricing as if they were a monopoly.

Cash transfers Government grants in cash that can be used for any purpose.

Central bank A government-established agency that controls the nation's money supply, conducts monetary policy, and supervises the monetary system.

Civilian labor force The number of persons employed plus the number of persons unemployed.

Command economy An economy in which the what, how, and for whom questions are answered by central government planners.

Common property resource A resource that belongs to all; characterized by absence of a private party's right to use the resource exclusively.

Comparative advantage The advantage a country has if it can produce a good or service at a lower opportunity cost than its trading partner.

Comparative disadvantage The disadvantage a country has if it produces a good or service at a higher opportunity cost than its trading partner.

Competitive industry An industry in which (1) there are many buyers and sellers, (2) no individual buyer or seller can affect the price of the good, and (3) equilibrium price and quantity are determined by the interaction of the buyers and sellers in the market place.

Complements Goods that are used together. An increase in the price of the original good results in a decrease in the demand for its complement.

Composite index of leading indicators A weighted index of 11 leading indicators: presumably it is a more reliable predictor of economic activity than a single leading indicator.

Consumer price index (CPI) A weighted average of the prices of goods and services purchased by a typical urban household.

Consumer sovereignty The production of goods and services in response to individual demand.

Consumer surplus The difference between the total benefit (expressed in dollars) received from the consumption of a good and the total amount paid for it.

Consumption of fixed capital Allowances for depreciation of the na-

tion's structures and equipment and for accidental damage to them.

Contraction phase The phase of the business cycle during which real GDP, employment, productive capacity use, and profits decrease while unemployment rises.

Contractionary fiscal policy A decrease in aggregate demand brought about by a decrease in government purchases, an increase in taxes, or both.

Contractionary monetary policy An action by the Federal Reserve to decrease the money supply.

Coordination Process that makes consumption and production plans consistent, ensuring that quantity demanded equals quantity supplied.

Cost-minimization The attainment of an objective at the lowest possible cost.

Cost-of-living adjustment (COLA) clause A clause in a labor contract that allows wage rates to increase automatically as the CPI rises.

Creditor A person to whom money is owed.

Currency (cash) Paper money and coins.

Cyclical unemployment Unemployment caused by the drop in economic activity that occurs during the contraction phase of the business cycle.

Deadweight loss The portion of competitive total surplus that is lost by consumers (and producers) but not turned into monopoly profits; it simply disappears (also called net social loss).

Debtor A person who owes money.

Decrease in demand A situation in which, at each price, consumers

plan to purchase less of a good; it is depicted by a leftward shift of the demand curve. It may also be interpreted as a reduction in the demand price at each quantity of the good, thus emphasizing the downward shift in the curve.

Decrease in supply A situation in which, at each price, producers plan to sell less of a good; it is depicted by a leftward shift of the supply curve. It may also be interpreted as an increase in the supply price for each quantity of the good, thus emphasizing the upward shift in the curve.

Defensive medicine Medical procedures performed to reduce the risk of a lawsuit, rather than because of their medical value.

Deficiency payment A government payment to a producer equal to the difference between the target and market price of the product times the quantity of the product sold.

Deflation A continuing fall in the price level.

Demand curve A curve showing the quantity demanded for each possible market price, holding other factors that affect demand constant.

Demand deposits Checking accounts at commercial banks.

Demand price The price at which consumers will desire to purchase the exact quantity of a good or service that is placed on the market. It is the maximum price that a consumer will pay for one more unit of a good or service.

Demand schedule A table that shows how the quantity demanded of a good changes as the price changes, holding all other factors that affect demand constant.

Depository institutions Financial institutions that accept checkable and savings deposits.

Depreciation Under a flexible exchange-rate system, a fall in the value of one currency relative to another.

Depression A prolonged and very sereve recession.

Discount rate The interest rate at which depository institutions can borrow from Federal Reserve Banks.

Disposable income Household income less taxes; spendable income.

Distribution of income Apportionment of the total income of a society among its individuals.

Earnings penalty A reduction in social security benefits occurring when postretirement earnings exceed some amount specified by the government.

Economic efficiency The state that occurs when total social benefit minus total social cost is as large as possible.

Economic growth An increase in the economy's ability to satisfy wants.

Economic profit A return to a producer in excess of the minimum necessary to induce the producer to continue to produce the product.

Economic rent seeking Attempt by people to gain an economic advantage through production of new or better products or through production of products at a lower cost.

Efficiency improvement A change from the use of less than the best to use of the best technology—a movement to the production possibilities curve.

Efficient combination of goods and services A combination that yields the greatest amount of one good or service for any given amount of another.

Efficient output The level of production of a good or service at which marginal social benefit equals marginal social cost; thus, it leads to the largest possible total surplus.

Emissions reduction credit The right to produce additional emissions, earned by reducing emissions below a level specified by regulators.

Emissions tax A tax levied on polluters; also called a Pigovian tax after its originator, the late British economist A. C. Pigou.

Entrepreneur An individual who recognizes a potentially profitable opportunity, organizes a business firm to take advantage of it, absorbs the loss if the firm fails, and gains the profits if the firm succeeds.

Equation of exchange An equation showing the relationships among the money supply, the income velocity of money, the GDP deflator, and real GDP ($M \times V = P \times GDP$).

Equilibrium A state of rest of the market or economy. For an individual market, equilibrium occurs at the price where the quantity demanded equals the quantity supplied.

Equimarginal principle The last dollar spent on one activity should give the same marginal benefit as the last dollar spent on any other activity.

Excess demand A situation in which quantity demanded exceeds quantity supplied at a given price.

Excess reserves Reserves over and above required reserves.

Excess supply A situation in which quantity supplied exceeds quantity demanded at a given price.

Exchange rate The number of units of one currency exchangeable for one unit of another.

Expansion phase The phase of the business cycle during which real GDP, employment, productive capacity use, and profits increase while unemployment falls.

Expansionary fiscal policy An increase in aggregate demand brought about by an increase in government purchases, a decrease in taxes, or both.

Expansionary monetary policy An action by the Federal Reserve to increase the money supply.

Experience-rated insurance Health insurance in which premiums are based on individual or group characteristics that are correlated with the use of health care.

Exports Goods and services produced in this country and purchased by foreigners.

External benefits of education The benefits of education realized by individuals other than students and their families; this is an example of a case where private benefits are less than social benefits.

Feminization of poverty The growth in the percentage of poor families headed by females.

Final goods Goods purchased (or available to be purchased) for final use.

Fiscal policy Use of government purchases and taxes to achieve full employment and other economic goals.

Flexible (floating) exchange rates Exchange rates determined by demand and supply.

Free rider An individual who uses goods or services provided by others without paying for them.

Frictional unemployment Temporary unemployment arising from the normal job search process; occurs as individuals move between jobs or enter the labor market.

Full employment A situation in which all members of the labor force who desire employment are working.

Full employment rate of unemployment The frictional rate of unemployment plus the structural rate of unemployment; the lowest unemployment rate consistent with a nonaccelerating inflation rate. Also referred to as the natural rate of unemployment.

Fully funded insurance plan A plan in which annual benefits are financed by income earned on assets.

GDP deflator A weighted average of the prices of all final goods and services produced in the economy; also called the implicit price deflator for GDP.

Global budgeting Fixed budgets for groups of physicians and hospitals in an area.

Government failure The failure of government to achieve a desirable social goal.

Government purchases of goods and services The purchases of goods and services by federal, state, and local governments.

Government transfer payments Payments made to individuals or institutions by government that involve no production and exchange of goods and services.

Gross domestic product (GDP) The market value of all final goods and services produced in the economy over the relevant time span, usually one year.

Gross private domestic investment Firms' purchases of equipment, all purchases of newly produced structures, and changes in business inventories.

Gross replacement rate A measure of the adequacy of social security benefits as a source of income after retirement. It is the ratio of basic monthly retirement benefits to before-tax earnings in the year prior to retirement.

Human capital The knowledge and skills embodied in raw labor (numbers of individuals).

Hyperinflation Extremely high inflation rates.

Implicit price deflator *See* GDP deflator.

Imports Goods and services produced abroad and bought by persons in this country.

Income-tested transfers Government programs in which the amount transferred falls as the recipient's net income rises.

Income velocity of money The number of times the money supply is used to purchase final goods and services during a year.

Incomes policy Government action, other than monetary and fiscal policies, to restrain or control wages, prices, and other forms of income.

Increase in demand A situation in which, at each price, consumers plan to purchase more of a good; it is depicted by a rightward shift of the demand curve. It may also be interpreted as an increase in the demand price at each quantity of the good, thus emphasizing the upward shift of the curve.

Increase in supply A situation in which, at each price, producers plan to sell more of a good; it is depicted by a rightward shift of the supply curve. It may also be interpreted as a reduction in the supply price for each quantity of the good, thus emphasizing the downward shift of the curve.

Indexing The linking of benefits to the CPI so that they increase automatically as the CPI rises.

Induced retirement effect The tendency of social security benefits to encourage people to retire earlier than they would in their absence.

Inferior good A good that consumers purchase less of when their incomes rise.

Inflation A continuing rise in the price level.

In-kind transfers Government grants for specific goods and services, such as food, housing, and medical care.

Intermediate goods Goods purchased for resale or for use in producing other goods.

Labor All physical and mental abilities used by people in production.

Labor force participation rate The percentage of the working-age population in the labor force.

Labor productivity Output per unit of labor.

Land Resources found in nature such as land, water, forests, mineral deposits, and air.

Law of demand As the price of some good changes, with other factors constant, the quantity demanded of the good changes in the opposite direction.

Law of diminishing marginal product The law or principle that adding more of a variable resource to a fixed resource will eventually cause the additional output associated with the variable resource to fall.

Law of supply As the price of some good changes, with other factors constant, the quantity supplied of the good changes in the same direction.

Leading indicator A variable that generally turns down prior to recessions and turns up prior to recoveries.

Lifetime earnings profile The expected annual earnings associated with all years worked.

Loanable funds Funds, including those supplied by households and firms, that are available for borrowing by other households and firms and by government.

Managed care A health care organization or practice that intervenes in decisions made by health care providers to obtain or provide appropriate care at reduced prices.

Marginal benefit The value of the satisfaction received from the consumption of an additional unit of a good or service.

Marginal cost The opportunity cost of producing an additional unit of a good.

Marginal external benefits Benefits received on the marginal unit by all individuals other than the buyer.

Marginal external cost Change in cost to parties other than the producer or buyer of a good or service due to the production of an additional unit.

Marginal principle To maximize profits, the producer should choose the output that equates marginal revenue and marginal cost.

Marginal private benefit The value of an additional unit of output to an individual consumer; the maximum that a consumer would pay for one more unit.

Marginal private cost Change in cost to a producer due to the production of an additional unit of a good or service. It is the minimum that a producer would accept in payment for producing another unit of a good.

Marginal product The change in output associated with a one-unit change in an input, for example, labor.

Marginal revenue The change in total revenue associated with a one-unit change in the output sold by a producer.

Marginal social benefit The value of an additional unit of output to an individual consumer plus the value of any benefit received by other people. It equals marginal private benefit if all of the benefits of consuming a particular good go to the individual consumer; otherwise, it equals marginal private benefit plus any benefit that goes to other people in the economy. It is measured by the amount buyers and all other beneficiaries are willing to pay to consume an additional unit of a good or service.

Marginal social cost The opportunity cost to all people in the economy of producing one more unit of a good; it equals the marginal private cost if all costs are incurred by the individual producer. If some of the opportunity costs of production are incurred by other people, marginal social cost equals marginal private cost plus the marginal external cost.

Market demand schedule A table that shows how the total quantity demanded of a good changes as the price changes, holding all other factors that affect demand constant; it is the sum of the demand schedules of all consumers in the market.

Market economy An economy in which the what, how, and to whom questions are answered by markets.

Market effect An effect whose value is determined directly in a resource or product market.

Market failure The failure of a market to achieve a desirable social goal.

Market power A situation in which a firm or a small group of firms can affect the price received for their product, and new firms do not enter the industry in response to profit.

Medium of exchange Anything used to purchase goods and services and pay debts.

Member banks Banks that are members of the Federal Reserve System.

Monetary policy Use of the money supply to achieve full employment and other economic goals.

Money Anything generally accepted as final payment for goods, services, and debt.

Money income Earnings before taxes, plus private and government cash transfers.

Money supply Currency, travelers' checks, demand deposits, and other checkable deposits.

Monopoly An industry with a single producer of a good that has no close substitutes.

Moral hazard The tendency of insurance coverage to increase risky behavior by the individuals covered by the insurance.

National banks Banks chartered by the federal government.

National debt The aggregate of the federal deficits and surpluses that have accumulated over time.

Natural monopoly A monopoly that exists if demand and cost conditions are such that only one firm can survive in an industry.

Natural rate of unemployment The frictional rate of unemployment plus the structural rate of unemployment; the lowest unemployment rate consistent with a nonaccelerating inflation rate. Also referred to as the full employment rate of unemployment.

Negative income tax A federally funded, income-tested transfer program, often proposed as a substitute for existing income-tested transfer programs.

Net exports of goods and services The difference between exports and imports of goods and services; the amount by which foreign spending on domestically produced goods and services is greater or less than domestic spending on goods and services produced abroad.

Net private domestic investment Gross private domestic investment less consumption of fixed capital; refers to the portion of investment that adds to the existing stock of structures and equipment.

Net social loss The excess of social cost over social benefit over some range of production (also called deadweight loss).

Netting A regulation that allows a firm to add a new source of pollutant emissions to a plant if it can reduce emissions from other sources.

Nominal GDP GDP measured on the basis of current, or nominal, prices; reflects changes in both prices and quantities.

Nonexcludable good A good that it is impossible or extremely difficult to exclude nonpayers from consuming. It is one characteristic of a public good.

Nonrival good A good for which an individual's consumption of the good does not affect its availability for other people. It is one characteristic of a public good.

Normal good A good that consumers purchase more of when their incomes rise.

Official poverty threshold The annual cost of a nutritionally adequate diet multiplied by three.

Official poverty measure A measure of poverty according to which a person is poor who lives in a family whose income is less than the official poverty line.

Offset The reduction in emissions achieved by an existing source that permits the introduction of a new pollution source in areas not meeting air pollution standards.

Oligopoly An industry with only a few producers or sellers of a good.

Open market operations The purchase or sale of U.S. Treasury securities by the Federal Reserve.

Opportunity cost The value of the best alternative sacrificed when a choice is made.

Partial-cost payment The difference between the full cost of health care provided and the third-party payments for the care.

Pay-as-you-go insurance plan A plan in which annual benefits are financed primarily by current annual revenues.

Peak The highest point in the business cycle, during which real GDP is at a maximum and employment, profits, and productive capacity use are high.

Personal consumption expenditures Household purchases of durable and nondurable goods and services.

Physician-induced demand The portion of health care purchases determined by the physician, rather than by the patient.

Political rent seeking Attempt by certain individuals or groups to encourage government activity that will result in an economic advantage for them.

Pretransfer poor Individuals who do not receive enough income from private sources to escape poverty.

Price ceiling A government law or regulation that sets a maximum price that can be charged for a good or service.

Price index A measure of the price level for a given period relative to the base period.

Price support A minimum price set by government, below which the market price is not allowed to go.

Price taker A buyer or seller who has no influence on the price of a good but instead must buy or sell the good at the market price.

Principle of individual contribution An individual's insurance benefits are directly related to the size of contributions to the fund, the duration of and earnings on investments in the fund, and the individual's age of retirement.

Privatization Transfer of a government asset to private ownership and control.

Producer surplus Total revenue received by producers minus the total opportunity cost of producing the output.

Production possibilities All efficient combinations of two goods or services that can be produced by an economy when resources are fully used and the best technology is applied.

Productivity Output per unit of resource input.

Profit Total revenue minus total cost.

Progressive tax burden The result of a tax rate structure in which the tax burden increases as a share of income as income rises.

Property rights An individual's exclusive rights to use and sell a good, within certain constraints; the legally allowable uses of property.

Proportional tax burden The result of a tax rate structure in which the tax burden is a constant share of income as income rises.

Public good A good that is nonrival and nonexcludable. It is impossible (or extremely costly) to exclude nonpayers from consumption of the good; one individual's consumption of the good does not affect the availability of the good for other people.

Quantity demanded The quantity of a good that consumers are willing to buy at each possible price, holding other factors that affect demand constant.

Quantity theory of money A theory emphasizing that the money supply is the principal determinant of nominal GDP.

Quota An upper limit on the amount of goods that may be imported during any time period.

Rate of return The discount rate at which the sums of the present values of benefits and costs are equal.

Ration To allocate a limited supply of goods and services to people.

Real balance effect The change in consumption caused by a change in the real value of financial assets that have fixed dollar values; the change in real value may be due to either a change in the amount of financial assets or a change in the price level.

Real GDP GDP measured on the basis of constant prices; reflects only changes in quantities.

Recession A downturn in economic activity characterized by falling real GDP and rising unemployment; another name for the contraction and trough phases of the business cycle.

Recovery An upturn in economic activity characterized by rising real GDP and falling unemployment; another name for the expansion phase of the business cycle.

Regressive tax burden The result of a tax rate structure in which the tax burden decreases as a share of income as income rises.

Relative price The price of a good or service relative to the price of another good or service.

Required reserves Reserves that depository institutions are required to hold.

Reserve requirement The ratio of required reserves to deposits.

Scarcity The common situation for all economies, in which aggregate wants exceed the ability to meet them.

Social security All social insurance programs administered by the Social Security Administration, or (as in Chapter 9) old-age and survivors' insurance (OASI) program, alone.

Socialism Government ownership of the means of production.

Stabilization policies Government policies (generally fiscal or monetary) undertaken to maintain full employment and a reasonably stable price level.

State banks Banks chartered by state governments.

Structural deficit The deficit that would occur if the economy were at full employment.

Structural unemployment Unemployment caused by structural changes in the economy that eliminate certain jobs; unemployment caused by changes in technology or shifts in the demand for goods and services.

Substitutes Goods that satisfy similar needs or desires as other goods. An increase in the price of the original good results in an increase in demand for the substitute good.

Supply curve A curve showing the quantity supplied for each possible market price, holding other factors that affect supply constant.

Supply price The price at which sellers desire to sell an exact quantity of a good or service. It is the minimum that a seller will accept in return for selling one more unit of a good or service.

Supply-side policies Government actions aimed at increasing aggregate supply.

Target efficiency The degree to which transfer program benefits are confined to the poor.

Target price A guaranteed price for a product. The product is sold at the market price and the government pays the producer the difference between it and the target price.

Tariff A tax levied on a good when it crosses a nation's border.

Technical change Anything that results in more output being produced from a given amount of resources. Technological improvement plus efficiency improvement.

Technological improvement An improvement in best technology that allows more output to be produced with a given amount of resources—an outward shift in the production possibilities curve.

Third-party payment A payment for a good or service made by someone other than the buyer or seller of the good or service.

Total cost The explicit and implicit costs of all resources used by a producer during the production process.

Total revenue The price of a good or service times quantity sold.

Total social benefit The maximum that consumers would pay for a given quantity of a good; assuming that all benefits are private, it is the area under the demand curve between zero and the given quantity of the good.

Total social cost The minimum that producers would accept in payment for a given quantity of a good; assuming that all costs are private, it is the area under the supply curve between zero and the given quantity of the good.

Transfer payment A payment that is made with no expectation of something in return.

Transfer reduction rate The decrease in the amount transferred in an income-tested transfer program when there is an increase in net income.

Trough The lowest point of the business cycle, during which real GDP is at a minimum and employment, profits, and productive capacity use are low.

Tuition subsidy State appropriations used to subsidize tuition at institutions of higher education.

Unanticipated inflation Inflation that is unexpected or higher than expected.

Underground economy Economic activity that is either inherently illegal or not reported in order to evade taxes or for some other reason.

Unemployment rate The percentage of the civilian labor force that is unemployed.

Vault cash Cash held by banks and other depository institutions.

Voluntary Export Restraints (VERs) Agreements whereby exporting nations limit the amounts of goods that they ship to importing nations.

Vouchers Coupons issued by government that can be used by the recipient to pay for specific goods and services.

Wage subsidy A payment to a low-wage worker for each hour worked, equal to a percentage of the difference between a maximum wage and the worker's wage.

Wealth substitution effect An effect that induces workers to substitute one type of wealth (social security) for other types of wealth that could be financed by saving.

Workfare Government programs that require recipients of public assistance to enhance their employment prospects in exchange for public assistance.

INDEX